JEWISH
PARTISANS
OF THE SOVIET
UNION
DURING WORLD
WAR II

Cherry
Orchard
Books

JEWISH PARTISANS OF THE SOVIET UNION
DURING WORLD WAR II

Jack Nusan Porter

BOSTON
2021

Library of Congress Cataloging-in-Publication Data

Names: Porter, Jack Nusan, compiler, editor.
Title: Jewish partisans of the Soviet Union during World War II / compiled and edited by Jack Nusan Porter with the assistance of Yehuda Merin.
Description: First edition. | Brookline, MA : Academic Studies Press, [2020] | First edition was published by University Press of America in both hardcover and soft-cover: Volume I: ISBN: 0-8191-2180-0 (perfect-binding) and ISBN: 0-8191-2179-7 (cloth); Volume II: ISBN: 0-8191-2538-5 (perfect) and ISBN: 0-8191-2537-7 (cloth). | Includes bibliographical references and index.
Identifiers: LCCN 2020046256 (print) | LCCN 2020046257 (ebook) | ISBN 9781644694923 (hardback) | ISBN 9781644694930 (paperback) | ISBN 9781644694947 (adobe pdf) | ISBN 9781644694954 (epub)
Subjects: LCSH: World War, 1939-1945--Jewish resistance--Soviet Union. | Holocaust, Jewish (1939-1945)--Soviet Union. | World War, 1939-1945--Participation, Jewish. | Soviet Union--Ethnic relations.
Classification: LCC D810.J4 J48 2020 (print) | LCC D810.J4 (ebook) | DDC 940.53/47089924--dc23
LC record available at https://lccn.loc.gov/2020046256
LC ebook record available at https://lccn.loc.gov/2020046257

ISBN 9781644694923   hardback
ISBN 9781644694930   paperback
ISBN 9781644694947   ebook PDF
ISBN 9781644694954   ePub

Cover Photo: Jack Nusan Porter and his parents Irving and Faye Porter, after liberation, around May 1945, Rovno, Urkaine. Porter is wearing the "Partisan First Class" Soviet Medal he received from the Soviet government.

Cover design by Ivan Grave
Book design by Lapiz Digital Services

Publubed by Cherry Orchard Books, imprint of Academic Studies Press
1577 Beacon Street
Brookline, MA 02446, USA
press@academicstudiespress.com
www.academicstudiespress.com

DEDICATED TO

Yehuda Merin (1925-2010), with great love and affection,
and
to the memory of Binyamin West.

We miss them both very much as we do all the partisans and their spouses and children (if deceased) that I knew well: Abraham Lerer, Moshe (Morris) Kramer, Abba Klurman, Asher Flash, Avrum Puchtik, Dov (Berl) Bronstein, Avrum Bronstein, Dov Lorber, Sender Lande, Sasha (Charlie) Zarutski, and of course my parents, Yisroel (Srulik) Puchtik (Porter), and Faygeh Merin Puchtik (Porter-Arenzon).

**Dedicated to my parents
Irving Porter (1906-1979)
and
Faye (Merin) Porter (1909-2009)**

My father died
before the first edition
of this book was published.
May his memory be a blessing.

Do not judge your fellowman
Until you have stood in his place.
— Hillel the Sage, *Pirke Avot (Sayings of the Fathers)*

I believe
I believe in the sun even when it is not shining.
I believe in love even when feeling it not.
I believe in God even when He is silent.
— Inscription on the walls of a cellar in Cologne,
Germany, where Jews hid from the Nazis

CONTENTS

BOOK ONE

PART FOUR

PART FIVE

BOOK TWO

PART ONE

APPENDIX

BOOK ONE

ACKNOWLEDGMENTS

My thanks must first go to the Russian army for liberating my parents' home and to the Russian partisan movement for allowing my parents to fight with dignity and to avenge the deaths of my two sisters and the twenty-five members of my family who died a lonely death on a dark Sabbath eve in September 1942. Despite my personal disgust at what the Soviet leaders and bureaucrats are doing to Jews in the Soviet Union today, we must give credit where it is deserved, and it was deserved by the Russian people and the Russian army during World War II.

A special note of thanks must also go to the late Binyamin West, editor of the Hebrew version of this book, *They Were Many: Jewish Partisans in the Soviet Union During World War II*, published in 1968 by the Labor Archives Press of the Hapoel Hatzair Publishing Cooperative in Tel Aviv, in cooperation with the Yad Vashem Memorial Institute of Jerusalem. This present book owes a great deal to West's support and encouragement. I am sorry he did not live to see the English version.

Acknowledgments must also go to my cousin Yehudah Merin of Tel Aviv, who first showed me a copy of these memoirs and encouraged me to have them translated and published. I am especially grateful to Morris U. Schappes, Erich Goldhagen, and Joshua Rothenberg for reading the introduction and offering their critical advice. For various degrees of moral and intellectual support and advice, I wish to thank Leni Yahil; Shlomo Noble of the YIVO Institute of New York; Vladka Meed of the Jewish Labor Committee; Eli Zborowski of the American Federation of Jewish Fighters, Camp Inmates, and Nazi Victims; Moshe Kaganovitch of Tel Aviv; Yuri Suhl of New York; and Elie Wiesel of Boston University.

I should also mention the many partisan friends of my parents who were so generous with their encouragement and support: Moshe Flash (Montreal); Abraham Lerer (Cleve-land); Jack Melamedik (Montreal); Morris (Moishe)

Kramer (Philadelphia); Avrum Puchtik (Tel Aviv); as well as Chunek Wolper, Sasha (Charlie) Zarutski, Itzik Kuperberg, Berl Avruch, Yehudah Wolper, Joseph Zweibel, Vova Verba, Jacob and Berl Bronstein, Jacob Karsh, Abba Klurman, Isaac Avruch, Joseph Blanstein, Sender Lande, and finally Berl Lorber, a commander in the Kruk Partisan Detachment who fought under the *nom de guerre* "Malinka" and now resides in Seattle, Washington. The others live in Israel for the most part; some in New York; a few in Milwaukee, Denver, and the Soviet Union.

Many of the people, however, who worked on this book with me were born after the war. I would like to thank Laurie Smith and Danny Matt, for help with some Hebrew translation; Morey Schapira, for advice on "grantsmanship"; Seymour Rossel, for helping to rearrange the order of articles; and Doris Gold, for suggesting the title.

My thanks also to Miriam Magal and the Magal Translation Institute, Ltd., of Tel Aviv, who undertook the translation of the book from the Hebrew into English. They must be quite relieved to see it in print, as am I. This book took nearly eight years to see the light of day!

Finally, no words can adequately express my gratitude to my family: to my wife, Miriam; our son, Gabriel Alexander; to the Almulys, my in-laws; to my sister, Bella, and her husband, Mitchell Smith; to my brother, Reb Shloime, and his wife, Shushi; and, finally, to my parents. My parents were informal editors throughout. I am only sorry that my father did not live to see this book, but he knew it would be published one day.

Jack Nusan Porter

Boston, Massachusetts

May 1, 1981

It has taken some time (thirty years), but God gave me the strength to finally reprint these important volumes on the anti-Nazi resistance in the Soviet Union during World War II, or, as the Russians called it, the "Great War for the Fatherland." They were long out of print.

Demand has increased for these books, and few copies existed. In fact, Volume II in hardcover is so scarce that it sells for $208 on eBay or Amazon. In fact, I have only one of the few copies left of that volume. For some reason, Volume I is more common.

People have been asking for copies of these books for many years. I include an updated bibliography and filmography that follows this preface. I will deal with some of these issues in more detail in a follow-up book — *Like Sheep to Slaughter? Jewish Resistance During the Holocaust* — which will have many more essays and interviews that I could not put into this volume.

When I first compiled these stories, in the late 1970s and early 1980s, most of the writers were still alive. Many accounts and *yizkor* (remembrance) books had come out; the field was flourishing. Russia was still under Communist rule, yet material surprisingly was easy to get. I remember I had to pay for microfilms, books or films like *Sputniki: The Partisan Soldier's Guide* by sending the Lenin Library a similarly *priced* book in science or biology. Not money, but books were what the Soviets needed!

Today, most of the partisans have died, even Yehuda Merin, my cousin and the foremost organizer of the Volynian Jews in Israel, died two years ago (2010) at age 85. It was a great loss and proves my own vulnerability. I am now 68 years old, time is running out, and who will do this work except I. Corrections have been made. I promised Yehuda I would make them. My pardon if some still exist. I did my best.

I dedicate this book to Yehuda's memory and to all the others, both in Israel and North America, who helped me:

Binyamin West, Moshe Kaganovitch, Abba Klurman, Moshe Kramer, Avrum Lerer, Moshe Flash, Avrum Bronstein and so many others. My condolences go to their spouses and children: Idkeh, Esti, and Arick Shuster; Lyuba Merin and her children Mina and Yossi, and their children and spouses and al the other wives and children of the partisans.

Today, the old Communist rule is over. The Soviet archives are open to the public; there is little to hide; historians will be busy for decades. Still questions and doubts continue. Some feel these stories are simply Communist propaganda, and to some degree they are, but propaganda can still be true! These tales happened despite the embellishment.

Second, there are people who feel, shockingly, that what the partisans did was wrong: they killed innocent people (at times, true, but most were Nazi collaborators or relatives of collaborators); or they caused more destruction upon Jews, causing more lives to be lost (possibly, but they were all going to die anyway — better to die with dignity); or that these accounts are not really "scholarship" (true, they are not; they are the basis for scholarship; they are the lifeblood of scholarship); or that these fighters saw or understood only a small aspect of the war (true, but then any soldier only sees that; only the generals see the big picture) or that "spiritual" resistance is on the same plane as physical (not really; all the praying in the world did not kill a single Nazi — only a gun and bullets did that, but maybe it helped the fighter survive; in short, it didn't hurt; still, this has become a major debate today).

The political debates and scholarly conflicts continue.

I only want to set the record straight with these accounts. There is an old Jewish joke about fighting: Some Jews come to the rabbi and ask should we sit or stand when saying the Shema, a Jewish prayer — and the rabbi says that both sides are correct — you can either sit or stand — but what's the tradition, rabbi — what do we do? And the rabbi replied: the tradition is in the "fighting," in the arguing, that will continue *ad infinitum.* That's the "tradition."

May God bless all those who died and to all those who survived... and let the "fighting" continue.

Jack Nusan Porter, Ph.D.

December 2, 2012 (my birthday)

79 Walnut Street
Newtonville, MA 02460-1331

jack.porter1@verizon.net
www.drjackporter.com

As he was being carried away in an ox-cart to his death, Simon Dubnow, the great historian of Eastern European Jewry, shouted out to the people: *"Yidn, farshraybt!"* ("Jews, remember!" "Jews, record!") And the Jews have been doing that ever since. The Nazis attempted to exterminate two entire people — the Jews and the Gypsies. The Gypsies had no written tradition (thought they have a very rich oral one), and, consequently, one can find very little written on or by Gypsies. The Jews, on the other hand, follow the Eleventh Commandment: Thou Shalt Write.

Hiroshima and Auschwitz. These are the two touchstones of our generation. Not enough can be written on either one, yet there remains much ignorance, much ambivalence, and much callousness. The world is still puzzled by its perception that the Jews "allowed" themselves to go to their deaths without a struggle. Young people, especially young Blacks, are especially perturbed. They tell me that "if it ever happens here" they will get themselves a gun and fight. Their bravado exposes a deep ignorance of the Nazi era.

This book is an attempt to set the record straight. Though it can be read on various levels, it should be seen first and foremost as a *document*, an historical document gathered by Russian-Jewish intellectuals in 1948 at the height of antiSemitic hysteria, but written mainly by non-Jewish Soviet partisan commanders recounting the deeds of the Jewish fighters in their units. Furthermore, the original version of this collection was written in *Russian*, not Yiddish, despite the fact that it was a Yiddish publishing house that first produced it. Why was this book written … and why in Russian… and why, in most cases, by non-Jews?

In order to answer these questions, a brief history is necessary. The major portion of this book first appeared in Moscow in 1948 under its Russian title, *Partizanskaya Druzhba* (roughly *Partisan Brotherhood*), and was compiled by the editors of the Moscow-based Der Emes (in Yiddish,

"The Truth") Publishing House and the Jewish Anti-Fascist Committee (JAFC). This committee, composed of the cream of Jewish writers, poets and intellectuals, had as its primary duty the task of gaining worldwide support for the Soviet Union during the early days of the war when Russia stood almost alone against the Nazi onslaught.

There is a fascinating tale about this committee. In 1943 two of its leaders, the poet Itzik Feffer and the renowned Yiddish actor and director Solomon Mikhoels, went abroad on an official mission to the Jewish communities of the United States, Canada, Mexico, and Britain. This mission was decided on at the very highest Soviet Governmental level. Stalin himself not only authorized it, but also attached great political significance to it. Mikhoels and Feffer remained broad for about seven months; they toured forty-six cities in the United States and addressed audiences totaling over half a million people. From all accounts, it was an extremely successful tour. There is an apocryphal story that before leaving America, Mikhoels and Feffer were given a tank bought with money donated by the Jewish community, a tank with a large Jewish star on it. This tank was used by the Soviet Army during World War II.

In any event, Jewish trust in the Soviet leadership was high, but after the war, Stalin, for reasons not yet fully understood, no longer needed Jewish support, and during the final six years of his life the USSR was gripped by political terror and a series of purges. The Jewish Anti-Fascist Committee tried in its own way to disseminate information on the vital role Jews had played during World War II. This task was not easy: Jews were made to appear as traitors to the state and collaborators with the Nazis. The original editors of *Partisan Brotherhood* moved quickly to gather material in order to show the truth, that Jews were active citizens in the resistance and in the Red Army. This book was therefore addressed to a non-Jewish audience.

Jewish war veterans, some crippled, were mocked in the streets: "Where did you win those medals, kike? In a crap game? Did you buy them on the black market?" It was during such a time that the editors of the Der Emes Publishing House and the JAFC worked feverishly to collect these memoirs and to present them to the Russian-speaking public. The purpose of these memoirs was twofold: first, of course, it was to be a chronicle of Jewish participation in the resistance, but there was a more important reason — the JAFC had to prove that the Jews were not traitors and cowards during the war, but brave and loyal fighters for the "motherland." Jewish patriotism, in other words, had to be *documented* — not by Jews, but by non-Jewish army and partisan officers (some of them national heroes). This would give credence to the Jewish cause, a credence for Stalin to accept, and a credence for the Soviet people to honor.

The JAFC served as an important documentation center for the events and problems of Russian Jewish life during the war and for a few years afterwards. It also fulfilled an important mission by publishing the Yiddish newspaper *Einekeit* ("Unity"), which brought to the Jewish population much information about the Holocaust, especially news of the murder of Jews and the destruction of Jewish communities. *Einekeit* also printed authentic material about Jewish soldiers and officers who excelled in battle against the Nazis, whether in the front line of the Red Army or in the partisan movement.

The collection *Partisan Brotherhood* was prepared for print in Moscow on October 9, 1948. Apparently, there was not enough time to issue the book before all Yiddish cultural projects in the Soviet Union were abolished. Stalin began the purges of Jewish leaders and intellectuals: he closed Jewish schools and cultural centers, and he threatened mass pogroms against the Jews. Many of the most active embers of the Jewish Anti-Fascist Committee, including Mikhoels and Feffer, were later killed. The Der Emes Publishing House was closed in late 1948, but the book *Partisan Brotherhood* did appear in print in a limited edition.

Ironically, a few copies of the Russian manuscript were preserved by the Lenin Library in Moscow, and fifteen years later, an Israeli journalist, Binyamin West, heard about the book and was allowed to purchase a microfiche copy from the library's archives. In 1968 West's Hebrew translation of the book appeared in Israel. My cousin Yehuda Merin of Tel Aviv saw a copy and noticed that it contained a rare photograph of my father in a pose with his commander. Both my mother and father were active in a partisan group which fought in the vicinity of Rovno, Volyn, in the western Ukraine from 1942 to 1944. In 1974 I wrote to the Lenin Library and received a copy of *Partizanskaya Druzhba*. The English translation made by the Magal Translation Institute, Ltd., of Tel Aviv was done from the Hebrew version and checked against the Russian original. Additional material on partisan life was translated from other sources by the same institute. So one sees that this book has both a personal as well as a professional interest to the editor.

Jewish Partisans is a sociological account of the Jewish partisan movement in the Soviet Union. It is broken down into five parts, plus an introduction. The first part, "Prologue," consists of fiction the stories of Shmuel Persov, a Russian-Jewish writer, but it is fiction that is so lifelike that it is difficult to differentiate it from the true accounts that follow. Part Two, "Initiatives," begins with two versions of the partisan oath and continues with personal accounts of initiation into partisan warfare. Part Three, "Partisan Society," consists of memoirs written by non-Jewish Russian commanders and deals with the sociological structure of partisan life, including civilian camps guarded by such partisans. It also contains rare insights into two aspects of the underground: the role of women and the role of media (partisan filmmaking). Part Four, "Partisan Warfare," is composed of straightforward accounts of battle conditions and missions against the Germans. It also contains accounts of partisan warfare in the ghettos of Kovna (Lithuania) and Odessa (USSR). The book concludes with summary statements about Jews awarded medals of honor from the government written by L. Singer and a stirring conclusion by the great Russian writer and journalist Ilya Ehrenburg.

The book also contains maps of the region, several partisan documents, organizational charts of the partisan command, and the structure of an individual partisan group, as well as a sources section, a glossary, and an annotated bibliography on Jewish resistance and related topics. The order of articles has been rearranged for this volume.

This collection is both a literary document and an historical account. When these memoirs first appeared, they were used for propaganda, hence the somewhat "heroic" style of writing. Today these same memoirs are historical documents. I have tried, both in my introduction and in my notes, to point out any errors and to explain any excesses in the text. Corroborated by interviews with partisan survivors in America, Canada and Israel, this book is not exaggeration but, in fact, only touches the surface of heroism that took place during the war among Jewish partisans. I have attempted to be objective. I do not claim to be detached.

PREFACE TO THE FOURTH EDITION

I am very happy that Academic Studies Press has decided to come out with a new edition of my book. I would like to thank the editors and staff, Alessandra Anzani, Kira Nemirovsky, and Matthew Charlton. It was wonderful to finally have a great support group. Writing is so solitary.

Sadly, most of the partisans in this book have died, but I am happy I got them on tape, so to speak. Still, there are dozens of interviews at Yad Vashem in Jerusalem, at the US Holocaust Memorial Museum, and in archives in Europe where more stories await to be transcribed and translated. Many of these interviews are in Yiddish, Hebrew or Russian. There should have been more visual interviews, but the technology for that came too late—most of the men had died. The female partisans and survivors had a better chance of visual transcription.

Recent research has also begun to delve into the per¬petrators of the Shoah, those who went after Jews, Gypsies, and partisans. A recent example is the Netflix documentary *Einsatzgruppen*[1], as well as other films on Hitler and World War II. The *Einsatz* commandos were special killing squads who followed the German Army into the conquered Soviet territory in June 1941 in Operation Barbarossa after Hitler broke the Molotov-Stalin Pact and invaded Poland and Ukraine.

In this documentary, such prominent Holocaust scholars as Christopher Browning, Martin Dean, Jurgen Matthaus, and Christian Ingra described horrific tales of how the killings affected the SS and their collaborators—Ukrainian, Lithuanian, Latvian and other conquered groups. It cannot have been easy to shoot face-to-face these Jewish women and children—which, by the way, included my two sisters and twenty-five members of my family.

---

1   *Einsatzgruppen*: The Nazi Death Squads. Directed by Michaël Prazan, 2009.

So, while the tales are grim, I urge you to read on and experience the bravery and courage of these fighters who took revenge against the fascist enemy. May their memory be a blessing.

I write this on Tisha B'Av, the ninth day of Av, as we Jews memorialize the saddest day of the year for us—the destruction of the First and Second Temple in Jerusalem, as well as the Shoah, and all of the other ways the world tried to destroy us. And yet, through it all, we have survived.

Jack Nusan Porter
Newtonville, Mass.
Tisha B'Av, July 29, 2020

Introduction to the Original
1948 Russian Edition

This book, *Partisan Brotherhood*, offered for the reader's attention, tells of the struggle of the Soviet people during the Great War for the Fatherland which our country fought against fascist Germany. This was a war engaged in behind enemy lines, in territories temporarily conquered by Hitler's soldiers.

Basically, *Partisan Brotherhood* contains material about the military activities of Jewish partisans, and was collected by the Jewish Anti-Fascist Committee of the USSR. The collection consists of memoirs of former commanders and commissars of partisan units as well as testimonies written by Soviet writers. They tell of various events in the "partisan war" and give individual profiles of partisan heroes and heroines. Despite its varied sources, *Partisan Brotherhood* is a unified work. All the accounts included in this book are concerned with a single subject: namely, the friendship and unity of the Soviet people, a friendship which took shape at the very beginning of the 1917 October Revolution, was strengthened during the terrible days of the Civil War following the revolution, and which found its fullest expression in the Great War for the Fatherland against the German conquerors.

At the start of the war, during the first difficult days for our country, Comrade Stalin, in his historic Moscow speech of November 6, 1941, at a gathering of the Council of Workers Delegates, said:

> *The Germans built their war plans on the instability of the Soviet rear guard, and on the assumption that, following the first failure of the Red Army, conflict would break out between the workers and the farmers, and a division would take place among the peoples of the USSR. They thought that rebellion would spread and that the state would be split into factions. This would have facilitated the advance of the German conquerors up to the Ural Mountain passes. But*

the Germans made a grave error! The failures of the Red Army did not weaken, on the contrary, they strengthened the bond between the workers and the farmers, and intensified the friendship among the peoples of the USSR. Furthermore, they transformed the family of the peoples of the USSR into one strong camp which supported its Red Army and Red Navy with devotion.

The unity of the Soviet people was expressed with extraordinary courage during the war against the Nazis. Soviet people from all nationalities fought in partisan units, as well as within the lines of the Red Army. Those Soviet patriots who were left in territory conquered by the enemy, and who were able to take up arms, joined the partisans and fought bravely and devotedly for the honor, freedom and independence of their homeland. In the front lines, these "avengers of the people" included, together with the Russians: Ukrainians, Byelorussians, Jews, Georgians (Gruziny), Armenians, Latvians, Uzbeks, and members of other Soviet nationalities. All of them saw themselves as belonging to a single fighting partisan force.

These "avengers of the people" fought against the enemy and presented a model of brotherhood and friendship, of spiritual and ideological unity, among people who felt themselves as equals within their Soviet homeland. The struggle of the Jewish partisans against the Nazis is presented in this book as part of the overall struggle of all of the Soviet people, who rose as one to defend their country.

Shoulder-to-shoulder with partisans of other nationalities, the Jewish partisans fought against the Germans. They blew up bridges, destroyed military transports, wiped out reinforcements of the German Army, killed its officers and soldiers, and, with unyielding hatred, swept away the Nazi filth.

This book reveals only a few pages of the partisan struggle of the Soviet people. In this close-knit Soviet family, the Soviet Jews were loyal members, helping to protect the achievements of the Socialist Revolution.

October 9, 1948

Editor's Note

It is important to make a few comments regarding the style and rhetoric of this introduction. There is no question that the Soviet people engaged in a heroic struggle against the Nazis. They fought bravely and endured great losses; however, the Soviet peoples were not always the "close-knit family" they are portrayed as; they did not always present a "model of brotherhood and friendship, of spiritual and ideological unity." This was especially true during the early phases of the war when some Soviet nationalities, the Ukrainians and Latvians, for example, openly welcomed the Nazis, hoping that a German victory would liberate them from Soviet rule. However, the German occupation was often so brutal that it pushed these nationalities back into the waiting arms of the USSR. The role of the Jews within the partisan and regular army units is accurate; Jews placed fourth in the number of participants within these units, behind the Russians, Ukrainians, and Byelorussians. Despite occasional anti-Semitism within the partisan groups, Jews did play a significant role in the war. To demonstrate this fact is the true intent of this book, despite the rhetoric that appears.

ПАРТИЗАНСКАЯ
ДРУЖБА

ВОСПОМИНАНИЯ О БОЕВЫХ
ДЕЛАХ ПАРТИЗАН-ЕВРЕЕВ,
УЧАСТНИКОВ ВЕЛИКОЙ
ОТЕЧЕСТВЕННОЙ ВОЙНЫ

ОГИЗ
Государственное издательство «Дер Эмес»
Москва 1948

Facsimile of Russian original of the
book, Partizanskaya Druzhba
Source: Lenin Library-Moscow Taken
from microfilm copy

СОДЕРЖАНИЕ

★

Facsimile of Russian original Table of Contents
of the book, Partizanskaya Druzhba

INTRODUCTION:
JEWISH RESISTANCE IN THE SOVIET UNION

Jack Nusan Porter

The Myth of Jewish Cowardice

World War II cost four trillion dollars and the lives of over fifty million men, women and children, including not only six million Jews, but also eight million Chinese and twenty million Russians![1] When scholars attempt to describe such a Holocaust, words often fail.

There are many myths, falsehoods, and half-truths still associated with the Holocaust. One of the most controversial of these is that the Jews were "cowards" and that they walked passively to their deaths like "sheep to slaughter," to use a popular and by now tiresome phrase. The confusion, the accusations, the ambivalences still exist, especially among young people.

William Helmreich, a sociologist at City College of New York (CCNY), recently completed a preliminary study of forty-two Jewish undergraduates from several Eastern universities and found that the Holocaust was a subject very much on the minds of these students. Their reactions to the behavior of European Jews during the war are expressed in the following quotes:[2]

> *How did the Jews let themselves be led to the camps? Why didn't they fight back? If I was going to a camp, I think I would have fought back and refused to go.*
>
> — a 20-year-old junior at CCNY

> *The Jews sort of accepted it and went off to the concentration camps like sheep.*
>
> — an 18-year-old freshman at Yale

> *Why didn't they fight? Some did, but not enough. No one really had the courage to stand up. Not even the American Jews.*
>
> — a 19-year-old sophomore at Brooklyn College

*European Jews made the mistake of believing so strongly
in their religion that they could not see beyond it. And so they
behaved like a bunch of ...*

— a 20-year-old senior at Yale

The question of cowardice is a value-laden one and a very
difficult one to answer. The quotes above clearly reflect a
generation of young people who cannot empathize with
a situation that remains imponderable even to those who
experienced it, even those who did fight back. Soon after the
Eichmann trial in 1961 (which most of these undergraduates
may not even remember), a number of books and articles
appeared. Some blamed the victims; some defended them.
Today, fifteen years later, the debate is still not settled. The
victims are still being judged as cowards, even though more
and more research has appeared to make this debate futile.

Raul Hilberg, in his important book *The Destruction of the
European Jews*, notes an almost complete lack of resistance
on the part of the Jews.[3] Social historian Hannah Arendt,
in her book *Eichmann in Jerusalem*, has a theory of complicity, that the Jews aided the Nazis in their own destruction.
Furthermore, she describes Jewish resistance as "pitifully
small, incredibly weak, and essentially harmless."[4] Psychiatrist
Bruno Bettelheim also agrees with the "complicity theory"
and, in his book *The Informed Heart*, almost pleadingly asks:
"Did no one of those destined to die fight back? ... Only a
very few did."[5]

Ruth Kunzer, in a very perceptive piece on the literature
of the Holocaust, has this to say in response to Bettelheim,
Arendt and Hilberg:

*[Bettelheim's] thesis, as fashionable today as Arendt's on the
failure of thousands of methodically starved, systematically
brutalized and dehumanized human beings to revolt without
weapons and cooperation from the outside, suffers, in George
Steiner's perceptive words, 'from a failure of imagining.'*[6]

This "failure of imagination" is a failure to understand
that the real question is not why there was so little revolt,
but why, amidst the death and the destruction, there was
so much resistance. On reason why the myths and obfusca-
tions are perpetuated is because the actual role of the Jews

was suppressed, especially by the Russians and Ukrainians. Not only was Jewish participation in the resistance and the Russian army suppressed, but it was often portrayed as collaboration with the Nazis.[7] That is why this book, when it appeared, was so important — and why it, too, was suppressed.

It is also interesting to note that Arendt, Bettelheim and Hilberg are all German or Austrian Jews. Russian or Polish Jews were rarely prone to label themselves and their compatriots "cowards." Jewish theologian Eliezer Berkovits explains such accusations as examples of Jews alienated from Judaism who therefore defame the martyrs of their people in order to find themselves a more emotionally comfortable spot in the midst of a disintegrating Western society.[8] In other words, when such Jewish scholars as the three mentioned above talk of "cowardly victims," or of a "Jewish death instinct," or of "Jewish complicity in their own deaths," they in essence find an ingenious way out of facing a bitter truth: Auschwitz ushered in a final chapter in the moral disintegration of Western civilization. For these Western intellectuals, devoted as they were to the ideals of Western (and German) rationalism, this dissonance is too much to handle. So they find a scapegoat — the Jew — but, in reality, the label is turned inward because *they*, too, are Jews.

Bettelheim has written that the resisters were "very few" in number, and Arendt called Jewish resistance "pitifully small" and "essentially harmless."

Yet it was these "very few" who in the Warsaw Ghetto held of SS General Jürgen Stroop and his command of 1,000 SS-tank grenadiers, 1,000 men of the SS-Cavalry, two units of artillery, one unit of army engineers, plus armed units of the Latvian and Lithuanian SS, for nearly four months from April 19, 1943, to late August, 1943, with only a few rifles, a handful of grenades, and numerous homemade "Molotov cocktails."

It was the "essentially harmless" nature of Jewish resistance that forced even Goebbels to admit that "now we know what Jews can do if they have arms"[9] and in a letter to Reichskommissar Lohse in Riga, Wehrmachtkommissar Bremmer, on November 20, 1941, emphasized that:

> *... the Jewish population is in the forefront of propaganda, resistance, and sabotage against the Germans in Byelorussia.*
>
> *... in the cities of White Russia the Jews constitute the largest part of the population and the driving force of the resistance movement ... and everywhere, where reports about sabotage, incitement of the population, resistance, etc. have forced us to take measures, Jews were found to be the originators and instigators, and in most instances, even the perpetrators.*[10]

In another report to Reichkommissar Lohse, on August 31, 1942, Generalkommissar Wilhelm Lube, the *Gauleiter* (administrator) of White Russia (Byelorussia), made similar remarks:

> *In all the clashes with the partisans in White Russia, it has become clear that, both in the general commissariate territory which was previously part of Poland and that which was Russian, the Jews — along with the Polish rebel movement in the west and the forces of the Red Army in the east — have been the main leaders of the partisan movement.*[11]

We thus have documented proof that the Germans were both amazed and disturbed about armed Jews. In fact, in some ways the Germans were also *delighted* because Jewish resistance would clear the Nazi conscience of killing "innocent civilians" while giving them the excuse to accelerate their program of "solving the Jewish problem."

There were, however, many forms of resistance, and resistance took place under many guises and within different circumstances. It was both armed and unarmed, organized and disorganized, planned and spontaneous, passive and active, offensive and defensive, as well as moral, spiritual and psychological — and each form involved risk of life.

Passive resistance, known as the "white resistance" took many forms: escaping from ghettos, writing a diary, conducting Hebrew classes, praying, singing Jewish songs, studying the Bible, wearing one's *payis* (earlocks) and beard publicly, and carrying on a Jewish cultural and artistic life. Under freedom these acts are taken for granted, but living in the hell of Europe, these same acts were raised to the level of heroism.

Many people refuse to acknowledge the many forms of resistance. For example, there exists a special type of resistance based on a religious or moral principle (such as a belief in nonviolence) in which one could not and would not engage in armed resistance, preferring instead to suffer, or even to die, rather than comply with the demands of the enemy. The father and mother who walked calmly to their deaths, hand-in-hand with their little children, all the while believing in God's trust, in *Kiddush ha-shem* (the holiness of martyrdom), but up to the end, still maintaining *Kiddush ha-hayyim* (the sanctification of life) — their family together, their spiritual belief intact — this, too, was a heroic act.[12]

However, people have become hardened from watching too much violence and too many Westerns and war movies. They wish to hear only of *armed* resistance, the only *real* kind of resistance to them. Armed resistance took place on four major "fronts."

Ghetto Revolts

There were armed revolts within the major Jewish ghettos of Europe: Warsaw, Vilna, Bialystok, Lachwa, Minsk, Czestochowa, Slonim, Kleck, Bedzin, Neswizh, Braslaw, Glubokoe, and several other places. We know of organized Jewish undergrounds in Kovna (Kaunas, Lithuania), Cracow, Riga, Rome, Odessa, Paris, and Brussels, as well as throughout Czechoslovakia, Hungary, Italy, France, Belgium, Holland, Greece, and Poland.

Not all were able to carry out their plans — some groups were discovered and killed by the Nazis before they could accomplish their tasks. The urban underground and the armed revolts were essentially an extension of the general partisan movement — in this case, the partisans can be seen as *urban* guerrillas instead of *rural* guerrillas. There was a sink between them but quite often, and the Warsaw Ghetto uprising of 1943 was a tragic example: the Jewish rebels were isolated from the general non-Jewish resistance.

But generalizations about Jewish-Gentile animosity within the partisan movement cannot be made. An investigation of the particular circumstances surrounding each case must be undertaken. What held true in Warsaw between Polish and Jewish resistance groups would not apply to Paris, for example, where there was a great deal more cooperation. In Paris, Jewish underground groups managed to ambush and murder several high-ranking German officers; and in Cracow, Poland, they succeeded in blowing up a café where several German officials were killed. One could go into more detail about the uprisings in the Jewish ghettos, but many books have been written on the subject, and I direct the reader to them. (See the bibliography.) However, one final example of "urban partisans" must be mentioned.

There was even Jewish resistance within Berlin itself. Yuri Suhl, in his anthology *They Fought Back: The Story of Jewish Resistance in Nazi Europe*, devotes an entire chapter to the Herbert Baum Group, a youthful bank of thirty German Jews (nearly all of them were about the age of 22), who conducted underground acts of rebellion during the years 1937-1942. They were eventually infiltrated, discovered, and executed, and a monument to them stands in the Weissensee Cemetery in East Berlin today.[13]

Uprisings in the Concentration Camps

A second stage of resistance took place within the extermination camps themselves. Unlike the partisan resistance in the forests, resistance in the "death camps" and within the sealed-off Jewish ghettos were, in the words of Erich Goldhagen, a revolt on death row, a last-gasp effort against eventual extermination. There was no hope for success in overcoming the enemy and little in even surviving the revolt. Still, organized uprisings took place in the concentration camps of Auschwitz, Treblinka, Sobibor and Koldczewo, in the Camp at Janowska Street in Lvov (Lemberg, Poland), and in several other smaller camps.

One could say that to survive in these amps at all could be considered an act of resistance. However, in addition to the man acts of passive (spiritual and psychological) resistance, there were many acts of active Jewish courage. Sobibor is a good example. There, on October 14, 1943, a revolt took place that involved 350 people. Ten SS men were killed, and thirty-eight Ukrainian guards were either killed or wounded.

About 400 to 600 inmates escaped; nearly half of them died in the mined fields surrounding the camp, but the rest were able to survive and enter the forest to join the partisan groups already there.

Among the leaders of the Auschwitz underground which blew up a crematoria during the final das of the war were Jozef Cyrankiewicz, later to become Premier of Poland, and a young Jewish woman, Rosa Robota — one of many Jewish women who played an essential, though limited, role in the Jewish resistance.[14]

Jewish Participation in Allied Military Forces

Resistance in the ghettos and in the concentration camps were two relatively minor and ineffectual staging areas. Many more times effective, of course, was the Jewish role in national military forces and in the partisan groups which were often absorbed into the regular army units as the war continued. Wherever the Jews were permitted to take part in the general struggle within their own national armed forces, they engaged in them in great numbers.

In the allied regular armies and navies, some one and a half million Jewish solders and officers took part. Even the tiny Palestinian Jewish community contributed 26,000 soldiers to the allied cause. In the United States alone, a total of 550,000 Jews took part; of these, more than 1,000 fell in battle, and another 10,000 died of wounds. Great Britain contributed 62,000 Jews to the British Army — in addition to some 25,000 from other parts of the British Commonwealth, with Canada contributing 17,000 Jews in its army.[15]

As for Eastern Europe, according to official sources, slightly over 32,000 Jews fell in battle in the first few days of the September, 1939 *Blitzkrieg* — about 15 percent of the total casualties; and 61,000 Jews were taken prisoner — about 14 percent of the total of 420,000 Polish soldiers taken prisoner, which in turn was 52 percent of the total number of 800,000 Polish armed forces. Overall, some 150,000 Jews were in active service in the Polish army at the outbreak of the war.

In the Soviet Union, it is estimated that more than half a million Jews fought in the Red Army. Many of them fell in battle, while more than 100,000 were decorated for valor and devotion to duty. More than one hundred Jews (figures range from 105 to 147) were named "Hero of the Soviet Union," one of the highest designations.[16] Abraham H. Foxman, in his chapter on Jewish resistance in the excellent textbook *The Jewish Catastrophe in Europe*, cites two examples.

A Russian-Jewish lieutenant, Moshe Berkovitch, was twice awarded the "Order of the Red Star" for heroism. In hand-to-hand combat, he killed three German soldiers with his bayonet, choked two with his bare hands, and brought back alive a German officer as prisoner. And one of the greatest acts of courage was undertaken by three Jewish soldiers (Papernik, Ocheret, and Rimsky), all "Heroes of the Soviet Union," who tied bundles of hand-grenades around their bodies and threw themselves under advancing German tanks, one of many desperate attempts to repulse the Germans in the early stages of fighting on the Russian front.[17]

Jews also participated in the national armies of France, Greece and other occupied countries. Palestine not only contributed officers, soldiers, and doctors to the Allied forces, but also engaged in numerous, though ineffective, underground activities. Hannah Senesh was an example of a *halutza* (Israeli pioneer) who died at the hands of the Nazis. Palestinian underground members were also active in the illegal immigration to Israel of European refugees both during and after the war.[18]

Jewish Participation in the Partisan Movement

It was among the partisans that the Jews could be most effective, not only in engaging the Germans but in saving families and individuals from the embattled ghettos. Escape from the ghettos and the concentration camps led directly to joining forces in the forests, though, as will be shown, most Jewish undergrounds decided to stay within the ghetto and not abandon their fellow Jews until the very last minute. Jewish participation as partisans took place in every country that had a resistance movement. This introduction, however, will deal mainly with resistance in the Soviet Union, which ha the largest partisan organization in the war and the largest number of Jewish partisans.

In partisan warfare on Soviet, Polish, Slovak, Yugoslavian, French, Greek, Belgian, Dutch, Bulgarian, and Italian territory, one estimate of over 100,000 Jewish fighters has been made, but his figure is greatly exaggerated.[19] A closer approximation to the truth is a maximum of 50,000, with 25,000 Jewish partisans in the Soviet Union; 10,000 in Poland; 10,000 in France, Holland and Belgium; 2,000 in Yugoslavia; 2,500 in Slovakia; and over 1,000 in Greece, Italy, and Bulgaria. It is still an impressive figure and could go slightly higher, given the fact that the Jewish identity of some partisans was never made known to their comrades or commanders. The Jewish role should not be exaggerated, but neither should it be underestimated or disparaged.

Military warfare is only one aspect of resistance movements; other actions include clandestine political organization, intelligence gathering, propaganda and proselytizing campaigns, and diplomatic efforts to obtain outside assistance. Partisan warfare during World War II was geared for small-scale ground combat operations designed more to harass the enemy than to destroy him. Guerrillas can operate in almost any environment — deep in tropical jungles, within highly urbanized centers, or in dense forests and mountains. Some of the most effective partisan action of the war took place in the mountainous regions of Yugoslavia, Italy, and Greece and within the heavily forested and marshy regions of western Russia, the Ukraine, and Byelorussia.

Partisan warfare is rarely decisive in and by itself — its major goal is to badger and slow down the enemy and to engage in counter-propaganda and intimidation until regular army units are strong enough to engage the opponent. Normally, guerrilla warfare is employed by societies and groups too weak to defend themselves in open combat, but major combatants have often supplemented their conventional military encounters with elaborate guerrilla campaigns. This was the case especially among Russian partisans.[20]

Partisan organizations tend to be highly flexible and decentralized, and their tactics are usually confined to small-scale, hit-and-run forays against supply lines, police and military installations, small outposts, fuel depots, railroad lines, and other poorly defended targets. Because of their small size and limited military objectives, guerrilla units are often able to avoid open engagements with conventional armed forces and can thus occupy a disproportionate share of the adversary's military strength. In any study of resistance, the social and political context must be taken into account along with the usual military analysis.

Partisan Warfare in the Soviet Union

The Soviet partisan movement was established in the wake of the German invasion of the USSR on June 22, 1941 (Operation Barbarossa) and was, in both conception and scope, the greatest irregular resistance movement in the history of warfare.[21] It combined all the classic elements of resistance movements of the past with modern means of communication, transportation and modern weapons and, at its peak, involved a far greater number of people than had ever before been drawn into an irregular force. The exact total strength of the Soviet partisan movement will never be known, but the best evidence indicates that it reached a total of 30,000 men by January 1, 1942, rose to 150,000 by the summer of 1942, to 200,000 by the summer of 1943, and then declined slightly to 150,000 or 175,000 by June 1944 as partisan territory was retaken by Soviet forces. The partisan turnover resulting from casualties, sickness and desertions over a three-year period brought the total number who participated in the Soviet movement to about 400,000 or 500,000. These figures include only the partisans enrolled in regular, permanently organized combat units. They do *not* include a host of agents, saboteurs, demolition teams, as well as doctors, nurses, cooks and other support personnel. Of the former, some operated independently and, at other times worked together with the combat detachments.[22]

Reuben Ainsztein maintains that at least 20,000, and possibly 25,000, Jews took part in the Soviet movement. He notes that this is an impressive figure when calculated on a population basis in comparison to other Soviet nationalities and, furthermore, when one takes into account the fact that the Soviet partisan movement became an integrating force capable of absorbing tens of thousands of fighters in the occupied territories *only after the Nazis had destroyed most of the Jews of Eastern Europe.*[23]

In order to explain this phenomenon better, it would be beneficial to describe the stages the partisan movement underwent and the shifts in composition among its fighters.[24]

The movement was in a constant state of flux. In its first stage, almost immediately after the Germans attacked Russia, that is, in June 1941, a partisan movement was established behind German lines, partly through the independent activity of Communist party members, red Army officers, and Soviet noncommissioned officers. It depended heavily on party members, who comprised as much as 80 percent of individual units, while units averaging between 25 and 40 percent Communist party membership were not unusual. Up until the end of 1941 and continuing until the spring of 1942, the partisan movement could be characterized as a volunteer organization. The early bands were quite small; morale was low; leadership, too often political, left a great deal to be desired; and, consequently, little impact was made on the German army. Though they did not materially hinder the German offensive operations, they did make it difficult for the smooth functioning of the German occupation to take place, and they were successful, at least in some areas of Byelorussia and the Ukraine, in gaining the passive support of the inhabitants, while throwing considerable doubt into the minds of others as to the wisdom of collaborating with or supporting the Nazis. The number of Jews joining the partisans during this stage was small and insignificant.

The second major stage occurred in the spring of 1942 when the partisans began drafting men. The percentage of Communist party membership declined rapidly, though members were still quite important as instruments of Soviet control, as political officers (*politruks*) and as commissars. The number of Red Army stragglers increased greatly and, together with the drafting of peasants, would make these two groups account for about 80 percent of the total strength of the movement. The Central Partisan Staff was created on May 30, 1942, and Soviet officers were parachuted behind German lines to organize the growing number of partisans. Forming part of Stalin's Supreme Headquarters, this central staff would take another year or so to coordinate and impose a centralized system of control and command over the immense territory stretching from the front lines westward to Poland.

Most of the Jews who became partisans did so in 1942 and in the first half of 1943. Though the Germans were still very powerful and the partisans were still fighting for a foothold, morale was high. The partisan movement had come to life. The influx of Red Army officers and stragglers (some of whom had been fighting in small groups since July and August 1941) professionalized the partisans to a great degree. The draft gained momentum and continued until 1944. The most decisive and discernible shift followed the great losses the Germans suffered during their first encounter with the notorious Russian winter of December 1941 and January 1942, which weakened the underclothed Germans until, like a monstrous elephant attacked by jackals, the German army bogged down to wait for the warmth of spring.

The last stage of the partisan movement was also the turning point of the war: the Battle of Kursk in July 1943. From this point on, the Russians were on the offensive, and, after two brutal years of fighting, the Germans were pulling back. In August and September of 1943, following the failure of the *Wehrmacht* attempt to regain the offensive in their ill-starred "Operation Zitadelle," the Red Army launched a general assault of great force, and, at the same time, the partisans mounted their first large-scale offensive against the enemy's rear. Taken *in toto*, the partisan role in this offensive was not completely effective according to one analysis, but on the fact of it, it seemed highly successful.[25] More than 20,000 demolitions were set off on the railway lines behind the German's Army Group Center which bore the brunt of the Soviet attack. There was also extensive sabotage of railroad installations, highways, ammunition and gas depots, and signal facilities, plus an intensive propaganda and terror campaign that resulted in widespread defection among German native auxiliary troops and police.

At the end of 1943 until the end of the war, as a result of the Red Army's victories and the massive supply of arms by the Byelorussian and Ukrainian partisan staffs, it became relatively easy to join the partisans, but by then there were hardly any Jews left to take advantage of these changed circumstances.[26] Furthermore, the composition of the ranks had changed. In 1943 there was a new wave of volunteers. Many of these people were of doubtful quality; military and political collaborators plus managers and professional people who had tried to carry out their peacetime occupations under German occupation. Others either decided "to get on the bandwagon" or joined because they found life between the partisans and the Germans intolerable. The exact number of such people cannot be estimated, but it is likely that, especially in the Ukraine and in Lithuania, they became a significant element. Combined with the peasants who were drafted earlier in the spring of 1942, these new elements made discipline even more difficult. It was lucky that, by this time, the Russian army was on the offensive and the Germans were being turned back. Consequently, the ineffectiveness of the partisans at this stage was not a crucial factor in the outcome of the war.

Composition of the Soviet Partisan Movement

The major distinctive component groups within the partisan movement were the peasants, the Red Army stragglers, and the escaped POWs, all three of which comprised the largest segment of the ranks; these were followed by the urban continent, the intelligentsia, Communist party members, collaborators, and, finally, women.[27] The Jews fell within the categories of the urban contingent and the intelligentsia, with a smaller number being Red Army soldiers.

The Peasants

The peasants probably furnished between 40 and 60 percent of the total partisan recruits, and virtually all of them were drafted, many against their will. Since the partisans were able to move freely throughout most of the rural districts, it was relatively easy to enter the villages, select the men, and march them off as partisans. Though they wanted to be neutral, the peasants saw no other choice but to join the partisans, especially after the Germans began relinquishing their hold on the occupied territories. They remained a distinct group — passive, unenthusiastic, and untrustworthy. They were practical-minded opportunists with one overwhelming desire: to have the collective farm system abolished. Thus, at the beginning of the war, they were willing to tolerate the German regime if they could extract economic advantage from it. They disliked turning over their produce to the Germans, but they liked even less turning it over to both the Germans and the partisans. They were caught in a dilemma between German brutality, on the one hand, and Russian collectivization, on the other.

The Urban Contingent

While there were very few peasants who were convinced Communists, the urban working population was, on the other hand, strongly influenced by Communism. The Soviet program of industrialization had impressed the workers. Nevertheless, there were certain urban classes, such as the formerly rich and other *déclassé bourgeoise*, who were hidden sympathizers with the Nazis.

It is impossible to estimate the number that left the urban areas to join the partisans. Their numbers were small in relation to those of the peasants and former Red Army soldiers. Generally speaking, though, the urban contingents were sympathetic to the partisans.

The Intelligentsia

The term as used here refers less to the upper intelligentsia (professors, writers, editors, journalists), most of whom were evacuated and who, in any case, were few in number, than to the broad, lower reaches of the class (local doctors, teachers, administrators, and the subprofessional people — clerks, bookkeepers, and others). These men and women, because they thought in terms of their careers, were likely to believe that they had to choose one side or the other. From the partisan's point of view, they were valuable additions to the units. Their skills were useful; they were persons whose attitudes generally influenced others; and the Germans would in turn be deprived of their talents. A good many Jews, especially doctors, came out of these ranks.

The intelligentsia formed a sizable group in the early stages of the partisan movement, comprising most of the officer contingent and a segment of the rank and file as well. As the movement grew, this group declined in number, although it remained an important element in the partisans throughout the war.

Red Army Fighters and Soviet POWs

The German army took over three million prisoners in the first six months of the war; this figure grew to five million by the end of the war. Of these, about two million died in the POW camps. If, as can probably be estimated, one in ten avoided capture, then the total would come to more than 300,000 stragglers. To this, one must add the thousands more that the Germans released, chiefly Ukrainian and others who were considered anti-Communist. Wretched POW conditions forced many thousands more to try to save their lives by escaping. By January 1942, these former Soviet soldiers at large in the occupied territory probably totaled between 300,000 and 400,000.

The massive upswing of the partisan movement which followed the successful Soviet winter offensive of 1941-42 brought thousands of former army men into the movement until, by the summer of 1942, they formed the largest single increment. In July 1942, at the onset of the second stage, the Germans estimated that they made up 60 percent of the total partisan strength. These men became the backbone of the partisan movement. They had military training and experience; for the most part, they had neither family nor property ties in the occupied territory; they had definite moral and legal obligations to the Soviet Union; and their previous experiences in the POW camps led them to prefer partisan activity to life under the German occupation.

Communist Party Members

As was mentioned earlier, during the first stage of fighting, the partisans were overwhelmingly composed of Communist Party members. After the spring of 1942, when drafting recruits began on a mass scale, the Party contingent dropped sharply in relative numbers. The Party men, however, remained an elite group in the partisan movement throughout the war and were the most influential. At the same time, the Party segment was important chiefly as an instrument of

Soviet control, especially as political advisors and ideological indoctrinators. There is no indication that Party members acted on their own as an independent, spontaneous, creative, guiding force. Because of strict Party discipline, such independent action was out of the question.

Collaborators

The taint of collaboration fell on a great many people in the occupied areas. By definition, anyone who did not actively fight the Germans was capable of being suspected of at least being a passive collaborator. To nearly everyone, then, participation in the partisan movement was valuable as an alibi, a means of avoiding persecution as a collaborator. It gave one the proper credentials, but also gave credence to the belief that, at least in the final years of the war, all partisan groups were a crew of former collaborators, hiding in the woods in order to save their skins and putting up a feeble show of resistance.

The most significant group of collaborators were former policemen, army auxiliaries, and members of German-organized indigenous military units. These men had acted as the main antipartisan forces in the past. Estimates of their numbers ranged from 1800,000 to 2,000,000. Once it became clear that Russia was winning the war, the situation of these people became desperate. The partisans, in order to complete their demoralization, promised amnesty to all who would desert and join them. These efforts were very successful. Occasionally, entire collaborator units would desert *en masse*. Every German defeat, every German withdrawal, led to more desertions. And, in general, the promised amnesty was honored. The collaborators made useful recruits; they had military experience; they knew the terrain well; and they had important strategic and military information. By mid-1943, when the collaborators were prepared to desert in significant numbers, manpower was no longer a problem for the partisans. In the last year of the war, these men composed between 10 and 20 percent of the movement.

Women Partisans

Women made significant contributions in all areas of rebellion against the Nazis — in the ghettos, concentration camps and forests, and as support personnel in the regular armies. To the Germans, who summed up their conception of the role of women in society with the slogan *Kirche, Kueche, und Kinder* (church, kitchen, and children), the enlistment of women for combat duty was an outright abomination (although they were used for intelligence gathering in occupied zones). The Soviet government, as well as many other European states, was quite active, however, in recruiting women in various aspects of the armed forces. The USSR, moreover, publicized the participation of its women in partisan activity as evidence of superior dedication and resolution. Furthermore, with the loss of so many men, women were crucial in many areas of defense.

In almost every partisan detachment in the Soviet Union, there were some women members, although they usually numbered no more than 2 or 3 percent of the total unit and hardly ever more than 5 percent. They were used chiefly as scouts and intelligence agents. Soviet intelligence tended to rely heavily on women agents, particularly in partisan-infested territory where women made the best agents, since men of military age were liable to arrest on sight.

Some of the women had training as radio operators and nurses, and a large proportion of the doctors assigned to the partisan units were women. The doctors had officer status. Sometimes the women were assigned to combat missions along with the men, but it appears that, aside from intelligence missions, they were more often used as medical personnel, cooks and washerwomen.

Sexism abounded within the partisan ranks. Women served in service capacities in the majority of cases, and even for those women who did go out on missions to either engage the enemy or to blow up bridges, lay mines along train tracks, or gather food and clothing from local peasants, there were many times that the male partisans would ask the female partisans to wash the dishes or mend the socks after returning to the base camp! Then, as now, women had "double-duty" and were first seen as *women*, not as soldiers.

Few women were drafted. For the most part, they were volunteers, motivated by either political convictions (some were staunch Communists), a desire for adventure, or the wish to achieve some form of personal achievement in a society where satisfying personal success outside of the role of mother and wife was limited. Some women "draftees" were trained in espionage or radio communication on the Soviet side of the front, but these were usually Komsomol Youth members and were therefore politically reliable.

Earl Ziemke, in his chapter on the "Composition and Morale of the Partisan Movement" in John A. Armstrong (ed.) *Soviet Partisans in World War II*, maintains that the principal reason for including women in nearly every partisan detachment was that "a woman became one of the prerequisites of every major partisan officer ... along with his Nagan pistol and leather windbreaker!"[28] It was not unusual for the officers, from the brigade commander down to the battalion commanders, to "marry" the women enlisted in their unit. Needless to say, their wives — and most of them had wives who were worried sick over them — rarely knew of those affairs. The "lowly" rank-and-file partisans had to contend themselves with less convenient arrangements.

This resulted in a cynical attitude toward the women in the partisan unit. Jealously was common. Fights, some even leading to death, often broke out over the "possession" of a woman. Women became the property of the commanders, which by implication gave them officer status, and thus the commander's "wife" often lorded over the other women and the low-ranking men. This led to trouble.

For example, if the commander's wife wanted a blanket that belonged to another man's woman, she could incite a fight, and if that man rushed to his lover's defense, it could lead to insubordination and the man being shot — especially if the commander happened to be very drunk at the time.

In conclusion, one cannot minimize the heroic efforts of many women during the war. The Germans, though sexists in the extreme, nevertheless were quite happy to capture a woman partisan, because they were often exceptionally well informed and had valuable military information. Many a woman died a courageous and painful death rather than divulge her secrets.

The Organization of the Partisan Group

The popular image of the partisan unit is a small isolated group hiding in the forest or jungle. Actually, the partisan movement became highly complex. Starting with the Central Staff of the Partisan Movement in Moscow with its liaison officer to the Supreme Command of the Red Army, it contained subdivisions for political security, propaganda, cryptography, signal corps, cartography, finance, and transportation. From there it connected to various territorial command posts and on to operations groups in the enemy rear.

These operations groups were also composed of various subsections: security, signal corps, medical corps, propaganda, and finance. Operations groups had military subunits as well, which I will describe shortly, but they also had their political counterpart, the Area or Party Center, in which Communist Party work was carried out under the aegis of the Commissar. These would include Party "extension" work, illegal press, rumormongering, and various liaisons with the partisans. Under each Party or Area Center would be one or more District Committees, which in turn would contain one or more Party Cells and Blocks. The political Commissar was sometimes more powerful than the military Chief of Staff. At times, one man held both positions. (See appendix for charts.)

The basic fighting unit of the partisans was the *otryad* (detachment) which consisted of anywhere from 50 to 400 personnel each (counting actual fighters plus supporting troops). The *otryad* was further broken down into smaller units — platoons and companies, depending on the size of the *otryad*. In the spring of 1942, the partisans grew to the point where the detachments combined into brigades (*brigada*); that is, three, four or more *otryads* made up one *brigada*, and within each *otryad* could be from two to eight platoons. Later in the war, in 1943, brigades were usually organized into a *soedinenie*, a brigade group, with no American equivalent, though it comes close to a division.[29] Some of these partisan detachments contained large numbers of civilians. This was often a bone of contention between partisan commanders — whether to care for these civilians or not; Jewish commanders, of course, saw it as a duty to save as many lives as possible, even if the large number of civilians increased the danger of discovery. The Soviet Central Staff, furthermore, did not approve of the existence of separate Jewish partisan units and obligated the Jews and their commanders to integrate into the multinational partisan framework. Thus, such famous Jewish groups as those of Misha (Moshe) Gildenman, the Belski brothers, Yehezkel Atlas, Yechiel Grynszpan, Berl Lorber, and Nikolai Konischchuk, all had to eventually merge into the greater all-partisan central command and lose their distinctiveness as Jewish fighting forces.

Anti-Semitism in the Partisan Movement

Anti-Semitism is tenacious. It reared its ugly head even when Jews were no longer "sheep to slaughter" but valiant fighters. German propaganda followed the Jews into the forests and mountains. This propaganda had a considerable influence; it was directed at guerrilla units in general and at what the Nazis called groups of Jewish "bandits who stand at the head of the partisan leadership, direct its activities, and leave their Jewish mark on all its doings."[30] The Germans, of course, exaggerated the role of Jewish leadership in the movement, but not by much — Jews were at the head of approximately 200 bands of partisans and participated in all the underground Russian organizations, though not always as Jews. Quite often, their Jewish identity was kept hidden.[31]

One effect of the German propaganda against the Jewish partisans was that the Soviet Central Partisan Command decided on a quick intermingling of nationalities for fear that anti-Semitic farmers situated near the partisan bases would not consent to supply food and clothing to fighting groups made up of all Jews or led by Jews. But this was not always the case. Jewish partisan groups *were* sometimes sided by the population, but to be on the safe side, it was not long before most of these Jewish units, forced by the Central Command, ceased to exist as separate groups.

A good example is the Kruk Detachment mentioned in this book, which fought in western Ukraine, in the region of Volyn, from late 1942 to late 1944. This detachment consisted of over 200 Jewish fighters but was led by a Ukrainian Communist, Nikolai Konischchuk. He was allowed to lead, not only because he was a respected commander and knew the territory well, but because it was better "public relations" to have a non-Jew as the head, even though all his assistant commanders were Jewish. (There is a sad footnote to this story: Konischchuk, who went under the *nom de guerre* of "Kruk," was killed by Ukrainian nationalists after the war.)

Anti-Semitism among fellow partisans also existed, but it must not be exaggerated. There were many more philoSemites, especially among the leftist partisan groups. Israeli researcher Israel Gutman had this to say about the issue:

> *The partisan movement was not free of anti-Semitism. The extreme right-wing factions of the Polish underground viewed the Jews as "bandits" prowling around the forests. They took arms away from the Jews and even murdered many of them. The leftist groups took a less hostile stand toward the Jews. In Lithuania, Byelorussia, and the Ukraine, anti-Semitism was somewhat restrained after permanent contact had been established between the partisan areas and the Soviet high command.* [32]

For the Jew, no place was safe, but the forests were safer than the ghettos and the death camps. Still, the act of leaving the ghetto, especially with a family or the remnant of a family, was a difficult one. The environment was hostile, and Jews were often caught or informed upon and turned over the Germans for a reward. There were the exceptional few who risked their lives to save Jewish lives, but they were a small and brave minority.

Not al Jews and not all non-Jews were immediately accepted by the partisans. Women, children, the elderly, the invalid, and the sick were often rejected. Being accepted into the partisan movement depended first and foremost on one's physical strength and military experience, but if either of these was lacking, then the possession of a gun or rifle was sufficient. Yet here too, it was difficult for Jews to acquire arms; they had to resort to illegal purchase, robbery, or acquisition in battle. Many non-Jews would not sell guns to a Jew, or if they did, it was for exorbitant sums. This situation was especially grim in those ghettos that revolted and tried to find arms.

One of the greatest of all dangers to the partisans, to Jew and non-Jew alike, were the roving bands of extreme right-wing Ukrainian nationalists. At the head of these groups stood the nameless "Ottomanim" who fought against Poles and Jews, as well as against partisans. A more politicized group was the *Banderovtsy*, Ukrainian fascists who took on the name of Ukrainian nationalist leader Stepan Bandera. Under the standard of "Samostiina Ukraina!" ("An Independent Ukraine!"), he attracted many Ukrainians to his bands. The Germans offered the pledge of independence for a "free" Ukrainian nation at the beginning of the war, but they soon reneged after their initial victories against the Russians.

Extremely anti-Communist and anti-Semitic, the *Banderovtsy* killed their victims with fiendish cruelty — not with rifles or guns, but with axes and knives. Their motto was "Against the Poles! The Jews! And the Red Partisans!" It is no wonder that they were dreaded by the populations of Byelo-russia and the Ukraine, and became at times the number one enemy of the partisans. In fact, the Germans, caused fewer losses than these Ukrainian nationalists. Unarmed families were especially vulnerable to these bands, and the Germans paid large bonuses for the head of every Jew killed: a *pud* (a Russian measure of 16 kilograms, or about 40 pounds) of salt, a liter of kerosene, and twenty boxes of matches. Many Jews who had escaped from the urban ghettos or village round-ups fell into the hands of the *Banderovtsy*.[33]

Therefore, it was often a serious bone of contention between Jewish and non-Jewish partisans and their com-manders (and at times between two non-Jewish leaders) whether or not to offer help (food, clothing, and/or protec-tion) to these Jewish families. It is one of the sad and ironic chronicles of the war that, even in the midst of battle against a common enemy, there was such division and hatred *among* the partisans and *against* the partisans. It required the greatest of patience, self-control, and forbearance for the Jewish partisan to succeed in his mission.

Obstacles to Resistance

The major arenas of resistance, as well as the social struc-ture of the Russian partisan movement, have been described, and now we come to the question that still exists in many readers' minds: Why didn't more Jews resist? Why didn't they resist physically and militarily?

The reader must put aside emotional and intellectual arrogance for a moment and ask the question with a certain reverence for both the living and the dead. Those who were not there will never fully understand what happened, and those who were have no answers. As Jewish novelist Elie Wiesel so eloquently tells us: "Those who know do not speak and those who speak do not know."

What were the obstacles to resistance? There were many, and these obstacles held true for non-Jews as well as Jews. They held true, in some cases, for entire nations as well as entire families. First, it is obvious that resistance is an option not available to everyone. Physical resistance, by its very nature, is undertaken by only a small minority. Other forms of resistance are open to a far larger segment of the population, but here again, what of the very young, the very old, the lame, the sick, and those who were executed so quickly they had no time to resist? Are they to be labeled as "cowards" as well?

The major barrier to resistance was simply the incomprehensibility and the enormity of the crime. The magnitude and audacity of the killings psychologically overwhelmed the *world*, let alone the Jews themselves. Who would have believed that a culture that had produced a Mozart, a Beethoven, and a Goethe, could commit such acts? One's first reaction was to dismiss the entire idea as a cruel joke. Most of the Allied armies and their governments also rejected early repots as simply "propaganda."

Greuelpropaganda

Bruno Bettelheim describes three separate psychological mechanisms that were most frequently used for dealing with the horrors of genocide.[34] They are based on the belief that a supposedly civilized nation on a supposedly civilized planet could not stoop to such inhumane acts. The implication that modern man had such inadequate control over his cruelty was perceived as a threat to the individual psyche.

The following defense mechanisms were used" first, applicability to mankind in general was denied by asserting that such horrible acts (if in fact they did exist) were committed by a small group of insane or perverted persons. The Eichmann trial in 1961 clearly showed just the opposite: these acts were carried out with scientific and bureaucratic precision by thousands of quite ordinary people. Social psychologist Stanley Milgram has verified this phenomenon in his research: most people will harm their fellow human beings rather than disobey an authority.[35]

Second, the truths of the reports were further denied by ascribing them to deliberate propaganda; in fact, the Germans themselves, masters of the art, called it *Greuelpropaganda* (horror propaganda) and were quite aware that the more outrageous the atrocity, the more difficult it was for the world to believe, and the bigger the lie, the more likely it would be believed, but such lies had to exist in the realm of possibility and had to be based on already manifested myths and prejudices.

Third, the reports were believed, but this knowledge was repressed as soon as possible. In addition to the individual's psychological mechanisms, the Germans were experts in unnerving their victims, in bewildering them, and thwarting any plans for escape. The ploys they used are well known: they used code words which camouflaged their real intent — "relocation," "Jewish problem," "final solution"; they made people believe that the death camps were work camps; the victims were met by an orchestra at the train station; they were given bars of "soap" when they entered the gas chambers; and, moreover, the Nazis sent postcards to the victims' friends and relatives describing how "wonderful" the situation was and how well they were doing. In short, it was a time where morality was stood on its head: right was wrong, wrong was right, true was false, and false was true. This same thought was echoed by the French partisan leader Dominique Ponchardier:

> ... *It was by definition the era of the false: the false combatant, the false decent man, the false patriot, the false lover, the false brother, the false false. In a world of false noses, I was one of those whose nose was real and it seemed to me, as it did to all the "reals," that in reality we were all real cons.*[36]

This sense of existential unreality and dubious authenticity still plagues us today.

Collective Retaliation

The principle of collective responsibility baffled the Jews, prevented their escape from the ghettos, and helped suppress resistance. For example, in many ghettos when an escaped fighter was caught, not only he but his entire family, his neighbors, an even his work unit were killed. When a man or woman decided to resist, he or she knew that it would endanger not only his or her life, but that of parents, children, spouse, brother, sister, and acquaintances. Resistance could, of course, include escape, either from ghetto or concentration camp. Leon Wells, in his memoir *The Janowska Road,* tells the following tale:

> *Now the Untersturmführer (SS officer) begins his speech, directing it at us: "One of you escaped. Because of him these people will be shot. From now on for anyone who tries to do the same, I will shoot twenty of you. If I find out that you are planning an escape, all of you will be shot." After his speech, he turns to the chosen six, and shoots one after another ... when he finishes, he calls for four of us to pick up the corpses and toss them into the fire.*[37]

The Jews in the ghetto faced a great dilemma. If they left the ghetto to fight, they might save themselves but leave their families behind. If many fighters left the ghetto, the remaining population would be vulnerable. But if they did not resist in some way, they were denied the privilege of avenging themselves. The late historian of the Holocaust, Philip Friedman, succinctly summarized this dilemma in the following quote:

> *In the Jewish underground of Warsaw, Bialystok, and other ghettos, and passionate discussion was going on. What were they to do? Stay in the ghetto or leave it for the woods? It was primarily a moral issue: Were they entitled to leave the ghetto populace to face the enemy alone, or did they have to stay on and to take the lead in the fight when the crucial moment of the extermination actions arrived? After headed debates, the opinion prevailed to stay in the ghetto as long as possible despite the disadvantages of the position, and to leave only at the last moment when there was no longer any chance to fight or to protect the ghetto populace.*[38]

The Germans understood the Jewish psyche very well and knew very well where the Jew was most vulnerable. Closely connected to the principle of collective retaliation was the strong family ties among the Jews, and here the Jews were vulnerable. Ironically, what had been a great strength to the Jewish people now became a pernicious trap. The close-knit family structure made it difficult for one or two members to leave the rest behind, since it was extremely difficult for an entire family to escape the ghetto together. A decision to leave the village or escape from the ghetto or camp in the hope of reaching the partisans required a painful decision to leave a wife, mother, father and child.

In interviews that the author has had with his father, this theme is continually emphasized, and it is permeated with guilt, even if leavetaking meant the opportunity to take *nekumah* (Yiddish for "revenge") for the family:

> *Am I no different from my parents or my daughters that I lived and they died? No, we were the same. Why, then, did I remain alive? I may not have been able to help them if I had stayed, but at least we would have been together to the end.*

The Hope of Survival

As has been discussed, over and beyond all the concealed tricks, the half-truths, the devious ploys used by the Nazis to entrap the Jews (and the world), the most effective tool was the utter magnitude of their own evil. This led, as was shown, to numerous ways of adapting to the incomprehensibility of the time. One of the most elemental drives of the human being is to survive. Hope springs eternal. Many Jews felt they were not going to be killed; that they were too valuable; that the Germans "needed" their labor, their talents, or even their money. They would not risk the chance. They believe if they obeyed the law, then they would be spared. In short, resistance meant suicide; not to resist meant life, and why risk it? Hold onto life as long as possible.[39]

Orthodox Jews in many cases refused to take part in military resistance. Resistance to them was contrary to God's law; it was equivalent to a suicide mission, and suicide was considered a sin. Better that one trusted in God and His judgment. To the very end, they felt, one must do God's bidding, stay live, and not risk death. One's only objectives should be *Kevod Hashem* (Hebrew term for "religious honor") and *Kiddush Hashem* ("Sanctification of God's name, "religious self-sacrifice").

This form of nonviolent resistance (almost Gandhian in certain ways) has become a very controversial topic. Some readers will say that this form of passive resistance is not resistance at all — it is cowardice and human weakness, and, furthermore, it led to the deaths of many Jews who might have saved themselves (or died in active revolt) if they had not listened to the rabbis. A partisan, Moshe Flash, whom the author has interviewed, echoed these same sentiments:

> *Because of God and the religiously orthodox, many Jews died because it kept the people from fighting. The rabbis had a strong hold on the people. Because of that, I had to kind of leave my religion for a while and fight.*

Nonviolent resistance took many forms: there were prayer groups and Hebrew classes that would congregate in ghettos and camps in spite of heavy penalties; there were attempts to rescue Torah scrolls from burning synagogues, although many people were killed in the attempt; there were stories of Hasidim *who prayed and danced in religious ecstasy* until the last minute of their lives!

Are these acts of bravery or cowardice?

Lack of Arms, Lack of Trust

Among the most serious obstacles to resistance, once the psychological, theological, and family barriers were overcome, were, first and foremost, the lack of arms and, subsequently, the lack of communication between Jews and the outside world, and the lack of trained leadership. Yet it came down to basics: in any revolt, only a small minority are able to resist, and these few must have something to fight back with, and here the Jews were not always successful.

As Philip Friedman states in his article "Jewish Resistance to the Nazis":

> *A steady, uninterrupted supply of arms is a condition sine qua non for resistance operations. Most of the non-Jewish underground movements had received vast supplies of arms*

*and other material from their governments-in-exile and from
the Allied governments. But in no country was the Jewish
underground treated on an equal footing with the recognized
national underground organization.*[40]

Whatever the Jewish underground was to receive had to
pass through unfriendly national channels, and often the
requests were refused outright, as in the Vilna and Bialystok
ghettos, or came too late and in ridiculously small quantities,
as in the Warsaw ghetto. During the Warsaw ghetto revolt,
led by Mordechai Anielewicz, after prolonged and maddening
negotiations with the Polish underground, the Jewish partisan
finally received only fifty revolvers, fifty hand grenades, and
four kilograms of explosives. All this had to be used to fight
off entire artillery regiments and air attacks — and some of
the revolvers were defective and useless. One of the major
reasons why the Jews received so little aid from the *Armia
Krajowa*, the Polish Land Army, the largest underground
movement in Poland, was because its leadership was permeated with anti-Semites.[41]

Each gun, each grenade, and each rifle was worth its weight
in gold — because quite often each piece had to be purchased
in gold on the black market from illegal arms dealers and
army deserters, or had to be stolen from guards, soldiers and
peasants, or made in small clandestine factories and repair
shops.[42]

Aside from the lack of arms, there was often a lack of trust
and communication between Jews and the surrounding
communities. Some of this was due to anti-Semitism, and
some to outright fear of the Germans who would retaliate for
collaborating with the enemy (Jews, Communists, and partisans). In the words of Erich Goldhagen, Jews lived not only
like fish in a hostile sea, but like fish upon a hostile land. All
this hampered the effective coordination between Jewish and
non-Jewish fighting groups.

Added to all of this was a lack of competent Jewish leadership. Seasoned and established community leaders had been
ruthlessly deported and eliminated in the early round-ups.
Jewish intellectuals, professionals, political and trade union
leaders, former Jewish officers and soldiers, and religious

heads were among the first to be sent to labor camps or immediately killed under various pretenses.

Fortunately, the Nazis did not, in the first years of the war, pay too much attention to the young people and the women, and thus both the leadership and rank-and-file of the youth organizations (for example, Betar, Hechalutz, Dror, Hashomer Hatzair, and Zionist youth movements) survived and formed the cradle of the Jewish underground in the ghettos and, later, in the forests.

Evaluation and Conclusion

After the Eichmann trial some fifteen years ago, a myth emerged: the Jew as cowardly sheep. Will we soon have another myth to replace it: the Jew as mighty supermen? The truth, like life itself, like the war itself, is vastly more complex.

How should we evaluate the partisans themselves? Should we exaggerate their role during World War II? They are such a romantic group. Should we overestimate their importance? Should we glorify them? The answers, of course, depend on our purpose and on our role. Religious and political leaders utilize the glory of the past to bolster their belief system or maintain adherence to their regime to teach their people the lessons of the past and to give them inspiration for the future. But the role of the historian and social scientist is more difficult and much less grandiose: to tell the story as truthfully as possible. In the past, the Jewish role in the resistance was suppressed either out of ignorance or outright prejudice. Many Western historians were not fluent in those languages (Hebrew and Yiddish) which told the Jewish side and many eastern historians were motivated by political pressures or anti-Semitism. In either case, the true story never emerged.

It was left to Jewish writers to make sure that the vital role of the Jewish fighters was *not* omitted.

But what of the evaluation of these fighters? From a strictly military point of view, the Soviet partisan movement had a certain measure of success, as much as any resistance movement can have when opposed by a first-class military power, but the success was sorely limited by several factors, some of which have been described earlier. The partisans suffered from three major problems: irregularity, ineffectuality, and control.[43]

The problem of control was an important factor. A company or battalion of fighters is often extremely difficult to control from a distance of no more than several hundred yards. In comparison, the problem of effectively ordering 60,000 to 80,000 partisans in a given sector, broken up as they were in a number of loose-knit units a hundred miles or more behind the enemy's lines and a thousand miles from the central command, even with dependable communications, is almost insurmountable.

Second, there was the problem of ineffectuality. The partisans were never able to stand up to the crack regiments of the German army face-to-face, even in those areas and circumstances of their own choosing, and, furthermore, they were able to "deny" only that terrain which was tactically unimportant to the Germans at a particular time or which, because of manpower limitations, the Germans were unable or unwilling to occupy or clear. In those areas that the Germans wished to avoid, they would simply go around that particular sector. Despite the fact that the partisan bands were often extremely difficult to combat, still, the Germans, when they saw the need to clean up a sector of the rear and were not too committed at the front, were nearly always equal to the task.

Third, there was the problem of inexperience. Such inexperience, according to U.S. Army historian Edgar Howell, is the great weakness of most resistance movements, and the Soviet movement was no exception. The partisans were "irregular" in every sense of the word. They could never be equipped, trained and controlled like a regular army or approach a regular army in effectiveness and strength. Too often, the fighters were unenthusiastic and undisciplined. Leadership was often poor. Given these factors, it is no wonder that some military experts felt that the partisans were, by and large, a "third-rate militia."[44]

To say all this is not to gainsay the strengths of the partisan movement, most notably in the years 1943-44. It had a large pool of manpower on which to rely, manpower that was innately tough, frugal, inured to hardship, and often intimately familiar with the area in which it operated. Furthermore, the

partisans bruised the enemy, even if they could not vanquish it. Every rail break, every piece of rolling stock damaged or destroyed, every German soldier killed, wounded, or diverted, and every delay in the supply trains hurt. From a geopolitical point of view, the partisans were much more successful in preventing the Germans from ever fully going ahead with their occupation and economic administration of the conquered territory. The Soviet partisans and their political commissars were also a factor in spreading and maintaining Communist control over areas that were either hostile or neutral to the Russians. And, finally, the partisans permitted those people who joined them the dignity and the honor of retaliating against the Germans.

So, despite its many weaknesses, the partisan movement and the Jews within it played an important role. It was not simply that they allowed one to die, but to live with dignity.

PART ONE
PROLOGUE

THE PARTISAN TALES OF SHMUEL PERSOV

Introduction

Literature on the Holocaust abounds, but still there are serious gaps. We have military chronicles and political histories; memoirs of generals and of statesmen; theological essays and survivor diaries; firsthand and secondhand accounts of various stripes; bibliographies and surveys — yet with all the frenzied publishing, there are literally millions of non-Jews who do not know what the Holocaust is and thousands of Jews who do not know what it means.

One such gap is the role of Jewish resistance to attempted genocide and, in particular, *partisan* resistance. We know a great deal about resistance in the ghettos (especially the Warsaw Ghetto) and the concentration camps (especially Treblinka and Auschwitz) and about the role of Jews in Allied military units. However, the important Jewish contribution to guerrilla warfare is only now coming to light. Some books, such as John A. Armstrong's *Soviet Partisans in World War II*, contain only scattered references to Jews. It has been left to a very few (and of these, most are not scholars, but journalists and novelists) to compile and present the scope of armed resistance.

Four Jews who have attempted to do so are Moshe Kaganovitch, in his *The Wars of the Jewish Partisans in Eastern Europe* (in Hebrew and in Yiddish); Yuri Suhl, in *They Fought Back: The Story of Jewish Resistance in Nazi Europe*; Binyamin West, in *They Were Many: Jewish Partisans in the Soviet Union During World War II* (in Hebrew); and Reuben Ainsztein, in his 1,000-page *magnum opus, Jewish Resistance in Nazi-Occupied Eastern Europe*, the most comprehensive history of Jewish defiance written in the English language.

Still, there is much more to be done. For example, there are movies, novels, and plays that deal with the Holocaust, but the majority of these do *not* use the partisans as background. Yet, there is a large body of literature based on personal memoirs, written by Jews and non-Jews, most of it in Russian, Polish, Yiddish, and Hebrew waiting to be translated into English and published.

What follows are several tales by the Russian-Jewish writer Shmuel Persov (1890-1952). Persov was born in Putshev in the Chernigov region of Byelorussia. Until the age of thirteen, he studied in a *yeshiva* and later did "post-graduate" work with the help of the author-teacher A.N. Gensin. He was active in the *Bund* between 1905 and 1906 and later emigrated to the United States. However, with the onset of the Russian Revolution of 1917 he returned to the Soviet Union. He was murdered on Stalin's orders on August 12, 1952, along with twenty-five other Jewish authors and artists, who were among the most well known of Soviet Jewish intellectuals.[1] Because of Stalin's paranoid phobia about the Jewish threat to his regime, over 400 leaders of Jewish culture died by execution, torture, or prison hardship.

Persov produced many stories on Soviet life, including "Kornbroit" and "Royter Horn." Duing World War II, he wrote a great deal about Jewish partisans in the forests and ghettos. He devoted a book, *Dain Nomen iz – Folk (Your Name – A People)*, to this subject. It includes twenty-one factual accounts of Jewish resistance and of partisans who sacrificed their souls for the sanctification of the Jewish people.

Many readers may find Persov's style naïve, heroic, "propagandistic" — and it is, to some degree. During the course of the war, more than 90 Soviet writers were engaged in serving the needs of the war-related propaganda effort. As "troubadors" of a national epic, their words reflected the political ends they were called to serve. They were hemmed in by official Soviet ideology, and approved themes had to be handled in fresh and original ways in order to pass the censor. Jewish writers had an additional burden — they found it necessary to have to *prove* to their non-Jewish readership that Jews were

---

1 Editor's note: the original manuscript here is based on incomplete and misleading information about the case and actual circumstances of the trial, which have since been cleared up thanks to the release of previously inaccessible documents from Soviet archives, including trial transcripts. See J. Rubenstein, *Stalin's Secret Pogrom: The Postwar Inquisition of the Jewish Anti-fascist Committee* (Yale UP).

not cowards nor traitors during the war but, in fact, loyal sons and daughters in the fight against fascism.

In Persov's first tale, "Your Name – A People," the "people" referred to are not the *Jewish* but the *Soviet* people. The Jew as fighter, as partisan, had to be presented as part of an entire nation fighting for survival. In part, this perspective was so crucial because, at least at the beginning of the war, Stalin ordered the press and other media to omit the Nazi persecution of Jews and to emphasize the persecution of *all* Soviet peoples — Ukrainians, Byelorussians, Georgians, and others. Stalin wanted the struggle to be carried out in the name of the beloved land, the soil and home, and not as a mission to come to the aid of the Jews. It was for this reason that so many Jewish communities were caught unaware during the early part of the Nazi invasion of the Soviet Union.

After the war, the situation worsened. A complete change of line was imposed, and the true story of Jewish extermination and of Jewish resistance was suppressed. Furthermore, Jews were later to be pictured, under Khrushchev, as having been collaborators with the Nazis against the Soviets!

Shmuel Persov's tales must be seen against this background, as should the memoirs of partisan leaders Orland and Linkov that follow Persov, as well as all the tales in this book. Wartime and postwar Soviet literature must also be understood in the context of these enormous constraints. We will appreciate our own freedom as writers and readers today when we understand the pressures placed upon Soviet writers, intellectuals, and common citizens. Persov perished, as did many other writers, poets and thinkers, in the Stalin purges, but he had completed his task in portraying Jews as active fighters and devoted citizens.

Our present-day attitude toward the Soviet Union must be ambivalent; while the USSR continues to suppress Jews culturally and religiously, thousands of eastern European Jews were nevertheless saved by the Soviet army and navy in their valiant victory over Nazism. For this we owe the Soviet people and their leaders a bittersweet debt of gratitude.

* * * * *

A. *"Your Name – A People"*

The battalion was pulling back.

The Germans were attacking without letup on all sides. There was only one way left, the river shore. But there was no bridge around, and no time to throw a military bridge over; so the only possibility was to dash straight into the water and swim across to the opposite shore, but the partisans knew that the river was turbulent and deep.

Two Red Army soldiers who were good swimmers volunteered to examine the river in order to find a place where the water was less deep and the bottom firmer because, besides infantry, it was necessary to move the entire convoy and its vehicles. The commanders looked around with impatience at what was taking place beside the river. At any moment the Germans could mount an attack, and under these unfavorable conditions, the entire battalion could be wiped out. Time was at a premium.

One of the swimmers reached the middle of the river and began to go under. At that spot the waves were very high. The other went into the water once and twice, then disappeared for a few moments. Suddenly he surfaced...

At the river shore the tension mounted. An elderly man was brought to the commander.

"We have captured him; he has no documents," the guard said.

"Who are you?" asked the commander.

"I am a Jew..."

"I can see that, but I am asking you once again: Who are you and where do you come from?"

"From the town of Hachklovirt, from the Jewish section of Naye Leben, not far from here. The Germans have..." The old man burst into tears like a child. "I happened to be away from home on that day and so I survived. But the others..." He made a desperate gesture with his hands. "Even the babies were not spared by the murderers..."

"And what are you doing here at the front?"

"Do you think I know what I am doing?...I am roaming around...perhaps I could reach the partisans where I could find local peasants; they know me, and you...you seem to be Russian too, like me...you are taking me prisoner, at the point of the rifle...as if I were..."

At this point the commander was informed that the two soldiers had returned with the following information:

"This is not a river — only the devil knows what it is. The bottom is soft and full of pits."

"But to stay here is impossible," said the commander.

"Comrade..." The Jew came closer to him. "If you will allow me..."

"Don't interrupt me," answered the commander angrily.

But the Jew insisted: "I belong to this place. I was born here...I know this river like the back of my hand..."

And without waiting for an answer, he quickly began to take off his clothes. Standing there nude, the old man looked like a naughty little boy, as if he had stuck a beard to his chin to look funny. On his back were scores of sucking cup signs which looked quite fresh.[1] It was a dreary day and a cold wind was howling. Without hesitation he jumped into the water, struck out in the direction of the opposite shore, dived, and then surfaced at some distance. To those standing on the shoreline and watching the Jew, now diving, now surfacing, it seemed as if he were doing some tricks for them. Suddenly he came to the surface and shouted with joy:

"Here, this is the right spot." A soldier swam out to where the Jew was standing. "Yes, this is the place, the water is not too deep and the bottom is firm ground." The Jew swam to the opposite shore, moving in zigzags, diving in certain places, then surfacing again and, like an experienced instructor, gave directions to the soldier swimming beside him:

"Here! Swim to the right! A little more...that's it, that's it!" The Jew took the soldier across to the opposite side of the river and then swam back to where the battalion was waiting. When he came out of the water he was blue with cold and his teeth chattered. In order to warm himself up he started jumping around. The commander took off his military coat and said:

"Here, take this, old man. Put it on to get warm!"

The battalion crossed over with all the soldiers and the vehicles. Only the commanders and some platoons stayed behind. Turning to the Jew, the commander said:

"Are you warm now? It is high time we crossed over to the opposite side."

"Are you taking me along with you?" asked the Jew. Angrily the commander answered: "What a question! Come on, old man, hurry up!"

The Jew did not have enough time to stand up. One shell after another burst around him. There were groans from the wounded. When the commander looked in the direction of the Jew, he found him dead.

Those who had already crossed over to the opposite shore fired back at the Germans. The commanders started to swim across the river as fast as they could, taking along with them the wounded and the dead Jew. When the entire battalion was out of danger, a soldier buried the Jew in the commander's military coat, which was now soaked in blood.

At the open grave the commissar said the following obituary:

"This is his blood. He has shed it for us, and for the entire nation; and this will we say to him at our hour of parting: May your memory be blessed, old man…"

After a pause, the commissar asked: "What was his name?" Nobody knew. They all stood there in silence, abashed. Suddenly the commander raised his voice and said: "I know your name, o murdered brother. Your name is — a people!"

The battalion presented arms, fired three volleys, and then moved on.

B. Herschel, The Oven Builder

Six new men joined the partisan battalion. All were Jews.
Along with them they brought Herschel Rosen, an oven
builder from a Byelorussian small town on the river Sozh.
No one had appointed him leader of the group, but since he
alone was armed with a rifle, he was automatically accepted as
the head of all six. He had found the rifle in the forest where
he had been roaming around for weeks on end hiding from
the Germans. The other five Jews he met by chance in the
woods. All six had undergone the same disaster. They had
been thrown out from their place of residence. Wherever
the Germans went, Jews were murdered. Only those six
had survived. They had succeeded in running away and had
wandered about in the woods and on the roads until they had
reached the partisan camp.

Even in the early days of their joining the partisan battalion, the commander — who had been the mayor of the town
— assigned Herschel Rosen a very difficult task: to disrupt
work at the factory that produced woolen boots (*valenki*) in
his small town. This factory was known far and wide, and the
small town was proud of its high quality product. Now, why
should it be that those woolen boots should go to warm the
feet of the Germans?...Never! Herschel was very familiar with
the factory. He often was called there to build ovens.

"All right!" was his answer to the commander. "Only make
sure that all six get arms." But the company hardly had any
arms at all. In addition the partisans had to go out on a combat mission on the same day, so that in the end, Rosen was to
get only one more rifle.

Armed with two rifles, three bottles filled with kerosene,
and packets full of chaff and a few matchboxes, the five Jews
went on their first mission, with Herschel at their head.
Herschel, an excellent craftsman, had worked not only in his
small town, but had also done some odd jobs in the neighboring villages. He knew all the roads and paths in the area.

He led the group under cover of darkness through marsh-lands and sideways. The cold and strong autumn wind chilled them to the bone. Every rustle in the leaves frightened them. Slowly their eyes got used to darkness. Before long they had crossed the marshes and, far away on the peak of the mountain, lay the small town. Up there was the factory. Hershel knew that the factory was surrounded by a board fence. He even remembered the gap between the boards. When he built the ovens there, he had to bring red sand loam from the nearby pits into the factory. Here were the pits. Only now they had been filled up.

Herschel wanted to fall down to the ground and kiss them. In these its of red sand loam were buried the Jews who had been tortured to death, Jews from the small town of his birth. To cry? No! There was no time for that now. The time has come to take revenge on the Germans. Herschel starts to crawl forward, followed by the other five. Here was the wooden fence and here the spot with the two missing boards. Now the men were in the backyard of the factory. They were trying to hide in the shadows cast by the storerooms. Here was the opening to the factory. An armed German soldier was standing guard and whistling a melancholy tune to himself. The whistling suddenly stops. They fill his mouth with chaff and he falls to the ground. A few moments later he is lying there, dead. There were no other guards in the backyard. This fact had been known to Rosen even before he had run away from his small town. He assigned to each of the men their part of the work to be done. Two were assigned to the storerooms which were full of woolen boots. The other three had to set fire to the entire factory. He himself was to take care of the attic. According to their plan, all buildings had to be set on fire at the exact same time. Here is he, Herschel on top of the attic. He smells burned-up bricks. He passes his hands over the chimney which he built with his own hands before the war, pours some kerosene on them, and lights a match. Fire bursts out at once. The wind proves to be a great help to the partisans. Sparks are carried to the adjoining buildings and the sky turns red. The Germans start to put out the first only to be beaten back by the wind. The partisans take advantage of the pandemonium and go out the backyard through the same opening, escaping over the marshlands and back to the forest. All through the night the Germans kept firing after the escaping partisans. Some of them even reached as far as the marshes, but they did not dare to advance any further. Some of them were to flounder and die there. Only those who were familiar with every path in the area could save themselves from the marshes.

The six partisans with Herschel at their head, now armed with two rifles and one automatic rifle, came out slowly from the marshes into a forest, which became thicker and thicker the farther they moved away from the factory. The sky above was now red with flames. Formerly, this plant produced about six hundred pairs of woolen boots a week. After this operation the Germans did not succeed in running it for even a single day. It was burned to the ground with all its departments and buildings.

In the course of two years, Herschel Rosen, a vivacious and cordial man, was to turn into a ruthless partisan. His comrades would sometimes remind him of the job he did at the factory.

"My job is to build ovens for people, to make them warm, but to the Hitlerites I make it very hot."

He would answer with a sad smile. He was always very sad. For two whole years he could not walk freely into the small town of his birth. All fifty years of his life this oven builder had spent in only one place, his small town. There he had seen many days of joy and also of sorrow. When the Germans attacked his country, his hair turned white and the light went out of his eyes. But his hands were strong; they knew how to hold an automatic rifle and a mortar. His soul went out to the small town of his birth; there to see his home, the nook where he had spent his entire life. But the Germans had turned the small town into a stronghold. There was no access to the place. The small town stood at the peak of a mountain, overlooking the surrounding country. The Germans kept a strong watch over it.

Now the time came for the Red Army to recapture the small town. Once again it was to be in Soviet hands. Among the first to enter it was Herschel Rosen, the former oven builder, now turned partisan. It was impossible to recognize the streets and the alleys. Everything had been destroyed. Here had stood his house, beautiful and well kept. Now there was nothing but a heap of burned trees and bricks. The Germans had ravaged the house before they left. The heap was still smoldering. Had it not been for the foundation which had survived the flames, he would not have recognized his home. He had his own method of laying the foundations for the ovens. He had often bragged: "I can recognize my handiwork even with my eyes closed."

Having seen the destruction in his small town, Herschel turned to the mayor and said: "Send me into the ranks of the Red Army." The mayor answered: "You are right, Herschel, I will send you into the army. You will build the factory once again." Herschel was astonished and said: "You have found a good time to joke…" But the mayor replied seriously: "No, we have to rebuild the factory at once. Winter is at hand, and each pair of woolen boots is worth a good automatic rifle."

And Herschel the mason "went to war," to build the ovens of the burned-down factory and to provide the soldiers of the Red Army with new woolen boots.

C. Forty-Two

The attack was launched late at night. The partisans surrounded the village on all sides. Soon they would crush the German battalion like a worm. The sound of bullets was deafening. In the dark, gunfire flashed like lighting. From the door of a stable, a group of people came out towards the partisans. They were unarmed and approached with their hands raised above their heads. One of them held a white handkerchief. The commissar of the partisans gave the command to get them back behind the barn and to assign men to stand guard over them. At dawn, after the partisans had finished off the Germans, the commissar came to the stable. It was difficult to describe what his eyes saw in the light of day. Even on a person like him, who had seen so much in his lifetime, the scene had a terrible impact.

One of them, who spoke poor Russian, murmured: "We are Jews"… As they couldn't speak Russian, they were unable to make themselves understood. The commissar was in need of a translator. He sent for Abramel the tinsmith and the latter spoke to them in Yiddish.

"Who are you? Speak!" "Doctors, lawyers, engineers, artists, scientists, from Vienna and Budapest. The fascists made up a special company out of us and sent us to the Eastern Front as forced labor, to pave roads, to uproot forests, to quarry stone, to carry earth. We were a few hundred men, but the great famine and the terrible cold, the inhuman treatment, and the hard, unbearable work, illness, and epidemics — all these have taken a heavy toll on our men. We, the survivors, are still keeping on."

The commissar wanted to know where they lived. One of the learned men from Budapest smiled wryly and said: "Here, in the empty stable. The Germans forbade us to wear warm coats and to correspond with our families." "They were allowed only to die," said Abramel the translator. "What have they in mind to do?" the commissar asked Abramel the translator. To this, Abramel retorted: "Well, they have come out to meet us carring a white flag…" The commissar wrote down their names and took them along into the forest.

Thus, were forty-two prospective partisans to join our company.

The forty-two watched with excitement the operations of the partisans. A patisan who had fallen in the latest battle was being brought for burial. At the open grave all of them vowed to avenge the blood of their comrade. They raised the partisan flag and presented arms. In the morning, during roll call, the man on duty read the names of the newcomers. Partisan Abramel had taught them what to say when their names were to be called. "Answer like the others: 'Here'." The name of the comrade who fell the previous day was then called. A partisan who stood on the right answered: "He was killed in combat against the enemy." The newcomers asked Abramel to explain why the name of the fallen comrade was also called. "You are wrong," he replied. "Such a person never really dies…"

When the newcomers were sent to the bathhouse, they asked to wash separately, but it was difficult to comply with their request. As there was no alternative, they took off their clothes in front of all the partisans. The latter now had a chance to see on their bodies the wounds which had been inflicted by the Germans. The Viennese doctor said in a low voice: "for the slightest thing they beat us with sticks, like dogs." What could Abramel the tinsmith tell them? He had no words. He could only clench his fists and teeth and express his rage to fight. His wife and children were lying there in a common pit together with thousands of other murdered Jews…

He had never seen people washing themselves with such ecstasy. For over a year their bodies had not seen a drop of hot water. They were forbidden to wash in the German bathhouse. Even their toothbrushes had been taken away from them. After the bath they once again looked like human beings.

"Do you want to be together or to be divided up among other companies," asked the commissar. Partisan Abaramel answered: "Why do you have to ask them such a question?"

* * * * *

Among the partisans who operated in the woods of Bryansk, now sprang a Jewish group composed of forty-two men. The commissar addressed Abramel the translator: "They have to take the oath; translate the oath into Yiddish for them." That was no easy task for Abramel. The oath began with the words: I, a Soviet citizen, volunteer... But they were not Soviet citizens. Abramel had to think hard in order to put the oath into the proper form. He turned to the commissar and said: "What do you think of an oath in this version: 'I, a free son of my tortured people, volunteer'...?"

"That is fine, extremely fine," answered the commissar. The entire battalion with all its platoons stood at attention when each and every one of the forty-two men took the oath in Yiddish. The new partisans went about as in a dream. Only yesterday they were like human refuse, always displayed, to be laughed at and caviled, and today they were equals among equals with the veteran partisans, taking part in their training, listening together to reviews of the political situation, dressing like them, eating and drinking with all of them at one table. The commander of the Jewish group was a young Russian. It was he who taught them to use firearms and other weapons. He taught them partisan tactics, especially night fighting. "The nights are our faithful ally," he would tell them on every occasion.

But it was only during the night that some of them found it hard to move about or to aim their weapons exactly. Often they would fall to the ground. The commissar was present at their training. The faces of some of them looked haggard. He gave the order to excuse them from combat operations. They were offended. The accursed Nazis had taken their eyeglasses away from them and trampled them with their heavy heels, but to withhold from them the right to strike at the Germans — would they really have to accept that?

"We will see; get on with your training," answered the commissar.

A few days later a group of ground scouts went into action. When they came back they brought along with them a few pairs of eyeglasses. The commissar handed them to those who needed them most among the Jewish group.

"They took them off dead Germans. Try them on, please." The famous scientist from Vienna turned aside and wiped a tear. Abramel the tinsmith saw that and said: "Usually, comrade professor, partisans do not shed tears, but this drop in particular is extremely precious…" In the meantime they were not sent on combat missions. They fulfilled camp duties for the company. Wearing Russian woolen boots, German military coats, and winter caps with earflaps, the doctors and artists who had come from Vienna and Budapest could not be distinguished from Abramel the tinsmith or from the peasants and woodcutters of the Bryansk forests. Equals among equals, all together they led the unique lives of partisans. They took part in Red Army celebrations, and when they gathered in the earth hut which carried the pretentious name of "Central Partisan Club," those who came from Vienna and Budapest sang their own local songs. The partisans applauded them with great enthusiasm and asked for more and more!

On the day that followed the celebrations, the order was given to wipe out a German battalion. The partisan force was alerted. "Do you have the strength to go out on an attack?" asked the commissar.

The Jewish company with its forty-two men went out on its first combat mission. The battalion, which comprised one hundred and fity partisans, was assigned the task of wiping out two German battalions. The Jewish group, eld by the Russian commander, attacked from the right. At the beginning of the fighting one of the new partisans was wounded, but he bandaged the wound and kept on fighting. The group dispersed and began to crawl in the snow. Suddenly a partisan heard a low whisper in German. The Viennese scientists answered him in his own language. The Germans decided that these were their own men and all of them rose to their feet. The Jewish partisans fired a hail of bullets at them. Some of the Hitlerites fell to the ground, six raised their hands, and one acted as if he was going to surrender but immediately opened up with his automatic rifle. Three Jewish partisans were killed on the spot. The commander dashed forward shouting: "For the blood of our comrades…for our mothers and our wives, fire!"

The company charged at the enemy with fixed bayonets. Doctors, lawyers, scientists, artists stabbed, fired, threw hand grenades, as if they had done nothing but fighting all their lives.

After they had accomplished their mission successfully, the men of the company returned to the battle ground and brought back the three dead comrades. They buried them, as was the practice of the partisans, with a military ceremony, vowing at the open grave to take revenge on the enemy for the blood of their comrades. In the evening at roll call, the partisans on duty read the names of those who had been killed. Abramel the tinsmith, who stood on the right, answered gravely when the name of each one was called: "Fell in battle against the invaders."

Now the Jewish partisans understood that the killed were alive too, alive in the memory of their comrades and alive on the lists of the partisan avengers. Maybe some of them would fall in battle; nevertheless, the group would always number forty-two. For all forty-two had faithfully fulfilled the oath: "I, a free son of my tortured people, volunteer…"

D. REISEL AND HANNAH

Even as very young girls, Reisel and Hannah were close friends. Together they went to the same school and together they went to get their first identity cards. When the war broke out, they both went to the school for nurses in order to go to the front together.

But when the Germans came the two friends had to separate. The Jewess Reisel was forbidden to draw water from the same well Hannah drew water from. Hannah was absolutely forbidden even to look in the direction of Reisel. The Jewish girl had to carry the yellow sign on her sleeve. But that was not all. The Germans drove all the Jews into the ghetto, a few dilapidated houses beside a river. To leave the place meant death by a firing squad. To be seen in the market buying food meant death on the spot. If a non-Jew from White Russia brought to the ghetto a few potatoes or a loaf of bread, they put to death both the Jew and the Byelorussian.

Once, when the Jews were taken out for work, Reisel succeeded in escaping and, meandering through sideroads and sidepaths, reached her friend. Hannah was shocked at seeing the great change that had come upon the tall, blooming, seventeen-year-old girl.

"Hannahle," cried Reisel, "the world has collapsed upon me! I am going to hang myself…"

An idea flashed in Hannah's mind. "Reisel, we have to get to our men, behind enemy lines. We will run away together." Reisel was excited. She was ready. But she became sad immediately. Her Jewish eyes and kinky hair would give her away. Hannah calmed her: "Reisel, I will lend *you* my identity card."

"And you? How will you manage?" asked Reisel. "I, with my features…" Hannah wanted jokingly to lighten the load on Reisel's heart. For Hannah had the blond hair, the grey-blue eyes, and the typical face of a Byelorussian.

"But…"

"No buts," said Hannah. She removed Reisel's photograph from the identity card and glued hers in its place.

The two girlfriends then set forth on their way to the partisans. They took special pains to keep away from villages in order to avoid meeting people. On the third day they had to get some food. For this purpose they walked into a village. Here they were caught by policemen. The *starosta* (village head) released Reisel immediately. She had a real Byelorussian certificate. She was free; but he detained Hannah. Hannah made a sign to Reisel: "Don't stay here!..." But Reisel did not move. How could she leave her friend behind?

The *starosta* took Hannah for interrogation, and, as it was learned later, this was a grim interrogation. "Why," he shouted, "are you going about without an identity card? You must certainly be a Jewess at that!..." Hannah pointed at her outward appearance and mentioned her typical Byelorussian language. But he, the *starosta*, wouldn't hear of that.

"Here, look at her," pointing at Reisel. "She looks like a real Jewess, but when you see her identity card, you know immediately who she is. And you?... How old are you?"

"Seventeen," answered Hannah.

The Germans alerted all their commanders and police stations that from the small town of N. (here they mentioned the name of the small town), a seventeen-year-old girl had escaped from the ghetto one day before all the Jews there had been killed...

Reisel stepped forward. Hannah winked at her to keep silent. Reisel's knees weakened. Nudging her in the breast, the *starosta* pushed Reisel out of his office, and to Hannah he said:

"Yes, we have found you, my little bird... You are the Jewess we are looking for."

Reisel waited for her friend outside the village till the evening, but Hannah did not come. When darkness fell a group of children came out of the nearby forest. Reisel hid beside a broken tree. When it became quiet around her, the young girl fled to where her feet took her. On the next day she was again arrested, this time by two men in the forest. They asked her for her identity card. They scrutinized her face and her card.

"This is very suspicious," said one of them. "You look like a Jewess and your name is Byelorussian! Come along with us!" Through hidden forest trails he led her to a place where he handed her over to another policeman. In this manner she was to pass from one policeman to another until she reached the commander of a camp in the forest. Reisel told her what had happened to her, adding through her tears: "I should have told them I was the one who had escaped and that the identity card was Hannah's, and then…"

"Then they would have put both of you to death," interrupted the commander. "Now listen! You can no longer save your friend, nor your family which has been murdered. You had better stay with us here!"

Thus was Reisel to remain at the partisan camp. They gave her a rifle and taught her how to us it. Each shot sent a shudder through her heart. In the end she asked to be transferred to the company of field nurses, for she and Hannah had studied nursing.

"Of course, of course," the commander agreed. However, without her knowing it, the guard commander had decided to put her on guard duty.

The forest was thick and tangled. Up in one of the trees, a squirrel jumped and the branch shook slightly. Fresh snow fell from the tree. Reisel was startled. She held the rifle firmly in her hands. But at once she discovered the "culprit" and calmed down. Then once again she heard rustling among the trees and she shouted firmly: "Halt!" There was no answer.

A few minutes later she heard the rustling closer and more clearly. Reisel shouted:

"Who goes there?" Getting no answer, she fired. The nearby guard did not fire. She held the rifle with greater force. She was all ears. All around it was absolutely quiet. It turned out that the commander was testing the young girl. He had ordered all the guards around not to fire on hearing the girl's shots. He himself had slipped into the area assigned to her as if he were an enemy infiltrator.

"All right," he smiled to himself. "The girl has a sharp ear and she knows how to use a rifle." "Well, comrade fighter," he asked the girl when she returned from her guard duty. "Did anything happen while you were on guard?"

"Yes, something happened. I even had to shoot, but I didn't see any traces of the enemy."

Reisel kept learning the hard job of being a fighting partisan. Soon she was to finish her training. Along with the entire battalion she went out on combat duty. On the way the battalion encamped to get ready for action. Reisel looked around and saw a broken tree. This was the tree beside which she had hidden two weeks before. Nearby was the village... She went up to the commander and asked him to send her out along with a few fighters to reconnoiter the area. Perhaps she could find out where Hannah had gone... At dawn the commander assigned to a group of veteran partisans the task of "feeling the pulse" of the German battalion stationed at the village. One of them returned quickly with the important news that two weeks before, a partisan battalion had gone through the village and killed the *starosta*.

"But what about the girl Hannah?" asked Reisel with excitement. "I don't know anything about her," answered the partisan.

The Germans detected the partisan battalion and assigned to a well-equipped company the task of wiping it out. The partisan commander stood up and said, "It won't be the Germans who will wipe *us* out, but we, the Germans." All the platoons and companies were alerted. A small partisan company advanced forward to the small and distant bridge. Reisel could not understand what a handful of people could do. She was a little confused, and everything seemed to her as if in a dream. Only two weeks before she had waited her for Hannah's return. Death had stalked her everywhere she went. Now she was standing here, armed with an automatic rifle and hand grenades, ready to meet the despicable Germans as a woman partisan. Ten German tanks were detected approaching in the snow. They were coming nearer and nearer. But why wasn't the battalion shouting its battle cry: "Death to the invaders!"? Why weren't the partisans rushing forward or shelling them? The tanks were drawing close to the small bridge. Within one moment they would be on the bridge. Then all of a sudden she heard a number of explosions. The tanks stopped in their tracks. The Germans jumped out of the tanks firing in all directions. The partisans, who had mined the bridge, sprang up from their hiding places, fired at the Germans, and killed them. To Reisel this was the first and decisive lesson in the partisan method of war. Suddenly a comrade came from the liaison convoy with the news that, on the other front, the Germans had succeeded in breaking up the partisan battalion into a number of companies so that each company now had to fight it out on its own with the Germans. No help was to be expected. The commander ordered his men to lie down in the snow. When the Germans appeared he gave the order: "Fire!"

Reisel fired thirty-two rounds from her automatic rifle, replaced the clip, and once again sent bullets into the direction of the enemy. But the Germans too spared no ammunition. Their bullets struck close to the girl. Bullets whizzed past her head like flies. Wherever they hit they raised bubbles of snow. The enemy troops began to shell the partisans. It seemed to Reisel that a bullet would hit her soon, and then... "What are you firing at?" a comrade disrupted her train of thought. The girl had aimed her rifle at a spot from which the Germans were approaching with mad persistence. They did not crawl but went upright. She could see the ranks of the attackers were becoming more sparse. The battleground was covered with dead and wounded Germans. In the late afternoon hours, the fighting became less intensive.

The Germans did not like to engage in night fighting. But the night was the paratisan's best friend. The companies of the battalion joined each other again, and the commander got the battalion ready for a night attack. The Germans knew that the partisans would attack them at night. Reinforcements were sent to them in the form of two battalions and about one hundred policemen. They occupied all the brick hoses in the village and the entrance to the village. The partisans threw at them a large number of hand grenades. Reisel tossed her hand grenades with great skill. The moon came out over the battle area. It was easy to detect the places from which the Germans were firing. But the moon came to aid of the Germans too. They cut holes in the entrance walls to serve them as battlements. They shelled the entire village incessantly. One machine gun mounted to the left of the battle ground was particularly effective; so the order was given to silence it. The partisans kept on firing, but the Germans did not hold their fire either. Suddenly, Reisel began to crawl forward in the direction of the entrance. The Germans, who were throwing a great number of hand grenades, almost hit the girl. Bowing down, she ran up to the entrance fence, sped along it, and came up near the German firing position. The partisans held their fire. No partisan bullet should hit a comrade. Reisel mustered all her strength, and knocked strongly with the handle of her automatic rifle on the protruding barrel of the German sniper. The barrel was now twisted out of shape, and the machine was silenced.

The girl crawled back. Ten or fifteen steps separated her from the partisans. Suddenly she fell down, without even uttering a word. The automatic rifle dropped from her hands. She felt a terrible pain above her knee; her fingers touched the wet and hurting spot and then looked for her automatic rifle. But her strength failed her, and she couldn't rise to her feet. She felt someone trying to lift her and recognized two comrades of the company. Bullets and shell fragments whined around them, deafening their ears. One of the comrades was hit; another one took his place. The girl began to lose all her remaining strength, and she whispered faintly: "Enough, leave me here." The partisans did not concede to her request and they carefully took her out of the fighting area saying: "You have the right to pay for our lives with yours, and we do not?"

"Once it was Hannah who did it, and now you. Enough," she pleaded with them and passed out. She came to the next day. The commander bent over her bed and said, as if he were talking to his own beloved little daughter:

"My little child, a doctor is expected to arrive at any minute now from another company. We have settled the account with the Germans...two-thirds of them were wiped out yesterday. True, we also suffered heavy losses..." He sighed. Reisel once again began to pass out, running a temperature. She was seriously wounded. She heard voices around her. She felt that people were taking care of her. She imagined that she had caught sight of Hannah, but her eyelids were heavy as lead, and she could not raise them. Then she felt someone kiss her gently. She imagined that she sensed the breathing of Hannah on her flaming lips.

"Ah, what a dream…" She opened her eyes. "Hannah, is that you?" "Yes," was the reply. Hannah bent over her sick and wounded friend. Briefly she told her:

In the morning she fell into the hands of the *starosta* and in the evening the Germans phoned him and ordered him to transfer the Jewess to the small town of N, since the usual practice was that the murdered Jews should be buried in one grave. The *starosta* picked out two policemen to take her there, but a partisan company who passed them on the way slipped into the village in the evening. They killed the *starosta* and the policemen but she, Hannah, survived. In the partisan battalion she was acting as a nurse. The doctor took her along on all the difficult operations. Reisel could not utter a single word for joy. Hannah stroked her saying: "In a month's time you will again be in good health…"

"Take your identity card back," remembered Reisel. "That isn't necessary any longer. We are now among our own people doing together one united task. We are women partisans."

Both girls knew that, and they would not shirk from their task of saving the lives of partisan fighters.

REMEMBER!

H. Orland

In mid-winter he was recuperating in this sanatorium which lies in a thick forest near the Volga. Through the trees one could see a bare mountain from which was flowing water from a spa known all over the country. The sanatorium usually carried the name of the spa, but now the people call this place "The Partisan." The sanatorium receives people from behind enemy lines. Their exploits are recorded in books which are still kept under lock and key. The personal questionnaires lie there in bundles. The convalescents leave the sanatorium to resume their activities in the woods, villages, and besieged towns, where life hangs on a hair. They fight, thus avenging the sufferings of the people.

The wound in his lungs has already healed. His appetite has returned to him. After a silence which went on for two months, he can now speak a little with people and occasionally smiles to the boy with the amputated leg — a partisan ground scout from Polesia in White Russia (Byelorussia) — who is lying beside him. Only yesterday he had gone into the forest on a long walk with Horfina, an old woman from the vicinity of Bryansk. He had been leading her by the hand. During one of the bombing raids on the forest, the old woman lost her eyesight.

Today, early in the morning, the partisan spent a long time in the ward with the Ukrainians. He spoke with them animatedly and went silent when the nurse entered the ward. He then walked into the office and asked to be released, claiming that he had recovered enough to be able to leave the sanatorium. In order to get his papers ready, it was necessary to obtain the approval of the doctor in charge of him. He took the papers and went over to the white cubicle of the manager. The hospital's manager, a professor of worldwide fame, examined his heart. He offered him an aromatic cigarette, and both sat there smoking silently. At last the professor said:

"In my opinion your trip should be postponed."

The partisan inhaled the smoke deeper into his lungs, coughed for a long time, and did not answer a word.

"Your heart has weakened, and you are in need of complete rest," said the professor, who had not received an answer. The partisan looked down at his thin and smoke-stained fingers, sank deep in his thoughts, and did not hear the professor when the latter added: "The first strain on your heart may bring on complications."

The partisan kept silent. "A long time will pass before you can be of any use," said the professor seriously. Hearing this, the partisan raised his sad eyes to look at the professor. A stubborn fire was ablaze in them. He passed his thin long fingers through his grey beard. A coarse word hung on his lips, but he restrained himself and said nothing.

"I have to forbid you from leaving this place for some time," said the professor.

At this point the partisan stood up and said quietly: "Tomorrow I am leaving this place on the two o'clock bus which goes to the railway station. Doctor, will you please give me another cigarette." He lit the cigarette with the match offered him by the professor and began to talk at some length. He endeavored to pick out the right words, simple words, as people do when they are explaining things to the young.

"I would like to speak Yiddish. It will be much easier for me." The professor nodded approval.

"As you can see, I am a Jew," he smiled, wrinkling the skin of his face. He stood up and started to pace the floor nervously. He had to make a great effort in order to stand still; the professor sat in his chair and did not take his sharp dark eyes off him for a moment.

"I am not rejecting the whole idea, and I am not denying anything. Now it is clear to me that they are now after the weak, after those who give in, even those who have no horns or claws to fight back and to resist..." He shut his eyes and opened them again because of the deluge of thoughts that overwhelmed his mind.

"What do you call it, Doctor? Do you call it martyrdom? Why don't you speak, Doctor? Whole Jewish communities have gone like sheep to the slaughterhouse seeing before them the ten *Harugei Malkhut*.[2] Rabbi Akiva's head has cost us a very dear price... Jews have learned from him and followed his example."

His face had become ashen. He spoke in a whisper. "I do not refuse anything; on the contrary, I have taken upon myself things which are beyond my strength... The murderers tied me up and made me witness the massacre of the entire Constantin community. Woe to the eyes that saw such a slaughter! Afterwards at the open grave, they gave me a spade... and then, after the burial, they left me alone in the field and mockingly told me to march... May the Rabbi who buried our community keep marching on and on! I am a Rabbi, I am a teacher who saw ancient Constantin.

"Is it true that the people will remember only 'Thou shalt love...'" he said with difficulty. "Well, but where is 'Remember' — 'Remember what Amalek hath done unto you?!' In the Ukraine I met many Jews who still remember."

At this point fire flamed in his eyes, and suddenly it seemed to him that he was standing in the middle of the synagogue and with clenched fists was warning and warning: "If a Jew should forget till the day of doom what Hitler has done to the Jews, may his name be obliterated from the face of the earth." Jumping up, he put his hands on the professor's shoulders and said in a commanding voice: "Doctor, sign these papers! They are waiting for me out there by the River Bug!"

THE PARTISAN
MINE AND ABRAHAM HIRSCHFELD,
THE WATCHMAKER

Grigory Linkov

Our mines were causing great trouble to Hitler's soldiers, but to explode them from a distance was not worthwhile. For after the railway tracks had been destroyed in the mine explosion, much repair work was still needed, and that delayed the trains for many hours. Therefore, the Germans, that is, the railway managers and the policemen, sought special ways to get rid of the mines without having to explode them. But it wasn't always possible to find the right expert for such dangerous work. Then it happened that in the region of Mikashevichi a mine was removed in front of one of our demolition men — a mine which was thought to defy all experts. Later we succeeded in finding out the details of this interesting story.

In the Lenin area, in the region of Pinsk, the Nazis had arrested all the Jews who were unfit for work, put them into one camp, and executed them. The Jews who could work were put into a special camp located in the city of Slonim, where they were ordered to work in workshops, each of them according to his occupation. These Jews were told that their families had been sent over to Poznan where they would be kept till the end of the war. Among the craftsmen who worked at the Slonim camp was a watchmaker by the name of Abraham Hirschfeld. He did not work, however, at his occupation but was employed in repairing railway tracks and roads.

Then one day Hirschfeld was not sent out to work. He was called to the command building. There he was accorded special treatment — they served him breakfast consisting of a slice of white bread and a cup of coffee with milk. Abraham was surprised and became uneasy, fearing that such a human breakfast indicated a trap which the Nazis were setting for him. Actually he was not mistaken. After he had finished his breakfast he was approached by a German officer accompanied by a railway guard. They asked him about his knowledge and skill in electronics. Hirschfeld replied that he knew a lot about electrical circuits and that he would be willing to offer them his services in this field if he and his family were allowed to lead normal lives.

The Hitlerites assured him that they would take his request into consideration and asked him to follow them. They led him along the railway tracks. The railway guard went first, followed by the officer. The railway guard stopped and asked the guard something. The latter pointed at the track. "Well look here," the officer told Hirschfeld. "We want you to do this: here, under this track, there is a mine which cannot be removed. The whole thing is based on an electronic principle. You have to try to remove it. If you succeed, then we will bring your family back to you soon, and you will be once again free in your small town. But if you do not remove it, then you won't be in need of a family. Got it?!"

"Yes, I understand exactly what you mean," answered Hirschfeld, covered with cold sweat.

"Then you can get down to work; but let's get away some distance first. You see, there is a mound of earth here under the track between the sleepers." The railway guard indicated the spot with his finger. Hirschfeld nodded and didn't say a word. "This is the concealed mine we have been speaking about."

The three Hitlerites went away to watch him at some distance. Hirschfeld stayed on the spot. He stood near the mine and thought: "Who could have put the mine here if not the partisans? But they have laid it not in order that Hirschfeld should remove it."

Then, what was he to do? To come near the mine, pull the electric wire, and blow everything up, including himself? In this case the Germans would certainly shoot Adik, his mother, and his wife. "But if I remove the mine, that would be treason," Hirschfeld whispered to himself, not knowing what to do. The Hitlerites were now about fifty or sixty meters from him, watching his movements closely. "No," said the officer, "I think that nothing will come out of it, for the Jew will simply chicken out." After a short pause he added: "You have promised him too much, for his family has already been shot." "Wouldn't it be the same whether the family has been shot or not? And why not promise to someone a hundredfold of what we actually have if he has already bought a ticket to the next world." "Do you think that if the mine is removed, it will explode?" "Almost certainly. We have already lost twelve of our best sappers removing such mines."

"Well, but the time is up, and the man is not doing anything."

"Mr. Hirschfeld, get back to work! We are waiting for you." Abraham decided, nevertheless, to try and remove the mine. He had two arguments for that: first, the mine had already been discovered by the enemy, a fact which was sure to prevent the blowing up of a train. The Germans could actually explode the mine themselves and lay new railway tracks. In the final analysis that was not a difficult matter. Second, if he were to remove the mine, then it would not be regarded as a mine which no one could remove, and then the partisans would think that the mine was faulty and attempt to make a more elaborate mine.

Hirschfeld stepped with courage to the mine and began to study its wire connections. But no benefit could come out of that. Only the wires which had been laid on the railway track were visible. All the rest were buried in the ground. Very carefully Hirschfeld began to expose the mine. He worked a very long time at it. For two hours the Hitlerites sat at a distance, waiting or the explosion. But no explosion took place. Hirschfeld removed the mine. He had separated the electro-detonator from the explosive charge and put it aside. The danger of explosion was over.

"The mine has been removed and you can come near now. The danger of explosion is over," Hirschfeld cried out to the Hitlerites. They approached Hirschfeld gingerly.

"Well done, Hirschfeld!" the policeman said. "You will work for us as an instructor in dismantling mines."

Hirschfeld received this announcement with silence. On that evening he was given a meal like that of a German soldier. For the past two months he had not had such a human meal.

"You will work for us as an instructor in removing mines," the policeman's words came back to him. What was he to do? Hirschfeld thought. It was absolutely evident that the mine could be removed. The only thing to do was to cut one of the pipes which connected the detonator with the battery. But until you got to that, you could be blown to bits. In order to make it impossible to remove the mine, it was necessary to add one more battery and to use bigger pipes so that when one of them was pulled, the mine would explode.

Three days went by. Hirschfeld received the same meals as any ordinary Hitlerite. But they didn't bring his family back to him as they had promised. On the night of the third day, Hirschfeld stood at the door of his flat. In the nearby street Jews were being taken to work.

Suddenly he noticed that one of his old acquaintances turned his face to the other side when he saw him and did not return his greetings.

"Well, it has become known to one and all. My friends consider what I have done as treason, and as far as they are concerned, they are right," he thought to himself with some bitterness. "The instructor and mine remover." Suddenly he noticed that one of the Jews who passed by dropped something for him. A groan almost issued from his throat, but he stifled it in tie. When all the Jews and their guards had gone away, Hirschfeld looked around, and his heart contracted with pain as he picked up the crushed piece of paper. He hurried back into his room and with trembling fingers straightened out the paper. It was a piece of wrapping paper and bore the following lines, written in pencil:

Dear Abraham,

It seems that you have been given a job by the Hitlerites in return for which you are being fed like a human being. But we do not envy you. This act of yours is considered by us as an act of treason. By the way, do you know that all the members of your family have been shot?

— David

The piece of paper dropped from Hirschfeld's hands. A vacuum formed in his soul. A feeling of indifference to all that was around him permeated his consciousness, including his own life. He took out of his pocket a letter he had prepared some time before, added a few words in pencil, and walked out...

Next day Hirschfeld was seen once again on the railway tracks with a number of Hitlerites. He walked at the head of the group and spoke animatedly with the lieutenant of the technical troops. They were accompanied by an army man, a policeman, and two others.

Hirschfeld stopped near the mine which had been laid under the railway tracks and got down to work. The German lieutenant and two of his men proved to be men of courage. They bent down on the spot where the mine had been laid and watched every item that Hirschfeld brought out from the ground. After the mine had been completely exposed, he called the policeman to join them. At the same time a strong explosion was heard. Of the six men who had come to where Hirschfeld had been working, only one survived; it was the army man who had watched the job of removing the mine from a great distance.

These two cases were known to me quite well — that of removing the mine without the explosion and that of the Jew's death, together with the four Hitlerites, while tinkering with the mine. But I did not know the details. A week had passed from the second event when a package was delivered to me by a man I did not know. It contained a long letter written by Hirschfeld giving all the details of the tragic conditions of his life in the days of the Hitlerites. It also described the motives for removing the first mine and how he had done it at the Mikashevichi station. In the same letter was a drawing of what had to be done so that our mines could never be dismantled. There was also a final note written in pencil which said: "The murderers will no longer succeed in forcing me to remove our own mines."

We examined Abraham Hirschfeld's diagram and found that the details were accurate exactly to the point.

PART TWO
INITIATIVES

The following are personal accounts
of partisan initiatives.

The Partisan Oath

I, a citizen of the Soviet Union, hereby join the ranks of the Red partisans,[3] the avengers of the people, in order to vindicate the blood of parents, brothers, sisters, and children who have been brutally tortured by the Nazi fascists and to fight for my homeland and native country against Hitler, the bloodhound, and his henchmen, the blood thirsty invaders, and hereby take it upon myself:

To be a courageous fighter, disciplined, and always ready; To guard carefully the military secrets, the secrets of the state, and army property;

To carry out, to the letter, without hesitation, the orders of my commanders and all those who stand at the forefront of leadership;

Not to spare any effort, not even my life, but to devote myself to the last drop of blood to the struggle for my country;

And, if I happen to violate this oath, may the hand of my comrades fall upon me.

THE PARTISAN OATH

(A Second Version)

I, a citizen of the Soviet Union,[4] a true son of the heroic Russian people, swear that I will not lay down my weapons until the fascist serpent in our land has been destroyed.

I commit myself without reservation to carry out the orders of my commanders and superiors and to observe strict military discipline. I swear to work a terrible, merciless, and unrelenting revenge upon the enemy for the burning of our cities and villages, for the murder of our children, and for the torture and atrocities committed against our people.

BLOOD FOR BLOOD! DEATH FOR DEATH!

I swear to assist the Red Army by all possible means to destroy the Hitlerite dogs without regard for myself or my life.

I swear that I will die in frightful battle before I will surrender myself, my family, and the entire Russian people to the fascist dogs.

And, if out of fear, weakness, or personal depravity, I should fail to uphold this oath and should betray the interests of my people, may I die a dishonorable death at the hands of my own comrades.

FRIENDSHIP

D. Stonov

After an appeal made by the Soviet government on July 3, 1941, to the Russian people, we decided to organize a vast partisan movement behind the German lines. Who was the man behind the idea that "those who took part in the 1917 civil war in the past should themselves join the partisan camp at once"?[5] The idea occurred at one and the same time to friends Salai, Negreyev, Kamensky, and Korotchenko, as it usually happens among old friends, after each one of them had reached the inevitable conclusion that there was no other way out.

"Let's do it together, after we have decided on it with one heart," said Korotchenko. But suddenly he fell ill, and it was necessary to take him to the hospital. Later on, when his friends visited him, he reminded them: "If together, then of course together. Tomorrow I'll be okay. You've got to wait till I get well."

It was thus necessary to postpone the beginning of the activities. Until Korotchenko got well, his friends called at the headquarters of the partisan movement, found out all about the work to be done, and, when he finally recovered, they decided upon the day, more accurately the night, of the take-off.

The would-be partisans, along with their families, gathered at the flat of Alexander Kamensky. In the evening a car arrived at the gathering place and took them to the airfield. At night, the plane flew across the front line and dropped the men over the woods of Elensk in the region of Chernigov, north of Kiev.

In the beginning, the new arrivals from Moscow joined the partisan unit of Nikolai Nikitich Popudrenko. In this unit the 1917 civil war veterans acquainted themselves with the new conditions of partisan warfare. The new arrivals had rich organizational experience and, as Popudrenko's unit was expanding fast, every one of them was put at the head of an independent company.

Alexander Kamensky was made commander of a partisan company named after Stalin. Between the summers of 1943 and 1944, his company accounted for two thousand and thirty-five German soldiers and officers, blew up and burned about thirty tanks and forty-nine vehicles, besides derailing fourteen engines and one hundred and twenty railway carriages

* * * * *

Michael Zuckerman, partly clad, escaped right from under the muzzle of a German rifle straight into the woods. He knew that here, in this forest, he would find Soviet people, partisans, avengers of the people. Occasionally sinking in heaps of snow, Zuckerman roamed the forest. His strength began to ebb, but his will to live kept driving him on. When he came upon a small mound on the ground, he imagined that he could find potatoes in it to fill his stomach, but not too much, for one potato too many would bring about severe pains and vomiting. This feeling alone kept him alive and going. Then one day at dawn he saw a man with a thick beard who was wearing a short fur coat and carrying a rifle in his hand. The man called out to him: "Halt! Who are you?" but before he could answer his strength ebbed, and he fell to the ground.

The man, Alexander Masko of Koryukovka, the region of Chernigov, forty-five years of age, was a partisan from the Stalin company. He had just finished his look-out duty and been replaced by another partisan. He lifted Zuckerman onto his back and carried him to the forest, to an earth hut.

That was the beginning of friendship between Alexander Masko and Michael Zuckerman. Some time before it had been Masko who had fled from the Germans, carrying around his neck a piece of rope which had snapped.[6] Just like Zuckerman, Masko had seen death in the face. Perhaps because of that, the friendship between the two was so strong, so loyal. Under the difficult conditions of partisan life, Masko found time to take care of his friend. The doctor had done what he could, but the patient was in constant need of care plus a discerning eye and soothing hands. The throats of the hardy partisans constricted on seeing how Masko gathered red berries from the trees to feed his weakened friend; how he would walk, during the long

69

marches, close to the sled that carried the sick man, covering
him with his own fur coat, fluffing up the pillow under his
head, carrying him to the campfire to bring warmth to him,
and protecting his back from the cold.

At times a man may feel drawn to another not only because
of the great responsibility involved in a cause, but because of
the similarity of their trade. The friends lived in one earth
hut. Once Zuckerman woke up upon hearing some knocking
around the hut. Raising his head he saw Masko, his mouth
full of nails, doing some cobbling and, with the skill of a
craftsman, taking out one nail after another and hammering it
into the heel.

"Wait a minute," said Zuckerman with obvious excitement.
"Who are you, really?"

Masko, thinking his friend to be dreaming out loud, replied,
"partisan Alexander Masko, of the Stalin company."

"And before that, who were you?"

"Before that I was a cobbler working in a village."

"And I am a tailor," said Zuckerman.

When working, Masko wore glasses. Now, greatly surprised, he shook his head, and his glasses fell over his nose.
He strained his neck toward the sick man and looked straight
at him for a long time.

"Swear to it!"

"God is my witness."

Masko went over to his friend, shook him up, and burst out
laughing.

"Here, I'm looking at you now and cannot think for one
moment that you belong to our trade. Now the secret is out.
Why have you kept silent all this time? Now we can make
something so all the other partisan companies will be filled
with envy. Do you know how many cases of chrome uppers
and sole leather we have taken out of German hands? They
have been lying around here useless for so long..."

When Zuckerman recovered completely the two friends
began to work in their spare time, between battles and
between the moving around from one place to another.
Actually they did wonders, and accounts of their handiwork
reached all the companies stationed in the Ukraine. When,
for instance, partisans from other units met a fighter belonging to the company of Alexander Kamensky, they did not ask

him to what company he belonged, since his chrome leather boots simply gave him away.

One thing lay heavy on Zuckerman's soul. In battle he had to be separated from his friend. Zuckerman was a sharp-shooter and Masko dealt with machine guns. His side was a young fighter from the River Don region. Masko too was chagrined at having to operate separately. So the two talked it over and decided to bring the matter up to their commander, Alexander Kamyensky.

Upon receiving the fighters, Kamensky sat down in a relaxed manner, took off his cap, pushed his hair back with his fingers, and asked them to take their seats. Masko and Zuckerman understood that they were about to start a cordial talk. Kamensky called them the *Kozhtrest* (leather producers associates) and asked them about their businesses. "Are there shoes for all the men of the company?" he asked, adding some witticisms about cobblers in general, favorable remarks, until Masko found out that the commander himself considered cobblers the best people in the world. "It seems that he belongs to our trade..."

"I don't understand your complaint and request," the commander said to Masko.

"I have no complaints at all," answered Masko, "but I'd like to explain to you that between me and Michael there is such strong friendship that to fight separately is so boring..."

"There is a strong friendship between us," reiterated Zuckerman.

Alexander Kamyensky sank into deep thought. Friendship! Friendship was a frequent caller at his international company: A Cossack would befriend a Ukrainian, a Tartar, a Georgian, a Russian, a Byelorussian, a fighter from Tajikistan. These oft-recurring friendships did not appear only yesterday. Their roots went back to the historical days of the war for victory and the strengthening of Soviet rule. In the fire of the great war for the fatherland,[7] friendship was forged so srongly that it united men of different nationalities with close patriotic feelings. Through invisible cords this friendship was to continue deep into the partisan forests between one fighting company and another, so that when the Jew Kamensky was in a tight spot, other commanders hurried to his aid, Salai the Ukrainian and Negreyev the Russian.[8]

"Too strong a friendship," Kamensky whispered to himself, then said aloud: "Well, let it be as you wish!"

On the following day the two friends started to fight side by side, using the same machine gun. Soon word went round the company about the two cobblers, not only as good craftsmen but also as excellent sharpshooters. Their friendship was to weather many a test. Then finally came the ultimate test, the test of blood.

After prolonged fighting the company had to encamp in the small forest of Kusei where it was impossible to maneuver. The partisans were nearly exhausted from the demands of their struggle, and even the horses could not stand the hardships of having to move frequently from one place to another. The early days of May were cold and chilling. The wounded groaned and sighed. But it was impossible to rest to get some warmth around the campfire, or even to eat. Night came, and the scouts brought in the news that the Germans were concentrating considerable forces, bringing field guns, tanks, and armored vehicles. They were in control of all the roads leading to the forest. They had even called in the *Luftwaffe*.

The Kusii forest had an ill-fated reputation: in it had been annihilated a local partisan company, commanded by the secretary of the district committee of Dobryanka. It was necessary to get away from the trap. Alexander Kamyensky urged the men toward further effort. The company scouts found a path whereby it was possible to bypass all the German roadblocks. To this end the partisans began, under cover of darkness, to leave the forest of Kusii. The men were dreaming of the forest of Tupichiv, toward which they directed their steps, as a quiet home with a cozy hearth; a place smelling of good cabbage soup, with windows overlooking a quiet street. But how to reach this forest where they could have some rest and also continue striking at the Germans?

The path went by the village of Vladimirovka, which held a German garrison and police forces. An encounter with them meant a delay for the entire company in its forced march, a waste of precious time, with the possibility that the Germans would use reinforcements of both men and material, artillery and tanks. It was therefore necessary to divert the attention of the German garrison and police force from the partisans' march until the fighters were far enough from the village.

Before dawn, the two friends, Michael Zuckerman and Alexander Masko, took upon themselves this difficult and dangerous task. Marshes surrounded the village on three sides, and it turned out that to wade through them was the best way to reach the place without being detected by the enemy. The men took their machine gun and crossed the marshes, wading in the icy water up to their hips. They walked into Vladimirovka, reached the church belfry, and silently dispatched the German sentry. They climbed into the tower and opened fire with the machine gun. Pandemonium struck the village: the partisans had taken hold of the church!

Firing their rifles and machine guns, the Germans hurried to the church. The soldiers and policemen surrounded the daring partisans. But high above, the partisan machine gun went into action, sowing death among the Germans. The faultless warriors naturally picked out the most coveted targets, and after half an hour's battle the ground around the church was littered with German bodies.

The belfry shook under the pounding of firing and explosions, and it was coming closer and closer. The bullets tore into the stone wall, and yellow brick dust spread into the air. But even through this could of yellow dust, one could see through binoculars how far away, in the vicinity of Vladimirovka, the company to which these two men belonged was fast slipping away from the neighborhood of the inferno which was raging in that previously quiet village. It was an encouraging spectacle which gave the warriors greater strength to carry on.

Another hour of fighting between greatly unequal forces had passed, and the Germans finally succeeded in setting fire to the church belfry. The fire spread fast, and the smoke made it hard for the partisans to breathe. Now it was possible to think of beating a retreat, since the company had fulfilled its task, having safely by passed the village of Vladimirovka.

"Should we blast our way through?" asked Michael Zuckerman.

The bursts of machine gun fire and the general noise were frightening. At first Zuckerman was not surprised to find his friend leaning toward him for the reply. But Masko kept leaning farther and farther. Suddenly Zuckerman saw blood coming out of his friend's mouth.

"Alexander," shouted Michael.

The Germans increased their pressure, and Zuckerman could not bandage his friend's wounds quickly. Masko passed out. In the meantime firing had ceased for a short while. Then Masko opened his eyes and turned his face toward his friend.

"I've been hit," he murmured with difficulty.

"What did you say?"

"I've been hit. Listen, Michael, run for your life. Try to shoot your way out, perhaps ou can save our life. And please tell comrade Kamensky... please go, go, so long as you are alive..."

The two friends usually spoke in low voices, called each other by their first names, smiling at each other. Masko's words now enraged Zuckerman. He shook his hands vehementl and said out loud:

"What is this, Masko, are you out of your mind? Shut up!" Zuckerman carried his friend on his shoulder and started a fast descent from the belfry. It was quiet all around. Five Germans, the last remnants of the entire garrison, thought the partisans had reached a stage of exhaustion, and now they, the Germans, crawled to the foot of the belfry. That was what Zuckerman had expected. He hurled two grenades at them, one after the other. He also had his rifle ready, but there was no need for it. The Germans were dead. In a nearby forest, a cart was waiting for the two friends. It brought them, after a trip of several hours, to the forest of Tupichiv.

From now on Zuckerman was number one at the machine gun, and the man from the River Don region number two. Obviously, things began taking their normal course again, only the other way around. Now it was Zuckerman who took care of his wounded friend, Masko; now it was he who went along with the cart that carried the wounded man. Once again the two friends were dreaming of the day when they would not have to separate from each other again — not in battle, not at work, and not while resting.

* * * * *

This is the story of two rank and file partisans, but as the saying goes, one drop is enough to determine the quality of water in a well or a river. Deep friendship between people of different nationalities prevailed in the company. Life and struggle, hard as the were behind enemy lines, were permeated with a feeling of brotherliness which cemented together the entire company and urged its fighters on to battle. This feeling spread from the bottom upwards, and here, at the top, it was complemented by the friendly attitude of the company commander, Aexander Kamensky, and his chief of staff, Konstantin Kosenko.

The chief of staff began his military career in Kamensky's company as an ordinary fighter. He was young, enthusiastic, and faultless. Alexander Kamensky's sharp eye detected him in the early days when he joined the company and saw in him an extraordinary fighter. The company commander began to give him singularly responsible tasks, sending him to highly dangerous places, realizing fully that only fire could forge this unique young man. At that time we were engaged in continual fighting, one battle following hard upon the other. The company moved from the region of Chernigov to the regions of Bryansk, Kiev, and onward to the Poltava region. At the same time friendship also strengthened between Alexaner Kamyesky and Konstantin Kosenko.

Gradually the company commander began to call the young partisan "my son" and the latter called him "father." Friendship between these two men deepened from day to day. Official discussions ended with intimate and prolonged talks. Kamyensky not only imparted some of his experience to the man, but he also consulted him.

In the story of Kamensky and Kosenko we wee them in our mind's eye in their spectacular exploits. We visualize Kamensky, tall of stature, with his broad face, white hair, and narrowing eyes, sitting on the barrel of a fiend gun. Beside him a young man, with fresh and rosy cheeks. With a lofty military intonation, Konstantin Kosenko is reporting to his company commander about the mission that has been carried out. His speech is interposed with pauses, hesitations; for he would rather fight from dawn to dusk and from night to dawn, then imagine, even for one single moment, that Kamensky would not approve of his deeds. Kamensky is satisfied; he pats his friend on the shoulder and says:

"Here, Konstantine Konstantinovich! It has been some time since I wanted to appoint you my chief of staff."

Chief of staff! This is really the "brain" of the unit. It should also be remembered that we are not speaking here of a regular army, but of a partisan company, in which the commander himself takes part in the fighting. Quite often Kosenko had to leave his work at the staff office and join the fighters in the battle field. This is just what happened in the forest of Nova Basan in the Poltava region. The enemy had put around this forest a ring of steel and had every corner covered with tank-and-armored-vehicle fire, in addition to the *Luftwaffe*. The battle between these unequal forces continued for three hours, in the course of which the enemy closed and narrowed the encirclement. In the face of such a situation it was necessary to spread the forces out by concentrating them in different corners in order to break through the iron ring. Alexander Kamensky gave the order to divide the company into two parts, each of which was to act independently of the other.

"I will take command of one company, and you of the other," said Kamensky to his chief of staff. "Later on we shall meet and unite once again in the forest of Kobyzhcha. Goodbye!"

That was an unforgettable night because of the fierce battles that were fought. It was raining and darkness was complete. The flames bathed the woods in their eerie light. Huge trees fell with ear-shattering noise. Here and there the earth heaved and dirt flew up into the sky. In this flaming inferno the brave partisans blasted their way out. The carts and provisions were left behind. Al the men, the women, and even the sink and the wounded who were in this convoy took up arms and prepared themselves for the decisive fight.

A close check of the enemy ring of encirclement revealed to Kamensky's maneuvering company a suitable spot where it could deliver a resounding blow to the Germans. Both sides met in hand-to-hand combat a few times. A mine-thrower jammed, and its operator was killed. Under a hail of German bullets, Kamyensky repaired the mine-thrower and began pouring fire into the fascists. We won the battle and broke the ring of encirclement. It was dark all around us, and, thus concealed, we could move on to the forest of Kobyzhcha. Suddenly Alexander came upon a wounded partisan from the company of Konstantin Kosenko. The wounded man had miraculously escaped and his life depended on a hair. With great difficulty he told Alexander that the chief of staff had not succeeded in breaking through and that his company was under triple encirclement. Hearing this, Kamensky, who had just come out of a ferocious battle, went back into the turmoil to save his friend Kosenko. The battle was on once again. The forest blazed with the light of day. The "father" now himself wounded, was fighting to save his "son," and the "son," sensing this, summoned the remnants of his forces for the last battle of that night. The two parts of the company united again, the partisans were now hammering at one target from two directions... In order to get an idea of that cruel battle, it should be borne in mind that the enemy threw into it a large force of tanks, mine-throwers, and machine guns. But the brotherhood of the Soviet people was stronger than death. The fascists were smothered by the flames of their own tanks, and all of their overwhelming equipment was to no avail.

The night neared its end. The heavy raining did not cease. The reunited company wended its way to the forest of Kobyzhcha. In a cart drawn by horses newly captured from the Germans sat the two friends, Alexander Kamensky and Konstantin Kosenko. The young chief of staff supported the wounded commander. Around them were many friends, all members of one family: multinational, strong, and united. They marched along in the night, full of confidence in the battles to come, in victory which, like dawn, would overcome darkness; they marched along through the forests and the plains which had been drenched with so much blood, the blood of their brothers.

WITHOUT FIRE...

Shirka Gaman

In one small town the Germans did not leave any Jews alive, with the exception of a few craftsmen and invalids. They took out Ozer the blind man, put stones and wood stocks all around him, and shouted the command: *"Jude, rechts! Jude, links!"*[9] Ozer tripped and fell down, rose to his feet, fell down again, saying, *"Shma Yisrael!"*[10]

The Germans went into the house of Zemach the tinsmith and dragged his wife Rachel from her bed, where she had been lying for years paralyzed in both feet. Two of them caught her under the armpits and the others shouted:

"Forward! You wife of a swine!"

One day Zemach found her lying injured on the floor. When he lifted her up and put her into her bed, she told him quietly: "Zemach, please have pity on me, give me the poison." Zemach had somehow gotten some powder, wrapped up in a piece of cloth, for her, but every time he fed Rachel with the spoon, he forgot to put the poison into the dish... He stood at the entrance to his smithy, his hand in his pocket, his fingers holding the powder. He wanted to take out his smoking tobacco, but lately his hand had somehow been slipping to the poison powder...

Today would be the end. He would redeem her, his own Rachel, "and they would no longer torture her," he decided.

Suddenly he heard the sound of wheels outside. A drunken German had pushed a motorcycle into the smithy. Zemach at once saw that the sidecar was beyond repair.

"What can I do for you, Sir?"

"The sidecar should be repaired by this evening."

"Please, sir," said Zemach, and went to the coal sack.

"No, no, you shouldn't use any fire. A Jewish tinsmith should know how to bend iron without using fire," the German said, sitting on a coal sack. He took out his pistol and asked: "Did you understand?"

"I understand quite well," said Zemach.

"Shut up, you cur," the Nazi retorted.

Zemach pretended that he did not hear; he looked around the smithy as if he were looking for something, went over to the wall, took down a wide piece of sheet iron, examined it with his hands, and bent down as if he were trying to pick up something.

"Sit up, Jude," the German shouted. "How long are you going to keep up this loitering!" He bent to take the piece of sheet iron from Zemach's hands.

Zemach raised his hands quickly and, letting out his breath as if he were ringing down the heavy hammer on the anvil of the smithy, threw the sheet iron around the soldier's head, and pulled it tightly with all his strength, as if he was winding a rope around his neck.

The German soldier groaned heavily. Zemach kept twisting the iron he held in his hands, pushing the German's head to the floor, then dragged him to the wall, threw a coal sack over him, and left the smith, without closing the door behind him.

"Good morning, Zemach," greeted Hirsch the builder, who was passing by there by chance.

"Where have you come from, Hirsch?"

"From the forest of Yagila."

"How do the partisan boys feel there?"

"For the time being, very well. They are safe and sound."

"Come inside, please, I would like to show you something," said Zemach. He rolled back the coal sack from the dead German.

"Do you see, Hirsch?"

"I see. God bless the hands that did it! You will have to run away into the forest at once, to the partisans, to your 'sons.' Do you hear me?"

"Yes, I hear. Today there will be an end to all this. Today... One moment, please..." Hirsch looked at him in amazement. "Come on, Hirsch." He was ready to return to see his wife when they saw dark smoke rising in a thick column, and in the air hung the smell of tar.

"They have once again put the town on fire!" said Hirsch. "It seems that your house also is on fire, Zemach!"

Upon reaching the place of the conflagration, they found, that of his house and his paralyzed wife Rachel, only a heap of cinders remained. For one moment they stood there in silence. Then Zemach turned in the direction of the forest, and went to greet his "sons," the partisans.

Partisan Friendship

A.P. Fedorov
Hero of the Soviet Union, Major-General,
Former Commander of a Partisan Brigade

My brigade included fighters from various walks of life, different ages, men and women. Among them were Russians, Ukrainians, Uzbeks, Jews, Tartars, and Kirghizes. Within the partisan companies, with all the variegated nationalities, glowed all too brilliantly the brotherhood of nations, tempered by battles fought side by side, when our fatherland stood facing the danger of annihilation, when all had become brothers in the face of calamity...

Shmuel Gottesban

He had been a student at the Leningrad Institute of Physical Culture. During the war with the Finns he volunteered to serve in the Tank Corps of the Red Army. In August, 1941, the Germans surrounded Gottesban's tank. Seriously wounded, he was taken prisoner. At the POW camp, which contained some twenty thousand prisoners, the Germans tortured our men with hunger and thirst. They even killed some of them. Gottesban managed to escape. He was later to escape from Kiev, where he had been living for some time, when the Germans led pogroms against the Jews. He was arrested and imprisoned in a cargo-train full of people. The carriage window was tightly closed and, inside, it was stifling. Under cover of darkness, when the train started to move, Gottesban succeeded in breaking open the window, and, together with some daring companions, jumped off the moving train. A woman who was passing by showed them the way to the partisans. And thus, Gottesban reached our group.

A battle was going on at the outskirts of the town of Kovel. Among the fighters in the partisan company was Shmuel Mordechai Gottesban. In this battle he accounted for twelve dead German soldiers and officers. In another battle around the tracks of the Kovel-Sarny railway, when a group of Germans tied to outflank us and attack us from the rear, the first to detect them was Gottesban, who shot six of them with his automatic rifle. Gottesban was not only a sharpshooter, but also an excellent saboteur. He took part in blowing up six German transports, and, together with other partisans, destroyed six train engines and more than seventy train carriages loaded with military equipment.

In the Volyn area he worked intensively on organizing underground fighters. Gottesban had great authority among the men of his company as well as the entire battalion. For his exploits in battle, he was awarded the "Red Flag" medal.

Alexander Margalit

In the same company where Gottesban served, there was a platoon commander by the name of Alexander Mordechai Margalit. The partisans liked him very much and had a great deal of respect for him. He deserved it. He took active part in all the battles of the company. He himself accounted for the death of twelve German soldiers and officers. One of his remarkable exploits took place in the attack of the town of Bragin in 1943. Margalit's company had outflanked and attacked the German company in the rear, when the latter was engaged in providing aid for the garrison in the town. In this battle the Germans lost about thirty men and ran away. Among the partisans' booty were a field gun, two mortars, and two machine guns.

In the battle near Kovel, Margalit was at the head of his company, as usual. His fighters killed more than seventy Germans and took prisoner eighteen soldiers and officers. But Margalit himself fell in this battle. We all cherish his memory as a daring commander who instilled in his men love, hope, and sacrifice for their country.

Dusya Baskina

Mention must be made of one of our medical nurses — Dusya Baskina. There was virtually no battle in which she did not take part. She would bandage the wounded under a hail of enemy bullets and evacuate them from the field of battle. In this manner she saved the lives of forty-nine wounded fighters and officers. When on the move or while the force was camping, she would go around caring for those in need of medical treatment or giving a word of encouragement to someone who needed it.

Dusya Baskina was not only a medical nurse, but also a dauntless and expert saboteur. She took part in blowing up sixteen enemy convoys.

Some time before the war started, Baskina finished a course for midwives. She had occasion to use her knowledge while working with us. In the villages we visited, she came to the help of pregnant women about to give birth, at any time or hour, by day or night. She also had the opportunity to treat babies in enemy-occupied territory. Leaning her rifle against a wall and keeping an alert ear to any rustling sound, she worked fast, quietly, in a well-organized manner, as if she were in a hospital ward during peacetime. For her courage and daring exploits she was awarded two medals.

Boris Baskin

A scout's work constantly involves self-reliance and courage. Death stalks him wherever he steps. The brother of Dusya, the medical nurse, was one of our best scouts. At the outskirts of Kovel he was ambushed by the enemy. In the exchange of fire that ensued, Baskin single-handedly accounted for four dead Germans. He was wounded, but he kept on firing until his partisan friends came to his aid.

Joshua Hirsch Baskin

Joshua Hirsch Baskin, who had the same surname as Boris, also proved to be a daring fighter. He would receive radio messages and set them in type for partisan announcements. His radio messages came from Russia.[11] He set them in print and distributed them among the partisans. The news items he provided were more vital to them than bread.

Yefim Litvinovsky

He fought the Germans with all his might. Without any hint of joking, he called himself "Denizen of the Next World." Actually Litvinovsky arrived at our camp as a survivor from the claws of death. Whe war broke out he was twenty years old, lived in Kuibyshev, was a student, and studied singing. He entered the Red Army as a volunteer. In one of the battles he was wounded and taken prisoner. The Germans sent him from one camp to another until he was eventually transported to Sobibor. Today everyone knows how the Germans killed people in such concentration camps as Auschwitz, Maidanek, or Sobibor. When Litvinovsky related to us, as early as 1943, the stunning atrocities perpetrated by the Germans, when he told us of the fires arising from human bodies, of the "bath houses" where they killed the inmates, of the mass murder of thousands of children — a shiver ran down our spines.

Litvinovsky "managed" to be among those in charge of burning the bodies of those killed by the Germans. This "privilege" made it possible for Litvinovsky and his friends to take acdtive part in the revolt.[12] The day that the German guards went out for target practice, the inmates of Sobibor raised the banner of revolt. They broke into the armory and killed the Germans who had been left in the camp; but they could not break through the fences of the camp at the first attempt, as the gates were guarded by Germans with machine guns. Hatchets in hand, the rioters hacked out an opening in the barbed wire fences. Several were blown up by the German mines, but they had opened a safe path for the surviving escapees. The latter kept on firing, then ran for the woods. After hard and prolonged wandering, Litvinovsky arrived at our battalion together with his friend Tsadok Chaim Levin. Both had enough reasons to revenge themselves on the Germans.

And if patrol duty was a difficult and dangerous work, that of the runners, under the circumstances, was no less difficult and no less dangerous. We had runners both in the companies and in the villages directly under the noses of the enemy. They had to be continuously careful and on their guard. They did their duty at the risk of their lives.

We had a group of runners, young boys. At their head was a boy of fourteen, Aaron, son of a partisan woman whom we called "Dusya the Linen Seamstress," to distinguish her from Dusya Baskina. Aaron was a daring, well-disciplined runner. At the head of his boys, he took upon himself the most responsible missions. No danger stood in the way of those boys; as young patriots they carried out each mission on time and with great devotion.

Among the Jewish commanders we may also mention the company chief of staff, Levin, who had remarkable resourcefulness and a knack for drawing up splendid plans or the fight against the German armies.

A filmmaker called Michael Moshe Glieder took part in a number of outstanding exploits of our brigade. His men were included in the picture "The People's Avengers," for which he received the Stalin Award.[13] Twelve times he went out on sabotage missions. He took part in blowing up ten enemy convoys. Sometimes he would go into battle holding in one hand a movie camera and, in the other, a rifle. Another man who did a good job in our brigade was the photographer-reporter Yaakov Davidson. There were not many men in the brigade who did not take part in the battles themselves, but everyone contributed his own share, according to his occupation. Without these people our struggle would certainly have been a much more difficult task.

I have already mentioned the name of "Dusya the Linen Seamstress," who sewed for our partisans. Nothing wears out clothes faster than the continual treks through the woods. Particular importance was thus attached to the work of the tailors. Tirelessly, tailor Shcheglovsky went on sewing clothes. Under our peculiar conditions he knew how to sew convenient, durable, and warm clothing.

The hatmaker Sorin had his hands full of work. He was an outstanding artisan, and knew how to let comfort blend with warmth in the partisans' headgear, sometimes even pampering the idiosyncrasies of individual fighters.

Our partisans also owe a debt of gratitude to artisan Godes, a specialist in leather work. Wearing one of his leather coats drove away one's fear of strong winds or snowstorms and made one think nothing of lying in ambush hour after hour under heaps of snow.

To my regret I do not remember the name of the partisan who made sausage for us. I only recall that they called him Isaac. He was excellent at making sausage. Not at every grocery store could one find sausages of such quality as those prepared by this man Isaac.

Mention should also be made of our pharmacist, Zyama Ahron Noselevich. He was about sixty years old. His pharmacy he carried on one cart. Noselevich managed it in a remarkable manner. Whenever we camped he would had out medicine to the sick. Naturally enough our scouts would replenish his stock in the course of their patrol work.

The majority of our fighters were young men. Sometimes they would remember the old days, of peace, when they were fee to enjoy themselves, to travel, to listen to music, to dance, the throw an improvised party. But these memories were not enough for them. In the calm hours when it was possible to relax and unwind, we also knew how to make merry. To tell the truth we had some very fine musicians. Violinists Gurary and Schwartz had an uncanny sense of when they were needed. From memory they would play our favorite tunes, songs and dances. They also played works by Tchaikovsky, Glinka, Chopin, and Strauss.

Many Jews came to us along with their families. The men fought, but the elderly, the women, and the children worked in our rear lines. I remember well some of these families — Yakubovich, Karasik, Davidovich, Sirovsky, and others.

As partisans our duty was not only to fight the German invaders and their collaborators, but to do our best to help the local citizens by word *and* deed and, particularly, to save people, to free them from the hands of the fascist killers.

One day in the forest we came upon a group of people wearing tattered rags — old men, women, and hungry children. It was winter, and they were in danger of dying out there in the woods. We discussed the matter and decided to take them along with us. That was the genesis of our first civilian camp. As time went on two damps of this kind were set up. We took the sick and the weak to safe places. When they regained their strength, many of them joined our brigade as partisan fighters.

The inhabitants of the civilian camps did all they could to give us the help we needed. Each camp was attached to one of our battalions. When we were on the move, the people of the camp went along with our convoy under special guards. In sum, over five thousand Jews passed through our amps. They stayed with us for about ten moths, and almost al of them were eventually taken to "The Great Land," namely — the Soviet Union.

When we freed populated areas our brigade would first release the prisoners. Thus on freeing Koriukovka (District of Chernigov) we released twenty-five Jews; in Sofievka (District of Novozybkov), eighteen; in Leyubeshov, eight; and several Jewish people in other places.

*   *   *   *   *

I have a strong desire to mention one more friend. He did not belong to the partisans, nor did he belong to the civilian population, but meeting him was a great joy to all of us; in January, 1944, our men met for the first time scouts from the Red Army who had penetrated deep behind enemy lines. The commander of this group of Red soldiers was Leonid Leontyevich Levitas, a native of the Ural Mountains. He was a fine man.

THE AVENGERS OF THE MINSK GHETTO

O. Cherny

The winter of 1941 was hard and forbidding. Already on the tenth of October the first snow started falling. Great and biter suffering fell to the lot of those who happened to be in the region swept by the German attack…They had lost contact with the Soviet army.

It was also difficult for Israel Lapidus, in the region of Vyazma, which had been encircled by the enemy. For several weeks he was to roam through the woods, seeking escape from the Germans. He did not succeed in finding the partisan nest and thus had to direct his steps towards Minsk, the town where he had grown up and worked and had concerned himself with public affairs. It was in this town that he joined the Red Army in the early days of the war.

Wearing a peasant winter coat and a yellowish beard, Israel Lapidus arrived at German-occupied Minsk. Barbed wire encircled like a belt the narrow and ancient streets of this old town. Death was beginning to be felt from behind the fence of the ghetto, where seventy thousand Jews were leading a life of desperation. Nonetheless Lapidus began to look for an opening into the ghetto. In those days Minsk ame to a standstill as a town at five in the afternoon. Only intermittent firing and the monotonous marching of the German guards disturbed the eerie silence.

For quite a long time Lapidus kept loking for a way to get into the ghetto. Near the felt factory on Kolkhoznaya Street he saw an empty lot and the pits that indicated the sites of former buildings which the Germans had burned down. He crawled a few scores of meters, crossed the ghetto boundaries, and was in.

Was there at least a single relative alive? How many citizens of the lively and boisterous Minsk region had Lapidus known? He reached the house of his relatives. They had survived. From them he heard the blood curdling account of the Germans' first pogrom against the Jews on November 7, 1941. His parents and son were among those killed by the Germans on that day. He hurried to look for his wife and found her, along with his surviving firstborn son.

Filled with a deep desire to avenge himself on the Germans, Lapidus decided to ether a partisan company, take it out of the ghetto, and add it to the forces engaged in the people's war against the fascists.

Lapidus also found his old friends: Davidson, Losik Gantman, Kravchinsky, and together they went about organizing the partisan company. It was difficult to operate in the ghetto. But Lapidus found out that the spirit of the ghetto people had not weakened and that their will to act had not died out. He looked deep through each and every one of them, trying to visualize how the man would act in the forest, under the singularly severe conditions of partisan life.

Many of Lapidus's friends, workers in Minsk, were now in the army. Most of the ghetto people had never held a gun before; but everyone of them had had his own tragedy, and the all-consuming fire of hatred for the Germans kindled in their hearts. Everyone was dreaming of taking up arms. But Lapidus picked only those who were fired by the desire for revenge. He sought people known for their self-restraint and self-control. In his mind's eye he saw the interminable tests to which the partisans would be put.

Cautiously and with great care he enlisted men into the company. The ghetto abounded with spies and German agents, and it was necessary to make all the preparations in complete secrecy. Lapidus asked typesetters Oppenheim and Rappaport to get him the necessary equipment for a printing press. They renewed their contacts with old fiends living outside the ghetto, and they helped them get the type they required. To smuggle all the equipment out of the ghetto could be done only by hiding the parts in one's pockets or concealing them under one's clothes. That was a tough and dangerous job, but by the end of winter the partisans had set up their own printing press, with a sizable stock of paper, ink and type.

The first bulletin put out by the national avengers was directed at the ghetto Jews. It called for resistance and planted in their hearts hope for the day when Minsk would once again be a liberated Soviet city. Those who read the bulletin felt the taste that a thirsty person has for water from which he is given only one sip.

* * * * *

Winter passed amid tense preparations. Smuggling arms into the ghetto became extremely difficult. It called for great effort to get the twelve grenades three pistols, three rifles, and about five hundred cartridges they now had. They guarded them like the pupil of their eye.

The weather was still cold. The trees were still bare of leaves, but the winter was now over. With the help of the underground Bolshevik organization, Israel Lapidot was able to pick out forty-eight people for the partisan company. Then the decisive day arrived. On the morning of April 10, 1942, when the groups of workers leaving for their daily work outside the ghetto boundaries were lined up in neat rows, the forty-eight people met on Rakovskaya Street at a predetermined spot. They could not be distinguished from the other inmates of the ghetto: the same yellow patches[14] on the chest and on the back, the same sacks with the work tools on their shoulders, but among the tools there were rifles, and in their pockets they had grenades.

With no hitches they made their way through Shpalernaya, Respublikanskaya, and Shornaya streets, turned up Novomoskovskaya Street and, from there, onto the road leading to Slutsk. They had hardly left the outskirts of the town when they tore off of each other's clothes the yellow patch that symbolized forced labor and slavery.

On the Slutsk road the group was divided into smaller groups of two or three persons walking ahead at some distance from each other. At the head of this small sale exodus walked Lapidus, his wife, and their firstborn son.

After they had covered some forty kilometers down the road, the would-be partisans gathered once again, only to find out that not all of them had made it to that spot and that the daring operation had taken its first toll.

Turning in the direction of the villages of Rudkovo and Kolodino, the company tarried for some time in the forest.

The peasants of these villages knew Lapidus well, and he realized right from the outset that the company would have a fighting chance only if it could establish close ties with the local population.

From a peasant woman, Marusya, in the village of Rudkovo, Lapidus learned all that he needed for the first leg of their march. This piece of information helped him to acquire the right orientation for the conditions prevailing in the woods. Marusya had her own intentions in relation with the ghetto people. Some weeks after the partisans had started their activities, she approached Lapidus with the request to admit her into his company. In the forest the partisans went about pitching tents for themselves, since it was too early to think about more permanent quarters. In the ghetto there still remained many people who wanted to go into the forests. Before long Lapidus sent over to them three partisan women, Patent, Duker, and Borzin. The peasant women dressed them in their traditional dress and gave them two carts loaded with potatoes: one for Borzin and the other for Patent and Duker. The women reached Minsk safely and once again slipped into the ghetto. Although they had never done any reconnaissance or intelligence work, they fulfilled their mission faultlessly. According to a list which had been prepared by Lapidus, work started on organizing a new group, which in turn succeeded in evading the German claws. The women led the ghetto people over the familiar road that brought them to the forest adjoining the village of Rudkovo.

Meantime the company had become lager, and a name had to be found for it: a name which would be close to the heart of everyone. Someone suggested they call the company after the great Russian commander Kutuzov. The suggestion was accepted unanimously. A few days passed, and to Minsk went once again two women partisans of the Kutuzov Company, Patent and Duker. They were dressed as peasant women and carried false identity cards.

Near Shatsk the two women were stopped and taken to the Gestapo, where they were interrogated for several days. The two women did not disclose the name of a single partisan. The Gestapo started torturing them, but still the Germans could not extract anything from the brave women, and they killed them. Lapidus then sent Asya Binder to the ghetto to bring out another group. With commendable courage she followed the path which had earlier brought death to her two friends. On reaching Minsk she carried out the dangerous task she had been entrusted with. On many occasions women from the Kutuzov Company continued slipping into the ghetto on vital and dangerous missions.

Here is an example of the self-sacrifice revealed by woman-partisan Leah Borzin, who was formally declared a ground scout within a short time of her joining the company. On one occasion, when the partisans were about to mount an attack on the small town of Uzlyany Leah Borzin succeeded in slipping into the local German command. There she got all the necessary information the partisans needed. But she was arrested after she had succeeded in getting out of the building, and was taken to the Rudensk station where she was subjected to torture for a long time. Still, she did not reveal anything. With unspeakable cruelty they stabbed her in the eyes and then hanged her in the town square.

As a result of the viable relations which were established with the aid of reliable friends, the Kutuzov Company received new fighters every day: men and women who had succeeded in escaping from the ghetto or from the surrounding villages, which were groaning under the German yoke. When the company numbered about one hundred partisans, Lapidot began combat operations. The first attack was launched on the village of Khotlyany. In this village there were twelve policemen who lived off the peasants like leeches. The artisans attacked the village under cover of darkness, cut off the telephone line, and killed the traitorous policemen. They took possession of a German store and distributed among the peasants all that was in it: sickles, scythes, shoes, grinders, and the like.

The operation succeeded without any casualties and kindled the enthusiasm of our fighters. The partisans then asked to be taken on further operations. They mounted a sudden attack on the village of Doshchenko as they had done on Khotlyany before, setting fire to all the documents of the local management which listed the debts of the peasants. In the estate of Samoilovo, formerly a *kolkhoz*,[15] they shot the German manager, dispatched the policemen, captured twenty-six horses, some thirty cows, and ten tons of seeds. The sheep, the goats, and the bread they distributed among the peasants.

* * * * *

Thus relations were strengthened between the partisans and the peasants. Often they would come to Lapidus with the request to be accepted into the company, which was multinational right from the start, one of the numerous companies whose name was to become a household word all over Byelo-russia.

The company led a life of brotherhood: on dark nights the fighters would go out on combat missions. They were through marshes and through snow, dressed in camouflage coveralls, looking alike. They would meet in huts, where the burly Siberian Danila Stolbov listened to the stories of an old cobbler from Minsk, Wolf Lusik; and the Ukrainian woman Galina Kraiko watched with unconcealed excitement Lapidot's son, Misha, growing into a brave partisan and acting out theatrical characters. All of them were drawn close together by their abysmal hatred for the enemy.

With dogged persistence the partisans learned how to use arms. They had to master not only the Russian rifle but also the other arms captured from the enemy. The blacksmith from Minsk, Tokarsky, set up a workshop in the forest, where he repaired the arms taken by the partisans. It was necessary to get explosives, and the partisans learned how to take the dangerous but vital material out of the dud shells they found in the woods. The company laid ambushes, destroyed railway tracks, and attacked command posts, and well as regional and district garrisons which had been set up by the enemy.

During the first fifteen months the Kutuzov company derailed twenty-one train full of German troops, laid fourteen ambushes, and accounted for hundreds of dead German soldiers. The company inflicted heavy casualties on the Germans, destroyed their bases, and put the Osipovichi-Minsk railway tracks out of commission.

The partisans weathered hard battles. Those who had come from the ghetto were honed to a fine point in these battles.

Student Misha Lapidus was doing a fine job destroying enemy vehicles: he would jump on the top of a vehicle and shoot straight at the Germans inside it. The boy Abraham Zhitelzey was outstanding in throwing hand grenades. Lazar Lasin, a sixteen-year-old boy, derailed about ten trains. Pima Schneider had many explosions to his credit. They all struck at the fascists. These boys had come from the ghetto and had been school children only a short while before. But the old did not lag behind: the company included sixty-year-old Lei Strugach and the old cobbler Vorobeichik.

Fine yet strong ties stretched from the forest near Rodansk to numerous villages in Byelorussia. The partisans distributed among the peasants news from the *Sovinformburo* (Soviet News Agency) and held political discussions with them.

The contact between the company and the ghetto of Minsk was kept viable mostly through the daring spirits who escaped to join us. Thus the partisans were to admit into their lines the three brothers Golub who had escaped from the ghetto on their own and who, in their first battles, proved to be dauntless fighters. One of them fell in battle with the enemy, and the remaining two kept on fighting until the final victory over fascist Germany.

The ray of hope emanating from the forest near Rudensk was so luminous that even small children used to run away from the ghetto in their search for the site of the partisan company. They had all undergone nightmarish experiences at the hands of the Germans, who had killed their parents in front of them. Desperation had made them faultless fighters, and sixteen boys and young men, ranging in age from seven to fourteen, eventually succeeded in slipping out of the ghetto, hungry and unclad. They wandered in the woods for a long time. Peasants took them into their homes, fed them, and brought them into the forest to the partisan camp.

The Kutuzov company saved all those that could be saved and supplied arms to all those who could fight. Though it lost many fighters in the course of its numerous battles, many of these fighters, who had come from the ghetto of Minsk, eventually succeeded in seeing their hometown once again.

After the war these former partisans returned to their work in the factories; some even went back to resume their studies.

Rolling up their sleeves, they began to work on rehabilitating the economic and cultural institutions of their capital. And today, in the rebuilt and revived town of Minsk, you may once again see old Leib Strugach, or the invalid cobbler Schafsal Vorobeichik, and the Lusiks, both father and son, along with Israel Lapidot himself, who has in the meantime resumed (Communist) party work. The former partisans often remember the stormy nights, the long treks from one place to another, the battles, and the reconnaissance missions. These recollections are certainly of great help to Misha Lapidot, who has now become an actor in the Byelorussian theater, when he acts out on the stage real characters of the heroes of the fatherland's great war.

PART THREE
PARTISAN SOCIETY

In the Forests of Bryansk

V.A. Andreyev, Major-General,
Former Commander of a Partisan Unit

The Shchors Partisan Battalion, of which I was Chief of
Staff, was composed of Communist party members, Red
Army soldiers, Soviet workers, and ghetto survivors from the
Bryansk region of Byelorussia. Our battalion consisted of two
group: one, the underground group, was active in the district
of the town of Kolodnya under the command of Filkovsky,
and secretar of the party's regional committee, and the other,
led by Vasily Rysakov, had already begun its activities around
the village of Uruchye.

For a long time I had only heard of Filkovsky through
hearsay. It was impossible to get to see him or the other
underground fighters because of the distances that separated
us and the difficulties involved in conspiracy. This situation
continued for a long time, but, as the saying goes, "happiness
would not have come had it not been for disaster."

The Germans turned a crack punishment squad against
us. This squad came upon the tracks of our unit. A group
commanded by Filkovsky engaged the enemy in battle.
Twenty-five men fought off an entire German battalion. As
the defensive operations were organized in the woods, it was
possible for the underground fighters to hold their ground till
the evening. Under cover of darkness they slipped away from
the enemy and fought their way to our camp.

This was the first battle for the Filkovsky group. Generally
speaking he was no military man, abut in this battle he proved
to be a dauntless and ingenious commander. He made good
use of the arms at his disposal — two machine guns, two
automatic rifles, a few bolt-action rifles, and one mortar —
giving the impression that a much larger military unit was
fighting it out with the Germans.

The first engagement of the Filkovsky group with the
enemy cost the life of an outstanding fighter and Communist,
Emelyanov, the N.K.V.D.[16] representative. The Germans,

however, suffered heavier losses — they had forty killed and many wounded. Among those killed was their battalion commander.

I first met Filkovsky in his earth hut, which had been originally intended for thirty people but at the time provided shelter for over a hundred. He was about thirty-five, of medium height, and strongly built. His homely features indicated intelligence, and his chestnut hair was combed back. His eyes, also hazel, had an aggressive, manly expression.

Filkovsky was wearing a black woolen shirt tightened close to his body with a military belt, from which hung a TT pistol. His woolen trousers, also black, were tucked into crafted peasant felt boots.

I was to learn later that during the short time that the underground movement had been active behind enemy lines under the leadership of Filkovsky, it had undergone many trying experiences. As early as October, 1941, the Germans had destroyed the partisan base and spread rumors that the party leaders, together with the regional Soviet officials, including Filkovsky, had been caught and put to death. By so doing, the Germans wanted to spread confusion and demoralization among the people. The regional committee had thus o issue a declaration to the inhabitants of the region to the effect that the Soviet leaders and the party associations were still active in their region in the occupied areas and were continuing their fight against the Germans and their collaborators. The regional committee called upon all the inhabitants to join the fight. The proclamation was signed by Filkovsky.

In our battalion Filkovsky, who had been promoted to the rank of commissar, was treated with deep respect. He was my age. He had worked in a tailor shop at Bryansk and had been an active Communist party member for ten years. According to his friends he had done excellent work in the prewar days. Now behind enemy lines, he worked with great enthusiasm. But often he seemed uncommunicative and, at times, even irascible. In the beginning I could find no explanation for such streaks of character.

"What's wrong with him?" I once asked Mazhukin, the chairman of the regional executive committee — and he recounted to me the tragedies of Filkovsky's life. When war started Filkovsky moved his family — his wife, three children, and a female relative — eastward, a distance of only two hundred kilometers. Being in a strange place was no easy matter: they had no home to live in and the children fell ill. At the same time the Red Army stemmed the German advance at the Sudost river. In Vygonichi, the people assumed that the Germans would not advance any farther, and they began to bring their families back. On October 5, Filkovsky's wife, children, and female relative returned to their home, and on the sixth of the same month the Germans occupied the entire region. The Germans began a search for Filkovsky and his family. As Filkovsky was then busy organizing the underground movement, his friends took care of the members of his family, smuggling them from one village to another to hide them from the Germans. With the approach of cold weather they were living temporarily at the small village of Pavlovka. It was here that the Germans caught them and put them to death in a most atrocious manner.

Filkovsky blamed himself for the loss of his family and had no peace of mind. I did everything, together with some friends, to help him get over his grief and take his mind off his personal tragedy. As head of the battalion staff, I always let Filkovsky take part in drawing up the plans for all the fighting operations of the battalion. He would get down to work with enthusiasm, get the fighters ready for battle, provide the propagandists with the necessary instructions, write announcements and leaflets. On such days he would forget his personal tragedy and change to such an extent that it was difficult to recognize him.

While continuing our raids on enemy garrisons, we carried out demoralizing operations on the railway tracks. At the beginning of January, 1942, Filkovsky gave two of his partisans, Glebkin and Tishin, the task of sabotaging the railway tracks. The demolishing charge was prepared in a very primitive manner — a box was made out of some boards, filled with mines, and put on the tracks. The operation succeeded. The train, which was filled with German soldiers heading for the front, advanced at a high speed, and about ten carriages were blown up.

This successful operation meant a great deal to the battalion. Filkovsky suggested holding courses in sabotage activities. At the same time we were joined by First Lieutenant Vorobyov of the engineering corps, whose unit had been surrounded by enemy forces, but he had succeeded in escaping to our lines. It was he who began to impart to the partisans the know-how and skill involved in sabotage work. The comrades were highly elated at the beginning of their "studies." But Filkovsky put an end to that premature joy.

"For the time being you are only acquiring knowhow. But we have no demolition charges. What're you going to use for demolition work?"

Actually the lack of explosives made the situation difficult for us. But Vorobyov suggested that we take the tracks apart. A great number of our men, led by the commanding commissar, went out on this operation, which succeeded without the use of explosives.

"We now have something to report on to the partisan center," Filkovsky informed his men, beaming with joy. On that very night he wrote a telegram and sent it through our transmitter to the frontline headquarters. Two days later we heard a summary of the news items broadcast by the Central Soviet Information Bureau which said, among other things, that "the partisan company led by R. and the secretary of the regional committee F., acting in the woods of Bryansk (Bryansk region), derailed an enemy convoy heading for the front and inflicted heavy casualties on the enemy forces."

Filkovsky had great concern for the local population, which was gravely suffering from the occupation forces. He addressed the people constantly through encouraging leaflets written in a cordial style. These leaflets he wrote together with his propagandists. When we had freed some villages from the Germans, Filkovsky would hold a general meeting of the inhabitants. The speeches and discussions usually ended with a general get-together party.

"Comrades, let's not be downhearted. Let's sing!" — thus would Filkovsky address the gathering. "Out with your har-monica," he would call out to a member of his company, Gutorov, the harmonica man, who was also one of his propagandists.

And Gutorov would begin. He would begin with *Kassyan* and then play the *Ermak*. Filkovsky would start singing. The multi-voiced choir would follow suit. In the end Gutorov would play the music of *Stradanya* ("Agonies").

"Let's dance!" And taking off his coat, he would lead the dancers.

It could only be that this man had once been a first-class dancer. He stomped wonderfully with his feet and invited into the dancing circle one fighter after another. He then gave his place to the singing girls. To the tunes of the harmonica, one of them started:

"Germans came to our village,
My song died out.
They burned my house down, took my father away
And hanged my beloved........."
The other singer answered her, in song too, improvising:
"In the Nazi claws
We led lives of imprisonment.
When the partisan came
Our spirit came to life as a miracle!"[17]

At the end of such get-together parties, the partisans would feel a great relief after the day-to-day hardships of living in the woods.

Month after month saw the growth of the partisan movement in our region (Bryansk region). By the beginning of May, 1942, we had five companies fighting alongside us, numbering nearly two thousand men. I was appointed brigade chief of staff and commander of the Bauman company.

Our companies performed heroic deeds. Filkovsky was a remarkable company instructor. In the summer of 1942 he was awarded a number of medals, including the "Red Flag" and the "Red Star".

* * * * *

The activities of the Bryansk partisans caused much concern among the Germans. They started to bring punishment squads into the region, increased their patrol activities, and attempted to infilrate our lines in order to cause us as much harassment as possible. I shall recount in detail one such fascist provocation: it happened in those days when the

Filkovsky group had not yet joined our battalion. A young woman by the name of Irina was brought into our camp. She told us about her Jewish descent, that she was born in Berdichev (Ukraine), that she had not been able to escape before the German occupation and had thus been driven out into the ghetto, together with her parents. She had succeeded in escaping to Vygonichi where she came under the German order of r the registration of all Jews, without her being able to evade it. But owing to her mastery of the German language, the Germans had made her work as an interpreter for the Gestapo at the high command.

It may be pointed out that I had come across Irina's name before she arrived at our company. In December, 1941, one of our scouts, a villager from Kolodnoe, delivered a secret message to the commander of Rysakov's group. The message read: "Dear comrade, a friend is writing to you. Conditions have forced me to work for the Germans, but you have to know that I have worked, am working, and will continue to work only for our country. I shall do all I can to cause harm to the Germans. Give me whatever mission you want, and I shall prove my loyalty."

"What do you make of it?" the commander asked me, showing me the note. "Isn't this a provocation?"

"It is not unlikely," I answered, then asked: "How did she find our runner? And who is he? Can we trust him?"

"He is no doubt one of our men," came the commander's confident reply.

As we came to learn later, the runner had gone on a mission for us to Vygonichi during a snow storm, and he could not leave the village for three days. One day at dusk, while he was crossing the railway tracks, a young woman he did not know came up to him and asked:

"Where do you come from?"

"What's the matter?"

"I'm asking you, where do you come from?" the young woman said firmly once again. Then she went on. "I work at the German High Command. Here are my certificates. Do you have documents? Let me see them."

The runner was confused and showed her his passport, as a resident of Kolodnoe.

"Are there any partisans there?" she asked, lowering her voice, and looking around her.

"No."

"There are," she insisted. "I know. Don't pretend to be naïve. You are a party scout."

Surprise confused the runner, and the young woman said to him in a firm voice, pushing an envelope into his hand:

"Deliver this to the partisans. If it doesn't reach them, I'll know where to find you, and you'll have a bitter end. I remember your surname, and I am familiar with the village. I'll find you wherever you go. Is that clear? And if you should decide to come with this message to the German commander, I know what to say, and then — you—," and she pointed at the sky.

Afterwards the young woman told the runner that she was a Jewess and that there was nothing to worry about.

"Let's put her to the test," I suggested to the commander. "Let her kill the German commander."

After some consideration we decided to put her to the test by giving her a lighter mission. We suggested to her, through the same liaison man, that she establish contact with the workers of the hospital at Vygonichi and commandeer medicines and instruments for us and, later on, that she bring us doctors. Among the workers of this hospital, we had friends who had worked for the army and had been taken prisoner. Needless to say we did not tell the unknown young woman that we had already revealed our plans to the doctors who were waiting for an opportunity to come over to us.

Shortly after giving that mission to the unknown young woman, the women doctors were safely with us. They were POWs Lydia Unkovskaya and Lyuba Todortseva, to be joined soon afterwards by Stera, the daughter of Moshe Tyomkin. They brought along with them a great many instruments and other hospital items. Two medical nurses came along with the dotcors. The whole thing had been organized in the best manner. According to the doctors, the young woman, who had won the confidence of the German commander, succeeded even in arranging transportation for the hospital equipment to our base.

We kept wondering at the zeal, courage, and ingenuity of the unknown young woman. We decied, however, to give her the mission to kill the German commander. We were told that she eagerly took it upon herself to carry out this task. She acquired a pistol without any difficulty and, at a convenient moment, shot the commander in the back and killed him.

As it now was dangerous for the unknown young woman to remain in Vygonichi, we helped her come over to stay with us. To our regret we found out a few days later that the German commander was still alive and that she had killed another Hitlerite. She had fired in the dark and had missed. The man she killed had a silhouette similar to that of the commander. "Well, to hell with the commander; the Germans would certainly have sent another one in his place. But one more dead fascist," Rysakov soothed her. "A woman of valor! It's good that you yourself managed to escape!"

Irina was an asset to our company. In that crowded and stifling earth hut, she cleaned, ironed the men's linen, laundered, mended, and patched. Systematically and thoroughly she learned to use all sorts of weapons, and she missed no opportunity to take part in the operations of the company. Owing to her contacts in Vygonichi she even succeeded in getting for the battalion about ten rifles, several pistols, flare rockets, and flare-gun cartridges of different colors. She made only one mistake, and that was when we were sitting around the camp fire. She was playing with some flares when one went off, a green one. It went up and exploded above the camp exactly when an unidentified plane was flying over the woods.

Irina was also an excellent interpreter. She had a good command of both German and Russian and helped us in translating German documents. Thus she was able to render a great service to the partisan forces. This young woman got on well with all the men, especially with a young man called Tsibulsky, who was known for his courage in battle and gaiety in everyday life. He would play the violin, and Irina would sing, a fact which may have brought them closer together. He was active in the company, like his girlfriend, and showed an interest in everything.

However, we were lucky to learn that Tsibulsky was a prominent German spy, who had been sent to our company by the Gestapo and by the head of the investigation department at the police station of Bryansk, Tsibulsky's despicable brother. During his stay with our company, this spy succeeded in causing us great harm — he brought about the capture of many of our runners and liaison men. At the questioning, Tsibulsky admitted all that had already been known to us.

After we had executed Tsibulsky our men kept close watch on Irina. She sensed it and demanded from the commander that he sentence her to death if he did not have faith in her. "I cannot keep on living like this," she told him firmly.

Some time after that incident two new comrades arrived at our camp. One of them, Dmitry Yemlyutin, who was about thirty-five, had a quick and nervous manner of speaking and was also a chain smoker. He was a representative of the sabotage department of the N.K.V.D. and had stayed on his mission behind enemy lines. The other, Isaac Bentzionov, who was quite dexterous and also a heavy smoker, brought me and Rysakov the following message: "You have a woman spy in your company, who poses as Jewess in order to cover up her tracks, but who in fact is a German. She was born in Bessarabia, has a good command of the Russian language, graduated from an espionage school, and has come to you for her first performance."

We at once understood that he meant Irina. We called her in for questioning, and when she realized that everything was up, she revealed everything. The liaison man from Kolodnoe, through whom she had made contact with us, was himself a distinguished spy. He had assumed the image of a Red Army soldier who had escaped encirclement and succeeded in wining the confidence of Rysakov. The entire store of his meeting with Irina and the delivery of the message was fictitious. The operation of bringing the doctors and hospital articles over to us had been approved by the Germans. They knew that the woman doctors Unkovskaya and Tyomkina were Jewesses and that they had been planning to cross over to our lines. But they decided not to kill them and not to interfere with their going over to the partisans. By keeping the doctors alive, the Germans aimed at giving their agent a status of authority among the partisans. Even the killing of the German by Irina had been the result of cool calculation. The murdered man had not been to the liking of the German commander, who was interested in liquidating him.

Besides a number of tasks, such as that of signaling to the enemy plane in order to expose the camp location, she had been given the task of finding and killing Filkovsky, the singer, and the other members of the regional committee.

"Why Filkovsky, of all people?" Rysakov asked the spy.

"You are naïve, young man. Our task is to kill off the head, and without a head there won't be any spirit," answered his low creature cheekily.

Some time later I met Filkovsky and told him the story about Irina.

"No wonder," he said. "The Germans are capable of committing any crime or provocation. There is only one conclusion: our fighters must always be on the alert."

Admittedly, the infiltration of German spies into our camp and our discovering them after some time had a bad effect on the general mood of the partisans. A recurring question at the time was: "Whom can we trust?" Our commander himself, a young enthusiastic man, was so affected by the stories about the spies that he turned into a morbidly suspicious man and decided not to admit into the company any new man in order to avoid future subversive acts. After one successful operation, when the inhabitants of a village we had freed expressed their desire to join us, Rysakov refused to have anything to do with them. On another occasion not only did he not admit a woman fighter into the company, but he also hurt her feelings in a cruel manner. This behavior on the part of Rysakov enraged Filkovsky, and acts of this kind were likely, of course, to have an adverse effect on the authority of the partisans among the local population.

Filkovsky gathered the company activists and told them: "Do we have the right to be suspicious of any Soviet man?" These were his first words. Though very angry he did not raise his voice. Calmly and with logical reasoning he expressed his opinion, and his conclusions influenced his listeners against anything that might give the battalion a bad name, since this might weaken the blood alliance between the partisan fighters and the local population. Turning to Rysakov, Filkovsky said: "The Party has left you here in order to strengthen the spirit of the people when the going is hard to encourage their belief in our cause, and to put them on the way to fighting the fascists. And what are you doing now? You are raising your hand against the most precious of our possessions — the Soviet people. The enemy, taking advantage of our carelessness, threw a few spies your way, and you panicked and began doing the wrong thing. That's just what the enemy expects. He has proved to be highly cunning, though not to the extent ou think he is. The party will not allow any man to smear the name of the partisan movement, let alone to let it die out. Whom do you want to disown, your Soviet people?"

Rysakov was sitting on the front bench. His lean face showed his deep feeling of shame. He listened attentively to Filkovsky's words, which were true at bottom, and when he spoke, he admitted his mistake.

Filkovsky announced: "I believe that Rysakov, the courageous commander, will acquire the qualities he now lacks as a Bolshevik partisan who derives his strength from the masses and whose feelings run true to the thoughts, wishes, and desires of the people."

In his own manner our commissar Filkovsky influenced the behavior of the partisan fighters.

Partisan Doctors

In February, 1942, when we were building up our company, we all lived in one single earth hut. As I have said, this hut was meant to house thirty people, but it served as a living place for over a hundred. At night it was so stifling there that the kerosene lamp and the candle butts blew out alone. Consequently, lice appeared in our camp and with them, typhus. The epidemic brought down one victim after another, and this had a bad effect on the partisans — much more than the German encirclement and their numerous punishment squads.

With the arrival of the women doctors who had been brought over to us by Irina, we at once began to organize the sanitary service. All three women doctors, Unkovskaya,

Todortseva, and Tyomkina, who had formerly worked in military hospitals, adapted quickly to the hardships of partisan life and were not troubled by the way things were going on at the camp. Rather at times I even believed that the hard conditions of everyday life, the absence of an elementary sanitary system, provided an incentive for them to work harder. The doctors were assisted by two nurses and one sanitary worker. At the head of the sanitary service was Doctor Lydia Unkovskaya.

Our collective efforts in the fields of sanitation and medicine did not succeed in checking the typhus epidemic. The disease attacked one of the doctors, Lydia Unkovskaya, and with her, one of the nurses. The whole burden now fell on the shoulders of Lyuba Todortseva and Stera Tyomkina. It became evident that as long as we did not improve our everyday manner of living and prevent overcrowding, we had no chance of overcoming the typhus epidemic.

"We should start building new living quarters and an isolation room for the sick and also tear down the earth hut — this is the only way to stop the epidemic," said Todortseva and Tyomkina.

We knew that digging the foundations, even with the help of explosives, was no easy job. One week would not be enough for this task. And how many new victims would the typhus epidemic claim in the meantime? We thus decided to bring into the woods a number of houses from the neighboring village. But how would we go about moving houses. There were Germans and policemen in all the surrounding villages. We could think of only one way out — to drive away the Germans from the village of Uruchye and from there to bring some houses into the woods.

Filkovsky brought the matter up for discussion, and the staff command drew up the plan for the task. We discussed the details, issued orders to the attacking parties, and got down to work. At sunset we called up all the fighters who were in good physical condition — forty men in all — and went out. The women doctors joined us too. We came upon the village in a pincer movement from three sides, firing white flares at the same time. The enemy was taken totally by surprise. The Germans did not stay to fight and they fled along the Sosnovoe Boloto road — the only outlet we did not have enough men to block. Only a few rear-guard units showed any resistance. By five in the morning Uruchye had been cleared of enemy forces. Our men found in the village a good supply of provisions, about nine thousand rounds of ammunition, and some fifteen rifles and machine guns. We decided to take out the houses on that same day. For this purpose we marked the large house of the village head — who was a traitor — the office of the *kolkhoz* management, the *kolkhoz* storehouse, and two uninhabited shacks.

In the dark and by the light of torches, professional house-builders among the villagers were authorized to mark the boards of the houses to be moved over so that it would be easier to put them in place afterwards. Fifty carts were used to haul the boards to the woods. On the next day we started work on setting up a new camp, and a few days later we erected in the woods a new partisan village, with a main road, a sector called "The Prospect of the First Earth Hut," a "Hospital Alley," a barracks courtyard named after Taras Bulba, and a site for the bathhouse. The *kolkhoz* villagers gave us bricks and some folk medicines, such as herbs for the sick. To the convalescent, they donated butter, eggs, and milk.

The epidemic began to die out thanks to the doctors' effort and the help offered by the people. Only one typhus patient died.

Often we had visitors from the nearby village, seeking our medical services. But more often it was our doctors who went out to the neighboring villages to heal the sick. It may be pointed out that a considerable number of the villagers suffered from bullet wounds caused by the enemy. The wounded were taken to the hospital by the doctors. For some time the hospital was stationed in the village of Gavan. With the approach of the Germans, however, it was moved back into the woods once again.

* * * * *

At the staff command of the partisan briades actie in the Bryansk area and numbering some twenty-five thousand fighters, worked Arkady Eidlin, a surgeon. He was in charge of the sanitary platoon and had to travel from one company to another, supervising and instructing, providing the necessary help for the young doctors in their work.

Not far from the village of Smelizh, in a thick forest, Eidlin set up an underground hospital. According to his instructions the partisans dug out the foundations and built a large hut, fifty square meters in area. Into this hut they brought homemade iron stoves. Windows were put into the ceiling for light. At night they used oil lamps. Parachute cloth taken from the enemy was used dfor covering the walls and the ceiling. The hospital was clean, warm, and pleasant. In it were grouped many severely wounded fighters who were on their way to the partisan center in Moscow.

The correspondent of *Partisan Truth*[18] Aronov was on the editorial staff of *Partisan Truth*. He had started out as a partisan fighter in the Voroshilov Company. On one of its raids the company captured typesetting letters and an Amerikanka printing machine. In cooperation with Zaytsev, the company commissar, Aronov started publishing a small newspaper called *Voroshilovich*. It was a good paper as they go, a fighting paper, printed on a quarter sheet. *Voroshilovich* soon had a good circulation among both the partisans and the non-fighting population. Needless to say, the paper necessary for printing was "provided" by the enemy.

When the decision was made to produce a central newspaper by the battalion, an editorial staff was picked from among the fighters, Bondarenko, Korotkov, Andreyev, Aleshinsky, and Aronov.

Under battle conditions the editors got down to work writing notes and articles, and they themselves set the type for the paper and printed it. In general Aronov wrote accounts of the operations in which he actually took part. In the course of a German attack, the editorial staff found themselves in a particularly dangerous situation. They managed to retreat under fire. Nonetheless, the newspaper came out on the day of the retreat. In the fall of 1942, his assistant, Comrade Sidorenko, who was later to die a hero's death, set up a well-defended base for the editorial staff. Here the *Partisan Truth* was to come out regularly for about one year.

Before they launched their attack in the direction of OrelKursk, the Germans decided to secure their rear lines against our raids. Amassing for this purpose a number of divisions and a great many tanks and planes, they renewed their attacks on the area held by the partisans. The partisans of Bryansk had to take part in a number of battles at which they were greatly outnumbered. They actually fought for every bush, destroying considerable numbers of enemy forces and equipment. The base serving the *Partisan Truth* was itself used as a stronghold. It was located in a marshland, highly convenient for defensive operations. The access road to this base saw a number of ferocious battles, joined in by the "Rule-for-the-Soviets" battalion which had been sent in for reinforcement. The fight went on for several days, during which the editors pitched in every now and then. In the end we had to withdraw, but the newspaper continued to come out regularly, as the printing type and machine had both been evacuated in time. Aronov continued to visit the fighting companies. He also kept on writing articles for the paper.

Lazar Bleichmann

I first met him during the months of March and April, 1942, in the village of Bely Kharpach in the Navlya region, where I had gone on a liaison and information-gathering mission. Lazar Bleichmann was in command of a company he had organized under the leadership of the Party regional committee.

The meeting was short. At that time Bleichmann was in control of an important section of the railway tracks in our region. The Germans launched several attacks to get hold of this section, throwing in the battle tanks and heavy artillery. But the partisans of the Navlya region held out and repulsed all enemy attacks.

Before long Bleichmann was appointed commander of the Furmanov Company. He started out by training men for sabotage work. In early July the Furmanov fighters succeeded in derailing a German train carrying soldiers and arms. Bleichmann himself conducted the battle.

Bleichmann's company was known for its defensive activities against the German attacks. In late June and early July the

Germans attempted to drive the partisans out of the woods of Ramasukha and the steppes along the back of the Desna River (northeast of Kiev). The first enemy blows fell on the Furmanov Company. At the same time there were two more partisan companies in the woods of Ramasukha. Bleichmann succeeded in establishing close contact with them for joint action against the Germans. The partisans repulsed all enemy attacks. The battalion chief of staff, Captain Gogolyuk, and myself visited the company grounds and helped in organizing defense activities.

The Furmanov Company acted for a long period as a well-knit, powerful unit against the Germans who fought at the outskirts of the woods. When the order for withdrawal was received, Bleichmann carried out an outstanding maneuver: he slipped unnoticed through the enemy forces and, on his way out, destroyed the police forces in the steppe sector in the direction of Trubchevsk up to the Pogar Area. Bleichmann also carried out a number of large-scale and spectacular operations along the Desna River.

For his military achievements, Bleichmann was awarded the Order of Lenin. The Order was awarded to him by Alexander Pavlovich Matveyev, chief of staff of the partisan movement.

Hungarian Jews

In the winter toward the end of 1942, the Felix Dzerzhinsky Company received orders to attack and oust the German garrison stationed around the village of Shilinka in the Bryansk region. The commander of this garrison, which was composed of Germans and Magyars,[19] was a Hungarian fascist called Major Parag. One day we received information that the enemy forces were planning to mount an attack on the woods of Bryansk from the southeast and that Major Parag was preparing roads for the withdrawal of the German forces, using for this purpose a large work gang of Hungarian Jews.

In the partisan company was a Hungarian, Paul Feldesh, interpreter, scout, and fighter. Through his help we succeeded in establishing contact with the Hungarian prisoners. Shortly afterwards the Dzerzhinsky Company raided the enemy garrison and killed Parag, whereupon forty-one Jews joined the partisan forces, expressing their desire to fight the Germans.

Thus the Felix Dzerzhinsky Company came to include a special Jewish force. The outstanding doctor Kovash Rezhe not only healed the wounded but also struck at the Germans, weapon in hand. In one of the battles he was wounded and fell down near the enemy. But he managed to escape. After long suffering he found his way to the Byelorussian partisans and joined them to fight our common enemy.

It is worthwhile to mention Nevai Laszlo, too, from Budapest, who held an LL.D. degree. Partisan Lastslo also did propaganda work for us. He wrote leaflets in Hungarian to be distributed among enemy forces. In these leaflets the Germans were called upon to kill their commanding officers and join the partisans.

The group of Hungarian Jews fought the German occupation forces with spectacular courage and took part in numerous battles. These former prisoners of yesterday had turned into popular avengers worthy of their name and kept up the fight against the enemy till the end of the war. Many of them learned Russian and served as interpreters in the interrogation of German prisoners of war.

The Partisans in Moldavia

In March, 1943, when the partisans of Bryansk established contact with the Red Arm, I was called to Moscow by the Center of Partisan Movement and ordered to provide assistance for the partisan fighters in Moldavia. I flew far into the rear of the enemy forces together with a group of officials belonging to the Communist Party center in Moldavia.

At the same time a number of small underground units had been active in the Moldavia area. We landed in Byelorussia. Our group included my chief of staff, Makar Kozhukhar, and a number of comrades from Moldavia. Our mission was to smuggle organized partisan companies from Byelorussia into Moldavia, where they were to serve as a core for the entire movement. Our unit was joined by many new fighters on the way, gained valuable fighting experience day after day, and eventually came to number three thousand fighters, comprising three brigades and one cavalry squadron.

The Moldavian unit contained many Jews who fought alongside fighters from other nations. I would like to make special mention of some of them.

During the "War of the Fatherland," Mark Shirokov, a Moldavian, joined the Red Army as a volunteer. He had been seriously wounded in the fight against the enemy. But when he heard of the formation of the Moldavian unit he expressed his wish to join the partisans, although his wounds had not yet healed properly. At first Mark was a company commander. In an especially ferocious encounter with the enemy while the company was still in the region of Polesia, Shirokov's men held their ground firmly against the German attacks. The fight went on for more than two hours, in the course of which Shirokov proved to be a gifted, faultless commander.

In Moldavia, Shirokov was put in command of a group of saboteurs. We had over one hundred groups of this kind in our unit. To give an example of the value of their work, suffice it to point out that more than two hundred enemy transports were put out of commission within six months. The Shirokov group had much to show for itself in these operations. Mark himself blew up five military trains. Along with his sabotage activities, Mark also took part in reconnaissance operations.

I must also mention the forty-five-year-old Michael Choban. He first went on patrol missions and at once proved to be a courageous fighter. In the fall of 1943, Choban was appointed my deputy in the technical platoon. Michael saw to it that the provisions and the fighting equipment of the unit were in tip-top condition. Like Shirokov, Michael Choban also was awarded two orders — the "Red Flag" and the "Red Star".

In conclusion, a few words about partisan Boris Rokhlin. He laid mines on roads which were in German hands, blew up several enemy transports, derailed enemy trains — duties he looked upon as simply "hobbies." He would often say: "We are partisans in order to blow up German trains." This was, in effect, the epitome of his military career.

MEETINGS AND EVENTS

MEETINGS AND EVENTS

A.P. Brinsky ("Dyadya Petya")
Hero of the Soviet Union,
Former Commander of a Partisan Unit

In White Russia

Our partisan company was first organized in the District of
Vitebsk, in the region of Lukolmsk Lake. Comrade Nelyubo,
its commander, actually had a fighting unit composed mainly
of peasants from the village of Ogurets.

In September, 1941, we succeeded in establishing contact
with Jewish workers from the neighboring small towns. A
month later we called a joint meeting with the representatives
of these small towns to determine the future line of action,
and it was decided to organize sabotage groups. Soon enough
we had a number of such groups acting in that sector.

The Lukolmsk group distinguished itself in sabotage work.
It was under the command of Isaac, a cobbler by trade. I
forget his surname to my regret. Besides the killing of two
Hitlerite officers, a captain and a major, they systematically
provided us with reconnaissance information, along with
medicines and bandages.

Before long we were to lose contact with these groups as
the company was forced to move to other regions. At that
time we had quite a number of Jewish fighters among us.
They had come from Lepel, Begoml, and Mstislavl. In those
days we had begun to receive from the neighboring small
towns a constant stream of refugees, including not only youth
in god fighting condition, but also old men, women, and children, and thus we had no alternative but to set up a civilian
camp.

To leave the small town was no easy matter. The Germans
had driven the Jews out into the ghettos and threw barbed
wire fences around them. Sentries were posted at regular
intervals, with order to let out only work groups accompanied

by Ukrainian policemen or SS men. We often received news
of killings already perpetrated or imminent. We did our best
to get the Jews out of the ghettos with all the means at our
disposal.

During this period we were forced to engage the enemy
in a difficult battle at the village of Neshkovo. In this battle
we lost twenty Jewish partisan fighters from our company.
Their bodies, which had been left behind, were later hung
high by the Germans in order to terrorize the surrounding
inhabitants.

On our way to the region of Baranovichi, I met a group
of some forty Jewish partisan fighters near the village
of Svenitsa. The group had contacts with the ghetto at
Baranovichi. We provided them with arms and suggested
that they bring out from Baranovichi as many people as they
could. The mission succeeded. The company, reinforced by
young men who had been saved from the ghetto, grew to
such proportions that it now had the strength to carry out
military operations by itself. With our help they blew up two
enemy transports and burned down a large bakery that provided bread for the Nazis.

In the Baranovichi region I met another group of Jewish
partisans in August, 1942. We held consultation with the
other companies which were active in our region. The largest
of these companies was the one named after Shchors. Before
long this unit had gown into an independent company and had
joined the brigade; it was commanded by Comrade Komarov.

I owe it to myself to mention here a Jewish partisan commander who fell in battle near Baranovichi. His name was
Sidelnikov. He had been a newsman before the war. He was
in command of a company which distinguished itself by
its military activities against the enemy, blew up scores of
German transports, and wiped out enemy garrisons in the
camps of Idritsa, Belaya, and others. The Sedelnikov company was widely known among the surrounding population,
and many came to join it. The company was soon to grow
into a brigade. In one of his brilliant operations, Sedelnikov
succeeded in releasing some two hundred and fifty Red Army
POWs from enemy camps. But, as I had just said, he died a
hero's death in the furious battle that raged near Baranovichi.

In the Ukraine

In September, 1942, we moved over to the western regions of the Ukraine. At the same time most of the Jewish inhabitants of these areas were being atrociously wiped out by the Germans. Here and there a few small ghettos survived. The few Jews who succeeded in escaping and had not fallen victim to German bullets had to wander through the woods, hiding from both German and Ukrainian police and murderers. With the approach of fall these people had only tatters on their backs, suffered from hunger, ate uncooked potatoes, were afraid of being seen on the roads, and avoided lighting camp fires.

It was necessary to start setting up civilian camps. The first camps of this kind were erected in the region of the villages Ozery and Svaritsevichi in the province of Vysotsky. Here was active the partisan group under the command of Misyura. His second in command was the Jew Bokalchuk, a dauntless young man, and his adjutant Moshe Bromberg. The Jews of this group numbered about ninety. I gave the order to set up a new camp for all the refugees from the neighboring woods who came to us singly or in groups and delegated the Misyura company to guard it. To all the able-bodied men, we gave arms.

We soon had a second camp in the vicinity. Again I issued an order, this time to the Kurochkin-Obukhov group, then active in that region. The new camp, which was organized by Kurochkin, comprised some two hundred persons. Out of his camp a fighting group was formed which was soon to grow into an independent partisan company. This in turn grew into a brigade, comprising about seven hundred men, mostly Jewish. The brigade systematically disrupted the telegraph lines of the Germans, occasionally raided their food storehouses, disarmed three police stations, and blew ip enemy transports carrying soldiers and military equipment.

The partisans under the command of Kurchev, Misyura, and Bokalchuk began their military activities almost without any weapons, but were soon to supply the neighboring companies with military equipment out of the booty that fell into their hands in their battles against the enemy.

In the month of January and February, 1943, a number of daring raids were carried out in this area on police stations, ranches, and German administration buildings. In these raids the partisans took many horses, cows, and foodstuffs which they later distributed to the neighboring inhabitants. The raids were led by Nachman Silberfarb, Bokalchuk, and Bromberg.

At the head of one company stood a daring commander, Boris Yakovlevich Bazykin. He carried out many daring raids on German garrisons. Bazykin's company was distinguished for its attack on the Strashievo station where an armored train stood at the time. Bazykin's fighters dispatched the train guards and blew up or otherwise dismantled about 400 meters of railway tracks. In addition, this company blew up eight transports, destroyed three bridgeways, and wiped out a number of village administration offices. Bazykin himself fell in a battle which took place in the region of Vladimir-Volynsky.

In the Kruk Company

The Kruk company was active in the area of Volyn (western Ukraine). Kruk himself was a Ukrainian, his real name being Konishchuk. When the Hitlerite invaders occupied Volyn and began their murderous persecution of the Jews, Kruk went about organizing a partisan company. In the village of Griva, where Kruk had been head of the village council until the outbreak of the war, there lived only six Jewish families. Kruk turned to these families, and the first to take up the challenge was the Zwiebel family — the seventy-five-year-old man, his four sons, and his brother. From the neighboring village of Leshchinovka, eight men joined the company, headed by the brothers Hannan and Shimon Koval.

There were also volunteers from the town of Manevichi.[20]

In the beginning there were only seventeen men. The military equipment at their disposal was sufficient for eight men only, but this did not deter Kruk and his group from going into action. They headed for the woods and began assembling people who had gone there to hide from the German murderers. Occasionally Kruk would himself slip into the ghettos of the neighboring small towns, and release the prisoners who would later join the ranks of the partisans. Before long the company numbered one hundred and twenty men. Eventually it was to comprise about seven hundred fighters.

Kruk's company acquired its arms in the same manner as other partisan companies: at the expense of the enemy, by attacking small German groups and seizing their weapons. As the company added more fighters, it widened its field of activity. Its men were active in the areas of Volyn, Rovno, and Brest. The company was well known for its sabotage activities: it blew up more than one hundred military transports, burned down two sawing mills, and destroyed tens of kilometers of telegraph and telephone wires.

Many partisans belonging to this company sacrificed their lives for the fatherland.

The Civilian Camps

The civilian camps caused us much trouble, but they also brought us great benefits. In our unit there were four such camps, comprising over a thousand Jews. We also had camps for Ukrainians, to which were brought families which faced death, and one for Poles, who had fled the terror of German and Ukrainian fascists.

We stationed the camps in the heart of the woods, in faraway spots, and on islands in marshland country. When we moved to a new place, we took the camps along with us. With the approach of Nazi punishment squads, we moved the camps to a far-off safe place.

In the early days we sent to the civilian camps all those we could save from the German holocaust. Among them were men, women, children, and the elderly. Gradually, after our companies had acquired additional weapons and military equipment, all the young and middle-aged men and women joined our fighting companies. At the camps were only the old men and the children. But even they did not sit there doing nothing. The old women patched up the partisans' clothes, did the washing, and knitted socks and mufflers. The old men mended the shoes, did some tailoring, and a little furriers' work. The children tended the cattle and collected seeds which were essential to protect us against scurvy.

The Jewish camp of Kruk's company rendered us an invaluable service. They had a big farm. The civilians mowed, sowed, gathered wheat and barley. The camp grounds under Kruk's command included a flour mill and a bakery which provided the fighting company with bread. There were also a considerable number of cows, sheep, goats, and horses. The buildings also included a hospital for sick and wounded partisans. But the most important thing for us at this camp was the workshop which built military equipment. From German dud (unexploded) shells our men took out the explosive charge and prepared their own bombs and mines.

The workshop was located deep in the forest near Volskaya Volya (in western Ukraine). It provided us with more than fifteen tons of explosives. This work involved constant danger and was shared by men and women alike. Chief among them were Wolf Rabinovich, Abraham Goldes, Gershon Grinberg, Israel Hirsch Flas, Arka Kirschenbaum, and Friedel Melamed. In the course of preparing the mines we lost sixteen-year-old Peisya Raiter and thirteen-year-old Shlomo Biedermann, both from the small town of Manevichi.

At the head of this camp was Isaiah Zwiebel, a highly practical man, who organized the very complex life in this camp with remarkable wisdom and vigor.

Mention should also be made of two brothers who stayed at Kruk's camp, Liezer and Abraham Lisovsky. The latter was the company's chief technician. He was the man with the golden touch. He not only repaired rifles and pistols but also designed and built machine guns and automatic rifles.

Boris Gindin and Others

We had a great many courageous fighters and commanders who spared no effort in their fight against the enemies of our fatherland. It is impossible to recount the exploits of them all, but there were many unforgettable men among them. When the war broke out Boris Gindin was only a junior lieutenant who had just graduated from military college. He was nineteen years old, and under his command an infantry platoon engaged in defensive operations near the town of Grodno. He fought in the city streets of Minsk and, to escape encirclement, organized a partisan company in a very short time. At our camp he was in command of a Jewish platoon. At the head of this platoon, Gindin blew up eleven enemy trains and destroyed five bridges. One of his platoon fighters, Volodya Zwiebel, holding a string of hand grenades in his hands, threw himself under an approaching German rain and blew it up at the price of his own life.

When our battalion moved to the Ukraine, Gindin's thirty-seven-men platoon spearheaded its movement. It was difficult to march through the woods and the marshes. Each fighter carried about twenty kilograms of explosives.[21] We went twenty days on this march, but in the end our orders were carried out in full. The men reached their prearranged point through the towns of Kovel, Shepetovka, Sarny, Lutsk, and Vladimir-Volynsky. Before long Gindin was made second-in-command to Kruk, and shortly afterwards he was appointed chief of staff in Loginov's company. Within eleven months of military activity, from April 15, 1943, to March 15, 1944, Loginov's company blew up about one hundred and fifty train engines, killing some twenty-two hundred German officers and soldiers and wounding about four thousand. It also destroyed many enemy tanks, vehicles, and a large quantity of fuel and provisions.

Many partisan Jews also fought in Max's company. I remember in particular the fighter Melamedik, from the small town of Manevichi. He blew up three enemy trains and died in a raid on a police station.

When the war broke out, another Jew, Minich, had been working as a bookkeeper in the town of Rafalovka. He was soon to turn into a fearless partisan and was held in great esteem by his comrades in the company. He took part in blowing up nine enemy trains and two bridges. Minich, too, fell in battle, in the vicinity of Rafalovka.

The commander of a Jewish platoon, Bronstein, blew up eleven German trains, three vehicles, a large bridge, and burned down a sawing mill.

Yeshayahu Segal, who came from the small town of Manevichi, was our instructor. He was a dauntless partisan who knew every square inch of the forest. He was good at sabotage and was credited with blowing up seven German trains.

I would like to speak of another one of our partisans who was distinguished by his manners and deeds. Rabbi Lipe, the son of Todres Yosilevich, from the village of Luninets. The partisans simply called him Lipe. One of his friends hit the nail right on the head when he called him "The God of Israel's Vengeance." He was of medium height, had a dark beard, wore a deerskin mantle, and a warm cap. Carrying an automatic rifle across his chest, and with a string of hand-grenades hanging from his belt, he naturally did not look much like a rabbi. He had a good command of Russian, Polish, and German. At the beginning of the war he was thirty-five years old. In the ghetto of Luninets he called upon the Jews to rise in revolt against the fascists. The Jews of Luninets had no previous contacts with the surrounding population; they also had no weapons. The rabbi succeeded in escaping from the ghetto. After much wandering he established contact with the partisans, and with their help he released many of those who had been trapped within the ghetto walls. But he could not save his own family, since he was first and foremost concerned with saving others. His wife and children were killed by the Germans.

I appointed Lipe Yosilevich platoon commander because of his courage, wisdom, and logical reasoning. The partisans were satisfied with this appointment. "Our Lipe won't betray us," they used to say. As a matter of fact, whenever he went out on a mission, he would first take every military detail into consideration, and during the fighting itself he provided a good personal example of fearlessness and coolness under fire.

Once, two German battalions engaged in battle with a partisan company which had Lipe among its fighters. The partisans were highly outnumbered, and the fighting was fierce. But the partisans pushed back the Germans and began to chase them. In order to run faster, Lipe threw off his boots. The fighters did the same, and, barefoot, continued their chase. The Germans suffered heavy losses, but Lipe was seriously injured in the pursuit. The partisans evacuated him from the battlefield and on the first plane had him flown to Moscow and to a hospital.

Women Partisans

Among the Jewish partisans in our unit were many women, especially young women, who, rifle and hand grenade in hand, fought shoulder to shoulder with the men and were among the first to distinguish themselves in battle. From the very beginning of our struggle in White Russia, we had among us an outstanding woman partisan, Liza Lyanders of Minsk, who was fearless and full of life. She took part in all the battle operations, kindled by the desire to take revenge upon the enemy.

At the small town of Vizno in the region of Slutsk, the Germans had a storehouse of provision. We decided to destroy it. The task was entrusted to Liza Lyanders and a young partisan, Kravchenko, a Ukranian. We dressed them as bride and bridegroom and drove them to Vizno for their wedding ceremony. The Germans were surprised to see that their guard had been killed and the storehouse set on fire. They pursued the "newlyweds" for eight kilometers, but the young couple and their guests succeeded in eluding the pursuing enemy. Liza not only took part in the fighting, but she also killed two collaborators with her own hands. She did not shirk any kind of work: she sometimes even did the washing and worked in the kitchen.

Other outstanding women fighters were Rina Guz and Musya Bernstein, together with the sisters Raya and Ida Brat of Manevichi, the elder only nineteen years old and the younger only sixteen.

A fearless partisan woman was Dora Silbert. In the beginning she worked in the kitchen, then as a typist at the office of the chief of staff. But Dora could find no satisfaction in such jobs. Eventually she was to take part in the blowing up of four military trains, aside from a number of battles with the enemy. She fell in a battle near the town of Vladimir-Volynsky.

In battle also fell Raya from Pavurin. I forget her surname. She was an exceptionally fearless young woman and took part in several attacks on police stations.

Partisan life was not easy for all of us, but it was particularly difficult for the young women. Besides taking part in the fighting, they also treated the wounded and the sick and did the washing and the cooking. Occasionally we were short of food and wore "raffia" shoes and whatever clothing we could find.[22] The young women did not complain and stoically endured the shortage. One thing they would not tolerate, however: not to be given arms.

Here is a request I received from Rina (Rifka) Guz: "Dyadya Petya! My military record shows four enemy trains destroyed. You know fully well that I have military privileges, and my privilege to get arms is no less than that of the others. Give me an automatic rifle, I hereby request you, dear Dyadya Petya!"

The favorite of the entire partisan group was fourteen-year-old Luba Melamedik. She worked as a cook and at the same time tended the sick and the wounded. She would see one of our men walking around in a soiled shirt and would immediately have him take it of and wash it for him. Her cousin, Yuri (Jack) Melamedik, was a fighter in Max's partisan group under the general command of Anton Brinsky ("Dyadya Petya").

Partisan Doctors

I owe it to myself to say a few words about our doctors. They were extremely remarkable partisans. Our hospitals were often located in far-off spots, constantly under guard. When on the move we would usually take the sick and the wounded along with us, or, if the circumstances so dictated, we would leave them behind in the woods. Despite the difficulties involved we saw to it that the hospitals received the best available foodstuffs. Medicines and bandages were acquired in our raids on the enemy, which is also how we got our weapons. In many places we were in contact with doctors, pharmacists, and nurses who would give us all that we needed. In the small town of Rozhishche in the district of Volyn there worked a Jewish doctor who posed as a Czech.[23] He did a great deal for us, keeping us supplied with medicines and instruments.

Another physician, Dr. Melchior, had run away from the ghetto. His entire family had been wiped out. He was a great doctor and an excellent organizer. He served as a doctor in one of our brigades. Our men started to come down with typhus and dysentery, and we also had the seriously wounded.

Dr. Melchior had not a single death among all the cases he treated. He himself would go out to get medicines and other materials, serving not only the partisans, but also the local inhabitants. He also went out to visit the sick in the neighboring villages, thus enhancing the respect and authority our partisans had with the local population.

A great deal of love and appreciation went to Dr. Wiener of Lvov. He worked with Loginov's company. His family had also been wiped out. Wiener did not stop at simply providing medical treatment, but also insisted on taking part in military operations. He was a real "national avenger."[24] He was credited with scores of partisan survivors and scores of Germans dead.

The senior doctor of the second brigade was Dr. Rotter of Stolin, in the district of Pinsk. His wife worked for us as a dental surgeon. The companies of Mahmed and Doroshenko had such experienced personnel as Dr. Kurtz and his wife.

Despite all the difficulties our doctors carried out the most complicated medical operations under fire. Young Dr. Mirmelstein carried out a serious operation of this kind on partisan Nikolai Zayats and saved his life.

There is also much to say for our medical nurses. I would like to make special mention of only one: Rubinstein was her family name. She was an elderly woman who tended not only the partisans, but also the local population. Despite her age she worked tirelessly; innumerable fighters were brought back to health, thanks to her efforts.

* * * * *

I have not told the entire story. All of us, from the simplest fighter to the unit commander, fulfilled his duty to our country. We felt a special concern for Soviet citizens who had suffered from Nazi plunder. A great number of Jews were also saved from the murderous claws of the Hitlerite beasts, and they were in great need of our help. A great many inmates of German prisons, upon joining the family of partisans, soon became fearless fighters and commanders and fought with honor for their beloved country.

A CIVILIAN CAMP IN THE FOREST

Pavlo (Pavel) Vershigora

Introduction

Pavlo Vershigora was born in Moldavia in 1905. He was an actor and a stage-manager. In World War I he was a commander in one of the partisan battalions under Sidor Kovpak, the commander-in-chief of the entire Soviet partisan movement. For his outstanding service as a partisan commander, he was awarded the title: "Hero of the Soviet Union."

In 1946 Vershigora published a book under the title *People with a Clear Conscience*, which includes historical accounts of the exploits and battles of the battalion against the German fascist invaders, besides personal glimpses of gifted and capable commanders of partisan units.[25]

Here is an excerpt from his writings:

...It was only by a miracle that a Jewish ghetto had been left in Skalat (not far from Tarnopol) early in the summer of 1943. Behind the barbed wires were Jewish craftsmen — tailors, shoemakers, saddlers. The Germans had put off for them the day of their doom — they forced the Jews to work from dawn and well into the night on a starvation diet. The partisans, the Karpenko fighters, released them from the ghetto, over three hundred people who later appeared in the forest, including old men, women, and children. They were a mass of tortured people wearing tattered clothes.

Their appearance in the forest in the midst of the partisan camp caused no little embarrassment. We understood quite well that if they were to remain in the town, the fascists would have killed them all on the following day. But we could not take these wretched people along with us since we were a military unit about to go out on difficult missions. "How could such a mass of weak old men and miserable women stand the rigors of combat operations?" we asked ourselves; but there was no way out. Commander Kovpak ordered one of his aides, Pavlovsky, to have the weak carried on carts while the strong were to talk behind the fighters' columns.

Among the fighters some Jews must be mentioned, such as Misha Tartakovsky, Volodya Lapopin, and others. Tartakovsky served as an interpreter in the interrogation of German prisoners of war.

Right at the beginning of the motley march, Kovpak brought into a single line all the Jewish men and women who had come from the ghetto of Skalat and told them: "Now I would like to have a serious talk with you. We are military men. Our aim is to do valuable military deeds. And though I must regret it, I cannot accept you all into the unit. So every one of you has to consider his abilities and adapt himself to this military life whether it suits his strength or not. The decision is in your hands. This is how I am presenting the question, straightforward and fair. Those who want and can carry arms will stay with us. Those who hate the fascists will stay with us. Those who have no fear of death and are ready to sacrifice themselves for our country will stay with us. And those who lack them? Thus will I say straight and to the point. Do not go! As for those who stay behind, we will send them to the villages and find accommodation for them with the peasants. We will leave some food supplies behind. But if you join the ranks of the unit, you will have to take the oath, and if then you find yourselves incapable of doing the job, don't take us to task. We have one law for all, no matter who he is; Russian, Ukrainian, or Jew. This is an agreement. Think it over till evening. Talk it over with the elders. I will send for your answer before evening."[26]

PARTISAN ALEXANDER ABUGOV

A Witness

Alexander Abugov was a partisan in White Russia and the Ukraine in the years 1942-1944. He was in command of a reconnaissance company and accomplished many exploits as a Jewish fighter.[27]

Before the war he was a physical training instructor in Odessa. He was recruited into the Red Army at the beginning of the war between Russia and Germany in June, 1941, was taken prisoner and spent four months in POW camps — first in a deep ravine near the town of Uman (Ukraine) and later in POW camps in Vinnitsa (Ukraine), Shepetovka (Ukraine), Brest-Litovsk (Byelorussia), Kobrin (Byelorussia), and Kovel (Ukraine). During this period many Jewish prisoners of war were killed. Abugov was not killed, because he had succeeded in concealing the fact that he was a Jew. After numerous attempts he escaped from the camp at Kovel to the neighboring forests. Through his wanderings in the woods he succeeded in reaching a partisan unit not far from Pinsk, led by the commander Dmitry Popov.

Here are excerpts from his testimony to the Yad Vashem Memorial Authority in Israel:[28]

Upon reaching the village of Svaritsevichi (near Rovno), we decided to encamp in the forest for the night. Our ground scouts went out to reconnoiter the area as we were not familiar with it. I well remember that it was cloudy and that the falling snow was mixed with rain, so that it was both wet and cold. Not all the partisans had winter clothes.

End of November, 1942. At dawn our sentry heard the sound of someone working with an axe and decided to go in the direction of the noise. On approaching the spot, he saw two men dressed in tattered clothes and unshaven. They were cutting dry pine wood. The sentry, who was a Siberian, could not form any idea as to who those two men were. When they saw him they began to run away. He was wearing a short

German coat, and they thought him to be a German policeman. He ran after them, shouting in Russian that he would
not do anything to them if only they would tell him who they
were. Finally he caught one of them and began to shake him.
The man would not utter a word for fear. At this moment
the sentry saw at some distance some huts from which thick
smoke was rising. In the meantime the man who had escaped
noticed the red ribbon on the cap of the partisan, who told
him: "Don't be afraid of me. I am a Soviet partisan." On hearing this the man told the partisan that he was a Jew.

Both went to the huts where the partisan sentry found many
Jews. At first they were afraid to come near him, but after
he had assured them that he would do them no harm, they
came to him slowly and began to speak. He learned that these
were Jews who had come from various villages from Serniki,
Dubrovitsa, Svaritsevichi, Vichevka, Gorodnaya and others.

The sentry told us of his discovery when he returned to
the camp. Upon hearing that there were Jews in the forest,
I went to see them. I may take this opportunity to point out
that no one in the company knew anything about my nationality. They thought I was a Russian. On seeing the huts where
these Jews were living, I was overwhelmed with deep emotion. Remembered my sufferings as a prisoner of war in the
German camps and how the Jews were wiped out. I thought
to myself that there was a chance that these Jews, who were
dispersed in the woods, unorganized, would come out alive
from this hard war and that they would not be able to defend
themselves under such difficult conditions in those tattered
clothes — a camp of four hundred people. They came around
and asked hundreds of questions. I did not have the answers
to all of them. Only then did I have a feeling that drew me
close to my people. The "Jewish spot" was revived in me.
Until the time I was taken prisoner and during my life in the
forest I did not have such a feeling because all that time I had
lived among Russians, studied with Russians, had Russian
friends; and for this reason I did not find it difficult to conceal my nationality both in German prison camps and in the
company of partisans.

Among the Jews we found in the woods, I saw many young
men who had side-curls. I took out my razor and shaved them
on the spot, for I always kept my razor with me.[29]

Upon returning to camp, the idea flashed in my mind to get these people organized. For this purpose I had either to stay with them or to persuade the commander not to continue our advance eastwards. This latter possibility was out of the question for two reasons: first, the entire company would fall into the hands of the Germans who were getting ready for an extensive combing operation in the woods, mainly because of those Jews hiding in the forest; second, the company was moving eastwards to join the Red Army and so it could not be delayed in the woods. Thus the order was given to get ready to pull out on the following day. One of our guides had to take us across the river Goryn, but I decided to desert my company in order to organize a new partisan company out of the Jews in the forest, out of those who could carry arms and fight. In my company there were friends who agreed to stay with me in order to continue the fight behind enemy lines. They were Anatoly Korochkin, Serge Korchev, Genia Vodovozov, and Fedor Nikonorov.

The company pulled out at night, and we went together to the village of Svaritsevichi where we destroyed a German police command. Then the company continued its advance to the village of Ozyorsk, which lies on the road to the river Goryn, and then to the village of Hilin, where we deserted it quietly and went back to the Jewish camp in the woods. We were five Jews.

On the following day we began to set up a new company of fighters. We gathered more than twenty Jewish young men. They were: Y. Boris, Asher Mankovisky, Shmuel Purim, Nahum Zilberfarb, Zvi Liebherz, the brothers Moshe, Efraim, and Anshel Landau, Leibel Fleischman, who was known as Zamorochensky, and others. (All of them are now in Israel.)

* * * * *

We lived in earth tunnels in winter and in huts in the summer. These we set up in the forest and camouflaged them as best we could — living two in each dwelling. They were covered either with snow or with moss so that even in daylight one could not tell that partisans lived there, as they looked like small mounds.

Serge Korchev was appointed commander of the new company, which expanded with the addition of new people, both from among the Jews and the local population. One of them was a peasant called Misyura. He was a daring fighter who brought a pistol along with him. In order to strengthen our company so that it could start its military operations, we admitted into our ranks every man who could carry arms; Ukrainians, Jews, escaped prisoners of war, and others. Among them also was a Jewish young man by the name of Bakalchuk.

Two weeks later a Jewish woman came to me and said that half an hour before two Jewish boys had come into their shed from Ozyorsk, beaten up and terribly wounded. One of them was called Asher Turkenich; I forget the name of the other. The veins of both were cut, and on the bodies of both of them were many wounds. One of them was in critical shape. Asher had fewer wounds.

The two boys, who were about twelve or thirteen years old, had hidden in a shed not far from the village of Ozyorsk. Two Ukrainians had detected them there. On a night in December, 1942, when the two boys had lit a small fire for themselves, a Ukrainian forced his way into the shed, caught one of the boys, and started to stab him wildly. When he thought that the boy was dead, he threw him away and rushed at the other, Asher. But Asher succeeded in freeing himself from the murderer before the latter could inflict heavy wounds on him and escaped. The Ukrainian removed the boots from the feet of the near-dead boy and returned to Ozyorsk. When Asher returned to the shed about two hours later, he found it in shambles and saw his friend lying in a ditch, covered with snow. He pulled him out of the ditch and, with great effort, dragged himself and his friend to the Jewish camp in the forest.

The partisans bandaged the wounds of the two boys, but in the camp there was neither physician nor medicines. The seriously wounded boy suffered from blood poisoning and after lying unconscious all night, died in the morning. Asher Turkenich recovered, lived to see the day of victory, and today he is in Israel.

I decided to take revenge on the murderer. Leibel Fleischman and Moshe Landau said that they knew the man

and were ready to go along with me to the village and show
me where he lived.

On the following day, a Sunday, we set out in the direction
of Ozyorsk, a distance of six kilometers from our camp. We
approached the village from the direction of the cemetery
without being detected. The Ukrainian lived in the house
before the last. All around it was quiet and empty because it
was a Sunday, and the villagers had gone to the village center
where the Sunday festivities were being held.

I left Fleischman and Landau at the entrance to the murderer's house and slipped quietly inside. I found his old
mother and his sister sitting there. They were very frightened
when they saw standing before them a partisan, armed with
a rifle and a cartridge belt. I warned them not to shout or try
to escape and asked them to answer my questions in a low
voice, otherwise I would shoot. I asked where the son was.
The old woman told me that he was celebrating in the village.
I wanted to keep on interrogating her, but at this moment the
sister opened a window, jumped out, and started running in
the direction of the village center. I ordered her to stop, but
she kept running. I realized that the entire operation would
fail if I let her alert the villagers, for they would come after
me and, upon catching me, would hang me by the foot, as
they had done to a prisoner of war who had fallen into their
hands, an event which was spoken of a great deal in the forest.
I could not lose one single moment, so I shot her in the back.
She fell to the ground. But the shot was heard all over the
village, and to my ears came the tumult of the approaching
crowd. It was then that I decided to set the house on fire.
The old woman jumped outside and began to shout. From a
distance I saw people running with a buckets in their hands.
I fired a shot in the air. When the house was in flames, we
stated running in the direction of the graveyard, about half
a kilometer from Ozyorsk. On the way we passed through a
solitary farm belonging to a peasant, a father of ten. I ordered
him to run to the flaming house, and if the old woman's son
appeared there, to give me a sign by baring his head. He
refused. I threatened that I would kill him together with
the members of his family if he did not obey my orders. He
agreed to do what I told him provided that the villagers did
not learn of it.

From the graveyard we saw everything that was going on in the burning house. A lot of people gathered there in an attempt to put out the fire. Before five minutes had passed I saw the owner of the farm remove his camp from his head. The sign had been given. I stood up and started to run to where the fire was. Young boys and girls who had been placed by the peasants around the house to serve as lookouts and to inform them if they saw partisans coming out of the woods, began to shout: "Partisans!" The crowd dispersed at once. I ran to the farmowner and asked him where the murderer was. He pointed to a young man. I went after him, but the peasants came to his defense, and formed a barrier between us. I fired a few shots. The peasants around him dispersed. He ran into a back yard and hid inside a shed full of chaff, closing the door behind him. Apparently he thought I hadn't seen him. I ran to the shed and burst open the door. The young man stood near the wall and wanted to lunge at me; but I caught him in the chest, holding my loaded rifle in my right hand. He began to plead with me, begging for pardon, and assuring me that he was innocent. At that very moment Fleischman arrived, and I asked him if that was the murderer who had cut up two young boys. "Yes," he answered. At first I wanted to tie the murderer and take him into the forest so that Jews could kill him. But there was no rope around. In the meantime a lot of people had gathered outside. I was afraid that if I stayed there a little longer, I wouldn't be able to leave the place alive. I fired straight into his belly. He slumped to the ground, murmuring: "You have already killed me." But I answered: "No, now I'll kill you so that you will stop killing and robbing other people." I reloaded the rifle, brought the muzzle close to his neck, and, while he was lying there slumped against the wall, I fired again, and the bullet killed him.

Coming out of the shed, I noticed a crowd of peasants closing. I fired above their heads, and they dispersed. All three of us ran back to the forest. The farm owner caught up with me and gave me a bottle of *samogon* (a home-made alcoholic drink) to express his thanks for killing that knave. Some time later this peasant was to become our liaison-man.

Next day we ordered the village head to call a gathering of all the local inhabitants to hear an address by the partisan commanders. I was the first to speak. In my speech I warned the villagers that if another murder took place, no matter whether the murdered man was a Jew, a Tartar, a Georgian, or a person of any other nationality, we would put the torch to the entire village and shoot all its inhabitants, irrespective of whether they were guilty or innocent. I ordered them to offer aid to all prisoners of war and to all Jews that happened to reach the village. In this manner I emphasized the national aspect of the Jews in particular.

Before long many Jews were to reach Ozyorsk, and the peasants received them with marked hospitality. They fed them and hid them in their homes during the search raids of the German police. The Jews who hid in that village lived to see the day of victory.

Our company had by now grown to a force of eighty fighters, mostly Jewish young men. A short distance from the company, a Jewish family camp was set up in which were grouped all those Jews who could not carry arms. Earth huts were built for them. In order to obtain the necessary equipment, I went out with a number of fighters to the village of Gorodnaya where we confiscated from the peasants the Jewish possessions they had looted, loaded them onto three carts, and brought them to the family camp. We also brought along two cows, one for the partisans and the other for the non-fighters.

Gradually our company started its combat operations. We destroyed police stations and killed local inhabitants who had collaborated with the Germans.

* * * * *

...At the beginning of March, 1943, we received the information that a large partisan unit under the command of Fedorov-Rubensky was about to reach our area. Our ground scouts had met theirs. Some time later we received a letter from Fedorov in which he invited the commanders of our company to go over to their camp for talks. The letter was worded almost like an order. Three of our commanders, including myself, went to his headquarters in Zolowa. Fedorov suggested that we join his unit, since, according to an order sent down form Moscow, all the small companies

had to be united into one large unit. This union had its
advantages. We were formally recognized as partisans, maintaining contact with Moscow and receiving from it arms and
ammunition. However, it was agreed that we remain in our
present place. From now on our company was to be called the
"Voroshilov Company of the Fedorov-Rubensky Unit."

As a result of the union, some changes took place in the
command of the company. Company commander Korchev
was transferred to the unit headquarters, and his lieutenant,
Misyura, was appointed company commander in his place.

Misyura was a local peasant. He was thoroughly familiar
with the area, besides being a daring and aggressive partisan.

I may point out here that he did not discriminate between
his men on the basis of their nationality, and he helped
numerous Jews.

As head of the company staff, I was appointed commander
of its ground scouts. Korchev who, as already mentioned,
was assigned to the unit headquarters, tried to persuade me
to move to his quarters so that we could both work together.
At that time I got married to the partisan Chaya Landor,
and this marriage was not to the liking of Korchev, for he
did not want me to get tied down to a family. A number of
orders were even issued in connection with my transfer to
the unit headquarters, provided that I would leave my wife
with the company. For my part, not only did I not agree to be
separated from my wife, but I also did not want to leave the
Jewish family camp of which I had taken so much care for so
long. If I were to accept that transfer to the unit headquarters,
I would have been forced to leave for good. In the meantime,
strong relations had formed between the Jews of the camp
and myself. I took great efforts to stick to my original opinion, and I am happy to point out that the great majority of
those Jews survived and are today living in Israel, the United
States, and Canada.

Toward the middle of March the company resumed its
military operations, now under the command of Misyura. We
laid ambush to the Germans on the road running through
Gorodnaya-Butovo-Vichevka-Serniki where they moved
frequently. We stationed ourselves close to the entrance. At
dawn we saw a great number of German soldiers outflanking

us on the right and the left. It was clear that someone had warned them. One of my ground scouts, Baruch Menkovsky, who was stationed at the top of the fire-brigade tower in the village, noticed that the Germans were advancing straight to the village. When he informed me of that, I reported the news immediately to Misyura at Vichevka. He felt not quiet at home at this place and decided to engage the Germans in battle. That was absurd. The Germans had twenty times as many soldiers as we had. They were armed with sub-machine guns and mine throwers and were all around us. From my bitter experience I knew that they planned to encircle us. I tried to persuade Misyura that all we had to do at the time was to hold a position near the bridge through which we could withdraw into the forest at any moment. But he would not hear of it, and ordered me to stay at the spot, together with my platoon, which comprised only twenty-five men. I refused to obey the order and moved to a place close to the bridge. Company commander Misyura was angry at me, but he had no choice other than to follow me.

We dug in at a convenient point. To our right and let were marshlands, and the Germans could not mount an attack on us from the rear. Soon we were engaged in a battle which continued all day long. Under cover of darkness we succeeded in withdrawing through the road running between Vichevka and Butovo. On the way we saw from the direction of Butovo rockets which lighted the way for the Germans who had been sent to reinforce their colleagues with whom we had been engaged in battle near Vichevka. Without undue delay we laid ambush to the Germans. We lay in the ditches on both sides of the road. When the German carts reached the spot where we were hiding, we opened up at them from a distance of ten meters. In our crossfire many Germans and horses fell. We could not continue the fighting as we were tired out and highly outnumbered; so we returned to the forest, where we stayed for the night. In the morning we went back to the point of th ambush where we found only dead horses, a few rifles, and a pistol. From the cart owners who returned form the battle, we learned that they had picked up twelve dead and twenty-two wounded soldiers.

We returned to base without any casualties, only to be informed by our liaison man in Butovo that the Germans had returned to the village, grouped the peasants and their children in a circle, poured kerosene on them, and set them on fire. We at once jumped on our horses and galloped to the village. But we were late. The Germans were no longer in the village, and the peasants had turned into cinders. I saw only dismembered bodies. One woman was lying there with her child in her arms, both having been burned together. In this manner, about thirty-five people were burned alive.

In April, 1943, the Germans mounted a massive attack on the village of Svaritsevichi, after they had bombed it from the air. We had warned the inhabitants in time of the danger that faced them, and they had succeeded in taking refuge in the forest. The Germans burned down their entire village.

Anti-Semitic Tendencies in the Company

After Fedorov had appointed a new chief of staff and a new commissar for our company, anti-Semitic winds began to blow in its rank. The company consisted, among others, of Jewish girls and Jewish partisans' wives. They were among the first partisans to join the company before its union with Fedorov's unit. The women mainly took care of the cooking and the washing and looked after the wounded.

One day an order was issued by both the chief of staff and the commissar to expel, within twenty-four hours, all the Jewish women and girls from the company. I went down to the staff command and tried to prove to them that the order was unjustified, that the work of the Jewish women was of great benefit for the company, that they were looking after the wounded, and, therefore, no one had the right to expel them from the partisan company and, by so doing, to expose them to certain death. To my regret I realized that my arguments did not make any impression at all. I therefore informed them that I was leaving the company too. The rumor spread at once among the partisans. My scouts joined me, along with some partisans. In all, I had around me twenty-seven people, including the women and the girls.

When night came we left the company, armed only with our rifles. We went deep into the forest. In the morning the company command found out that we had left, and they at once reported to Fedorov's headquarters that I had deserted, together with a group of partisans and had even taken rifles along with us, although they knew all too well that the rifles were our own property. The headquarters sentenced me to death and issued an order to the effect that any partisan could kill me on the spot. Since they knew where to find me, they used to send, day in and day out, a messenger whose task it was to persuade me to go back to the company. I told them that I would go back on the condition that the two anti-Semites who wanted to do me evil were removed. To stay at that place was of course dangerous, and so we left the forest to where the company of "Dyadya Petya" was encamped.

The Company of "Dyadya Petya"

"Dyadya Petya" was a Russian *polkovnik*[30] by the name of A.P. Brinsky who was dropped behind enemy lines together with twelve men toward the end of 1942. He organized a partisan company out of escaped prisoners of war who had been hiding in the woods of Manevichi (Maniewicz) in the territory of Rafalovka-Manevichi (western Ukraine). The entire company did sabotage and demolition operations.

Upon reaching the company of "Dyadya Petya" who had heard a lot about me and my scouts, we were admitted into his company without delay. He assigned us to the various groups within his company. I was assigned to the group of Moshe Bromberg of Svaritsevichi who specialized in dynamiting operations. The group consisted of twelve men. Within two weeks we succeeded in blowing up three trains carrying German troops and ammunition on the railway tracks running between Rafalovka and Manevichi.

In May "Dyadya Petya" was called back to Moscow to be awarded decorations for his partisans. But before he set out, he filled out a questionnaire concerning my combat operations, and upon his return he brought back a copy of the order to award me the medal "Za boevye zaslugi" (for military successes) which was presented to me in Moscow at the end of the war.

In the same month we accomplished a difficult task. We had been assigned the job of blowing up a bridge not far from Manevichi. We divided our men into two small groups consisting of six fighters each. One of them was ordered to outflank the bridge from the left and the other from the right. The access from the left was covered with a tangle of shrubbery. When the group was within thirty meters from the bridge, it was met by a hail of bullets. The Germans had detected it. The group who had deployed to the right heard the firing and hurried to the bridge to support the other group. A pitched battle followed. The Germans suspected encirclement and withdrew immediately.

To their luck the night was dark, and we could not see the direction of their retreat. In this battle Moshe Bromberg was fatally wounded by a fragment of a hand grenade. When we put Moshe on the cat he was still alive, but he did not survive the rigors of the trip. He was awarded the Order of Lenin posthumously.

The first operation aimed at blowing up the bridge thus ended in failure. A few nights later, however, we repeated the operation and this time succeeded. We even had time to remove the railway tracks.

Some time later I was given a new assignment. "Dyadya Petya" appointed me the commander of the guards at the village of Galuziya, which was only one kilometer distant from the station of Manevichi. These guards were in charge of all the access roads leading to the company command. In June, 1943, I was asked to report to the command. In the courtyard I met many ground scouts whom I knew from Fedorov's company. I got off the horse and walked in the direction of the village. Here I met Major-General Begma who had arrived in April by plane from Moscow at the partisan landing strip in Lamachichi, bringing along with him many decorations and orders for the partisans in the Ukraine and Byelorussia. He had been appointed chief of staff of all partisan units in these areas.

At the headquarters building I also noticed Korchev, who was standing near "Dyadya Petya." I trembled all over but regained my composure immediately, saluted, and informed the general of my arrival. As I was to learn later, Korchev could not reconcile himself to the fact that I had deserted the company for which I had been sentenced to death by the firing squad. However, he had maneuvered the general into coming here in order to get me back into his unit. In answer to the general's questions, I recounted to him all that had happened, pointing out that the expulsion of the Jewish women and girls from the company had resulted from the fact that they did not consent to be the mistresses of the commander.

I added that both the commissar and the commander would often send the brothers and husbands of these women on highly dangerous missions. In this manner they endeavored to break their spirit and thus make the women surrender to them. General Begma chided me for not having reported the incident to him directly. To this day I remember the words he said: "I hereby annul the death sentence, and I order you to return to Fedorov's unit." After a talk with "Dyadya Petya" I went back to the unit on horseback with my wife. They received me with much joy.

Vanka Moryak

Next morning I was asked to report to the commander at the general staff. Around the table sat Begma, Korchev, Fedorov, and Kysya, the unit commissar. They asked me for the assignment I preferred. My answer was: fighter. On the following day I was asked to fall out of line and, in front of all the fighters, was appointed commander of the ground scouts of the entire unit.

I reorganized the unit. Some of the scouts I transferred to a number of companies, and many men of these companies I took into my group. I made a special effort to transfer into my unit as many Jews as possible. Upon finishing the reorganization of my unit, I was given a new assignment: to go on a sabotage mission with a group of three hundred men under the command of Korchev to the vicinity of Pinsk. In this area I felt quite at home as I had operated there as a partisan in former years.

Upon reaching the place, we found an armed camp comprising eight hundred men. It was under the command of a Russian nicknamed Vanka Moryak. We didn't know what they did exactly. The earth huts they lived in were arranged in wide squares — with furniture and carpets. Among Moryak's men were a Jewish doctor and two Jewish girls who were the mistresses of their commanders. We had come to them in order to use their camp as a base for our operations. But Moryak was soon to inform us that he did not like the idea that in his vicinity partisans would start blowing up trains since the Germans would soon put him under siege. We answered that we had been sent there by a large partisan unit and that the only thing we could do under the circumstances was to move away from his camp.

We went in the direction of the village of Gnevchitsy. There I was familiar with all the trails, and thus I could lead our group directly through the forest. On reaching a distance of about one kilometer from Moryak's camp, we saw on the roadside a destroyed earth hut among an assortment of old objects, groats which were spread all over the place, and a tablespoon. It was evident that no partisans had dwelt here. One could assume that Jews had dwelt in this place and that something had happened to them.

Upon returning from the mission I went up to the Jewish doctor to get from him details about the abandoned earth hut. At first he wouldn't say anything, but when I revealed to him that I, too, was a Jew, he told me that Moryak's men had murdered the Jews who had been living in that deserted place, sparing only him and the two Jewish girls. He spoke in a whisper, as he feared Moryak's men, adding that not far from Gnevchitsy there still lived some Jews who were hiding from both the Germans and the "Moryaks." On that very day I went to the earth hut dug into the ground, and found beside it bodies of men and women strewn all around. They were covered with moss and fresh snow. On the next day, on our way to perform another operation, we saw another earth hut about five kilometers from Moryak's camp. At some distance stood a sentry, who began to run away on seeing us. I had four Jews with me, and they called out to him in Yiddish not to run away. He stopped and guided us to the earth hut where we found a few men and women and a wounded man lying on the floor. Here is what the wounded man recounted to us: "In this earth hut, which was near the camp of the 'Moryaks,' lived thirteen Jews — ten men and three young women. All of them were residents of Ivanovo. In order to obtain food, they used to wander to the neighboring villages. One day three Moryak men came to the earth hut, including Moustafa, the notorious bandit. They dragged out one Jew some distance from the earth hut, pushed him to the ground and stabbed him to death with their bayonets. In this manner they killed all the Jews who were in the earth hut — one after the other." Even he, the wounded man, they wanted to stab to death. But the bayonet which was aimed at his heart wounded him in the shoulder only, without touching his heart. When he came to, it was already dark. He crawled until he reached this earth hut, a distance of about five kilometers from the scene of the murder. At this place lived the Leibovitz family, who took him into the earth hut, looked after him, and dressed his wounds. Some time later, when Fedorov sent one of his companies to this place under the command of Michael Nadalin, the wounded man was admitted into its ranks to fulfill various missions assigned to him by the company. He met Moustafa a number of times, but did not take revenge on him.

As I learned after the war, the doctor sued both Moryak and Moustafa. But they, in their defense, argued that the Jews had stood in their way on their combat missions. Moryak later worked for the N.K.V.D. (The Leibovitz woman who treated the wounded man and thus saved his life is now living in Israel.)

In the region of Pinsk we blew up, on several occasions, the railway tracks running between Pinsk and Brest, attacked police stations, and laid ambushes on the roads. For these operations I received the commendation from the general staff.

The Struggle to Capture the Landing Strip

At that time the military operations centered on this landing strip, not far from the village of Luninets. Here landed the planes that brought the partisans arms, ammunition, and various other supplies, and took the wounded back with them. The Germans knew about this landing strip and attacked it, but we resurfaced it after each bombing attack, because it was so vital to us.

After we had returned from the vicinity of Pinsk, I was sent to the landing strip along with a company of ground scouts in order to protect the planes that were to be flying in a great deal of military equipment, including 76-mm field guns. Immediately after the planes had taken off with the wounded, the Germans started a combined operation against the landing strip, from the air and with tanks. The bombardment continued for twenty-four hours. The Germans then entered the village, but they found it in ruins. All the inhabitants had gone into the woods.

In retaliation Fedorov decided to strike at the German garrison in Rakitno, which, according to my knowledge, numbered three hundred men. We shelled them all night, but their positions were well fortified. At dawn we were severely attacked by German planes. We had to withdraw. Under a heavy barrage of fire we crossed the river Goryn in the direction of the village of Hilin, but here too we could find no rest. My ground scouts detected in the area Germans who had just arrived in four military trucks. We attacked them immediately and wiped them out, taking only three prisoners. After they had been interrogated through our interpreter, Meilech Bakalchuk, all three were handed over to me to be shot. One of them pleaded with me not to kill him, because he had children. I asked him: "Then why do you throw Jewish children into a well alive?" I killed them all on the spot.

After this battle we proceeded to Zolotoe, where we massacred a group of *Banderovtsy*.[31] The company of Misyura also fought against them. On one occasion, while my company was encamped in the village of Vichevka, it was attacked by the *Banderovtsy* who wanted to free two German prisoners of war. The partisans, who were taken by surprise n their sleep, ran away to save their lives. The *Banderovtsy* made a search of the houses and found a Jewish sanitary worker by the name of Matilda who had not had the time to hide. They cut off her breasts, engraved the Magen David sign with a knife on her chest, and hanged her on a stock of wood which had been lying on the ground. In this battle, thirteen partisans were killed. The *Banderovtsy* took back the two German prisoners, some carts and horses, ammunition and food supplies.

The partisans, for their part, took revenge on the *Banderovtsy* while the latter were asleep in the forest five kilometers from Gorodnaya. The same scene occurred, only this time the partisans had the upper hand.

At this time we attacked an armored rain on the railway tracks running between Kovel and Brest. Our 45-mm gun succeeded in a second shot to set the train on fire, and this forced the Germans, about thirty soldiers, to jump off it. Being mounted, I attacked them with my ground scouts and finished them off.

As a result of all these battles, all the German garrisons along the way to Rovno were wiped out.

When the war was over, General Begma offered that I stay on in Rovno and serve as chairman of the urban committee on physical culture. I went to Kiev, where I received the necessary certificate and started to work. About two months later I was invited to see Korchev, deputy chairman of the district committee. He confided to me that before long, all Jews would be removed from important positions. To his pleasant surprise, however, I showed him my identity card in which my registered name was Abugov, Alexander Leontievich, a Russian. Under Korchev's recommendation I was soon to be transferred to the district committee on physical culture. That had a real advantage in those days — the chairman of the district committee was excused from military service.

The conditions of the Jews went from bad to worse. Jews were dismissed from the positions of factory managers and from other enterprises. My wife's family and all my brothers-in-law, who had been with me in the partisan unit, began to talk me into leaving the Soviet Union, especially when it was possible to go to Poland as repatriates. In the beginning I was against the idea, but later on I decided to try my luck and leave Russia, for which I had done and fought so much.

After many wanderings through Poland, Czechoslovakia, Austria, and Italy, we finally arrived in Israel in 1949.

THE PARTISAN FILMMAKER

O. Savich

For one entire year Michael Glieder fought in the partisan camps under the command of Major-General Alexei Fedorov and also at the camp of High Commander Sidor Kovpak.

In describing his life as a daring fighter, Fedorov wrote:

"Comrade Glieder, fighting shoulder-to-shoulder with other fighters behind enemy lines, accomplished his missions with great success, attacked enemy companies as a fighter while also fulfilling his duty as a photographer. In his active participation in blowing up railway racks which served for German transportation, he sometimes came as close as fifty paces from the tracks and there lay in ambush for the German train and all the soldiers and ammunition it was carrying, in order to see with his own eyes its approach and explosion and to photograph the entire event at once."

Sidor Kovpak describes Michael Glieder both as a photographer and a fighter:

"Michael Glieder demonstrated extraordinary heroism at the camp. He also did a highly significant work by directing his camera at the combat activities of the camp, as well as at the acts of cruelty of the Germans against the peaceful population. Documentary evidence is attached to his work as a battlefield photographer. He was also a courageous fighter against the German enemy. On May 12, 1943, during one of the hardest battles, he stayed at the forefront all the time, organized the crossing of the camp over the river Pripyat, and served as an example to the other comrades. At the same time fighter Glieder filmed with his movie camera the accomplishment of this difficult and dangerous task."[32]

* * * * *

The first year of the war of the fatherland and half of the second year were spent by Michael Glieder, a movie-technician, in the Red Navy. In March, 1943, he was called to Moscow to make a documentary film on the activities of the partisan movement. The man required for the job had to be deeply familiar with the Ukraine. Without asking many questions, Glieder agreed to drop over the combat area of a partisan company behind enemy lines. He did not reveal, however, that he had never dropped by parachute before and that he had only seen it done by others. Thus, Michael Glieder was to arrive in Sidor Kovpak's famous unit.

The unit was having a very hard time. The Germans had surrounded it and were endeavoring to drive it into the triangle between the Pripyat and the Dnieper rivers. The partisans attempted a breakthrough by crossing the railway tracks. That was the first partisan battle in which Glieder took part. As he could not do any filming in the dark, he fought as an ordinary soldier. The breakthrough did not succeed. The partisan forces were heavily outnumbered. Kovpak decided to cross the Pripyat, and the preparations for the crossing went on all through the night. At this point the width of the river was two hundred and forty meters. The current was so strong that a temporary bridge could not meet the requirements, as it had also to withstand the passage of fieldguns, vehicles, and food supplies. All went into the cold water. The bridge was almost ready, but the ropes did not hold. Then Glieder remembered how bridges of this kind were thrown over the River Amur, and he suggested that wedges be driven into the bottom of the river and fastened with wires so that each beam should have its own supporting point. After that had been accomplished, the bridge was ready by dawn. The partisans carried the loads and the field guns safely across. When the Germans eventually realized what was going on, the partisans had put some distance between them and the bridge.

A few days later Glieder filmed the historical discussions between the commanders and commissars of the five largest partisan brigades in the Ukraine, with the participation of the secretary of the Communist central committee, D.S. Korotchenko, and the chief of staff of the Ukrainian partisan movement, Major-General Strokach. Some time later Glieder was attached to the unit of A.P. Fedorov.

Fedorov's was a fast-moving unit. Its men marched for sixteen hours on end. On their way they saw villages which the Germans had put to the torch. Here it was not the local population that provided food supplies for the partisans. On the contrary. It was the partisans that gave the inhabitants food from their own provisions. After the unit had defeated a German garrison in a battle in which Glieder took part, both as fighter and cameraman, it proceeded to the region around the railway tracks running between Kovel and Sarny. It was necessary to disrupt in this region all German communication lines which carried troops and arms to the front. Once the partisans were encamped in the forest, they at once went out on sabotage missions.

Glieder wanted to film at any cost an actual blowing up of a train by the partisans. Twelve times he went out on missions which resulted in ten blown-up trains, but only once did he succeed in filming such an event. In the meantime he had turned into a remarkable photographer of sabotage activities under the guidance of such a skilled artist as Pavlov, hero of the Soviet Union. The explosions shot by Glieder from a distance of sixty meters from the embankment have remained unique in the annals of movie photography.[33]

Fedorov's men fulfilled their mission: they totally stopped all enemy movement in their region, and the Germans were thus forced to send reinforcements through Romania. No night passed without demolition explosions. Fedorov was proud of his saboteurs. People used to say that German trains "run only with their wheels upwards." In the intervals between one sabotage operation and another, Glieder filmed the everyday life of the company. He succeeded in shooting some four thousand pictures.

With the approach of winter the partisans started digging pits for the camp earth huts. But the Germans surrounded the camp and forced them to leave the place, cross the river Styr, and engage in battle. The Germans bombed the surrounding woods in their search for Fedorov's people. Along with the unit fighters, there was a civilian camp made up of Ukrainians and Poles who had been saved from certain death.

In the meantime Glieder learned how to lay mines and to read traces; he learned everything: the tactics of partisan warfare, reconnaissance work, how to build earth huts without using nails, and, also, the art of interrogating German prisoners.

* * * * *

Not everyone who took part in the prolonged events of the partisan war remembers all the details necessary for recreating a vivid picture of past happenings. The power of observation, a phenomenal memory, and the diary he kept helped Glieder in postwar days to write an excellent book in Fedorov's unit.[34] In this book he gives a detailed account of how the partisan celebrated at their camp on the 7th day of November, 1943, the First of May, and Red Army Day; and how they celebrated the coming of the new year, 1944. He describes the celebrations, the parades, the evening of "personal activities." In his book on the battles and the sabotage operations, Glieder does not forget to give the accounts of individual fighters who contributed their share toward the final victory. He delineated a pageant of vivid partisan characters, their commanders, and their commissars: Kovpak, Fedorov, Rodniev, Druzhinin, and others. On roads, sabotage missions, and in newly liberated population centers, the partisans met many civilian citizens, rural and urban, old and very young, men and women. The great suffering that fell to the people's lot under the yoke of the German invaders did not destroy the belief in the victory to come. In each and every place young people and adults joined the partisan camp. The women were ready to give everything they had to feed the fighters, and the children did all they could to help along. When the Red Army front was approaching Fedorov's region of operations, it was decided to move the wounded across the front line, along with the sick and the "civilian camp." But it turned out that the wounded and the sick did not want to be separated from their companies. They had made fast friends among their comrades, and they had been dreaming of one ceaseless struggle until victory was achieved. Even some of the civilians found it difficult to be separated from the main force; they were leaving their saviors behind enemy lines.

All these situations were captured by Glieder on his movie film.

Glieder succeeded in shooting a particularly spectacular event: In January, 1944, a Red Army patrol penetrated for the first time into Fedorov's region of activities in order to establish contact with the partisans. Naturally both the Red Army soldiers and the partisans were apprehensive of a possible mistaken identity and thus gingerly approached each other. But when the partisans saw the stars on the headgear of the strangers and recognized the Soviet automatic rifles, they fell into each other's arms shouting, "Comrades, dear comrades!" Then the Soviet troops embraced the partisans, and the latter hugged the welcome Red Army soldiers. Many wept. The tears disturbed Glieder the photographer.

The Red Army soldiers and officers spent the night at the unit's headquarters. They were fed well. The partisan girls washed their underclothes. In the evening a concert was given in their honor.

However, it was not easy for Fedorov's men to be united with the Soviet army. The days of ordinary activities returned to the partisans: blowing up of railway tracks, roadside ambushes, insignificant skirmishes. Unexpected rains came in that season of the year. The earth huts were wet, and it was impossible to move along the roads. The last large-scale operation in which Glieder participated took place in 1944, on the twenty-sixth anniversary of the Soviet army. On that night the partisans noiselessly dispatched the front guards of the Germans and entered the village of Nesukhoezhe where there was a great concentration of enemy forces. The battle was long and hard. The partisan ground scouts were heavily outnumbered by the Germans, some of whom were firing from stone-built houses and properly sited firing positions. Nevertheless, only a few scores of Germans came out alive. About one thousand German soldiers and officers were either killed or taken prisoner. Fedorov's men captured enemy storehouses full of military equipment.

Following that battle the partisans made a breakthrough to their camp, reaching it after twelve days. They marched only in the dark, covering about forty kilometers in a single night. The Germans tried to follow them, and enemy planes dropped bombs on the roads and forests ling on their party. But the partisans arrived safely back at their camp, bringing all their wounded along with them.

In March, 1944, Fedorov and unit commissar Druzhinin were called back to the center in Kiev. Glieder crossed the front line back to Moscow. His photographs were published in scores of movie journals. They were included in the movie on the Ukraine produced by Alexander Dovzhenko and went into movies about the partisans which were produced by Beliyev.[35] But in Mocow Glieder was to hear of his great tragedy: his only son, his brother, and his son-in-law were among those who fell at the front.

Before long Glieder accepted an offer to go out to the Slovak Corps: Producer Kupalin was shooting a film on Czechoslovakia. Thus Glieder was to become the movie-technician of the second brigade of the paratrooper air force. He filmed the brigade in training and, later, its first battle near the Polish village of Pelniya. In this battle Glieder pulled out from under a hail of enemy fire eighteen wounded, a field gun, and four vehicles.

At the same time an insurrection broke out in the Slovak army which had been set up by the Germans and its quisling government. A "liberated zone" was formed near the towns of Banská Bystrica and Zvolen. The front command thus sent the second brigade of the paratrooper air force to aid the insurgents.

The first group with which Glieder flew landed safely in the liberated zone. But owing to bad weather, there was some delay in airlifting the entire brigade. In the meantime the situation of the insurgents was worsening. The area under their control was not large enough and the insurgents were still inexperienced soldiers under equally inexperienced commanders.

The German attack was not late in coming. The brigade was moved into battle one part at a time, and so its full forced was not brought to bear on the enemy. In the first encounters the insurgents had the upper hand, but the Germans received great reinforcement, including airplanes. A great panic spread among the insurgents, and gaps began to show in the front itself. Elements of the brigade and the partisans put up a heroic fight, but they did not have the strength to withstand the pressure exerted by the enemy. The Germans captured Banská Bystrica. It was then necessary to leave the "liberated zone."

All the roads were blocked with numberless troops and refugees who had escaped from the advancing Germans. The road was hard and mountainous. The Germans bombed the roads with singular ferocity and disrupted all communications between the units that stood in their way.

In the tumult of retreat, brigade commander Prikaril called Glieder to him and said: "Although I am a veteran soldier and have seen no few battles I my life, I am not familiar with partisan war tactics. We are now expecting a highly unusual war, far beyond our strength. You are the only one among with the necessary experience. There is no other way but for you to take part both in command and in tactical operations."

The brigade numbered only one hundred and twenty fighters at the time. It was mandatory to move them away from the battlefield at once as the Germans were by now close at their heels. Glieder buried his movie camera in the ground. A difficult forced march began over the mountainous terrain, but a heavy downpour saved our lives by making it difficult for the Germans to bomb the retreating forces. The going was singularly tough over those steep hills with the arms and food supplies. The horses fell down. On our way we met soldiers form other units. They joined the retreating column.

At long last, high up on some mountain peak, in the earth hut of the commander of the partisan company, a meeting was held between the brigade commanding staff and the headquarters of the partisan movement in Slovakia, with the participation of members of the Czechoslovak parliament. In the course of discussions it was decided that the brigade should serve as a combat unit. Its commander was advised to take in troops from other units, besides volunteers from the civilian population, and switch to partisan tactics. Glieder was appointed commissar of the brigade. There was no time for arguments. Glieder said: "Thanks for the honor and our faith in me" and went straight to work.

The brigade by now numbered five hundred and sixty fighters and thirty-two officers. Glieder addressed them briefly. In his speech he did not try to hide from them the difficulties of the struggle ahead and asked all those who had doubts, fears, or misgivings to fall out of line. No one budged.

Once again they headed for the mountains, which were now clothed in thick fog and swept by strong winds. The fighters slipped, fell down, rose to their feet, and later rested and warmed themselves by the fire. The Germans cordoned off all the villages that lay in the valleys to prevent the brigade from passing through them. One battalion was instructed to move in another direction. The partisans had to eat their remaining horses; and as they had almost run out of bread, each one was given only one hundred grams.

The only way out was through the high mountain of Chabenec with its permanent cap of snow. They kept on the ascent under a hail of fire. Snow kept falling. Strong winds threw the marchers down as they walked. Their clothes were covered with sheets of ice. But they did not come down from the peaks. They let the wind erase their footsteps behind them.

Then the descent into the valley began. Even now the people would slip and fall. Glieder felt that he could not move one step farther. He was saved by a solider called Sidor, who pushed a stick into the commissar's hands and pulled him behind him. They crossed a number of streams and rivulets. In the dark the people fell into icy water. Parliament member Schvirman was exhausted from the effort and passed away in the valley.

The main column suffered relatively few casualties, but out of the second group, which numbered one hundred and three persons, only twenty reached the valley. The rest froze on the way. All the survivors had their weapons with them.

The people stopped at a mine known by the name of Lum. Down below spread the villages of Dolná and Horná Lehota. The commander sent a group of partisans to these villages to fetch some food supplies, and the villagers gave them generous amounts of food. The next day another partisan group blew up two tankers at the Ľupča station, captured a seed storehouse in the village, and handed the stock to the villagers.

New groups of soldiers and volunteers from the nearby villages kept joining the brigade. Glieder held talks with representatives of the local authorities. All were on the side of the
people. Armed battalions quickly formed in the villages. The
local population provided the brigade with food supplies and
gave its commanding staff valuable information.

On several occasions the Germans announced that the brigade had been beaten, that it had dispersed, but at the same
time they put up a reward of half a million kronen on the
heads of commanders Prikrila and Glieder. Once, when all
the battalions had gone out on missions in various directions
and the brigade headquarters were left without cover, the
Germans mounted a sudden attack on them. A fire exchange
ensued. The Germans were only twenty meters from
Glieder's earth hut, and so we had to escape into the forest.
Luckily, we suffered no casualties.

On the following day the command staff succeed in joining one of the battalions. But the joy was short-lived. The
Germans repeated their attack, and once again we had to
move away. A few officers tried to persuade the commander
and the commissars to stop the struggle. The answer was a
categorical "No!" To turn a regular army brigade into a partisan one is no easy matter. This was particularly difficult for
the officers, who had been taught according to the old school
of strategy and tactics. The brigade command staff demaned
operations that were usually carried out behind enemy lines.
To bring together dispersed, temporary units, with mostly
incomplete cadres into one army unit at combat level, whose
duty it was to spearhead the battle of the people in that
region, was not easy.

The brigade headquarters were now stationed in an isolated
hut high in the mountains. Communications were gradually
established with all the units, and provisions were supplied
regularly. The local inhabitants helped in everything. They
succeeded in establishing contact with the patriots in the
neighboring towns, including the people of Bratislava. The
runners became everyday heroes in their devoted work.
Many presents were received from the local population for
Christmas. In one village the presents were collected openly,
ostensibly for the German troops, and then delivered to the

brigade. The Germans were then told that the partisans had attacked the vehicle that was carrying the gifts to them.

With the help of the brigade, a resistance movement was organized against the Germans in various settlements. The headquarters had contacts with twenty-one local authorities and ten underground armed organizations. On the first of January, 1945, the brigade comprised three full battalions. There were enough arms for all the fighters.

The healing of the wounded was a serious problem. The brigade medic, Regach, went about in the mountains endeavoring to visit the huts of all the units. The wounded and the sick were sent to the hospital at Podbrezová. Hospital doctor Robert Kristik, an enthusiastic patriot, hid the partisans and treated them as he did the local residents.

* * * * *

At the conference of party workers in the district of Brezno, where reports were presented of the activities of the armed battalions, and a discussion was held of the ways to be followed for stepping up the resistance of the people and integrating it with that of the brigade, Glieder represented the fighting forces. The meeting was held in the forest, at a distance of two kilometers from the German guards. Among the delegates there was also the priest Bartel who fought the Germans with a rifle in his hand within the ranks of one of the brigade's battalions. On the day the conference was held, the brigade saboteurs derailed a German train, attacked another one, and thus disrupted train traffic at the station of Ľubietová.

In the meantime the Red Army was approaching the region of the brigade's operations. On quiet nights one could hear the rumblings of the field guns. The Germans were getting ready for evacuating the region. In early February, 1945, the brigade was thrown into the battle front. The need for ground scouts and runners was so great that Regach, the medic, did runner missions. The same medic would write down a summary of the news items sent by the *Sovinformburo* (Soviet News Agency) and duplicate them. On the first of February, 1945, the first battalion of the brigade engaged in battle a large German unit and succeeded in wiping them out. That was a battle to remember.[36]

Fearing that the brigade might strike at their rear, the Germans made several attempts to defeat it before it withdrew from this region. They failed in their efforts to do so and were forced to station there strong units of guards made up of frontline troops against the "town people." After the Soviet Army had advanced so close as to make possible a coordination of operations with the brigade, one battalion after the other joined the battle against the enemy.

Some time later an order was received from the commander of the Czechoslovak corps instructing us to cross the front line. The order was carried out without any special difficulties. The high command of the Soviet army and the Czechoslovak corps, which had no accurate information about the brigade, could not rely on the latter's fighting ability. It was therefore surprised to see before it a full-fledged combat brigade. General Svoboda embraced both Prikila and Glieder and said: "Thank you, thank you! God bless you!" Glieder informed him with some excitement that the brigade command had promoted and demoted a few officers, perhaps without being authorized to do so. Answered the general: "I confirm all your orders!"

* * * * *

Glieder's mission had come to an end. The frequent treks throughout the mountains had affected his health. For a long time he lay ill; but on recovering, he went back and dug out his movie camera from its hiding place. It still contained the film with the pictures he had taken before he had gone back to the role of partisan.

His photographs were integrated into the movies: "The War Day," "Our Moscow," "Avengers of the People," "The Ukraine in Its Struggle," "Czechoslovakia." Together with the director, Glieder received an award for the picture "Avengers of the People." A great honor was bestowed on him: he filmed the parade at Red Square.

Michael Glieder, he gifted movie-technician, daring and courageous partisan, justifiably carries on his chest a chain of orders and decorations, both Soviet and Czechoslovak.

WOMEN SPIES

*Grigory Linkov ("Batya"), Hero of the Soviet Union,
Polkovnik,[37] Soviet Partisan Commander*

On his way back from a combat mission, Commander
Anatoly Tsyganov brought along with him seven new fighters, including two women. One was young and beautiful, so
everyone called her "The Bride." Tsyganov said that the new
fighters had helped his company raze two farmsteads and a
large alcohol factory with a considerable stock of products for
the invaders.

I had a great liking for Anatoly Tsyganov since the time
of our joint activities behind enemy lines. I took his words
seriously. This time his company had fulfilled with great
success the combat mission which had been assigned to it
between Baranovichi and Minsk, with the active participation
and daring acts of the two women fighters. According to him
"The Bride" had done outstanding work. The other women
had taken part in disarming the guards of the farmstead in the
region of Nesvizh and proved to be quite a good fighter.

But I was not convinced by the proof that Tsyganov
adduced concerning the fighting ability of the two women.
The Hitlerites at that time were doing their best to find out
the partisan bases, and for that purpose they used mainly
women. Women spies could reach us only as members of
partisan companies, where they had been accepted as loyal
members after they had concealed all their contacts with the
Gestapo. The participation of women in razing a farmstead
and an alcohol factory which had already been in the hands of
the fascists was not proof enough of their loyalty to the partisans. In order to gain full confidence, one had to do something of great importance against the invaders.

I gave orders that I wanted to see the papers that the
women had carried on them, if there were any such papers
at all, and also to check up on certain biographical details
concerning them. In the evening two passports were brought
to me, one bearing the name of Yelizaveta Vasilyevna Alexova

and the other bearing the name of Vera Shamenskaya. The two passports had been issued in Minsk at the beginning of 1942, that is seven months before they came to us. Alexova was registered as a Russian and Shamenskaya as a Pole. I also learned that both spoke good German. It was presumed that Alexova had worked as an interpreter for the Hitlerites.

I could not sleep all night for fear that women spies had come into our partisan base. In the morning I made up my mind that I should not have any suspicions concerning the validity of my doubts. Accompanied by a few handpicked young men, I went toward Alexandrov's position where all the "newcomers" were grouped together. I had decided to talk with them, interrogate them thoroughly before issuing the order to have them executed.

The first one to be called into the earth hut was Alexova. I asked her to tell me how she had found her way to the partisans. I listened to what she was saying every now and then. She spoke in a quiet, composed manner while she related to me the story of her life. She gave details of her work for the fascist commander in Minsk as an interpreter and how she had decided after a quarrel with him to run away to the partisans in the forest, a thing which she did at the first opportunity.

Her words gave me the impression that she was lying all along. I could not make up my mind. "To hell," I said to myself. "Doesn't this girl think that she is endangering herself by giving such evidence?" Perhaps all of this was a skilled move played by an accomplished woman spy who knew how to treat her own life with indifference?

While listening to Alexova I did not ask any questions and did my best to give her the impression that I was satisfied with the story she was relating to me.

"Well, you may go now and do whatever you like," I told her, and I let her leave my earth hut.

Alexova went out. I gave the order to bring in Shamenskaya. I also ordered that upon her entering the earth hut, Alexova was to be arrested at once.

Shamenskaya sat calmly in front of me as Alexova had done before her.

"Tell me, please, how did you get here?" I asked her, looking straight into her eyes.

The woman was disturbed. I had the impression that she was considering what to say and what to hide. I waited with patience for everything she had to say:

"I am Shamenskaya, Vera Mikhailovna, from Poland," the second woman started slowly. "Till the war broke out and during the war, I had been living in Minsk. When the Hitlerites came to our town I did not know where to go. Many Germans knew Polish, and I knew a little German, so I had no difficulty in finding a job as a waitress at a restaurant."

I listened to her without moving my eyes from her lips.

"Once," she went on, "I had a quarrel with the manager of the restaurant. Because of that I was fired. On the same night I ran away into the woods to the partisans."

"How long were you in the woods together with Alexova?" I asked.

The woman cast a frightened glance at me. "We...we... were together for about six months."

"Perhaps you could tell me something about this woman?"

Shamenskaya's tension mounted. To go on lingering was dangerous. Feeling uncomfortable, she blushed and became increasingly excited.

"I don't know this woman at all, and I cannot tell you anything about her," said Shamenskaya, fighting her inner feelings.

"Well, then, it is all clear to me now. I'll have both of you shot," I said very quietly.

Shamenskaya stood up in consternation. The soldier who was standing at the entrance to the earth hut aimed his rifle at her. The woman paled and clung to the wall, her strength ebbing. I made a move to leave.

"Comrade Commander, allow me to add a few words to what I have just told you," Shamenskaya said calmly.

"Speak," I stopped, waiting for her confession and the self-incrimination of the spy who got caught in the cobweb of her lies.

"Pardon me, Comrade Commander, but all that I have told you is one big lie," she said and began to sob. "I...we...

thought that everything would be all right as it has been so far...but know I realize that I shouldn't keep on doing this... both of us, this young woman and I, are Jewesses..."

Without realizing it, the soldier lowered his rifle.

"She is a distant relative of mine, and I can tell you a lot about her. Everything. All I have told you has been due to the fact that our passports are false."

This announcement made me mad. I wanted to curse her, but I restrained myself.

"And how can you prove that you are a Jewess?"

"Among your men are three Jews, and if you will allow me to talk to them, they will testify that both of us are Jewish women."

"How do you know that we have three Jewish comrades here?"

"Can't anyone tell that they are Jews?"

At the position commanded by Alexandrov there really were three Jewish fighters, but one couldn't tell by the looks of two of them that they were Jews. Only I knew that they were Jews.

"Well," I said, "let it be as you say."

Commander Shlykov was instructed accordingly. A few minutes later the three testified that the two women were Jewish and that they had run away from the ghetto of Minsk into the woods. This evidence, of course, did not assuage my suspicions. Indirectly we checked up on them in the ghetto of Minsk, including their deeds in the battlefield. The facts proved that they had told the truth.

PART FOUR
PARTISAN WARFARE

DAVID KEIMACH

Grigory Linkov ("Batya"),
Hero of the Soviet Union, Polkovnik,
Former Commander of a Partisan Unit

I was appointed commander of a paratrooper company. Although this company had already undergone special training, I still had a host of worries, chief among which was the absence of a political commissar.

September, 1941. I am traveling by streetcar in the blacked-out streets of Moscow. I am trying to think of a man who would fit the role of commissar, sifting and weighing the qualifications of Communists I know. I was reviewing an imaginary list of names, but the role of commissar, which is essentially a difficult and responsible one, calls for specific traits and qualities.

Suddenly I feel a piercing gaze directed at me, and before I had time to look around, I heard a voice saying: "Grigory Matveyevich, why haven't we been seeing you of late; where've you been hiding?"

A young, tall man with dark hair and black eyes gives me a warm handshake.

"David, it's so good that we've met! How're things going at our laboratory?"

David Keimach and I were both engineers. Until recently we had been working together in a science laboratory. We both had a record of Party work too.

"What's this talk about the lab?" David said sadly. "It's still there. Nothing has changed much with us. Even the enemy bombs are obligingly missing us. But sitting home is no easy matter. I believe that my place is at the front. I don't feel like working at the lab these days."

I looked into David's face with great interest. Like him, I had had the same feeling in the early days of the war.

"Is it correct, Grigory Matveyevich, that you have been appointed commander of a paratrooper company?" Keimach inquired in a low voice.

"It is correct!"

David looked at me, a hint of jealousy in his eyes, and said, "How lucky!"

Suddenly I had an idea! This is the man I've been looking for — our political commissar.

"David, would you join my company as commissar?"

"I?" For some time he was deep in thought. "You aren't joking?"

"Is there anything to joke about here?"

"Then I'd gladly accept the offer. Do I have to send in an application?"

"Questions of this kind cannot be solved on a streetcar. Here's my phone number, and if you don't change your mind, ring me up three days from now."

David called me three days later and told me that he was accepting the offer to join my company.

I notified my immediate superiors. I told them about David, the man, his traits and qualifications, and asked their permission to have him appointed political commissar of my company. A few days later David appeared at the company barracks, happy and proud of the confidence we had shown him. I, too, was glad of the fact that he had joined us — I was about to set out on a long and difficult road.

I had known David for a long time. He was the son of a tailor from Odessa. At sixteen he had joined the Komsomol, was active at the trade association, and later was a delegate to the municipal council of Odessa. In 1929 he was admitted into the Party as a student at the Institute for Machinery and Construction in Moscow. On receiving his degree he did postgraduate studies at the Institute and later became scientific assistant at one of the faculties there. I knew his curriculum vitae as well as I knew my own. An excellent worker, a good and sensitive friend, an ideal family man. Now we were once again to work together under difficulty conditions of war behind enemy lines. I could not have wished myself a better commissar.

On the night of September 17, 1941, our company was air-lifted in seven cargo planes heading for the front. We didn't make it this time. Heavy rain and a strong head wind stood in our way. The paratroopers could not jump according to plan. Tens of kilometers apart, one from the other, many fell straight into the hands of the enemy punishment squads and, in their first encounter with them, died a hero's death. David Keimach and I also landed a considerable distance from each other.

For twelve days I had to wander alone in the woods and the inhabited areas, looking for my men and my commissar. At the same time David was trying to locate me, accompanied by a small group of paratroopers.

With the approach of autumn, the trees lost their leaves and shrubbery became sparse. There were long spells of rain. Behind us, like a shadow, doggedly moved the German punishment squads. We made ceaseless effort to locate the reminder of the men, sustained by boundless stubbornness and our belief in the rightness of our cause. One evening, while I was sitting in the hut of a Byelorussian farmer, the door flew wide open and Keimach appeared. Wearing a tattered and soiled shirt, with a wild growth of hair, tired out, he fell into my arms, beaming with joy. Peering from behind him was a young man, a physical training instructor by the name of Zakharov.[38] We embraced each other warmly, shed-ding tears of joy. From that moment on we were together once again, now behind enemy lines. We had no contact with Moscow. Almost without any military equipment, we none-theless were strong in spirit, as we had to keep up the fight against the enemy. We started organizing the company in the woods. At the spot to which Keimach later took me, there were about ten people from Moscow and some thirty men, local inhabitants who had been recruited by the commissar in the course of his wanderings.

Many of the inhabitants of the neighboring villages wanted to join the company. But there were all around us people who had betrayed the motherland, who had sold themselves to the enemies of the partisans and had even begun to serve as their secret agents. It is no easy matter to look into the soul of a person and to know his true identity. But we had to know who was for us and who was against us. In those difficult days of getting the company organized, Keimach fulfilled his job with an unusual sense of responsibility. He had an uncanny knack for looking through people and telling a great deal about their character and personal qualities. It was an easy matter for him to ferret out provocateurs and secret agents who attempted to infiltrate our lines. He never misjudged a new fighter who joined the company: "This man is on our side; you can trust him," he would say.

David Keimach had a liking for youth. At the camp when he was resting, he would be surrounded by groups of young people who loved him too and confided their deepest secrets to him. He knew when to have a talk with a person and when to give encouragement. Among the youth he looked young himself, laughing unreservedly, his eyes beaming, his cheeks crimson with excitement.

In the fall and winter of 1941 the Germans pretended to be settling down for a prolonged period in the occupied territories. Our scouts came back from a neighboring village with the unsettling news that the Germans were building a schoolhouse there.

"A schoolhouse?" Impossible!" said David. "Who told you they were building a schoolhouse?"

"All the people are talking about it. All the villagers, retorted the excited fighter. "Comrade Commissar! The Germans have announced that a school is to be built in the village so that our children will be taught the German language. The announcement has been officially made through the head of the village. They are building schools in other villages too. In the village of Rudnya (Byelorussia) the foundations have already been laid. It follows that these creeps intend to stay here for good."

"No, someone has misunderstood the facts," said Keimach. "For the present the Germans cannot afford it. Their attack has caused them great difficulties."

Keimach asked me for permission to go out to the village. Accompanied by the reconnaissance men who had brought the news, he went out to Rudnya under cover of darkness and returned quite pleased.

"Well, I knew it. It's not a *school*. Only a stronghold. That's what the Germans are building. In some places they are laying brick foundations for their heavy artillery — the Germans are unsure of their position in these places, and they are getting ready to defend themselves."

Keimach sat down and wrote a leaflet to this effect. The men had it duplicated and distributed in the surrounding villages.

The days passed. We had succeeded in organizing a company made up of 120 fighters. We kept wandering in the woods from one base to another, harassing the Germans with our daring surprise attacks. So far these had been only small scale operations; however, we managed to saw through the beams of a bridge which fell apart under the weight of a German tank; here and there we assassinated a fascist mercenary, the head of a village or townlet or a collaborating policeman; we cut off the telegraph wires; we lay in ambush along a road. The blowing up of a large bridge on the River Essa, on the road between Lepel and Borisov (Vitebsk and Minsk regions) finally drew the Germans' attention to us. So they sent a battalion of field soldiers, heavily equipped with artillery and mortars. We now had to withdraw to a valley full of marshes. For hours on end we had to wade, waist-deep, in cold water, which was covered with a thin layer of ice, holding our weapons up in the air and carrying the wounded on our shoulders. Thoroughly wet and freezing with cold, we finally reached a dry island where we could make campfires to get warm and dry.

The three of us — David, the local chief of staff, and myself — held a council of war and decided to divide the company into two parts: one would be led by me back to our former base in the woods of Kovalevichi (Byelorussia) and the other would be led by David to a well-guarded point in an impassable terrain in the direction of Lake Palik (Byelorussia). After the decision was made, we hugged each other and said goodbye. Who knows, we might never see each other again.

I gave my men the order to set out on our way, and we were soon once again waist-deep in the icy marsh water. Evening came. David, the light of the campfire dancing eerily on his face, sat tense, staring in my direction. When he saw that he had caught my attention, he took off his hat. Again I wondered at the sublime patriotic feeling of this man, who had left behind a nice job, a loving wife, and beloved son — all that so he could go through freezing marshes to a cruel struggle and perhaps even get killed.

At the first village we reached after coming out of the marshes, the people told us that the entire region was full of German soldiers. Two divisions, one of them having been pulled back from the front to rest and regain its strength, were all over the place. It was beyond our power to fight them. As it was, the Germans had already cut us off from the men who had supplied us with useful bits of information, arms, military equipment, and provisions. We were surrounded by fascist forces bent on annihilating us at any price.

While wandering through the woods, I began sending runners to Keimach's base. Two groups, each made up of five fighters, were killed on the way. Some days later, while patrolling the area with my company, I came upon the body of fighter Zakharov, loved by one and all, who had fought it out with the Germans to his last breath. Beside him lay the body of Chapai, his closet friend.

The third group we went out for reconnaissance came back to report that our base at lake Palik had been destroyed and that bodies of partisans were strewn around it in the snow. The local villagers gave contradictory accounts about Keimach. One said that he had been killed in a fight with the Germans, another asserted that, together with a handful of fighters, he had broken through the German encirclement and escaped through the front line.

It would be difficult to describe all the hardships of that first winter in the woods. Often it occurred to me that we had better cross over to our main forces and then drop once again behind enemy lines, reinforced by a new company, with a transmitter and new military equipment. However, I dismissed this idea. After every attack, which cost us some of our best men, we went out once again on the roads, blew up bridges, sniped at the "Fritzes,"[39] and cut telegraph wires.

Our base in the woods of Kovalevichi was named *voenkomat* (military center), on account of the great number of farmers who came to it wishing to join the company in the fight against the hated enemy. Despite the German atrocities (which were aimed at terrorizing the inhabitants), despite the deep snow and the ambushes along the roads, we continued our raids on enemy units, thanks to the splendid relations we had with the people in the surrounding villages, relations long since established by Commissar David Keimach. In the meantime we were getting low on ammunition and were totally out of explosives to sue for mining the access roads. Our raids on the Germans had to be cut down accordingly.

In March, 1942, our fighters came back from patrol duty to report that they had come across a group whose men were well dressed and equipped with automatic weapons. The men called themselves guerrilla fighters and expressed their desires to establish contact with our company. At first I suspected this to be a trap set by the Gestapo. A few days later, however, I found out that the people I had suspected had met the chairman of the local *kolkhoz*, a fellow by the name of Ozoronok, with whom we were on good terms and told him that they were underground fighters sent out by Moscow to look for the Batya's company. They then demanded to be shown the way to our base. Ozoronok told them that he knew no one by the name of "Batya," thinking, as I had done before him, that they were Gestapo agents. He ran to the village head and told him about the paratroopers so that Germans themselves would search for and trap their own spies. But the head of the village caught on and said to Ozoronok: "You can catch the paratroopers yourselves. There's one under every bush!"

To my great surprise I was to hear some days later that I had been mistaken and that a new sabotage group had actually arrived commanded by Commissar Keimach. Everything happened the way we read in fairy tales. On March 27, 1942, I once again had the chance to meet my old friend. Needless to say, we spent the whole night in friendly talk.

"How is it that you decided after all the bitter experience of last fall to drop in here again?" I asked David. "You must certainly have heard that we had all been wiped out and that I was dead."

"That you were killed — well, I heard that. But, how can I put it...I somehow knew that you were alive. You may have noticed that I'm not saying that I believed it. To say that I believed wouldn't be enough — I knew it."

"Well, suppose it was so, but what chance did you have to find me here, in this area crawling with German punishment squads?"

"Here we are! I did find you, and I would have found you under any circumstances. In the first attempt the people helped me, and now they have done so again. You see, I didn't go into the 'desert' — I went to the people. 'Here's the commissar,' the people said, 'the soul of the company.' How can a soul live without a body?" he joked. "A soul has no peace without a body. It is…unpleasant. I wanted all along to drop in on you from a plane, from the heavens down to earth…"

We soon resumed our partisan activities. David was once again at the head of the fighters.

The Germans committed a number of atrocities in the villages. In their attempt to put an end to partisan activities before the coming of spring, they kidnapped and shot every man they met who looked in the least suspicious to them.

The people flocked to our military "center." Tirelessly, David picked out new fighters. At the same time we held sabotage courses at our central base to teach the new recruits the ins and outs of this business, of blowing up trains and cutting railway tracks.

When the snows began to fall, we decided to hit the enemy's transportation lines. The first company, with its forty fighters, went out in the direction of the Vileyka-Polotsk line (Molodechno and Vitebsk regions) and were led by Shcherbina and Keimach. It was difficult for me to say good-bye to Keimach, my closest friend, but we couldn't help it — on our most important operation we had to send our best men and Keimach was one of our very best.

On the first of May, the Shcherbina-Keimach company sent in reports of having blown up three German trains full of soldiers heading for the eastern front. In these operations more than two hundred Germans were killed. The last of these three sabotage operations were carried out by Keimach, accompanied by five fighters. After they had mined the railway track, they went back quietly into the woods. David did not know that after the second operation against the Germans the latter had alerted a large number of forces and brought a punishment squad to comb the woods for us.

David and his men were in high spirits. They sat on a nearby hill covered with green bushes, overlooking the tracks. They watched while the train chugged its way along the tracks and directly onto our mines. They then saw pieces of the railroad carriages flying up into the air. They heard the groans of the Germans and saw huge columns of black smoke rising from a smashed-up tanker going up in flames.

Having enjoyed the results of his work, Keimach ordered his men to move back. The fighters crawled down the hill, but when they reached the woods they started moving at a fast clip and covered a distance of about three kilometers. Afterwards they quietly made ready for some needed rest. They made a fire and took off their clothes and leggings in order to dry. The water in the field cauldron had started to boil when suddenly they heard the rustling of branches. The Germans had surrounded their camping site. Keimach at once ordered them to get their hand grenades ready and move away to the other end of the forest. He also ordered that the campfire should not be put out. When the branches moved in the nearby bushes, Keimach commanded: "With the grenades, fie!" Six hand grenades were tossed into the bushes. The sounds of the explosions and the whine of the splinters stunned the "Fritzes" and forced them to "hit the dirt." Keimach's men opened up with automatic fire and broke through the German encirclement.

Taken aback, the Germans did not fire at the partisans. They were afraid they would hit their own soldiers. Not waiting for them to recover their senses, Keimach and his men put some distance between the Germans and themselves.

Only later did the fighters understand why the commissar had ordered them not to put out the fire when the Germans were advancing towards the partisans' camp. The reason was that the attention of the Germans was directed toward taking the partisans by surprise and wiping them out. To have put out the fire would have given the Germans a clue. That's what they thought, but they had guessed wrong. Some hours after, Keimach and his men were back at the base. Only one fighter had been slightly scratched. After some time, when I moved with my company to another area, I saw to it that the Keimach-Shcherbina group would be attached to a special fighting company.

Keimach did not want to be separated from Shcherbin. His company began to assume large responsibilities, acting on a sector of hundreds of square kilometers in area. When Vasily Vasilyevich Shcherbina later fell in battle, David took over. He had by then become famous as the commander of an invincible partisan unit — a reputation which served as a banner for the local population in the fight against the Germans and their collaborators. The fatherland recognized Keimach's military exploits by awarding him the Order of Lenin and the medal of "The War of the Fatherland, First Class."

David did not live to see the happy day that signified victory over fascist Germany. The plane in which he was flying on his way back to Moscow, in September, 1943, was shot down by Germans in the region of Vileika, and David died.

For me that marked the loss of my best friend; for the Soviet country, the loss of a loyal son and a brilliant defender.

His memory will live forever in the hearts of all those who met him, especially in the hearts of those who lived and worked with him.

THE PARTISANS OF THE KAUNAS GHETTO

M. Yellin and D. Galperin

Men of the Underground

It was the fall of 1941, far behind enemy lines, and the whole of Lithuania was groaning under the yoke of the fascist invaders. Thirty thousand Jews, inhabitants of the town of Kovna, were behind barbed wire. Pogroms, arrests, imprisonment, and cruel trials had uprooted thousands of people. But the German oppressors demanded fresh sacrifices every day. The condition of the survivors was desperate.

But the Soviet people who were imprisoned in this fascist concentration camp did not fall victim to despair. Under the direction of the Communists, there appeared within the ghetto a number of underground groups, each one different from the other, all with the single aim of waging partisan warfare. The head of one such group was a young Jewish writer and Communist by the name of Haim Yellin. Under stringent conspiratorial conditions the individual groups united into one antifascist organization in the ghetto of Kovna. This organization was first headed by a committee of five comrades and, later, by a committee of seven.

The fighting organization initiated highly important underground work in the entire ghetto. The number of its members grew from day to day and so did its influence on the rank and file within the ghetto. A powerful transmitter was set up, and it was well camouflaged. Day in and day out, news summaries were received from the Soviet information bureau and were transcribed onto leaflets and distributed in the ghetto. Every Soviet victory at the front, every important event in occupied Lithuania, every Soviet celebration was reported in articles and leaflets.

The underground started sabotage activities against enemy transports, storehouses, factories, buildings, and such places where Jews were brought from the ghetto for forced labor.

To such places the underground sent members who had succeeded in carrying out a number of incendiary demolition jobs. Every day had its act of sabotage, which, though small or insignificant, cause some trouble to the Germans: the partisans changed bills of lading on train carriages, mixed up cargo designations, sabotaged engines and machines, cut off telephone and telegraph wires, punctured tires.

The main task of the organization was to channel the able-bodied ghetto dwellers to the partisan companies. For this purpose scores of organization members slipped out of the ghetto and, at the risk of their lives, went out on reconnaissance missions to establish contact with others and to get arm. Communist members like Shmuelov, Milstein, and Yoffe, as well as Komsomol members such as Slavyansky, Tė-itel, Borodavka, Stern, Lipkovich, and Rachel Katz, were the first to give their lives in this highly dangerous work. At last the persistent efforts of the organization achieved its objective: contact was established with Gesya Glazerite, whose nickname was "Albina" and who had been sent to engage in underground activities behind enemy lines. "Albina" would often ask Haim Yellin to come over to her hiding place in Vilna, where she would put him in contact with the partisans active in the Rūdninkų wood. The commander of the partisan brigade in this forest, Genrikas Zimanas, who was secretary of the southern committee of the Lithuanian Communist Party, issued instructions to send people from the ghetto of Kovna to the partisan company which was to be formed under the name "Death to the Invaders!"

Those who went over to the partisans were in need of arms. Thus the underground people broke into a German storehouse to the center of town, directly opposite the Gestapo building, took out rifles and military equipment, put them into sacks, loaded them onto a waiting truck, and brought them to a hiding place. In this way it was possible to obtain a considerable quantity of antiaircraft weapons from the German storehouse. Sometimes it was necessary to attack in the open. One such operation, which yielded sizeable booty, was carried out in the forest sector of Kaišiadorys.

The path to the partisan base was a long and dangerous one. Forty-three out of the first hundred men who left the ghetto for the woods did not reach their destination. They were killed by the Gestapo. Eleven were caught and sent to "Ninth Fort," a death camp for people from Lithuania and other countries. They were ordered, together with other prisoners, to unearth the bodies of some seventy thousand people who had been killed in that place and to burn them. The eleven underground members who were taken there were later to initiate the great daring escape of the prisoners of "Ninth Fort" under cover of darkness, on the night of December 25, 1943.

In order to prevent the killing of ghetto fugitives on their way to the partisans, the underground organization brought fighters in trucks to predetermined spots. The usual practice was to have an organization member, dressed in German uniform. Arrive in a truck at the ghetto gates and take out people for "night-shift work," using false documents. The truck would then take them some 120 kilometers away from Kovna where special guides would be waiting to take them to the partisan base. Among these guides was partisan Nechemia Endlin who at the same time served also as liaison officer for the party underground. For five months on end it was possible to send partisan fighters right to the gates of the ghetto, but in the end the Gestapo discovered the trick and laid an ambush for the partisan truck. At a short distance from the ghetto, a bitter battle broke out between both sides. Only part of the group of fighters succeeded in shooting their way out and coming back; the others died in the fighting.

The preparation of one transport cost us the life of the organization leader in the ghetto, the brave fighter Haim Yellin, who insisted on supervising all the work involved in sending partisan companies to the ghetto to help in taking many ghetto prisoners out into the forest hideouts.

In the Forest

In the early days of November, 1943, Constantine Rodionov, following an order from the Northern Committee of the Communist Party, began organizing the "Death to the Invaders" company, whose chief duty was to receive into its ranks the fighters from Kovna. The company was stationed in the Rūdninkų wood under the command of the secretary o the regional committee of the Lithuanian underground, Genrikas Zimanas ("Yurgis"). He had the full respect and love of the partisans as well as the local inhabitants, who played an active role in helping the avengers of the people.

In the beginning the "Death to the Invaders" company suffered from serious shortage of arms and military equipment. Besides, the number of fighting men was small. Before long, however, new partisans joined it from among the fugitives of the ghetto of Kovna. They brought along with them arms, equipment, medicines, bandages, clothing, and other things they had received from the underground while still in the ghetto. To everybody's joy, a powerful radio-receiver set was brought into the partisan base, and the people in the woods could now listen to the voice of the Moscow broadcasting station. They heard the voice of the head of the Lithuanian communists and partisan fighters, Comrade Antanas Sniečkus. His calls of "To Arms!" added much strength and alertness to us all.

The company, complemented with armed refugees from the ghetto of Kovna, could now carry out highly complex fighting tasks. This company from now on was to take part in large-scale operations which were planned in cooperation with other companies operating from the Rūdninkų wood.

In the village of Kaniūkai, some thirty kilometers from the partisan base, the Hitlerites had a stronghold. They ambushed our units and fired at them from their hideouts. The "Death to the Invaders" company was ordered to wipe out this source of harassment and murder. Thus a partisan group crossed forests and marshlands under cover of darkness, approaching the village at dawn. All of a sudden a rocket flare poked a finger at the gray sky. That was a sign for the beginning of the attack. Twenty fighters of the "Death to the Invaders" company, headed by their commander Michael Trushin, stormed the village. The Germans took shelter in the houses and returned fire with rifles and machine guns. The partisans had to fight from house to house and to use hand grenades and fire-torches in order to drive the fascists away.

Partisans who had come from the ghetto of Kaunas — Teper, Ratner, Volbe, and Tzadikov — headed the attack on the fascists under a hail of enemy bullets. Leib Zayatz, a burly

young man, broke into one of the houses after he had run out
of ammunition, forced a rifle out of the hands of a Hitlerite,
and opened up on the enemy. The Germans were wiped out;
this fascist nest was put out of commission.

In their fighting missions, the partisans of the "Death to
the Invaders" company often had to go through the village of
Strielčiai. The Germans used to station guards in the village.
They even provided arms for the villagers to help them in
attacking the partisans. So the company sent a group of fighters to the vilagers and asked them to hand in their arms. The
peasants gladly did what the partisans requested, and German
weapons were turned against the Germans themselves.

A reconnaissance group of the "Death to the Invaders"
company reported unusual activity on the part of the
Germans in the nearby village of Žagarinė. Our mounted
scouts brought in more detailed information about the setting
up of a reinforced siege garrison in Žagarinė. The "Death to
the Invaders" company mounted an attack on the Germans in
full force. Taken back, the Germans began to run away from
the village. The partisans put the barracks to the torch, blew
up the water towner and the railway station, destroyed the
railway engine garage, put tow railway engines and a number
of full and empty railway carriages out of commission, dismantled a considerable length of railway tracks, and threw
the rails into the marshes. They also blew up two wooden
bridges for good measure. The road back was cut off from the
Germans.

On another occasion a partisan reconnaissance party
repoted that a great number of arms was to be found in the
hands of the nationalist German Lithuanians in the village
of Gudakiemis in the district of Onuškis. The partisans
now faced the double task of beating the German force and
getting the arms. Leib Zayatz, Leizer Silber, Israel Yoels,
Solomon Abramovitch, and Abba Diskant had enough reason
to revenge themselves on the Hitlerites. No wonder, then,
that they covered the entire sixty kilometers in exceptionally high spirits. The skirmishes they engaged in on the way
did not cost the partisans any losses. Upon arriving at the
spot, they surrounded the house of the gang leader who was
having a good time with his friends. The partisans had only

a few rifles and pistols. Leib Zayatz ordered at the top of his voice: "Mount the machine guns; the sharpshooters, after me!" The gang leader and his friends ran down to the cellar, thinking that they were surrounded by a large company. A few hand grenades thrown into the cellar did the job. A great amount of booty was taken and carried on carts to our base: it included fourteen rifles, about forty thousand rounds of ammunition, a machine gun, a radio-receiver set, rockets, and other military equipment.

The Struggle Along the Railway Tracks

An everyday practice of the partisans was the blowing up of enemy transports. Leizer Tzadikov, the first partisan to arrive from the ghetto of Kovna, stated out by sabotaging railway tracks. In the vicinity of Vievis, some eighty kilometers from our base, he derailed an enemy convoy carrying military and technical forces heading for the front. In the same area he blew up two more transports. The boy Meerov, who was among the first to join the company, blew up five enemy transports. He fell in the sixth attempt.

Boris Lopyansky carried out four sabotage operations on the railway tacks between Vilna and Vievis. Shimon Bloch had four to his credit, two of which were a hundred kilometers from our base, on the way to Pravieniškės on the Kovna-Kaišiadorys line and near Gaižiūnai on the Kovna-Jonava line. His permanent assistant for military operations was Moshe Puchekarnik. The woman partisan Chaya Shmuylova and partisans Silber, Eidelman, Feitelsohn, Vilenchuk, Eida Pilovnik, Birger, and others blew up German transports and carried out with great success the fight along the railway tracks.

Along with three comrades Yaakov Ratner blew up an enemy transport driven by two engines. The fascists went after him. The valiant partisans kept running in an area swarming with Germans. On the way back to the base, they also had clashed with a large group of fascist policemen. Yaakov Ratner was wounded in the leg and in the left hand by a fragment from a hand grenade. He fell. It was already dark. The Germans swept the area with search lights and found the wounded partisan. They began to advance toward him. Ratner let them come close to him and then, with all the strength he could still muster, threw two hand grenades and opened up with his rifle. The Germans were confused and ran away. With his last strength and reached a peasant shack, crawled in, and passed out. The peasants gave him first aid and dressed his wounds. On the following day he was picked up by the partisans and taken back to the base.

The destruction wrought by the partisans left a dent in the German war machine; several kilometers of dismantled railway tracks, the loss of scores of German transports full of soldiers, military equipment and fuel, kilometers of cut telephone and telegraph wires, and other losses. These were the blows that the partisans struck at the enemy in that most vital element: the communication lines between the front and the rear.

A Well-Knit Family

New forces were added to the company that was formed from refugees of the ghetto of Kovna. The "Death to the Invaders" company grew larger and larger. Under the supervision of Constantine Rodionov ("Smirnov"), two new Kovna companies were formed: on January 11, 1944, the Vladas Baronas company (commander, Karp Ivanov-Semyonov; commissar, Michael Belkin), and on March 13, 1944, the Vperyod ("Forward") Company (commander, Captain Tseyko; commissar, Haim David Ratner). The bases of all three companies were not far from each other, and in the first one was located the joint command. The construction workers of the brigade worked hard under the supervision of Moshe Sherman in setting up partisan camps. They built earth huts, a camp bakery, and a bathhouse.

It was only natural that partisan arms would always be kept in tiptop condition. Leib Sher set up a workshop for this purpose. In it he tested the weapons and repaired them. Among the partisans who came over from the ghetto of Kovna were other specialists. In their spare time the tailors made new clothes and mended the old ones; the cobblers were kept busy making boots and leggings. There were also excellent fitters. The two academic degrees that Chuna Kagan had received from two colleges did not stand in his way in proving that he was also a good mason. Israel Gitlin set up a printing press at the barracks of the "Free Lithuania" company. It served a useful purpose for putting out propaganda literature for the local population.

The underground organization in the Kovna ghetto sent over to us a number of experienced medical nurses. Zoya Tint and Riva Epstein remained to look after the Kovna companies. Other nurses were received at the "For the Fatherland" company and the "Free Lithuania" company. The ghetto organization saw to it that Soviet planes dropped us ammunition, equipment, literature, provisions, and medicines.

At the base itself one could feel a true spirit of brotherhood. The Lithuanians, the Russians, the Jews, and the Poles came to each other's aid with unbounded warmth. They were ready to sacrifice their own lives in order to save their friends. Once, partisan Ivan Dushin volunteered for a dangerous mission in order to save a partisan group from encirclement. Chaim Volbe saved the commander of Goryachev's group from certain death: when a German was taking a bead at the commander, Volbe sprang up from his hiding place, charged at the German, and killed him on the spot. On another occasion, Commander Goryachev evacuated Volbe (who was wounded at the time) from the field of battle under a hail of enemy bullets.

Moshe Milner and Sofrony Orlov were once surrounded by a Greman company while on a reconnaissance mission. In order to make it possible for his friend to escape and deliver the information they had obtained, Milner engaged the Germans in battle. Eventually he was left with only four bullets in the chamber of his pistol, which he had received as a present from the ghetto organization before he left for the woods. Milner shot three bullets into the enemy, the fourth he reserved for himself.

On the way back from a successful mission in December, 1943, a group of partisans were ambushed by the enemy near the village of Gailiūnai. In their escape the partisans turned onto a river which had frozen over a short time before. Commander Trushin was in charge of the crossing. Enemy bullets kept whizzing past him. Pesach Gordon-Stein fell and was killed by the pursuing enemy. The remainder succeeded in crossing over to the other side of the river in order to hide in the woods. Sharpshooter Aaron Gafanovich covered the successful crossing. The commander brought up the rear, but the much trampled ice finally collapsed and he went under, up to his chin in the freezing water. Partisan Lopyansky, who had been out of danger, ran back to save his commander. The ice broke under his weight. Above his head the bullets kept whizzing. Lopyansky succeeded in catching the drowning commander by the hair, pulled him out of the water, and dragged him away from enemy fire.

Daring and Courage

Ten kilometers from the main base in Viečiūnai stood the nerve center of the Germans. At that spot several narrow-gauge railway tracks crossed the Vilnius-Grodno road. Here also was the Forest Authority. A reinforced German garrison was stationed in the town.

The three Kovna companies — "Death to the Invaders," "Forward," and "Vladas Baronas" — decided to attack this fortified crossroads. They divided into small groups, set up ambush units along the way, and advanced in the direction of the garrison. A well-aimed bullet fired by the unit commander, Trushin, accounted for the German guard. It also indicated the beginning of the attack. Shouting "Hurrah," the partisans stormed the barracks area through a barbed wire fence. The Germans were held in a crossfire. Krakinovsky pounded at the German command with an antitank gun. Gafanovich, Nemzer, and Pasternak fired at the Germans with machine guns. The surprised Nazis jumped out of the houses in their underclothes; some ran about carrying suitcases, reluctant even at such a moment to be separated from their loot. The bodies of the murderers rolled on the ground and among them were six officers. Other Germans who showed any resistance were cut down.

Suddenly firing started from the direction of the barracks. Hirsch Smolyakov was the first to throw a hand grenade at the German machine gun and lead an attack on the barracks. Padison, Tzadikov, and Bloch also charged at the head of their groups. The fighters of the Strom and Eidelman group surrounded the staff headquarters. Lopyansky broke into the building through a window and killed the German machine-gunner with the butt of his rifle.

One by one the houses of the garrison fell into the hands of the partisans. At the same time a partisan group was in pursuit of the Germans, who had escaped in the direction of Rūdninkai. The effective fire power of our groups was cutting down the Germans when, all of a sudden, a truck appeared on the scene full of armed fascists who had been sent over from Vilnius to help the forces under attack. The handful of partisans now had to fight it out with a large enemy company. The "avengers of the people" entered into this unequal battle in order to enable the main partisan forces to reach the base safely, together with the booty and the German prisoners they had taken. The partisan rear guard returned fire until the last round of their ammunition. One after another, the partisans fell. The last survivor was Teibel Vinishskaya. She was wounded. Rising her hands she turned toward the Germans, who were overjoyed to have a partisan woman fall into their hands. When they came closet to her, she released the grenade she had kept in her hand, killing herself and six Hitlerites surrounding her. Of the sixteen partisans who died a hero's death near Viečiūnai, thirteen were members of the party underground of the Kovna ghetto. The partisans vowed to avenge the blood of their fallen comrades. On the day after the battle, a group of fighters followed a German truck on the way from Viečiūnai to Vilnius. In it were seven German officers who had been wounded in the previous day's battle. The partisans blew it up. They landed one blow after the other until this enemy garrison was taken out of Viečiūnai.

While on one of their military operations, partisans belonging to the "Invaders" company caught concentration camp commander Nikolayunas, a hangman who had killed numerous Soviet prisoners. They put him to death on the spot.

Once six partisans of the "Death to the Invaders" company were on their way to the Kaišiadorys station. They stopped for a day's rest at the village of Žalioji. Suddenly they were detected by a local anti-Communist who informed the Germans. Protected by a small tank, a carful of armed fascists arrived at the village. The partisans put up a brave fight. They blew up the tank with a grenade. But they were surrounded and greatly outnumbered. All the partisans fell in the fighting. Toward evening the Germans were seen setting up a gallows in the small town of Onuškis. The next day the inhabitants of the town saw six nude dead bodies on the gallows. Those were the bodies of the partisans who had fallen the day before.

The murder of these six brave fighters was a great loss to our company. When news of it came to the base, the commander of the "Death to the Invaders" company issued Order No. 39, which read:

> *While on a military mission, a group of six partisans, under the command of Comrade Lopyansky, was surrounded by Hitlerite killers in one of the houses in the village of Žalioji. After intensive fighting, all the members of the group fell.*

> *Comrade Lopyansky, who was born in 1921, was an exemplary partisan, who was recommended for a state decoration for his battle honors.*

> *Partisan Shmuel Martkovsky, who was born in 1922, Leizer Tzadikov, born in 1916; Mates Goldberg, born in 1922; Solomon Abramovitch, born in 1914; Itzik Miklishansky, born in 1923 — they too were fearless partisans, loyal to their fatherland.*

> *Eternal glory of victory to the fallen heroes!*

> — *(signed) Company Commander Smirnov*

For the First of May celebrations it was decided to mount an all-out attack on the Rūdninkai road junction. Peretz Klyachko, Frieda Rothstein, and Rachel Lifshitz slipped in the early morning over to the bridge going through the small town of Merešlėnai and blew it up, together with the guards who were on it. This operation served as a sign for the beginning of the attack. Fire was opened on the German garrison. Michael Pasternak, an excellent sharpshooter, sent seventeen discs into the enemy. Sarah and Moshe Rubinson, together with Aaron Vilenchuk, kept firing for three hours or more at close range into the exit doors of the fascist barracks. At the same time the railway station went up in smoke and fire. Boris Stern, Solomon Breuer, and Vasily Zaporozhets destroyed the telephone station. Other partisans laid mines on the roads which were to be used by the Germans to send in their reinforcements. Anton Bondar, Chonye Padison, and Katriel Koblentz blew up the munitions factory. The companies returned to their base without a single casualty.

Now, the First of May celebrations had a special flavor. The privileged partisans were singled out for state decorations, and offered the deep appreciation of the high command. Among the outstanding fighters to be so honored were forty-nine partisans from the ghetto of Kovna.

Shoulder-to-Shoulder with the Byelorussian Partisans

The Vladas Barnas company received orders to move over to the woods of August and to continue the fight there. On the way the fighters encountered a number of ambushes, and an intensive fight took place near the small town of Valkininkai. The company, more experienced now in the fight against the enemy, passed through these ambushes without suffering any casualties. Aaron Gafanovich alone accounted for three fascists, took their arms, and added six more prisoners to those already taken. At the predetermined point the company carried out a series of operations: they destroyed a bridge on the River Marykha in the vicinity of Kapčiamiestis and the bridge on the road running between Kapčiamiestis and Grodno. The blowing up of both bridges was credited to partisans Klyachko, Yoels, Deutsch, Lifshitz, and Shilin.

The operations in central Lithuania were etrusted to a group of partisans from the "Death to the Invaders" company, under the command of Stepan Kulikov, a well-known partisan favorite whom they nicknamed "Lyotchik" ("flyer," and two experienced partisans, Tepper and Goldblatt. The group was active in the district of Ukmergė in the vicinity of Pagelažiai, setting fire to a tractor loaded with arms. Together with the tractor, eight Germans also went up in flames. German guards from the nearby POW camp hurried to the aid of their colleagues. The partisans took advantage of this development and attacked the remaining guards. They released Soviet prisoners of war, who in turn joined the partisans. In Siesikai the partisans set fire to large storehouses for bread, destroyed in several places a narrow-gauge railway track running between Jonava and Ukmergė, sawed off the telephone and telegraph poles, and took a great many head of cattle from the Germans. The commander of the Hitlerite police of the Ukmergė district Keturaka, was also shot and killed. The partisans later distributed Soviet publications in Lithuanian, together with the newspapers Tiesa (Truth) and Už Tarybų Lietuva (For Soviet Lithuania).

When the Germans were on the run out of Lithuania, the partisans blew up a bridge on the road leading from Taujėnai to Ukmergė, destroyed a fast tank and another small one, fired at enemy convoys, set ambushes, and prevented many Germans from getting out of Lithuania alive.

At the time the Soviet army mounted its devastating attack against the Germans, which brought freedom to White Russia and to the greater part of Lithuania, the "Vperyod" ("Forward") company, under the command of Captain Tseyko and Lev Solomin (Petrovich), went into the woods toward the southwest, which extended from Kazlų Rūda up to the former German frontier. Partisan Nehemiah Endlin who had trekked hundreds of kilometers of Lithuanian soil with his outstanding knowledge of the roads of the country, was entrusted with the task of serving as guide on this difficult march.

On their way out from the Rūdninkai wood, the partisans faced many difficulties. The Vilnius-Grodno railway tracks were under heavy guard every inch of the way. Dugouts and mine fields stretched along the entire length of the tracks. Endlin went out to reconnoiter the area. Close to Rūdiškės, he led the company on purpose along a road which was heavily guarded by the Germans, counting on the assumption that they would not expect the partisans in this area. When the Germans eventually grasped what was happening, it was too late. In the meantime the company had succeeded in getting into the forest.

Now it was necessary to cross the river Neman. Though there were a number of suitable points for crossing, Endlin found that we had better choose the same path once beaten by former partisans. And, indeed, the number of Germans here was greater than in other spots, but in such cases it was more important to count on the aid provided by the local inhabitants, who had already come in contact with the partisans and knew how to provide the necessary information. The high command accepted Endlin's suggestion. The peasants of that area brought out all the canoes they could find, even wooden boards and drinking troughs. The moon came out to light the way for this motley armada now floating on that languid river.

June nights are short. In order to make it to the company's destination, it was necessary to be on the move at dusk and at dawn. Not far from Marijampolė, the partisans were ambushed. They at once flattened themselves on the ground and opened fire with machine guns and antitank weapons. Their bullets checked the enemy attack. The partisans then commenced crossing into the forest, but all of a sudden an order was given by Endlin: "Run back; follow me!" The partisans obeyed the order and started running back. Endlin's keen senses, which had been honed to a fine point under the trying conditions of partisan struggle, did not fail him. He had sensed that an ambush had been set. The partisans were soon to realize that he was right: from the forest, hundreds of Germans came out "on the double," followed by vehicle moving at great speed. Apparently, after intensive firing by the partisans, the fascists eealized that they had come upon a large partisan unit, which was now about to attack them. It was only natural, after this incident, to expect an encounter with the enemy near the railway tracks running from Kovna to Marijampolė, where the partisans were likely to cross. In this case, too, the local peasants reported heavy German guards along the tracks. The peasants also reported that the ambushes were called back at eight in the morning, and guards were stationed at two-hundred-meter intervals. This valuable information helped the partisans decide to make their crossing in broad daylight. Thus at ten in the morning, the company crossed the tracks. This move elicited amazement and admiration from the peasants. Days later, after a march of some 230 kilometers,[40] interspersed with occasional fighting, the company went into the forest allocated to us, and there it set up its new base.[41]

A short time before this operation, a number of fighting groups had been sent out to establish contact with the partisans of White Russia. These groups also reached their destinations after some fighting with the enemy. When the Red

Army launched its June offensive, the Kovna partisans stayed behind in White Russia in order to fight shoulder-to-shoulder with their comrades, the Byelorussians. In the company commanded by Major Shostakovich, special distinction was accorded by Alter Feitelsohn. In the operation that took place near Molodechno, on June 21, 1944, he used a mine-layer to destroy the enemy's firing position, and the partisans succeeded in taking this area without casualties. Yaakov Kave was among his Byelorussian comrades when, in the course of a single night, they destroyed the railway tracks over a distance of forty-five kilometers.

The Freeing of Soviet Lithuania

The Soviet Army advanced quickly toward Vilnius. The Germans made great efforts to ensure for themselves a "quiet" rear line at any price. They sent reinforced units into the forests: guns, mine-layers, and even called in air strikes. With calculated maneuvering the partisans avoided any premature encounter with the enemy, deploying their forces for the military operations that lay ahead. The "Death to the Invaders" company received instructions to drive the German forces out of the small town of Rūdninkai and its surrounding villages when the Red Army began its attack on Vilnius. Armed gangs of Byelorussians and Poles collaborated with the Germans. They laid ambushes against the partisans on the roads leading to Rūdninkai and often attacked them. In one particularly intensive battle the partisans beat the gangs. The small town of Rūdninkai was later freed from enemy forces. Red flags were raised on the houses. Both liberated and liberators sat together in a joint meeting.

New missions were now given to the partisans. The Red Army surrounded Vilnius with a ring of steel. Shoulder-to-shoulder with the army the partisans fought. The "Death to the Invaders" company, together with other companies, crossed the river at Baltoji Vokė and fanned into the outskirts of Vilnius. Near Aušros Vartai the partisans engaged the enemy in violent fighting. The fascists had barricaded themselves inside the houses, but the partisans liberated one house after another, one street after the other. On July 13, 1944, Vilnius was finally freed from the German invaders.

The partisans helped put out fires and establish order in the city. They stationed guards on the roads leading to the old capital of Lithuania. Woman partisan Bella Ganelina happened to be in charge of the Vilnius checkpost at that time and had the privilege of supervising the passage of Lithuanian government leaders, under Premier Justas Paleckis, through the checkpost. Premier Paleckis was also head of the Presidium of the Supreme Council in Soviet Lithuania.

After Vilnius had been liberated from the Germans, the "Forward" company was still fighting it out with the Germans in the woods near Kazlų Rūda. The partisans were in control of the railway tracks running between Kovna and Marijampolė. A number of enemy convoys on their way to the front were ambushed and wiped out. Shimon Bloch and his group fired at the Germans during the latter's crossing at Seredžius. The partisans destroyed enemy vehicles, blew up a tank, and captured, among others, four Gestapo men dressed as civilians who had run away from Vilnius. Shaya Vershovsky, Boris Stern, and Pesach Sadovsky laid mines on the roads and set traps at vital crossings. One German tank fell into one of these traps.

In the course of the military operations of the Forward company, a number of its men died a hero's death, among them Chaim David Ratner and Yaakov Levi, fearless fighters and loyal sons of the Communist Party. Chaim David Ratner belonged to the underground organization in Kovna right from the time it was founded; he stood out as a great fighter and was eventually appointed group commander. Up to the time he was sent out on a mission to White Russia, Ratner served as commander of the Forward company.

Yaakov Levi, who had begun his partisan life as an ordinary fighter, became well known for his exploits in the underground and was eventually to become one of the best liaison men in the ghetto organization. Levi was one of the closest comrades-in-arms of Haim Yellin.

The Forward company came in contact with Soviet paratroopers in the woods of Kazlų Rūda. Together they reconnoitered the area of the German batteries and passed on information to the high command of the Soviet army. The partisans noted with satisfaction that the Soviet planes had accurately bombed the spots they had marked out for them. In the meantime the battles around Vilnius were coming to a close. The Forward company advanced to the city of its origin, Kaunas. The commander told Endlin: "You have been the guide for the company so far, so keep on showing us the way ahead too! Lead the company on to Kaunas!"

Endlin led one hundred and thirty-seven fighters. Upon reading the Neman River, the partisans saw the towers and chimneys of Kaunas. The liberated Soviet town lay there before them, ready to receive its fighting sons.

TALKING OF FRIENDS

Yu. Zbanatsky,
Hero of the Soviet Union,
Former Commander of a Partisan Unit

When the war broke out I was a high-school teacher in the picturesque town of Oster, on the Desna river. In the fall of 1941 I organized a partisan company behind enemy lines. The company operated in the vicinity of Kiev and gradually grew into a might partisan unit. I would like to relate something about the lives and exploits of a few fighters who belonged to the company named after Nikolai Shchors.

* * * * *

The first snow had fallen. It had been falling throughout the night, and we, three partisans, had been on our way to the village for a meeting with some comrades when dawn broke on a white world all around us. The comrades were Red Army soldiers who had escaped from a German hospital for prisoners of war located in Oster. We met at dawn. All three of us were at the point of exhaustion and nearly frozen. We had to stay at the village till night so as not to draw the attention of the Germans.

We were put up in a hut at the edge of the village. Our new friends were good-natured and after some time they were to be made commanders of partisan companies.

One of them drew my attention in particular.

"Are you a Jew?" I asked him.

"Yes."

"Were you at the hospital?"

"Yes."

I began to take an interest in the destiny of this fellow. Boris Pinhasovich had lived in Kiev. He was a Red Army soldier right from the first day of the war. His platoon was driven back to Kiev by the advancing Germans. In the region of Oster the platoon was engaged in defending the people who were leaving Kiev. In these battles Boris was seriously wounded. Bleeding, he lay in a foxhole for some days, and one night was found by the children of the village. An elderly woman took him to her house and nursed him. The village peasants treated many wounded fighters in this manner. The Germans issued an order to bring all the wounded to Oster, where they had set up a hospital for them. Had the Germans known that Boris was a Jew, his life would have been in danger. But the doctors did not reveal his nationality. When Boris had enough strength to walk a little, the chief physician sent him out with the hospital cows, and he took advantage of this opportunity to escape.

On the first day of our meeting with the new partisans, they had to fight for their lives. The German police who had gone after the escaped soldiers from the hospital surrounded our hut. The situation was quite serious. We had many people, but not enough arms to go around, a total of three rifles, three pistols, and few hand grenades. Nevertheless we opened fire. In the fighting, the commander of the police company was wounded and his men dispersed. We took the arms they threw down and returned safely to the company. In this encounter, Boris Pinhasovich proved to be a cool and fearless soldier. At cone I had the feeling that this man would make a good partisan and bring us great benefit, both as a daring fighter and as a politically well-oriented man.

He had a phenomenal memory. After he had spent some time with the company, he began to lecture us on politics. In the course of these lectures he would cite accurate quotations from Marx, Engels, Lenin, and Stalin, all from memory. His words captured our attention, since in those days we had no Soviet books or newspapers. In battle, Pinhasovich acquitted himself as an outstanding fighter. On one occasion the Germans formed a brigade out of Soviet prisoners of war and sent them to fight the partisans.

The brigade soldiers approached the station of Yanov, where they learned about the hideouts of the partisans. Whereupon, they at once attacked and killed the Germans, took their arms, horses, and military equipment, and started coming in our direction. They reached the village of Sorokoshichi on the Dnieper. A group of our fighters, including Boris Pinhasovich, were in the area. On hearing of the new arrivals, and without knowing anything about them, twenty of our partisans went out beyond the village. The strangers sent a delegation to us. We met at the outskirts of the forest. Company Commissar Molodchenko received the delegates and held a lengthy conversation with them but, of course, was not in a position to believe every word they said. He suggested that they lay down their arms. This proposal raised some doubts and anxiety in the minds of the delegates. Sensing this, Boris Pinhasovich and his friend Georgy Khachaturian volunteered to go out to the new arrivals in order to see for themselves who they were. Despite the possibility of a provocative action, Boris and Georgy ventured out in the company of a delegate to the newcomers.

* * * * *

Pinhasovich was soon to be appointed director of political affairs in a company of the new battalion, which included the new arrivals. The battalion was stationed in a forest sector in the vicinity of Karpilovka.

This was a small town. Suddenly a large German unit approached the place in a pincer movement. The new partisans were flustered at first, but the veteran partisans led the new ones in the attack on the Germans. Boris led the attack. The German major was in command of the enemy company was killed. Confusion prevailed among the enemy forces. The battlefield remained in our hands.

I well remember another battle with the German garrison of the small town of Rybotin-Korop in the vicinity of Chernigov, where the Germans had built construction wood factories. The partisans occupied the place and destroyed all the plants that the Germans had built. The enemy garrison, numbering some five hundred soldiers, was taken. About two hundred bodies were left by the Germans on the battlefield. Boris and his company were outstanding in this battle. Some time later Boris Pinhasovich was appointed commissar of a new company named after Voroshilov. Boris succeeded in setting up a fighting collective which was to justify its existence in many a future large-scale military operation.

Meantime the Soviet army had reached the Desna
and Dnieper rivers. The Soviet information bureau had
announced the liberation of Konotop and Bakhmach. So
we decided to come to the aid of our fighting forces in their
crossing of the rivers. After this decision had been taken, the
Voroshilov company dug in at the southern outskirts of the
village Maksim on the Desna, between Chernigov and Ostir.
A German brigade, reinforced with heavy and medium tanks,
moved along the shore of the Desna. The Voroshilov company was the first to engage the enemy in battle.

Greatly outnumbered, the company fighters were ordered
to stand their ground at any price until the arrival of the
other companies. Boris carried the battle into the center of
the village and took charge of defending the positions that
eventually repulsed all enemy charges. His understudy and
close friend Michael Lukyanovich Derevyanko, an excellent
machine-gunner, inflicted heavy casualties on the enemy. The
battlefield was littered with German bodies. Changing their
tactics the surviving Hitlerites lay on the ground and sent
their tanks forward. Derevyanko inserted a disk with incendiary bullets into this machine gun and engaged the enemy
tanks single-handed. At the same time partisan antitank
guns manned by the Shchors company and led by Gabriel
Adamyenko started firing. This company had been moved to
the battlefield to relieve the Voroshilov fighters. Boris arrived
on the spot and urged his men to attack the enemy. The
Germans retreated in their vehicles up to the small town of
Sokolivka. A great number of Germans drowned in the Desna
in their attempt to cross over to the other side.

A few days later the partisans established contact with
the advancing Soviet soldiers. In the villages of Maksim,
Gnilusha, Smolin, and Morovsk, the Soviet armies were carried in the vehicles which had been prepared for them by the
partisans and the inhabitants of these villages.

The Voroshilov company hurried to the Dnieper River.
Around the villages of upper and lower Sivki and Zhary, as
well as Navozy, we made preparations for ferrying Soviet
army units from one shore to the other. Boris Pinhasovich
worked with remarkable zeal in ferrying the armies to the
left-had shore. In the meantime, the right-hand shore was

strongly defended against any sudden attack on the part of the Germans. The Soviet army safety crossed the Dnieper. The partisans took part in the battles with the Germans on the right-hand shore.

Boris Pinhasovich was highly respected by the company fighters, who loved him and had faith in him. He was on particularly friendly terms with Georgi Khachatourian and machine-gunner Michael Derevyanko. The machine-gunner that Boris held so close to his heart was killed near the village of Maksim. His death brought great sadness to Boris. Michael was buried by his comrades in the village of his birth.

Comrade Pinhasovich was awarded three state medals, including the "Red Flag" decoration.

Rasya

Once one of our partisan companies was on its way back to base after a military operation. A snowstorm was raging in the area. The front sled stopped; something had gone wrong with the harness. In the midst of that snowstorm, at dusk, a human figure was seen moving about, disappearing every now and then in the eerie light that preceded darkness. It was a woman. She was running. In her attempt to catch up with us, she often stumbled and fell in the gathering snow, only to rise and try again.

"Help, help, good people!"

"Where're you running in such weather?"

The woman replied:

"I've been saved from certain death. I'm a Jewess. I've been looking for you, partisans."

The partisans took her onto the sled, covered her with clothes, and fed her. All that time the woman was shivering with clod and excitement. After she had regained her calm, she told the partisans about her prolonged search for their camp.

Rasya was her name. Her Ukrainian husband, Tretyak, was in the Soviet army. When the Germans started their extermination of the Jews, she fled to the countryside, leaving her young daughter with her mother-in-law. The *kolkhoz* people hid Rasya, but she began to miss her daughter terribly, and so decided to go back to her. On reaching her home she was told by her sobbing mother-in-law that the Germans had taken her daughter away in her nightgown, loaded her on to a cart and brought her to the cemetery (and, presumably, shot her).

Rasya was badly shaken. At first she thought of committing suicide; later on she decided to avenge the murder of her daughter. And now her wish had come true. She had never held a rifle in her hands, but when it was suggested that she join the partisans to do the housework, she firmly refused.

"Give me a rifle," she said. "Teach me how to use it. I want to kill at least one fascist. To take my revenge on the enemy; this is the wish of my life."

Rasya was admitted into a fighting company. She became a partisan. With alertness and loyalty she did her duty. She spent long hours lying in ambush along the roads, far from base. With great patience she bore the hardships involved in partisan life.

In the numerous battles against the Germans in which she took part, Rasya proved to be a daring and fearless fighter.

Paulina

I remember with good feeling the friendly old woman with the rose, sunken cheeks, the tight mouth, and the dark eyes. She was neither sharpshooter nor scout, nor even a woman who fired a rifle in anger. She was merely the cook of a partisan company. The fighters simply called her "Mother," Aunt Paulina, or Paulina Abramovna.

I remember how Paulina received the weary fighters when the came in for lunch. She greeted them with love and motherly concern. Every now and then the restless cook would ask them if they were enjoying the food, if they wanted some more, or if they needed salt. When she saw that one of the fighters was not eating well or was preoccupied, Paulina Abramovna would go up to him like a worried mother, inquiring and carrying on a conversation to take his mind off his problems, even to the point of having him eat his food, ask for more, and leave the table in high spirits.

The events in the life of Paulina Abramovna ran similar to those that marked the life of Rasya Tretyak. She too lost relatives. Soviet people helped her find the partisans. There, Paulina Abramovna found a new family, respect, and love.

THEY WERE MANY

Nikolai Konishchuk,
Commander of the Kruk Partisan Department

Until the war began I was the chairman of the Village Council in the district of Kamen-Kashirsky, in the region of Volyn (western Ukraine). On July 28, 1941, I began to form a group of partisans. Quickly I made connections with the Jews from the village of Griva and the small town of Manevichi. Our partisans succeeded in rescuing about two hundred Jews from the village and the nearby settlements — men and women who, afterwards, joined my unit. I will tell about several of them who especially excelled.

The scout Avraham Blanstein came upon a group of twenty Germans. He fought against them until he fell with a severe wound. The Germans grabbed him and brought him, dripping blood, to the Gestapo headquarters in KamenKashirsky. Here, they tortured him cruelly: they stripped his flesh and broke his ribs. The Germans demanded that he point out the location of our camp, "The Jewish Unit," as the fascists called my unit. But Avraham bore his suffering with supreme bravery and did not reveal anything to the Germans. He died a true partisan, a loyal and devoted son of his Soviet homeland. Avraham's brother, Hershel Blanstein, also fell in battle against the Germans.

Among other partisans there was Asher Flash from Manevichi who was a guard at the partisan camp, as was Sender Lande, who was also a guard at the nearby civilian camp that was protected by the partisans. Susel Shepa, also of Manevichi, went out on numerous missions and blew up train tracks and bridges.

Pinick Berman, who fought under the command of Anton Brinsky ("Dyadya Petya") in other groups as well as mine, won may medals for his heroic deeds. The nephew of Asher Flash, Moshe Flash, was a brave fighter and also went out on many missions during his time in the partisans.[42]

Volodya Zweibel was an excellent partisan saboteur. He died a hero's death. So did Disak, a Jew from the Rovno region. His murder cost the Germans dearly: in his last stand he wiped out six of the fascists.

Abba Klorman, along with his group, blew up eight trains, killing two hundred Germans who were heading toward the front. Aside from this he destroyed twelve tanks and new fewer cars. He was an alert scout and an excellent commander of his unit.

Joseph, the brother of Avraham and Hershel Blanstein who were both killed, blew up eleven German trains and destroyed eight cars and several tanks.

Yitzchak Kuperberg, along with his unit, blew up seven trains carrying military equipment and wiped out approximately eighty Germans.

Berl Lorber (called "Malinka") was the commander of a unit composed solely of Jewish partisans. This unit destroyed twenty-four German trains, eighteen engines, forty coaches, four large bridges, and three hundred Germans. Lorber and his fighters also ruined twenty-eight kilometers of telegraph and telephone lines.

Miriam Blanstein, a daring scout, took part in the partisan struggle from 1942 onwards. She helped carry out many acts of sabotage, blowing up German trains which were heading toward the front.

Yitzchak Zafran was born in 1928. This young partisan joined equally with all the rest in the attacks upon German garrisons and trains. He carried out the most difficult and most dangerous missions assigned to him.

Shaya Zarutski was always in the most dangerous places during a battle. When an especially important mission had to be undertaken, a mission requiring extreme courage, Zarutski was one of the first to come forth and volunteer. More than once he went out to scout three hundred kilometers away to check the places where we could capture arms and military equipment.

Isaac Avruch was one of my most devoted and loyal partisans. He accepted every difficult assignment no matter what it entailed and took pat in many acts of sabotage against the German conquerors.

Vova Avruch was our mine technician. He emptied German bombs which did not explode in order to equip our unit with explosive material. He thus supplied us with a large quantity of explosives from the German booty we captured.

Israel Puchtik[43] (called "Zalonka") appeared in our unit with his own weapons. He killed several Germans with his own hands and took their rifles. He was appointed to lead one of our units and, along with his comrades-in-arms, he blew up eight German trains. Many times he went out on scouting missions, attacked German command posts, and destroyed bridges.

Hirsch Grinberg, like Vova Avruch, extracted caps from air bombs which didn't explode. In this way we obtained explosive material which was sorely needed. Greenberg invented an original method which simplified and speeded up this work. Many German bombs thus became the source of death for the Germans themselves.

Lena Blanstein also worked in our "mine factory." She prepared approximately one thousand mines, using very primitive methods. This courageous girl also went out on scouting missions armed with her weapon. She fell during an air-attack on our brigade.

Leiba Flyam was our radio broadcaster. He coordinated the communications with other partisan groups and also with central headquarters in Moscow. He also worked actively on making our mines and took part in many battle operations.

Joseph Zweibel was the leader of a division. Together with other partisans he blew up trains carrying Germans and destroyed bridges. Also, Yankel Zweibel led a unit which blew up ten German trains.

Shimon Wolper was one of the organizers of our unit. Once I assigned him a mission to go to Maniewicz to save the Jews who still remained there. Wolper returned with thirty-two men and three women. All of them became active fighters in our fighting force.

I have mentioned the names of a small number of the Jewish partisans — those who fought and headed my unit. This small list could be expanded tenfold. There were many like these "Avengers of the People." With entire families Jews escaped from the preying teeth of the enemy, penetrated into the forests, and fought a life-and-death struggle against the conquerors.[44]

IN THE TUNNELS OF ODESSA

Shmuel Persov

On October 16, 1941, Odessa came under German and Romanian occupation. Soon after that, the remainder of the Jewish population, except those who did not succeed in escaping from the town in time, was gathered in the courtyard of the local prison, ostensibly for registration purposes. In this courtyard, hundreds of people were to die each day of cold, hunger, contamination, and disease. Many of these prisoners were shot at the whim of the German sentries.

On October 26, about twenty thousand Jewish prisoners were taken out of the prison courtyard to the storehouses of the artillery corps and burned alive. But in the course of this transfer, a small group of prisoners succeeded in slipping through the gate and disappearing. Among them were Hirsch Fuhrman and his family. Having been born in Kuyalnik, Fuhrman went to this small town, to his former neighbor and boyhood friend, Vasily Ivanov. The latter had connections with the Party underground organization. After Fuhrman had recovered a little, he was asked by Ivanov to gather all those who would be willing to answer his call and to bring them to him.

Fuhrman succeeded in gathering about twenty-five persons who, like him, had escaped from the hands of the German and Romanian murderers. Not unlike the majority of the inhabitants of Kuyalnik, Vasily Ivanov was a stone-cutter, extracting clamshells from tunnels for the buildings of Odessa. Here, in Ivanov's backyard, was the opening into those tunnels and to the stone layer below. Ivanov used this entrance to hide the ghetto fugitives.

Even before Fuhrman had appeared at this place, Ivanov had hidden a few rifles and pistols in one of the underground recesses. The arms strengthened the morale of the people and encouraged them to join the ranks of the partisans. It was then decided to set up a fighting company. Fuhrman, a veteran of World War I, was chosen to command it. For his aides he chose the brothers David and Grigory Bobrovsky. Mogalevsky, a former corporal in the Czarist army, undertook to teach the would-be partisans how to use the firearms and to conduct battles. He was also appointed head of the guards. Before long Fuhrman's partisans joined the company of Badaev, which chose Yaakov Vasin for their aide. This company, too, found shelter in the tunnels of Odessa.

The new united company occupied only a small recess in the tunnels. Here they had a fireproof safe where documents were kept and, beside it, a barrel containing fuel. This barrel was guarded day and night, for, in the eternal darkness of the tunnel, even the person most familiar with its endless labyrinths was doomed if the light went out.

On the first night after the union of the two companies, the partisan group came out of the tunnels under the command of Vasin and staged an attack on German-Romanian guards who had been stationed near the tunnels.[45] The partisans were greatly outnumbered, but they took the unsuspecting guards by storm and forced them to run for their lives, But reinforcements soon arrived, and the partisans had to fall back to the tunnels. Upon reaching the opening Vasin found out that one fighter, David Krasnostein, was missing. Under a hail of enemy bullets Vasin crawled back to look for his friend. He found him wounded and brought him back to the tunnels.

David Krasnostein belonged to the Badaev company right from the early days of its formation. Besides him, there were the fighters Elik Zasovsky and Khariton Liebensohn, a member of the Odessa Komsomol, who took part in the first partisan attack on the Romanians on October 16, 1941. Danya Semberg was one of the best ground scouts of the company. On one occasion a Romanian company surrounded four of our scouts, including Semberg. The stubborn and biter fighting that ensured resulted in six dead Germans and the four partisans returned safely to the company.

* * * * *

The former ghetto fugitives now turned into capable fighters and began to take part in combat missions of the united company. The brothers Bobrovsky, the members of the Fuhrman family, and others, proved to be daring fighters. Rita Fuhrman, the vivacious and intelligent eleven-year-old girl who had in the meantime picked up some Romanian, served as a runner. On many occasions she was called upon to carry out highly dangerous missions. She fulfilled them with flying colors.

Rita usually left the tunnels early in the morning. The partisan on duty accompanied her to the exit. Here he gave her the password. Late in the night, under cover of darkness, Rita returned. One of the comrades would be waiting for her at a predetermined spot.

At first the German and Romanian invaders tried to let the people believe that all the stories about partisans hiding in the tunnels of Odessa were fictitious and that there were no partisans at all in these places. But after the enemy had come to realize that many of their soldiers and officers were falling under partisan bullets, they began to announce in the bulletins they distributed that, though there were actually partisans in the tunnels, they were nevertheless left there without any light, water, or air, and therefore, they were doomed to die.

In order to intimidate the local population, the German murderers killed forty-two people, forty men and two women, in the village of Nerubayskoe, near Odessa. They then declared that these were the partisans they had caught inside the tunnels. The dead bodies were laid in a row on the street, and their burial was forbidden. Nevertheless, the villagers succeeded in burying them in secret, and now a tombstone stands at their mass grave.

The blows the partisans directed at the enemy became more frequent. The invaders did not succeed in stopping the partisan attacks. Out of blind rage, the Germans brought a field gun to the entrance of a tunnel and fired into it point-blank. In retaliation the partisans attacked the nearby enemy barracks and wiped out almost all the solders they could find.

The Hitlerites then decided to use gas for driving the partisans out of the tunnels. When this foul intention became known to the partisans, the latter mobilized all their manpower to collect stones and sand. Within a few hours an impregnable wall was put up at the tunnel entrance, which prevented the gas from getting into the tunnels. The invaders poisoned the wells that provided water for those who were hiding underground. But this, too, had no effect on the fighting spirit of the partisans. They dug two wells in the tunnels to a depth of thirty meters. This, of course, was no easy task, as they had to blow up a continuous stone layer. But nothing could make the Soviet patriots surrender to the invaders. The tunnels were connected to the surface by vertical shafts thirty to forty meters deep, from which stone had been quarried in former days. Now these shafts served as the only source of fresh air for the partisans. The invaders sealed off the shafts, and the partisans now were in dire danger of suffocation. But they opened the shafts once again. The Hitlerites then took a most stringent measure: they now used cement and mortar to seal off the shafts. The invaders sealed off about four hundred tunnel entrances. The partisans underneath walked scores of kilometers in the labyrinths in search of new exits. The extensive search was to bring about the desired result: exits were found at a distance of many kilometers from the main base. The partisans could now resume their combat operations.

Walking about with torches in their hands in the endless labyrinths, the partisans marked the walls with predetermined signs such as circles, lines, and letters which could be understood only by those who had been brought into their secret. These abstruse signs served as road markers.

* * * * *

On one occasion Badaev's fighters discovered on the walls signs which were unknown to them. This indicated that there were other people in the tunnels. Badaev's people decided to meet them. The meeting was set for March 14, 1942, at 12 o'clock Moscow time.

But they had to take precautions. The approaches to the base were walled up, and in the walls openings had been made for rifles and machine guns, together with an "eye" for observation. This barricade was connected by telephone with the underground command at a distance of two kilometers.

The task of holding the talks with the strangers was assigned to Yaakov Vasin, deputy commander of the company, and to partisan Pavel Pustomelnikov. Behind them went a nine-man guard. The others were stationed behind them barricade. For two days and nights the men of Badaev stayed at the predetermined spot and waited for the "guests." Finally on March 16, a flame was seen approaching in the dark. Some minutes later the newcomers stopped at a certain distance from the barricade. The "parliamentarians" among Badaev's men approached the newcomers. Toward them stepped out three of the strangers.

"How many are you?" asked Vasin.

"As many as may be required," echoed the reply.

"And who are you?"

"Same as you."

"A long time in the tunnels?"

"Not less than you…"

This diplomatic dialogue would certainly have gone on in this vein had not Pavel Pustomelnikov cried out in jubilant excitement:

"Lazarev! Simon! You…?" and they began to shake hands and kiss each other. In front of Pustomelnikov stood Simon Lazarev, accompanied by Nikolai Krylevsky and Leonid Gorbel, secretaries of the underground provincial committee of the party. Lazarev was first secretary of the provincial committee and commissar of a partisan company. The commander was Nikolai Krylevsky. At that time the company numbered only seventy fighters.

After that exciting meeting Badaev's company united with the company of Lazarev.

One day the ground scouts came back with the news that the Romanians had laid mines at the tunnel exits. It was necessary to devote much time to unearthing those mines and then placing them close to the quarters of the Romanian guards. When fighting started late that night between the two sides, many Romanians were blown up by their own mines. But enemy reinforcements soon arrived, and the fighting went on till the morning. The Hitlerite forces suffered heavy casualties, but still, they had the upper hand, and we had to withdraw. A number of partisans did not succeed in reaching the tunnels but they eventually found shelter with the local peasants. On that same day the Romanians sealed off the entrance ot the tunnels at the spot where the fighting had taken place. On the following night the fighters that had remained outside cleared the entrance, and before dawn they were once again with their comrades. The Germans tried to win the partisans over with sweet promises, inviting them to come out of the tunnels without any coercion and surrender to the German and Romanian authorities. The partisans' reply to this "considerate" offer was to launch a number of new attacks. During the month of May, 1942, alone the partisans accounted for about forty-five dead and some sixty wounded enemy soldiers and officers.

The stock of food supplies in the tunnels began to run out, and in the end there was not enough food to go around. The partisans held a council of war and decided that under the prevailing conditions it was impossible to keep the fighters in the tunnels. So they decided to transfer part of Badaev's men to the partisans operating in the nearby forests of Savran, and the remainder were to be sent into Odessa for underground work. Only the provincial committee stayed in the tunnels.

In the fall a group of "illegal workers" was captured by the German butchers. On September 9, 1942, twenty-three people were brought before a fascist court, of whom sixteen were sentenced to death. Among those executed were partisans David Krasnostein, Ivan Petrenko, Danya Semberg, Ilya Zasovsky, Yekaterina Vasina, Shaya Feldman, Khariton Liebensohn, Frieda Khayt, and Zhenya Fuhrman.

For nine hundred and seven days the Germans and the Romanians were in control of Odessa. During all this time, Simon Lazarev and all the members of the provincial committee stayed in the underground tunnels and eventually survived the war.

With their exploits the partisans of the Odessa tunnels wrote a brilliant page in the annals of the Soviet patriots' struggle behind enemy lines.

SONYA GUTINA

S. Berkin

On a dark night in September, 1943, a runner came into the camp of the Shemyakin company, then operating around the town of Vetka in White Russia. He was taken to the hut of the commander. Immediately the group commanders were called to a council of war.

Before long the entire company was alerted. The men were read the order for the impending combat mission, to attack the Hitlerites and the police forces that were about to enter a village for the purpose of killing the Jews and the families of the partisans hiding there.

The partisans laid an ambush and massacred the Germans. One of the survivors of that village, a young woman, Sonya Gutina, expressed her desire to join the partisans. She was followed by others. Thus, Sonya, a former student at the Teacher's Institute, was to become a full-fledged partisan. She was soon to send a request to the commander to go out on a combat mission against the enemy.

Her baptism of fire was hard and grave. A partisan group that included Sonya Gutina went out on a ground patrol mission, but the Germans discovered and surrounded them. Six partisans engaged in battle an enemy force made up of thirty Germans. The exchange of fire lasted more than three hours. Sonya shot some enemy men, and when the Germans intensified their attack, she threw a number of grenades at them. They retreated, leaving behind thirteen killed and wounded. Out of the six partisans three were killed and one wounded.

A few days later Sonya once again went out on a combat mission, this time to blow up a troop train heading for the front. The partisans mined the rails and stated to conceal their tracks. That was a hard task, as the Germans had intentionally leveled the embankment to such an extent that any trace would stand out on it. Every ten minutes German guards patrolled to check the embankment. Sonya said to the group commander: "Now you go along. I'll do the job myself." A short while later they heard the approaching train. An explosion followed, and a huge flame lighted the entire area around it. The partisans retreated fast. Over three hundred German soldiers and officers were killed or wounded.

The Germans did not let it stand at that. They brought two SS divisions into the region where the partisans operated.

For three long months Shemyakin's company fought it out with the Germans in the forest despite the shortage in equipment, medicines, and food supplies. The siege was intensified. Shemyakin decied to make a breakthrough with his men. The attack started at dawn. Sonya went at the head of the attacking group. Our surprise charge carried us beyond the first German line of defense quite easily, but when the Germans opened up with their machine guns. These, however, could not stem the momentum of our attack, and the partisans scored direct hits at them. The company was safely out of enemy encirclement.

Then the fatal day came: Sonya went out with two fighters on a patrol mission. They were ambushed, and the two comrades were killed on the spot. Sonya hid behind a thick pine tree and kept firing while lying down until she ran out of ammunition. She started throwing hand grenades. After she had been hit by an enemy bullet, she lost consciousness.

Sonya was now in the hands of the Germans. They interrogated her for a long time, but she kept her mouth shut. They started to torture her. The fascist oppressors beat her up and smashed her hands. She groaned, but she did not answer their questions. For more than three days and nights they kept interrogating and torturing her. Finally they took her out to be executed.

On the way to the place where she was to be shot, the soldiers stopped at one of the houses to drink some water. With tears in her eyes, the housewife brought Sonya a glass of water.

"Don't cry, mother," said Sonya. "You shouldn't cry. They may kill me, but the people will triumph."

These were Sonya Gutina's last words.

THE DAVIDOVICH FAMILY

Mira Eisenstadt

When the Germans reached the outskirts of Novozybkov, recounts partisan Yaacov D., the Jewish population started to leave the place in a hurry. Only cart-owner Ziama Davidovich did not budge. His wife Hanna was bedridden with paralysis. "Go, Ziama," the invalid begged her husband. "Go and take the children, Dvora and Misha. Save their lives, Ziama!"

But Ziama answered: "I don't want to hear of it. Stop it, won't you?"

All the neighbors had left. The streets were empty. Sadness and boredom reigned all around them. One neighbor, a non-Jewish woman, Maria Stephanovna, offered to take the ailing Hanna into her home and to hide her there.

One night, when the German guns were booming all around the town, Ziama hitched his horse to the cart, took his daughter Dvora and son Misha on the cart, and left Novozybkov.

Whereto? Of course, to the nearby forest. There, Ziama Davidovich met a partisan company and joined its ranks. In the partisan tents he found a nook for himself and his two children and thus stayed with them under the command of P. Partisan Ziama of Novozybkov soon exchanged his whip for an automatic rifle and learned to use it quite well. But he was better at working with the axe. In pitched battles he would whirl his axe left and right, accompanying the movement with curses in Yiddish, without anyone being able to stop him.

His daughter Dvora, a young girl of sixteen, was called "Nurse" by the partisans. On quiet days she would cook and do the washing for the entire partisan company. But on battle days she served as a medical nurse. Crawling on the ground she would reach the area where the fiercest fighting was taking place and drag back the wounded partisans whom she would later nurse back to health during the long nights.

Thirteen-year-old Misha also had something to do. He was a skillful, clever, resourceful boy who was soon to become the liaison runner of the partisan company. With remarkable daring the young boy went on dangerous missions and always brought back the necessary information concerning the enemy front positions. The partisans liked him for his quickness and readiness to run at all times to the flaming front. Between battles he was something of a musical entertainer. He would compose songs on the Germans, on Hitler and Goebbels, composing and singing, accompanying himself on the har-monica, and all the partisans, even those who were seriously wounded, would laugh and have a good time. It was enough for one of them to say "Quiet! Misha is performing for us!" and the partisans would at once get into a festive mood.

The company had for a long time known that the town of Novozybkov had fallen into the hands of the Germans, but it had not heard as yet of their atrocities. The artisans heard of that later through their connections with the nearby inhabitants who would come and tell them of the Germans' heinous crimes, which were talked about far and wide.

One day a man from Novozybkov came to the partisans with the news that the Germans had srangled Ziama Davidovich's wife in her bed at the house of her neighbor Maria Stepanovna. Even Maria they didn't spare. They hanged her, tying a small board to her chest with the words: "I have hidden a Jewish woman in my house; I am an enemy of Germany."

It is impossible to describe how the news was received by Ziama, Dvora, and Misha. They sat dazed, uttering not a single word. Suddenly Dvora asked:

"Where did they bury my mother? Together with the rest of them?"

"I think so," answered the man from Novozybkov. How could he tell the girl that they had burned the body of her mother, together with the others, and had thrown the bones onto a garbage heap?! It was enough to tell that to Ziama Davidovich.

In the evening, sitting around the fire near the tent, the Davidovich family — the father and the two children — vowed before commander P.:

"As long as I am alive, and my hand can bear arms and blood flows in my veins, I will not cease from taking revenge on the fascists for our mother, for all the murdered Jews, and for all the people who were killed in our country. I hereby vow that only the blood of the German hangmen shall bring comfort to my heart."

The Davidovich family went on the warpath. Dvora left her work as a nurse and, together with her father and brother, held a rifle in her hand. She vowed never to return to her former work until she had killed ten Germans with her own hands. Terrible and ominous was Ziama Davidovich, who worked his axe to the utmost. Since that time he had stopped counting the number of Germans who fell under his axe.

Hard times came upon the partisans. Thousands of Magyar (Hungarian) fascists encircled the company. The partisans engaged the enemy in fierce bottles, until they finally succeeded in slipping through a narrow trail, while the Magyars kept firing at them from all directions. "The Death Trail" was the name that the surviving partisans attached to this path.

Dvora and Ziama Davidovich came out unscathed from these battles, but Misha, that clever and charming boy with the flaming dark eyes, died in horrible agony. A shell hit him in the belly, wounding him seriously. There was no chance to save his life, as no surgeon was to be found. The horses of the partisans galloped ahead in a storm in order to break away from that horrible front. "Shoot me," pleaded the seriously wounded boy. He repeated the words to every comrade who shot past him. Out of their great love for the boy, they could not raise a hand to finish him off. Nevertheless, someone quietly put a pistol beside the dying boy. The thirteen-year-old boy killed himself with his own hand, leaving behind his bereaved father and sister.

No smile came to their faces, and only occasionally could they utter a word. Even between themselves they used more sign language than words.

Partisans are known for their ability to observe how one of their comrades ceases to distinguish between life and death. That is what happened to the father and the daughter after the death of thirteen-year-old Misha.

Two years later the partisan company joined the Red Army. On that same day Ziama and his daughter filed a request to be accepted as combat soldiers into the fighting company. When they were offered a chance to go on a rest leave, they answered: "We haven't settled our account with the fascists yet…"

PART FIVE
EPILOGUE

SOVIET JEWS DURING AND AFTER THE WAR OF THE FATHERLAND

L. Singer

A considerable part of the defense of the U.S.S.R. can be attributed to Soviet Jewry. It is a fact that 123,822 Jewish soldiers and officers were awarded military medals and titles, and 105 Jews received the very highest distinction, "Hero of the Soviet Union," for their bravery and heroism against the German invaders. Judging by the number of soldiers who were given awards, the Jews ranked fourth or fifth place, after the Russians, Ukrainians, and Byelorussians.

Among the heroes of the Jewish people who distinguished themselves in battle were: David Dragunsky, a tailor's son who was twice awarded the title "Hero of the Soviet Union." From the rank of *polkovnik* (colonel) in the early days of the war, he became *general-polkovnik* toward the end. Of the same rank was Yaakov Kreiser, also a "Hero of the Soviet Union" and a member of the Jewish Anti-Fascist Committee; others include tank-commander David Katz, the daring pilot Michael Plotkin, submarine crew-members Israel Fisanovich and Caesar Konikov, artillery commander Israel Baskin, the young Red Army soldier Hayim Diskin, the pilot Paulina Gellman, Alexander Matrosov, and the cart-industry worker in Birobidjan, Joseph Bumagin.[46]

Along with other Soviet patriots, Jews fought within the ranks of the partisans in great number. A great many of them provided examples of fearlessness and self-sacrifice. With deep respect and appreciation, twice "Hero of the Soviet Union" Major-General Sidor Kovpak, commander of the largest partisan detachment in the western U.S.S.R., writes in his memoirs about his highly esteemed tank commander, Abraham Friedman. With great love, twice "Hero of the Soviet Union" Major-General Alexei Fedorov, commander of the Partisan Union, writes about Shmuel Gottesban, who, with his own hands, killed twelve German soldiers and officers on the Kovel (Ukrainian) front. *Podpolkovnik* (lieu-tenant-colonel) A.B. Brinsky, another "Hero of the Soviet Union" (who fought under the nom de guerre "Dyadya Petya," Uncle Petya), recounts the heroic deeds of the Jew Sedelnikov, a commander of a partisan company. Sedelnikov was a household name among the local population and drew so many men to the company that within a short time it became a full-fledged brigade.

Furthermore, the commander of the Boevoi partisan detachment which operated in the district of Leningrad, was a Jew called Novakovsky, the son of a small-town manual worker. The company of Nikolai Konishchuk (called "Kruk"), which fought in the western Ukraine in the area of Rovno, consisted almost entirely of Jews from the surrounding countryside. Many were admitted along with their families.

In special independent units, as well as in mixed groups, Soviet Jews fought in the forests of the Ukraine, White Russia, Lithuania, Latvia, and Moldavia. Among them were outstanding fighters, commanders, political commissars, ground scouts, liaison men, nurses, doctors, and communication experts. Long is the list of Jews who distinguished themselves in the battles for the war of the Soviet fatherland. Their intrepid exploits can provide material for many books.

Our Place

Ilya Ehrenburg

The Jewish people were not wiped out in Egypt, nor were they destroyed by the Romans, nor even by the zealots of the Spanish Inquisition. To destroy the Jewish people is also not within the power of Hitler, although human history has never known of such a brazen attempt to kill an entire people.

Hitler brought to Poland and Byelorussia Jews from Paris, Amsterdam, and Prague: professors, diamond-cutters, musicians, old men, and babies. The Nazis are killing them there every Sabbath. These Jews are being suffocated with gas after the modern achievements of German chemistry have been tested on them. They are killing them in full ceremony, against the background of an orchestra playing the tune of *Kol Nidre*.

The Germans have razed to the ground those places they had temporarily occupied in Soviet Russia. Not a single Jew was left of those who did not escape in time or did not join the partisans — all the rest were wiped out. They were annihilated in Kiev, Minsk, Gomel, and Kharkov, in the Crimea peninsula, and in the Baltic States. For two years the German army fought against unarmed women, old men, and helpless children. Now, they have announced with arrogance that they have killed all the Jews, down to the very last one.

But the Jewish nation lives! Hitler the madman does not realize that it is impossible to destroy our people! True, there are fewer Jews today than there were before the war, but the value of each has risen in comparison with what it was before. It was not with laments alone that the Jews reacted to the despicable slaughter, but with arms. Every Jew vowed to himself, to his conscience, and to the ghosts of his murdered brethren: "We may die, but we shall annihilate those abominable murderers!"

The Jews are not over-zealous in fighting for its own sake. They do not enjoy displaying their "muscle" in order to show off. Despite the onrush of the forces of evil, they do not cease to believe in the power of human understanding. They are the People of the Book who illuminate the darkness with their brilliant contributions. When the terrible days came these men of thought and toil, who had been tortured in the ghettos for hundreds of years, proved to be daring, unflinching soldiers.

Jews do not weep! Jews do not boast! Jews struggle and fight! I will not try to recount the number of heroes. Blood is not to be weighed on the balance wheel; heroic deeds are not material for statistics. I would like only to say that the Jews who fill the ranks of the Red Army and Red Navy are fulfilling a mission, a mission which every civilian, every patriotic fighter, must fulfill — they are killing the Nazi beasts!

Jews are fighting in tanks as if tanks were their natural home; in the midst of winter, Jews glide on skis; Jews are sailing in submarines; and Jews, who are known far and wide as experts in watchmaking, have now proved to be experts in warmaking. When I happen to speak with a German prisoner of war, I am eager to tell him: "Look, I am a Jew." I take great pleasure in seeing his dreadful look, the look of fear in the distorted face of the vaunted "Superman," now trembling in his boots...

Stalingrad, the river Don, North Africa — all this is only a beginning. The war will return to the place where it began. We, the Jews, understand only too well our rights: to sit in judgment of those who murdered the old and the young.

On the cobblestones of Victory Boulevard in Berlin, we shall engrave the names of Kiev, Vitebsk, Kerch — the names of towns where the "brave" Germans buried alive thousands of children. These names shall cry out: "Let sleep never come to these hangmen and to their offspring. May they never know peace of mind!"

BOOK TWO

DEDICATED TO MY TWO YOUNG SISTERS

I never knew them.
They must have been a terrible threat
to the Nazi machine.

Chaya Udel Puchtik
(Age 4, killed September 23, 1942)

Pesel Puchtik
(Age 2, killed September 23, 1942)

PREFACE

A nation, especially its young people, needs heroes. No child wants to believe that his parents were cowards or that they went — to use a tiresome and by now vulgar phrase — like sheep to slaughter. Soon after the Eichmann trial, a decade and a half ago, we were deluged with books and articles on the Holocaust. Some blamed the victims. Some defended them. Today this debate is futile in the extreme. The question becomes: what are the motives of the writer, not the martyr?

For the Jews, World War II was massive in its scale of death and power, towering and complex in its elemental balance of good and evil, majestic and stirring in its multi-leveled simplicity. Everything can be found within its confines… if only one wants to look or it. If one wants to find cowards, one can find cowards; if one wants to find collaborators, one can find collaborators. If one wants to find weakness and degradation, one can find that also. However, if one wishes to find heroism, one can find that in great measure. If one wants to find rebellion, one can find rebellion; and if one wants to find strength and nobility, one can find that as well.

I want to look for the defiant and for the heroic. I want to look for resistance… of all stripes: passive, active, spiritual, moral, military, and political. I have looked and I have found it. The documents in this section serve as testimony. I have a deep personal interest in them: my parents were both active in the underground movement in Volyn, western Ukraine, in the Kruk detachment mentioned in these articles, from 1942 to 1944.

When one talks to Jewish partisans, few of them strut and boast of their achievements. Most will tell you their fascinating tales and then remain silent. They will fill you with chronicles of revenge and then they will weep. They will tell you to pass on their tales to future generations.

The first half of the book originally appeared in Moscow in 1948. Its Russian title was *Partizanskaia Druzhba* (Partisan Brotherhood) and was compiled by the Jewish Anti-Fascist

Committee and the Moscow-based Der Emes Publishing
House. This committee, composed of the cream of Jewish
writers, poets, and intellectuals, had as its primary duty the
task of gaining world-wide support for the Soviet Union
during the days when Russia stood almost alone against the
Nazi onslaught. After the war, their task widened to include
the gathering of material on the vital role Jews played during
the war.

Under the megalomaniacal paranoia of Stalin, anti-Semitism was whipped up in the post-war years, 1945-1953. Jewish
war veterans, some crippled, were mocked in the streets:
"Where did you get those fancy medals, kike? In a crap game?
Did you buy them on the black market?" It was during such a
time that was to see the purging of Jewish leaders and intellectuals, the closing of Jewish schools and cultural centers,
and infamous "Doctors' Plot" and threat of mass pogroms,
that the original editors of *Partizanskaya Druzhba* worked
feverishly to publish these documents. They succeeded just in
time because soon after their 1948 publication, many of them
were killed or jailed. The Der Emes Government Publishing
House was closed, and the book was suppressed.

Miraculously, a few copies were preserved, and fifteen years
later, Binyamin West was allowed to see a microfilm copy that
the Lenin Library had in its archives. From this copy, West
made his translation; and from this same copy, Magal made its
translation into English.

So, one must thank the Lenin Library, and one must also
thank the Russian people, the Russian army, and the Russian
partisan leaders for their devotion and their valor in saving
the lives of many Jews in Eastern Europe. I know that this
statement will not rest easy with some readers. The Soviet
Union today is seen as a villain, but I speak of the Russian
people and the Russian soldiers, not the Russian leadership.
One must always make that distinction.

These writers are not scholars. They speak as they do for
two reason: first, it is war and this is fighting propaganda, and
two, they wish to prove to Jew and non-Jew alike that Jews
were neither "cowards" nor "traitors" but loyal citizens and
devoted patriots.

These selections are among fort-four testimonies gathered by the Israeli journalist, Binyamin West, in his book *Heym Hayu Rabim (They Were Many: Jewish Partisans in the Soviet Union During World War II)*, Tel Aviv: Labor Archives Press, Department of Soviet Jewry Affairs, 1968. Miriam Migal and the Magal Translation Institute, Ltd., of Tel Aviv did the translation.

* * * * *

The second half of this book was collected more recently, in the past five years or less, and deals specifically with my own family and friends and with a particular region of Volyn, Ukraine, the partisans and the family camp in the area of Gorodok, Manevichi, Lishnevka, Kamen-Kashirsky, Rafalovka, Griva, and Povorsk. This section was edited and compiled together with my cousin Yehuda Merin of Ramat Gan, Israel. It dovetails nicely with Part I.

What is intriguing about this second section is that it is reminiscent of the movie *Rashomon*. One views the German-Ukrainian "action" (the mass killings of Jews) from various perspectives and then the response — hiding, going into the forests, and slowly organizing into fighting forces. It was on September 22 and 23, 1942, that an action took place outside Manevichi that led to the killing of twenty-five members of my immediate family, including my little sisters, Chaya Udel, four years old, and Pesel, two years old. My mother hid and was saved; she later met my father in the forests and they worked in the "family camp and the fighting units of Kruk, Max, and others. The Jewish "family camp" is a unique and fascinating aspect of Holocaust history, and I am happy to present various perspectives on it in Part II. I, by the way, was born later on December 2, 1944, after the area was liberated by the Russians.

* * * * *

This book should be seen as a continuation of Book I; the two books complement each other. At a time when some misguided scholars are saying that the Holocaust never happened or happened in ways different than we are led to believe, it is refreshing to hear these voices. The people have actually participated. They are, in a sense, living legends. In another generation, their voices will be stilled, never to be heard from again. The recent world gathering of Holocaust survivors poignantly brought home the message that time is running out. It is up to us, and especially those of us who are the sons and daughters of survivors to carry on, to continue the legend, because soon, very soon, the only thing left will be these stories, these living legend, for us to hold onto.

* * * * *

These two books owe a great deal to many people. I have mentioned some of these people in the preface to Book I. I would now like to add the names of those who not only helped "build" this book but also those who contributed financial assistance to make these two volumes possible. If I have forgotten someone, please forgive me. The list is so long.

To Yehuda Merin, for compiling many of the interviews in Part II.

To my editor and proofreader, Abby Solomon, who labors over nearly everything I write and always finds a way for it to read better, my deepest thanks.

To the translators of this volume: the Magal Translation Institute, Ltd., of Israel for Part I; and to Ann Abrams, Esther Ritches, and Esther Kluger, for translating the Hebrew and some Yiddish into English. Ann Abrams is, however, responsible for most of Part II. I am truly grateful to her.

For the maps, my thanks to Marta Braiterman for a difficult job well done. She not only drew the maps, but translated them from Hebrew as well.

To all my friends at Communication Graphics in Brookline, Massachusetts, for their efforts and skill for all the work they have done for me. They are a patient group of people, and I am grateful to make their names public: Jerrine Larsen, Dudley Glover, Norma Larsen, Patricia Gould, Susan Gould, and Janice Thalin.

To all the people who consented to interviews and to their families.

To VAAP, the Russian Copyright Office, for permission to publish Part I of this Book and all of Book I.

To Jack Elbirt and the Federation of Volynian Jews of the USA, for permission to publish sections of Part II.

To the following supporters:

Celia and Avrum Stzundel

Jacob Sredni and Family

Dr. Samuel Porter and family (in memory of Boris Porter and Chana Seltzer Levenson)

Hinda Porter

Leonard Lieberman and Family

Benjamin Lande and Family

Jacob Karsh and Family

Sophie and Lou Kaplan and Family

The Schoenfeld Family

Young Judea of New England

Barney Porter

Sarah Singer

Marie Kargman

Dov (Berl) Lorber

Shulamit Goldman

The Snow Family (Mina Snow)

Abba Klurman

Charlie (Sasha) Zarutski

Morris and Sophie Kramer

Harry Steinbaum (in memory of Michel and Bella, and their two children, Pessie and Avrom; Mordechai Steinbaum from the town of Vishgorod, Ukraine; with loving remembrance from their son and brother, Jacob)

Rubin Kirzner (Slivka) and Family

Avraham and Berl Finkel

And finally, to those who purchased copies of this book for themselves and their friends, my thanks. Lastly, to my wife Miriam, my son Gabriel, my mother Faye Porter, my brother and sister Shlomo and Bella Porter, my in-laws Joseph, Reli and Lea Almuly, and all my friends. Thanks. And, thank you, dear reader.

Jack Nusan Porter
Brookline, Massachusetts
March 2, 1981

THE TEN COMMANDMENTS
OF THE HOLOCAUST

Jack Nusan Porter

1: - .Thou shalt remember everything and understand nothing.

2: - .Thou shalt record everything — memoirs, diaries, documents, and poetry.

3: - Thou shalt teach it diligently to thy children, for, as Rabbi Emil Fackenheim has said: the survival of Israel is now a sacred duty.

4: - Thou shalt teach it to the Gentiles and to their children because thou art often at their mercy.

5: - Thou shalt not heap abuse upon the children of the ungodly. Though the wicked are to be punished, their children must be forgiven.

6: - Thou shalt not judge the victims.

7: - Thou shalt not place one set of idols (the heroic) above another (the cowardly). They are to be judged equally before the Lord. As Reb Eli Wiesel of Sighetu has said: there is a time to remain silent, so therefore know when to be silent.

8: - Thou shalt not lose faith. Amidst all thy doubt and confusion, I, the Lord your G-d, am here among thee.

9: - Thou shalt not dwell heavily upon the sadness of the past. Rejoice, for thou hast survived while thine enemies have perished.

10: - Thou shalt not turn away from thy brothers and sisters; instead, reach out and build a paradise on earth so that life and love can prevail.

PART ONE
JEWISH PARTISANS
IN THE SOVIET UNION:

LATVIA, UKRAINE,
AND BYELORUSSIA
1941-1944

THE KOVPAK MEN

P.Ye. Braiko, Hero of the Soviet Union,
Major, Former Commander of a Partisan Battalion

Sidor Kovpak was one of the chief organizers and central comanders of the partisan movement in World War II. He was twice awarded the supreme title: Hero of the Soviet Union.

He was born to a poor peasant family in the village of Kotelva (Poltava region) in 1882. From 1941-1944 he fought as a partisan together with Commissar S. Rudnev, behind the lines of the enemy occupational forces — first on the steppes of Bryansk (Byelorussia) and later on the right shore of the Dneiper, at Polesia; he crossed the Desna, the Sozh and the Pripyat rivers at the head of his fighters. In the summer of 1943, his battalion was sent on a mission to the Carpathian Mountains and destroyed on the way a large supply of oil intended for the fascist armies on the Ukrainian front.

In 1944 Kovpak was wounded and had to return to the Soviet Union. His duties were taken up by Lieutenant Colonel Pavel Vershigora in the unit called "The First Kovpak Ukrainian Partisan Division."[1]

In the fall of 1942, Kovpak's famous battalion was given the task of crossing over to the right bank of the Ukraine and Byelorussia. This occurred after the battalion had carried out a great many operations in the woods of Bryansk. In those days Sidor Artyomovich Kovpak's name had become a household word all over the scorched lands held by the Germans. Ukrainians, Byelorussians, Jews, and people from other nationalities flocked to him. Every one of us started his career way down in the ranks; only later, when an individual's aptitudes, know-how, and military ability had been established, was he promoted to a responsible position.

Grigory Lubensky

When Grigory Lubensky arrived at our company, we had heard nothing about him — he was just like any other man. He was tall, well built, with dark hair and eyes; he wore glasses because he was short-sighted, though he did not use them all the time. Apparently his eyes hurt him. He was well educated and had graduated from the faculty of history or literature. We asked him to join our transport platoon, but he refused. So we had him join one of our platoons as a fighter.

Winter came. Our battalion had reached the region of Ivankov and was moving to the southwest, carrying out some small-scale missions and engaging the enemy forces in frequent skirmishes; in the course of these we learned something about partisan warfare. Our military experience, however, was complemented and enhanced through the day-to-day analysis and discussion of our operations. During one such analysis session — I was then chief of staff of the Krolevets company — we found out that the commander of one of the subsidiary units had panicked at a critical moment. It was left for Lubensky to save the unit from defeat. There are situations where the absnce of a preordained commander brings to the fore a "natural" one. The men who took part in that fight realized that Grigory Lubensky, who had justifiably taken over the command, was a man of great willpower and ingenuity. The men who fought alongside him had faith in him. I thought to myself, "Well, we may as well entrust him with the lives of our fighters."

I had many occasions to see Grisha Lubensky at decisive moments. He had the knack of quickly grasping the gist of a situation. Before long I was to make him company commander and, some time later, platoon commander.

We came back from Byelorussia, crossed the Polesia, and the regions of Zhitomir and Kiev. We went out from Knyaz — a lake near Kiev. In the village of Blidcha in the Ivankov region we blew up a number of bridges on the river Irpen. The Germans threw into the battle against us a battalion of young soldiers, who were soon to be called "good-for-nothings" by Kovpak. This battalion, which numbered six hundred soldiers, began its attack in the woods from the direction to Ivankov along the right shore of the river Teterev. They sent ahead two armored cars that suddenly appeared close to our positions in the sector of the third battalion and opened fire. In the wake of the armored cars came the German attack.

Our fourth battalion held defensive positions on the right flank of our third. When the Germans began pressing hard upon the third, we decided to strike back at the rear of the attackers by outflanking them from the right, rolling them back to the river in order to wipe them out. The task was entrusted to the second and third companies. The latter, containing Lubensky's fighters, kept pressing them without letup. The Germans stared jumping onto the ice. Soon the thin ice gave way and they went under.

We were drawn to Lubensky not only because of his courage, but also because of his great education. We had no newspapers or books, so we had a great appreciation for any interesting story. Loubienisky was an excellent storyteller. He presented every complex thing in a simple, popular manner. His listeners took a liking to what he said.

But the Germans did not calm down. They concentrated great forces and started chasing us. We had to cross the Teterev and after a number of crossings camped at the village of Nova Krasnitsa close to the railway tracks running between Chernigov and Ovruch (north-central Ukraine).

Everything went well till the latter half of the next day. On that day our patrols told us that the Germans had concentrated great numbers of infantry in the neighboring village. We could quickly have pulled out of that place and moved away, but that very night we expected some planes from the Soviet Union, which were to bring us ammunition and take back our wounded for treatment. So we had to stay.

The German attack came soon after we received news of their intention to mount it. We had to join battle before we could dig in. The fighting was conducted under difficult conditions which were inconvenient for the deployment of our forces. Aside from their overwhelming manpower, the Germans also used mine throwers. The severest blow was aimed at the third company, which included, as I have already mentioned, Lubensky's unit. This unit bore the brunt of the main German attack. Before long, the company was beaten, leaving only Lubensky's unit with its twenty fighters to face an attack by an entire German battalion.

At that time I was at the other end of the village, engaged in a fight against the Germans. When a runner came up to us and told us that the third company had been beaten, I sent a reserve company to the aid of Lubensky. This improved things a little for him, but the situation still was very critical. The Germans kept up their attack without giving Loubienisky's men a chance to dig in. The battle had been going on for three hours, well into twilight — it had been a clear, sunny day in March. The men had been bled white, but they kept on fighting. Lubensky kept his ground with astonishing determination. We looked forward to the arrival of the Russian planes. And then, from far away, came the persistent din of plane engines. The fight, conducted under such difficult conditions, had been justified in the end. At that spirit-raising moment, new came that Lubensky was wounded. I at once sent a carriage to bring him to the plane, which had landed meanwhile, in order to evacuate him to a hospital on Soviet soil.

A mine splinter had entered Lubensky's chest. Dusya Usachenko, one of our bravest nurses, had bandaged his wound while the fight was going on, but the wound was a serious one, resulting in quick death.

We had lost one of our best comrades, a distinguished fighter, and a brave commander.

Misha Rubinov

I want to tell you also of another partisan, Misha Rubinov, who, like Lubensky, was in my consideration the incarnation of nobility, attained at times by the great sons of a nation.

Michael Elhanan (Misha) Rubinov was extremely young. He was born in 1921 in the small town of Timkovichi, in the Minsk region. He had finished only ten grades when he joined the army. When the war broke out he was a sergeant. His company was surrounded by the Germans, but he succeeded in escaping and, like many others, found his way to us. He at once asked to join our reconnaissance company.

I was in charge of picking out the men best fitted for patrol duty. I asked a great deal of them. This energetic little guy seemed to be the right man for the job. His quick, precise movements showed outstanding drive and nervous energy. It would seem that Misha Rubinov liked the job of being a soldier and did not flinch from danger.

I worked diligently and consistently with my reconnaissance men to prepare them for their job I took a liking to Misha Rubinov right from the start. When I went about training him, I realized that I had made the right choice. The other scouts also liked him. But unfortunately they soon began to suspect him of being overbearing and supercilious. Some partisans had gone on a patrol mission and had not fulfilled the task entrusted to them. When debriefed, they did not tell the truth. Rubinov, who had been with them on that mission, came up to me and told me what had really happened. This was not to the liking of his comrades, but I decided to use this incident as a lesson to all those going out on patrol duty.

I told my men, with considerable emphasis, that reconnaissance in war was a sacred job, especially in guerrilla warfare, and that loyalty and falsehood could not dwell together. The men understood what I was driving at. They also stopped being angry at Misha when hey came to realize that there was no justification for suspecting a daring and intelligent fighter like him of wanting to lord it over them — that such thoughts were not fitting for a man who had no fear of danger and was ready to risk his life on highly dangerous missions.

I asked my men not to shy away from the enemy, even when outnumbered. Misha Rubinov proved once and again that he knew what military daring meant. I do not remember any attempt on his part to shirk a mission — on the contrary he would always volunteer for the most serious and daring missions.

I decided to take him on as my liaison man: I was in need of a scout with initiative and courage. Misha Rubinov went through the entire partisan war with me till the end. He did not know fatigue. Sometimes they would wake him at night and tell him, "Misha, we've got to move!" And he would answer without hesitation, "I'm ready!" Readiness for battle ran in his blood. He never asked for more men to go than were needed for any action. He would get the details of the mission, mount a horse, and move out. Armed with an automatic rifle, a pistol, and many cartridges, he would get to places which seemed to be accessible only to a mouse.

During the battle that raged in the village of Nova Krasnitsa, when Lubensky's company was almost entirely cut off, it was necessary — before sending reinforcements — to find out everything about the situation. That called for a man of great daring. I looked around to ask who would do it. "I am going," said Rubinov — and disappeared. He reached the other end of the village at a fast clip, and, under a hail of machine gun bullets and mortar shells, crawled to where Lubensky was conducting the fight, received the necessary information, and came back. He was a very fast runner.

The more I got to know Misha Rubinov, the more I came to rely upon his accuracy and ingenuity. When I sent him on a mission to the battalion staff, I would not tell him exactly what to say. I would merely say, "Tell them what is necessary," and Robinov would give them only the most essential information.

In May 1943 we had to cross the railway tracks between Gomel and Kalinkovichi (Byelorussia). The Germans had thrown great forces against us. The battle went on till morning, but we could not get to the railroad tracks. We were nearly surrounded by the enemy: part of the company was on the other side of the tracks, entirely cut off from the main forces. The companies of the fourth battalion engaged the Germans in battle. When it became evident to the battalion staff that it was impossible for us to cross the railway tracks, they decided to pull back to minimize losses. Rubinov came back running from the field staff, holding in his hand the order to withdraw. It is easy to say "withdraw" when there is no contact with two companies, cut off by the enemy.

"I'll go to them and tell them to pull back. Please let me!"

"Where do you want to go? They are cut off."

"That's nothing. I'll get over to them and get them going."

Rubinov had to report back to the battalion staff, but he started to talk me into sending him to the cut-off companies. He did his best to persuade me that anyone could get to the field staff, which was not the case with the encircled forces. I agreed to what he said. Ruhad a feeling that binov ran towards the Germans.

In that terrible hail of rifle and mortar fire, I realized that I had given Misha a difficult and dangerous task. I kept listening to the firing and looking forward to his return. I was afraid he wouldn't make it, but I also had a feeling that Rubinov could not fail — it wasn't like him; he wasn't cut out for *that*. In war, personal success is tied up with daring and self-confidence. Forty desperate minutes passed, fraught with great concern for the man out there among the bullets and the shells. Then all of a sudden he appeared, followed by the second and third companies. It turned out that he had found a gap in the German encirclement and could not only *get* to the two surrounded companies but also get them *out*, without having to fire a shot at the enemy.

The German high command now began to trumpet the liquidation of the "Kovpak Gang" and the killing of their chief commanders, Kovpak and Rudnev. But before the Führer got down to the business of awarding medals to his generals and officers for their brilliant exploits, Kovpak's men were again behind the enemy lines, in southern Ukraine. Our appearance at a place where the Germans had never dreamed of seeing us at all was heralded by our blowing up the bridge over the railway track connecting Tarnopol with Volochisk, on a road which till then had been beyond the range of partisan activities and had served as a main artery of supplies for the enemy forces deployed in the direction of Orel-Kursk.

The German command did all it could to prevent the infiltration of partisans into the Carpathian region. The enemy turned against us eight mountain companies, including two "Norwegian" ones, an SS Galitchina division, and several SS battalions. That was the beginning of a series of cruel battles, in which we were invariably outnumbered. On the second of August, our battalion, surrounded by fascist armies, was engaged in battles in the region of Mount Sinichka. The Germans kept bombing with a dogged determination to break through to our field command and the vehicles in its possession.

In these battles Misha Rubinov proved once again to be a matchless warrior. During one German bombing of the peak, he came to me running under a hail of artillery and mortar fire.

"What's new at the HQ?" I asked him.

"The commissar has issued an order to hold on to the peak at any price. Runners have been sent in all directions. Tonight we have got to break out of the encirclement."

A few minutes later the runner of the second company came to me and, in a shaking voice, announced:

"Comrade *Kapitan*, the second and third companies have evacuated the heights and are now on the retreat. The company commander is in need of reinforcements. The Germans have received new forces. They are crawling up towards us like so many insects."

I could send no reinforcements, so I decided to go to the company and stop the retreat.

"Comrade *Kapitan*, permit me to join you," said Rubinov. "You have got to run back to the field command!"

"No, at such a time they don't need me up there," he insisted. "Will you permit me?" Without waiting for an answer, he followed me.

When I arrived at the battle scene, I found the second and third companies pulling back down the slopes of the heights in their retreat. The first and fourth companies, however, were still holding their ground. The summit of the peak had not been taken, neither by us nor by the Germans. Poising for a new attack, the Germans kept pouring artillery and mortar fire on the heights.

There was no time for hesitation. I ordered the commander of the second company to take the summit at once, then called upon the commanders of the other companies to do the same thing.

When the German shelling stopped, we launched a counterattack against the enemy battalions. A hall of machine-gun fire was directed at the summit. The absence of return fire had encouraged the Germans. When we were only about fifty meters from the summit, the enemy mounted an attack on our forces. The second company opened fire. The Germans halted their advance and hugged the ground. Upon a signal from me, companies two and four attacked the enemy from the flanks. The Germans were confused and began to pull back. Shouting "hurray," companies two and three joined the attack.

Misha Rubinov, who was with me in the field, ran with his feline dexterity to the second company at the beginning of the attack and joined the fighters. Within one minute, he was at the head of the company, conducting a running battle with the retreating Germans. They opened up with mortar fire, but they could not stop our advance. After a few minutes, the Germans were thrown back from the heights, leaving on the slopes behind them heaps of dead bodies. I halted the advance of our fighters, as we could not afford to follow the routed enemy for long. The main battle was over. Only sporadic mortar fire came from the enemy's direction.

Rubinov sped back to me, paying no attention to the enemy mines. Suddenly a shell hit the ground close to Misha. He fell to the ground, then rose to his feet, went a few steps forward, then fell down again. When I reached him, the nurse had already bandaged his wound. Beside her stood and number of fighters. Rubinov was breathing hard, and a gurgling noise came from his throat. Blood ran in thin streaks down his chin from the nose and mouth.

"Is the wound serious?" I asked with concern. The long eyelashes of the nurse moved close together, and she whispered:

"He was hit by a splinter. It penetrated a lung."

I looked at Misha's face, into his blurred eyes. They expressed anxiety. I at once understood what he was worrying about — this wise young man was afraid we would leave him in the mountains. I said:

"Misha, don't be afraid. Everything will be all right. Until the wedding, the wound will heal — it will heal. We will again dance together."

I tried to soothe him. I looked at his face, which had paled, and into his wet eyes, which had lost their vaunted brilliance, and I thought to myself, "How this man has changed!" I gave orders to carry him to the sanitary platoon where the doctor could look at his wound. There might be need for an urgent operation.

During the night we discovered a gap in the enemy lines, and our battalion could finally untangle itself from the encirclement. We carried out the wounded on stretchers we had hurriedly made out of tent materials.

Toward morning, there was an improvement in Misha's condition. He was able to speak and even to smile. After a few hours he announced, "Why should four men exert themselves for me, when I can go on foot with the help of one or two comrades?"

"Are you crazy?" rebuked the nurse. "Lie down and keep still!" But Rubinov would not listen to her. He sat up, leaning on one of the fighters, stood for a moment, and started to walk.

Though severely wounded, Misha regained his strength after a few days, and his wound healed on the march. When I think of this "miracle," which also happened to many other wounded men, I cannot help wondering at the immense vitality of the Soviet fighters.

Toward the end of our careers as partisan fighters, Misha was promoted to liaison officer. He was constantly active, full of life, and he had been since I first met him. He had taken part in all the operations of the Kovpak battalion. His glorious exploits against the German occupation forces eventually earned for Michael Rubinov some medals — "The Red Star," the "Order of Glory, Third Class," and the decoration of "To the Partisan — Homeland War, Second Class."

MY COMRADES IN ARMS

M.G. Salai, Former Commander of a Partisan Unit

The partisan group under my command, which toward the end of 1942 was dropped by parachute over the Elinsky woods in the vicinity of Chernigov (Ukraine) close to the front, numbered only thirty men. Its appearance behind the enemy lines brought us new volunteers every day. By March 1943, my company numbered about 300 men. Two months later I had become the commander of a large unit.

The unit comprised four companies, had considerable military provisions and equipment, a huge quantity of arms, and even field guns. Like that of other partisans, our equipment had come from the Germans. We roamed over 2,500 kilometers behind enemy lines; we were active in the districts of Chernigov, Kharkov, Zhitomir (Kiev region), Poltava (Kharkov region) and Polesia. We blew up seventy-six German army transports as well as arms and military equipment; we destroyed thirty-eight tanks, 173 vehicles, and thirty-one field guns. As a result of our military operations, seventeen garrisons and thirty-one police stations were put out of commission. In the battles with our unit the Germans lost about 9,000 soldiers, nearly one full division.

Right from the outset, our unit consisted of men from various nationalities. Its thirteen organizers included Russians, Ukrainians, Byelorussians, and Jews.

Ilya Shklovsky

Ilya was one of the most resourceful fighters of our unit. Though not young, he was extremely daring. That is why he was soon to be appointed commissar of the Shchors company.

Once, when we were in the woods of Tupichiv in the district of Chernigov, Shklovsky came up to me and said: "May I have your permission, Michael Gordeyevich, to attack the village of Glebovo? According to the information brought by my patrol units, a number of prisoners of war have been sent

out there, and we have got to release them. In the course of
this operation I'll take from the German horses, cows, and
provisions. Much of what the Germans have commandeered
may be found in the village of Glebovo."

I looked with wonder at Shklovsky. In Gleibovo there was
a ranch full of armed Nazis. In order to reach it, one had to
cross the Chernigov-Gomel road. The Germans guarded
this traffic artery with reinforced units so that it would not be
vulnerable to partisan attacks.

"Are you mad, Ilya?" I asked.

Without batting an eyelash, Shklovsky started lecturing
me on his plan for the attack on Glebovo. He had thought
the plan through; before he asked for my permission, he had
worked out all the details of the attack with his chief of staff,
Alexeyev.

"With a company of sixty men," said Shklovsky, "I'll cross
the road under cover of darkness, when the German, may he
cough out his soul, is fast asleep. As to the way back, we will
fly on wings of eagles, on the horse we shall take from the
Germans, who will have no time to know what is going on
around them."

As the plan of the attack has been worked out by Shklovsky
down to its smallest details, there was nothing left for me but
to agree to its implementation.

"Well, go on," I said. As a matter of fact, I was afraid for his
life.

That evening, a group of fighters set out under Shklovsky's
command. The night passed. At dawn my worries mounted.
Shklovsky had promised to send me word about the situation
at the end of the operation. Nothing had been heard from
him so far. Out of sheer anxiety I sent out a group of patrols,
but they returned to the camp without having found anything
new. In the end, toward evening, news came from Shklovsky:
"Everything is okay!" He himself arrived soon afterwards
together with his company. His fighters were mounted on
horses. They brought along with them about one hundred
horses. They also brought a sizable supply of provisions, followed by a herd of cattle.

Shklovsky was shivering with cold. I poured him a glass
of vodka. He calmed down and told me in detail all about

the raid. In order to reach the road, they had to go through the village of Veliky Listven, about one kilometer and a half from the regional center of Tupichiv where a garrison of 250 German soldiers was stationed. In the village of Veliky Listven itself, there was a police company of thirty to forty men. Shklovsky, at the head of his men, routed the police unit, cut off the telephone and telegraph lines leading to Tupichiv, and destroyed a storehouse full of provisions. The company then hurried back across the road and broke into Glebovo at midnight, quietly dispatching the armed guards.

Once in Glebovo, Shklovsky stormed the house which seved as the living quarters of the chief of the police and the German majordomo, a man by the name of Kiznyak. The chief of the police was killed on the spot, and the talk with the handcuffed majordomo was cool and easy. He pointed out the hosues occupied by the German soldiers. The first thing we did was to release the prisoners of war, and they immediately joined us in our operation.

At dawn, Shklovsky's company left Glebovo with wagons full of provisions, and a herd of cattle. "The whole thing went as I told you it would," Ilya concluded. "We came back galloping on the German horses. As you see, we rode fast."

I kept silent. Together with Shklovsky we began looking into the booty. There were many horse-drawn wagons, like a big Ukrainian marketplace. In one of the wagons sat two women and their children.

"What's this?" I asked. "You know all too well that we do not include in the company women and their kids!"

"I couldn't do otherwise," answered Shklovsky. "I had to bring them along."

It turned out that they could not leave the women by themselves. One of them was the wife of a commander in the Red Army; the other, a chemical engineer, Maria Gordon. Both had children. Al the time we stayed at Glebovo, we didn't know that Maria Gordon was a Jewess. It might be interesting to see how Shklovsky came to know about it. Before the company left the village, Shklovsky ordered that Kiznyak, the local German majordomo, be executed. All of a sudden, both women came running to him. One of them said that she was a Jewess and that Kiznyak had known about her and had hidden her. She also said that he had treated the Russian prisoners well.

Shklovsky checked up on what Maria Gordon told him and found it to be true. Whereupon he not only waived his order to put Kiznyak to death, but also ordered him to destroy all German possessions in the neighboring village, to release the prisoners of war, and to bring them along to the Shchors partisan company. Kiznyak carried out the order.

Once Shklovsky heard that a ship was to leave Kiev and sail out on the Dnieper to Chernobyl. As usual, he came to me with a carefully worked out plan to attack the ship.

"You see, this is their first ship," he said. "All this time the Germans have been hesitating about sailing on the Dnieper. Now they've finally decided to do it. I'd like to make it clear to them that this time the risk involved is not worth it to those who call the cards. Grant me permission to do it. Come on, be a friend. I'll be back before you can bat an eyelash…"

Once again this business of not having time to bat an eye. I decided to joke a little myself and asked, "Are you returning on that ship?" "What for?" he replied seriously. "I'll destroy it."

Shklovsky did not succeed in destroying the ship, for it was armored. As usual, Ilya had taken with him a rather small company, about sixty partisans. Under cover of darkness the company came close to the Dnieper and dug in quietly. In the morning the ship appeared. When it approached the line where Shklovsky's men had dug in, he gave the order, "Fire!" The partisans opened up with machine guns and antitank guns. The Germans had been eating breakfast peacefully, without any thought of an imminent attack. It is impossible to describe the shock they experienced when Shklovsky let them have it with all the weaponry at his disposal. In this operation scores of Germans were killed, and the ship turned around and scuttled back to the shore it had sailed from. Much to our regret, it succeeded in escaping the blows of our shells.

On the right-hand shore of the Dnieper, a group of Germans stood guard over a storehouse. We succeeded in wiping out the guards and blowing up the storehouse. Courage and self-sacrifice were the characteristics of Shklovsky's exploits as company commander. These qualities

stood out particularly in times of crisis. For instance, in
the battles against the Germans on the river Teterev, in the
district of Kiev, Shklovsky was cut off from his battalion and
surrounded by Germans. He was outnumbered, yet he broke
through the German encirclement. He struck at the enemy
effectively by ambushing them in places they never thought
of. In the districts of Chernigov and Zhitomir, he wiped out
several armed enemy columns in this manner. He was particularly successful in destroying hundreds of German vehicles
on the roads leading to Chernobyl and Dolginichi-Ovruch.

I have recounted some of the exploits of the company
whose commissar was Ilya Shklovsky. He carried out many
operations. In all of them, he was a daring, courageous man.

Isaac Sosnovsky

In Korop, in the district of Chernigov, lived a Jewish cobbler who was the father of a large family. In the next village,
his fifteen-year-old son tended the sheep and goats of the
kolkhoz. Every morning at the first light, the boy took the
livestock out to pasture, despite the unease that was being felt
on account of the Germans' approach to Korop. Once, on his
way back home, he met an old woman who advised him to
run away, never to come back to Korop. "The Germans have
wiped out your entire family, and they will kill you, too." The
boy turned to the woods. At home, only death was waiting for
him. He wanted to live. But one could live only by struggling
against the murderers, shoulder to shoulder with the "men
of the forest," the partisans, of whom the boy had heard. For
a long time he wandered about in the woods, looking for
those men, seeking shelter in the accommodating trees by
day. He had no fear of animals — he had learned to fear only
the two-legged creatures who swaggered around in dark blue
overcoats.

He spent many nights searching for "the men of the forest,"
only to be found in the end by one of our patrols. The men
called him Isaac Sosnovsky. He was emaciated and exhausted.
They thought it only fitting to let him work on the transports, but he would not hear of it.

"I didn't come to you to save my skin," Sosnovsky asserted firmly. "I want to strike at the Germans."

They had no alternative but to put a rifle in his hands. In April 1943 his company was camping in the woods of Elinsky. It was getting ready to cross the river Snob while fighting it out with the Germans. The latter were making all the necessary preparations to encircle us and, for this purpose, had brought considerable forces into the region. In order to check the German advance along the axis of the Turya-Tichonovichi line, we stationed at Ivankivka a company made up of thirty fighters. Among them was the boy Isaac Sosnovsky.

On April 12 my brother Ivan Gordeyevich Kruglenko-Salai set out for the village of Ivankivka to see how the company was deployed. At the same time, about 500 Germans mounted an attack on the village. Under the command of Kruglenko-Salai, our fighters, highly outnumbered, engaged the enemy in a desperate battle. The Germans opened up with deadly fire from machine guns and mine throwers. The entire village was set afire. That was the first battle the boy had ever seen, but he acquitted himself as a hero. Not far from that spot there was a bridge, and Sosnovsky, together with the fighter Selekhov, was entrusted with the task of blowing it up. At the risk of their lives, they succeeded in carrying out their difficult mission, and by so doing they checked the advance of the German invaders.

The fight went on. Isaac Sosnovsky was now put in charge of defending the command post. An enemy mine hit the post, killing two partisans and seriously wounding Kruglenko-Salai. Sosnovsky evacuated the chief of staff from the battlefield: on his way back he kept up the fight until the partisan group he belonged to succeeded in rolling back the enemy in this sector of the battlefield too. In their attack on Ivankivka, eighty Germans were killed...some sixty wounded. Eentu-ally they had to withdraw. While committing atrocities, the mounted another attack on our men with new reinforcements with a view to encircling our company and forcing it back to the river Snov. Under these conditions we had to fall back.

We went through marshlands, floundering and often sinking into the treacherous water. The Germans guessed that we were heading for the river, so they brought tanks and machine guns to the shore, and on seeing us, opened up with all they had. In order to divert their attention, we set up a dummy bridge near the farm of Shevchenko and under cover of darkness began to cross the river near the village of Kirillovka. We had gone eight kilometers into the water when it began to get light. I ordered the main forces to move away toward the forest and, together with a small group of fighters we went back to retrieve the field gun which had sunk into the water. It took us a long time. Our repeated efforts eventually succeeded in saving the gun. By then I did not know in what direction our main forces had gone and where they had camped. German soldiers and policemen roamed that vast forest. All of a sudden I saw a horseman galloping at a terrific speed. It was Isaac Sosnovsky. Having been anxious about my prolonged absence, Commissar Negreyev had sent him to search for us. We followed Sosnovsky and before long were with the company again. When the Germans learned of our having broken out of their grip, they began chasing us, but by then, it was too late.

After a long night trek, we finally reached the woods of Zlynka in the region of Bryansk.

Following that episode, Isaac was made a scout, and what a scout at that! In the forest of Kusii we were again surrounded by the Germans. For two long days we warded off their attacks, but we could not break through the ring they threw around us. It was necessary to feel our way about; we sent Isaac Sosnovsky, together with comrades Koshel and Chernysh, to the village of Kusii, where we believe the major forces of the enemy were stained. The daring scouts went right into the lion's mouth, obtained the necessary information, and came back safely to us.

At the village of Aleksandrovichi, four of our scouts encountered a company of German soldiers who had two armored cars with them. Our scouts flattened themselves to the ground and opened fire. The exchange of fire went on four over an hour. Two scouts, Sosnovsky and Vysotsky, crawled up to the armored cars and tossed hand grenades into them. One car blew up, and Vysotsky was seriously injured. Isaac managed to help him; for 400 meters, he crawled doggedly with this wounded comrade on his shoulders until they were both safe from enemy fire.

Once at the village of Golubichi, when three partisans — Sosnovsky, Koshel, and Dunayev — were on their way back from a reconnaissance mission, a company of Magyars (Hungarian) Nazis came into the village at the same time. Our scouts wore police uniforms, and the Magyars, without suspecting them to be partisans, started calling out to them: Pan, Pan, come here." Sosnovsky and his comrades went up to them and, at point-blank range, opened up with their automatic weapons. Six Magyars were killed on the spot, and the rest beat a hasty retreat.

Whenever I looked at Isaac Sosnovsky or listened to his reports, I always saw before my mind's eye that tortured boy who had come to us in order to strike at the Germans. To tell the truth, I never thought at the time that Isaac would become a real partisan and an outstanding scout. In our unit, he grew up and gathered strength. Three medals were awarded to Sosnovsky — the man, not the emaciated boy: a brave young man, a robust, gifted scout, a fearless avenger.

Major

It started out as a joke, when someone called Isaac Meitin of the quartermaster service "Major." Then it went on all the time — "Major," "Major." People even began to forget his surname. As for the partisans who kept joining our unit, they did not know that he had any other name.

"Major" was my assistant in the equipment and materials department. He was fifty-two when he joined the partisans. As a matter of fact, he had first been a partisan in the civil war in the Ukraine, but when he heard during the "war of the fatherland" that I was in charge of a partisan sabotage group, he came to me with the request that I "make him a saboteur." "How would that be possible, when you're doing responsible work now?" I chided. "Well, you're right But as a partisan, I'd like to be an ordinary man," he said.

I thought about the matter for some time and then decided to put him in charge of supplies. At first the major was offended, but he realized that a partisan in charge of supplies and services is not just a caterer.

In the Elinsky woods we were short of provisions. The neighboring villagers were considered partisan sympathizers, so we did not want to take any provisions from them. Major suggested that for this purpose we should go to the distant villages. "We've got to live of the police and the traitors," he said, "and there are many of them in the region of Korop. May I have your permission, Michael Gordeyevich, to go to these places?"

As a matter of fact, I hesitated to give the major permission to go on. It involved great danger. But later on he succeeded in presenting strong arguments for his case, and I agreed. Of course he gave me his word to be careful. Thus he eventually set for in the company of twenty partisans, all armed with automatic weapons. Now you can imagine the extent of my anxiety when on the following day one of our patrols brought me the news that in the vicinity of Korop a partisan group had been wiped out. Thus, it would seem, we had lost the major. I waited, angry at myself for having agreed to let him go on such a dangerous mission. I sent scouts out to search for the missing men all over the surrounding area. One hour followed the other. One day followed another. On the morning of the fifth day, I could not believe at first what I saw. There, in front on me, was the major, sitting in a covered wagon drawn by three horses and behind him a long line of horses, cows, pigs, and even prisoners. The major reported: "I've brought eight wagons full of provisions, plus horses, three cows, and two pigs. We're a little late in coming back, for we did some baking on the way, since we were short of bread and it takes time to build a new bakery. That's why we did what we did."

With great relief and joy, I poured him a large glass of vodka, but the major refused to drink. "How can an old man drink vodka?!"

In the evening the major gave us a detailed account of the raid: At the village of Tikhonovichi, his provisions company chanced upon two peasants of that are, who knew well the roads leading to Korop. During the night they reached the village, disarmed the policemen and killed them, took provisions, horses, cows, pigs, and even baked some bread.

The partisans left the village in the morning by another road. At a distance they saw a company of Magyar (Hungarian) S.S. units. The major had enough time to hide the wagons. He left three partisans to guard them and he himself, together with the rest of the partisans, lay in ambush.

When the Magyars came within effective firing range, the major's company opened fire. Four enemy horsemen flew up from their horses, and the others ran away.

Another encounter with the police took place not far from the village of Tikhonovichi. Some of the policemen were killed and the others escaped. In a third clash, in the village of Antipovka, the major suddenly came upon a German garrison. He could not withdraw, and it was impossible to wait. So the men decided to fight their way through the village. That took aboaut an hour and a half. The German garrison was partly defeated, and the major took twelve soldiers prisoner. Incidentally, they were our first prisoners.

In the partisan unit itself, the major was on excellent terms with Karmazin. His friendship started on a "productive basis." Karmazin was our sausage man, and the major wanted to feed the men properly. Often they would both go out to fetch food in the wagon hitched to the three horses. For this purpose they sometimes went to the Nezhin woods region. Those were hard times, as we had just broken out of an enemy encirclement and did not have anything with which to feed the men. The little supply of food at our disposal we had to throw away in that operation. When the major and Karmazin entered the village, the Germans started firing at them from an armored train. What to do? The partisans were hungry, and the major could not reconcile himself to that fact. Paying no attention to the shells bursting around them, the two friends began to gather provisions. They were inside the house of a farmer when they heard someone cry out: "Run for your lives, the Germans are in the vegetable patch!"

The two came out of the house, jumped onto their provisions-laden wagon, and beat a hasty retreat to their base, firing back at the Germans.

This was our "Major," the man of the supply service.

Naumov

A resident of Koriukovka, former surveyor Naumov was in command of our sabotage group. His large family — his wife, two sons, two sisters, father, and grandmother — had been shot by the Germans. Actually, he had been among those taken out to be put to death but fortunately the enemy bullets had missed him — they "spared" him. Naumov was pushed to the ground by the falling bodies of those shot beside him. He fell and for several hours lay under the corpses of his close relatives. Some time later he succeeded in getting out of his blood-curdling "hiding" place. He looked for the partisans for a long time, and eventually reached us.

The sabotage group also included Levin, Moroz, and Marusya, nicknamed "Pevuchaya" on account of her lilting voice. Our saboteurs set forth at once in the direction of the railway tracks connecting Bakhmach with Kiev, with the intention of blowing up an enemy transport. They were not lucky this time. During the night they laid mines on the tracks, only to have those mines removed by the Germans the next day. This laying of mines by our men and their removal by the Germans afterwards was repeated a number of times.

What were we to do now? The saboteurs held a "council of war." There were several options. Naumov proposed going back to camp. Marusya was of the same opinion. But Levin and Moroz were firmly opposed: to return to camp without having achieved anything — that was a sign of weakness. Naumov held to his opinion: "We didn't succeed this time, but we'll make it later. We cannot stay forever in this damned place."

"Not forever, only until we wipe out a German transport," Levin kept on repeating. "We'll be the laughing stock of the whole camp. They'll say, 'There go "good-for-nothing" saboteurs.'"

This argument convinced Naumov. Once more the partisans laid mines, now on two railway tracks, and pulled back to hide on the far side of a hill overlooking the spot. They crouched there waiting, shivering with excitement. Then, like music at a boisterous party, the sound of chugging, so much cherished and awaited, came to their ears. It grew louder and louder The men held their breath. Suddenly came the expected, earsplitting explosion. At the same time, another train was approaching from the opposite direction. This one hit the other set of mines.

In one operation, two transports were wiped out.

It is easy to understand the great joy felt by the sabotage group upon returning to the camp.

Alexander Kamensky

As a boy, he had already taken part in the civil war.[2] In the course of my frequent meetings with Kamensky, who was to become one of the important figures in the country's economy, I had the impression that he had forgotten about his own clashes in the past with the "Whites" and the "Greens" in the Ukraine. However, in the early days of the great war of the fatherland, who should drop in on me but my old friend, a man with gray hair. With his first words he tried to convince me that both of us had to join the partisan fight behind enemy lines.

"And what about your factory?" I asked Kamensky. "After all, you are its manager!"

"Down at the plant, they can manage without me," replied Alexander. "You see, Michael Gordeyevich, who but us who took part in the civil war, should be first among the partisans?"

I remember quite well how Alexander Kamensky started on his way as a partisan. At the village of Brecha, there was a Magyar garrison at the time. According to the information we had, the garrison numbered about one hundred men. It stood in our way to the other shore of the river Snov. Consequently, we had to strike at it.

One night, Alexander Kamensky went out to the village of Brecha accompanied by thirty fighters. He had decided to storm his way into the village fro the direction of the river, taking advantage of the hard ice. But as it was the end of March, the ice had thawed close to the shores. Dunayev fetched a board, put one end of it on the shore and the other on the edge of the ice. After a few paces on the board, the ice went under and Kamensky and his men sank in icy water. But they managed to outflank the village, and wet and shivering with cold, got on the shore once again. The Magyars were asleep in the schoolhouse. The partisans surrounded the place and opened fire. Having been taken by surprise, the Magyars escaped, many in their pants. Eighteen Magyars were killed and twelve taken prisoner. The partisans burned down the enemy command and took a great quantity of arms. As time went on, Kamensky's company became bigger and bigger, having been joined by some twenty peasants. He himself was a modest, righteous man, of a quiet nature, but daring and courageous. In the vicinity of Zlynka he destroyed seven police stations, and only afterwards requested me to put him in command of the company.

"I won't be a bad commander!" he said in his simple and direct manner.

Actually, Kamensky was an excellent commander of his company, which was named after Stalin. One day I received an urgent order to cross over to the right-hand shore of the river Desna. The order came late in the night of September 9, 1943. Time was at a premium, so we decided to start moving early in the morning. On September 10, we began crossing the Desna. First to cross over with his company was Alexander Kamensky. His men had succeeded in setting up some defensive positions when all of a sudden, as if they had been watching us al this time, German horsemen appeared from the nearby forest. The other companies were still on the left-hand shore of the Desna, and we could do nothing to help Kamensky and his company. We sat there, clenching our fists and watching the battle.

It was a terrible sight. The German horsemen attacked Kamensky's company at a fast gallop We heard all too clearly the automatic rifles and machine guns of the Germans. From that distance we watched as Kamensky's company held its breath in the face of approaching death. But Kamensky warded it off just at the last moment, with the firm hand of a competent and experienced commander. He let the Germans come close so as to open up with lethal fire. For a few long minutes it was impossible to tell the outcome of the battle, but suddenly we realized that the German horsemen had fallen back. The crossing of the whole unit over the river Desna went on without a hitch, with not a single casualty to our forces.

Alexander Kamensky always knew how to find the right men. It was thus that he found one by the name of Artyom, who helped the unit cross the Desna. At the Dnieper, too, he hit upon a peasant by the name of Fileiko, who was to help us in our hour of need. The Dnieper, this vast body of water, held a surprise for us. It was so wide we could not see the opposite shore. Feeling dejected, I stood y the water and stared ahead. Alexander and his Fileiko came up to me. We met one another. Sensing my low spirits, Fileiko turned to me and asked, "Why are you so sad, Commander?"

"How can one manage not to be down in the mouth on seeing this wide Dnieper? Even a sparrow cannot cross safely to the opposite shore."

Obviously Fileiko was not of the same opinion. He scratched his head, narrowed his eyes cunningly, and said, "Don't worry, Commander. By the first light of day, we'll all be on the opposite shore. We have our 'major' with us, Isaac Meitin."

The major's first concern was how to move our provisions and cows. He went over to Fileiko, spoke with him excitedly about his "cargo," and began to count the horses, cows, horsemen, and wagons.

"My cows will be lost," said Meitin in a sad voice. "They won't be able to cross the Dneper." To him came Fileiko's reply, with that same narrowing of the eyes:

"Don't worry. By the first light of the morning, we shall all be over there."

Our guide made only one mistake: the date of the crossing. At dawn, enemy planes appeared and started to bomb us. They kept at it al day without letup. The major, with all his cargo, could not cross over. He had to spend the day in the forest. Fileiko stayed by him and under cover of darkness helped him cross the river with all his earthly goods.

The partisans in the company under Alexander Kamensky were on friendly relations with each other. As a matter of fact, similar friendly relations characterized our whole unit. The reason for that was to be found in the warmth and cordiality which characterized the relations of the partisans among themselves. The sense of brotherhood existing between Alexander Kamensky and his chief of staff, Konstantin Kosenko, was a model for all the partisans to follow. I know of occasions where one saved the other at the risk of his own life.

IN THE STRUGGLE FOR SOVIET LATVIA

Otomārs Oškalns, Hero of the Soviet Union,
Former Commissar in a Latvian Partisan Brigade

Our partisan company was called "For Soviet Latvia." Its origins were in White Russia, where it numbered only a few fighters. Later, when it moved north to Latvia, it soon grew into "The Latvian Partisan Brigade." It was then under the command of Vilhelms Laiviņš. I was its commissar.

This brigade included many Jewish fighters, both soldiers and officers, who with heroism and courage fought side by side with us to save the country from the fascist yoke. I shall now proceed to tell you something about a number of them.

Raphael Blum

Blum was the commissar of the second company and, some time later, the commissar of the expanded partisan brigade. Comrade Blum, "The Bespectacled Politruk," as he was called by the partisans, played a guiding role in our life and struggle. He was a young man with a technical education, a gifted newsman, and a singer. When the war broke out, he volunteered for the Red Army. Later the Komsomol[3] center in Latvia sent him over to our brigade for political orientation.

Upon arriving at the partisan camp, Blum took a rifle in his hand, and his personal example whipped up the people's enthusiasm in their struggle against the Nazis. On the most dangerous missions, you could see from a distance his tall body, which stood out even among us Latvians who are well known for our height. He was always to be found in the first rows of the fighters, never flinching in the face of whining bullets. This naturally brought him love and popularity among the partisans.

"I've grown so used to bullets," he would say with a boyish smile, "that I carry forever a bullet in my shoulder. Even a scalpel could not separate us from each other."

This "token" (the bullet) Blum had received upon crossing the Latvian border along with ten other partisans, in the direction of the Lubāna forests. They kept marching on for eleven days and nights, making special use of the protective cover of darkness. On that memorable march they occasionally came face-to-face with Germans as well as Latvian Fascists.[4] But the group always succeeded in storming it sway through the enemy forces and established friendly relations with the peasants of the Lyuban district. Blum was an oft-invited guest at the villagers' celebrations, where he was received with unmitigated pleasure on account of his wonderful voice and vivacious personality. In this manner he succeeded in finding his way to the hearts of the village youth, and thus we were able to obtain the information we needed for our struggle. These youths were ready to come along with us through thick and thin. When a battle was going on, Blum would spring from one fighter to another, encouraging this one with a joke and showing the other how to take deadly aim.

"You've got to know," he would say, "that every partisan bullet is a digit in our account with the Germans. Each figure has to be put in the right place, like a digit set down by a competent bookkeeper. And the more accurate our digits, the greater the sum total will grow in the final reckoning."

The brigade commander and his colleagues had a great appreciation for the exploits of Blum. He himself was very modest. Whenever there was talk about a new heroic deed of his, he would put a stop to it with the following retort:

"As a matter of fact I thought fighting would be much more difficult, but it turned out to be easy. I often wonder whether I haven't been born for just this sort of thing: to be a partisan and to settle the account with the fascists."

Blum had good reason to take revenge. Once, while sitting around talking of various things, Blum suddenly picked up a pencil and started adding up all the catastrophes he had gone through on account of the Hitlerite tyrants. His father, his stepmother (and the best of stepmothers at that), a sister, a brother, two female cousins, and a number of distant relatives... "We had all lived on such friendly terms with each other... and they have wiped out such a family."

Here is a characteristic feature of Blum's altruism. When the partisans were being inoculated against typhus and there wasn't enough vaccine to go around, he stepped aside in favor of the other partisans. Eventually Blum himself came down with typhus fever and was about to die. But his immense desire to live tided him over the danger, and came back to our lines, fresh and vigorous again.

Toward the end of July 1944, we began to hear the artillery of the advancing Red Army; we had been looking forward to them for so long. Blum went out with a group of partisans and drove back the Germans and their collaborators from the region of Bērzpils, then put up red flags in every corner. The Red Army forces which reached this region a few days later found it clean of enemy forces.

This is only a brief outline of Raphael Blum's life. When you watched his behavior under fire, you could see that he was a born fighter, a well-tempered soldier, who had spent all his life in carnage and incessant fighting. But that is how he looked in the midst of fighting. When relaxed, he was a young man full of the joy of life, good-natured and sharp-witted, with a touch of romanticism.

For his achievements he was awarded the order of "War of the Fatherland, First Class," the "Partisan Decoration, First Class," and the decoration "For Victory over Germany."

After the war he returned to his former occupation, exchanging his rifle for a writer's pen and becoming the editor of a Latvian paper called "Soviet Youth." As editor, he worked as tirelessly as he had done in his partisan years, which he considered the highlight of his life.

Leib Kassel

I would like to tell you about another outstanding partisan in our brigade, the chief of staff of the Third Company, Leib Kassel, who was nicknamed "The Landlord of Žīguri."

Kassel really earned this nickname. He virtually held in his young hands the entire region of Žīguri, a vast, vital, and strategic area in Latvia. The name "Žīguri" became well known to the Nazis, connoting railroad derailment, blowing up of bridges, and incessant ambushes.

Until the outbreak of the war, this young man, a Komsomol member, had worked in a weaving factory. When the

Germans occupied Riga (the capital of Latvia), ne was among
the last residents to leave the city. Together with a group of
young workers, he traveled through Latvia and Estonia, up
to Leningrad. After the Latvian Division had been organized,
Kassel joined it as a volunteer and took part in all its battles.
Twice wounded he later went over to the company of Latvian
partisans.

Seven times a plane carrying Kassel and his six partisan
comrades attempted to land in the district of Abrene in
Latgalia only to return without landing. The Germans had
learned to recognize its distinguishing signs. On the eighth
attempt they succeeded in landing, but the partisan group
that Kassel was to join had in the meantime been beaten.
Thus, the partisans found themselves in unknown territory;
they were strangers to both the place and the people. But
partisans usually do not lose their head; they dispersed at
various points in the district and began to fulfill their mission
unaided.

Leib Kassel arrived in Žīguri and started operating with
great enthusiasm. He had a highly variegated task: to prepare
the local population for the expected arrival of the Red Army,
to activate the peasants toward the ultimate struggle with the
German invaders, to draw the inhabitants toward joint action
with the partisans, and to organize the security forces.

"I look back with satisfaction on those days," Kassel once
told me. "They were good days. They taught me to hate the
enemy from the depths of my soul and to develop a strong
love for the Jews. They enriched my knowledge of nature and
of life. I had spent all my former days in a town and could
not distinguish between a pine and a birch. As a partisan I
learned, like an animal, to recognize tracks in the marshes or
in the grass; to determine the nature of sounds coming from
a distance, to crawl like a snake, and to run like an antelope."
Kassel would not take pleasure in speaking about himself.
He was a modest man. But the distinguished orders of "The
Red Flag," "The Partisan Decoration," and "For Victory
Over Germany" pinned to the chest of this man proclaim his
exploits. One of these exploits may be related here as a case in
point:

It happened near Kachanovo late one May night in 1944.
Kassel and a group of fighters had come on a visit to this

village, which was the administrative center for the region. They decorated the entire village with red flags. The enraged Germans mobilized one full division to wipe out the company, some 12,000 soldiers against 100 partisans! Kassel did not think much of that. He knew the woods around this region like the palm of his hand. He spread out his partisans behind tree trunks over an area of one square kilometer with the order to open fire on every fascist they saw. The Germans began to move shakily in the forest, step by step, thinking it to be full of partisans. Kassel's fighters shot the enemy soldiers one after the other, at the same time outflanking the enemy and appearing at his rear. In this way a great many Germans fell without a single loss to the partisans. The Germans, with their overwhelming numbers, took to their heels. The operation was carried out with remarkable skill and it will live long in the annals of our partisan struggle as an example of matchless bravery and remarkable tactics.

In his exploits in the woods, Kassel, in the company of his fighters, would call at villages which had been sense of the outrages of the Germans and their Latvian collaborators. In the course of such "visits," the partisans would attack police stations or the administrative quarters of the districts. They would release prisoners destined for hard labor camps and release prisoners destined for hard labor camps and hold court-martials for the traitors of the people. Once, when Kassel and a group of partisans were holding a court-martial of this kind against an anti-Communist traitor, a large unit of German gendarmes came into the village. The partisans did not lose their head; while their comrades, who stood guard at the outskirts of the village, fought it out with the Germans, the court-martial went on according to partisan protocol. However, when news came that the guards were incapable of keeping their ground much longer, Kassel ordered his men to shoot the traitor and leave the village.

As already mentioned, Kassel knew how to organize his information service in the best possible manner. The peasant girls would put at a predetermined spot, packages of cheese, buter, and eggs, with messages attached to them. For their part, the peasants brought along potatoes and, in separate sacks, maps of the surrounding area. The shepherds would bring along packs of German printed material, together with

SS printed material, and receive from Kassel leaflets for distribution among the local population. Thanks to such organization, Kassel knew all about what was going on around him. He would systematically send this information to Moscow, three times a day, to central Army headquarters and usually within three or four hours after receiving his information, the high command would send in planes to bomb the places and the factories he had marked out for them.

On several occasions, Kassel went deep into the rear lines of the enemy. Once he even reached Riga, dressed as a German officer, in order to establish contact with the people of the ghetto, among whom was his own father. When Kassel approached the city, one of the guards recognized him, but before the soldier could do anything, he shot the fascist dead and jumped onto a car that came along. He immediately put his gun to the temple of the driver and streaked out of danger...

Sasha Gurari

"Foundling" was the nickname of the Jewish boy Sasha Gurari in our brigade. The story of his life is a multi-colored account. In the early days of the war, the ship in which he was sailing after he had left Leningrad hit a German mine and sank. The waves carried Gurari to the island of Dagö in the Bay of Riga. There, the Germans arrested him and put him in a POW camp. Sasha was born in Ukraine, and he told the Germans that he was a Ukrainian, thus saving himself from a quick death. For two long years he suffered in this camp, and in August 1943, he eventually succeeded in escaping.

Our reconnaissance men came upon him one summer night when he was asleep in the field. Before long this boy, with such dreamy, tender features and short stature, had turned into a fearless fighter; he fought like a lion.

Once Gurari, with the commander of our group and a number of partisans, went out on a mission to wipe out a gang of SS. The mission was carried out properly, but it cost us many casualties; out of the entire company, only the commander Pashko and Gurari remained alive. Since Gurari's wounds were superficial, he carried the commander on his shoulders, took him up into an attic he found along the way, and dressed both the commander's wounds and his own; they both stayed there for the night. In the morning, our reconnaissance men found them and brought them back to our camp.

I remember another incident which is so characteristic of Gurari's ties of friendship. In one of the battles against a strong group of SS, Partisan Istomin, a close friend of Gurari's, was wounded. Gurari went on fighting with his usual fierceness and courage. When the fighting ended and the Aizsargi had run away, we did not find Gurari among us and were greatly concerned for his life, thinking that he had been killed. While searching for his body, we heard some firing in the area, and a few minutes later saw Gurari running in our direction from the woods holding a smoking rifle in one hand and a ... cap full of strawberries in the other!

"It wasn't easy bringing back my strawberries from those mongrels," he said, breathing heavily, his eyes looking for his wounded friend. Then he went over to Istomin and started feeding him the fruit he was holding in his hand. Istomir looked at Gurari with a deep sense of gratitude and apparently felt better. Gurari was so pleased and so moved, that he started dancing around.

"That's it! I knew that all you needed was strawberries." Sasha Gurari was a colorful personality in our company. He was very particular about his clothes and walked around in highly polished boots. He even washed with scented soap, which he knew how to come by under any circumstances. He had a strong liking for Ukrainian folk songs, as well as sports and wresting. His skills in sports helped him in his hand-to-hand fighting with the fascist enemy. Like a panther, he would dash at his prey. In one battle, against a punishment squad, Gurari accounted for eleven German soldiers and saved the company from encirclement.

During his career as a partisan, Gurari was wounded three times, but he never stopped fighting. For his achievements in battle, he was awarded the order of "The War of the Fatherland, Second Class."

Zina

Gusta Jacobson, or "Nurse Zina," as she was called in our company, was liked by all. She was a medical nurse, but when necessary she picked up a rifle and fought shoulder-to-shoulder with her comrades.

This fragile young woman adapted with unusual ease to the difficult conditions of the partisans and their struggle. I often had occasion to see her in battle. She was a fearless young woman, cool and hardy. She would evacuate the wounded under a hail of bullets, and many partisans owe her their lives.

I well remember one particular incident: in the midst of a battle, our machine gun stopped firing. We had counted heavily on that machine gun. Zina told us that she would try to find out what was the matter. It turned out that the machine gunner had been seriously wounded. She bandaged his wounds, took his place him behind the machine gun, and resumed the firing until she herself was replaced by another partisan. Such was "Nurse Zina" in battle.

While the men were resting, Zina would often think up all sorts of entertainment for the company. Before the war she was a scout instructress and new a lot of games, songs, and legends. At present, she is working at the Komsomol youth center in Riga, and you can often meet her there, along with several elderly bearded men who sit there with her for hours. Such visitors usually make one wonder, since they do not look like Komsomol members at all. But "Nurse Zina," who is now once again Gusta Jacobson, tells the inquirers:

"These are my partisan friends, the dearest men of all…"

Grigory Gerchik

In the pageant of Jewish partisan fighters in the Riga region, one particular commander stands out in my memory: "The Black Bandit with the Golden Teeth," as he was called by the Germans. He was known far and wide as a fearless partisan, and the Germans put up an award of forty liters of vodka for catching him alive! Such a prize meant a great deal in those days. Not many people could whip up enthusiasm to catch him, even for such a reward, for it was impossible to catch him anyway. Gerchik was an expert at lightning-speed, hit-and-run raids. He had an uncanny sense of orientation and was adept at disguise.

Thanks to this latter skill, he often succeeded in getting far behind enemy lines. Once we were surprised to find an officer wearing a German uniform in our camp. The partisans could not understand how this could happen, but were soon relieved to find that it was none other than Gerchik himself.

Once, Gerchik and his adjutant Stanislav put on SS clothes and went about as ordinary citizens. On their way, they saw two German officers, dressed as hunters, coming out of a car. Gerchik and Stanislav went up to them and engaged them in conversation. A few moments later the two men had shot and killed what turned out to be a German general and his adjutant.

Here is another incident. A reconnaissance man brought the news that some 350 Germans and two armored vehicles had come into the village next to the forest where Gerchik and his soldiers were stationed, in order to collect bread and cattle. Gerchik's company had only fifty fighter and could not engage the enemy in open battle. They had on the outskirts of the forest; when the Germans came out of the village loaded with provisions and leading a large herd of cows they had taken from the peasants, they opened up with all the firepower at their disposal. The Germans took to their heels, some even jumped into a nearby river, leaving behind all the provisions and cows they had taken. Gerchik gave back to the peasants the cows and the bread that the Germans had taken from them. This incident had a great impact on the peasants' attitude toward the partisan movement; within a short time about 600 new volunteers joined our companies.

On another occasion, Gerchik and his company arrived one night at a village and thought to get some rest after a long and tiring march. At midnight, they learned that the Germans were approaching. Upon entering the village, the Germans were received with partisan fire from all directions. Most of the Germans were killed, but seventeen were taken prisoner and brought to the company field command.

Gerchik was an experienced soldier. He had taken part in the battle with Finland as a commander of a skiing group.

In the early days of the war he served in the Red Army, was taken prisoner, then escaped and reached a partisan company. He spent ten months fighting with us. During this period he accounted for some 60 Germans, blew up a score of enemy tanks and 400 trucks, and took about 200 prisoners. For his exploits in the partisan movement, Gerchik was awarded the order of the "Red Flag."

* * * * *

In our brigade there was a young man by the name of Kan. I forget his first name. He was born in Jelgava and worked as a diver. Being jovial and quick-witted, he was soon nicknamed "Witty Kan" by the partisans.

On a certain mission, the company to which Kan belonged had to cover a distance of thirty kilometers. The going was tough. The men were tired from previous fighting, and they expected more. Seeing the sinking spirits of the men around him, Kan decided to inject some life into the tired fighters. All through that seemingly endless thirty-kilometer march, he told them jokes. The partisans said later that Kan's jokes took their minds off this dangerous and weary trek.

Kan was not simply a merry young man. During a battle that the partisans started immediately after that long trek, Kan killed four Germans with his own hands; this time he was not joking. To our regret, however, he himself was killed in that same battle...

* * * * *

The six partisans I have written about here do not cover the entire list of Jewish comrades who fought in our brigade and provided examples of courage and fearlessness. I shall forever remember the names of Aron Khayit and Alexander Eidus, who blew themselves up in order not to fall into the hands of the enemy; also the names of Sima Friedland, Alexander Galperin, Brocha Kretser, L. Gelfand, and many, many others who died heroes' deaths in the fight for our Soviet fatherland. In every instance, the Jewish partisans showed they knew what they were fighting for; they were excellent comrades and fearless soldiers. In the battle against the fascist monster, they pitched in with all their spiritual strength, with all their fiery hate for the enemy.

In conclusion, I would like to add that the Soviet government awarded me the highly coveted order — "Hero of the Soviet Union." I proudly wear another order — the "Golden Star": not with pride alone, but also with humility, realizing that the gold of this star has been steeped in the blood of heroic partisans. Among them, the Jewish partisans occupy a distinguished place.

IN WHITE RUSSIA

P.P. Kapusta, Major-General,
Former Commander of a Partisan Unit

In July 1941, while getting my battalion out of enemy encirclement, I was seriously wounded in the leg. I could not move and had to stay behind the lines of the German forces. For two days I was hidden by the peasants of the village of Starye Falichi, and then they moved me by cart to the small town of Starye Dorogi, where the doctor dressed my wound. From there I was later taken to the hospital in the city of Slutsk.

Before I was taken prisoner, I heard Stalin on the radio, calling upon the Soviet people to set up a movement of partisans to fight behind enemy lines. Thus, while at the POW amp, I began carefully, but conscientiously, to gather a group of people who thought the same way I did. We set ourselves the task of escaping from the camp and hiding in the woods, with a view to setting up a partisan company there. In the spring of 1942, our plan was put into operation. We escaped from the German camp under a hail of bullets and slipped into the woods. The roads were rugged and movement was difficult. We headed for the woods of Staritsa. We were fourteen men, including a Jew by the name of Zubarev. In the forest of Staritsa, among the first to join us was Leib Gilchik, an inhabitant of the Kopyl region. When the Germans occupied the region, Gilchik headed for the woods in search of the partisans. His wife, a Russian, and his children stayed behind in Kopyl. When the Germans heard that Gilchik had gone into the woods, they killed his wife and children.

First of all, it was necessary to get the men well armed and equipped. Zubarev and Gilchik helped me a great deal in this task. The former proved to be a first-rate scout and the latter, an outstanding commander. Both knew well the region where we had started to operate. We had no maps, but the familiarity of both Zubarev and Gilchik with the region filled in the gap. They knew every path in that area, including the woods.

Before long, Zubarev had brought the intelligence service to such a level that I knew what was going on over a radius of sixty kilometers. On no occasion did he lose his way in that vast region, nor was he late in delivering a message, nor did he deliver in accurate information.

Zubarev was very young, only twenty years old, and remarkably diligent. He knew how to acquire authority among the partisans as well as with the local population. The latter supplied him with valuable bits of information. In the beginning, when it was highly essential to acquire military equipment, the local inhabitants showed Zubarev several places where we could find caches of arms.

Leib Gilchik was older than Zubarev. He was born in 1907. Like Zubarev, he was very alert, had his own way with the hearts of people, and had a friendly countenance. I entrusted Gilchik with the task of establishing contact with the inmates of the ghetto of the small town of Kopyl. With the help of the ghetto's eldest man, Kogan, it was possible for Gilchik to gather the youth around him. Furthermore, he even got into the ghettos of the towns of Nesvizh and Kletsk and succeeded, after meticulous preparation, in releasing thirty persons from them.

At first I thought to distribute the ghetto people among the partisan companies, but I dropped this plan and asked Gilchik, who had a great sense of responsibility, to form a new and independent company out of them. For its initial equipment we allotted a few rifles, assuming that the recruits themselves would take care of getting additional arms. For the position of company commissar, I appointed Senior Air Force Lieutenant Razuvayev. And so, within a short time, our company had grown into a 140-man unit, nearly all of them Jews. The men of the company proved that they knew how to get more arms and proved that they could use them too.

No longer prisoners of the Germans, we were now a fighting company of fourteen men, heading for the woods. All of a sudden, we were attacked by a large group of gendarmes and policemen armed to the teeth. They did not succeed in driving us out of the woods and eventually retreated, sustaining heavy casualties. Soon it was known all over the region of Slutsk that a large partisan unit was active in the forest of Staritsa.

Volunteers began to flock to us, and by May 1942 I had become the commander of a brigade named after Voroshilov.

We did all we could to establish contact with the other partisan groups operating in the area. With the help of Vasily Ivanovich Kozlov, chairman of the Presidium of the Supreme Council of the Soviet Socialist Republic of Byelorussia and later commander of a partisan company, we succeeded in establishing contact with Moscow and with the headquarters of the Byelorussian partisan movement. Kozlov also helped us in making the necessary arrangements for publishing leaflets to distribute among the local population and in organizing Komsomol groups.

In order to give my unit greater mobility, I divided it into a number of companies, each headed by an officer under my command. We then went on to draw up a plan for attacking the town of Kopyl. However, we did not succeed in carrying out this plan, since the Germans soon brought in a large force against us, with further reinforcements sent in from time to time. My grapevine brought me information that SS companies had been sent over to Slutsk and Kopyl in order to wipe us out. And, indeed, on May 1, 1942, at seven in the morning, the SS troops mounted an all-out attack on our unit. My companies were spread out all over the region of Slutsk. The brunt of the attack fell on two companies under the command of Gilchik and Dunayev. The outnumbered partisans engaged the attackers three times in hand-to-hand fighting. Nikolai Vasilyevich Dunayev was killed in this battle, but the Germans suffered heavy losses, including more than 740 killed. They also lost three field guns, three tanks, and fourteen vehicles. Gilchik's company proved its military mettle in this battle. The task entrusted to it, of not letting the enemy get into the woods, was fulfilled.

Before long news reached us from our scouts that the Germans had received new reinforcements. In those days we were suffering from ammunition shortage, so I decided to move to another location, more suited to our struggle. We thus went to another forest near the small town of Pesochnoe. The persistent efforts of the Germans to drive us out of the woods were doomed to failure and, suffering heavy losses, they discontinued their activities against us. Our units, however, went on with their raids on German garrisons, blowing up enemy convoys and bridges and destroying factories which were engaged in war material production for the Hitlerite army.

By order of the "hangman" Kube, Hitler's deputy in Byelorussia, all the police forces in this area were mobilized to strike at the "Kapusta Gang" and wipe it out. Zubarev, director of my "grapevine," knew how to obtain the correct information in time. On December 8, 1942, at four in the afternoon, the Germans were to mount their attack upon us. I deployed my forces so that one fighting unit was sent out about two kilometers ahead of our main force. This unit would engage the enemy in battle before the time they had set for it and before they could come close to our main force.

Gilchik's men bore the full brunt of the battle. Advancing toward them were the 64th SS battalion and two police battalions. The fighting continued for a long time. The partisans stood their ground, vowing not to withdraw. They fell to the last man, having fulfilled the task they had been entrusted with. German prisoners later told us that the Hitlerites eventually wiped the group of partisans, but they could find not a single round of ammunition, or even a single rifle, indicating the partisans had fought to the last bullet. As we learned later, two partisans who had succeeded in eluding the enemy buried their partisan rifles and machine guns in the snow, then put an end to their own lives, as befits loyal Soviet patriots.

Gilchik's company was to move a distance of eighty to ninety kilometers in order to reach its objective and cross the road between Brest and Moscow, which was heavily guarded by the Germans. This march seemed to me both dangerous and difficult, so I decided to go with the men myself. Under cover of darkness we reached the railway racks, with Gilchik and I traveling at the head of the company. Suddenly we were discovered by enemy guards. Our men took cover and we opened up with all the firepower at our disposal, killing all the guards. Our booty included a number of machine guns, hand grenades, rifles, cartridge cases, tents, all of which we took back into the forest.

* * * * *

That is the end of my reminiscences of Zubarev, Gilchik, and their company. In May 1943 I was given the task of relocating to the region of Białystok, in order to spark partisan struggle behind enemy lines.

It was necessary to pass through numerous points in the enemy's rear line, over an area of approximately 1,000 square kilometers. We succeeded in crossing five railway tracks and twelve roads after eight battles with the enemy. On the way between Baranovichi and Luninets we destroyed an eighteen-kilometer length of railway track, blew up a number of fortified German gun emplacements, and wiped out police stations which happened to be on our way.

Upon reaching the woods called Lipichanskaya Pushcha, I divided the fighting force into three companies and gave each one a well-defined task. When we went through the district of Białystok, we found hardly any Jews in the entire area; the majority of the Jewish population had been wiped out. We then went about organizing underground groups of Communist youth. There were only a few Jews who had been saved by the non-Jewish population. We received highly valuable information from the local people and passed it on to Moscow.

The Germans had terrorized the entire population. Often they would send among the people traitors and spies posing as partisans, so that we had to act with extreme care. Nevertheless, in every area we had a liaison man, a loyal citizen, who carried out all our instructions.

In conclusion, I would like to say a few words about a liaison woman, one of the best. She was a young woman, short of stature, modest, well built, who spoke German well. She was a resident of Białystok, where she lived under a false passport and called herself Maria Ivanovna Mrozovskaya. Her real name was Liza Chapnik. Only two years after the German invasion, she decided to devote herself to the fight against the fascists. In order to help us in our struggle, she found work at the German command.

A brigade commander of my unit, Nikolai Voitsekhovsky, received an order from me to set camp near Białystok. He moved with great care through a forest not far from the town. Then word came that there was a trusted person in Białystok, and young woman, who was in close contact with the local underground. That was Liza Chapnik. Voitsekhovsky could thus entrust her with the task of getting the information he needed and to find among the German personnel people who would be willing to carry out our instructions. This highly complicated task was efficiently fulfilled by Liza Chapnik.

The Red Army was nearing Białystok. The retreating Germans had reached a state of disintegration. With Chapnik's help we could find out what they did before they left the town, especially the places where they had laid mines. We got the plan in time to hand it to the Red Army commander who was approaching the town. Thanks to this information, our army also succeeded in finding military equipment and enemy storehouses.

THREE FIGHTERS OF MY UNIT

Y.Y. Melnik, Polkovnik,
Former Commander of a Partisan Unit

The unit under my command was organized in the days when Sidor Kovpak, who had been fighting in the Sumy area, moved over to the woods of Bryansk. At this time it was suggested that I join Kovpak's struggle in that region, set up new partisan groups, and strike at enemy communications.

Comrade Kovpak helped me very much in organizing my unit. He put at my disposal a partisan group for his unit that had considerable expeience in local fighting conditions. With the full help of this group, my first fighting units were organized: "For the Fatherland" company, "Red Partisan" company, and "Death to Fascism" company, which together numbered 300 fighters. Our base was to be in the Khinel Forest. The village of Lomlenka in the Yampol region turned into something like headquarters for us. It was from here that we started our struggle against the German invaders. Not only fighting operations fell to our lot. For instance, the Hitlerlites sent our skilled youth to Germany for forced labor. We took a variety of measures to prevent such practices. We would attack the Germans who accompanied them and liberate the young men, who would then join our companies. We killed the Germans without mercy, at the same time caring for the people of the districts through which we used to pass in our fight against the German hordes. Thus, we were to distribute to the local inhabitants some 10,000 tons of bread, 141 tons of sugar, thousands of head of cattle, 3,800 sheep and pigs, besides a great deal of salt, which was in great demand by the peasants.

In the beginning we worked in small groups, but before long we had grown into a large unit. As time went on, from October 25, 1942, to March 26, 1944, our unit had covered more than 6,000 kilometers. We fought the Germans on the soil of eight regions, crossed thirty-eight rivers, including the Desna, and Dnieper, and the Southern Bug. We also crossed forty-eight railway tracks. In the 114 battles we went through, our unit accounted for over 12,000 enemy soldiers and officers, derailed eighty-two regular trains and armored trains and shot down five enemy planes.

From these figures alone, it is possible to have an idea of the self-sacrifice, courage, and daring of all the men of my unit. In the following accounts, however, I shall speak of the exploits and heroism of only three partisans: a telegraph operator, a doctor, and a reconnaissance man.

Telegraph Operator Joseph Isakovich Malii

I had met Joseph Isakovich Malii in Stalingrad. This small, lean man was working as a telegraph operator at one of our military units. The men of this unit always spoke of him as a skilled technician. When it was decided that I fly over with a group of comrades behind enemy lines, I immediately thought of Malii and asked him directly:

"Are you ready to drop behind enemy lines?"

He answered briefly and to the point: "I am!"

Upon reaching the rear of the enemy forces, we gathered in the woods of Khinel. Before long, Malii had established two-way communication with Russia. He worked tirelessly, with remarkable coolness and precision. He was always alert and calm. Our unit went on expanding, and it was necessary to equip all the companies with radio transmitters. Comrade Malii took it upon himself to train telegraph operators from among the partisans. In 1942, under difficult fighting conditions in the woods, Joseph Isakovich held courses for wireless operators; and, indeed, in three months — November, December, and January — he succeeded in giving proper training to five women operators. Some time later these operators were allocated to the companies under Naumov's command, and they were to render great service to the fighting forces in the regions of Sumsk, Poltava, Kirovograd, Odessa, Vinnitsa, and Zhitomir.

In February 1943 I received orders to move on to the district of Chernigov, north of Kiev. Malii came over with me. On the day that followed our arrival at the specified place, which was nine kilometers from Kholmy, a regional center in the region of Chernigov, my intelligence service found out that one full Magyar division was stationed in the town, while the nearby villages contained police battalions. I instructed Malii to contact Moscow in order to pass on to the Ukrainian headquarters our request for military equipment. That was a tough job. The request had to be made in such a way that the Germans would not be able to decipher it and consequently find out the spot where we expected the equipment to be dropped by parachute. For two full days, with no rest or sleep, Malii kept working on the final form of our request. In the end he found a way out, and the message was sent. Before long the planes appeared over us and dropped the military equipment we had asked for.

On our second crossing of the region of Shatovka, we were once surrounded by large enemy forces and ford to move into open country. Here we came under heavy German attacks; but even under these conditions, Malii worked with his usual precision. We had a number of transmitters. Malii organized work on these transmitters and regularly sent out our messages to the "Big Land" (Central HQ in Russia). While on the move in his operation, under the most difficult conditions, we lost three transmitters. Malii always kept his in excellent working condition, and we always had contact with the fatherland. In our third crossing, in October 1943, Malii was also to render us great service through his regular radio communication.

In battle or when on the move, a transmitter would go on the blink. Malii knew how to repair it in a short time. Once a transmitter component broke and communication stopped. Using the transmitter of a nearby company, Malii devised a new part. Contact was established once again in the camp. On another occasion, when we could get no batteries from the "Big Land," Malii used an accumulator from a broken-down car and thus kept the transmitter working. Malii asked me to instruct our fighters that upon destroying enemy vehicles they should do their best to keep the engines intact.

Joseph Isakovich Malii stayed with us for nearly two years. He accompanied the unit throughout all the fighting. For that, he was awarded the "Order of the War of the Fatherland, Second Class," "The Red Star," and "The Partisan Medal, First Class."

At the end of partisan warfare, Malii stayed on in a military unit. I am certain that he kept on working with his usual conscientiousness and loyalty. He will always remain in my memory as a man of impeccable character and loyal in his duty.

Dr. Yaakov Bolach

When we were on the move in August 1943, two doctors joined our forces. I forget the name of one of them, but the other was called Yaakov Emmanuelovich Bolach. He was fifty-five years old. Both doctors escaped from the town of Kerch by the skin of their teeth, the Germans having wiped out more than half the Jewish population. Bolach was of great benefit to us. He healed the sick and operated on some of the wounded. He knew how to fight typhus. We improvised a primitive bathhouse on the river Ubort. We dug out a hole in the ground, put inside it an iron petrol barrel, and covered it with wooden boards. In this bathhouse it was also possible to disinfect clothing. We did not have a single case of typhus. Our doctor provided medical aid not only for the fighters but also for the neighboring inhabitants, putting in endless hours of work. At times he would help women in childbirth in the villages where the Germans had stopped all medical services.

The "Big Land" could not provide us with the necessary amount of medicines. We made up for the shortage by obtaining the necessary items from German hospitals and pharmacies. Nevertheless, we sometimes lacked medicines and supplies, particularly bandages. For this latter purpose we sometimes resorted to parachute cloth. Bolach's out-patients from the neighboring villages, who owed him a great debt of gratitude, began to provide us with bandage material, sometimes made of high-quality linen.

Yaakov Emmanuelovich had a vivacious, pleasant nature. In the evenings he would come over to us at headquarters, to the campfire, where the fighters and their commanders usually gathered. When he arrived, joy would spread all around us. I often joined him in the dancing to bring joy into the hearts of the young men. The difficulties and the pain involved in partisan warfare did not snuff out his joy of life or lessen his love for the people.

Scout Yevgeny Volyansky

In the early days of 1943, when our unit was encamped in the region of Khinel Forest, we received great help from Red Army Lieutenant Yevgeny Volyansky. He was born in Odessa and soon moved to Zhmerinka. Since October 1941, Volyansky had served in one partisan company after another, which had been organized from among the Russian soldiers who had escaped enemy encirclement. He was sent over to the scouts' company as its deputy commander.

In the Desna region the Germans stood in the way of the river we wanted to cross and actually encircled us. We had to find a way out. At the head of the patrol group was Volyansky. Four of our attempts at reaching the river were thwarted by the enemy; and it was only thanks to Volyansky that we succeeded in breaking out of the encirclement without any casualties, even without being detected by the enemy.

The Germans attached great importance to alcohol factories. They used alcohol for their tanks and vehicles. It was only natural that the partisans would want to destroy these plants. Once, while stopping at a regional center in the area of Chernigov, I sent the Chervony company to the village of Kriski on some military mission. Volyansky was among its men. There was an alcohol factory in that village. The dauntless scout not only found out where the distillery was, but also supplied the fighters with accurate details on how to get to it and how to dispose of the guards. Volyansky himself took two comrades along with him, slipped into the factory building, laid explosives, and blew up the alcohol tubs.

On another occasion, when we were camped near the Pripyat River, Volyansky went out with a group of partisans to the railway racks running between Gomel and Kalinkovichi. These tracks served as a main line or communications for the German army in the Bryansk front. Naturally, the tracks were heavily guarded by the Germans. After through reconnoitering, Volyansky crept up to the tracks with the men, at a point four kilometers from the Goleniche station. A passenger train went by, followed by an eight-man German guard. Volyansky waited for the guard to move away and then went to work with his men on the tracks. He laid two demolition charges at a distance of twenty meters from each other. The partisans were hardly through when an armored train was seen chugging its way from a distance. The partisans moved away from the tracks, slipping into the nearby woods. Still trying to catch their breath from the intensive effort, they heard two ear-shattering explosions. Fragments of both train and tracks went up into the air. The tracks were put out of commission for five days.

On other occasions, Volyansky and his scouts would slip into an enemy-held village, find out all about the German forces there, and come back to base to draw up the plan for the attack.

Yevgeny Volyansky was awarded the "Red Flag" order, the "War of the Fatherland" order, First Class, and the "Partisan Medal," First Class. After our companies had ceased their operations behind enemy lines, Volyansky expressed his wish to fly over to the Carpathian Mountains where he could resume partisan warfare against the Germans. His wish was granted. For his military exploits in Czechoslovakia, he was awarded a Czechoslovak decoration.

VICTOR SPOTMAN

Y. Kuzshar, Hero of the Soviet Union,
Major-General, Former Commander of a Partisan Unit

In the spring of 1943, a special-missions company was formed in our unit. The man appointed as its commander was Victor Spotman, a young officer who had long proved his military mettle. For that he had thrice been awarded state decorations. There was no important military operation in which he did not take part along with his partisans. In everything he did, he showed not only courage, but also understanding and ingenuity.

Here is one of his exploits. In early June 1943, there arrived at Rechitsa a German division, including tanks and armored cars, two battalions of gendarmes, and even airplanes. Our unit was encamped at a distance of twenty-five kilometers from Rechitsa. On the eve of the enemy arrival, our men succeeded in downing a reconnaissance plane. In it they found a map showing the exact location of our company and the headquarters of our unit. It was evident that the Germans would launch a heavy attack on these spots, which were now known to them. With the help of our own combat reconnaissance and intelligence teams, we succeeded in finding out the date of the planned German onslaught — June 13, 1943. On the night of this day, our partisan unit left its camp and, after a forced march, took positions behind the line that was marked out on the enemy map.

At exactly six in the morning, the Germans started shelling the spot we had evacuated. Before long this shelling was complemented by an attack mounted by German infantry and tank units. We laid strong ambushes along the roads flanking the woods and sent out a fighting outfit of lookouts to the village of Uzhnozh. When the Germans appeared, the outfit fired at them and forced them back to the outskirts of the forest. The Germans, having recovered from the initial shock, went after the lookout outfit, but they were forced back once again by the fire of our ambush.

In order to collect their dead and heavily wounded, the Germans sent out a large infantry unit. At the same time, the partisan ambush had received significant reinforcement. Thus half an hour after the first shot had been fired, a great battle raged between some 3,000 fighters on both sides, using automatic rifles, machine guns, and mine-throwers. Before long, the field guns joined the battle.

At the head of his company of sharpshooters, Spotman controlled the central sector of one side of the forest. At this sector the Germans poured a dense fire from mine-throwers. Spotman's unique familiarity with the place made it possible for him not only to stand his ground, but also to prevent loss of life among his men.

After the first German attack had petered out, Spotman moved his men fast from the outskirts of the forest to a distance of about one hundred meters inside it. The company had hardly taken its new position when enemy mines started exploding at the outskirts of the woods, at the exact spot where the partisans had been before. The explosions died down after some time, and Spotman ordered his men to go back to the outskirts of the forest, where the ground had been deeply marked by the exploding German mines. At the same time the enemy directed its mines and artillery fire into the forest, where the partisans would have meet a bitter end had they stayed.

The Germans launched another attack. They went in close lines, walking upright, feeling certain that there was no one to oppose them at the end of the forest. When they came to a distance of about fifty meters from us, Spotman and his men opened up with a crossfire of machine guns, rifles, and mine-throwers. The Germans fell back. Four times they attacked the outskirts of the woods, leading two charges at the spot. After Spotman's counterattack, they eventually ran away. Despite the large concentration of German infantry, arms, tanks, and armored vehicles, one end of the forest still remained in our hands.

Full of resentment, the Germans burned down the village of Uzhnozh and filled up the wells with earth. But they were soon to retreat, leaving behind them hundreds of dead and wounded.

TYPICAL BIOGRAPHIES

I.A. Belsky, Hero of the Soviet Union, Former Commander of a Partisan Unit

As one who took part in organizing a partisan movement in Byelorussia, I was often behind enemy lines in the districts of Minsk, Polesia, Mogilyov, and Pinsk.

The partisan movement was small in its early days; the first groups organized consisted of ten, fifteen, and twenty men each. The future commanders of the units personally picked out the men, gathered information, and saw to the provision of supplies and arms. In the vicinity of the Sorochi district, aided by the chairman of the *kolkhoz* named after the ten-year anniversary of the Byelorussian Soviet republic, I organized a partisan company made up of twenty-eight men. For its commander I appointed the Jew Berdnikovich, who had formerly been a postal employee. The company still had no arms, so I gave Berdnikovich one of my pistols and he set out, at the head of thirty hand-picked fighters, to get arms for the company.

By the approach of fall there were scores of such companies. But the situation in general was not clear to me. So I sent one of my aides, Roman Katznelson, to Minsk in order to bring over Berenzon, whom I had come to know in the course of our working together some time before. I met Berenzon and Katznelson in the winter in the district of Lyuban and sent them on a long reconnaissance mission: to find out the forces that were trying to work with us and to indicate what could be done for a more comprehensive organization of the partisan movement. They called at seven districts: Slutsk, Starye Dorogi, Dzerzhinsk, Zaslavl, Pukhovichi, Rudyansk, and Minsk, and also visited the town of Minsk itself. They were gone about a month and a half, doing propaganda work besides reconnaissance. They called upon the people to carry out resistance operations behind enemy lines.

Then one day I heard that Katznelson died a war hero.

279

In October 1941 we got ready for our first operation. We formed a striking force of about 180 men out of three companies and put it under the command of Dalidovich, the commander of one of them. And thus though greatly outnumbered, we attacked the German garrison.

The battles we waged attracted new men into our fighting units. We set up a chain of workshops for making and repairing arms. Each workshop was manned by ten to fifteen workers. In these workshops we had 110 craftsmen in all. The Germans bombed us, but many of the bombs were duds, so we took out their powder and used their explosive charges. In May 1942 we received a transmitter and could thus send out the announcement that we had some 5,000 partisans active in our region.

At about this time I met in the woods two people, barefoot and in taters, a man and a young girl. The man, whose name was Abraham (I forgot his family name), had been a photographer in Gomel. He was about forty-five. The girl had been a high-school pupil in Bobruisk, and was called Mania Mintz. They had escaped from the Germans into the forest, where they fed on potatoes boiled in a German steel helmet. Mania cold walk only on her toes, as the soles of her feet were bleeding. I brought them to one of our companies.

We allocated Abraham to our supplies platoon. He was entrusted with the task of caring supplies to the company from the neighboring villages. This was highly dangerous, as he was likely to fall into the hands of the Germans. Often he would move under a hail of bullets. But he did not flinch. Mania, for her part, worked in the kitchen for nine months, then asked to be given a combat task. She was attached as a demolition fighter to the Gastello company and took part in many combat missions.

I appointed Alter Kustanovich as my adjutant. He had been left behind enemy lines to organize the partisan movement. His wife was killed by the Germans. Accompanied by one partisan, he destroyed and burned an enemy truck, killing the ten German soldiers who were in it. I could not think of a better adjutant. He did not seem to sleep at all. He stationed the guards and lookouts in their positions. In battle he patrolled the area and was responsible for establishing contact with the neighboring companies. He did everything fast, accurately and without fear.

Physician Nahum Shvets entered the woods in the early days of the war. In the district of Glusk he joined a partisan company under the command of Stolyarov. It was here that I met him in December of 1941 and had him transferred to Dalidovich's company. He healed and operated on the sick and wounded of both the partisans and the neighboring population, even serving as obstetrician in emergencies. At the same time he trained the cadres of medics we so badly needed. Before long Shvets was put in charge of the sanitary service for the entire unit.

Simon Reznik, an ordinary fighter in July 1941, was later made commissar of one of our companies. He was only twenty-five and took part in at least four battles, destroying twenty firing positions near Lomovichi, blowing up the bridge on the river Drissa, and destroying the Parichi station. He was wounded in 1944 and airlifted to the "Big Land."

Schulman, the commander of one of our companies, came to us in 1942. Till then he had been hiding in the woods for about one year. At first he served as an ordinary fighter, but he soon established himself as a daring partisan who won the respect of his colleagues and thus was appointed commander of his company. He was given the task of blowing up railway tracks. Some time later he set up a company of saboteurs under his command. His company accounted for many German trains destroyed on the tracks running from Bobruisk through Vyazye to Osipovich.

The following is a typical account of one Jewish family.

To my regret, I cannot remember its name. At the time we knew the people by their first names only and that is how we remember them. Till the outbreak of the war, this family had lived in Urechye, in the region of Starye Dorogi. Later on the family was brought over to us. Abraham, the head of the family, was put in charge of supplies. His wife worked in the kitchen. Their son, Georgy, was a mounted scout. Under our instructions, he twice accompanied convoys headed for the

"Big Land" through the front lines. On his second mission he stayed there and joined the Red Army. Abraham's sixteen-year-old daughter, Ida, worked at our headquarters. When later we established contact with the Red Army, we sent her to school.

In 1941 I met Khinits. In that year the Germans had killed his wife. He took part in many battles and sabotage operations as an ordinary fighter. Later on he set up a new company and was made its commissar. He personally accounted for eighteen dead Germans. He kept fighting until 1944.

There were many Jews in my unit, both fighters and commanders. Here I have mentioned the names of only a few. But the stories of their lies, their fates, and their participation in the partisan movement are typical of all the sons and daughters of the Jewish people who, along with the other peoples of our Soviet fatherland, rose up in arms against the enemy during the difficult years of German occupation.

Two Partisans

*V. Klokov, Hero of the Soviet Union,
Former Deputy-Commander of a Partisan Unit*

Young Zelig Kadin was seriously wounded in one of the battles. A fascist bullet had shattered his hand, but Kadin did not leave the company He only moved from the platoon of sharpshooters to that of demolition fighters.

Zelig's wound took a long time to heal. The shattered bone of his hand did not join well, but he kept taking part in combat operations. Holding a grenade in his hand, he would go out in the company of his comrades to face the enemy, charging ahead and killing Germans. Months passed, and the bone in Zelig's hand did not heal. So we decided to send him back into the Soviet hinterland. The parting was hard on all of us, and we often remembered our "Zaika," as we fondly called him in our company.

* * * * *

Simon Yudovich joined the partisan company in September 1942. He had succeeded in escaping from a German POW camp. I came to know him well in August 1943 when I was appointed deputy company commander, and Yudovich was appointed commissar of the sabotage platoon. Being aggressive and full of drive, he at once adapted to his new job and elicited both respect and friendship from the men of the platoon. Even while serving as a commissar, Yudovich kept up the hard task of saboteur.

I remember well one event in particular. It happened in early November 1943. The company had used all the explosives at its disposal. Only seven kilograms were left, enough for one demolition operation. So far, we had accounted for ninety-six blown-up trains and had a strong desire to show a hundred for the October celebrations. But how to do that? We decided to switch over to using one-kilogram mines. Such mines were usually laid on the tracks a short time before the approach of a train, a highly dangerous operation to the life of a saboteur. One ship would mean premature explosion. We used these mines to blow up three more trains. The blowing up of the hundredth was entrusted to partisan Sobolyev. But he did not succeed. After the mine had been laid, something went wrong and it exploded. His entire left hand was lost, along with four fighers of his right hand.

Only a few days remained to the celebrations of the October Revolution. The honor of blowing up the hundredth German train fell to Yudovich. Under cover of darkness he went to the specified spot. Back at the camp we waited for Yudovich with mounting impatience. At long last he appeared. He approached us with the long-familiar glint in his eyes. The comrades surrounded him and congratulated each other on the hundredth enemy train, a present to the saboteurs and the entire company in honor of the celebrations.

This account of Simon Yudovich may well be concluded by an outline of his character in combat: in the course of the partisan company's struggle, Yudovich proved to be a patriot loyal to his fatherland; he took part in many battles against the fascist invaders and himself accounted for seventeen dead Germans. In fighting he showed courage, fearlessness, and leadership.

As commissar of the sabotage platoon, Yudovich often led the sabotage operations on the railway tracks. He himself derailed eleven German trains containing soldiers and equipment. His sabotage work accounted for eleven engines, seventy-six railway carriages full of soldiers and equipment, and over 320 killed and wounded German soldiers and officers. In addition, he took part in destroying fourteen German trains carrying soldiers and equipment on the tracks running between Kovel and Rovno, in the western Ukraine.

COMMISSAR NAUM FELDMAN

A. Pismenny

When Naum Feldman was fourteen years old, he left Zhuravichi, the small town in which he was born, and went to the town of Gomel in White Russia. Even then he was a good tailor and thus was soon to find work at the shop of a local craftsman. After the October Revolution, Feldman began a new life. He dedicated his life to the skilled-workers movement and began to study. Before long he joined the Bolshevik party.

In 1918 the Germans occupied White Russia and the Ukraine. Huge fires lit the skies over the small towns and the villages, and the blood of peaceful citizens flowed like water. Feldman joined a partisan company together with a group of Gomel inhabitants and soldiers who had come from the front. The company was formed in the village of Fedorovka (region of Gomel), and there its headquarters were set up; hence its name: the "Fedorovian Partisan" Company. Its commander was a former railway worker, Yakovlev. In those early days the partisan struggle was still taking its first steps, but the Fedorovian company, which numbered only forty men, struck hard at enemy installations. It was in this company that Feldman acquired the experience that he would need many years later.

When the Red Army started to get organized, Feldman volunteered, joined the First Gomelian Proletarian Battalion, and took part in the battles on the western front. Later on he was to reach Warsaw along with the Soviet cavalry corps.

More than twenty years passed. It was now 1941. The great war of the fatherland had begun. The enemy was at the gates of Minsk. In the backyard of the house where Feldman lived, there was a gathering of neighbors and friends. The weather was hot, and the air was filled with the smoke of the numerous fires that were raging around. The rolling of artillery fire was coming nearer and nearer. All were apprehensive of what the next hour might bring. Feldman said: "Anyone not connected with the defense of the town must leave Minsk for Moscow immediately on the main road."

Along the wide asphalt road they walked, ashen with struggle, thirsty for water, carrying on their shoulders packages of meager household utensils. Enemy planes zoomed fast above them, and the thousands of wandering refugees — women children, and old men marched on the burning asphalt. When dawn broke, they were approaching Borisov. At the same time the Germans dropped paratroopers, thus block in the way of the escaping refugees.

With the passage of time Feldman was to witness many formidable events, but this first encounter with the enemy left an indelible mark on his memory. The Germans fired indiscriminately at the defenseless people. They killed old men, women, and children. When the carnage had subsided, they gathered the survivors and forced them to run back to Minsk.

Feldman survived. When the firing started, he had jumped into a ditch. He had crawled to some shrubs along the road and escaped into the nearby forest. As a veteran partisan he immediately began to think of fighting the enemy and the need to rally the people and get them organized in partisan companies. Naum Feldman returned to Minsk. For some days he went into hiding in the home of a friend. To appear on the street was out of the question: many people would recognize him. In those days the Hitlerites issued an order that all men between the ages of sixteen and fifty had to have their names registered. Feldman did not show up for registration. One day he secretly went out of the street to find out who had remained in the town. He was caught by a German guard and sent to a concentration camp. At first this camp was in a faraway cemetery not far from Minsk. Later the partisans were moved to Drozdy, where the garbage dumping grounds had previously been. And from Drozdy, they were taken to the Minsk ghetto.

Feldman knew many of his fellow prisoners in the fenced-off neighborhood, and he looked for men ready for the struggle ahead. He was to find them. The Party's underground committee in the ghetto was composed of sixteen comrades. Its secretary was Naum Feldman.

With the help of ghetto people whom the Germans took out to work in the town, Feldman and his friends succeeded in establishing contact with the workers of the Voronov printing house. The latter called a meeting between the underground group and a printer who worked at the German department. Through this printer they got type, paper, ink, and the parts of a printing press. The thirst for true information was so great, and the ghetto people were in such a pressing need for a live word, that the underground group decided first to put out a bulletin.

In October 1941 a meeting took place between Komsomol member Kaplan and the writer Smolyar, a brave and experienced man of the underground. Kaplan introduced Feldman to Smolyar. Before long the ghetto underground group had established contact with the Party underground committee in Minsk and willingly accepted its authority.

But even before contact was established with the Feldman group in the ghetto, working relations had been established between the town committee of the Party and the partisan companies operating in the forests around Minsk. These companies were in need of aid and support. They needed men, clothing, and medicines. The underground committee suggested that the Feldman group provide equipment for the partisan companies. In many workshops Feldman had supportes who rallied to the call of the underground people. The wallets of the workers served for hiding medicines, bandages, pieces of cloth, and the like.

In accordance with the instructions of Smolyar and instructor Michael Gebelev, men were taken secretly out of the ghetto to join the partisan companies. Arms were also collected from the inhabitants and smuggled to the partisans. Some of the arms were captured from the Germans. But all this was not enough for Feldman. Together with Communist Joseph Lapidot, he decided to set up a new partisan company.

In the beginning it was necessary to set up a base in one of the neighboring forests for the company in the making. During the long nights of the fall, he thought the plan through. For the first reconnaissance Feldman picked out fifteen men, putting them under the command of his son, Victor, who was only sixteen years old.

The group left the ghetto unharmed, but the reconnaissance operation did not succeed. For about one week Victor and his men wandered about in the region of Dukora, only to return without having accomplished anything. But the lack of success did not weaken Feldman's will. In the ghetto there were rumors that strong partisan companies operated somewhere in the regions of Zaslavl and Koidanovo.

"We must first set up a base close to them," thought Feldman, and once again sent his son out on reconnaissance.

But now he sent along with him a young woman, Natasha Lifshitz. Before the outbreak of the war, Natasha had been studying in the ninth form. Now she was to be revealed as a daring young woman who soon adapted to the hard and dangerous task of a ground scout. Lately she had gone thrice on missions to Minsk. On one of these missions she was caught by the Gestapo, but she bluffed her way out. She took them along to a house where she told them she lied. She knew that the house had a backyard open on both sides. She slipped away through this backyard, leaving the Gestapo guarding the entrance...

Natasha first accompanied Victor on a reconnoitering mission when they both were still inexperienced. For five days they kept looking for the partisan groups — in vain. They returned to the ghetto empty-handed. Upon hearing that the Pokrovsky company was active beyond Dukora, Feldman once again sent out three men: Komsomol member Ovrutsky, vivacious and liked by one and all, along with Pesin and Tyumin. They had succeeded in reaching the village of Lushitzi when they came upon a company of policemen. Battle broke out between the two unequal forces, and two ground scouts were killed. Wounded Tyumin buried himself in a heap of snow and some time later made it to the ghetto.

However, the unsuccessful attempt did not weaken Feldman's determination to move his men out of the ghetto. He went about making further preparations with greater thoroughness. Despite the alertness of the Hitlerite guards, people left the ghetto on the tenth of April, heading ostensibly for their daily chores, under the leadership of Commander Israel Lapidot and Commissar Feldman. On reaching the road to Slutsk, the people divided into groups. Some time before, guides had been posted along the road to show them the way. Thus, by being passed from one guide to another, they found their way to their destination in the distant forest.

The group headed by Feldman consisted of twenty men. They had gathered together, surmounted all the difficulties, and were only a few steps from the meeting with the second part of the group, led by Lapidot. Then, all of a sudden, German mounted guards loomed up, charged at the Jews, and killed sixteen of them. Feldman was forced to go back to the ghetto with the few men who had survived the attack.

What spiritual strength, what self-control and persistence were required of Feldman so that he should not sink into despair in the face of all the losses and failures. Since Feldman did not succeed in establishing contact with Lapidot and his group, he once again met with Smolyar and members of the underground committee of the Party in that town. This time the committee took it upon itself to see that the men were taken out of the ghetto. At kilometer nine, the Feldman group was met by experienced guides who directed the men to the forest of Staroye Selo, where the company base was to be set up.

There were neither tents nor earth huts. Everything had to be built from scratch. At the same time, the people started their combat training. Till the end of May 1942 the Feldman company was busy collecting arms, preparing provisions, going on reconnaissance missions, and establishing friendly relations with the inhabitants of the surrounding villages. That area was the fighting grounds of other partisan companies as well. Sometimes the Feldman partisans would join them and have their first taste of battle against the enemy.

The relations with the ghetto and the urban committee became stronger and more viable. More peole joined Feldman's company. On the first anniversary of the war, on June 22, 1942, the underground committee sent Simon Grigoryevich Ginzenko to the Feldman company. Wounded, he had been taken prisoner by the Germans and brought back by Natasha Lifshitz. Ginzenko was appointed company commander and Feldman company commissar. Firing in the woods never ceased, and Ginzenko taught the men how to shoot. Feldman, Ginzenko, and their friends began to make careful preparations for their first combat mission. For this eventuality the company had already gathered some sixty rifles, eight machine guns and countless cartridges and grenades.

Shortly before the attack was mounted, Feldman went around the camp and told his friends: "Well, brothers, tonight we go out on the road. The saying goes that every beginning is hard, but we shall come through all right."

On the grounds of a former *kolkhoz*, not far from Koidanovo, the Germans had set up a large ranch. It was decided to destroy this ranch. In it was stationed a very strong garrison. In three groups the partisans closed in on the German stronghold. Ginzenko gave the sign by firing his pistol, and the waves of partisans charged at the enemy. The German garrison was taken. Some time later, after the ranch had been re-taken and rebuilt by the Germans, it was once again attacked by Ginzenko and Feldman.

The partisans later launched several attacks on the German farm near Rakov, and many times they derailed German military trains, drove back convoys, and wiped out garrisons in villages and small towns. The company, having been honed to a sharp edge in constant fighting now bore the name of the indefatigable Budyonny.

In mid-1943 the Feldman-Ginzenko company received a large shipment of explosives. Now it was possible to carry out sabotage operations on a much large scale.

It was the beginning of 1944. Along the entire front the Red Army was chasing the retreating enemy forces. Before the attack on Minsk, it was necessary to cut off all railway communications on the tracks running between Stolbtsy and Koidanovo. The high command entrusted this task to a brigade named after Stalin.

In three companies the partisans set out for the railway tracks. The Feldman-Ginzenko company found a base for itself in the forest of Ivenets after it had covered fifty-eight kilometers in a single day. In the evening the Feldman-Ginzenko men arrived at the predetermined spot. From a distance they could see a German convoy, consisting of tanks and other heavy equipment. They had no time to mine the tracks. They had to act fast and wipe out the convoy at any price. Feldman gave the order, "After me!" Grenade in hand, he ran out to the tracks to meet the convoy. Anti-tank grenades flew in the direction of the engine. Until this encounter Feldman had accounted for fourteen blown-up convoys. This one would be the fifteenth. The heavy German engine was blown from the tracks, followed by the carriages, one after the other. The entire tracks were demolished.

The Feldman company kept up the fight until all of White Russia was liberated from enemy forces. In the course of its military operations the company accounted for over 2,500 dead Hitlerites and hundreds of derailed enemy railway carriages.

THE LERMONTOV COMPANY

S. Davydovsky

In September 1942, after the German hordes had reached Stalingrad and driven a wedge in the foothills of the Caucasus Mountains, a company named after Lermontov mounted a heroic attack on the large village of Kamennomostskoye in the Kabardinsky region. The partisans crossed the Malka River, stormed the village, and drove the German garrison out. The company blew up the command of the German tank unit and carried out other important operations. In the village streets and on the shores of the Malka River were strewn some four hundred German corpses.

The razing of Kamennomostskoye, which lay at an important crossroad near the front, caused much worry to the Germans. They sent punishment squads after the partisans.

The twenty-fifth anniversary of the 1917 October Revolution drew near. To celebrate the day, partisan groups, along with the Lermontov company, launched an attack on the populated center of Khabaz, forty kilometers from Kislovodsk, where there was a German transit base. The attack was of course preceded by large-scale reconnoitering missions. Besides the Lermontov company the partisan companies of Novoselitskoye and Baksan areas were involved. The access to Khabaz was so difficult that the mounted partisans had to reach the place on foot.

On the night of November 2, 1942, the partisans, holding onto each other's hands, descended the jagged slopes leading to Khabaz. They split into three groups and, on reaching the predetermined spot, opened fire. The Germans first pinned the partisans down with machine guns and mortar fire. Then, at the head of a partisan group, Company Commander Grigory Davydov stormed the German command. Shouting "Halt!" at the German sentry, he killed him with a pistol shot. On the roof of the command building there was a group of

German officers. Some ten anti-tank shells were enough to blow up the entire command building.

The fighting went on for over two hours. The German garrison was wiped out. On the walls of the houses the partisans hung handwritten leaflets devoted to the twenty-fifth anniversary of the October Revolution. The leaflets asked the population to keep up the struggle against the Germans and closed with the words: "We have struck at the invaders. We are striking at them now and will keep on striking at them till they are wiped out completely." A short time later German reinforcements arrived. They were made up of a sniper unit which pushed our company back. In this battle, machine-gunner Vanya Kussinko was outstanding in the hits he scored. He was wounded four times. Sixteen-year-old girl partisan Motya, who until the outbreak of the war had been working at the molybdenum complex, lifted the wounded partisan and carried him on her back for a distance of two kilometers. Other outstanding comrades were Alexander Romanenko, Fedor Bogatov, Prokofy Kolesnikov, and partisans who had taken part in the Russian civil war following World War I. The partisans laid mines in the way of the retreating Germans and later hid in one of the ravines.

For one whole day the Germans combed the valleys, the paths, and the mountains, but they could not find the partisans. In order to launch the attack, the company had to cover some 200 kilometers on the way to Khabaz on such steep mountains as Mt. Kinzhal, Mt. Koshtantau, and Mt. Katyn-Tau, close behind the German front. In their ascent the partisans held on to the tails of their horses, and in the descent they used ropes and belts. The conditions beame extremely bad at the foothills of the Caucasus Mountains. The region of the Baksan ravine contained a large population which was forced to leave with some 40,000 sheep and goats and a huge amount of ore: wolfram and molybdenum. All that could have fallen into the hands of the enemy. The Germans occupied the vehicle storehouse and dug in on the slopes of the Elbrus. After they had established control over the population centers of Zayukovo and Kyondelen, they tightened their siege of the ravine in Baksan. There was only one way out: to overcome the snow passages at Daut, Balk-Bashi, and Khurzuk, which are nearly impassible in winter. After two days of efforts to hold their ground no the summit of a cliff, the men started their descent. During this passage it was essential to keep proper distance between the men. The fall of one into the abyss would bring others along with him. Close watch had to be kept over the movement of snow masses. In this manner, for five days and nights, some 20,000 people were to pass through these treacherous regions — one long, endless chain of partisans and local inhabitants who had left their settlements. The company covered fifty kilometers in these ravines and descended to Svanetiya. From this point the partisans went into Megreliya, then to Kizlyar, and the outlying territory behind enemy lines.

In Kizlyar, Grigory Davydov-Koltunov was appointed leader of the southern group of the partisan company. This group was assigned the task of destroying the unpaved roads and the enemy communication lines on the railway tracks of Ordzhnikidze. After many battles between the partisans and the Cossak armies (probably the traitorous Cossak troops that collaborated with the German forces), the partisan commander wrote: "These men fight like lions." The fighting took place under extremely difficult conditions, on the sands of the Kizlyar steppes.

The Lermontov company was international in its composition. Shoulder-to-shoulder fought Russians, Kabardians, Armenians, and Jews. Among the fighters were many who belonged to the independent professions. Outstanding in battle was the engineer Urshavsky and the professor at the local spa, Andreyev. Despite his age, Andreyev never parted from his rifle.

Of particular interest is the biography of company commander Grigory Davydov-Koltunov. As a child he had studied in the *cheder*[5], in the town of Starodub in the district of Chernigov. In his adolescence he graduated from a drama school and for some time acted in a Jewish theater. Later, he was director of the arts department in the district of Ivanovka.

THE COMMANDER OF THE BOEVOI UNIT

V. Gerasimova

Leningrad is the city of a myriad of heroic exploits. It has been entered in the annals of the great war of the fatherland as a unique city, whose millions of inhabitants hovered between life and death for over two years. People in years to come will continue to extol the rave inhabitants of this important city its glorious fighters, and the faultless men of the Red Navy.

But there was another force, another brilliant army, whose exploits are worthy of being entered in the book of glory concerning Lenin's city; the partisan force in the Leningrad region. It was the men belonging to this force, in those dark days when the destiny of this large city was being determined, who neutralized large enemy forces by holding them in a tight vise of partisan warfare, bled them to exhaustion with their iron will and resourcefulness, undermined their morale, and annihilated them. Suffice it to say that in order to fight the partisan companies operating in the Leningrad region, the Germans had to throw some 40,000 of their elite troops into the battle, particularly in the decisive days of the fight to capture the city. At the time apparentl, almost the entire region was in the hands of the occupation forces. It seemed that at the outskirts of the northern capital, Hitler's men were about to begin their victory celebrations. These celebrations, which they so eagerly looked forward to, had been hysterically hailed by the fascists' newspapers, heaflets, and broadcasts. But those very fascists, with their premature bragging, kept asking apprehensively: What are the partisans up to in the region of Khvoynaya? Of Pestovo? What region would they capture now? Where is the Boevoi company operating at present? And Grozny company, where is it?

In all these grim and disquieting questions that the Germans asked about the intentions and actions of the partisans, one name kept recurring on their lips, the name of Partisan Commander Boevoi – Dmitry Ivanovich Novakovsky.

Now, after the war, when you see Dmitry Novakovsky at the head of a large industrial plant in the Soviet Union, in his spacious and well-lighted office at a large desk, it is difficult to visualize him in the partisan struggle, with his thick growth of hair, yellowish beard, leather coat, and fur cap. That is how he looked in those days, which were not so long ago.[6] Behind this man lie years of hard fighting, interminable shortages, hunger, cold, sleepless nights. And now he sits, a very quiet man, bright-eyed, clean-shaven, smiling.

Engineer Novakovsky began his military career in the early days of the war. In those days he had already decided to join the ranks of those who fought behind enemy lines. Before long this quiet man of the industrial sector, who had been born in the region of Chernigov, was to make his appearance in the woods and the marshes of the forbidding northern district. But the man was strong of spirit and did not give in to the hardships of the bleak environment. As a Bolshevik, he showed no weakness even for a single moment.

In the beginning only a few dozen people belonged to the company commanded by Novakovsky. But with the expansion of its combat activities, more men joined its ranks, especially after the local inhabitants came to realize that Novakovsky was their staunch defendant. Hundreds of people flocked to him: people who had left downtrodden and ruined villages or had escaped from enemy-occupied towns. But in order to win the full confidence of the local people and to serve as an emblem of persistent struggle against the invaders, the company had to wage further battles against greatly superior numbers of enemy forces, battles of glory and heroic exploits.[7]

Even in the early days of its formation, the Boevoi company, then numbering only about eighty men, attacked a German punishment squad made up of 400 men. This disparity in numbers between the two fighting sides called for a high degree of resourcefulness, courage, skill, and even cunning on the part of the partisans, as physical strength alone would not suffice. There was a need for a great measure of sacrifice and even self-effacement, a quality which characterized the people of the Boevoi company under their commander. That was the first encounter of a company made up a newly formed fighters with an enemy armed to the teeth.

The operation was set for the twenty-fourth anniversary of the Red Army.

This brilliant operation, carried out on a pitch-dark February night in 1942 according to the plan drawn up by Novakovsky and under his command, is interesting for its combination of cool calculation and revolutionary, passionate courage. And that, in effect, was a characteristic feature of Novakovsky's spiritual makeup.

News had reached the company that the German command was sending a large punishment squad to the region of the village of Tyurikovo. The company had also learned of the task that had been assigned to this squad: "To burn down villages and ruthlessly wipe out the entire population, including the children." The partisans also learned that the punishment squad would be under the command of the tyrant hangman Fashisky, who had become notorious for the acts of cruelty he had perpetrated in White Russia and the Ukraine. The partisans refrained from direct encounters with the numerically superior forces. Then the fighting started with a trivial and unexpected act, though it showed a great measure of self-control and resourcefulness.

It happened that nine armed German soldiers were approaching a barn full of hay, carrying pitchforks on their shoulders, to get some fodder. In the same barn were a number of partisans, including Novakovsky. A single shot would have alerted the entire area. Apparently there was no way out. The commander whispered an order to catch the fascists. We lay there waiting. "When the Germans came near, we caught them without a single shot," reminisced Novakovsky with a broad smile on his face. We extracted from the Germans detailed information about the deployment of the punishment squad in the village of Tyurikovo. They also divulged the information that the squad would start its attack on the following day. Last but not least, they gave the partisans the password to Tyurikovo, "Pan Shpitsky."

Novakovsky found that he could not afford to lose a single moment. He had to strike at the Germans while they were still unfamiliar with the place and could be taken by surprise. In the evening the partisans tore up a white overall, tied on their sleeves white arm bands similar to those worn by the

German police, and went out on carts to Tyurikovo. To the sentry's challenge of "Halt!" they answered, "Pan Shpitsky." Thus the partisans could get into the village. Once inside, they quietly deployed for the next move, as they knew where to find the enemy. Novakovsky went to the schoolhouse which, according to the information supplied by the partisan scouts, housed the command of the garrison. The men in this building had not gone to sleep. Novakovsky tossed an anti-tank grenade through the window. According to the predetermined plan, that was the sign his comrades had been waiting for. The village shook under the noise of explosions. The barracks went up on flames. Desperate howls, shrieks, and curses shouted in a foreign language came from inside the smoke and flames. The Germans who attempted to escape from the burning houses were cut down by the well-aimed partisan bullets — the wounded were killed with the butts of the rifles. The commander of the punishment squad, "Pan Shpitsky," whose name had been of such a great help to the company, was captured alive.

In this first battle, the Boevoi company killed some 200 Germans and took fifty-two prisoners. Its booty was also sizable: field guns, machine guns, vehicles, radio transmitters, etc.

The news flashed through the villages and small towns of the Leningrad area: "Our men are striking at the German beasts." But that was only the "first swallow." Following the fighting in the village of Tyurikovo there came an attack on the village of Siverskaya and others on the villages of Stanki, Krutets, Zvanka, Pritchi, Kryazhi, etc.

Regular army battalions were often aided by the partisans. On one occasion, the enemy attacked a Soviet army battalion stationed at the village of Krutets. The battalion was greatly outnumbered, and through the situation was desperate, the fighters and their commanders heroically repulsed the enemy attacks. When the Boevoi company heard of this, it outflanked the attacking German unit and, just when the Germans were drunk with the prospect of the approaching victory, landed a sudden blow on them. The Germans threw down their weapons and beat a disorderly retreat.

Forged by the fire of continued fighting against the Germans, the feeling of partisan brotherhood became stronger in the company from day to day. Surrounded by the enemy, separated from the "Big Land" (Russia), the partisans came to the rescue of each other at the risk of their own lives. Novakovsky could thus be found carrying his best friend and military aide in his arms and donating blood to him. Prokhorov, his daring friend, was to save Novakovsky from certain death on many other occasions. An outstanding feeling of brotherhood tied together these two courageous men...

Cruel are the laws of war. The struggle against the enemy called for great sacrifices. When the company attacked the village of Zuevka, the first to charge was the platoon commanded by Kozhornin. This unit wanted to carry out the task it had been given, to burn down the storehouse with all its military equipment and to kill the general staff. The Germans attempted to pin the partisans down with hand grenades and machine-gun fire. Nevertheless, the mission was carried out; both the storehouse and the German command went up in flames. But the redoubtable commander, Kozhurkin, was fatally wounded and died on the battlefield.

Novakovsky's fearless comrades went shoulder to shoulder with him into battle. His consistent and firm willpower forged them into one united fighting force. His close friends were Prokhorov, Kozhurkin, Belozyorov, Nikitin, Petrov, and Lavrentyev. His name and those of his aides will ever be dear and close to the hearts of the *kolkhoz* farmers in the region of Leningrad.

The Germans burned down the village of Pritchi for its relations with the partisans. But the latter were soon to get into the outpost that the Germans had built on the ruins of the village, where they apparently felt secure. The avengers of the people threw antitank grenades at the outpost, and the village that the Germans had burned down became their own burial ground.

In celebration of the Red Army anniversary, the German garrison at the village of Tiyrikovo was wiped out. In honor of the First of May, the partisans struck at the German

garrison in the village of Kryazhi. On that international holiday of the workers, the dauntless fighters accomplished many
heroic exploits.

* * * * *

In the woods and the marshes of the Leningrad region, the
"victorious" Germans were being constantly harassed by the
partisans. In only two months and ten days — from the 20th a
of February to the 30th of April 1942 — the Boevoi company led seven sorties against the enemies and killed a great
many German soldiers.

During this same period, sabotage groups blew up the
railway tracks running between the stations of Vyazye-M.T.
Sakh and Shimsk-Porkhov, derailed a German military train
between the stations of Morino and Polonka, cut telephone
communications on the line connecting Pritchi to Gorky, and
captured a great deal of booty and many storehouses.

Here is an excerpt from a letter found in the pocket of a
killed German soldier:

"We are fighting in the heart of partisan country. It is my
duty to tell you that many friends who arrived here with me
are now among the dead or wounded. It is better to be at the
front than here. There I know the distance separating us from
the enemy. Here the enemy is everywhere; he is all around us;
he is watching us from every nook and cranny; and his bullets
usually find their targets."

Thus were the Germans, who had lorded it over the area,
to feel the punishing hand of the partisans. As for the local
peasants, they could get both aid and protection from them.
Communists Novakovsky did not spare any opportunity to
prove to the peasants that he was their faithful protector,
theirs and that of their cause. On one occasion, word got to
the company that the fascist robbers had entered a village
lying in partisan territory and had taken all the livestock
and poultry. The company, headed by one of its commanders, soon arrived at the scene, wiped out the robbers, and
returned all the loot, down to the last chicken, to the owners.
This incident was illustrated in the cartoon that appeared in
Boevoi's own newspaper, drawn by the young and talented

partisan Nikitin, depicting birds flying out of the laps of dead Fritzes (Germans).

* * * * *

All the facts concerning the murders perpetrated by the Germans were thoroughly examined by the company. Evidence of torture, murder, and theft was entered in special certificates signed by partisan representatives and the *kolkhoz* people. Here is one such certificate concerning the cruel acts of the fascists, as written down at the scene of the crime:

We, the undersigned, have written this certificate concerning the murderous acts of the German fascists in the village of Karpovo. The certificate has been written by Molin, head of special platoon of the Boevoi company; Nikitin, head of the general staff; Petrov, member of Krasny Oktyabr *kolkhoz*; Fedor Petrov, Michael Grigoryev, and Yevdokya Petrova:

On the night of the April 1st, a group of robbers belonging to the SS punishment squad broke into the village of Karpovo, headed by German officers. They found the inhabitants fast asleep and set fire to all the houses and other buildings in that place. In addition, they mounted a machine gun and opened fire up and down the village. Besides their barbarian acts they killed the woman Marfa Vasilyeva, aged sixty-five, and fifty-one-year-old Michael Gavrilov. The entire village, comprising twelve houses, was burned down. The survivors of this brutal massacre are now leading a life of poverty; they are living in three wooden bath houses..."

(Signed)
Head of the Special Platoon of the Boevoi Company
Chief of Staff
Kolkhoz Members

These criminal acts did not go without reprisals. With firmness and ingenuity the partisans picked out the traitors among the local inhabitants, an operation which called for a large measure of equability and self-restraint. Novakovsky recalled how partisans dressed as German officers came to a village head, who was a traitor. It was necessary to finish off this traitor quickly, for he knew the hiding place of the partisan company. On seeing these German officers on this friendly visit, the head of the village offered his services to these "officer masters" and accompanied them to the path in the woods that led to the partisan headquarters. Needless to say, this was his last trip.

The bewilderment of the traitor's wife increased when, some hours after her husband had gone out with the "German officers," there came the Germans whom the head of the village had promised to show the way leading to the partisans. They had arrived too late. The man who could have shown them the way lay dead in a secluded path in the woods. The partisans applied the same treatment to other traitors.

All these activities enhanced the authority that the company wielded over the local population. Like a lodestone, the company drew to its ranks the best of the village people who were suffering under the yoke of occupation in the Leningrad region. The company soon grew to such proportions that it was necessary to divide it into units according to regions. Along with the stepped-up momentum of the attacks the company launched against the Germans, there came the idea of setting up a partisan territory under Soviet rule behind enemy lines. In the summer of 1942, the partisans drove the Germans out of this vast area, which comprised about 2,000 villages. The Germans were forced to evacuate all the points they had captured in this territory. On the soil thus cleansed from German filth there streamed once again the usual Soviet way of life. Here, behind enemy lines, returned the *kolkhozes*, the schools, the activities concerned with information and culture; newspapers and leaflets. In addition, an unbelievable operation under German occupation was carried out by Novakovksy: through the front line he sent about 200 carts laden with food supplies to the beleaguered city of Leningrad. On the way, many carts joined the expedition. Everyone tried to add something, the last onion, the last egg, but the main thing was "to send food to the people of Leningrad," Novakovsky was to sum up later.

Such was this Company Commander Novakovsky, a commander who generated respect and faith and allowed the people to participate in his exploits. This approach gave him the strength and courage to go through difficult situations with unflagging zeal. Once, while saving himself from the Germans who had suddenly appeared nearby, he was to wander in the woods, lightly dressed and seriously wounded, for twelve days, tired out, hungry, and frozen with cold. But he held his own in the face of death.

In these modest words Comrade Novakovsky said of himself, "I was born to a working Jewish family. My father learned to read and write by himself, thus remaining uneducated for the rest of his life. The outside world was an invincible barrier to him. He led a hard life, a life of degeneration; but we, his children, are doing creative work which is both interesting and valuable. My brothers work at large aircraft industries, and my sister is a newswoman."

But I am not speaking of my own lot," adds Novakovsky, "or of the fate of my relatives, although even in this is reflected all that is new and important in human life in our country. When I saw burned-down villages, tortured children, violated women, I realized and kept in mind only one thing: it is worthwhile to sacrifice everything so that all this should never happen again; so that emancipated humanity should never allow the warmongers to raise their heads. Of all this I thought when I saw with my friends around a campfire in the depths of the forest or when I hid within impassable marshland. These were also the thoughts that passed through the minds of my fellow partisans who took part in the national war."

EDITOR'S NOTES

[1]This short biographical sketch is taken from the *Soviet Encyclopedia*, 1951 edition.

[2]The civil war in Russia after the October 1917 revolution. The "Whites" or "Belaya Gvardiya" supported the Czar; the "Greens" were Anarchist forces.

[3]Komsomol was the youth group of the Communist Party.

[4]Latvian collaborators.

[5]Jewish day school.

[6]This was written in 1948.

[7]Again, one must understand the minor exaggeration that the "heroic style" of these memoirs engenders.

PART TWO

JEWISH PARTISANS
IN VOLYN AND POLESIA, UKRAINE
1941-1944

IN THE FAMILY CAMP
UNDER MAX'S COMMAND

Pesel Librant (Bronstein)

Long before the first "action,"[1] an attempt to organize
and flee to the woods was made. Once, by chance, in Asher
Halperin's house, in the restaurant downstairs, I ran into
a group of men: Asher Halperin, Shmerel Paul, Avraham
Slivka, my husband, Zev, and others. They did not allow
me to be present at the meeting. I asked my husband for an
explanation, and he told me that they were planning to escape
together with the boys, without women. I told him the children and I wanted to accompany him. To my sorrow nothing
came of this escape plan. Most were captured during the first
action, and the rest of the 370 Jews were shot in the "Horses'
Graves."[2] A miracle happened to my husband — he wasn't
captured.

My husband, my son, and my brother worked in the sawmill next to the woods, and they began to plan an escape.
On the last Friday before the liquidation of the ghetto, my
husband and son parted from me and from my other three
children. Bitter crying began. "Why us? Why do we have to
die?" My husband hugged them and said, "Please don't cry,
children. You are dear to me, and I will not abandon you."
And, indeed, he went to the sawmill with my oldest son,
Yaakov, and returned home the same night. Meanwhile, there
was a commotion on our street. Jews were being rounded
up from every street. Representatives of the *Judenrat* also
appeared and said, "This is the end for us all."

My husband began looking for separate hiding places for
each one of the children. One could grab onto the huge tree
in the yard, one could go underneath the stairway. I was
against this and said that we had to hide together, and we
started to go up on the roof. We lay stretched out motionless,
and all we heard was the forced gathering together, amidst
beating and cursing, of the Jews in the street.

The next day (on Shabbat), at dawn, I went down with my son Yaakov, who hadn't left me and I saw them assembling the Jews amidst shouts and threats; gradually thee was quiet in the street. We hard until late at night only the drunken voices of the Ukrainian and Polish murderers who were celebrating their victory by drinking whiskey. Suddenly, we heard whispers, "Pesel, Pesel," and it was Faygeh Puchtik (Merin)[3] who had been hiding inside a cask in the stable; she came with us up on the roof. Later we heard a little girl's cry and the cry of Itka Rozenfeld, who was led off by the police. They had been hiding but were discovered. Itka tried to calm her small daughter. "This is our fate," she said.

The next day at four A.M. at dawn, we climbed down from the roof and began to leave the town. We crawled across the railroad tracks and went into the woods. We hid among the bushes the entire day. In the evening, on the way to the house of Slovik, the Polish forester, we met a farmer from the village of Manevichi who was amazed that we had been able to escape. He gave us a piece of bread, but we greatly feared that he'd hand us over to the police force.

Upon our arrival at Slovik's home, barking dogs confronted us and Slovik came out to meet us. He did not tell us that there were other Jews hiding at his place; only later did we see my brother Shmuel's daughter, Dvorah Sherman, who had managed to escape. And also, there were Chava and Hershel Kuperberg and their daughter, Raizel. They had been hiding in a farmer's attic. (The Germans searched there, stabbed around with their bayonets, and injured the girl.)

At sunset Slovik led us to a shed in the middle of the woods, where we would stay through the night. In the morning my brother-in-law, Dov, and another person arrived and took us to the woods.

At the place to which we were led, we met the Michal Brat family with their four children, the Shmaryahu Guz family with their two children, and the two sisters Dinah and Dvorah Zilbershtein. Slovik instructed us to remain in the place throughout the day. In the evening he brought us to another hiding place. When I wanted to know why he was transferring us from one place to another, he replied, "You must believe me, if I had not transferred you, you would have

been caught. Because the police searched your hiding places."
He allowed us to collect potatoes from his fields and warned
us not to take any from other fields.

With the passing of time, after many hardships and prolonged wanderings, during the rainy and snowy seasons, we
were brought to the camp that was next to Max's fighting
unit.

The Organization of the Family Camp

Max's family camp was separate from the fighting unit,
about four kilometers from it. The guard duty and internal
schedules were set up in accordance with the partisan commanders. Avraham Puchtik served as the camp's commander.[4]

I remember an incident from a time I was on guard duty
with "rifles," with Yankeleh Guz, when a reconnaissance unit
from the fighting units — Kartukhin's, Nasekin's, and Max's
— started to approach our camp on horseback. When we
heard that riders were approaching, we called to them to halt,
and we asked them for identification. They were favorably
impressed by this manner of guard duty, and they mentioned
us in their dispatches. Standing on guard duty was an obliga-
tion or all those who could use weapons, women, men, and
youths over the age of twelve.

The first stage of our getting organized continued for four
months, and we were sustained by pilfering from the fields
and cellars of the Polish peasants. One day, partisans from
Max's unit came by and told us that we had to move to the
woods by the village. One peasant was supposed to give us
shelter for a while, until we reached the woods. But the peasant left us in the forester's house (it was winter) without food
and frozen from the cold. Only after ten days did Itka and
Rachel Brat arrive with two partisans who brought us bread
and led us to the partisan camp. We did not know the camp's
routine, and we began to "get organized," cooking potatoes,
etc. And then Max appeared and started shouting: "All misery
is on my head!" and ordered our removal from the camp.

They began to look for a suitable place for us, and they
"settled us" on a piece of ground amidst swamp and marshes.
We started digging bunkers. Water began streaming into
them. We covered the walls with cowhide.

Gradually the camp became productive: a herd of cows and oxen grazed — a source for meat and milk; we prepared young pig meat and smoked meat sausages that we gave out to the camp and to the partisans. We had bread and made toast for them. For me civilian camp then was without any shortages.

The family camp's residents would go out to the fields of those peasants who were liquidated, according to a list by the partisans, and would harvest and gather the produce from their fields and gardens. The Jewish fighters would frequently come to the family camp, bringing with them clothing, food, and all kinds of goods that were important at that time. The young partisan men's attitude toward us, and especially toward the children, was warm and friendly. They, too, benefited in the camp from the homey atmosphere, which they needed so much. Here they changed sheets which we laundered for them and washed themselves in the bathtub that was set up in the *zemlaynka*.[5] After a short time, the camp was spotted by Germans who discovered it from their planes. We left the place. German tanks began to attack the camp, bomb it, but they didn't enter it. Upon our return we found the *zemlaynka* destroyed, but, amazingly, most of the cows survived, scattered about the woods and local villages.

During my entire stay in the woods, although I prepared dishes of sausages made out of pig meat, etc., I never tasted this meat. While I cooked I would tie a handkerchief around my mouth and had someone else taste the dish. I remember when we were moved from the woods to a fighters' camp, they cut up pieces of pig meat for everyone. Max found out that I didn't eat pig meat. He threatened that if he found a piece of pig meat in a dish he would kill me. The children go frightened and passed the piece of meat behind their backs when we were searched.

On Passover eve, 1943, we received flour from the partisans. We prepared dough and rolled it out with a bottle on a board and baked *matzah* on the campfire in a frying pan. The men *davened* by heart in a *minyan*.[6] During the entire holiday we prepared dishes from potatoes and didn't eat *chametz*.[7]

On Yom Kippur eve we made candles out of wax, using linen thread as a wick, and in this way we commemorated the memory of the martyrs. Mostly everyone fasted. That same

Yom Kippur I had given a jar of borsht and chopped meat to my twelve-year-old daughter, Zisel. She was then grazing the three hundred head of sheep. At dusk she brought all the food to me. "It's a commandment to fast on Yom Kippur," she said. We observed all the holidays in a special way, and prayers were said by heart, as much as possible.

I remember a Jewish refugee, one of the refugees from Manevichi, who got sick and died after he had received "treatment" from a peasant. The camp's Jews gave him a Jewish funeral and wrapped him in linen material for a shroud. Any piece of material like this was then a rare commodity. Several other Jews died, including Hershel Kuperberg and Kahat Finkel, who Max himself killed and then hid, as we didn't know for a long time that he had been murdered. His son, Avraham Finkel, searched a long time for him until he found him, shot.

Often we sat together at the campfire, telling stories about the past, and here and there would be a joke or a song in Yiddish, Polish, Ukrainian, or Russian. The youths and the children would begin, and the adults sometimes joined them. I remember Avraham Gorodetzer, who would sing songs in Yiddish filled with humor and joking, but he always ended with a sad song; then a silence would take over and gradually everyone left for a night's rest.

Children in the Camp
(For Avraham Merin, in blessed memory)

In our camp there were more than twenty children, the youngest three years old. They included children orphaned of both a father and a mother. These children, although they had "matured" and behaved as adults in every way, were in need of some "family care," such as bathing, haircuts, and more. (Shimon Mirochnik, who was in the fighting unit, brought me scissors from an "operation" as I had asked.) We cut their hair, and washed their clothes, and gave them showers in a bathtub set up with a barrel from above, with the water warmed up on a boiler. We women helped one another, knitting gloves, socks, and scarves. Chava Puchtik, especially, excelled at this. But, sadly, there were those who evaded all types of work.

It is especially worthwhile to mention Zisla Brat, who had a strong position, because her two daughters, Ida and Rachel, were in the fighters' camp. She took care of everyone, especially the orphan children, and demanded an equal share of the staples or clothing that the partisans, mainly the Jewish ones, brought for the camp's residents. I once heard her say to her partisan daughters: "Take care of the orphans. We, thank God, have a father who takes care of us."

I also remember the first "hot meal" (soup made out of flour), which she served us when we arrived at the woods, frightened and frozen from the cold.

I also remmber the good deeds of Avraham Merin, the son of Yosef and Mindel. He was the only one from his family to survive, and he reached our group after walking through the local woods and marshes with Zecharya Viner for a long time. (They were both killed, as soldiers in the Red Army, close to the victory day.)

One evening, as we sat frozen from the cold in a *zemlaynka*, he took of his jacket and covered my son with it, When I said to him, "Aren't you cold, too?" he replied, "It doesn't matter, these are small children and I'm able to tolerate it." Avraham excelled at preparing all kinds of medicines and ointments from plants. He actually saved my foot that had been completely swollen, with an ointment made out of pig fat and the sap of a pine tree. The ointment really worked wonders and helped many people who suffered from *chiryi*, pus-filled infections that resulted from our declining sanitary conditions.

Leaving the Woods and the Soviet Homeland —and Going Home!

In the winter of 1943, we got reinforcements for the camp. The Slovik family, headed by the Polish nobleman who had saved hundreds of Jews, was forced to leave its home, and came to our camp. First, Kapzik (Casimir), the son, arrived and then the entire Slovik family. It was thought that Slovik's deeds and actions had been followed for quite a while, but he was mainly forced to move because of the *Banderovtsy*, who harassed the Polish settlers.[8] We received them joyfully and with open arms. He and his family got along well with the Jews, who had only appreciation and gratitude for him.

(After the war the family received an agricultural farm from the Polish government and lived near the *otryad*[9] commander, Max, who rose to the rank of general and mayor.

We left the woods when the Red Army arrived in our region. Our house in Manevichi was burned down with the entire row of Jewish houses on our street. At the beginning of 1943, we had seen the flames of fire from the woods and were actually glad. We went to the nearby town of Rafalovka. We settled into the home of Simcha Brat, who had survived with his family, two daughters and a son; Michal and Zisel were also there with their four children, Itka, Rachel, Moshe, and Leah'la.

Once, late at night, when we were all sleeping closed up in the kitchen, we heard knocking on the door. We became very frightened. There had been many incidents of *Banderovtsy* murdering Jews who had returned from the woods. We were unable to indentify the voice. Was it that of my husband, Velvel, who had been conscripted into the army? Kola, the partisan, who was with us at that time, moved cautiously whith a weapon in his hand and opened the door. And there in the doorway stood a tall soldier on crutches. With difficulty, I saw that it was my brother-in-law, Avraham. The children at first were very frightened, but then became happy. I began to take care of him in order to rehabilitate him, physically and economically. His disability enabled him to move about freely on the roads and take "business" trips.

At the en of 1944 we succeeded in leaving, in a legal manner, for Chelm, Poland, as we wanted very much to go to Israel. We all went. Simcha Brat took provisions for the road — a cow and a harness of horses. I brought two sacks of flour.

We arrived in Atlit in November 1945.[10] We could breathe easily. We had finally, truly, come home. My family and I moved to Kibbutz Ramat HaChovesh. My daughter, Shoshana, joined a youth group at Kibbutz Yagur in Israel.

A Partisan's Testimony

David Blanstein

On Friday, 22 Elul, 5712, the night of the slaughter, I decided to lee from the town, come what may.[11]

I had previously heard that a number of Jews from Manevichi and Griva were already in the Borovno Woods, next to the villages of Lishnevka and Griva. I crossed the Lutsk direction, the main road, and the Sosnovka road — a road that went through Shlomo Verba's yard.

Zev Verba's mother, when she saw me leaving, asked that her son Zev go along with me. On the road, I met up with Urtziya Chazon, who was serving as a policeman. I arranged with him to direct us as if we were going to the sawmill. En route, the boy Zev Rabinowitz joined us. At first I tried to send him away, as his appearance was so very wretched. But he refused to leave, so I allowed him to join us.

As I crossed over to the eastern side of the town, I saw Shmaryahu Zafran and Yehoshua Kanonitz. We were a group of eight in all. We walked in the direction of the sawmill and, from there, to the Karasin road. We crossed over the fence of the roll mill and started running in the direction of the towns. On the way, some more people from Manevichi joined us, and we ran about four kilometers into the woods. At my own initiative I assumed command of the company, and I showed them how to gather together all the food and divide it equally. Everyone listened to me. Thus, I took for myself, the only gun with its six bullets that had belonged to Yehoshua Kanonitz, in blessed memory.

I asked specifically for everyone's agreement to obey me, and they agreed. In the late night hours, we reached the yard of the landlord Sandutzin. There we filled our bellies with carrots and took provisions with us for the road. We continued in the direction of the village of Lishnevka. There I met the peasants who had had some contact with the Jews who were already in the woods with Kruk.[12] At last I received a number of messages, including one saying that they wanted contact with me, because I had served in the Polish Army in the cavalry and had become very familiar with all of the forests in the area due to commercial relations with the local peasants.

When I arrived at the village of Lishnevka we were a group of sixteen to eighteen men, including Pinchas Tina, Yitzchak Kuperberg, Asher Flash, Yosef Guz, and Chunek Wolper.

I asked the liaison peasant, Maria, to deliver a message to Kruk, saying we were waiting next to the bridge over the Stokhod River. During the day, I attended to the confiscation of bread from the shepherds in the fields.

The following night, we met with the company from Kashevka by the bridge. The brothers Abraham and YisraelHersh Blanstein and others informed me that Kruk was preparing to abandon twenty of the comrades, because their fate would be bitter without arms and, even more important, without familiarity with the region. Yitzchak Kuperberg came up to me and kissed me: "Only in times of trouble," he said, "is it possible to recognize a human being, and that is you, David."

The messengers returned to inform Kruk of our arrival. Kruk himself arrived and led the entire group to the edge of Nabruska, deep in the woods. Thee we decided that a portion of the men would go out together with our men to gather some food for the group, without revealing its whereabouts. Kruk had good reason to do this. According to him, an embarrassing incident had occurred in Troyanovka because of a Jew who had been captured by the Germans and had led them to the hiding places of all of Troyanovka's Jews.

We got ourselves organized in the woods. A month later I told Kruk that we had to move to another forest, because the peasants "smelled" that Jews were living there. It is worth mentioning that the only arms in our possession were Yehoshua Kanonitz's gun and a few *obrezy* (sawed-off shotguns). Kruk brought us to the woods surrounding the village of Serkhov. There we counted more than thirty people, mostly from Manevichi and the local villages. There were also a number of women among them. I approved Yitzchak Kuperberg's request to bring back his parents and sister who were in Koninsk (Okonsk) with Slovik,[13] and I sent a number of men with him. They later brought back with them Chava, Hershel, and Elka Kuperberg.

The group of Jews with Kruk and Yosef Zweibel nbered in the tens, consisting mainly of the Zweibel and Rozenfeld families and the Lishnevka Jews. In the Serkhov woods, we made an effort to collect food in anticipation of the coming winter. We would dig pits in which to store potatoes and cover them up so that the peasants would not discover them. We dug more than twenty-two pits. We brought the potatoes to new "habitations" in the middle of the woods and covered them wit the forest's vegetation for camouflage.

We had in our possession three sawed-off, defective rifles, Kruk agreed that I should come to him to fix them. I reached his cap after a nightlong journey, and the rifles were fixed and ready for action.

On the way, I fired some test shots. The rifles really worked. Upon my return, I found out that a peasant had arrived at the camp on the pretext of looking for oxen. I could see that danger was lurking here; he wasn't really looking for escaped oxen, but rather searching for the hiding places of the Jews. One night after we had returned from an operation, Chunek Wolper was on guard duty. We all lay down to sleep when suddenly, a shot was heard. It was Chunek's shot that saved us. A hail of bullets came down on all sides. I gave the order to flee and disperse, and the company fled. We had with us a refugee from Terespol by the name of Aharleh, whose leg was swollen from an erysipelas he had contacted. We had carried him on his back to the camp, but at the time of our escape he held onto my coat and ran behind me. The power of the will to survive!

We ran the entire night. About three kilometers from Kruk's camp, we stopped. I went to him, by myself, and told him about the attack on us. Kruk decided that it was necessary to also move his camp immediately, because he was certain that the police would follow us. He knew the local woods well, and with his leadership we tread many kilometers into the thick of the woods to a new campsite.

We went out to the villages to find out who the attackers were. It became clear that they had been Germans, together with the Ukrainian police force. There was no doubt that this had been the work of the peasant who had been looking for oxen.

After three months we decided (Kruk, myself, and the others who were armed) that it was important to set up a fighting unit, and that those unfit to carry arms — women, old people, and children — in all about 100 people, would organize a family camp that would be under our protection. I went over to the fighting unit. We collected food and clothing or the family camp and from time to time brought them whatever we could.

The family camp was situated close to the fighting unit and began to organize a life it would be worthwhile to describe at a later time. We Jewish partisans gave a lot of attention and concern to the family camp. Each time we returned from an operation we went into the camp, as we brought with us equipment and food.

The fighting group began its operations by coordinating with other units, and we concentrated mainly on bowing up trains. I personally took part in blowing up thirteen trains.

Outside of other operations, we knew that in Manevichi there were many who had taken pat in the murdering of Jews. We had a list of fifty-six murderers we decided to liquidate, and I admit and confess that with my own hands I liquidated eighteen. With this I fulfilled the martyrs' will and testament — to avenge their spilled blood. It was not easy! However, in the beginning we severely punished the murderers, according to our own decision — that of the unit. Later we had to get permission from Dyadya Petya's partisans' headquarters, to which our unit, along with Max and Kartukhin's unit, belonged.[14]

We made the effort and also received permission to avenge the blood of the Jews of Troyanovka, who were murdered by the peasants of Gradisk.

I knew the residents of the village due to my business dealings with them, and I requested to join the partisan group under the command of Berl Lorber ("Malinka") and Yisroel Puchtik ("Zalonka"), together with thirty partisans. We liquidated about twenty murderers and left in every house a notice

written in Russian, saying that this had been a retaliatory
mission for the Jews of Troyanovka, who were caught and
murdered by them.

Once when we were on our way to an operation near the
village of Stobykhva, we found inside a house six or seven
Jews, men, women, and children, who were all skin and
bones. We took clothes off ourselves and dressed them and
left them food. I do not know what their fate was, because
they were far from our base.

During our entire stay in the woods, individuals who were
hiding in the woods or with the peasants joined our family.
It eventually numbered more than 100 people and included
women and children, young men and young women.

A Good Ending

With the liberation from the woods, a new chapter of
wandering began for me: conscription into the Red Army.
Many of my friends who were conscripted fell in battle on the
way to Berlin. I decided to reach *Eretz Yisrael* at any cost. In
Rovno I made contact with Abba Kovner's group, and I went
with their help to Lublin. I volunteered for public work in the
Jewish community there, and I was assigned to organize an
orphanage.

I began gathering children who had been hiding with Polish
peasants; sometimes I had to use armed force to take these
Jewish children from them. There were also incidents where
the children themselves did not want to leave the peasant's
domain. At the inception of the orphanage, there were about
thirty children, and several months later, when I left, there
were sixty-four. I tried to instill in them a love or *Eretz Yisrael*
through the study of Hebrew, using placards, etc. But this
idyll did not last long, because I was threatened by the danger
of imprisonment. The men of the "escape" decided that I had
to leave.[15] I went to Romania, got married, and immigrated
to Israel with my wife. As of today I am a "lord" in my nation
and in my land, and we have three children and three grandchildren. Let them multiply!

Stages in the Organization
of the Partisan Fighting

Abba Klurman

The organization of the partisan fighting began, in fact, only in the fall of 1942, when Jewish young men went out to the woods and became the nucleus for the formation of partisan units. Word spread through the town that there was an organization made up of refugees from the Soviet rule who had remained in the rear lines when the Red Army retreated.

The reason for these people staying behind was hazy. It was very doubtful that they had stayed behind in the occupied area in order to organize a Soviet underground in the German military rear line, as the rumors stated. I suspected that the rapid disintegration of the Red Army at the beginning of July 1941, after the unexpected German attack, was the cause for their remaining behind. A local incident is imprinted in my memory that points to the friendship that prevailed or, more accurately, that was nurtured between the Germans and the Russians, especially in the border regions; because of this it is possible to infer that the Russian officers had no idea about the clash with the Germans. In any case they had not planned on preparing staff officers for fighting in the Germans' rear lines after retreating which they had not dreamed of doing in the first place.

On June 19, 1941, I was taking part in a party organized by Soviet officers for the German officers, who had come to us to attend to moving the Volksdeutsche from the occupied Russian regions to Germany.[16] At the same party, Soviet military officers were uttering threats in the ears of Jewish girls who refused to dance with German officers.

It is worthwhile mentioning that one night before the outbreak of the war, in the city of Brisk (Brest-Litovsk) on the Bug River, German trains, filled with soldiers, crossed the border, disguised as merchandise for the Soviet Union. The cars were not expected at all. When the war broke out, commando units with improved military equipment jumped from the cars and at-

tacked the city of Brisk. An additional fact is that, at the very least, in the region of my hometown, Kamen-Kashirsky, there was not any prepared organization to deal with the possibility of a war in the rear lines, one of the cardinal principles in the partisan organization; the remaining Russians fled from the ghettos. This occurred, in essence, between the first action and the final liquidation (during the period between May-October 1942).[17]

The plan for the "final solution" in the areas taken from the Russians by the Germans in 1941, as distinguished from the plan for the final solution in the territories taken by the Germans in 1939, was base on two concrete liquidation operations, the last one being complete:

> 1: - Psychological preparation for annihilation that came about through selective murdering.
> 2: - Complete annihilation in two actions.

This also confirms again and again the fact that the Germans had no trouble finding collaborators in carrying out the annihilation. These included the Ukrainians, who had been the Jews' neighbors for generations. The Germans found in them active collaborators who were ready to carry out the murder of a people. The final plan for destruction of the Jewish population in all the other occupied regions was carried out by removing the Jewish population from their home towns on various pretexts, such as assembling them for "work camps." In the Ukraine and Byelorussia, on the other hand, the Jews were publicly annihilated with the help of the local residents, who did not take the trouble to prepare alternative plans if there were to be mishaps or mistakes in the annihilation operation. One piece of evidence that confirms that there were preparations for massive annihilation is that in July of 1941, four weeks following the occupation, the Jews were put to work preparing the ground, digging pits, etc., near the Jewish cemeteries where, in fact, the murders were carried out.

The Jews — Combat and Creative Potential

With the grouping together of Jews from all levels, from those who were educated to the lowly maidservant, there was great creative potential. With their strong desire to justify the essence of their existence, this potential was doubled and tripled, helping the fighting units. And there was a nucleus of communal life in the middle of the woods. While there was no agricultural or economic base, every one of the camp's residents carried a load of knowledge and the desire to create, help, and contribute. They also contributed to keeping up the moral framework between the partisan fighting unit surrounding the population.

The beginning of the partisan organization was based on the ethical behavior of the Russians who fled from German imprisonment, the pro-Soviet Ukrainians, or the Poles who did not sympathize with the Germans and had been forced to flee to the woods. One can see in this period the first stage of individual, or of small groups, who began the armed struggle against the Germans and their allies. Their behavior was different from that which existed in the area. It was an area where all kinds of gangs swarmed whose common denominator was looting and plunder, murder and rape.

The second stage was still based on violence, murder, and rape by the fighters on the civilian population. But there began to be restraint, a slowing down of lawlessness, and gradually there was a governing force from above which took the trouble to unite the ranks of the fighter; it did so successfully.

The third stage was defined by cooperation, tranquility, and humane relationships in private and family life. And it was the "Jewish camp" that contributed to this, and as I pointed out earlier, it was one of the significant factors that led to a repairing of relations between the partisans and the local population.

Kruk — Anti-Semitism in the Midst of the Partisans

One of the central figures in our otryad was, without a doubt, Kruk. And it is not surprising that our opinions about him are divided. On the one hand, he received almost every

Jew, even non-combatants, under his auspices; on the other hand, he also killed Jews, including youths, because of a breach of discipline (though he also killed Ukrainians for this reason). All in all, he was a primitive man, illiterate, but imbued with an instinctive sense for absolute justice and fine organizational ability. In my humble opinion, there was not a trace of anti-Semitism in him. On the contrary, I would dare say he was, as we nicknamed him, one of the "righteous of the nations."[18] In fact, he also was not a Communist. The combination of Kruk and Jews was formed because both parties were looking for partners for support.

The anti-Semitism among the partisans mainly derived from the Russians' belief in some idea of freedom and equality, at a time when they imagined and remembered the Jews to be merchants and exploiters. It is possible that we felt guilty for following after a Gentile out of indecision and a certain fear. We could have gotten along as well without them.

Kruk killed as a result of the pressure of time. Generally people acted then according to the senses alone, and life or death was a trifling matter, a game, nothing else. Kruk was the one who would order fighters to guard the citizens' camp, when we had left them on their own and mortal danger awaited them. Through his inspiration we also left them a lot of food.

Still, it must be emphasized that it was not Kruk, Max, or Moscow who organized these partisan units but the young Jews discussed in this book.

IN THE FOREST WITH GRANDFATHER

Micha Gazit

And this is what I want to do — all the survivors of the Holocaust probably do the same — I want to preset a vivid picture and revive all those moments in my life which I still remember from childhood and boyhood.

The 1940's. Europe is fighting and bleeding. Germany is victorious everywhere, and one can feel that the "vision" of a thousand years of the Reich, the reign of the "pure Aryan race," will come true. Not a single country in Europe could oppose the Germans; not a single army could resist the stream of the German armored forces or their trampling boots. But for us, this was not simply occupation. It was a question of life and death. Our lot was different from that of all other defeated nations that were allowed to live. And what on earth was it we wanted? All we wanted was to be left alive.

I can still vividly remember the escape into the forest. Beaten and frightened, we were like those creatures who fled from a rapidly spreading fire; we ran wherever we could, in all directions. In front of us there were the great Polesia forests, the marsh land, and the rivers streaming through enormous areas. It was a dark and rainy night in the autumn of 1942 when my uncle Joseph sent us strict orders to escape quickly, because the next day we all would be sent away and slaughtered. We left quietly in the dark of the night, under the watchful eyes of the German and Ukrainian guards. We were moving in circles, afraid of meeting people, because the hatred all over the Ukrainian villages was enormous. All that night we walked in the midst of the deep forest toward the meeting spot which my uncle had decided on earlier.

In the early morning we made our first stop. We took slices of dry bread and sugar cubes, which we still had with us, out of our bags. And so we lay al day long, waiting for new orders telling when to move. Suddenly god news arrived — there was a group of partisans gathering in the neighborhood village. (Later the group was named the Kruk division.) This Kruk knew my uncle vey well; when in trouble, they used to help each other. And so the partisans started organizing their people in the forests.

This first nucleus developed into a company, which in the course of time became a place of security for all the Jews who had survived and had run into the forest. And in the forests connections were created between distant people strangers became brothers. Brothers sharing the same fate — stress, cold, hunger — comrades in arms. This was the covenant of blood crated by the war. Jewish partisans, a symbol of our new pride, which since the days of the Maccabees had been buried somewhere deep in our subconscious. Jewish partisans, the first sing of the renewal of the people's youth and a sign of good tidings of revival. This is what I thought and imagined in those harsh days. I, a Jewish boy of twelve. But the partisans did not realize what they really were.

The Jewish partisans fought a battle of revenge. There was no enthusiasm in those dreary days, death was luring everywhere and it was terribly real; you could feel it close at hand. The fighting was hopeless and nobody thought of survival — only revenge. In the long and dark nights, they were marching toward their missions — exploding of trains and fortifications, disrupting of communications, destroying of bridges, hitting the enemy in the rear. They were marching in long lines, carrying outdated arms and wearing rags. They were walking silently, and only in their faces could one discern the stubborn bitterness and the burning eyes thirsty for revenge.

We, the camp of women and children, were accompanying them with loving eyes and wishes for success and safe arrival home. Every parting was like a last one — every pressing of the hands was a last one. We were anxious, because they were like those uncrowned Olympic champions whose records spoke for themselves. The partisans' records boasted of killed Germans, of damaged trains and, most important, of the disruption of the supply-road, so essential for the enemy — the main road to Kiev. Every delay of these loaded trains bound for the front was a great victory. The number of graves of our dear comrades was increasing day by day. This was the price for victory. The forest became very precious to us. Among those thick trees covering enormously wide areas we found our home. This was our rear area our country. We penetrated into the most secret corners of the forest, into places where it seemed man's foot had never trodden. It was virgin soil into which we injected life.

There lived among us in the forest a wonderful man, an outstanding person. It was Grandfather Shlomo Zweibel, of blessed memory. His glorious beard and his typically Jewish appearance symbolized for us the Jewish tragedy of this war. I vividly remember those days when Grandfather used to wake up early in the morning, when the forest was still dark. Grandfather used to prepare himself for his personal talk with the creator. He would put on the *tefilin* and *talith* and would raise his head up high — he would stand and murmur his prayers in whisper and devotion. And then, in unity with him, the entire forest would wake up.

The birds began singing while circling over the tops of the trees; on the branches sleepy squirrels would spring drops of cold dew still glistening on their long tails. From beneath the trees a strange and different voice would burst forth, by no means less pure than that above. One could listen to prayers like *Ma Tovu Ohalecha* and "God of Abraham, Isaac and Jacob…", "To Jerusalem thy city thou shalt return to mercy…" and "We sinned, we offended."

And the trees stood still, like that holy congregation on Yom Kippur, a big and diverse crowd. Back home on Yom Kippur, the crowd was clad in white, and here in brown. And here in the forest too, Grandfather would pass in front of the Ark of the Law, and his lips would utter prayers and psalms. This was prayer never before uttered in such a way and in such surroundings. And I do not know if such a pure prayer will ever be uttered again. During all those years Grandfather's food consisted of potatoes only, because there was no kosher food. He used to retire into the forest, light his small fire, roast his few potatoes, and eat them slowly, as if he were eating delicacies. And he felt replete, more replete than anyone else. How could he? Only God knew.

And when the partisans were leaving the forest for their operations, they always remembered Grandfather Zweibel and always brought him something kosher, which they had stolen somewhere. They did it because Grandfather was loved by all. Not only did they love him, but they also guarded him as a most dear human being. When Passover approached, Grandfather would contemplate very hard how he could keep all the rituals, those rituals which he kept strictly his whole life. The partisans remembered the holiday, bringing him kosher dishes and fulfilling his special holiday needs. In those remote days there was some consolation in what the partisans did.

Out of the dreariness, in the midst of the daily bloodshed, acts of chivalry of the individual and the group hovered prominently. And it was those deeds which lit the few sparks of light in the darkness surrounding us.

The hardest time for us was the winter, the cold winter of the Ukrainian forests. Typical for the winter were the horrible storms, hurling the forest violently and sweeping out all those creatures who inhabited it in warmer days. And then the heavy snow would fall and accumulate on the branches and on treetops, till the trees themselves would fall down, unable to bear their heavy burden.

And we were wandering within this cold dreariness — we and the hungry wolves, both of us looking for food, both of us chased, as it seemed, by the same demons. The wolves cherished some special sentiment for us. During our stay near them they did not touch us, they only revealed some "playfulness" toward our food.

And in those cold days the Germans would enter the forest on purpose. They would raid the depths of the forest to find our hiding places and to finish with us. They thought that in the winter it would be easier to stare and freeze us. And then came the days of trial. There were days during which we felt completely lost. We would run in all directions. We would run thousands of miles without rest, passing frozen swamps and mountains of boggy snow, and from time to time we would groan, fall down, breathing heavily, stand up again, and stubbornly move on and on...

There were nights in which, after running a lot, we would gather in one place, a heap of human bodies, wet and hurt. Nobody would utter a word. We would lie almost unconscious, and only the strong among us would from time to time wake the sleeping, because even a short sleep in the snow could have ended in the everlasting sleep. Sometimes we would sit and sometimes lie down, and the snow would be our pillow. We would also stare at the skies, at the distant glittering stars.

There would be times we would strive to fly high up into those distant and benevolent worlds of enormous light, shining on God's angels who hover in the light and fly close to His holy chair. At midnight the moon would appear and shine brightly. Its face would be sadder than ever, because it was bereaved. The moon would bewail those of her sons who in the past would sanctify it every month and welcome it with happiness and joy. And here in the forests there was nobody to welcome it; now it also was bereaved. And so it would move on and sink into far distances. And you would feel as if you wanted to tell the moon something, to send with the moon a message for your distant brothers, if they survived, if any were still alive. You wished to send them the blessing, "Be strong and of good courage."

But there were also nights without the moon, dark nights of snow and storm. We would grope in the dark without compasses and in no particular direction, walking stooped, horror looking from our eyes and accompanying our steps. From the far distance we could hear the howling of the wandering wolves and echoes of the trees breaking in the wind. The snow would utter deaf rattling's when our feet pressed its white smooth rugs. From time to time we shook the snow from our backs and dried our eyes, which were running with tears of cold.

At the end of the line we could discern Grandfather, his beard frozen in splinters and his back stooped low, bearing the burden of his years. On his back he carried a bag from which a fringe of the *talith* was dangling in the wind. Did he then see himself as one who wore the last *talith* in Israel, as one whose *talith* did not guard him anymore that day, as that day he did not wrap his back to pray? From time to time Grandfather would raise his eyes, as if looking for something, as if hoping for a day which was so far away — he would look for tomorrow to come and rescue him from this dreary existence which seemed as endless as the *galut* (diaspora) itself. He would look for his God who had long ago forgotten to look down at him from heaven and to see.

Translated by Esther Kluger of Israel

A TOWN IN THE WOODS

Abraham Puchtik

In underground trenches in various places in the Volyn and Polesia woods, Jewish "towns" blossomed during the period of the Holocaust. They were the citizen camps under the control of Russian and Jewish partisans.

In the citizens' camp in the Kukhotskaya Volya woods, there were about 150 souls, sometimes more, sometimes less, because there were reunions of families or friends. People came there from ghettos in the Rovno region. There were entire families, portions of families, and individuals. Most were men who were fit for fighting and hardships, but there were a few old people and children who required help and care.

We dug our bunkers for our quarters. We called them *zemlaynkas*. These quarters were camouflaged, and a guard was posted over them, day and night, from the partisan camp, which was under the leadership of "Dyadya Petya" (Anton Brinsky). Individuals and families with some kind of weapon were taken in by the partisans.

When we began to set up, the number of partisans was small and their weapons were few. In time we accumulated more fighters, some of them having escaped German imprisonment. Thus, arms that had been taken as booty from the Germans and the *Bulbovtsy* (Ukrainian nationalists) were added to what we had. Our partisan unit was in contact with other units, and in time of need we cooperated with one another.

As was taken for granted under those circumstances, the partisans' job was to provide arms, food, shelter, and means of transportation. The operations were carried out against the Germans and their allies. Until the outbreak of the war, I lived with my family in the village of Galuziya in the area of the town of Manevichi.. I had had business relations with the local villages. During the Soviet rule I was director of the flour mill near the village of Galuziya and as a result, I became an expert in the work of running mills. A number of months after the German occupation, in the autumn of 1941, we were expelled to the Manevichi ghetto. We hid with village friends before the first "action" began, and we were not harmed.

We knew that in order to survive we had to flee to the woods. Among those who were fit for this dangerous mission was a portion of my family — my wife, Chava, my son, Yitzchak, my daughter, Itka, and myself. My mother, my sister, and my two small daughters stayed in the ghetto.

We fled to the woods. We built a hut and I got in contact with my village friends. I got food from them, as well as a rifle with ammunition.

We wandered far into the woods searching for the partisans. In one of northern Volyn's spacious forests, we succeeded in reaching a group of Russian and Jewish partisans. Thanks to the rifle, I was accepted into this group. The commander was responsible for getting food or the citizens' camp that was part of his organization. I was among the most active members. My son, Yitzchak, became part of the fighting brigade.

Concern for food was implicit in the term, "to organize," which meant taking from the villagers. To accomplish this, a group of armed partisans would go out and, in a show of strength, would obtain food, fuel, matches, house and kitchen utensils, and more. At the camp we were concerned with cleanliness, discipline quiet, and mutual aid. Women took care of housework. My wife mainly attended to child care.

During the partisan operations, certain villages were taken, including the place where "my" flour mill was from the days of Russian rule. The mill was full, and the *otryad* commander ordered me to operate it for the local villagers, as a portion of the flour was reserved for our people. During the four months of the mill's operation, in the summer of 1942, I managed to collect enough flour for our people for the winter season.

The *Bulbovtsy* "smelled" the mill one day. We stopped operating it. After a fierce battle, the enemy retreated and we again operated the mill, but after ten days we were forced to leave it. It fell into the hands of the *Bulbovtsy*, who burned it.

The second winter in the woods (1942-1943) we had an abundance of flour, four cows, and potatoes, but mortal danger awaited us. The woods were swarming with Germans and Ukrainian police. We had to leave and move onward in order to join up with another partisan unit. We left behind the cows and loaded up our wagons and horses with old people, children, food, and clothing. The rest went on foot and, following four armed partisans the march set out. We trudged along that entire night, a winter's night, but in vain. We did not meet any partisans. In broad daylight we hid among trees and bushes. That short winter's day was interminable for us. Near us the villagers moved about, engaged in their business, but fortunately we were not noticed.

In the evening we went, four Jewish partisans, to the nearby village of Zaliznitsa in order to collect provisions. There we found an empty barn. Our men went inside and gathered grain for four full days. There were *Bulbovtsy* in the area. Other partisans that we met told us that the enemy had not discovered our living quarters and that the cows were still there. We returned "home" to our trenches.

A strong fighter joined our ranks — Dvorah. She went on the most difficult missions. To our sorrow, she fell because of treason. One of the *Banderovtsy* infiltrated our ranks, and he handed her over to the enemy. There was also an incident of a killing based on settling a personal account. The Polish partisan commander, Max, shot a Jewish partisan, Kahat, because in his day, a man by the name of Kahat had killed the commander of the Polish police force.

For some reason there arose in the partisan headquarters a desire for valuables, and an order was issued to give jewelry and ready cash to headquarters. Those who violated the order could expect the death penalty. I, at the risk of my life, was involved in trying to prevent the implementation of this order. I worked at obtaining food for our camp. One day I arrived at the flour mill in Karasin. The mill belonged to a Pole who was murdered along with his family by he *Banderovtsy*. I operated the mill after I received permission to do so. Someone informed on me, charging personal fraud in

my job, and a search was conduced accompanied by an interrogation of witnesses. It was then I learned that this had been
a case of intentional slander and nothing else.

It was the beginning of spring, and the Red Army had
entered the region. From our camp youths were inducted into
the Red Army and some of them fell in battle. A few of our
people were killed after the liberation by the *Banderovtsy*. We
endured many more hardships. But most of the people of the
"town" in the woods survived. And some of them, including
myself, reached *Eretz Yisrael.*

THE FIRST DAYS IN THE WOODS

Zev Avruch

One evening (19 Elul, 1942) we decided to flee from the Manevichi ghetto, in spite of the mortal danger involved in the escape.[19] Whoever was caught was shot on the spot. Our goal was to reach Kruk, the organizer of a partisan group in the area.

Parting from our parents was very melancholy. They gave us some light valuables, all that they had, mostly threads that we could exchange for bread. We left and had to stop for a moment. We heard the weeping voices of our dear ones. We fled. But the voices followed after us and still follow me till this very day.

My sister, Faygeh, took a chance and approached the house where Kruk was known to be hiding. She was successful. We walked in the dark of night into the thick forest, my sister, Faygeh, my brother, Berl, and I. The fear that took hold of us was an old one. The same fear was with us every time there were people who chased after us and who, from time to time, overtook us. It was similar to that primal fear one feels fleeing in the dark of night in dense woods.

At dawn we reached the village of Leshnevka. Here we met the brothers Avraham and Hershel, natives of our city. In the village there was a peasant acquaintance of ours. He allowed us to stay one day in his barn. In the evening we headed for Kruk's house.

Kruk was a Ukrainian Communist, a native of the village of Griva. During the Soviet rule in eastern Poland, he served as head of the village of Griva. With the retreat of the Red Army, Kruk moved to Kiev. He went through training there, received some kind of arms, and was dropped by parachute near his village. His objective was to organize a partisan detachment from the local residents. He hid in different places, and changed his outer appearance as much as possible. He moved about the villages and tried to persuade the young Ukrainians to join him and organize a partisan group — but in vain. He had success with the young Jews, but Kruk refused to take anyone without weapons. He postponed fulfilling his plans and meanwhile worked in units. At night when he arrived at his living quarters, he wasn't pleased that we had come to him without arms, but he agreed to take us. In his outer appearance, he was a partisan "to the hilt," dressed in leather clothing and equipped with a rifle, pistol, and ammunition. He also had binoculars in his possession.

We went out to the road. He told us that in the woods was a group of young Jews who had fled from the villages even before the Jews had been moved to the Manevichi ghetto and to other ghettoes.

His partisan leadership training began with instructing us in how to gather potatoes into sacks that he had prepared. This seemed strange to us — to go into a strange field and gather the fruit of someone else's labor. After we had gathered the potatoes, Kruk drew his pistol, and under the threat of killing him, demanded a sheep. Berl, my brother, carried the sheep on his shoulders to the woods. Kruk knew every tree and path in the woods and led us to a place that was surrounded on three sides by uncrossable swamps.

On Kruk's partisan territory we met with families and individual Jews. Kruk appointed himself commander; his first order was for two volunteers to go to Manevichi and persuade the Jews to flee to the woods. The volunteers were my sister, Faygeh, who disguised herself as a Ukrainian, and a lad by the name of Yechezkel from the village of Lishnevka who looked like a young Ukrainian.

The two of them arrived at the town, but to our great sorrow, they were late for the designated meeting time. This was on Shabbat, the 23rd of Elul, in the morning. On that day the Jews of Manevichi were shot and thrown into prepared pits.

Individuals who escaped reported that on Friday night, they led the Jews to the killing site. The Jews cried and shouted and waited for the help and salvation that did not arrive. They shouted and commanded those who would live to avenge their blood. This command somehow reached us.

And, indeed, we fulfilled their holy command. We fought in the partisans' ranks against the cruelest enemy of our people that history has ever known.

EXEMPLARY FIGHTERS

Shmaryahu Zafran

One day when we were in the village, working at the threshing floor, Linda, the peasant's wife, came back from the city and told us that the Germans, with the help of the Ukrainian militia, were taking Jews out of their homes and into the street, making them lie face down on the ground, and cruelly beating them. Every now and then trucks would arrive to take the Jews to the "Horses' Graves" on the outskirts of the city of Manevichi. There they forced the Jews to dig pits, and afterwards, shot them as they stood on the edge of the pit; those slain would fall directly into the pits.

She burst into tears. "Even though I also don't see Jews as people, this is too much already," she said, wiping her nose with her hand, and she made us leave, for fear of the Germans.

We stayed in the woods near the village until the evening. Despite the strict curfew, we succeeded in slipping by the German guards, and we arrived home, where bitter news awaited us: Our father and brother-in-law, along with more than 360 Jews, had been killed.

Upon hearing this terrible news, the idea of revenge crystallized in my consciousness. I hid. I found out that several other youths were in hiding. I went out one evening and talked to Yehuda Melamedik (who later, as a partisan, was killed in a heroic situation) about leaving for the woods. The two of us talked to Zev Verba, David Flash, and Shimon Miroshnik. We had only one pistol, which had been repaired by Yehoshua Kanonitz after he found it in a grove. It was clear to us that it was impossible for us to leave as a group, and so we decided that everyone would leave on his own.

We designated the nearby village of Galuziya as our central meeting place. After many hardships, we finally were able to leave the town David Weinshtein helped me. After a while, we all met in the woods, everyone sharing a story about how he slipped by the police guard posts.

Before leaving home, my sisters, although not my mother, were opposed to my fleeing. My mother was indeed afraid that, God forbid, I would be killed in the woods, but she immediately stopped crying and wished me well, "Go safely, my son, and avenge the spilled blood of your father, your family, and of all the Jews." And there is no farewell more difficult than this, when you sense very clearly that you will never see your mother again.

Successful Operations

Our division received a directive ordering an operation in the direction of the city of Sarny; one of the objectives was to obtain, along with some others who had crossed the border near Zhitomir, automatic weapons that Commander Kruk had hidden. One partisan, who had been among those who had hidden the weapons, came with us. The journey took place without a mishap. Some of the weapons were found, but most of them were apparently taken by the local peasants.

On the way back, we (two squadrons) blew up a train and wooden bridge over the railroad tracks, and the third quadroon set up an ambush not far from a village in the area. Our central meeting place was in a grove net to the village. The operations were successful above and beyond our expectations. We left without a scratch. We fond a hiding place, and it was only the next night that we began to move in the direction of the base.

In one of the villages lay a contact man for the partisans who was known in our headquarters. We made a detour to the edge of the village and learned to our joy that the chief of police of Sarny was staying overnight in the village with three policemen.

The chief of police had a mistress who lived near the village, and from time to time he went to visit her. We were given a briefing on the houses where they were staying for the night. We divided into several small groups and simultaneously surrounded the houses where the Ukrainian policemen, who loyally and diligently served the Nazi regime, were staying. I had the fortune to be in the group that surrounded the house where the chief of police was staying. After continuous negotiations, the chief of police surrendered and came out with his hands raised.

The policemen surrendered long before this. We confiscated their weapons and quietly, without creating a disturbance, left the village. Regretfully, as we were drunk with victory, we forgot the rules of caution and our men began robbing the collaborators. We hitched two wagons to horses, and loaded them with everything at hand, from food to clothing. We liquidated the collaborators and left the village two hours before sunrise, going in the direction of the woods and swamps of Strashov, where there were Polish strongholds on the former Polish-Russian border. There were two Jews in this division, myself ("Verny") and another young Jew ("Zaichik"). In our group there were several Ukrainians who agitated against he Jews and caused serious arguments among us on the subject of the Jews. We stationed ourselves about a kilometer from the village, on the road leading to another village. We gave food to the forest watchman's family to cook for us. We placed a guard on the road leading to the forest watchman's house, and the fighters lay down to sleep. I stood guard during the second shift, at sunrise. At the same time the unit commander awoke and asked me to go into the forest watchman's house to see if the food was ready. I explained to him that I had gotten up to relieve the guard. He saw the company was fast asleep, and he said, "It would be a shame to awaken them, they did such a nice job, I'll go myself." And he got up and went.

Dangerous Missions

I stayed there a little bit longer, as I had five minutes left. On the way to guard duty, before I reached the guard, a burst of fire from automatic weapons was suddenly heard, followed by light shelling. We immediately hit the ground. After ten minutes, all was quiet. I ran back to the fighters who were in a state of alert. I told the deputy commander that the commander had gone to see the forest watchman. The deputy asked my friend, the Jew, and another Ukrainian to go and find out the source of the shots. To my shock, the Jew Zaichik refused to go, pleasing a stomachache. The Ukrainian claimed that if the *zhid's* (this disgraceful nickname was prohibited by law in the U.S.S.R.) stomach hurt, then his les hurt. I felt an urge to save the Jewish respect, and I volunteered to go. The deputy commander, a Russian from Siberia and anti-Semitic in every bone in his body, embraced me and asked: "Who else besides "Verny" volunteers?" Silence took hold of everyone. I left. I went toward the watchman's house. At a clearing in the woods, I began crawling, and what do my eyes see?

The commander is hanging, with half of his body on one side, and the other half on the other side of the fence, and about twenty meters away from him, his short rifle is lying on the ground, pointing toward the woods, and his pistol is hanging with the holster over it. I crawled slowly. I took the rifle with me, but I left the pistol there. I didn't want to stand up, because hundreds of Germans were swarming next to the house. Some of them poured something (apparently gasoline) on the house; others were busy lining up families with their faces to the wall; another group of soldiers got ready to take them out to be killed — and perhaps there were those who were being interrogated with threats. I went back and reported and turned in the rifle. The deputy ordered me to go back and try to remove the pistol as well. He sent a Russian fighter after me to see if I really would try to remove the pistol, or if I would try to slip away.

I crawled. When I reached the hanged commander, I stood up in one motion and removed the pistol, while leaving the belt and the holster, and I crawled back. The Germans didn't sense my presence, as they were busy with the forest watchman's family and were preparing to burn down the house and the entire farm.

At the edge of the woods, I met up with the watchman's son, a youth of twelve, who managed to slip away and escape to the woods. About 150 to 200 meters into the woods, I met the Russian who had been sent to follow me.

The youth told us that an hour after we had left the house, the Germans surrounded the entire yard, took positions, and stayed there, as if they were waiting to ambush the partisans who were about to arrive.

The deputy came to see me, complaining that I hadn't brought back the pistol's holster. He ordered me again to make a round and find a place from which we could escape from the siege. The forest watchman's son helped me, since he was familiar with every path. We found just one exit — through the swamps. I led the division, with the watchman's son and I walking at the head of the line. When we were in the heart of the swamps, and the rest of the partisans were a ways behind us, the Germans sensed us and opened fire. The shots didn't reach us, as they were directed to the middle and tail end of the group. Miraculously, not one of us was hit. The same day we walked, with the boy's guidance, through swamps and woods until four in the afternoon

We rested. When it became dark, the boy showed us the route, and he himself turned right toward a village, to his relatives. After two nights of walking we had to cross the Styr River. This time too, I was sent, along with one other, to carry out a mission: I was to liquidate two guards with a silencer, and blow up the *budka* (shack) that was next to the bridge, along with the German soldiers inside. The operation was successful, and we safely returned to the base.

Hand-to-Hand Combat

The first snows were already covering the area. The cold penetrated our bones. And, worst of all, the snow showed our footprints, enabling the Nazi enemy to find us more easily.

It was very difficult to be careful, to walk exactly in the footprints of the first person in order to prevent the enemy from assessing the number of fighters. But there was no choice. We were obligated to carry out whatever was imposed on us.

The Chief of Staff, Dyadya Petya, ordered an increase in operations, this time in areas that, until then, we had not worked in and were, therefore, unfamiliar to us. The targets were railroad tracks, bridges, and telephone lines that connected the towns of Brest-Litovsk-Pinsk, Kovel-Sarny, and Kovel-Rovno. Several of the best lads joined us, including the Jews Yitzchak Kuperberg and Zev Verba from Manevichi and Hershel Blanstein from Lishnevka. His brother Avraham had been captured by the Germans when he was badly wounded in a special mission and had been tortured to death.

After several successful operations on our part including one battle with the Germans, where we liquidated a great number of them, the commander and some of his fighters dressed up in the slain German's jackets. Treating the rules of caution lightly, we moved at twilight on the King's Road, instead of waiting for complete darkness, drunk from our victories. The commander, in a German jacket, entered a peasant's house next to the village of Golovno. We were there about a half an hour, drinking milk and resting a bit when German soldiers surrounded the house and opened with automatic fire. As the commander ordered us, we threw a few grenades through the windows, jumped outside, and waged hand-to-hand combat.

I don't remember much about that battle: After shooting at the first figure I encountered, I received a blow from behind with a rifle butt and lost consciousness. I awoke with a terrible headache upon hearing from afar Hershel Blanstein's voice calling out in a whisper, "Verny, Verny." I recognized Hershel's ("Tupoi's") voice, and I tried crawling, since I was badly wounded, in its direction.

The silence of the battle's aftermath prevailed, but Volodya the Gruzin (the Georgian) (he appeared to me to be a Jew), pulled me back and begged for help. He was badly wounded in the left hand. He had chosen to be my guardian and always helped me. With his guidance I tended to his wound. We tried to remember which direction "Tupoi's" voice had come from, as Volodya had also heard it, but we couldn't locate it. To this day, his voice echoes in my ears — those were probably his last moments.

Volodya told me that he had jumped through the window. When he saw that, with his first burst of fire, a figure had fallen, he came up behind the second figure of a short German — the one who struck my head with his rifle butt — and had turned the rifle around in order to stab me with its bayonet. Volodya immediately filled him with a round of bullets and killed him. And he still had time to see the German that shot him. Volodya got so excited about his wound that he didn't even check to see if I was still alive. The snow apparently awoke me from my faint.

We continued on, using the northern star to guide us to the base. We entered the woods after two hours of walking and crawling. Since it was very difficult for Volodya to walk, we had to lie down and rest once in a while. Volodya lost a lot of blood. When we went into the woods, looking for a hiding place, we found three of our fellow partisans. They had reached the same woods before us. We were happy to see them. That night we met up with more of our men unexpectedly. A battle almost broke out between us, but we identified the familiar voices, including those of the Jewish lads. But Hershel was missing. My heart ached for him. We also learned from them that his commander had received a mortal chest wound and had lived another eleven hours before passing away. They, the lads, buried him in the same fearful place in which we had hid the entire previous day.

One of our lads hinted to me that he had almost been shot by our Jewish lad, who thought he was a German. The German jacket he wore was the reason.

After several nights of walking, we got back to the base, weak and depressed from the blow we had received — that it was due to carelessness on the part of the commander that we had made two precious sacrifices — Hershel, and the commander himself.

The news that Yehuda Melamedik from Manevichi, from Max's (Józef Sobiesiak's) otryad, fell in battle hit us like a thunderbolt on a clear day. He was one of the best young men, a brave and modest fighter. We met him when we were in Manevichi and were planning an escape to the woods to fight the Germans and their allies. He was fearless. Once in a while, news of his excellence in battles or in blowing up trains reached us. I met up with him only a few times in the woods, and only by chance; either when his unit was returning from operations or when ours was. We would exchange impressions and information. Our fateful battle was at the village of Karasin.

The mission was to capture the Karasin police force, which was made up of Ukrainian nationalists, enemies of the Jews. They were like bones in our throats. They overlooked a part of the region that we partisans controlled. Melamedik was in a house in the village with only three other fighters and poor weapons, when a strong unit of Ukrainian police surrounded him. Yehuda Melamedik was left on his own in the fighting

sector and fought until the last bullet. The enemy's hand
grenade downed him. We went to him at nightfall, a crushed
partisan fighter. The partisans and his sisters, Rivkah and
Luba, stood erectly on his fresh grave.

Little Luba was one of a kind. She was loved by all. Twelve
years old, she helped the wounded and sick, washed clothes,
cooked, and baked. Wherever help was needed, she was there.

Yehuda's death leaves a deep wound in our hearts to this
very day. He was a young and daring fighter. He was eighteen
years old when he fell.

The Legendary Image of Raya Flos

I will briefly tell of a young heroine — Raya Flos, the
daughter of the pharmacist from Povorsk.

A beautiful girl, she was a fighter who went through the
seven fires of hell because of her beauty. She fell in a German
ambush. The Germans found her at dawn, while she sat leaning on the wall of a barn with a weapon in her hand, asleep.
They alerted their commander, astounded by her beauty. The
German commander exclaimed, "A beauty such as this!" The
Germans held a military funeral for her and fired shots in her
honor by her grave. I heard of what she had been through and
her life with the partisans from Moishe Edelstein, her friend,
with whom I became friendly. Testimonies of her death and
heroism were eliminated from the mouths of peasants, and
they were forbidden to talk of her. Even the great Russian
writer Ilya Ehrenburg wrote one of his stories about Raya
Flos.

Moishe Edelstein

He died a hero's death in a battle with the Ukrainian
Banderovtsy. After we left the woods, he was buried, in a park
in Rovno, in the section for the Soviet Union's heroes and
received the title, "Hero of the Soviet Union." I went more
than once to his grave in the park to be alone with his memory. There were not many young men like him as a fighter,
a human being, a comrade in distress. He had been modest
in his actions and quiet. His only desire had been to avenge,
for the sake of his parents, his family and for his wife whom

he had loved and who had loved him. A comrade at arms, a Russian, had tried to steal her from him. She had preferred to die rather than betray her beloved Liba Moishe.

In 1944 I had to go with Moishe to Chernovtsy to organize an illegal immigration route from the liberated regions to Eretz Israel. He was more suited for this job than any other young man, but he more and more requested to go on "clean up" missions and retaliatory operations against the *Banderovtsy*. It was from one of these operations that he didn't return. My trip to Chernovtsy was postponed for a month because of his death. Yaakov (Ilyusha) Zweibel went with me in his place.

The Tragedy of Kahat Finkel

A fighting figure worthy of mention was Kahat Finkel of Manevichi. We, the town's children, knew him and admired him for his brave disposition even before the war, when Polish rioters would attack old Jews and pluck out their beards. Kahat, the simple wagoneer with the warm Jewish heart, dealt them severe blows. The Poles knew that Kahat's hand would get them, and so they became very cautious. Only after the war, was it clear that he had been taken out and killed by the *otryad* commander, Max; his gentile comrades-at-arms had set a trap for him, because he was brave, honest, and a Jew.

The Heroic Death
of Two Young Friends

Zev Rabinovitz

I'm not going to tell about the heroic deeds of the Jewish partisans. I don't want to tell about the number of trains that were destroyed, nor to list, one by one, the bridges that were blown up. I my eyes, it was the missions of Jews who died for *Kiddush Hashem* (Sanctification of the Holy Name), including the small children, who were the real heroes. And it was they, in their bravery, who brought us to the State of Israel. Anyone who says otherwise doesn't know what he's talking about; nor does he know about the souls of the martyrs.

I would only like to relate what happened to my two dear friends who fell, whose only thoughts, desires, and dreams were for revenge. They wanted revenge for their parents, relatives and friends who were murdered; they wanted to revive their dreams for a nation among nations, living on their own soil, in our own State of Israel. We were youths then, and it is for our nation's youth and for Israel's youth that I'd like to tell my story.

I don't remember exact dates, as they have all gotten mixed together in my mind. It was around the spring of 1943. German planes flew over our woods and fired into them. The company scattered to find cover, when suddenly Major Mahmed appeared, calling out, "Stay where you are!"

Zev Avruch ("Volovich") and I continued running. "Stop!" the major shouted, "or I'll shoot!" He had a mauzer (a type of rifle) in his hand. We stopped and said, "This afternoon we are going to start an interesting job. I will teach you to look straight into the eyes of death."

The "interesting job" was, after several unsuccessful attempts, setting up a workshop for this extracting of explosive materials from heavy shells that the Red Army had left behind when it retreated. It was necessary to release the "head" of the shell, to heat the shell in a cauldron of boiling water, and to pour the explosive material into molds that each

344

weighed five kilograms about 12 pounds). The fighting *otryad* (detachment) brought the shells to its camp.

After we spent a number of days extracting explosive material, Syomka Biderman, a twelve-year-old youth from Manevichi, came to see us, saying: "I've had enough of working with Shimon and of taking care of horses. I'm staying with you. I know that another person is needed, and I will be that person, volunteering out of my own free will!" And so our group of three youths worked. And there was more: Even Nechamka, the cook, treated us with great respect. Syomka would laugh, "She's giving us better food, because she sees our going to the world to come and she wants us to request a good place for her in the Garden of Eden and to be a champion in the right for her before the Master of the Universe."

Eight shells were left, which the major forbade us to touch as they were too dangerous, in his estimation. He was an expert in these matters.

We prepared a new transport. Meanwhile, we were resting in the evening, sitting with the company, when the major arrived. He looked around and called me, as he was accustomed to doing, by my Jewish family name, Rabinovitz. (In the camp, they felt that he was a Jew.)

"What a nice moonlit night — we need explosive material. Come, and we'll try to release one of the forbidden shells. Go by yourself so that if, heaven forbid, there'll be an accident, there will only be one sacrifice, for the sake of the parents and for the sake of your people." (He always added "for the sake of your people.")

This was Passover eve. After about an hour, I returned and reported that I had in fact succeeded in releasing the "head" from one of the shells. The major was actually radiant from happiness.

"Go to the company, Rabinovitz. Tomorrow you will work and prepare whatever is possible."

The next day he came to visit us. He inspected the shells. He ordered us to put one of them, the rustiest one, aside and not to touch it. "That's an order!" This was on the second day of Passover. Syomka said to himself, "What a shame, we cold extract about eight kilograms of explosive material from this shell. It would be possible to blow up an entire train with this, and perhaps also the Germans inside of it. What a shame to leave it. But the order was not to touch it.

The next morning Major Mahmed arrived with Kostin, the partisan commander from headquarters. Syomka was humming a song. He stopped humming.

"Good morning, boys! Syomka, why did you stop singing?" he asked.

"My stomach hurts," Syomka replied.

"O.K. I'll bring you a pretty girl!"

And to Kostin, "Look, they say that Jews are cowards. But look at the dangerous work these Jewish boys are doing! Who else would do that?"

And to us, "And for you, boys, I have news. A revolt broke out in Warsaw. Courageous Jews rose up and struck at the Germans. They are standing bravely against many Germans. That's what they're saying on Moscow radio. Listen, don't touch this shell! That's an order!" Mahmed repeated, warning us. The major and Kostin let our workshop, satisfied. Syomka again walked around the shell, mumbling, "Eight kilograms of explosive material! Aren't we here to take revenge?" he says to us a childish smile and serious adult expression mixing together on his countenance, and he left us. Not a lot of time had passed, when a loud explosion was heard. There was fire and smoke. I thought that the Germans were attacking. But then we heard Syomka's voice, "Mama, Volovich. Ratevet." ("Mother, Volovich! Help me!")

All around, the explosive materials that we had extracted and were cooling in molds were burning. The major came running, and shouted, "Flee!"

I shouted, "What a waste of material!"

"Do what you want!" Mahmed shouted.

Volovich ran to bring help. We removed the explosive material, turning over the cauldron of water we had used for extracting the material. We quickly removed the shells from the boiling pot. Only after this did we put out the fire.

Syomka was lying on the ground with his guts spilled out. He was completely torn to bits and his eyes were blinded. He was just a lump of flesh without legs or hands. Only his mouth still pleaded, "Save me, shoot me, take revenge. *Shma Yisrael*" ("Hear, O Israel"). These were his last words. The major took out his mauzer and asked Kostin to shoot Syomka. Kostin turned his head and shot him. Silence prevailed. Only his final words still echoed through the woods and, to this day, in my years: *"Nemt nikomeh* ["take revenge"], *Shma Yisrael…!"*

We brought Syomka to a burial place in the afternoon. We, his two friends from work were not allowed to take part in his funeral. We had to continue working. There was an urgent need for explosive material.

That same day a group of Jews from Troyanovka arrived at the camp. The major introduced us to a youth who was sixteen years old, tall, and of a strong character. His name was Payskeh. We became friendly. His entire family had been killed. His brother was killed in a battle with Germans and Ukrainian police and he joined us to avenge their blood.

The major ordered us to move the workshop a distance from the camp, so that spot wouldn't remind us of Syomka. Volovich was meanwhile transferred to Sokolov's unit, one of the tough and distinguished units.

We were again a threesome. Are'leh would prepare the boxes, and we went on with the shells. Time passed. We acted more carefully and never worked together. We made some improvements in the pouring of the material. The major would visit us every morning. One morning Payskeh was singing some song. When the major appeared, he stopped singing.

"Why did you stop singing, Payskeh?"

"My stomach hurts."

"I'll bring you a pretty girl," said the major.

In the afternoon, Are'leh and I released the heads, and Payskeh transported the material in the wagon hitched to horses. Suddenly, Payskeh appeared without the wagon and horses. There was an alarm, he says, and they took the horses from me. Just at that moment, I was releasing a bomb head.

"Let me. I too want to test my strength. I too have an account with the Germans. I too am a Jew! They killed m-m-mine, too. All the Jews of Troyanovka and Manevichi." Tears welled up in his throat, but he choked them back. No fighting man would cry.

I gave him a shell and moved away from him. Then, all of a sudden, there was a thundering explosion! Without a moan or a groan. Silence. There wasn't a trace left of Payskeh. I managed to hear just one word from his mouth: "Revenge!"

Syomka had been torn apart widthwise, and Payskeh, lengthwise.[20] Together they were length and breadth as it were. The remains were collected and brought to the burial site.

The group continued on with its work. Yisroel-Hirsh Flash, twenty years old, from Manevichi, was brought to us. They transferred me to Volovich's unit. I recall that, before this we had tied to remove explosive material from a German shell, and we were nearly poisoned; our faces turned a pale green like a lime, and our tongues turned completely blue. It was only with difficulty that we were saved from this poisoning.

Flash continued to direct the work in the workshop. He lied to see victory and died immediately afterwards from tuberculosis, which he had contracted at his job at the workshop.

I also remember two wonderful Jewish girls, Faygeh Avruch and Chasyah Blanstein, who perished after they had left the woods, when the train the two of them were traveling in to Kiev was bombed by Germans.

The two of them had worked tirelessly in the hospital that was set up in the camp. They would meet us joyfully and warmly when we returned from field operations. They especially gave attention to those youths who were lonely or without family.

And I remember David Blanstein and the slap he gave my cheek when I joined him in my flight to the woods, and I was just a youth. "Go home," he shouted, "to father and mother!" And in spite of this, he took me to the woods with him and helped us as much as he could. He was dedicated to us and concerned with us, just like a father.

DEEDS OF A CHILD

Tzvi (Vova) Verba

With the retreat of the Red Army, an atmosphere of uncertainty prevailed. We were living in fear. My father and my five brothers and sisters and I fled and moved in with a Ukrainian peasant acquaintance, in an isolated house outside of a distant village. We had thoughts of fleeing, following the Red Army's retreat (from the German attack). But father was confused and unable to make a decision. We returned home to the town.

We viewed those first days after the Russian retreat as a great tragedy for the Jews of Manevichi. Even I, a boy of nine, sensed that something frightening was happening, and that it was just the beginning of an impending disaster. And, indeed, it happened. My father, my brothers Shikel and Motel, and my brother-in-law were taken, together with another 370 Jews, on the pretext that they were needed for work. But they did not return. (They were all shot.) And so, as the only "man" left, I became the head of the family.

Once I was caught without the yellow patch. They took me to the police station. There were other Jewish children there. An interrogation began, accompanied by blows from the Ukrainian policemen. I was rescued from the blows when a policeman recognized me and released me, saying, "I knew your father; he was a decent man."

I recall an incident when the Germans passed through the houses and held searches. They searched my pockets for gold jewelry. A shuddering passed through my body that is now difficult for me to describe.

They began to round up the Jews on "the other side." I said to myself, "They're going to take all of us out and kill us!" I hid in the cowshed of a Ukrainian neighbor, Sovotnik, without his wife knowing about it. At night I would go out to the garden and gather vegetables. I returned home after four days and found all of my relatives from the village.

In the meantime my three sisters began working in Polska Gura. Every day girls would go out to the town to work and in the evening return in a cargo train, tired but satisfied. A German from a military engineering squadron promised the girls that he would warn them when the situation became critical, and in fact, one day at sundown, he informed my sisters that they should flee at all costs, because the day of liquidation was near.

This information spread quickly, but people were helpless and lacked the desire to flee. And where could they flee? My sister Rivkah and I fled with Hershel Trager and his daughters, Polya and Vitel. Traer decided to go by foot to Rozhishche. We walked day and night without water, going around villages and eating sugar beets from the fields. I decided to try my luck as a child. I entered a number of houses and asked for food. In most houses, they gave me a piece of bread, while shaking their head sympathetically. But in one house, a peasant came out to meet me and wanted to "wrap me around his pitchfork." I ran away with all my strength, and he ran after me. I succeeded in slipping away and arrived safely at the place where the Trager family and my sisters were waiting for me.

We reached Rozhishche and found a city empty of Jews. Hey all had been liquidated! We returned to the Manevichi woods. Near the town, we came across the pits of the Jews of Manevichi who were murdered. To be sure (was this not a bad dream?) we went back and found that in the pits were Jews shorn of their beards, robbed of their souls. We broke out into bitter crying. Our group divided up. Trager, who was familiar with the surroundings, pated from us and went with his daughters, and I remained with my sister, Rivkah.

The Woman Angel Tanya

I'm returning to a time when we were wandering about in the vicinity of Manevichi. My sister, Rivkah, and Vitel Trager would go out by themselves to check the possibilities for obtaining Aryan papers, and to learn of the fate of the rest of Manevichi's people. Rivkah found out that her sister Tzviya had escaped and was hiding with a Polish woman, Tanya, along with our sister Krayndel and her daughter.

My sister Rivkah and Vitel were caught and brought to Manevichi, where hundreds of Jews were concentrated. These were Jews who had managed to flee but were caught by the peasants. The Germans spread rumors that no harm would befall those who were still alive, and so a number of Jews were persuaded to return voluntarily, since the conditions in the woods were intolerable. Among those who returned was my aunt from Cherevakha.

However, and I my sister, her two-year-old daughter remained with the Polish peasant woman, Tanya. Tanya gave us a hiding place in her home, in a *khutor* that contained two houses. The peasant from the second house was an enemy of Tanya's aristocratic family (her husband, and their two sons, one fifteen, and one twenty years old). Tanya laid down the rules and made the decisions in the home. They greatly feared that the hostile Polish family would inform on them, especially since more than once, Ukrainian police and Germans had visited their house.

We hid inside a bunker under the floor. We entered it from a closet; a camouflaged exit was a distance inside the garden. At night Tanya would open the bunker, and we would go out and get a breath of air, then immediately go back into our hiding place.

One day, some people came to Tanya's house, while we were below in the bunker. Suddenly, little Bronya burst out crying; my sister and I tried with all our might to quiet her, pulling our hair out of nervousness and holding onto one another, because we knew that the danger was great, not just for us, but also for Tanya and her family. Tanya decided then to bring us to the woods.

Tanya's sons prepared a bunker for us in the woods, covering its entrance with a decaying log. Tanya continuously supplied us with food. For Tanya, having us was like a holy mission, which she desired with all he might, to the point of her own self-sacrifice and that of the members of her family. Her attachment to my sister Tzviya, who had stayed there before we arrived, was so strong that she wanted, in this way, to compensate for her loss.

Looking in a mirror of those days, when a man suspected his friend or a son informed on his father, when murders and looting were common occurrences, Tanya's behavior was really unusual. To this day, I go over and over again in my mind what her motives could have been for endangering her life and that of her family in order to save us.

Tanya would visit us frequently in the woods and provide us with our food and clothing. This continued for about a year. Later, when the Ukrainians began to abuse and kill the Poles, Tanya fled with members of her family to the town. So we remained alone in the woods and were forced to worry about our survival.

At night we would go out to look for food in the fields. We gathered potatoes, beets, and carrots. We had to accumulate food for the winter. I would light a fire, striking a piece of steel on a stone. Many times, while we were searching for food, we would meet up with Ukrainian murderers who tried to capture us; they also fired shots at us.

We began to become accustomed to life in the woods. I was familiar with every path for a radius of tens of kilometers. I would walk about with my niece. At a number of kilometers from our bunker, railroad tracks crossed the woods. We would hear the noise of the trains, and very frequently we began hearing explosions. We suspected that this was the work of the partisans, and we were right. The partisans were active despite continuous guarding by the Germans and Ukrainians of the railroad tracks.

The railroad tracks formed almost naturally the border between the *Banderovtsy* and the Soviet partisans. It was like an agreed-upon boundary. Our bunker, unfortunately, was on the *Banderovtsy* side, and it was dangerous to cross the railroad tracks to get to the other side. The partisans refused to receive us in their ranks. (Once partisans visited Tanya, and she urged them to take us, because we were threatened by liquidation. They did not consent, saying that they did not accept anyone without firearms. Also, they did not like the idea of a little girl.)

And so we remained stuck in the middle of an area filled with dangers. Meanwhile disturbances started up against the Poles. Ukrainian nationalists murdered entire families in a most cruel manner, cutting off their heads with axes I found corpses with wooden stakes stuck in their heads.

I taught the little girl how to be familiar with the paths and the area surrounding the bunker, so that she, on her own, could find the way to it. The girl quickly adapted and acted with the utmost caution in the woods. Hearing a suspicious noise, she would hide among branches or bushes, and it really was difficult to find her. My sister also became very familiar with the woods.

I the man, nine or ten years old, also went astray once in a great while. Fear grabbed hold of me when even I lost my way to the bunker, coming back from my frequent trips to gather food from the fields the Poles had abandoned or from their homes where I sometimes went to look for clothing they had left behind. In the winter of 1943-1944, I would more and more frequently meet up with groups of young Ukrainians who came to the Polish villages to loot and take apart the houses, and I would slip away from them. I learned to plan my visits in such a way as not to run into them. My sister would always be afraid when I went out to the villages and often asked to come along with me.

Subsequently we went out together, from time to time, with Bronya on my back, holding onto my neck with her delicate fingers. Tens of kilometers. I walked along in this way, with my niece fastened to my back like a knapsack. We would only go out at sunset, when there was relatively less danger.

One time, as we approached a Polish village, we sensed that there were people around. We began to go back the way we had come. When we crossed the dirt path, we noticed a wagon full of Ukrainians who began shouting at us to stop. They jumped out of the wagon and began chasing us and shooting. As the bullets whistled around us, the girl, her fingers wrapped as usual around my neck, stammered, "God, help us…" Apparently her prayer brought us help. We succeeded, fortunately, in reaching the woods, which were thick and impenetrable. The murderers lost track of our footprints. We were saved.

When we were alone in the woods, we dreamt and trusted our dreams. We knew to interpret the dreams as if something was guiding us in our flight. It happened more than once that we dreamed we had to leave the place, because danger awaited us. We would leave, and after a while, when we returned, we found out that indeed there had been uninvited guests there, who took with them all the food we had prepared for the coming of winter.

We began hiding the food in a number of places inside the wood. One time I dreamt that I saw three snakes and that I had to kill them. The next day I found two snakes, and at sundown the same day I found the third snake. To this day, I don't know how to explain this phenomenon. Did the merits of our ancestors stand us in good stead?

It happened that heavy rain soaked the burnt rag which served us for lighting a fire; only after desperate efforts for a full day did I finally succeed in lighting it. There is no describing the great amount of joy I felt. At night we would hear the howling of wolves, and entire packs came near the bunker. We were afraid they might get inside, and so by means of fire, I would, with difficulty, chase them away.

I recall an incident that won't leave my memory. I knew, generally, where birds, squirrels, and all kinds of wild animals built their nests. One time I climbed a tall tree and found inside a nest three fairly large fledglings. I removed them, with difficulty, and prepared a tasty meal that was particularly enjoyable to the girl, who had not tasted a meal fit for kings like that in quite a while. The parents flew about shrieking around the bunker in their search for their fledglings. This went on for a number of days. A deep shuddering took hold of us, for our sin in stealing chicks from their parents. We feared that perhaps we would pay for the theft.

This difficult life, the war for survival, and the struggle for our lives, continued for a year. Somehow, the will to stay alive fixed itself in us — we wanted to tell what happened to us. It was a desire that stayed with us during all our days of wandering in the woods.

On the Way to the Woods

Spring of 1944 was late in coming. Snow still fell. The Germans retreated from our area. We did not know this, but we sensed something different in the air. We did not hear any more explosions by the railroad tracks, but we were afraid to leave our hiding place. Only a month after the German retreat, a Ukrainian hunter discovered us when his dogs led him to our bunker. On seeing us, he became frightened and began to run away. We called to him, and he told us that the Germans had retreated, but he advised us to still stay in our hiding place until the atmosphere had calmed down a bit in the area. We decided to leave the spot, fearing that perhaps the Ukrainian hunter would decide to liquidate us.

We started to walk in the direction of the town. My sister Krayndel walked with great difficulty, because he feet were swollen and wrapped in rags. On the way we went into a house, where the peasant who received us served us food. We warmed ourselves in his home. I recall how Bonya, three and a half years old, was like a little hunted animal, looking around as they brought food to the table. Her whole being was frightened, as if she had fallen into another planet.

We arrived at the town and did not recognize it. On the entire main street, only a few houses remained. Our houses were not there, not the one on the main street, not the one on Teatralnaya Street, near the woods. There were only ruins, foundations covered with thorns and grass. I did not find Jews in Manevichi. We found out from the Ukrainian peasant that only in the town of Rafalovka were there a number of Jews.

I do not remember how we reached Rafalovka, whether by train horse, or foot. Once there, we entered a house where Jews lied; we were like a miracle to them. How was it that we survived on our own, and that only now, more than a month after the Germans' retreat, had we left the woods? Truthfully, the reception was not enthusiastic. Everyone was concerned with himself and his family. In this house we were given a small corner into which we settled, and my sister began working as a cook in a kitchen in Rafalovka. I fell into bed. I was sick with typhus fever, and I was taken to the hospital in Rovno. The Germans continued to shell Rovno every evening. The shellings actually helped me. I would go into the kitchen and gorge myself with anything I could find. I recuperated. The resiliency I had acquired in the difficult conditions in the woods stood me in good stead. During my illness, no Jews came to visit me. I returned to Rafalovka, and I found my sister and her daughter relatively healthy.

I was then an experienced man, twelve years old, and I began to "trade" in all kinds of merchandise in the train station with the soldiers going to the front. Once a woman came down from a car, speaking Polish to me, hugging me, with tears in her eyes, and whispered, "I had a little brother; you are a brother to me." She left me a gift as a memento and continued on her way. I recall her waving to me with her hand as she moved further away, going toward the front.

We reached Israel through Youth Aliyah in 1947. I enlisted in the Hagana at the age of sixteen. In clashes with the Arabs and the British, a number of my young comrades fell. With the declaration of the State of Israel, I served in the regular army of the Israeli Defense Forces (Tzahal), and I participated in the battle for the liberation of the Galilee in Israel.

I DECIDED TO DEFEND MY LIFE

Asher Mirochnik

At the outbreak of the German-Russian War, we were only children, twelve and thirteen years old. We feared what was coming, and entire days we sought advice about what to do, if...

The first German columns arrived in the town on motorcycles. Out of the curiosity that accompanies fear, we gathered in groups, we children, around the Germans, in all five or six soldiers. After a short rest, they left the town.

After one or two days, the Ukrainian police began to get itself organized, and a relative quiet prevailed. The towns-people, the youth, began organizing the herds of cattle to go out to graze outside of the town. (Almost all of the town's residents owned a cow or two, which they had to take out to graze.) Generally, we four youths would herd the cattle early in the morning with the falling of the dew and go out to the fields and woods. At nightfall we would return, laden with mushrooms and all kinds of blackberries. This was at the end of the summer, near the beginning of the fall. In fact it is possible to say tha the food the women and children gathered in the daytime was the Jews' main sustenance.

There was, however, plenty of food for the craftsmen blacksmiths, tailors, shoemakers, carpenters, wagon makers and others, since the peasants paid them with food products. Once, as I went out with a herd of cattle, Zelig Khizhi — a Hebrew teacher and neighbor — accompanied me. Suddenly I saw an S.S. policeman, who had reached the entrance to the town. The Ukrainian and Polish peasants bragged to us that on this day they were about to slaughter all of the Jewish men. On hearing this, I asked Khizhi, the teacher, to stay with the herd of cattle, and I would run to the town, but he would not agree to stay by himself, deciding that he would be the one to return to the town. I asked him to tell my father — with urgency — to get out of the town and go to the woods.

The teacher did meet my father and passed on to him the things that I told him. He told my father that I said there were things, it wasn't clear what, that were likely to occur. But his manner of telling this, and even his trustworthiness, did not influence my father, who at that time was working in the smithy of our blacksmith neighbor, Hershel.

My father did not take Khizhi's words seriously, and when I returned home at sundown, my mother told me about the tragedy. Father had been taken out of the blacksmith shop and, along with 370 other Jewish men, was brought out to the fields to the "Horses' Graves." This was the first action.

About two months after this, a peasant came by, bringing a letter in my father's handwriting, in which he asked that we send him winter clothes and warm underwear. I urged my mother not to believe what was written in this letter, because it was apparent to me that it had been written under coercion before his murder, but my mother wanted to believe that my father was still alive. I heard stories of the atrocities that had taken place for the Ukrainian shepherd youths (who had heard about the murders from their parents). I recall being told about Binyamin Eizenberg, the blacksmith-locksmith, who was nicknamed Nyoma the hero. He struggled with an S.S. officer, and his head was cut off, and he, Nyoma, a body without a head, continued running for a ways, until he fell.

After the liberation, when we left the woods, I was walking with my friend Zev Avruch to the site of the murder, and there we found skulls with hair lying in the field and uncovered pits with the soil falling into them. About fifty meters from the brothers' grave, we found a huge skeleton without a head, and we knew that this was Nyoma's corpse. No one had even taken the trouble to bury it in the dirt, and it stayed unburied out in the field.

Life had to continue. I recall that the responsibility of taking care of the house, which had belonged to my mother and my sister Chaya'leh, became mine, and so I began searching for food.

In spite of the strict prohibition on leaving the town and going to a village, I would go out by myself to the surrounding villages, to peasant acquaintances, collecting anything I could get. There were peasants who remembered my father, who helped out once in a while by giving a loaf of bread, a bit of flour, or potatoes. I would slip back into the town with a sack on my shoulder. In this way we got through a very difficult winter.

In addition to my wandering through the villages, I engaged in "vital" work for the German army, which was in need of sleds. Hershel-Leib, the blacksmith, was given a quota for the preparation of sleds for the German army. I filled the place of my father, in blessed memory, and helped the blacksmith in his work in exchange for a bit of food. I remember the quotas that were given to the town's Jews, when they had to collect fur coats, brass utensils, gold and silver, and also sums of money. These Jewish policemen worked very diligently in their search for these things.

The Forester Slovik

With the arrival of spring, news reached us about partisan units that were conducting raids on police stations and killing people in them.

At the Manevichi police station, they began building bunkers around the building with double thick walls made out of logs. The peasants, as well as the Jews, worked at this task (the few men that were still alive). A group of about fourteen youths, twelve to thirteen years old was organized to remove the outer layer of the logs. Every day we went out to the woods, accompanied by Senka Melamedik — he was our group leader, as he had worked before the war as a tree-sorting expert.

We went by foot six or seven kilometers to the Koninsk woods. We received a quarter of a kilogram of bread in exchange for this work, but our main profit was in the mushrooms that we gathered in the woods.

When we went out to work, we sometimes met with Jews who had fled from the surrounding towns: Kolki, Melnitsa, and others. They told horror stories about the total liquidation and destruction of the towns' Jews.

We began to contrive plans of escape, and we prepared bunkers as hiding places. In order to camouflage our work in preparing bunkers, one or two people would withdraw from the group and prepare the bunker while we tried to fill their

quota. The preparations continued for a long time. I personally prepared a bunker in our house underneath the floor. I
decided to myself that I would defend my life at all costs.

I knew that the youths who were eighteen to twenty years
old were organizing themselves in order to leave for the
woods, but it was impossible to join them. It was known that
a group of adults had attempted to leave in organized form
and had failed. The police apparently knew about their plan
of escape and began shooting as they left for the woods. A
number of the company were killed, and the rest returned to
the town.

The hangman's noose began to tighten more and more
around the town's Jews, who were concentrated in one section. The Jews living on the other side were brought over to
us on a Friday and were settled in the Jews' homes.

The day before this happened, they forbade the group to
go out to work in the woods. On Friday night, a Ukrainian
policeman, an acquaintance of my father, in blessed memory,
who was grateful for ast acts of kindness, knocked on our
door and begged my mother to leave the town in any way
possible. My mother felt helpless, saying, where could she
flee? To the woods? Who and what awaited them there? My
sister Dhaya, sixteen years old, resigned herself to her fate
and did not want to be separated from my mother. She said
that, apparently, her fate had been decided, and she had to
accept it.

Helplessness and despair enveloped us, and we spent a
sleepless night. When morning broke, I peered through the
window and saw that they were beginning to take people out
of the houses on one side of the street. The street was filled
with the crying and wailing of women and children, along
with the shouting of policemen who brandished rifles and,
mercilessly and indiscriminately, dealt blows, as they hurried
the women and children along. I opened the bunker that I
had set up and begged my mother and sister to go down into
it. My mother complied with my request. She was prepared to
join me, but my sister, who for some reason — maybe because
she had resigned herself to her fate — was set in the opinion
that if it had been decided for her to go, then she would go
and not resist. It was difficult for me to comprehend those

personal motives which prevented her from going into the bunker. But by taking this stance, she influenced my mother to remain with her and not leave her by herself to Fate, from which she saw no escape. I pleaded with them, and with all the people who were in our home at that time, to go into the bunker, but in vain! The only one who joined me was Sima Guz's daughter, who was seven years old, but she immedi- ately came up out of the bunker saying it was stifling inside. Avraham Gorodetzer went down into the bunker with his three daughters: Zelda-Zavit, sixteen years old, who imme- diately came out of the bunker, when she could no longer tolerate the oppressiveness inside.

Upon seeing the police approach our home, I jumped into the camouflaged bunker and closed it over me. I heard them take out my mother, my sister, and all the rest of the people who were in the house. During the entire day, searches were conducted in the house, and we, inside the stifling bunker, heard the shouts and curses of the Ukrainian policemen, who took great pains to find people in hiding.

We passed that difficult day of the slaughter in the bunker. At midnight I was the first to leave. I looked for and found a bit of food, and I put it into a sack and called to those in the bunker to come outside. We began running toward the woods. Every road and path between the houses and yards was familiar to me, and so I led the group, which numbered forty people, including myself. My intention was to get to the same bunker in the woods, which my young men friends had set previously.

As we were crossing the railroad tracks that were close to ponds and marshes, we met up with Tzvi Kuperberg, his wife, Chava, their daughter, Elka, and Dvora Sherman. According to them, they were heading for Slovik, the forester's, woods. We continued in the direction of the bunker.

At two in the morning, on Saturday night, we — Avraham Gorodetzer, his two daughters, and myself — reached the bunker in the woods. When we went inside it, I realized that some of the young men had been there before me.

We stayed all day Sunday in the bunker. Its entrance was quite far away, through a channel we had dug during the time we had worked in the woods. It was ten meters long.

The entrance to the channel was underneath the trunk of a very old tree. The bunker itself was a pit, which we covered with tree stumps, branches, and dirt. Grass grew on top of it, so it couldn't be distinguished from its surroundings. Air came in through the channel. The bunker could accommodate the fourteen youths working in the group.

A utensil with water was set up in the bunker, and we brought a bit of food with us which we had gathered when we fled from the house. During the entire first day of our stay, we heard the herds of cattle and the conversations of the shepherds, as they walked on top of the bunker.

That same night, we decided that we would go out at dawn and look for Jews who had managed to escape and join up with them. We also decided to go see Slovik, the forester. Slovik got frightened when he saw us, fearing that we had been seen coming to his house. He asked us to go into the nearby woods, promising that he would come to see us. After a while, he came. We suspected that he would alert the police. He calmed us down, promising to bring us a group of Jews who were staying in the woods. Supposedly, they all passed by Sovik's house, and it was he who brought them into the depths of the woods.

Slovik walked in front, and I was about one hundred meters behind him, for the sake of security. We did this in case there was to be trouble, and we'd have to flee. We still weren't free of the suspicion that he possibly wanted to hand us over to the Germans.

In the morning hours, we arrived at a plowed-up field of fodder. The area was open. Slovik crossed the field and entered the bordering woods, while we stayed at the edge of the other woods. (The field, about one hundred meters long, divided up the two woods.) From afar, we saw Moshe Rosenfeld going out to meet Slovik, and our fear dissipated.

We joined Moshe Rosenfeld — a sixty-year-old Jew, after Slovik instructed him to take us to the group of Jews. I am sorry to note that Moshe Rosenfeld hesitated to bring us to the group and started to argue with Slovik. Rosenfeld, of course, gave in in the end and did not stop us from going on.

Despite Moshe Rosenfeld's opposition (which may have been due to hunger, the threatening conditions, and the danger of death), we energetically continued on according to Slovik's directions, and two kilometers away, we found a group of Jews. Thee were about seventy people, including four to five of the friends we had worked with in the woods. They told us that the previous night, on Sabbath eve, they had managed to flee from the town, along with Senka Melamedik, who was shot as he climbed over the fence at Porotzki's farm; the son of Elka and Mordecai from Novaya Ruda was also shot.

Our arrival caused arguments and anger over whether we were entitled to join the group. Sensing we had food with us, the men took it from us, sat down, and finished it. This was lie a bribe to stay with them. The group had been living without food, or means of livelihood, with no contact with the outside world, with the exception of Slovik's son Kazik, who would come by to transport the group from one place to another. Sometimes he would also bring a bit of food, but not one bit of this reached the small, weak ones in the group.

After we had been in the woods or a number of days, I organized the five youths in the group. They were: Yehuda Melamedik, Senka's son, Yehuda'leh Lorber, and others whose names I don't remember anymore. We decided to go out to the village of Volchitsk to ask for food from the peasants.

When the five of us went out on the dirt road leading to the village, a Ukrainian forest guard caught us and wanted to take us to the police. At that time it was being publicized that, for every Jew captured, dead or alive, they would pay in salt, which was a precious commodity.

At first it wasn't clear where he was leading us, but on the way the Ukrainian bragged to me that he would receive eight sacks of salt for us; it was then that I understood his intentions. I managed to communicate to my friends with signals that we had to get away at the first opportunity and not allow ourselves to be taken to the police.

When we came into a tangled grove, I gave the signal, and every one of us fled in a different direction. The guard got flustered, because he hadn't expected that we children would dare run away. He fired two shots, and we fled while the breath of life was still in us. I reached the group in the woods first and related what had happened. After waiting for a day, we went to look for my four friends, but with no luck. It was only after two days that all four of my friends returned to the group, each one coming separately, with a story to tell of his hardships from the escape.

We stayed for about a week and had to get organized again to find any kind of food. We left at night and arrived at the village at midnight. We knocked on the doors of the cottages and asked for food. Sometimes the door would open, and a peasant man or woman would take pity on us and give us a piece of bread or some potatoes; other times those who saw us slammed the door while uttering curses and insults.

In spite of setbacks, there was a lot of booty. Every one of us carried away half a sack of precious food. In the meantime, family camps began to get organized and take care of themselves.

One night most of the people left, and Avraham Gorodetzer and his daughters and I stayed by ourselves in the woods. During this time, I began to become very familiar with the surrounding area. I became very well oriented to the woods and developed a kind of sixth sense and was able to find the Jews who were scattered about in a short amount of time and join them. This happened many times. I regret having to recount an embarrassing incident. I was struck by one of the men, because I had dared to join the group, and the situation became threatening, but then, in time, the adults came to see that they could derive benefit from my being so familiar in the woods, and they began using me as a guide.

Once I took Michal and Zisel Brat and their son Moshe to the village of Serkhov, where they gave their valuables to peasant-acquaintances. In exchange, they received food and then they returned to the camp. I also received for my trouble something to refresh myself. I became well known as an outstanding guide. I also served as guide for Avraham and Chava Puchtik and others.

The winter drew near. We got ready for it by digging a "winter palace." Those who had relatives in the fighting unit began moving with their family to the family camp, which had started to be organized by Max's and Kruk's fighting units. In the end, I remained alone in the woods, next to the farm of the Surma brothers, who were Polish blacksmiths from Koninsk.

I was helped by them. They always warned me in good time of peasants that were wandering by, of the appearance of policemen, and more. One day, during this same period, I met up in the woods with Rachel, the widow, and her two small daughters who had succeeded in hiding and escaping. I invited them to stay with me.

The Long Road to the Citizen's Camp

At the first snowfall I decided to leave for the town and to ask the Pole living in our house for the clothing and valuables that we had left with him for safekeeping. I dressed as a villager in a coarse woolen jacket and shoes made out of tree bark and went "home." Except that in the interim, his place of residence had been moved to another house, to one of the "choice" houses. I found him. He had moved to Dr. Stokalski's house, on the other side of the town, near the Ukrainian police station that had located in the house of Geler, the dentist. I arrived there in the afternoon. They were startled to see me and urged me to leave the house immediately and come back at night. I went to a grove, and hid there in the bushes until nightfall.

Walking at night inside the town, our outside of it, was an activity laden with mortal danger. At dusk a curfew went into effect, and those who violated it were shot without warning. The main difficulty was in crossing the railroad tracks, where Germans and Ukrainian police stood guard. I finally succeeded in taking advantage of the sentry moving away, and I went over the crossing. The town's paths and yards were lit up well, and so I safely reached the Pole's house. With all of this, they gave me a guest's reception. They served me a warm meal. They returned some clothing to me — mostly rags that could hardly be used any more. "This is all we have left," they said. I managed to return to my hiding place in the woods and gave the clothing to the Surma family. They told me that the Germans had issued a directive to the villagers, forbidding them to walk in the woods with its accumulation of three consecutive days of snow. They didn't want them to cover the footprints of the partisans and Jews hiding in the woods.

Rachel went into the Surmas' house, the girls stayed outside by the campfire, and I went into our hut. I was exhausted and fell asleep.

When I woke up, I saw four armed men in front of me, pointing their rifles at me. But they told me not to be afraid of Red partisan-comrades. They told me that when they came into the woods they saw a woman from afar who began to run away when she saw them, toward the hut. They chased after the woman, because they had had a bad experience with a peasant woman from the village of Cherevakha when they were going out to a sabotage operation on the railroad tracks. The peasant woman had alerted the police, and the partisans had been forced to retreat until they came to the Koninsk area.

I offered them roasted potatoes that were in the hut. They said that they belonged to the partisan unit under the command of Nasekin, and they were involved with mining railroad tracks. In the meantime, Rachel and her daughters returned to the hut. The partisans proposed that I serve as their guide and bring them to the railroad tracks. I happily consented to their request. I was ordered to prepare knives from strips of metal, in order to dig into the frozen ground.

I asked the Surma brothers for metal strips to be used for making these knives, needed to dig potatoes. I knew that they had such things. Surma gave me a number of knives. The same night, I led the partisans to the railroad tracks, where peasants stood guard, 250 to 300 meters away from one another. A campfire marked their presence. One of the partisans strangled one of the guards, and another partisan and I moved quickly to plant the mine. At first I was ordered to plant the mine on my own, but one of the partisans objected to sending a youth to do a job that was dangerous and unfamiliar. At any rate, I set up the mine so that the long cord was attached to it, in order to activate it.

I planted the mine with the partisan's guidance and stretched the cord to the entrance of the woods, a distance of about 200 meters. We managed, with difficulty, to reach the woods as the train approached. The partisan and I stayed at the entrance to the woods with the cord, while the remaining three retreated to the depths of the woods.

I pulled the cord when the locomotive was on the mine. A loud explosion was heard, and the locomotive and eight cars filled with soldiers were hurled into the air. I wanted to run and grab a gun, but the partisan reprimanded me and ordered me to run quickly after him to the woods. This was the first act of sabotage that was carried out in the Manevichi region. And later on I would be proud of that.

We returned to our hut, and the partisans promised me that they would report my participation in the blowing up of the train to headquarters. After several weeks, a few partisans from Kruk's unit came to see me with an order to have me join the partisan unit. To this day, I don't recall if Rachel and her daughters were taken into the family camp.

In Kruk's camp I was told essentially what had happened. At Nasekin's headquarters, charges were made against Kruk that his unit wasn't carrying out enough sabotage operations, while a single youth, hiding in a hut in the Koninsk woods, had blown up a train with his own hands. Apparently, it was then that it was remembered that I was staying by myself in the hut, and they came to take me to the unit. The news about the first bombing spread quickly through the partisan units. I was then fourteen years old, and I was taken to the family camp. I joined up with the guard unit of the camp.

Once, while I was on guard duty on the road leading to the family camp I saw from afar two partisans from Nasekin's unit approach. I saw hands waving about as if they were arguing. The two partisans saw me and began to come over to me. I knew one of them, Ostrikov, who had been with me during the blowing up of the train. He recognized me and began talking with me, asking how I was and if I would show him my sawed-off rifle. I didn't mistrust him and handed him the rifle, when suddenly he said, seriously, "We are Germans dressed up as partisans. You are under arrest!" He hit me over the head with the rifle butt and brought me over to the guard of the fighting unit. I saw that blood was dripping all over the guard, and that he didn't have any weapon. They had, through deceit, taken away his rifle too.

This was Fayvel Zafran from Lishnevka. They made us kneel one behind the other, with me in font and Zafran behind me. Suddenly, as I turned my head around, I saw one of the partisans loading his rifle. They simply wanted to kill the two of us in one shot. Two shots would alert the partisans in the camp. When I realized what was happening, I jumped up and ran quickly into the woods, in order to reach the camp and inform the Jewish partisans about the two murderers. Just as I arrived one shot was heard, and I knew that Fayvel had been killed. And, in fact, a Jewish partisan was murdered by the Russian partisans. One of them was a Jew from Odessa, by the name of Bazykin, who had concealed his Jewishness, by actively taking part in the murder of Jews. One day he was murdered by *Banderovtsy*, who were conducting business with a group of partisans. The Ukrainians among them were released and he, the deceitful Jew, paid with his life.

A New Life

Life began anew. The fighters among us went out once in a while on sabotage operations, and while the groups changed, there almost always was a fighter squad in the area.

It was decided to set up a frontal guard unit with patrols, next to the *sezonka*. I was assigned to be in the patrolling and guarding unit and I stayed there until the second hunt, and the end of 1943.

During the second hunt, I left our base. All of the conscripts joined the liberation campaign of the city of Rovno's partisans. When the town of Manevichi was liberated, I moved there, where I joined the Lorber family ("Malinka"). I lived with them until I was conscripted into the anti-*Banderovtsy* unit.

I left the town, and after continuous hardships, I reached Israel. I took part as a combat soldier in the War of Liberation, the Sinai Campaign, the Six-Day War, and the Yom Kippur War of Liberation.

A COMMANDER PRACTICES
WHAT HE PREACHES

Asher Mirochnik

Life in the family camp was conducted according to schedules set by the military camp; there was a division of labor,
with order and discipline.

One day we learned that the Germans, surely with the
help of the Ukrainians, were planning a hunt in our area of
the woods. And it was then that something happened that
I am unable to forget. Yankeleh Wolper, who was twelve or
thirteen years old and a relative of the three Wolper siblings,
asked if he could join the fighting unit, which was beginning
to retreat.

It was said in the camp that everyone was responsible for his
own skin, according to his familiarity with the forests. If he
knew the dangers of the forests, he could survive.

Yankeleh approached commander Kruk and asked for permission to join the partisans. I heard with my own ears Kruk
ordering him to leave, warning him that if he tried to ask
him one more time, he would shoot him. And indeed, when
Yankeleh approached him again, pleading with him to let him
join his relatives, Kruk shot him without hesitation with his
automatic rifle. Yankeleh was left lying on the snow, lifeless, one hand under his head, and one leg raised. When we
returned to the base after the hunt, we found the boy's corpse
in the same position, covered with snow — only his eyes had
been gouged out by crows. This incident shook many of us to
the core, and I am unable to forget the sight to this very day.

A HUNGRY BOY

Asher Flash

Chanukah 1942, the beginning of the winter. The first snow has fallen. It is the start of our organizing in the woods, with Kruk as the leader of the group. The youths only had a few weapons. There was still no division between the fighters and the non-fighters. It was simply a camp of refugees who were afraid to leave the woods and made do with the little food that Kruk, whom they had appointed as commander, and the Jewish youths brought them.

We also had with us a group of youths and children who had managed to slip out of the surrounding towns and escape to the woods. Among them was a ten-year-old boy, Yideleh (Jack) Melamedik, Senka's son from Manevichi. With no one to take care of him, he suffered greatly from hunger and didn't have the strength to endure it. Suddenly, Yideleh began disappearing from the camp. Once, twice, three times. Once in a while he returned with a bit of food in his sack. It became apparent that he was going out to the village of Galuziya, where his father and grandfather had been born, and finding peasants who still remembered past acts of kindness from his grandfather, Avraham, and his father Senka. These people fed him and once in a while gave him some provisions for the road.

Kruk found out about this. He was horrified to hear that a small Jewish boy was going out alone to beg for food, fearing that he would be caught and would tell the police the location of the camp, or, that they would follow his footprints.

As one of the adults in the camp, he summoned me and told me that it was necessary to frighten the boy so that he would no longer dare to leave the woods; if he didn't obey, he would have no choice but to shoot him.

On Kruk's orders, I took the boy and led him to the outskirts of the camp. There I ordered him, with my help, to dig a pit. When the pit was dug, I told him to get inside of it and lie down. Yideleh, in his innocence, went into it and said to me, "Reb Asher, how can I lie down, I'm cold..."

I told him to come out, and I warned him that this time I was only frightening him, as Kruk had ordered, so that he would stop going out on visits to Galuziya. But if he slipped away one more time from the woods and ran to the village, Kruk would kill him and bury him in that very pit.

This incident affected Yideleh, and he no longer went out on independent missions to the village. Yideleh (Jack Melamedik) stayed alive for many years and is today living in Montreal, Canada.

FROM A PARTISAN'S NOTEBOOK

Dov (Berl) Bronstein

For many hours we held council. What should we do? Escape? Where to? With whom? And we didn't have even one weapon. One of the obstacles that hindered an early and organized escape from Manevichi was the danger to the families. The Germans and the Ukrainians distributed warning notices saying that an entire family would be held responsible for one person's escape. Fear began to enter our hearts. Hints from the Ukrainians about liquidating the Jews increased.

Klimchak, the old Ukrainian, and his son lived many years amidst the Manevichi Jews. They acted decently toward us, and at times were very helpful. Jews brought some of their possessions to the Klimchaks for safekeeping. Most of the possessions stayed with them, for most of the Jews were liquidated, but there was never a time when Jews who had been hiding in the woods or in villages would come to them for the return of property, and they would not comply. They sent me personally a message by means of peasant, saying that they wanted to send me all of my belongings.

Before the second "action," the elder Klimchak came to me and suggested strongly that I flee to the woods and hide there for several months, until the war's end. It became clear that I was not the only one who received this advice from him.

He visited most of his Jewish acquaintances and advised them in the same way. The Klimchaks truly acted despite a great deal of personal danger; they were even endangered by their son Andryusha, who was in the Germans' service and, later, an officer with the *Banderovtsy*.

The atmosphere that prevailed in Manevichi was one of depression, and people were wary of one another. We were meeting frequently and consulting on the issue of fleeing to the woods. Encouragement to flee came, in fact, from the head of the "Tudnikim" group, a German who was living in Yeshayahu Zweibel's house during the years 1941-1942. He extended friendship and help toward us, although he did so in a disguised manner. The German did not agree with what was about to happen, but he was forced to take part in the Germans' and Ukrainians' program of annihilation. But he immediately passed on a communiqué about it to Yeshayahu Zweibel and Pinchas Tina, in blessed memory, who worked near him in the woods, preparing trees for transport. He, the "Tudnik," did not know enough to specify an exact date, but he warned that the event was likely to happen in the upcoming days. The news was passed on. The Zweibel family (Yeshayahu, Sarah, Esther, and Ida) and the Singel family (Aryeh, Malka), as well as Pinchas Tina, were the first who fled.

I worked then at a sawmill in Dovzhitsa making oak wood brackets and loading wooden sockets for railroad racks, along with my brother Zev, Chaim Sherman, and Shmaryahu Guz. And then my sister-in-law, Ethel Finkel, arrived with her baby in her arms on the 19 Elul 5701 (1942) and shouted that the city was surrounded by police and Gestapo and some people were shot while trying to escape by way of Porotzki's fence. We tried to flee in the direction of the old church, through the old graveyard, but were fired upon. We went back. We tried again to cross through the Lyudova, but here too, we were heavily fired upon. We walked the entire length of the Torgovaya street. Here a Ukrainian policeman tried to stop us by directing us to our workplace. We gladly went, because from there, we began to escape to the woods in the direction of Koninsk, to Yasenty Slovik's house.

Slovik was known as a religious man, well-liked, with a decent attitude toward the Jews. His house was near the section of woods that belonged to him. His son Casimir was a forester during the German period and behaved as his father did, endangering his own life for the sake of saving Jews. Consequently, all those who fled sensed instinctively, without speaking to one another, that refuge was to be found with Slovik. And it was not surprising that nearly a hundred people were concentrated in the woods near his house during the first days after the slaughter, and that those who reached his home survived and later got organized into a family camp or who joined the fighting unit later. I stayed with Slovik only one day; he received us pleasantly, fed us, and told us about a number of Jews who were hiding in different parts of the woods.

The same evening, we four men departed in the direction of the horse gear traders in Lesovoe. We reached the home of the Surma family, seven brothers, the oldest of them being Franek. Franek fed us until we were full and presented us with a revolver and fifteen bullets, in spite of the fact that Shmaryahu Guz, who was one of our foursome, had not acted well toward him in the past. Shmaryahu removed his wedding ring and gave it to Franek. The latter refused to take it, but Shmaryahu insisted.

We went to see the Polish shoemaker, Puchtovski, in Lukov. We asked him to help us in getting Jews out of Manevichi. This was on Wednesday, 20 Elul. (On the 23rd of Elul, 1942, the slaughter was carried out.) The shoemaker agreed to this, and even revealed to us that two Jewish sisters, Dvorah and Dinah Zilbershtein, were hiding with him. They immediately joined us, and we returned to Slovik's forest. Slovik went to check on the possibility of saving more Jews, and, indeed, he brought, in a wagon covered with hay, Raizel Guz, Shmaryahu's wife, and their two children, Itkah and Yakov. They had been hiding with Klimchak, and Slovik got them with his help.

The Power of Arms

The means for survival in the struggle against the murderers of the Jews was arms; it is impossible to underestimate the importance of the Jews having weapons during the Holocaust period. The wretched Jew stood condemned to death — but with weapons in his hand, he stood erect and saved face — his own and that of his people.

My group had a pistol and a Polish rifle. With these loaded weapons, we arrived at the village of Sobeshchitsy, in order to obtain food. We knocked on a peasant's door, and several Ukrainians, with axes in their hands, appeared in front of us. When they saw weapons in our hands, they lowered the axes, claiming they had thought us to be Jews. These gentiles were not able to imagine Jews with weapons. We looked like Ukrainians in every way. "And what would you have done, if

Jews had shown up here?" we asked. And the reply was, the same that had been done to the Brill family with its three members. "Three Ukrainians handed them over to the police and, in exchange, received thirty kilograms of salt!" We took the gentiles outside, took the axes away from them, and, using our weapons as a threat, got from them the addresses of those who had exchanged Jews for salt. We ordered them to dig a hole, and they were shot and thrown into it. With great effort, we also caught those who had received the salt, and they too were shot. We set fire to the house of one of them, the fire spread through the village, and the church bells were rung. The news spread quickly: "Jews are avenging their brothers' blood!" And, therefore, our operations deterred the "Jew Hunters."

We had Polish friends who were clearly anti-German. Young Ukrainians also joined up with them. We met with a few of them and explained to them that at the present time, the Germans, with the Slavs' help, were liquidating the Jews, but after the Jews, they would subjugate and liquidate the Slavs as well. The common enemy was spoken of here — the cursed Germans and their followers.

We convinced them and received a Polish rifle and thirty bullets. I practiced with the rifle and felt ready to use it. The first opportunity came immediately; about ten Ukrainian policemen, under the command of a German sergeant, occupied an area at the crossroads between Polska Gura and Koninsk. We passed through the area and then we heard "Halt! Don't move!" The company fled, and I stayed behind with the loaded rifle, hidden away. I shot the policeman, Vaska Zaruk, whom I had known for a long time. He was hit in the knee and shouted, "Save me!" The police left the area and got a horse and wagon in order to transport the wounded for medical treatment. (His children survived the Holocaust.)

In a Snow Pit

A refugee family from the occupied territory of Poland, two brothers and two sisters, lived with my uncle Yosef Merin in Manevichi. At the time of the first action, they caught the oldest brother, Tzvi, and beat him until he spat up blood. Fortunately for him, they let him go. During the second action Tzvi managed to escape to the woods. Tzvi's sister, Chanakeh, was already standing naked in a pit, ready to be shot; but at the last second, the German told her to run away. She snatched up a dress from the pile and fled. She crossed over the railroad tracks and got as far as Lesovoe.

As she wandered about, there in the bushes, she noticed a man's shadow. They played "hide and seek," she and the shadow. Chanakeh would alternately emerge and hide until she decided to look at the "shadow," close up. And then they met. Shouts of joy shook the surrounding silence. It was her brother, Tzvi.

At night they found shelter with the Poles. After several days, the two met up with another Jew from the Kovel area by the name of Mundek. The Poles somehow hid them from the Germans and their allies. Until one day, Max (a partisan leader) happened to meet them and they, these Poles, entreated him to take the Jews from them, to save them from German atrocities. The Germans had one penalty in those days for both the Jew and those who hid him: death.

Mundek had arms. Like the Polish residents, he, to, cooperated with the partisans in everything asked of him. Among the things we needed were batteries for flashlights, and equipment for radio communication with Moscow. One time the Shtalitsy commander, Narovsky from Manevichi, brought us these items. He got them from the pharmacist, Belinsky, in exchange for meat. We arranged that on one Sunday evening, we would come and get the items we had asked for. Narovsky was late in arriving. We waited for him. Having nothing to do, I went through the rooms, and I suddenly saw a woman quickly get into bed and cover herself. When I asked who she was, the woman of the house replied, "My daughter." We sat down at the table to eat and in front of me was a hole-ridden curtain covering the doorway of the room where the woman was lying down. She turned away from the bed, looked at me, and seemed to recognize me. After I finished eating and was already outside, Narovsky came out and said to me, "Someone wants to see you." For a second, a trembling passed through me. Maybe it was someone from my family.

I went back into the house, and suddenly I saw Chanakeh Goldberg.

"Why did you hide in the bed?" I asked.

"I thought you were German policemen."

"And where are the two boys who were with you?"

"Not far from here," she said, and burst into tears, begging us to take them from there and save them from certain death.

At that moment, Narovsky came in and added, "This is an opportunity for them to go with you. We very much fear a surprise visit by the Germans. If they suddenly show up, they will kill all of us."

I instructed my friends to go to see Franek Surma, and I went out with Chanakeh to bring the two boys. After we had gone quite a distance on foot, I asked Chanakeh, "Is it much further?"

"No," she answered, and burst into tears.

"And why are you crying?"

"God knows if they are still alive," she said. "It's already two weeks that food hasn't touched their mouths, since the first snow fall, and I have been unable to go see them."

"And who provided them with food before the snow fall?"

"Kalish," she said.

I was startled to hear his name. The same Kalish appeared on our blacklist for liquidation. Only the previous week, our men had liquidated one of his sons, and then I heard that Kalish made a hut on top of a pit for them and equipped them with a saw and an axe — vital things for forest dwellers — in addition to eating utensils.

"I myself," says Chanakeh, "sew, and two weeks ago, I went out to sew for the Poles in a village and stayed with them."

"Is it much further?" I asked her.

"No, very near," she replied.

That night I wore a long fur coat. I had a rifle and a satchel with bullets. I was already drenched with sweat, and I did not see the place where the boys were to be found. At last, we reached the woods. Chanakeh began shouting, "Tzvi, don't be afraid. Berl is here." I looked. The size of the hiding place was perhaps the size of a small table, and snow was piled on it, at least half a meter thick. The boys tried to get out, but they were not successful. I decided to go to Kalish's house, a distance of several kilometers. I awoke him from his sleep.

He hitched two horses and took two shovels with him. We quickly removed the snow from the makeshift shelter and brought out the two frozen boys.

It was hard to say whether they were alive or dead. I seated them in a sleigh, and we went to the Surma family. In the house, a wave of warmth engulfed them, which they so much needed. The mistress of the house put a large bowl on the table with cheese in sour cream and a loaf of bread. All of this was devoured in an instant. I refused them additional portions because of their health. After they had sufficiently warmed themselves, I transferred them in the sleigh to a more secure location, where we were staying temporarily. Food was not scarce then. Meat and bread were hanging on the trees.

After ten days, I transferred them to Kukhotskaya Volya, where we were more established. We had orderly trenches, makeshift showers, and almost an abundance of food — really the "comfortable life." After several days of rest and intensive bathing in our showers, they were transferred to a citizen's camp, where they stayed until the end of the war. The two of them immigrated to South America. Chanakeh married Shaiya Flash. They, too emigrated to South America, and during their visit in Israel, they also visited me.

Blood Revenge Operation

Here a few memories about the first of the Ukrainian partisans, the founders of the partisan unit in our vicinity.

In 1933, the young people of several villages got together in the area and requested a permit from the Polish government to demonstrate on the first of May. The permit was not granted, but the Ukrainians demonstrated anyway. Police from Karasin and Manevichi were summoned, and a special train of police arrived from Kovel. Tempers flared, and one of the demonstrators threw a rock at the face of the Karasin chief of police. He was hit, and some of his teeth fell out. He shot and hit one of the demonstrators. The commotion grew. Arrests and quick trials began. Many of the demonstrators were sentenced to three, four, five, and ten years' imprisonment.

After some years, with the changeover of power in 1939, all the prisoners returned home. The government was now in the hands of the Soviets. Property owners' lands were in the hands of the Soviets. Property owners' lands were confiscated by force in accordance with local orders.

Kolkhozes and agricultural communes were established. The May 1st demonstrators from earlier years got jobs as directors of the *kolkhozes*, food warehouses, and other things of that nature.

In 1941, with the outbreak of the German-Russian war, the Russian army retreated; the local directors and pro-Soviet workers of the city of Kharkov followed it. There they all received instructions to go back to their hometowns and to organize a partisan movement.

One day, four residents of the village of Manevichi returned home. But on that same night, they were arrested by their friends, the demonstrators and prisoners of May 1933, who decided to collaborate with the Germans. The four were transferred to the prison in Kovel, and there awaited their turn to be taken out to be killed, as was the custom of the Germans in those days.

During their time in prison, the four became acquainted with two other young people from the Kovel area. In prison, they also met Sohar, who advised them to escape as their end was approaching. He promised them he would turn a blind eye to their escape. The next night, they sawed through the grid, wove a rope from their clothing and, one by one, lowered themselves to the bottom; from there they crossed the fence and fled to their two friends.

On the same day, they obtained two semi-automatic rifles with ammunition, and all six arrived at our regiment. Another four were equipped with arms, and together they began functioning. In the beginning, they operated on a small scale but consistently. They liquidated informers, Ukrainian police, and plunderers of Jewish property. For a while, the Pole, Max (Sobiesiak), myself, and several other Jews joined them. The small, restricted unit grew. We went over to the localities of Kukhotskaya Volya and the Sazanka, where already the first units of *Polkovnik* (colonel) Brinsky (Dyadya Petya) which later became the central command, and Kruk's unit, were located.

The pressure on Dyadya Petya from the partisans in Max's unit for retaliatory missions increased to the point of agitation. And then, one day, Max returned from the high command with the news of Dyadya's agreement to the hoped-for campaign. Immediately we thirteen fighters went out to the road. From Kruk's camp, another three Jewish fighters joined us: David Blanstein, Zev Avruch, and Yosef Tanenbaum. Still that same night, we got not too far away from the village of Manevichi. We hid there until sunset the next day, maintaining a position where we could see, but not be seen. I was responsible for the execution of the operation. But when the zero hour arrived, I didn't know where to begin.

After I had thought it over I went to the nearest house and ordered the mistress of the house to go and call the village leader. But she came back, claiming that the leader was not home. I ordered her to go a second time and not to return without him. When the two of them appeared, I sent out two men to secure the road leading to the village from the town of Manevichi, in case Germans or the German police would come and surprise us. The order was to shoot at the Germans and retreat. I sent three of our men to the church at the crossroads in the center of the village. I divided the rest of the men into two groups, one under David Blanshtein's command, and the second under my command.

I arrived with my men at the first house and removed my sheepskin. Then Syrkov came up to me and said, "You'll be cold. Wear something else that's lighter." I remember my heart was beating loudly. My hands shook. The depressing thought did not leave me: How is it possible to enter this house and kill for no reason? Suppose I know the people. But the moment the murderer of Jews, who was renowned, appeared before my eyes, even I became a wild man and shot him.

We went on front there to the village leader, who was collaborating with the Germans, and we liquidated him. The leader's wife, Marya, managed to escape through a window. Shaiya Flash was on guard outside, and he shot at her, but he did not hit her. At the same moment, our group arrived, bringing with them the leader's daughter and her husband. We were thrown into a moment of uncertainty. We deliberated. The husband was my neighbor from the town of Manevichi. He fell at my feet and begged for his life. I still did not touch him. Meanwhile, his wife too pleaded that we let him live. According to the information we had received about her, she too deserved to be killed. Her husband became hysterical. I pitied them and warned them not to leave the house.

We continued on to another Gentile, known as an arch executioner of Jews. His friends were there also. We shot them, one by one. From there, we went to several more houses in the "blood revenge" operation. At the end of the campaign, we met up with a second group.

In summary, we liquidated at that time forty-one German collaborators and all those who were with them. The rest fled. The next stage in that operation was confiscation of their property, property that had been stolen from Jews. We also took oxen, cows, and horses that were hitched to wagons and were there for the taking. The convoy continued for a distance of three kilometers. The next day at dawn, we arrived at headquarters to report to Dyadya Petya.

The young men who were among the founders of the Partizankeh were largely involved in this operation. It was these same young men who, in his time, conducted conversations with the Ukrainian police commander, Slivtziak, who had, with his own hands, murdered partisan families.

Nadya the Cook

We left Slovik's woods and found Kruk with his partisans. We situated ourselves not far from him and went to work.

My house in the town and Yakov Bergman's house were close to one another. I knew that in his house there was a cook by the name of Nadya. She was originally from Russia, and she had connections with the Ukrainian police, for whom she was cooking. One day we went to see Vasil Baron in Manevichi. We asked his wife to put us in contact with Nadya. We wet up a specific day and hour for this meeting.

We arrived, five partisans, at the agreed-upon location. Two of us secured the location on the road, outside the house and I waited with two others outside. The meeting in the village of Lukovka was brief and to the point. We proposed to her that at the next meting, she come with several Germans, if this was possible.

Eight of us arrived at the next meeting, at eight o'clock in the evening. We waited until ten-thirty. We looked through binoculars and saw about twenty-five Germans approaching. We immediately left the area.

We contacted her again, and she began to shout about how we had not come to the meeting. Of course, we apologized and let it pass. We set up another meeting next to the brick factory that was near Manevichi. This time she came with ten Germans.

A third meeting was agreed upon. This time, we advised her to obtain a bit of poison and put it in the food of the Ukrainian police. She agreed to carry this mission out, on the condition that if she would have to run away as a result of this deed and would reach the woods and there meet up with the Jews, she would want to blow them up with a grenade, even if she were to die with them. I wanted to kill her at once, but my Gentile friends would not let me. Because of this transgression, I was transferred to another location.

Nadya took the poison with her and the word spread that at a sawmill in Cherevakha, she had poisoned twenty-five Germans and afterwards fled, along with two Cossacks, in the direction of Moshchitzki Buglovoki's farm. There she met the staff patrol, and they took her to the woods.

The person responsible for the kitchen in those days was Ostshenko Moriniak and his son Kolya. After a few days, when she had become familiar with the surroundings and was slightly known by the partisans, they made her responsible for the cooking. And then suddenly, she was caught red-handed with the same poison in her hand, intending to put it in a pot of milk. She was immediately taken to a special unit — Base 5 — under the command of Major Mahmed (Melamed). In spite of the strict guard that was placed on her, she managed to steal a rifle and escape.

That same night, I went off with Shaiya Flash. We were traveling in two wagons with sacks of flour from the village Galuziya to Base 5, when our horses suddenly became alarmed. I jumped out of the wagon — and saw Nadya in front of me. When I asked, "Where to?" she pointed her rifle at me.

I did not get flustered. I grabbed her rifle with one hand
and with the other, pulled her hair. I told my friend Shaiya to
inform headquarters of the incident. Immediately, Mahmed
appeared from the other direction and, without much delay,
drew his pistol and shot her. At that moment, the commander
of the special unit, Vasilenko, also arrived. On seeing what
had occurred, he turned around and caught the two Cossacks,
Nadya's friends. He found them sleeping, took them outside,
and shot them.

The Wedding Operation

During operations at railroads in the town of Manevichi, a
train with salt, a vital commodity in those days, was among
those damaged. This enabled the villagers to steal considerable amounts of salt.

After this operation, we learned that in the adjacent village,
Vyrka, there was to be a wedding on Saturday night where a
Ukrainian policeman was to be present. I reported this to the
captain and he ordered that we kill the policeman. Toward
this end, we obtained two horses, which we returned after a
few days. The informant, a policeman, hid at his brother-in-
law's home (Sak), because he refused to cooperate with us, the
partisans, and he agreed. When Jews walked about the woods
and villages, knocking on the doors of villagers for a piece of
bread, a potato, or any kind of food to satisfy their hunger,
he would give them something and even ordered his younger
brother to transport Jews behind the village and send them
to the woods. When I showed up at their house I was warmly
received, despite the fact that the first time he saw me, he was
completely shaken. I calmed him down and assured him that
humane deeds were rewarded. The members of the household began to hug me and kiss me with great emotion. They
set a table fit for a king, given the conditions of those days,
and eventually, with great difficulty, I was able to take my
friend out of the house.

We went out on the road in the direction of Vyrka. In the
middle of the road, we saw from afar a flashing light. We
decided to find out the explanation for the light. When we
reached the site, we saw one of our liaisons boiling whiskey.
He urged us to drink with him. And so we finished a full liter

of liquor. Dead-drunk, my Russian friends arrived at Vyrka, and there was no one to go with me to the "wedding." I situated myself at the village elder's home. I put my Russian friends to bed. I assigned Yitzchak Segal to guard duty. I left my rifle in the house and took one of my drunken friends' submachine uns. Shaiya Flash and I went out to the school in the village, where the wedding was being held. When I called out, asking if the policeman was among those present, they answered that this man did not exist. But next to one of the tables, I noticed unusual movement among the people. I called out his name a second time and fired into the air. I approached; it became apparent that the people were trying to hide the policeman under the table. I ordered him to throw down his arms. Shaiya Flash grabbed his rifle, and the police-man crawled outside. We tied his hands with rope and moved from there to the elder's house.

On the way, we received 11,500 gold rubles from him. I joined my company, and before dawn, we reached Sazanka, where the commander Chunek Wolper was staying. There, we took him out of the wagon into the bushes and shot him, according to Dyadya Petya's orders.

The Eighteen Fat Cows

We were informed that a herd of cattle that belonged to the Germans was grazing in the village of Galuziya. Eight of us went and waited not far from Manevichi's church, until the shepherds returned from lunch. Upon their arrival, we immediately surrounded the herd. The shepherds quickly scattered in every direction, but we managed to catch a few of them. We picked out eighteen cows. I gestured to a young boy shepherd who was about fifteen, and asked him, "You know me; what's my name?

"Yes" he answered, "your name is Burku."

"And do you know my friend?"

"Yes, Segal," he replied.

"And now, go and tell people that Yitzchak and Burku con-fiscated the cattle."

The shepherds informed the Germans about the deed in the meadow. The Germans immediately sent forces next to the small wooden bridge on the road leading to Galuziya to block the partisans' retreat. I succeeded in outwitting the Germans. Instead of sending the cattle to Galuziya, as the Germans imagined I would, I sent them to the Optova woods; and then I, with two others, arrived at the cemetery of the village of Galuziya and ambushed the Germans. When they reached the small wooden bridge, which had been burned down for a while and was not passable for vehicles, we opened fire on them. Upon hearing shots, a reinforcement arrived from the village, from the flourmill that was run by one of our men, Avraham Puchtik. After this, an advance unit from a frontal position joined us, from the village of Serkhov.

The Germans were forced to retreat. We maintained eighteen fat cattle for quite a while. We held a feast for kings.

The Jewish Partisans and the Local Population

The Jewish boys from Kruk's unit excelled at forcibly entering homes of villagers and confiscating clothing, food, and the like, which was the most natural thing for them. As Jews from the area, they knew about this or that peasant's role in plundering, or in the murder of Jews. They essentially returned Jewish property that had been stolen for the good of the citizens' camp. But headquarters did not view this kind of behavior favorably, and tragic events occurred. Complaints were made to Kruk about his Jewish fighters, and he took severe measures against them. Malinka (Dov Lorber) was once stood up at a formation, and his commander and friend Kruk slapped him in front of everyone. Malinka was forced to restrain himself, because he knew that opposition would lead to severe consequences, for him and for others.

Once a Jewish fighter from the unit took a pair of boots from a peasant from the village of Gorodok. This matter was brought to the attention of Kruk. The fighter denied it, but his things were searched, and the boots were, in fact, found. Kruk, seething with anger, drew his pistol and was about to shoot the Jewish man.

With great difficulty, Yosef Zweibel succeeded in convincing him, for his sake to not shoot the fighter. Afterwards, Kruk apologized to him, speaking as a close friend, saying that all of the slander was coming from his Jewish comrades, and so he had no choice but to react as he did.

Once, a peasant by the name of Dmitry, who served as a liaison in our unit, made a complaint to me. This peasant had a warm relationship with the camp's Jews. He and his sons would take the children from the camp to their homes, giving showers and feeding them. In those days, a lot of significance was attached to such things.

He complained about a partisan from Kruk's unit who had confiscated a sewing machine, a pair of oxen, and a wagon from him, pointing out that he wasn't angry about this and wasn't asking that the things be returned to him, because the matter could cause reactions and retaliations.

I knew that I was obligated to act in a quiet manner, so that the matter would not reach headquarters and Dyadya Petya, who closely watched over the integrity of the partisans toward the village population. I consulted with Kruk, and he ordered that the confiscated items be quietly returned to their owner.

And there was another incident. I was ordered, as head of a group of fifteen partisans, to confiscate all the belongings in a distant house in the middle of the woods, that were to be used for a wedding there.

We arrived in three sleighs, after a three-hour trip. We found many goods — boots, clothing, coats, and a lot of food that was prepared for the wedding.

Everything was loaded onto the sleighs, and we got ready to leave. Suddenly the peasant remarked that "if only Nikolai (Kruk) knew, they wouldn't be doing this to him." And the peasant told me about a battle between four partisan-paratroopers from the great army and one hundred police and Germans. They all fell, except one wounded man who reached the peasant's home, and he, the peasant, hid him in the attic and gave him medical treatment. I knew that he was telling the truth, and I ordered that the things we had confiscated be returned, but the peasant asked that we divide them up, fifty-fifty. And so we did. Then he pointed out a place not far from there where they made *samogon* (a liquor). We supplied ourselves with twenty-five liters, and with great difficulty, I prevented the partisans from getting drunk. I had to threaten them with my weapons to prevent this. In the past, tragic incidents had occurred when a company got drunk and fell into the hands of the *Banderovtsy*. When I reported this to the commander, Captain Anishchenko (Dyadya Sasha), he came up to me to kiss me on the head. "You acted in a manner worthy of a Soviet partisan."

A Ukrainian partisan slandered a peasant, because he was courting the peasant's daughter, and she didn't return his love. Disappointed, he decided to take revenge in this base manner.

Once, while on reconnaissance with the objective of attacking the Karasin police, we passed by Zamostye and went on to the road leading to the Polish forester, Tsibulsky. The latter sensed us coming and, thinking we were Ukrainian police, jumped out of the window and fled. The next day, about twenty of us paid a visit to the forester, with an order to confiscate all of his property. We didn't find him, only a woman, whom we thought to be his wife. We loaded up everything, and one of the partisans, Yeshayahu Shalosh, called to me in Yiddish, "Berl, *lomir gayen...*" Upon hearing this, the woman was jolted and shouted, "Are you Jews? Please don't do this for the sake of the Pole who rescued me. I am a Jewess from Lutsk."

We returned the things and later established very friendly relations with Tsibulsky, who served as a liaison. He greatly excelled at this job.

Germans Following Max's Blood

When we found out about the German hunt in the woods that was to occur at the beginning of the frost and snow season, we immediately got in touch with Kazik (Casimir) Slovik, and he contacted the former school principal in Manevichi who had been a forest watchman during the German rule. The two of them contacted Slipchuk, the Ukrainian chief of police.

Slipchuk was willing to meet with us, the partisans. We agreed upon a location not far from the town. From the partisan side, three Ukrainian youths, Max, and I appeared. On the way to the meeting, a youth from the village of Griva who served in the Ukrainian police force came out to meet us. He was also said to be participating in the upcoming hunt, and he told us its approximate date (February 2, 1943).

The policeman took a hat with a particular sign on it from the sleigh and asked that, during the hunt, we wouldn't fire at him and then he too would not fire on us. He also advised us to leave the area for a while until things calmed down. The meeting with the chief of police took place in a tense atmosphere, because it was the same chief of police who, thirty days previously, had ordered the murder of partisan families and Jews, including the families of the three partisans sitting there with us. These three requested that we liquidate him, but the order that Max received from Dyadya Petya was unequivocally, "Don't harm him." The three left after many pleas and words of persuasion. When we returned to the woods after reports and clarifications, it was decided that we leave the woods and station ourselves in the village of Svaritsevichi, which was under the command of Fedorov-Ryvnya.

The retreat from the woods took place on Saturday night, the 10th of January, 1943, at midnight, north of the village of Kukhotskaya Volya. We stationed ourselves for a few days in a local school in the village of Svaritsevichi. Shaiya Flash, Yitzchak Segal, and I were sent out to secure the road leading to Dovrovitch. Meanwhile, it was decided at our headquarters to send out patrols in the vicinity of our base, which we had left only a number of days earlier.

The mission was assigned to Max, who already held the rank of captain. He joined up with me and two other partisans, and we went out to the road, which was full of surprises. The first of them occurred when we crossed the Styr River, which was icy and slippery. One of the horses slipped and was torn in half. He was shot on the spot. I tied ragged sacks onto the second horse's feet, and in this way, we crossed the river. Further along the road, we confiscated a peasant's horse that we chanced upon on our route. The same night, in the freezing cold of -32° Celsius, we traveled 120 kilometers to the village of Belskaya Volya. We entered one of the houses, whose owner (Yosef) was a foodseller for the German government. He complained to us that a while ago, partisans had burned 3,000 tons of kernels. We tried to clarify among us whose unsuccessful operation this had been, and reached the conclusion that this had been one of Kruk's unit's operations. We were hungry and frozen, tired from the journey and from lack of sleep. Yosef put a bottle of vodka on the table, which emitted a burnt odor.

I ordered him to bring spirits and dessert at once. After the meal, we continued on to the sawmill in the village that belonged to a Jew by the name of Mikolitch (he is today in Israel). Near the sawmill were wooden shacks that were the workers' quarters. Max set up a resting place for us there for the day. I pointed out to him that it was not a suitable place for resting, but he did not heed my warning. We unharnessed the horses and went to rest. Everyone went. One of the two partisans urged me to also go and rest so that I'd be able to continue on, but I was unable to fall asleep and went outside. I sensed that imminent danger awaited us.

While standing outside, I heard a loud racket coming from the center of town. I asked the first man I met on the road what the noise was, and he said, "To tell you the truth, I don't know if those are Germans over there, or partisans."

I weighed these words carefully; I did not want to lose the good reputation I had won in a short time as a fighter and an implementer in the young partisan movement. I thought that maybe they were in fact partisans. But very quickly I realized that other partisans besides us could not be here in the area at that time, and that I must quickly and immediately wake up my comrades. I followed the Germans' movements and saw them dividing up into two groups. In one there were seven Germans heading toward the village of Serkhov, and in the other were five Germans going in the direction of the village of Vyrka. It was clear to me that we were surrounded. Just at that moment, a young girl from the household burst into the house shouting, "Holy Mary, we are surrounded!" Partisans burst out of the house, including Max, who was barefoot, and this was in -32-degree cold. He fired from his automatic rifle to the right flank and ordered me to strike at the left side. We waged a battle in this way for twenty minutes.

And then I sensed that the ammunition had run out, that the bullets in my satchel had been used up — and so I gave the command to retreat in the direction of the grove. Completely exhausted, we reached a tree that had been uprooted in one of the storms and, as a result, blocked the road. A lot of blood dripped from Max's legs, and the

Germans pursued us following the bloodstains. Max removed his shirt and tore it to pieces, in order to bandage his legs, and we went to a clearing in the woods. A pile of hay was there. I took two grenades from my satchel, and we decided to prepare for the final battle. We observed from afar that the Germans were getting closer and closer to the uprooted tree — and when they didn't see the bloody footprints, they turned around and retraced their steps.

We continued on toward one of the houses, where we ended up the day, and at night we went on in the direction of the village of Serkhov. We stayed with a Pole by the name of Diknesky, and he told us about the Germans, who, during their retreat from the woods at the time of the hunt, captured a Jew from Chelm by the name of Chaim. The Pole also told us about the battle we had waged the previous day in the village of Belskaya Volya. We went on from there in a sleigh, which we had confiscated for our use, and reached the village of Koninsk. The next night, we traveled to headquarters to report to *Polkovnik* Brinsky (Dyadya Petya). I received an order to take ten of the best young men and to try to find out who had informed on us in the village of Belskaya Volya. And if the investigation were successful, we would liquidate the informers and confiscate their property. Anything that could not be taken, we would burn.

The road was a good one. We arrived quickly and immediately began the investigation but we came up against a stonewall. No one talked. We arrived at the house where we had recently been, but we were unable to single out anyone. The members of the household received us nicely, returning a blanket and fur to me. I urged them to tell me what they knew, but in vain.

We returned to the sawmill and to the families where we had originally been. We searched the houses and every type of potential hiding place. We discovered some things, mainly precious strips of leather that really had been stolen by the "tenants." I returned to report to *Polkovnik* Brinsky. He smiled and said, "Next time they will kill you, because you didn't kill all of them."

Fifty-Six German Casualties

During the war, great importance was attached by both of the fighting armies — but especially by the Germans — to transportation. The Germans transported most of their equipment and manpower to the front by means of the railroad. Because of this, emphasis was placed in the partisan movement on disrupting the transportation system whenever possible.

Two men were assigned to this task from each unit. We stationed ourselves in the Galuziya woods, with the purpose of making sudden attacks, mining the railroad tracks, and carrying out acts of sabotage. We would visit the tracks every other night, or when we had early information about German soldiers being rushed to the front. The information was leaked to us by Ukrainian and Polish workers, the signalers who had worked during the Polish and Russian rule until 1941. In this way, we received information about a train with German army officers, making its way to the front. Nine of us men went out for the mining operation. We sat near the tracks for three consecutive days. At the estimated time of the train's arrival — at ten at night — we went up on the tracks with a large mine, set up to be pulled by a cord. It weighed seventy kilograms. When we finished setting up the mine, the patrols signaled us that a guard unit was approaching to check the tracks. We didn't know whether to remove the mine or leave it, as it could be discovered. The danger was great. I suggested that we leave it, because a few weeks earlier, a partisan from Kruk's unit had been killed in a similar operation.

We were still discussing this matter when the train approached. We pulled hard on the cord, and a powerful explosion, whose echo was heard over a forty-kilometer radius, shook the air. The entire train was turned over on its side. Only from the last cars, shots were head, fired wildly. We went off in the opposite direction in order to mislead them so that they wouldn't follow our path of retreat. The next day, we learned there had been hundreds of casualties and many wounded. This was March 23, 1943.

We returned to headquarters. I was sick, my whole body was covered with wounds, and I was forbidden to leave the woods. They set up a bed for me behind the trenches, in the bushes, and there I received medical treatment from Dr. Melchior. Once, while I was lying down, half awake, half asleep, I heard someone coming. I quickly opened my yes, and *Polkovnik* Brinsky was standing in front of me. He calmed me down, asked how I was, and we began talking. I said, "What brought you to see me, Comrade *Polkovnik*?" And he told me not very good news. "Headquarters' patrols brought word that tomorrow the Germans plan to confiscate 300 head of cattle in the villages of Karasin and Zamostye; I'd like to stop them from doing this," *Polkovnik* said.

"You are putting this on my shoulders, Comrade *Polkovnik*?"

"I'm not happy about disturbing you when you're sick, but there is no other way. Take a mine from headquarters, get a shell from Kruk, and at the village of Galuziya pick out whichever men you choose — and go safely!"

I did as I was commanded. I equipped myself with a mine, asked my older brother, Velvel, to hitch a god horse to a wagon for me, got the shell from Kruk and went out by myself to Galuziya. On the way I made all sorts of calculations about how to carry out the operation in the best possible way. I got an idea. I figured that some of our comrades must have lived there, after they had escaped from prison but before joining the partisans. And I was right. I met eight of them in one of the houses, sitting around the table eating and drinking. I joined them, and we began to work out a plan of action.

At dawn, when we were ready to go, it rained, and there was a flood. But we continued on. The mine, as well as the shell, got wet. I sent a local youth out to the road leading from the village of Manevichi to Karasin, telling him that the minute he saw the Germans, he should quickly run back and tell us. Our messenger met a peasant who was returning from Manevichi, and he told him that the village was full of Germans and Ukrainian police, and hat they were said to be heading for Karasin. We acted according to this information, opening fire with every weapon we had.

In the villages, panic ensued. The Germans fled back to the city, and the villagers in Karasin led the cattle to the central location as they thought that it was Germans who were firing the shots.

The villagers, some delighted and others disappointed, stood openmouthed when they saw us. The village leader, who had brought his two oxen, was shot on the spot, and we confiscated his oxen. We picked out fifty-five cows and set the rest free. Some of the villagers asked us to kill their cows, so that the Germans wouldn't take them and eat their meat. We fulfilled their request.

A Chapter of Events on Passover

Passover eve, 1943. Two Poles from Guta-Stepanska came to us, and asked Max, our commander, for help in setting up a Polish partisan movement. Max consented. He chose twenty men and went out with them to the road, a distance of about 120 kilometers. In Guta-Stepanska, it became clear that the situation was not improving. The local residents, the Poles, either were unable or did not want to defend themselves with their own resources. Many Poles also lived in the town who had fled their hometowns and Polish villages and settlements that had been established during the Polish rule were found there. In these people's neighborhoods, there were also Ukrainian villagers who were notorious for their hatred of the Poles, no less than that of the Jews. These Ukrainians were persuaded by the Germans to make names for themselves among the Poles, after committing murderous deeds against the Jews. The Ukrainians would torture the Polish mad and make them die unusual and unnatural deaths. They would throw Poles upside-down into wells of water and do other brutal acts.

The Ukrainians' cruel actions spread alarm and fear amidst their Polish neighbors, and the Poles fled to the city. The overcrowding in the houses increased. There were about fifty people crowded together in every house — women, children, and babies. The pandemonium was great.

Max called together the city dignitaries and tried to talk with them. Taking into account the existing conditions, he tried to incorporate them into the partisan network. We suggested that there be a cooperative guard duty over the town, day and night (a suggestion that *Polkovnik* Brinsky did not agree to). In the end, it was decided to send a different unit, under the command of Porotchnik (a lieutenant in the Polish army), who was a native of Guta-Stepanska. Twenty of us went with him. We crossed river and railroad tracks that were closely guarded by the Germans. After we safely crossed the railroad tracks and arrived at Galuziya, the *Shtalitsy* (similar to the Gadna youth corps in Israel) reached a commander who supplied us with wagons and horses — and we went on to Guta-Stepanska. Together with the Polish fighters' commander, we outlined a plan of action. There was an explicit and severe order given not to fire unnecessarily, because all of the residents knew that an open fire was a signal for them to defend themselves and ward off any kind of an attack, whether it be by Ukrainians or Germans.

With our appearance, the Poles' sense of security increased tenfold. They led counterattacks on the Ukrainians, who imposed fear on the area.

We found out that in the Guta vicinity, two Ukrainians were moving about, one of them more than two meters tall, that they were armed with machine guns and were assigned to an area extending over a square kilometer. Quite a lot of murderous acts were credited to them. We immediately investigated their security techniques. It became clear that they were very simple. The two of them regularly left the center, each one going in the opposite direction, and then they returned to the center. We divided up into two groups and lay an ambush for them.

When they came near the edge of the section, we surprised them in such a way that they had no time to activate their weapons. We tied their hands from behind and, bound, we brought them to Guta, to the former post office. There we imprisoned them in one of the rooms and posted a guard over them. We went out to eat. To be on the safe side, Yitzchak Melnitzer and I went back and tied their hands and feet with wires.

The post office serviced the Polish headquarters, so it buzzed with people all hours of the day, but during that day, it did even more so. The Poles wanted to punish the two murderers by "lynching" them, and when we returned, the two looked like corpses. The next day we brought them to Solyonye Bolota, salty water marshes, where we buried them alive.

Once when I returned to the center of town, near the church where a meeting of the local Polish high command was taking place, presided over by the Commissar, I suddenly heard six shots from the direction of the village of Vyrka. One of our fighters was hospitalized in this village. I suspected that he had been liquidated. I burst into the church and reported the shots to Porotchnik. He sent a Pole with me and a pair of horses hitched to a wagon, and we went off in the direction of the shots. I broke into the house, where I found Vanka and a young woman with him who made a strange impression on me. I observed her closely, and I had no doubt in my heart as to her origins.

When I asked her who she was, she burst into tears. I calmed her down. I asked her if she lacked anything, but she insisted, "I don't lack anything except freedom." She also told me that she had been with the *ksiądz* (Polish priest). I thanked he for the help she had extended to the wounded man, and I extended my hand in a parting gesture, when she again broke into tears and begged me to take her with me, pleading that I should not leave her there. I said to Vanke, "I'm taking you home." He started to cry, "How am I going to be able to make it through a long and very dangerous route such as this?" We had to cross over railroad tracks and the Styr River.

I calmed him down. I told him that I had another sick person, Dyadya Malyshov, and also two wounded people from our woods. I took leave of those who were in the house, and we went with the Pole to the road leading back. When we arrived at Solyonye Bolota, I saw many people gathered together, blocking the road. We had to walk around in order to get over to them. There we met about twenty Polish youths, armed with automatic weapons and several hundred citizens surrounding the two youths, who it became apparent, were partisans. When I asked them why they had fired, they answered that they were testing out their weapons. I interrogated the two of them as to who they were and what they were doing and it became clear that they were partisans from Suborov's unit. I suggested to Yitschak Segal that we take action against them, that is, take their weapons from them. I wanted to show them what Jews were capable of doing.

In a matter of seconds we had their submachine guns, and I made them sit in the wagon. We had just started moving, when we saw from afar their commander approaching. They reported to him and pointed to us. Their commander asked me what had happened. I answered, "I don't know you, either. Come back with me to our commander, Vanka Danilchenko." After some brief clarifications their weapons were returned, and they were set free, in the midst of warm handshakes. They, the *Suvorovtsy*, were impressed by our actions, especially when Vanka told them that Yitzchak Segal and I were Jews. He also told them that, when they were in a village staying with peasants, after the disintegration of the Red Army, they had established ties with Jews, who were always desirable candidates for the partisan movement.

This was during Passover. We were coming into the village, when two youths came up to me and asked me if I'd like to see how Jews conduct the Passover-night Seder. We went to the edge of the village, Yitschak Segal and I, and went into a barn. The people were startled. I immediately calmed them down, "Don't be afraid. We are Jews too. Continue?" It pained me to see their fear, and my eyes filled with tears. Silence prevailed. Old people, men and women, held a Seder. I asked them if they needed help. "Only *Haribono Shel Olam* (The Almighty God) can help us through all of this in peace," they said. We wished them a good holiday and parted from them with tears in our eyes.

After two days, I left the place. I received an order to transfer the sick ones to headquarters, which was, so to speak, home. I brought with me one of my Ukrainian fighter friends, Lazar Kadek. Three more wounded people from another unit joined us, among them a young woman who was slightly wounded. They had gone out, ten of them, on an operation and come up against Ukrainian nationals. Seven fell during a battle with them. Those who remained asked to go to Guta-Stepanska, which was in the direction we were going. I received under my command twenty Poles, who were to help us cross over the railroad tracks. I divided the Poles up into two groups. The first one posted itself on one side of the tracks, and the second on the other side, across from the bunker's entrance. Kadek and I crossed over to the second side and took a position across from the bunker. The wounded young woman appeared to help us, with a submachine gun in her hand. The wagons with the wounded and sick safely crossed the railroad tracks.

Before we were done with one obstacle, we had to face a second danger. The nationalistic village, Lozki, stretched out before us. I stopped the caravan of wagons and, with my friends, slipped into the village to check out the situation. We immediately noticed two villagers moving about, with sticks in their hands. We took them to the wagon with us and tied their hands from behind. We learned from them that their job was to go to the church and ring the bells if partisans appeared in the vicinity of the village, and then the weapon-owners would organize themselves and fire at the partisans. Fortunately for us, this plan was frustrated. We made the prisoners go up on the wagons and slipped out of that place, in the direction of the village of Babka. There, in one of the homes, I obtained a pitcher of milk and a loaf of bread. I threw the two prisoners out of the wagon and continued on to Guta-Stepanska, where the young woman had stayed with her two wounded comrades.

From Guta-Stepanska, we continued on to Krymno. There we had a frontal position with four men. From the large amount of information we received, it was clear that a German unit that had left the town of Rafalovka was pursuing us. Very quickly, we approached the Styr River and went up on the bridge, which was temporary and small, and apt to move and get closer to the edge of the river which we wanted. Our men from the frontal position, under cover, brought the sick down to the shore, to the bushes, and we camouflaged them. The Germans got as far as the river, stayed there a bit, and retraced their footsteps.

With the Germans' retreat, I freed the Poles on their wagons and horses. I took, in place of them, two wagons and horses from our unit. I gathered the sick together and traveled to headquarters, to report to Dyadya Petya. In spite of the late hour — two in the morning — he listened patiently to the report, asked questions, and advised me to sleep at headquarters and not go "home." He even gave an unequivocal order not to wake me in the morning. When I got up, he invited me to eat breakfast at his company. Meanwhile, the doctor visited the sick, and he, too, reported on their condition. One of the sick was in critical condition. (He later died.) Vanka was out of danger and remained alive.

I went "home" to the mother-unit under Max's command. They held a nice reception for me. I also reported to Max about his Polish brothers. He made many endless comments, but generally received everything in a good and sympathetic manner.

During that time rumors circulated, saying that there were those who wanted to poison the captain, that is, Max. Max was invited to celebrate the Polish holiday, Easter, that was coming up at that time, to stay with Tsibulsky, in the village of Karasin. Max informed me of this and added that he would not go without me, because I was responsible for him and would not cause him any harm. We arrived at Tzivolski's house. I couldn't stare long enough at the abundance of food that was laid out on the table. In the midst of eating and drinking, our host told us that in the town of Manevichi there were close to 20,000 Germans. It wasn't clear what they were planning to do — attack us or attack the Ukrainian nationalists in the vicinity of Kolki.

After the meal, despite the fact that Max was in Goloby, we headed for Koninsk, to our friend, a Pole by the name of Casimir Slovik. We were sure that he already knew about the Germans' plan. Slovik was already waiting for us, impatiently. He had been sure that someone would come in light of the situation.

He knew that the Germans were going to Kolki. I was relieved. It was difficult to speak with Max, as he was dead drunk and in a deep sleep. I politely postponed the invitation to have breakfast, saying, "I must report to headquarters, and I have a thirty-five kilometer journey ahead of me." Without rest or sleep, I reached headquarters the next day at eight o'clock in the morning and reported to Dyadya Petya about what was going on in the region. That was the end of my operations during Passover.

Another incident occurred earlier, when we were staying with Slovik in the woods. We once returned late at night, after an intensive operation, and we were very thirsty. When we passed by Lesovoe, I knew that there was a spring of water among the bushes. I put my gun down, stretched out on the ground, and scooped up water from the spring with my palms. My friends did as I did. Suddenly in the quiet of the night, I heard a moan and then a groan. My sharp sense of hearing, which had developed during that time, led me in the direction of the groans. With my rifle extended, I advanced a few more steps. I was stunned. On the ground lay two dying men. I immediately recognized them. They were Yosef Tanenbaum and Dr. Melchior, the two refugees who had fled the German occupation of Poland and had come to us in 1939.

I lay them down in the wagon and brought them close to the partisans' central meeting place. I told them how we had found two Jews, one of them a doctor, but they adamantly refused to receive them in their ranks. The reason was this: when the partisans were getting organized one of the fighters, Lazovy, was hit badly in the stomach. They sent a messenger to the city and requested that this same doctor come to treat the wounded man; he refused. Because of this, they were not willing to receive him now. (By the way, the wounded man recovered and prepared a rifle for me, with bullets, during the time he was still in the ghetto.) I argued with them and raised man different points and reasons for taking the two in. I argued that if the doctor had really left the town at that time, it was likely that he wouldn't have had enough time to reach them, and the Germans would have killed him on the road; secondly, our struggle with the Germans was still our chief concern, and we still needed a doctor. One of them shouted in an angry voice, "If you feel that we must receive him — go and bring both of them!" I quickly ran and brought them.

Later on, when we moved to Kruk's area, where there were also Russian partisans, Dr. Melchior served as the Brigade's doctor and lived with us, the fighters. When I once brought him a piece of soap, he was delighted. In 1944, with the entry of the Red Army, Dr. Melchior left the woods and moved to the city of Rovno. I, along with a number of other Jews, had to go across the Bug River, which was under German control.

And so, we reached the Bug River that was then a line of battle.

In 1945 I arrived in Lublin and worked there with "Antek" Zuckerman in the *Breicha*[21] movement. Later on, at the end of 1946, I was in Israel. Once, in Jaffa, in the milk factory, *T'nuvah*, a man passed by me like a shadow and disappeared. I asked one of the workers at the place if that was not a doctor by the name of Melchior. At that instant, she called out "Mr. Melchior, someone's looking for you!" He came up to me, brought me coffee and cake and told me, in answer to my question, that his brother the doctor had been looking for me for a long time. He had even been at Kibbutz Yagur, looking for me there.

One day I met with the doctor. He could not control his emotions and burst out crying. We sat, together with his wife and brother, and talked at length about those days and the problems of that time. One day he later passed away. May his soul be bound up in the bond of everlasting life.

An Evening of Dancing and A Hunt for Murderers

On one spring day in 1943, Dyadya Petya came to see us. He advised Max to take on the command of the advanced position in the village of Serkhov. Max, on his part, appointed me local commander. He placed under my authority fifteen men, including two Jews. The villagers of Serkhov were among the worst in the area due to their long-time hostility toward the Polish government. The residents were also distinguished for their cruel hatred of the Soviet government and, particularly, of the Jews. When we reached the place, I chose a house close to the woods, next to a Pole.

With Anishchenko's visit, the reason for the gang of murderers, the *Banderovtsy*'s hasty disappearance became clear to me. Using the weight of my position as local commander, I ordered that a general meeting convene in the school on Saturday night. The school was filled from wall to wall, but the wanted murderers did not show up. On the spot, I announced that the next day, on Sunday, an evening of dancing, accompanied by an orchestra, would be held in the same place. I warned them that whoever didn't come today and also didn't come the next day would be punished.

The next day, four men from the *Banderovtsy* arrived. Also, some musicians came. I immediately sent out patrols to the village to set up the situation. When Manchi from Povorsk arrived, we went into the school. I instructed the musicians to play energetically, to make merry and make noise. My instructions to the comrades were, for each of them to go up to one of the wanted men and arrest him. During a break in the music, I went up on the stage and announced, "In the name of the Soviet government, and by orders of the partisan movement — the *Banderovtsy* are under arrest!" Our men stood paired up with each of the wanted men, and the order was given, "Hands behind your back!" They were tied up right away. The large crowd began to escape through the doors and windows. At the entrance to the house, two wagons were waiting, and we loaded them, two by two, onto the wagon.

We brought them to an advanced position in Galuziya, where Vaska Butko was the commander. He was one of the young men I had brought to the woods. We ate supper there. Vaska advised me to rest a bit after the capturing mission. I put off his advice, expressing the desire to spend the night in the company of the murderers. He cleared a house of its inhabitants, and there we "hosted" the murderers — the enthusiastic German collaborators. Among them was one by the name of Ritz Sopol, a blatant sadist and murderer of many Jews. He dealt murderous blows to my cousin's husband during the first action. I got a wooden stake from the yard and went inside to settle an account with him.

I started to strike him. I struck him one blow after the other: "This is for Nyoma." "This is for this or that Jew" It was a long list, because he had killed many a Jew with his own hands. After this, I moved on to the other one. Joachim was his name, and I continued in the same manner. "Tell me," I asked him, "how many Russian soldiers did you kill?"

"I didn't count," he replied, "maybe fifty." I shot him on the spot and threw his body outside, into the bushes.

The next morning, Max arrived. We loaded the three of them onto the wagons and went to the woods by way of Serkhov. Some of Serkhov's residents were Poles. Max wanted to show them his deeds, as a Pole — that one of the murderers has been killed, and the other three awaited a similar end.

Upon our arrival in the woods, the three were sent to bases, where they were tied to trees with ropes. As was later found out, one of the three, Ritz Sopol, asked the partisan guard assigned to him to loosen his rope a bit. He did the rest of the work himself. (By the way, the aforementioned partisan guard was a former soldier in Vlasov's unit and had served in the German police force.) We found out that the escaped murderer was walking about, armed. I was warned about this. We continuously laid ambushes for him in every possible location, but with no results. One he sent his cousin to me, asking that I stop looking for him, "for the good of both of us."

In the meantime, an order from Dyadya Petya arrived. He wanted us to bring back alive one of Kaplatz's two sons, who was operating as a nationalist, and the other, whose name was Shashka. Four of us went out to lay an ambush next to Kaplatz's house. We sat in the bushes from nine o'clock in the morning until late at night, with no results.

The next day my comrades asked if they could leave the spot, saying that they were hungry. I urged them to stay a bit longer, and I would take care of the food. I moved a few hundred meters away, into the bushes and came to a clearing in the woods, enclosed by a wooden fence. This spot was used as a plant nursery by its owner. From a distance, I could see the murderer moving about inside of it. I quickly retraced my steps and reported tom friends that he was definitely armed with a submachine gun. I cautioned them not to act hastily. We had to close in on him from every side and fire in such a way as to not hit one another.

When we got close to the fence, the first one to jump inside was Pavka (Pavel) Metkalik, a seventeen-year-old boy, our friend Silvestr's son. Pavel advanced a few steps and shouted to him, "Hands up!" while pointing his gun at him. He, the murderer, came out instead under the bundles of grain that were piled up in the nursery and jumped Pavel, grabbing his throat. On seeing this I shot him from behind and fired a few more rounds into the air. The murderer fell, rolling in his own blood. On hearing the shots, his wife and daughter came running, and they began to wail. I advised my friends to go back and set an ambush for the two sons. But they suggested, in contrast to this, that we take a break and rest a bit.

We returned to our command post and began planning the liquidation of Shashka. One evening we went to his house and told his wife that we wanted to meet with him and have him join the partisans and be like "one of the guys." His job with us would be to take care of the horses, to feed and water them — in short, a job that was not difficult.

The next evening we met at the designated spot, at the home of Vanka Vavluk's father, who I had once brought out from Guta when Vanka had been sick. Andrei Shashka was pleased with my offer. We filled up two large sacks with straw and loaded them on our wagon, hitched two horses and left for the woods with the murderer. On the road, I exchanged a few words with my friend Vanka, as to which one of us would liquidate him. Vanka proposed that I do it.I, in contrast to this, offered the task to Vanka. And going on like this we came to a point not far from our command post, Sazanka, which was under the command of Chunek Wolper. This was an area where, from then on, firing shots was absolutely prohibited. Sitting in the wagon next to this murderer, Shashka, I pushed my rifle barrel under his arm and shot him. Wounded, he managed to jump out of the wagon, and got a few hundred meters away. We chased after him and overtook him. And thus came the end of yet another wanted murderer.

I reported to Dyadya Petya that we hadn't succeeded in bringing Kaplatz back alive, because the moment contact was made with him, he tried to assault us with an ax. For that reason we had to shoot him.

"That's good, too," the *Polkovnik* replied. "And what about the other one, Shashka?"

"He, too, is dead," I told him.

"You are a *molodets* [a clever guy]," he said. "Come on, let's drink something."

From there, I went to report to Max as well.

The next day, as I passed Sazanka, I saw that they had buried Shashka, and a cross was waving about over his grave. I kicked it over and sent the cross flying. We learned that, not far from Sazanka, in Lishnevka, Shashka's brother lived. With the cease-fire, this brother came out to see what had gone on, and he discovered the corpse of his dead brother. He buried him and notified the man's wife about it. She, upon seeing me in the village, began to wail and shriek. I wasn't able to pass through the village, and I was forced to imprison her in one of the houses. She escaped at night and threw herself into a well.

In the woods and at the command posts in the village, there was one set procedure in regard to guard duty. We never sat in a house without a guard outside. One time we were sitting down to eat, and we heard our comrade's voice outside, "Stop. Who's there?" I hurried outside to see what had happened. Despite the darkness, I could make out several horsemen. I shouted to them, "Who are you?"

"*Fedorovtsy!*"[22]

"And who are you?" asked their commander.

"From Dyadya Petya's *otryad* [fighting unit]," I replied.

The commander came up to me and dismounted' we shook hands. We clarified some details and he presented me with two letters from headquarters that were intended for me, in which I was requested to help them obtain food. They were five partisan fighters, patrols from a large unit of 4,500 fighters, armed with the best weapons for partisan warfare. Their purpose was to become familiar with the rear line of the German army and to incessantly harass it. With the breakdown of resistance on the eastern front and its disintegration, we were ordered by the military command to leave our base in the Briansk woods. I took several men from my command post, and we went with these partisans, the *Fedorovtsy* to the village. There we confiscated several sacks of potatoes and a few wagons for them. They thanked us warmly and left.

The next day the patrols came back, along with another two hundred men and with two more letters from headquarters. This time I was asked to assist them in a sabotage operation at the railroad tracks by my own hometown, Manevichi. I received a saddled horse from them, and we left for the village of Galuziya. There, at the command post, we had thirty of our men. Also, our flourmill operated there, supervised by Abraham Puchtik.

Before the war, he had owned the mill. There we found all the comrades sitting at the tables and eating breakfast. Someone welcomed me loudly, "Good morning, Burko!" I recognized him. He was a Ukrainian, the police chief of the town of Karasin, and was on our blacklist. His actions of chasing after Jews were numerous and reached the Trochenbrod woods. By chance he joined up with the partisans, during one of their encounters with the Ukrainian police. He was captured by our comrades, by the brick factory near Manevichi. I called the *Fedorovtsy* commander outside and told him about the Ukrainian policeman. The commander ordered that he be brought inside the stable. There we put him on the ground, and two partisans beat him with sticks until he breathed his last.

Outside, a young woman by the name of Pasha, from the village of Vyrka, passed by. She had worked in the town of Manevichi for many years. And whenever partisans appeared in the village, she would report to the Germans. This young woman received heavy blows, and was warned not to chatter anymore.

We left Galuziya and went towards Koninsk, to the woods. We set up huts there. For several days I slept in the same hut as the commissar. This spot served as a temporary base for sabotage operations on the railroad tracks. Night after night I went out with a different detachment, each one numbering thirty men, on sabotage operations.

One Sunday morning Max turned to me, asking me to get him a liter of vodka from Slovik. I had one of the *Fedorovtsy* come with me, and we went to the address. The owner of the house received us warmly, inviting us for breakfast — after all, it was Sunday. We left with two liters of vodka.

We left Slovik and went to see Franek Branovski with the same request. And again, there was the same refrain, "It's Sunday!" We ate and drank there, too. We finished off a bottle and went on our way. We returned — and I was shocked at what I saw. About forty fighters and nurse-medics in wagons hitched to horses were preparing to leave for an operation. I reported to the captain, presenting him with the vodka he had requested. He thanked me and added matter-of-factly, "The time has come for you to take the blood-revenge that you have desired so much. You will be able to settle your accounts with those who, one time at night, when you came by chance into their village in search of food, ran to take our weapons from you and hand you over to the Germans," and he handed me the "blacklist."

I pondered over how to each our destination, Polska-Gura. There were several possibilities. One of them was to go from the Manevichi side, but it was possible that the Germans would ambush us there in an area of the graveyard. I chose a roundabout path. We went along a marked route through parts of the forest and reached the village from the other side. From a distance I saw a campfire between the bushes. We quickly and cautiously approached the spot and met an old peasant grazing four horses. I immediately recognized two of them. They were the horses of Hazenkov, whose name was on the blacklist. I asked the old man what was going on in the village. He said that if partisans appeared he must immediately notify the village. We confiscated the horses and took the old man with us.

The first one we went to see was Hazenkov. When we appeared, the men began to flee. I signaled to the patrol-commander to open fire, and he immediately hit Bazykin, the leader of those who were fleeing. We entered his house, and I saw through the window that he was only wounded. I saw him gasping and trying to run away. "Pavel Pavlovich!" I shouted. "Here he is!" He rushed outside, mounted his horse, and chased after him — he rode over him on his own horse and trampled him. We took one of his sons with us and two other suspects. One, who was on our list but whose name for some reason wasn't written clearly, slipped away from us. This was the very man who had plotted to steal my gun, during my stay in the village with my brother Zev. The luck of a Gentile.

When we went outside, we ran into an acquaintance, Chavador Kolev. "You didn't stop the main organizer, the most dangerous of the murderers — Stakh," he said tome. "But he already escaped to Polska-Gura, to the Germans." It was too late to chase after him by foot or by vehicle because of the tangled growth on the road.

We left with the three murderers. I looked behind us and saw our prisoners' wives walking along. I stopped at the edge of the woods.

"What do you want?"

"Our husbands," they said.

"O.K.," I said, "you will get them if you bring us vodka."

They agreed. We waited for them. We got the vodka from them, and told them that we would set them free after an interrogation.

We changed our direction and assed through the Polish village of Optova. A heavy rain accompanied us to the entrance of the village. The sun set, and the shepherds brought their flocks home. When the shepherds saw us, they began to run away, thinking us to be Ukrainian nationalists. I recognized among those running away a girl whose father was a forest guard. He had hidden several Jewish children, until they were taken by us. I called the girl by her name so that she wouldn't run away. She turned her head and shouted, "Matka-Boska, I didn't recognize you!"

We were about fifty men. We stationed ourselves at the village school. We immediately assembled all of the village's residents. I was asked, among other things, if we would spend the night at the village. When we agreed to this, they began bringing us food and drink. Later on, about forty men offered to stand guard around the village. Our commissar and the captain were getting worried bout us, as they didn't know our whereabouts. When at last we appeared, the joy was great. We set tables and got ready for breakfast. I personally submitted complaints about inaccuracy and vagueness, in relation to the fifth murderer, who has slipped away from us. I handed over our prisoners to Davydenko, from the special unit. He interrogated them, and later killed them.

With Commander Kostin

I was with the *Fedrovtsy* for two months. I was credited with the blowing up of twelve cargo trains carrying military equipment that were on their way to the eastern front. They transferred Max to another location, and a lieutenant by the name of Kostin took his place. People who knew him, from Kartuchin's unit, said that Max's men were lost. He, Kostin, was a professionally military man and not well suited for the living conditions and the fighting in the woods. I took advantage of Max's absence and went to the village of Serkhov, where a Pole lived who was involved in pillaging and plundering in the town of Manevichi. Two *Fedorovtsy* called him outside. I made him sit in the wagon, and we went to the woods. There we took him and tied a rope around his neck. As it says, "Who by strangulation and who by stoning."[23]

The new commander, Kostin, sent Shaiya Flash with an order for me to return to the unit. I was standing talking to the commissar of the *Fedorovtsy* at the same moment that Shaiya gave me the message by heart and in Yiddish. The commissar was amazed. "We slept in the same tent together for two months, and I didn't know that you were a Jew. I'm also a Jew" he said. "Send your weapons back to your unit, and stay here with us."

"I was one of the unit's founders," I told him, "and so, I'd like to remain with it." I returned, then, to the unit and stood before Kostin. "I'm here, as you ordered!" I said to him.

"Bravo, very good!" He warmly shook my hands.

I had known Kostin since 1942. I met him at one of Kruk's meetings where we became acquainted and together became familiar with routes for operations in and outside of the forest. Among those invited were Captain Kartukhin, who sat with Lipa (a Jew), and Kostin, Max, myself, a few others from our unit, the *Polkovnik* Brinsky, and several assistants. As we sipped a healthy amount of vodka, we began talking. Kartukhin said, "I personally wouldn't take twenty Russians partisans in exchange for one Lipa." Max said, "I wouldn't take twenty Russians partisans in exchange for one Barku." The last of the speakers was the *polkovnik*, whose words were brief and matter-of-fact. Among other things he said, "From now on, Berl Lorber and Burku (Berl Bronstein) are entitled to come with Kruk and Max, respectively, to the main headquarters at any time." The Russians had often complained, generally, that Jews were cowards. If they were captured by the Germans, they said, they would give out information about the partisans. At two o'clock in the morning, the meeting ended, and I brought the *polkovnik* home to headquarters.

Kostin read out his orders to a formation in order to become familiar with them, despite the fact that he was familiar with most of them from before. We had with us some of the thirty soldiers from the Red Army who had escaped from prison with him. There was also a group of Jews, more or less unified, that could not adjust to the way he ran the unit. A delegation visited his trench and in an unambiguous manner, he said to him, "If you want to succeed in your job, leave the Jews alone, because otherwise they'll go over to the *Fedorovtsy*, and without them you can't do anything." He freed me from all other duties I had, and I would accompany him just about everywhere. We frequently went to Brigade headquarters, and to *Fedorovtsy* headquarters. One time he wanted to make a detour and visit Kruk's civilian family camp.

Yeshayahu Zweibel, the one in charge of the camp, welcomed us. He spoke with Kostin about the conditions in the camp, the daily schedule, and employment of the people, the diet and the future of the orphaned children, widows, and old people. Friends from bygone days surrounded me, as well as Jews who just wanted to see me and hear from me what was new. Kostin asked me what the people in the family camp wanted. I replied to him, that they didn't believe that "the residents of the camp under our command live better than they do." He looked at me in a kind of amazement and said, "Do, then, let's go visit our civilians' camp while we're in the neighborhood!"

Immediately we went up to the road leading to the camp. I introduced him to Zisel Brat, and they talked among themselves. I, as much as I could spoke to those standing around me, and hinted to them that now was a chance to improve their situation. Immediately a request was raised to Kostin that he put in an order for meat and salt. Kostin turned around and pointed at me, "He is guilty! Aren't there enough calves in the woods — slaughter them and eat them and he'll soon bring you salt!"

The visit came to an end. We returned to our camp, and I related the details of the visit to Mitka, who was in charge of the food. His family also lived in our civilian camp. It was decided between us that after supper we would bring two sacks of salt to the civilian camp. Kostin himself wanted to make sure the salt was delivered to his satisfaction.

In the meantime, events occurred one after the other in the woods. The Germans did not accept their defeat on the Stalingrad front and tried, from time to time, to pursue that partisans and liquidate them. We learned that the Germans sent out from the front an antitank division that numbered about 18,000 soldiers, and they were getting ready to lay a siege on our woods. I got in touch with Major-General Fedorov to hear his opinion on the subject.

It was decided that we stay where we were and go to battle with the Germans. The surrounding outposts in other places were strengthened and reinforced as much as possible — and we waited or whomever would come. At one of the outposts, a battle took place, a few against many, with little ammunition. We were forced to retreat, but first two squadrons were sent in an attempt to ward off the invaders, mainly to staff for time so the sick and wounded could be transported to a secure place. The only path for retreat was in the direction of the Styr River where, on the other side, Germans swarmed with Ukrainian nationalists all waiting for us. As we neared the river, they opened fire on us. We retreated about a kilometer in order to assess the situation.

A peasant came up to us. I brought him to the commander immediately. Under interrogation, he said that he was from the surrounding area. But I knew his place of residence. The commander, Nikolai Bezruk, hit his face with a whip and ordered that he be liquidated, because it had become clear that he had joined those retreating into the village of Ozertsy and had informed the Ukrainian nationalists of our actions.

We approached the Styr a second time, with intensified strength and laid out a bridge using logs. We arrived at Svaritsevichi, where we had encamped during the first siege. Our situation was now much worse. The Germans destroyed everything in the woods — trenches, living quarters, food, and they poisoned the water, set fires in the woods, and threw oil barrels from planes to increase the burning.

In spite of all of this, we returned "home." Our trenches were completely burnt. So we temporarily lived in lodgings at headquarters. The overcrowding was great, and I slept in a wagon. The nights were cold, autumn nights. Rain and snow were common. One night, after strenuous activity, I fell asleep as usual. I felt a strange heat, but I continued sleeping. That same night, snow fell and completely covered me, and if Captain Anishchenko hadn't happened to be going by awakened me to tell me good news from the front, I would have slept like that until the morning and maybe would not have gotten up at all. The next day I got a place to sleep inside a bunker, like everyone else.

One night they woke me up at two in the morning, with an order to present myself immediately at headquarters. On the way there, I saw six horses tied up in a strange manner; the saddles were also not in line with our standards. In any case, I went on. I stood before Captain Malin and received instructions to bring back six *Fedorovtsy* patrols, who had gone off their path to call for help for those under attack and now couldn't find their way back to their base. About 3,000 Ukrainian nationalists attacked the partisan camp, "Vanda Vasilevska," in the village of Cherevakha. I jumped onto one of the good horses, at the head of the patrols. "Forward, after me!" The distance from where we were to Fedorov was about ten kilometers, and then night was dark and dismal. I couldn't see the horse I was riding on, nor, for that mater, the road. After we had gone about six kilometers, the patrols recognized the road; but I reached Fedorov's headquarters long before them, despite the fact that I was stopped several times by sentries. In the end, I appeared before the General-Major. After a short report, General Fedorov ordered that tea be prepared. In the meantime, the six arrived, and he couldn't control himself and burst out shouting, "With patrols like you, the nationalists will eat us alive! They'll reach the woods before we have time to move!" And to the liaisons, who stayed permanently next to headquarters, he said, "Battalion 5 and 9 — go fight the nationalists!" To me he said, "Finish your team and you're permitted to leave! And tell your officers to set up ambushes on the side roads, in order to obstruct the path of undesirable Ukrainian nationalist elements."

Despite all of our preparation to forestall the danger, the nationalists succeeded in penetrating our frontal outpost in the village of Lishnevka. Our forces retreated. Our second destination was the village of Karasin. They also made a breach there, and our forces retreated from there as well. From Karasin, they continued to Serkhov. This outpost was controlled by the *Fedorovtsy*. In time, they reinforced and drilled their troops and waited for the arrival of the nationalist force — and then, the *Fedorovtsy* opened fire with machine guns and light artillery. The attackers withdraw and retreated.

They didn't expect such a strong reaction. A reinforcement of about eighty men was sent from headquarters; their objective was to obstruct the path leading to Galuziya. And that is what happened. When the nationalist attackers met up with heavy fire at the Karasin outpost, they were forced to retreat in the direction of Galuziya. I knew the roads were uncrossable swamps on both sides and, in the middle, a bridge made out of logs. We lay down on the sides of the road, and when the nationalists approached, we shot them in a crossfire. We took just six of them prisoners. They claimed that they were Russians, former soldiers from the Red Army, and that they had no idea what Ukrainian nationalists were.

During one of the battles with the Germans in the area of Lovoshov, the partisans took a woman doctor and a girl prisoner, and brought them to headquarters in Karasin. With the approach of the second siege on the woods, Sashka Voronov, who was in charge of that station, asked Kostin what to do with them. Without much thought, Kostin ordered that they be liquidated. And so they were. They took them out to be killed next to the lake, in the Zamostye area. When the battles against the Germans and Ukrainian nationalists had scaled down, our operations and those of the *Fedorovtsy* were resumed — and then two bodies were discovered — those of the woman doctor and her daughter.

During the *Fedorovtsy's* investigation, the blame was placed on commander Kostin, and he was arrested by the special unit. During the preparations for the civil New Year, 1944, I packed a parcel with food and vodka and sent it to the division commander, Kovlov, for the imprisoned Kostin, but he sent it back to me. I took the parcel a second time and went to the General-Major Fedorov. I strongly requested that he allow me to bring the parcel to Kostin. He hesitated and said, "This time I'll let you, but don't go to see him anymore. You're permitted to come to see me whenever you want, even after midnight." I sat with the general, and we talked a bit, drink, and were all feeling pleased, but the one who was the most pleased was Kostin's love, Katerina Grigoryevna. Kostin's life was saved, thanks to *Polkovnik* Brinsky , who at that time was in Moscow, where they asked him for his opinion. Kostin was freed, given a hundred men under his command, and went across the Bug River to establish a partisan movement in the center of Poland.

The Partisans Ward Off Attacks and Capture

Kostin's position was filled by the former commander of the special unit, Vasilenko. During those days, we were supposed to receive supplies from Moscow by air. The problem was how to parachute them down. The woods were virgin forests. There were many ponds and swamps, and also there was the population, but we were mainly anxious about the Germans. We went out to locate a site according to Moscow's directives, but it became clear that the distance was great, and we were afraid that we wouldn't be able to arrive on time. We contacted Kruk, who was settled deep in the woods, and together we located a clearing in the woods not far from the Sazanka. Following agreed-upon signals from the ground, the pilot dropped the "goods." We got ammunition, arms, medicine, and clothing and also radio technicians and officers. We received such consignments several times.

One night a captain was parachuted to us with new equipment. When we entered the base, there were three of us: the commander Vasilenko, the captain who had parachuted, and myself. The two officers talked among themselves about every subject under the sun. I listened, but did not take part in the conversation as long as it did not concern me. Vasilenko said to the captain-paratrooper, among other things, "You see, this is an outstanding partisan, and what a pity that he's a Jew."

I didn't remain quiet, and I said, "Comrade Commander don't be sorry I was born a Jew and I'll die a Jew!"

"You see," Vasilenko said to the captain, "a Jew and proud of it."

With the collapse of the front at the Moscow-Stalingrad lines the Germans tried without much success, to present themselves as a power that was still able to stand up under the pressure of the Red Army at the front and the partisans in the rear. In fact, the situation was just the opposite. While the Red Army forged on at the front, the partisans tried, successfully, to occupy key points along the length of important, almost exclusive, railroad tracks.

One night it became known to us that our division, which numbered more than thirty men in the Rafalovka area, had succeeded in repelling the Germans and taking back the town. On hearing this news, the staff commanders, including my commander, Vasilenko, went out to the place. Among those going to Rafalovka was the chief of staff, Provishka, a captain who had served in the Bug region until the outbreak of the war. With the deterioration of the front, he was imprisoned by the Germans, but had managed to escape, and he joined up with the partisans. In Rafalovka he learned that the unit he had served in was a distance of eight kilometers from there, and that his good friend from his days of military service was there. He decided to meet with him at any cost. The meeting of the two friends was emotional. Tables were set. Afterwards, the regular army captain took us into the supply depot and equipped us with some arms. In a discussion with the regular army captain, he expressed annoyance about the actions of the partisans in the area of the civilian population. "There's too much taking people out to be killed," he complained, "and too little training." We asked him to be more tolerant, and said that in time it would be decided who was right.

We went to Rafalovka to see a film about the life of Vanda Vasilevska. The movie hall was filled with soldiers from the captain's unit, and, by his request, the soldiers gave their seats to the partisans. We concluded the day's events with a good sleep at the division where the conquerors of Rafalovka were staying.

The next day the general-major from the city of Sarny came by and addressed us. Among other things, he said that Stalin had ordered that assistance be offered to partisan units in need of it, and that the partisans held 50 percent of the credit for the victory over the Nazis. On account of the assistance that he had to offer us, he requested meat from us, saying he would pay us in tobacco, salt, and other — "good things." We got cattle ready for him, and I was responsible for bringing it to a designated place. I went with the cattle into villages that were under our control and under the Red Army's control. In one of the villages I again met with the captain from the "regular army." The conversation again turned to the hostile civilian population. Now he agreed with me. The captain's being in agreement about the Ukrainian population's hostility was not incidental. A truck with soldiers passed by Vladimerets and met with fire from an ambush. Some of the soldiers were killed, and the wounded were burned along with the truck.

After a number of days I went out with some of the men to patrol the Povorsk area, to gather information about the Germans — if they were still in the town, what their conditions were, etc. We had just approached the village of Chersk, when everything became clear to us. We changed our direction, and went to Manevichi, my town. This was my first visit in two years. The house I had lived in and had built with the sweat of my brow, the home where I knew happiness, still stood in its place, but it was all in ruins, with the doors and windows broken into a wide open. I didn't go inside. My heart ached. I pulled out a hand grenade that was with me, but my commander prevented me from doing this. Looked all around at the nearby houses and saw smoke rising from the chimney of one house, where a Polish policeman had formerly lived. I approached it, and a Pole, Stephan, who in our time had helped us a bit, came out to greet me. He asked that I allow him to live with me in the house. I agreed. I arranged a few more visits before we went on to the village of Manevichi, and the next morning we returned to the base, to the woods.

Upon coming into the base, I saw unusual movement. My commander, Vasilenko, had received an order to find a hundred men and go with them across the Bug River. He had wanted me to go along, but the staff captain, Anishchenko, opposed this. And so I stayed temporarily.

With the liberation of Rafalovka the mainland communication with Moscow was renewed, although with limited dimensions. In any case, people came, mainly by train. They transported the wounded to hospitals in the Russian rear lines, children were transported and partisan commanders went. Stalin had invited the commanders for consultations about the continuation of the campaign. Our commander, Dyadya Petya (Brinsky) was also invited, and I was the only Jew among the escorts to the train in Rafalovka. I parted from them in friendship. I suspected that Brinsky was a Jew. He stayed with me, and the two of us returned to the woods.

The woods were in turmoil. The traffic was like that in a beehive. In every place, people were packing; they were rushing about and whispering secretly. The family camp's residents had received instructions to be ready to leave the woods and to go in the direction of Rafalovka. Young men, especially Jews, were released from the fighting units and were attached to the family camps. Some of the Jews stayed to guard the camps, in case we'd have to return. They divided up and organized the young fighting men into new units; they prepared plenty of food, arms, and ammunition, for the trip across the Bug River.

On March 23, 1944, we left for our destination. The men were among the best, and most of them had secondary duties in addition to fighting. There were a few Jews, myself and my nephew Yaakov Bronstein among them. The road was difficult, the snow that had fallen in the last few days had melted, and so there was mud. Progress was slow. Worse than this were the Red Army's regular units' conditions. The weapons were silenced, standing in the street corners without shells; trucks got stuck in mud up to the ales, and couldn't move. Rifle cartridges were dropped from single-engine planes that flew almost as low as the treetops. Once in a while, these planes — *kukuruzniki* — were shelled by the Germans. Also we, who were in a convoy about a kilometer long, were harassed by German planes. Through all of this, we reached the vicinity of Ratno. Despite the shortage of ammunition, and means of transportation, and food, the Red Army soldiers succeeded in capturing Ratno, but the general in charge of this section of the front ordered an evacuation of the area, fearing German raids. And indeed, the Russians had just evacuated the town, when a squad of German bombers appeared, turning the city into a heap of ruins.

Our objective was to cross the front, which wasn't solid nor clear of Germans, in the opinion of many in the Russian high command. Even more severe was the situation across the Bug River, which our patrols returned from. (Because of this we made rounds close by the front.) During the nights, against the background of the sky, we clearly saw the firings of rickets that bombed the German centers. In return, the Germans shelled the Russians with heavy mortar from the air. The Germans tried to recover from their defeat the entire length of the front and took advantage of the Red Army's supply hardships.

We reached the vicinity of the city of Kovel. The *Polkovnik* Nazarov, who had been parachuted to us while we still were in the Kukhotskaya Volya woods, was with us. Nazarov met with a general from the Red Army in one of the houses in the village. I and another, Vanka Tretyakov, went out to get food for the horses. The villagers in the vicinity of the front left their homes, especially the men. The villages themselves were ghost towns. We gathered barley, oats, etc.

At one of the houses, a little girl opened the door. I asked her, "Are any of our men here?

"Yes," she answered, "they're sitting over there with Russian soldiers, playing cards."

We went back and reported to *Polkovnik* Nazarov. Immediately, a squad went out and brought them to head-quarters, with their hands tied. After I related to the captain the content of our conversation, he ordered that we kill them. We stayed for several days in that place.

Not such good news reached us about the partisans under the leadership of Kovpak, who had suffered heavy losses in the Carpathian Mountains. An order from Moscow was issued to transfer all the partisan units that were close to the front to the army command, in order to reinforce and fill in the thinning columns. They left us alone in the mean-time, because we were thought to be a military unit. Captain Brigada approached me and in a friendly manner asked me if I wanted to go home. I replied to him "Your decision is final." His answer was "Go home!" In the afternoon the secretary, Kolia Tzitzel, called him and ordered him to make up official papers for us. We were three Jews. We received arms and ammunition for self-defense. Each one had a rifle with bullets. After a walk of several kilometers, we met up with the Red Army's guard. We were interrogated; they read our papers; and afterwards released us. And so we went on to Lyubitov.

The next morning we continued in the direction of Povorsk. There were only three of us when we arrived at the town in the evening. Right at that time, a train was about to leave or Manevichi, our destination. The cars were all full; there wasn't even room for a pin. And suddenly I heard some-one calling me, "Bronstein! Bronstein!" — and who do I see but the *nachalnik* Maneko, who had served from 1939 in our town, Manevichi. He asked me where I was coming from and where I was going.

"Don't you see the arms?" I said.

"You're a clever guy if you could stay alive! You want to go home?"

"Yes," I answered. He went up to one of the sets of steps of the car, removed a few villagers from there, and put my nephew Yaakov and me on the steps.

In Manevichi I entered Leib Singel's house. I met several Jews there. The next morning I went to see my house. It was difficult for me to go inside, to cross the threshold, and I turned toward Shimon Blanshtein's house. Finally I went over to my house.

One morning I went out to the street, and heard that Tzigenski, my father's neighbor, was arrested by the N.K.V.D. I stood before the police, presented the three doc-uments I had with me to the commander, and said, "I am a local resident." He looked over the documents. One was from our unit, written in Russian, the second was from General-Major Fedorov, also written in Russian, and the third was written in Polish, from Gryunvald unit, under Max's leader-ship. The chief of police, Grichenko, took out thirty rubles and handed them to me. Very politely, I pushed away the money and said to him that it wasn't for that that I had come to see him. "With your permission," I said, "there's a man here in prison who is one of the city's righteous men, and it is my wish — with our approval, of course — that you release him despite the 'sin' that he committed, as it were when his son fled with the Germans. This man Tzygansky deserves freedom for his deeds and for the information he passed on to us, the Jews, during the occupation."

"If so," he said to me, "come with me to the prison house," and Grichenko opened the door for me.

Tzygansky's property extended over half of the town and was surrounded by a high wooden fence, which was almost uncrossable. He had a spacious garden of fruit trees. In the shade of trees the Jews found a hiding place fortified for them, and there they found a loaf of bread to break their hunger. He had served as the town's leader during the Polish rule. "At the request of your good friend, I am releasing you!" the chief said to him. Tzygansky hugged me tightly, and the two of us went straight to his home. He and his family did not live in their own house, but with their housekeeper, Yaldovska, not far from the flourmill. When his wife saw us from afar, she ran to meet us, falling on my neck and bursting into tears. "I'm crying from joy and grief," she said. "If it weren't for you, who knows if he would have stayed alive. God is repaying us for our helping the Jews."

I Avenge the Enemy, and Illegally Immigrate to Israel

I found out that Olek Sokhachevski was working as a telephone operator. I immediately informed the N.K.V.D., and he was arrested. Later on, one of Dombrovski's sons was arrested. Both of them were strong collaborators with the Germans. On my third day in Manevichi, I invited several Jews to go to our relatives' graves. At the first ditch, a terrifying picture of the martyrs was revealed to us. We cried a lot and said *Kaddish*.[24] When we turned to go, several Red Army soldiers appeared and asked what had happened. I told them. They looked, and their eyes filled with tears.

I received permission to use the horses. We removed some cement blocks from Feyvel's (Olinik) house and brought them to our relatives' graves, and Feyvel, who was a builder, built two gravestones with our help.

I received an order to present myself at the recruiting station. I attended to the order in order to stay — as indispensable — at the place. But I found no rest. Men, Jew-murderers were moving about freely. I contacted the N.K.V.D. and put Simon in prison. His crime was very great and serious, at least in regard to the Jews. Among other things, he handed Itka Ferdman over to the Germans. I was called to Rovno to testify against him and succeeded in getting the better of him. I had just returned when a N.K.V.D. man informed

me that Olek Sokhachevsky had managed to escape and was
working in Kovel in a workshop repairing railroad cars and
locomotives. I turned to the N.K.V.D. commander on this
matter, and we brought Sokhachevsky to Manevichi. When
his mother found out, she began looking for people who
would testify, because she said her son Olek didn't do harm to
anyone, and it was all a complete and utter lie. And in fact, a
woman was found who testified. The N.K.V.D. commander
told me that apparently she received a pay-off from his
mother. Olek was sent to prison in Lutsk.

During the time I was working on the railroad, I developed
a strong desire for revenge. This was natural. I was the voice
and prosecutor against those who were guilty. One night,
a Gentile town resident approached me, one of those who
had signed a petition for the Germans to carry out the first
action, in which three hundred and seventy men were killed.
His name was Yaakov Yalotsky, and I immediately recognized
him. He asked me different questions and invited himself
over for breakfast. I was quiet and then immediately informed
the N.K.V.D., and, on his way home, he was arrested. He
was released on account of his wife, who worked as a cook
in the kitchen there; she had good relations, in bed, with the
officer's corps. I didn't let up on them. I reproached the arm
corps for their weakness, and I mocked them for being able to
sell their homeland for the sake of a woman. My words apparently influenced them, and I was called to testify. To begin
with, I was briefed by the deputy commander of the N.K.V.D.
Afterwards, they brought in Yalotsky. His face became white
as plaster when he saw me. The commander came in after
him. He reprimanded his deputy for leaving the submachine gun near the accused man. Before he was interrogated
Yalotsky said, "Even if you hung the submachine gun on my
nose, I wouldn't know what to do with."

"Quiet!" the commander reproached him. He was transferred to the Lutsk prison. After several weeks I was called
upon to testify against him at a military court. At first he
tried to be evasive, unintelligible, and later he began to be
unruly, trying to deny any connection to his deeds. The judge
became irritated and sentenced him to the maximum penalty
for a crime against humanity: death.

The Germans, meanwhile, resigned themselves to defeat. They tried, even before the death throes of the Third Reich to confound the Red Army's victory. They incessantly bombed the railroad tracks, the supply trains, the anti-aircraft artillery batteries and, for the hell of it, the peaceful population. And there were many who were hit. Then too, the constant struggle to stay alive continued, as it had before, during the time in the woods.

Once I was called to the city of Kovel, to stand before the officer in charge of manpower. After presenting my documents, the deputy to the officer in charge turned to me, "You can speak Yiddish with him," and added, "I can't believe, and no one will believe, that a Jew did everything that's said about you in the documents."

One day, a committee was established consisting of Polish citizens who wanted to live in Poland, under the leadership of Tzygansky, the same Tzygansky that we had freed. I had a word with him, and we agreed, that if there were problems in releasing me, he would act accordingly. My officer-in-charge was not opposed to this but my release had to come from Kovel, from the same Jew in charge of manpower. When I appeared before him a second time, he started shouting at me. I calmed him down and told him, "The Polish committee was established by the Soviet government which is your government."

I appeared before the Polish committee and received a letter from them. I brought the letter to the officer in charge of manpower in Kovel, and I left the room slamming the door. He sent his secretary after me, to ask me to sit down, and a smile came onto his frozen features. He apologized to me. "I know that where you are headed is not Poland, but rather, Palestine. I wish you a successful journey and much happiness in your work and in your life. It's my wish and request, that you leave your documents with me. It would be a pity if they got lost."

"These documents are more precious to me that gold," I replied. "They tell of my readiness to die for freedom more than once."

I shook the hands of all those present in the room and left for my journey. He accompanied me a few hundred meters.

With his hand still grasping mine, he again wished me well. In the end, tears welled up in his eyes. "I am a Jew," he said.

I returned to my workplace, because I had to make up for a few days of work. Once, I met a woman who was by herself. She quickened her steps toward me and asked me directly, "Are you a Jew?"

"Yes, and what do you want?"

"I am a partisan," she said, "and it is my wish to reach Poland. Please, help me!"

I directed her to *selsovet*, where Berl Lorber (Malinka) worked, and I gave her several thousand rubles. She spread the word about my "Jewish heart," and caused masses of Jews to come to me. They, the few who remained after all the different hardships and annihilations, were searching and searching. There were those who were searching for a relative who was still alive, for a survivor of a family split apart, for a next of kin, for a road, a path, for any kind of crack — "so long as we get to Eretz Yisrael (the land of Israel)."

We sent a man to a certain address in Warsaw. He knocked hard on the door. For some reason he became disappointed and left in despair, but the man who was inside went after him on the steps, and when he caught up to him, he asked him who he was looking for. The unknown man introduced himself as a Jew, despite his Aryan appearance. "You found the man you were looking for," he said. "I am Yitzchak Zuckerman, and my alias is 'Antek.' Return to Lublin, and prepare the people. I'll come in a week!"

On the designated day, a crowd of several thousand Jews assembled for a meeting, in which one of the main items was the election of an action committee. From out of the crowd came cries of "Bronstein! Bronstein!" I tried to slip away and exit through the back door. Nothing helped. I was elected to the committee along with Berl Lorber (Malinka) and a rabbi from Pinsk.

Our first undertaking was to prepare a list of names. Using a password that we received from Antek, a group of Jews was sent to Krakow and from there, via Czechoslovakia, Hungary, and Romania — to Israel. Another time I received an order to organize a group of partisans and assume its leadership.

We went out, about eighty men, and came to the Hungarian-Austrian border. After a short rest, we approached he road heading in the direction of Austria. But there was a roadblock in front of us, and next to it were armed Russian soldiers. We retraced our steps. All of a sudden, two Russian officers appeared, and asked us for two watches and a pair of boots. Two Jews from Lithuania contributed the watches, and the boots were donated by Shimon Wolper. The Russian guards removed the roadblock between the Alps and pointed out the road where we could go. They left — and three other soldiers appeared. They asked us for three watches. After some bargaining, they received what they asked for, and left us alone. We walked a bit of a way, until we reached a small train station, and from there we traveled by train and reached the city of Gratz; we went to the hotel Weitzer, where once Hitler — may his name be blotted out — stayed. After a short rest in the hotel, we went to a camp that was under British rule.[25]

We had just managed to get a bit organized when there was a search. They were looking for weapons and were preventing the organizing for immigration to Eretz Yisrael. Antek from Poland arrived at this camp, and in front of a meeting that numbered about 2,800 people, he introduced me as a partisan, as a fighter against the Nazis, and as one who was worthy to lead the first group immigrating to Eretz Yisrael under the revered name of the commander of the Warsaw Ghetto uprising, Mordechai Anielewicz, of blessed memory.

The stream of refugees who left Eastern Europe was increasing, and there was an urgent need to organize and direct all of those people, who were so different from one another, but were unified by one desire — to leave the European soil which was saturated with the blood of Jews. A considerable portion of these operations are to be credited to the soldiers from the Jewish (Palestine) Brigade, emissaries from the *Yishuv*,[26] and to anonymous individuals who did their job tirelessly, through the day and through the night. Many Brigade officers endangered their positions, and perhaps their lies, in their search for Jewish orphans and those baptized into Christianity. Among those, I especially want to make note of Mordechai Sorkis, who did a lot of work in this area. He set up for our use two covered trucks, after we were forced to leave a train, when we were later in Italian territory, in the Alps. We arrived at Mastero, where a Jew from England worked as director of the train station, and he arranged for two railroad cars with a locomotive to transport us to Aquacento, in Italy. At this place, there were already forty people. I knew some of them from before.

One day I met with Dov Karpuski, a man from Kibbutz Ein Harod who came as an emissary from the *Yishuv* to organize people for illegal immigration. His objective was to take out of the camp, which numbered about eight hundred people, only one hundred selected individuals who would be able to endure the hardships of the journey. The response was beyond all expectation. About two hundred people signed up. One evening we left in the Brigade's truck for a deserted coast in Italy. At a certain distance from the shore, a "boat," as it were, came to anchor, where nine rooms of couches were set up, to sleep, and we lay down on these. One January 12, 1946, we moved out of that place, on our way to the final destination, Eretz Yisrael.

The journey to the island of Crete was tolerable, but later on, the sea raged and our boat was about to descend into an abyss. We were given over to the mercy of heaven. Food and drink were at a minimum. They forbade us from going up on deck. The oppressiveness was unbearable. The resentment grew, but for the most part, the people gritted their teeth and suffered in silence. The main thing was to get there!

The small ship approached the city of Haifa. The city's lights glittered. The distance was now only about sixty kilometers.

At night we would have to go down to the shore. And then, suddenly, we were surrounded by warships of the British Navy. For twenty-four hours, negotiations were held between the Jewish Agency and the British Mandate government. We were taken to the Atlit camp, where we were imprisoned behind a barbed wire fence for three weeks. Upon our release we went, forty people, to Kibbutz Yagur. We were finally at home in our own land.

MY LIFE UNDER
THE UKRAINIAN-GERMAN OCCUPATION

Dov Lorber (Malinka)

On the 22nd of July, 1941, Hitler's Germany ordered its troops to march into Russia without declaring war and on the same day, Russia declared a full mobilization of her armed forces.

I left my post at the Karl Marx arsenal in Cherevakha, a village near Manevichi, and joined the mobilization point in Manevichi, Ukraine.

Almost every youth from Manevichi, as well as from the surrounding villages, gathered there and waited impatiently for the command to tell us where we would be transported.

Hitler's troops easily passed through the Russian borders and quickly forged deep into Russian territories, destroying massive Russian forces. The situation was very chaotic.

The next morning, we were loaded onto trains and sent to the Russian-German border which at that time was established at the River Bug, between Poland and Russia. Arriving in Kovel we were stopped. There was no road further up the line because the German forces had forged ahead without stopping. Our leaders decided to transport us deeper into Russia and on the 24th of July, 1942, we were already in Sarny.

The atmosphere in Sarny was hectic. Thousands of people were wandering the streets, not knowing where they were. Everyone was asking each other what they were doing and what they were going to do. Many decided to go on further and others decided to go back and see their family, or to take their belongings and escape deeper into Russia. I joined a group of peasants from our area who decided to go back to their homes to see their families and in a few days, I was back in Manevichi.

Arriving in Manevichi, I met the Russians but they were ready to leave. The panic was great and the Jewish population was very frightened, not knowing what was awaiting us.

At that time, I was staying with my cousin Gittel Pliatch and I told her that I was planning to leave the village with the Russians and go deeper into Russia. Her opinion was that regardless of how bad the situation would become in Manevichi, one would still be in one place and she didn't believe Hitler would kill us all for nothing. She talked this into me to such an extent that I changed my mind and remained in Manevichi.

In a few days, the Russians left the village. It became anarchic. Since there was no legitimate power, the Poles and Ukrainians declared themselves leaders and established a militia. Their reigning decree was that the town would now become a free for all, and that everyone could do what they wanted with the Jews. All of the peasants from the surrounding villages came pouring into Manevichi, robbing what was possible, accompanied with beating and threats.

For three days this wild ecstasy of rape, robbery, and murder continued and on the fourth day, it was quiet. While many of the Manevichi residents remained without a shirt on their backs, the same occurred in the surrounding towns. Degraded and humiliated by this fine piece of work, we sat and waited for our murderous rescuers, the Hitlerites (Germans), to come and bring order.

In a few weeks, a few dozen Hitlerites came. They supported the existence of the Polish-Ukrainian militia and gave them instructions as to what kind of evil decrees they could enforce against the Jews.

Then began the bitter persecution against us Manevichi Jews. Through the Ukrainian-Polish leaders, and with instructions from the Hitler murderers up to the liquidation of our dear friends and families who were killed for the sanctity of the name of God, our conscience will always haunt and hate these murderous Ukrainians, Poles, and Germans.

Written on January 28, 1959

* * * * *

Life Under Occupation
During the First Liquidation in Manevichi

Under the reign of terror and persecution, day-to-day living was very difficult. Every day there arrived new evil decrees against the Jewish community. One lived with the hope that perhaps a miracle would occur and Hitler would be crushed. Unfortunately, the miracle came too late. Various rumors were spread how the Germans were persecuting Jews in the surrounding cities and towns. The news came that the Germans were recruiting all the men from the surrounding small towns to work, and the town of Manevichi was also included.

On a beautiful early morning, the murderous Germans attacked our village and began capturing all the men, disturbing each house and corner. The Ukrainian police helped them. They caught about three hundred men, loaded them in trucks, and took them away to the next village, Cherevakha — driving them to the *Ferdishe Mogiles,* 'Horses' Graves', a field outside the village, where three ditches were prepared. The men were unloaded from the trucks, undressed naked, and sadistically beaten. Many of them, while still alive, even had slices of skin cut out of them. They were then systematically put to death.

The Germans filed up two ditches with bodies which were still alive — twenty people to a layer, one layer on top of the other, shooting them in the head as they were lying. This was done in such a manner so that no one in the village could hear any shooting. The last ditch, they covered with the remaining earth, and any earth left over they took in trucks with them.

I believe I was the first to have discovered the details of this horrible murder carried out by the Ukrainian police and the Germans.

Before the Germans came into Manevichi, while riding through the village of Cherevakha, they took with them a group of peasants with shovels. They dropped the peasants off outside the village and ordered them to dig the ditches. These same peasants witnessed the cruel scene, and they were also the last ones to cover the graves with earth.

Because I knew these peasants well, I had a chance to find out the details even though the Germans threatened them to remain silent. Finding out what happened sent a shiver through my soul.

Returning to Manevichi, I told my relatives about this but they did not believe it. Why? They heard no shooting.

My aunt, Pearl Pliatch, talked me into going with her to see the ditches and learn the truth. Her two sons, my cousins Shlomo and Yehuda, both died in the action and I remember that it was a Saturday dawn, how we snuck away and went to see where the murder took place. It was terrible. The earth was split, and the blood poured from the surface like a well.

My aunt fainted. I revived her. Broken-hearted, we turned back, assured that our sons and fathers and relatives were no longer alive.

Although we didn't keep the tragedy a secret and told everyone about this, many didn't believe us and lived on with the hope that their husbands, sons and fathers were still alive somewhere.

The Germans used to send Jewish spies to the *Judenrat*, a group of Jewish leaders in the surrounding towns, with lies and stories about how they saw their relatives working in factories or on the railroad tracks. They suggested that everyone send packages of food and clothing, and more than one family believed this and really did send things back with the Germans. The reason the Germans did this was to calm the community and keep the people from organizing any resistance. And this is how it was. The whole village was murdered by the Germans and their graves can be found outside the village of Manevichi. We will never forget how our friends and families were barbarously killed.

February 1, 1951

* * * * *

The Liquidation of the Jews in the Villages around Manevichi and Our Escape into the Woods

The inhuman treatment by the Ukrainian police made life unbearable in Manevichi.

I had planned to escape to the underground together with the Chairman of the village of Cherevakha, however I lost contact with him and he was killed by the Germans as a Russian spy. Because of this, I decided to leave Manevichi and go to the village of Lishnevka where my family lived.

Life there was easier because one didn't come into daily contact with the police, but the situation was still bad. The police from the nearby village of Karasin often came to terrorize Jewish families.

Lishnevka was a small town where, before the First World War, nearly 200 Jews lived. After the war, the Jews from Lishnevka settled in the surrounding towns, however, six families came back.

Their livelihood came from stores, free enterprise, and anything else they could trade. A few families made a living spinning wool and another family was in the blacksmith trade. All of them had children who totaled about forty. There was also a teacher with whom the children studied. On *Shabbos* and weekdays, there was always a *minyan* (quorum) and the *shul* (synagogue) was located at the home of Yaakov Aryeh Gold who was a pious Jew. He was also a *Torah* reader and a *moyil* (circumciser).

The Jews from the villages would come here for the High Holidays. The relationship between them and the peasants was friendly until Hitler's occupation; then the situation quickly changed for the worse. The peasants waited impatiently for the day when their Jewish neighbors would be annihilated.

Two weeks before Rosh Hashanah, 1943, on a lovely summer day, the news came that the Germans were taking Jews from the nearby village of Karasin. Knowing that after this, came us, I and the other youth in Lishnevka scattered into the surrounding woods. There were twenty-one of us ranging in age from fifteen to thirty years old.

After spending the day in the woods, we returned to the village in the evening to find out what happened to the rest of our families. We discovered that the Germans did not come to Lishnevka that day, and we found our parents and the small children of the village waiting for their destiny, knowing that tomorrow it would surely come.

We decided to return to the woods and while lying in a silo, waiting for dawn, the door suddenly opened and my name was called. I recognized the voice of Shimon (Chunek) Wolper. I answered him and he told me that he was looking for me and wanted to tell me a secret. He said that Joseph Zweibel from the neighboring village of Griva came to him with a peasant and wanted us to join the partisans. He didn't know what to do and wanted me to met with them and come to a decision. After meeting with them, it became clear that the peasant was the former mayor of Griva who was in the underground all along and with whom Joseph Zweibel had a secret contact.

Having decided to go underground with them, we immediately left to find the others and take them along. The blacksmith and his family didn't join us because the Ukrainian peasants in the village needed him there and promised to explain this to the Germans.

Joseph Zweibel suggested that since we ha no food nor clothing, we should remain until the next day to confiscate what we could from the peasants and thus a group of us, under my leadership, remained hidden in the silo. I sent another group into the woods to capture whatever goods they could.

On the second night, we decided to meet at a certain spot outside of Lishnevka but the Germans had already been there. They took all the Jews and seeing that more than half were missing, they threatened to kill everyone on the spot unless the rest were found. They eventually took everyone with them to Manevichi, leaving the blacksmith and his family and giving him twenty-four hours to find those who were missing and to bring them to the police who waited in the village for us.

A peasant working near the silo where we were hidden noticed that someone was inside. He opened the door and shouted for us to come out of the hay. Having no choice, we came out. He warned us against hiding there and told us that we were sentenced to die. I denied this, saying that the Germans were merely concentrating us in one place in Manevichi, begging him to let us stay until nighttime when we would go to Manevichi ourselves. He ordered us to leave the silo and we started running through the woods and the open fields. Luckily, the Germans and the police didn't notice us, and we hid in the bushes until dark when we were to meet with Joseph Zweibel and the mayor of Griva, Nikolai Konishchuk, alias Kruk.

When night came, we went to the designated meeting place and along the way we stopped to see a peasant to learn what happened to our families. He told us that Abraham Meyer, the blacksmith, came to see him and if any of us should appear, he would like to see us. I sent two of our men to him. They came right back with the blacksmith's son who warned us to go back. He said that the Germans were taking Jews from surrounding villages to Manevichi and if we didn't return they would kill our families. He also said that the police were waiting for us.

In the meantime, we met with Kruk who came to get us. A discussion started as to what we should do now — to return to Manevichi or go into the woods. In a few hours, we divided into two groups. One decided to return; the second decided to go into the woods. I, my here brothers, the widow Mechamke Glupstein with her two sons and two daughters went into the woods. The blacksmith's family, the Zafran family, and my father decided to return to Manevichi. We agreed that when the situation because very serious and they had to escape, they should come back here to the spot where we said good-bye and where we would return every night. We took the group that was returning to Manevichi that they should tell everyone that we would be in the woods near Griva and Lishnevka.

We said goodbye and departed with the hope that shortly we would see each other alive again. We all knew in advance that the gathering of the Jews in one place was simply a prelude to killing them.

March 4, 1959

* * * * *

My Impressions and Experiences with Kruk

Nikolai Konishchuk was a peasant, born in the village of Griva, in the Kamen-Kashirsky district. He came from a wealthy family and had a wife and children, but had barely

finished a few classes in elementary school. He had been
active in the underground Communist Party of Poland.

In 1939, when Russia occupied the section of Ukraine that
belonged to Poland, he became chairman or mayor of the village of Griva. In 1941, when Germany occupied the area, he
escaped deep into Russia. In Kiev, Kruk and all of the leaders
of the surrounding area were mobilized by the Soviets. They
were taught methods of sabotage against the Germans and
were sent back to their districts to organize partisans groups.
Kruk had to filter back through the German lines, often
meeting difficult ordeals with SS troops and with Poles.

Almost all of these underground leaders fell in battle and
only a few survived long enough to return home.

Kruk could not return to Griva because the people there
hated the Russians as much as the Germans, and he remained
hidden, only having contact with his family.

Among Kruk's few good friends was Joseph Zweibel who
came from the same village. Kruk used to meet often with
him and if the situation became critical, Zweibel and his family planned to flee into the woods with Kruk.

This is what happened. Seeing that the situation in
Manevichi was becoming serious, Zweibel ran away and met
with Kruk in Griva. Both of them came to us and asked us to
come with them to the woods.

Kruk knew the area in the surrounding woods amazingly
well. He was a sensitive person with a sense of humor and a
smile on his face. He liked wearing a military uniform with
a gun at his side and although he never served in the army,
killing came very easily to him.

At the start of our co-existence in the woods, he was very
humble about himself and once even proposed that I should
take over the leadership, but I refused. However, toward
the end of the partisanship, he became more egotistical and
aggressive against his aides and comrades. He once even
killed a twelve-year-old boy who was found in a civilian camp
during a siege and who wanted to be in the infantry. Kruk
also reprimanded a fellow from Kamen-Kashirsky for hiding
some bread which he shared with some civilian friends. He
once had an argument with me over a potato which one of
the gentile partisans said I tried to steal. Kruk shot at me but

I somehow avoided getting hit, and Miriam Blanstein, who lived with him as his mistress, finally calmed him down. She feared the same thing would happen to her brother who was once a foreman in my factory because he was also accused of this crime together with me.

There was a time when the commander of the Nasekin partisan unit, who was a Jew-hater and killed many Jews in White Russia, tried to influence Kruk to kill all of the Jewish partisans but Kruk refused. The Nasiekin commander, however, did not give up on the idea, and we were constantly in danger of an attack by him. By a miracle, General Dyadya Petya came from the main headquarters for an inspection, and the plans of the Nasekin commander were foiled. General Petya found out about this plan and removed the Nasekin commander and sent him to the Soviet Central Bureau in White Russia. There were rumors that the commander was tried and received a death sentence, but this was never confirmed.

A few leaders of the main headquarters could not tolerate Kruk. They did not think he was qualified as a military leader, and he was virtually ignored on the field. He was always criticized for not disciplining his men and because his men were unruly with the people in the surrounding villages. Most of all the leaders disliked the fact that Kruk had a civilian unit. He was often referred to as the "Jewish Messiah."

There was once a complaint lodged against me at headquarters, saying that I disapproved of Communism and this endangered my life. Kruk defended me saying that this was not so and that I was a dedicated partisan. Kruk told me that the squealers were Yitzchak Segal, Mordechai Hersh's son, and Shaya Pliatch. Until today, I never knew why they did this. I had no misunderstandings with them though I knew they were once in the Jewish police force of the *Judenrat*, and they never repeated the charge again.

The reason that Kruk kept close to the Jews was well understood. With us, he was commander of a unit where everyone respected him. Without us, he would have been an ordinary partisan and would have gotten no credit for his initiative to organize a unit which had such a just cause to fight against the Nazis.

Though Kruk had his good and bad moments with the Jews in his unit, we must be thankful to him for his determination to take every Jew into the unit, and they respected him for that.

February 9, 1959

* * * * *

The Approach of the Partisans

The first group of us who went into the woods consisted of eleven men and women: Kruk, Joseph Zweibel, Dov Lorber (Reb Malinka), David, Abraham and Yehezkel Blanstein, Nechamke, Miriam, and Bailke, and the children Joseph and Melech.

Kruk took us deep into the woods to a small island in the mud which was covered with twisted bushes. Having been disappointed and depressed and finding it hard to survive, each of us lay down under a tree trunk. We lay lifeless and didn't speak to each other, thinking about how slim our hopes were of surviving here in the woods. Finally, Kruk began comforting us and told us that we would find a way out. He said we would have to obtain weapons, and he knew many peasants who had them and would be happy to exchange them for any goods that we might be able to steal. If this would not do, we would find other means of arming ourselves.

The first week, Kruk acquainted us with the area, showing us all the side roads and how to reach the surrounding villages. We used to steal food from the fields and gardens. We also made contacts with friendly peasants, having had close ties with at least one prelate in each village.

Because it was hard for everyone to go out each night, we decided, during the second week, to split into two groups and each night we alternated. Kruk managed to steal two rifles from a few villages and Kruk carried one with him. The rest of us wore sticks tied with rope.

During the second week, after completing our work, we blew up our food supplies, taking only necessities like salt and sugar and destroying the remainder of our products so that no one else could use them. We felt that we were gaining ground and each day we became more aggressive and eager to take revenge on our enemies.

Remaining in the woods another two weeks, we learned that most of our families were dead. A gloom befell us and there were tears running down our faces, Each of us wondered why we were still living when everyone else had perished.

Eventually, we calmed down, and Joseph Blanstein and I went to the place where we were supposed to meet with our friends from Lishnevka to see if any of them survived. When we arrived, we met no one there. Going further toward Lishnevka, we met a group of people outside the village who were walking in a row. Because they looked suspicious, we lay down and commanded them to remain standing, shooting into the air. I thought they were peasants coming from work, so I decided to go farther toward the village. As I passed them, I heard one of them call my name and realized that they were the first group of our friends to escape from Manevichi. Among them, whom I remember were: Itzhak Kuperberg, Zev (Vova) Verba, David Blaustein, Asher Pliatch, my father, Kononitz, Chunek Wolper and his wife Blumeh, and others.

I had agreed with Kruk earlier that if we were to meet any people we knew, we would not bring them to our hiding place but settle them elsewhere. This was done in case the Germans should attack, we would not be together but scattered in different places.

I hid these people in the woods outside Lishnevka and told them that tomorrow night, Kruk and I would come and settle them in a safe place. I took my father and Blumeh Wolper with me and on the second night, Kruk and I and the rest of my group came back and settled them in another hiding place between Lishnevka and Nabruska. We supplied them with food and told them not to go anywhere until we returned the following week.

The night before the liquidation of the Manevichi ghetto, many people escaped into the surrounding woods. Others ran to look for us around Lishnevka, knowing that we were located there. Every night, new people arrived including Joseph Zweibel's family and most of the other Lishnevka

folks. In a few days, we counted about eight people. We settled them near us.

On one hand, Kruk was happy that more people were
coming, but on the other hand, he was concerned because
it would be hard to support so many unarmed people. The
time came for us to go meet the first group of friends, whom
we settled outside the village of Nabruska. On our arrival, we
learned that the Germans were planning a raid. The reason
for that was that they didn't listen to our orders and went into
Nabruska to steal several things fro the peasants. The peasants recognized that they were Jews and told the Germans
where they were located.

We immediately took this group away and transferred them
to a second area near our base and when the Germans came,
they found no one. Thus, we saved them from sure death.

February 12, 1959

* * * * *

The Organization of Kruk's Unit

After the liquidation of the Manevichi ghetto, new survivors
came to us every day. All of them knew where we were located
and after a few weeks we counted more than 100 people.

The first group headed by Kruk, decided to divide up
everyone and send them to three separate places. Thus, the
Germans would not find us in one spot. This situation was
also more suitable since we had no weapons and could not
defend ourselves.

We nominated Kruk as commander and I was his representative. Our hiding place became the chief headquarters where
the orders were given to all three groups.

In time, we took several guns and other goods from the
peasants. We also carried out acts of revenge against those
peasants who had collaborated with the Germans. We killed
them.

The peasants in the surrounding areas were afraid because
they heard that a large army of partisans were nearby. They
told this to the Germans, seeking their protection, but the

Germans didn't move from their spot but barricaded themselves with tight security. They feared Jews with guns.

We also intercepted many goods that the peasants were giving to the Germans for protection, and they complained bitterly about this to the Germans.

We also began collecting food and material for the winter so that when the snow began, we would not have to go out and leave any signs of where we were. We captured a few horses and wagons to help us carry the goods.

After staying underground for about six weeks, we came out to meet with the other group of partisans who were located near us and about whom we knew nothing.

This meeting occurred on the way back from the mission where we killed a peasant who aided the Germans and confiscated his fortune. Arriving back at our base, I noticed a group coming toward me. I slipped under a tree, ready to shoot and noticed that their guide was a peasant who recognized me. He came to me and explained that the group consisted of partisans, Jews who escaped from the Germans, and they wanted to talk to me. They explained who they were and wanted to work with us. I immediately called Kruk and after a short discussion, we asked them to our base.

Fearing that they were lost, Kruk showed them where they were on a map, and then Kruk and I took them back to their base.

Their base was not far from ours and their commander's name was Nasekin. They also had a radio station and contact with Moscow. We explained our situation to them and told of our shortage of weapons. The commander connected us to the Central Bureau in White Russia and told us that he would get us weapons.

Since we knew the area better than they did, our group and their group of about thirty men decided to work together.

Their main task was to destroy the trains which were used to bring weapons, soldiers, and material to the battlefront. They had explosive material which they put under the train tracks and when the train came, it would explode. We also learned that a second group of these partisans, under the command of Kartukhin, was located, near the village of Povorsk and many of our Povorsk friends joined the group.

We agreed with Commander Nasekin's that on the following week, a group of us together with a group of their men would go to Griva and carry out a raid to take goods, since their group had almost none.

When the time, one Sunday evening, a group of our unit, together with a group from Nasekin's unit went to Griva. Arriving there, we learned that the commander and the police from neighboring areas were there. They were drinking in a certain house, surrounded it, and broke in. I remember like today that the Nasekin commander put everyone up against the wall and shot them all — about thirty people. Only a small child was left and the commander asked who wanted to kill him. Near me stood Joseph Blanstein, who was about fifteen years old. He appealed to me to let him do so, so he killed the child. The rest of the night, we badgered the peasants, gathering about twenty wagonloads of goods and stealing three guns.

February 14, 1959

* * * * *

Survival in the Partisans

Our leader Kruk was in danger of falling into Nasekin's unit. Their commander wanted Kruk to join his unit because he thought Jews were not useful in the partisans, and he felt they should be done away with. Kruk didn't accept his plan and refused to leave. Kruk told me of this: he was concerned that Nasiekin would attack us. Though we were not well-armed, I felt that we had nowhere to run and should stand up to this attack. I strengthened the guard around the base and we waited for the attack. Luckily, in a few days, Dyadya Petya came for an inspection. He was sent by chief headquarters, and his appearance saved us from attack. General Petya found out about this scheme and Commander Nasekin was sent to main headquarters where he was tried and sentenced to death.

Dyadya Petya remained with us for four months. He helped organize the fighters with instructions from Moscow. He installed military discipline. Because of our poor weapons supply and because we had people of various ages, we split the unit, making a civilian section for those who couldn't fight. We also had a number of girls who did domestic work and who occasionally accompanied us. The chief headquarters didn't like this but we proved their usefulness and they remained with us.

I knew Dyadya Petya quite well and often met with him. He was interested in Jews, and some thought he was Jewish himself though he never admitted it. His aides, however, did not like Jews, often made fun of us, and told lies about us. Dyadya called me to verify those lies, i.e., that we abused peasants.

I didn't understand where these rumors came from because they military police often checked out the peasants and they had no complaints against us.

Dyadya Petya decided the rumors were started by one of the other units and after this, he had a high regard for my work.

With winter coming, the Germans organized the Ukrainian police for a raid against us. We decided that all the partisans should leave the area and return after a few weeks. We went to the Sirnik woods and stayed in a village there. During this time we carried out acts of sabotage and ultimately acquired our first mine with orders to blow up a train. We learned where to place the mines, and Kruk and I and a group went to carry out the orders. We chose the area between Cherevakha and Manevichi.

Because of the snow, we had to place the mine on the tracks just before the train came. The tracks were guarded by the Germans and by peasants with two-way radios. The peasants also made fires near the tracks to keep them warm.

On the first night we couldn't get close enough to the tracks. The second night, we waited and when we heard the train coming, I and one of the Zweibel brothers wired up the mine. Concerned that the train was too close, he was careless about hooking up the wire and the mine blew up and he died. The train remained standing and although shaken, I got up and ran back to the group. Ashamed and saddened by this, we returned to our base having to report this unhappy event to chief headquarters.

February 15, 1959

* * * * *

Experiences in the Partisans

Because of this event, chief headquarters didn't want to give us any more explosives. Every piece of dynamite was as precious as gold.

Things came hard. We had to send people and arms to White Russia to main headquarters, and the roads were dangerous. It often took four to six weeks to do this because we had to carry everything on our shoulders.

One time, my group and I went to shoot up a train bringing men to the battle field near Manevichi. We ambushed some guards who were watching a railroad track. Most of them escaped except one who seemed dead. I suggested shooting him in the head to see if he was really dead. Upon hearing this, he jumped up and claimed to be a Russian who was our friend. We shot him anyway.

With the arrival of some Ukrainians and Russians in our unit, various new functions were created. There were also other Russians that didn't like having a Jew as their commander and once, while returning from a mission, they told Kruk that I tried to sabotage it. Kruk removed me as commander, and I was replaced by a friend of his from Griva.

A few weeks later, Kruk received orders to reinstate me so that our unit would be completely Jewish. I still kept a few gentiles so that I could send them on missions where Jews couldn't go.

My aides were: Joseph Blanstein, *Politruk* Zvoda, Yitzchak Kuperberg, and Zev (Vova) Verba as representative.

My first area of operation was between Vyderta and Kamen-Kashirsky. The Ukrainian police and the Germans rode back and forth daily. I placed mines along the road and once blew up a car containing a German general. His aide and a few people were killed, and he was wounded.

I was then given orders to go to Kamen-Kashirsky and destroy the viaduct. It was very risky and many tried to dissuade me but I felt that as a Jew, I was responsible for my brothers in the unit and wanted to go.

Nearing the village where the viaduct was located, I sent a messenger to inform me where the guard was, how strong it was, and who was guarding it. The next day, he returned and told us that the police held guard but the Germans controlled it. Two men guarded the building and ever two hours they changed. He told me not to go ahead, but I decided to risk it. Late at night, my group reached the main road which led from Kamen-Kashirsky to Kovel. The viaduct was about one mile away.

I left my group there with some explosives in case they had to defend themselves. I took with me Yitzchak Kuperberg, two others, and some explosives.

We approached the entrance of the viaduct and looked for an opening. We found one in the fence. We went to the door but it was locked so we knocked on the window, posing as police and asked the viaduct janitor for the key. He gave it to us and once inside, we placed the explosives under the machinery. We quickly escaped, taking the janitor with us, and the viaduct exploded. The Germans immediately began shooting at us but we safely ran away. Thus was destroyed the viaduct between Kovel and Kamen-Kashirsky.

February 19, 1959

* * * * *

After finishing with the Jews, the Germans started killing Ukrainians, whose names were given to them by other Ukrainians. They were labeled as Communists, and they and their families were taken from their homes and killed. We partisans did the same to the Ukrainian peasants who helped the Germans. We killed many in such villages as Lishnevka, Manevichi, Griva, and Novaya Ruda.

In the meantime, the Russian army was driving the Germans back and our task of blowing up trains became even more important.

In time, there came to our unit a Russian named Captain Mahmed. He solved our problem of explosives shortage by showing us that in the woods there were many used explosives that could be re-used. Our unit had the task of collecting these and by boiling them we could use them again. This process was very dangerous because many of the bombs were highly explosive, and people like Volfich, Avruch, and Siama were wounded, one of them seriously.

After a few months operating in the Kamen-Kashirsky area, our job was done and we moved to another place between Brest-Litovsk and Pinsk. This was the main connection to White Russia and the Germans transferred men and ammunition there. It took us two weeks to get there and we found many sympathizers and Russian partisans. It was, however, hard to hide since there were no woods.

The Germans guarded well the railroad tracks there; nevertheless, our first few missions were successful. We blew up about fifteen trains loaded with heavy weapons. Because of this the Germans stopped using those tracks at night and guarded them more heavily. We kept tearing up the tracks and they kept fixing them and eventually, their position was weakened.

That summer, the Germans began retreating and our acts of sabotage helped the Russians. We partisans waited for our final victory even though we had no family left. We knew that Jewish life was dead, and we understood that with freedom came pain. However, we fought with pride and defended our honor and we will never forget this.

February 25, 1959

* * * * *

In 1943, we saw freedom approaching. The Russians were driving the Germans from the occupied territories. Orders came from Moscow that Kruk's unit be abolished, and that we should join Max's unit which operated in Poland.

Kruk was against this and persuaded Dyadya Petya to leave him one unit. He selected the best men, including me, but I escaped to Max's unit. Max assured me that he would never return me to Kruk.

A few days later, Max's unit was ordered to Rovno to help free the city. When Kruk found this out, he wanted to have me delivered as a deserter, but this didn't happen.

In Max's unit the conditions were bad. We had to fight Germans and also bomb airplanes.

In 1944, we entered Rovno and were re-united with other partisans who worked together with us. Upon entering

Rovno, I gave orders to free the prisoners and then I returned to Manevichi to meet with any survivors. I met Lisenko, the former Secretary of the Communist Party. He asked me to take a party position but I refused. I returned to Rovno where I discovered that the N.K.V.D. unit of the Russian army had arrested my outfit. When I asked my commander why, he knew nothing about it, but I knew that the anti-Semites did not want Jews in the city.

Eventually, orders came that all partisans should join the Russian army. I was offered the rank of Lieutenant and was bestowed the Lenin medal and the 'Red Star'. Being considered a hero, they paid me and sent me to their headquarters. After all of this, I decided that I had nothing more to fight for and took a train to Sarny.

In Sarny, I was detained and searched. They kept me for four days and accused me of spying, and I was given over to the police. I somehow proved to them that I was not a spy, and they offered me a post. I promised to consult about this with the Secretary of the Communist Party. Instead, I jumped aboard a freight train and the next morning, I was back in Manevichi.

March 2, 1959

* * * * *

(Dov Lorber eventually left Russia and came to America. Until his death in December 1996, he resided in Seattle, with his wife, Chana and family.)

Translated from the Yiddish by Esther Ritchie.

At Their Death
They Ordered Us to Take Revenge

Dov Lorber

The relations between the non-Jewish fighters and the Jewish fighters were, so to speak, decent, but it is worthwhile to emphasize that this was only out of fear of the Moscow command, because there were many non-Jews who were willing to kill Jews who were their comrades at arms.

In particular they made charges and attacks on the fact that we set up the civilian camp. It was mainly made up of old men, women, and children, who were unable to actively participate with arms in our battle against the Germans and their allies.

This issue gave them (the non-Jewish partisans) no rest and they grumbled about it incessantly. But the Jewish partisans did not lag behind the non-Jewish partisans in ability and initiative; sometimes they even were superior to them, and the anti-Semitic partisans were forced then to take them into account.

The beginning of fighting with the Partizans was not easy for us. With the help of mock wooden rifles we had to persuade the local peasants that we Jews were a deterrent fighting force and were not to be disregarded.

With the mock rifles, we forced them to supply us with food, guns, and pistols. We burned down the "cooperatives" that the Germans had set up for their food supply, and the German produce designated for the Germans was taken. Also in battles in the village centers, we destroyed transports on the way to urban centers. The local population at first lived in fear of us, but after a short time they cooperated, for the most part, with us against the conquerors.

Our *otryad* unit, along with some of the men from Max's *otryad*, was successful in an expulsion campaign of German and Ukrainian police from the large village of Karasin, that was near the town of Manevichi. During the operation we burned down the police station that was built like a fortress. In this operation a number of policemen were killed.

We conducted a battle the entire night with the policemen of the village of Obzyr. The police station was built out of bricks, and with the light arms that we had, we could not easily take control of it. We were forced to end the battle, and we called on them to surrender. Their answer was that they would not surrender to Jews. The emphasis was on Jews, because in that entire area most of the partisans were Jews, and they very much feared falling into the hands of Jews "who knew no mercy."

Although we did not succeed in taking the police station, we spent the entire night in the village. We destroyed a lot of food and clothing, collected the medical supplies from the single pharmacy in the village, and destroyed anything that we could not take with us from the German estate that at one time had belonged to a Polish landlord.

We took advantage of every opportunity to settle personal accounts with the Ukrainian murderers from the local villages. Scores of peasants paid with their lives for collaborating with the Germans in the murder of the Jews. We carried out the first operation in *khutora* (isolated households) in the village of Zabara, where the head of the town council lived. He had been found to have extensively participated in the liquidation of the local Jews, especially in Kamen-Kashirsky.

We were a group of ten, armed with two rifles and pistol and rifle-shaped sticks. We reached his house before evening. Kruk and I went inside and found the village's head official, his wife and another peasant eating at the table. We ordered them to hold up their hands, and I ordered the official to go outside. We tied him up and made him lie on the ground. We demanded that he hand over his weapons, but he insisted that he did not have any weapons. We dealt him hard blows. After hours of torture, we shot him, without succeeding in getting him to say where he was hiding the arms. We were certain that he had a lot of arms, which we desperately needed. I was shaken by this retaliatory operation, because it was the first time I had taken part in killing a human being; but I knew that this "human being" had murdered my parents, brothers, and defenseless children in cold blood. We took the Jewish belongings that we found in his house and returned to our home in the woods.

We carried out another retaliatory operation after a short time in the village of Griva. The decision was made to liquidate not only a collaborator but also his wife and two children. At dawn several men from my group went to where he was staying. We knocked on the door of the peasant's house. He opened the door. We ordered him to get up on the bed that was by the stove. I ordered Yisroel Puchtik (Zalonka) to shoot him, but Yisroel was so nervous he was unable to fire. Someone else volunteered and shot the peasant and his wife. The two children, on seeing this, started to run. Outside, we took pity on the children, and I ordered that no one hurt them. I wondered, would their father have behaved in this way, he who was an organizer of the murderers of so many Jews?

Meanwhile we made plans to capture a peasant in the village of Serkhov. The peasants in this village were notorious. They had taken part in the murder of the Jews of Manevichi and the surrounding area. We knew that one peasant owned many weapons. We burst into his house suddenly, with the intention of surprising him. He was truly surprised. "How can this be? Are there really still some Jews left? And they even dare to break into my home! Jewish impudence!" We tried nicely to get him to talk and to develop a rapport with him. We felt that if we spared his life, he would supply us with arms, which were essential for our survival. We tried to convince him that we did not intend to harm him, that all we asked of him were arms, but he insisted, "I do not have arms." Suddenly, he jumped up and leaped through the window. One of the men was just able to wound him in the leg with his gun, but he kept on going. The men who were surrounding the house caught him, tied him up, and brought him back into the house. We started to torture him, and he insisted, "You're not going to get anything out of me, so let it be and just shoot me, for you're wasting your efforts..." A Jew, one of his fellow villagers, shot him.

In the town of Trebukhovtsy we killed the head official who had collaborated with the Germans and was known as a hunter of Jews who had escaped the "actions" and were hiding in the villages.

In the town of Ozertsy, we liquidated a peasant who had volunteered to lead Max's men — partisans who were disguised as policemen — to Kruk's Jewish brigade, and, indeed, he "very willingly" brought them directly to us. He managed to escape but was later put to death in his home in his town.

These operations served as a warning to the peasants from the surrounding villages to not harm the Jews that were in hiding.

In the village of Lishnevka we shot an officer of the local police whom we had forced to give us arms. Initially he refused, but then he agreed to bring us to a warehouse where the arms were hidden. Upon leaving the house, he started to run away. The first bullet that was shot, hit him and killed him instantly.

In the village of Novaya Ruda, we captured the town leader and brought him to our base for interrogation. After several days of interrogation we killed him.

In the town of Griva, we rounded up eight men who had collaborated with the Germans, including a few that had served on the Kamen-Kashirsky police force. They received the punishment they deserved.

We carried out more retaliatory operations in the area. Whoever we captured who had collaborated with the Germans paid for it with his life. We did all that we could to obstruct the Germans from moving about freely in the area and prevented them from obtaining horses and cattle.

We burned down bridges along the Stochod River during operations. We burned the agricultural land holdings (*folvarki*) that the Germans had confiscated, along with the cattle and grain in them. These holdings had belonged to Polish landlords during the Polish rule; with the Soviet take-over in 1939, they had been confiscated and turned into work farms. The Germans made them into an important supply station for the German army.

In the vicinity of the town of Rafalovka and others nearby, we burned down large storehouses full of grain that the Germans had confiscated from the peasants and had prepared to send to Germany. We also burned down a vodka refinery that operated continuously in order to supply whiskey to the soldiers. We severed all the telephone lines in the area, thus depriving the Germans of any means of communication. They were unable to repair the telephones.

The Germans did not dare enter the places where we were stained. We controlled wide areas of the forests and villages. The partisan guards made rounds and carefully watched over all that was going on in the area. We young Jews were the first to be in Kruk's partisan unit. There were fighters in it from every region of Rovno and the surrounding area. The command from our relatives, fellow townsmen, and woods-men was always with us: revenge!

We began to carry out this command on Ukrainian crim-inals. We knew that names and addresses of many of the murderers who had openly collaborated with the Germans. We systematically surrounded their homes in the dark of night, interrogated them, sometimes at length, sometimes briefly, sometimes demanding arms from them. We tried to convince them to cooperate with us, and we promised that no harm would come to them if they carried out our requests. But most of them did not do as we wished. When we were convinced of the abundance of their crimes, we shot them to death. We searched their houses and took arms, food, cloth-ing, and Jewish possessions (that they had stolen).

Among those we killed were nine peasants from the village of Griva, the former chief of police in the village of Lipiski, the leaders of the villages of Zabrody, Rudka Chervinskaya, and Novaya Ruda, and other peasants in the villages of Serkhov, Ozertsy, and others. Our operations created fear among our enemies, as well as respect.

We moved on to operations against both the German and the Ukrainians. We burned, as was previously mentioned, all of the bridges on the Stochod River, grain storehouses, cattle, and the like. We caused severe damage, and in time we adjusted to fierce hand-to-hand battles, and we succeeded in taking booty

Similar to the partisan unit was the civilian camp, a "town in the woods." This camp was made up of old people, women, and children who managed to escape. They lived in the woods and we took care of them.

This Jewish camp created a conflict between us, the Jewish fighters, and the non-Jewish fighters who were mostly Russians. But thanks to our heroic operations, we succeeded in overcoming the manifestations of anti-Semitism; they disappeared for the most part, from the area without causing damage to the town. We came to be appreciated, and in the surrounding area the word spread that the strongest partisans were the Jews, that sine the Jews had a particular account to settle with the murderers, their operations were the most dangerous.

The period of using wooden mock-rifles passed; we had gotten booty of arms and ammunition and could now function effectively.

One time we attacked the police station in the village of Karasin. We burned down the building and killed several policemen. We carried out a similar operation in the dark of night in the village of Obyzr. There we called on the policemen to surrender. They replied, "We won't surrender to Jews." They hid themselves in their brick protective building, and we did not have any explosive materials with which to blow it up. In spite of this, we stayed in the entire night. We took as booty a lot of food, clothing, and medicine, and we took or destroyed everything that was in the courtyard of the police station.

I was very familiar with the town of Obyzr. My grandfather Yaakov had managed the property affairs of the *poritz* (landowner). We continued liquidating German collaborators in every area, and scores of them were killed. From our headquarters we received an order not to shoot without a specific command. We evaded this order when we were convinced we had to attend to the murderers of Jews. I would like to mention an incident in the town of Troyanovka. In the summer of 1943, we attacked the German police station in this town. Many of the Germans were killed in an ambush, and the rest fled. My friend Yosef Halpshtein approached a peasant in order to look for Jewish possessions, and the peasant called him a "dirty Jew." Yosef shot and killed him. At headquarters I maintained that Yosef had shot the peasant after the latter had attacked him with an axe.

There were many more events during my time as a partisan, including the killing of many German soldiers. I have listed only a portion but through these events it is possible to show our humble part in the revenge against our enemies — the murderers of our people.

ABOUT KRUK — THE SECRET IS UUT

Dov Lorber

I first met Kruk in 1942, two weeks before Rosh Hashanah, at midnight, when he, along with Yosef Zweibel from the village of Griva, which is near Kamen-Kashirsky, came to the village of Lishnevka to encourage the village youth to go to the woods and establish a Partisan unit.

Nikolai Konischuk (Kruk) was a poor peasant, who lived in the village of Griva, and was very familiar with the area and the surrounding woods. In 1939, when the Russians had control of the western Ukraine and Byelorussia, Kruk was an active Communist and leader of Griva, even though he lacked education and had no military training.

In 1941, with the invasion of the German armies into Russia and the occupation of our regions, Kruk fled to Kiev, the Ukrainian capital. There the Russians organized all the Communist refugees from the western regions, trained them, and sent them back to their home towns so they could organize and establish a partisan movement.

Upon returning to his village in the occupied region, Kruk encountered many difficulties in carrying out the task the Russians had given him; the townsmen were anti-Communists, and he greatly feared that they would hand him over to the Germans. Because of this, he was unable to appear openly in the village, and he hid with relatives. In order to stay in touch with Yosef Zweibel, Kruk met him and set up a time when Zweibel would go with his family to the woods. As was expected, right before Rosh Hashanah, 1942, the Germans began to round up all the Jews from the towns and villages surrounding Manevichi; it then became clear to the Jews of Manevichi that the hangman's noose was tightening around their necks. Yosef Zweibel immediately contacted Kruk, and the two decided they had to go to the young Jews in Lishnevka and urge them to join them in going to the woods to

organize a partisan group. That night they arrived at
Lishnivka, met with Shimon Wolper, and presented their plan
to him, but he rejected it. The same night, they came to see
me in my hiding place in the barn. (As I mentioned this was
my first meeting with Kruk.) I agreed to their proposition
without hesitation and suggested that we go at once with all
the families to the woods. My plan was to save as many Jews
from Manievich and the surrounding area as possible.

At first, Kruk's behavior was decent and reasonable. The
reason for this was clear: All of his officers were Jews. The
Ukrainian youths not only did not like him, but they presented a moral threat. Because of this, and because he wanted
things to go well, he suggested to me that I be the group
commander. I refused, because I thought he would be a better
person than I for the position. He had military training from
his guerrilla warfare in the woods, he was familiar with the
local forest paths and villages, and he was a Ukrainian. I
agreed to be his second in command.

In time his friendly behavior changed, and he began to
show some antagonism toward the Jewish fighters in spite of
his knowing full well that without them he would not be a
commander for very long. After a number of months in the
woods, his personal behavior changed a lot; he chose for himself one of our women fighters to be his "house secretary,"
despite the fact that he was married and a father.

Most of the time he was in the base in the woods, thanks to
the fact that I had taken it upon myself to tend to the needs of
the two units — the combat unit and the unit made up of the
old people and women.

Later on we met a man wandering in the woods who was
hiding from the Germans. He had been an active Communist
in the village of Obzyr during the Russian rule. We decided
to take him into our unit. After a number of weeks, Kruk
decided to make him his second in command, appointing
me the unit's sergeant-major. Several months passed. Kruk
again honored his fried, the peasant from his hometown, and
appointed him in my place as the division sergeant-major; he
made me the commander of the combat division. Later, when
the combat division was divided into sections and I was its

commander, Russian soldiers who had fled from imprisonment were added to our company, and our *otryad* took on
a different character. Yet it did have several Jews in it, and
Kruk, despite his showing from time to time an impatience
toward them, was made to see that the Jews were a force to
be reckoned with. His behavior was much different from the
time of his first organizing efforts.

He began to live a life of ease in the woods, the life of an
"omnipotent" ruler. A dismantled house was brought from
the village of Lishnevka for him and was set up in the woods.
His "wife's" mother was the head cook, and she managed,
with difficulty, to supply him with food that he liked.

One day his true face was revealed. With his own hands
he shot in the woods a twelve-year-old Jewish boy, whose
only sin was that he had requested to go with his relatives,
the Wolper family, when they had to leave the base, because
the Germans and Ukrainians surrounded our woods. This
event shocked us deeply. Kruk clearly did not feel at ease on
account of this. His only explanation was that he was obligated to act as he did for the sake of discipline, that he had to
show that reality was truly harsh in the woods.

After a number of weeks in the Syrniki woods, we returned
to our original bases. There we found the youth's corpse, still
laying in the same spot where Kruk had shot him; because
of the pressure of circumstances he was forced to report this
incident to headquarters. To justify his deed, he ordered me
to go with him and serve as a witness to his merit in case
Dyadya Petya, the headquarters commander, declared him
guilty. But Dyadya Petya only reprimanded him with harsh
words, and with this, the matter was closed.

After a while a similar incident occurred; Kruk shot a young
Jew from Kamen-Kashirsky, because he stole some bread
from the kitchen to give it to the camp where the old people
and women lived. For this theft, Kruk killed him. He went up
to him and filled him with a round of bullets. The youth died
instantly.

During these days, a personal clash took place between
Kruk and me. I went out at the head of my division in order
to mine the dirt road leading from Kamen-Kashirsky to the

large village, Obzyr. German convoys and police passed daily
on this road to and from the village where the Ukrainian
police forces' main building was set up. The Ukrainians'
assignment was to confiscate livestock and food from the local
villages for the German army.

On a clear morning, we reached the dirt road that was on
the edge of the village of Verkhi, and we planted the mine.
We took a position behind bushes along the road, in tense
anticipation of the arrival of the executors of oppression and
destruction. And in fact, after several hours had passed, the
motorized column loaded with Germans arrived at the site
of the mine. We pulled the cord — but, Aha! The column
passed by and the mine did not explode. After we checked
the mine, we found that the cord had in fact been pulled. We
didn't understand exactly what had happened and decided,
come what may, to remove the ineffectual mine with the
utmost care, so that, heaven forbid, it would not deceive us a
second time.

Yitzchak Kuperberg and I succeeded in removing it.
Disappointed and embittered, we returned to our base in the
dark of night, with "His Highness," the mine. We wanted to
inspect it, find out why it did not explode, and learn a lesson
for the future. Because of this embarrassing incident, we
did not want to report to Kruk about our failure that same
night, and I decided to report to him in the morning. But
two Russians in our division went ahead of me and immediately reported the failure to Kruk, because I had, so to speak,
ruined the mission. Kruk, in a rage, drew his pistol and ran
toward my trench. Luckily for me, his "wife" preceded him.
Endangering her own life, she ran to tell me that Kruk was
about to shoot me along with her brother Yosef, who was our
unit's *politruk* (political commissar). I was ready to meet Kruk,
gun in hand, and then, the same woman who had risked her
life for us, appeared. She ran out to meet him and persuaded
him to calm down. And, indeed, he calmed down, went into
their house and spoke insolently to me, "I know that you
ruined the mission. If it had been anyone but you, I would
have shot him on the spot. From now on, you will not serve
in the position of division commander." He appointed in my
place one of the two Russian informers.

Kruk ordered that the horses be bridled, and he went to the staff commander, Dyadya Petya, to submit a report on the failure, and also on my removal from the post. The staff commander, after listening to his complaint and decision, ordered that the mine be brought to him. With characteristic patience, Dyadya inspected the mine and discovered hat the explosive material was not of good quality; for that reason the mine had not exploded. He ordered Kruk to immediately reinstate me as division commander, as the unit was completely composed of Jews.

Kruk summoned me, and embarrassedly told me to compile a list of thirty men I wanted. I requested that my division include two Ukrainians, very familiar with the surroundings, for the sole purpose of reconnaissance. I picked my friends Yitzchak Kuperberg and Zev Verba as section commanders. Each one of our thirty men faithfully carried out his assignment; together we performed great and sensational acts, comparable to that of David battling Goliath, as we struck out against our enemy. Our concern was to keep alive every Jewish fighter and ever person from the "family camps."

Besides the murders of the two Jews mentioned above, Kruk also caused the death of a Jewish family from Kamen-Kashirsky, that of a young Jew from Warsaw, and others. With these deeds he placed himself, in my humble opinion, in the same category as his Ukrainian brothers — a murderer of Jews.

THE FIRST ACTION:
MAHMED-MELAMED'S CHARACTER

Yisroel Puchtik

The first German patrol, thirty men on motorcycles, wearily entered the town of Manevichi. The Ukrainian population gave them a festive welcome. The Germans left their arms unguarded by the *village office*, confident that they were among a sympathetic population — Ukrainians and Poles.

The Ukrainian police quickly organized and inspected the stolen goods and booty of the town's Jews.

Six weeks passed, and 375 Jews, mainly heads of families, were forcibly gathered together and led to their deaths, into pits that had been prepared beforehand by the local peasants in the "Horses' Graves" sector. We do not have much evidence on what happened in the valley of death. From peasants who took part in this action, and from others who were spectators, we learned that the Ukrainian police beat people with beastly cruelty. All were stripped naked, dragged by the neck, and then pushed into the opening of the pit.

There were attempts at escape and struggle. It was told that Binyamin Eizenberg, a locksmith, killed two policemen, but then a third emptied an entire magazine into Binyamin's body — he was still walking until he fell dead, wallowing in his own blood, into the pit.

After this "action," the Jews were called upon to organize a *Judenrat* that would direct the affairs of the town's Jews, and would strictly concern itself with implementing the Germans' directives.

I left this place and went to my hometown of Gorodok. The town's peasants intervened on my behalf, so that the *Gebietskommissar* permitted me to stay with my wife, two children, and mother. My father had been killed in an "action."

* * * * *

At the beginning of our time in the forest, we carried out a number of punitive operations against Ukrainian nationalists (*Lysovtsy*), the Ukrainian police force, and other collaborators. But our dream was to carry out a serious operation against the Germans themselves. The opportunity for such an operation soon arrived: a mine, that was sent from Moscow to the partisan command, was brought to our company. A Soviet partisans also arrived, who taught us how to activate the mine on railroad tracks. Six Jewish partisans and the one Russian went out to execute the operation on the railroad tracks in the vicinity of Manevichi-Cherevakha. We attached the mine to the tracks, rigged up a long wire, and hid ourselves in a grove, ready to detonate the mine by means of the wire the instant the train passed. All of a sudden, we spotted from afar German troops coming directly toward us, and the young, strong partisan, "Volodya" Zweibel, was ordered to quickly dismantle the mine.

The mine exploded in Volodya's hands, and he cried out for help. The Russian officer blocked our way to him, pointed his gun at us, and ordered us to quickly retreat to the forest. Our helplessness to save our friend and our abandoning him on the railroad tracks jolted us into shock. Volodya's cries echoed in our ears for a very long time.

The next day a Ukrainian liaison informed us of Volodya's fate. The mine had severed his leg and wounded his entire body but he hadn't lost consciousness. The Germans cruelly tortured him, but he did not betray his comrades nor did he reveal the location of the partisan base.

After this tragic event with the mine, the anti-Semitic chief of staff, Kartuchin, decided not to give the Jewish brigade any more mines, based on the claim that they were cowards. This attitude caused a bitter mood to fall on the company, especially since we knew that the one who was at fault for the failure of the mission and the loss of a dear partisan was the Russian instructor. During this time, there was on the staff a captain by the name of Mahmed — he was dark-skinned, tall, and handsome. He had served during the years 1939-41 in the townlet of Poboresky in an artillery unit with the rank of captain-engineer. As the Russians' retreat, he decided to remove the cannon shells, so the Germans would not be able to make use of them. With the help of his soldiers, he buried them in pits in the surrounding forests. He himself was captured, but escaped and wandered about the forests alone, until he organized a unit of partisans. Once, when they were near the town of Kovel, they were attacked by Germans and caught in thick and continuous fire. Captain Mahmed successfully covered his men until they extricated themselves from the siege. This was one of the outstanding operations of Mahmed, but even this act of heroism did not serve to elevate him in Kartukhin's, the anti-Semite's, eyes. Kartukhin was suspicious of him because he was a Jew, although this was never proven the entire time he was in the forest.

Mahmed was transferred to the Jewish company headed by Kruk.

Here, too, Mahmed did not reveal his identity, assuming his Caucasus identity. In spite of this, he did not refrain from proving to his Gentile friends the great ability of the Jewish partisans. Mahmed organized the removal of cannon shells and their transport to Kruk *otryad*, and under his personal supervision and direction, the extraction of explosives from the cannon shells and the preparation of mines began.

This work was carried on intensely, with great expertise and no tools by Jewish youths from the civilian camp ("the family camp"). The process of melting down the explosive material was a very dangerous one. It was necessary to take apart the front piece that was made of copper and to remove another three metal rings to reach the metal explosive, that was as hard as cast cement. All of this work was done using only a chisel and hammer, thus creating a high risk of an unwanted explosion; accidents did in fact occur. Two youths, Syomka and Payskeh, were torn to pieces by explosions. They put the cannon shells in a barrel of boiling water, heated them until the hard explosive material melted, and then baked them into wooden molds that we smeared in a paste of flour and water so that the liquid would not stick to the wood. They baked sabotage-bricks that weighed two to five kilograms and used the explosive materials or mines. The girls of the camp made detonators from flashlight batteries they had obtained from Polish train workers in exchange for pork and other commodities.

Mahmed significantly improved the extraction of explosives and the activating of mines, making it no longer necessary to se a long wire to detonate the mine. Instead, a clock was used, and the danger in this operation was greatly reduced. These types of mines were activated with great success by Malinka (Dov Lorber), Vova Verba, Yitzchak Kuperberg, and many others from the Kruk *otryad*; the bombings of twenty trains, bridges, boats and more were credited to these "cowards."

In light of these operations, many partisans, our "comrades at arms" were compelled to recognize the ability of the Jewish company and to change their attitude toward them. The Jewish partisans and the "civilian camp" knew how to set up Mahmed's operation in every situation, and his contributions were always for their benefit.

With the victories of the Red Army and the approaching of the battlefront to our area, many partisans from the *otryad* joined the army, among them Zev Bronstein, Avraham Merin, Zecharya Viner, Schmuel Lupa, Avraham Gorodetzer with his two daughters, and many others. All of them died a hero's death in the capture of Konigsberg, Warsaw, and Berlin. (Gorodetzer's two daughters live in Israel.)

Mahmed, too, joined the army and went to the ford at the Bug River, while the Germans continued to hold the city of Kovel, where they had been for several months.

My wife and I settled with partisans in the township of Rafalovka. One day in the train station, I saw Mahmed I a major's uniform of the Red Army. In the forest his rank had been that of captain, even before the war. I ran over to him and called out excitedly, "Mahmed, Mahmed! What a hero of a soldier you are — already a major!" The officer looked at me in amazement. "Who are you? I don't know you." I apologized. I told him of the strong resemblance between him, the major, and Mahmed from the Caucasus, the captain that was with us as partisans.

The officer did not leave me and asked that I tell him even more about Mahmed. I told him briefly all that I knew of him. "He is my brother," the major cried excitedly, tears welling up in his eyes. "His name isn't Mahmed, it's Melamed. Our family lived in the Caucasus before the war, and he's my twin brother. We assumed that he was no longer living, and, here, he's alive and goes by the name of Mahmed." We parted with a handshake, *shalom aleichem* and "God be with you." The Jewish officer Melamed from the Caucasus was forced to conceal his Jewish identity not only from the Germans, but also, and especially, from his comrades at arms — the Russian partisans.

INTERVIEWS WITH JEWISH PARTISANS

Jack Nusan Porter

Irving Porter (Yisroel Puchtik)

This is an interview with a Jewish partisan leader, my father. Most interviews are carried out with people whom you don't know and with whom it is fairly easy to be objective. However, when you interview your father and when you talk about the destruction of your sisters (daughters) or uncles (brothers), all objectivity is thrown out the window.

It becomes a chronicle of tears and a necessary but painful task. This article is an edited version of an interview that lasted nearly four hours and took place in the living room of our home in Milwaukee, Wisconsin. Several times I had to stop the tape recorder when my father and I broke down into tears. Yet the chronicle continued because he understood how important it was that people, especially young people, know the true story of Jewish resistance during World War II. It was a story that I had to know. As his son, as a young Jew in America, and as a young adult living in this post-Holocaust era, I too had to know.

There are so many myths, falsehoods, and half-truths associated with the Holocaust. One of the most arrogant of these lies is that *all* Jews were cowards and that they *all* walked passively to their deaths.

Raul Hilberg in his book *The Destruction of the European Jews* arrived at the conclusion that "the reaction pattern of the Jews was characterized by the almost complete lack of resistance." Hannah Arendt in her book *Eichmann in Jerusalem* described Jewish resistance as "pitifully small, incredibly weak and essentially harmless." Psychiatrist Bruno Bettelheim in *The Informed Heart* pleadingly asked: "Did no one of those destined to die fight back? Did none of them wish to die not by giving in but by asserting themselves in attacking the SS Nazis? Only a very few did."

The myths continue, but what is the truth? Bettelheim says the resistors were "very few" in number; Arendt calls this resistance "pitifully small" and "essentially harmless."

Yet, it was these "very few" who, in the Warsaw Ghetto, held off General Jurgen Stroop and his command of 1,000 SS-tank grenadiers, 1,000 men of the SS-cavalry, plus two units of artillery for over two months in the spring of 1943, with only a few guns, hand grenades, Molotov cocktails, and plenty of Jewish guts.

It was this "essentially harmless" nature of Jewish resistance that forced even Goebbels to admit that "now we know what Jews can do if they have arms."

It was this "pitifully small" number of 25,000 Jewish partisans who fought in the forests and mountains — of Poland, Russia, Hungary, Czechoslovakia, France, Greece, Belgium, and Italy. Some of them formed autonomous Jewish national units — Jewish partisans led by Jewish command-ers. However, most of the partisan bands were mixed groups wherein Jews fought alongside Poles, Russians, Ukrainians, Frenchmen, Italians, and others.

Of the 25,000 partisans, there were a large number of survivors. My father was one of them. Irving Porter (Yisroel Puchtik), called "Zalonka" in the underground, was a leader in the famous "Kruk Division," led by the Ukrainian leader Nikolai Konishchuk (Kruk). They fought from mid-1942 to early 1945 in the vicinity of Manevichi, in Volynia, Ukraine, U.S.S.R.

This is my father's story. It could well have been the tale of his comrades now residing in America, Canada, or Israel and including such partisans as Dov Lorber (Seattle), Avrum Lerer (Cleveland), Moshe Kramer (Philadelphia), Isaac Avruch (Denver), Moshe Flash (Montreal), and Abba Klurman, Itzik (Yitzchak) Kuperberg, Vova Verba, Josef Zweibel, Charlie Zarutski, Avrum (Abraham) Puchtik, David Blaustein (Tel Aviv), Avrum and Berl Finkel, and many others.

My father was born in the little town of Gorodok in 1906, the same year and a similar *shtetl* to that of the fictitious Anatevka in the popular *Fiddler on the Roof*. In fact, after seeing the film I jubilantly asked my father: "It was a great picture, Dad, no?" he punctured my enthusiasm by saying, "Great? That's the way it was. It was no picnic."

We live at a time when our affluence and freedom lead us to glorify and romanticize the European *shtetl*, but it was nevertheless a hard and dangerous life. My father was one of eight brothers and sisters; his father was a poor shoemaker. After one major upheaval, World War I, he joined the Polish cavalry at the age of 21, one of the few Jews in that Army. After four years there, he worked as a textile worker, saving dowry money for his older sisters.

This delayed his own marriage to his childhood sweetheart Faygeh (Fay) Merin. They finally got married in 1937, two years before the Nazi Blitzkrieg into Poland. He later worked for the Russian Communists in a collective workers' union until 1941. The Germans came to the area in that same year and in 1942 he had to make the painful decision to leave his family, go into the forests, and join the partisans. I was born later in a bombed-out hospital, in Rovno, a small town near Manevich0069, on December 2, 1944, a few months before the war ended.

* * * * *

When the Nazis came, I was living in the town of Manevichi, a town of 2,000, at most 2,500 people. They first came in to kill the men; later they came on a Friday night to surprise us and took the women, children, old people, and the few men that remained.

We thought they were going to work camps, but found out that they were marched outside the town, told to dig a big hole, and then the Nazis killed and buried them.

When did you escape?

On Wednesday, two days before the came, I decided to escape. I threw away my jacket with the yellow piece of cloth that all Jews had to wear. I tucked my pants into my boots like a Ukrainian peasant, picked up a pail, and passed by the Ukrainian guards as a farmer — and then ran into the woods.

The Germans first came in 1941 to take just the men. They killed 375 of them. Later, in the summer of 1942, they came again — this time pushing women and children into the street.

They drove them out on Friday night. They knew the families were together and they would surprise them. They would kill the Jews, then have an orchestra and a big party, while they took Jewish property. When they finished one job, they'd go on to the net little town.

At this point, I made up my mind that I was not going to go like an animal. I was going to take revenge (*nekumah* was the word he used). I would run away even though it meant leaving my family.

On that Friday night in 1942, the Germans killed my two daughters (your sisters), my mother, my father, my four sisters, my grandparents — twenty-five members of my family. (His brothers, Morris, Boris, and Leon, had left home in the 1920s and 1930s for Chicago and Buenos Aires, Argentina.)

How did you feel about leaving your family?

To this day, I feel guilty. I don't feel bad about killing Nazis or taking revenge on Ukrainians (who collaborated), but I do about leaving my family. Am I no different from my parents or daughters that I lived and they died? No, we are the same. I may not have helped them if I stayed, but at least we would have been together.

What happened after you escaped? Did you find a group of partisans right away?

After I escaped into the woods, I hid for a few weeks, with a Gentile friend — a Ukrainian who lived in a different town. He gave me a rifle and 150 bullets. A rifle was worth gold; you couldn't pay a million dollars for one!

I told him I was not responsible over myself — I wanted revenge. My life was worthless. I would burn his house and kill him if he didn't give me a gun. He was scared so he gave me the gun.

I soon found a group of about 50 people who had just two rifles among them. Within three months, this group grew until it included 200 fighters (about 180 Jews and 20 Russians or Poles), 200 men who guarded the others, and between 500-600 women and children. We had a big job — to find food or early 1,000 people and to fight the Nazis.

How did mamma escape?

I found her two months after I escaped. When I was with the partisans I asked all the farmers in the area about my family. Did any live? One said that my sister's husband was hiding nearby. I went there, expecting to see a tall man, my brother-in-law but it turned out to be a "little man" who weighed only 60 pounds.

This "little man" turned out to be my wife. She was so small. She had escaped by hiding in a stall in a nearby barn. The Nazis didn't find her. By a miracle, she was alive. In the partisan camp, she became the chief cook. A miracle! Her whole family was killed. Everyone. She's the only one who survived. I took her in my hands. She was so light.

Why was the leader a non-Jew if most of the group was Jewish?

It was good to have a Gentile as commander because the Jews lived in small towns or big cities. They were tailors, butchers, business people; they didn't know the woods. Our commander, like other Gentiles, knew how to hunt and fight. He knew the woods. Later we wouldn't need him, but at the beginning he was needed.

What did you do in the partisans?

At first, we didn't do too much. But one day, a captain from a Russian partisan group about twenty miles away came over to us He had done something wrong and his "punishment" was to be sent over to the Jews.

This captain (Mahmed-Melamed) — who was later found out to be a Jew in disguise — told us that when the Germans invaded in 1941, they left behind piles of huge artillery shells, which the captain had found and buried. Each shell weighed over 100 pounds and was filled with gunpowder. With this gunpowder, we could make mines.

I was put in charge of this project along with twenty other men. We carefully took the shells apart so they were no longer dangerous, put them in long barrels, lit fires under the barrels, and heated up this powder to a liquid state. With this liquid, we made mines.

I would go out with a small band of men, and we would place these mines under railroad tracks, water or fuel depots, and bridges, and blow them up. All day long we would sit quietly in the woods; at night we would go out to set mines There was not too much face-to-face contact with the Germans; we could only slow them up and slow down the trains going to the Russian front.

We got food from the Gentile farmers, whom we threatened to shoot if they didn't give us potatoes, flour, or salt in good will. You must be careful in war. One is bitter and a little crazy. You do many wrong things in order to survive.

During the time of the underground, there is no law. It is like the Old West in America. We had to take food or rifles from the farmers. You had to use the gun to get food, to take his boots.

The farmer had enough food and three pairs of boots, and they probably stole them from the Jews anyway. So we had to use force, even kill a few if they didn't give or maybe burn their barns. Most of them gave. They were so surprised to see Jews with guns. They were scared of us. They gave.

This is what we did for over two and one half years. We survived.

What happened after the Germans retreated from your area (in late 1944 and early 1945)?

After the war, I worked for the Russians for a little while, but I wanted to leave Russia and go to Israel. I loved the Russian people; they saved many Jewish lives during the war. They even honored me with a medal for heroism.

I got forged passports from the *Breicha*, the Israeli underground, and began my journey to Palestine. I'll never forget my leaving. I told a Russian officer, maybe he was even a Jew, that I had fought for Russia and now it was time to fight for my own country, for Jews.

He shook my hand and wished me well and then he said: "Puchtik, go in peace, but remember, the Russian boot is a big one. The heel of Russia is here in Moscow, but in twenty years, the toe might be in Palestine." I'll never forget that.

My wife, child and I went by train from Poland to Austria. It took over a month and it is a complete story in itself. We went as Greek ciizens and it was a long and dangerous trip. (I understand that the present day exodus from Russia follows a similar route, by rail and the "Chopin Experss" from Warsaw to Vienna, but it's much less than a month to travel.)

From Vienna we went to a American displaced persons camp near Linz. There, we waited to go to Israel, but it was going to be a long wait because the British blockade was in operation and the illegal *aliyah* was starting. My wife was sick and I had a baby boy and the *Hagana* told us that the trip would be too dangerous for us. They were only taking single people or childless married couples.

In the meantime, we met an American captain who spoke good Russian. He asked me if I had relatives in America. I told him I had a brother, Morris Porter in Chicago. The American had someone who was going to New York put a picture of me in the Yiddish newspaper *The Daily Forward.* My brother saw the picture got in touch with the Jewish authorities and sent me money and a boat ticket. I came to American in 1946, first to Chicago, then moved to Milwaukee. I've been here ever since.

I still want to live in Israel but my children are unmarried. When they get married, I'll move to Israel.

How can you still believe in God after all that's happened to the family?

I can understand if young people don't believe any more in God, but I have reasons not to give up my belief. In fact, unlike some, I believe in God even more now that when I was younger. I saw miracles happen. Ninety-nine percent of the time my life hung on a hair! Bullets would fly all around me, but my body was never touché. Today, I am a strict Orthodox Jew. I don't work on Shabbos or on Jewish holidays.

Now let me ask you a few questions about today's generation of Jews. First, what do you think of the Jewish Defense League?

They make mistakes, but they do plenty that I like. They should search out and protect Jews. If an old woman is mugged, show the muggers your fist and they won't bother you again. But they should stay out of Israel's politics. They don't need them there. We need them here in America to take care of Jewish enemies.

America needs [Rabbi Meir] Kahane more than Israel does. We need protection, self-defense groups, in the parks and in the schools. People are afraid to walk the streets of the city. There's plenty of work for a JDL here in America, but not in Israel. Israel has its own police and army; they don't need the JDL's protection. And give them muggers a fist in the face. They'll think twice.

What can young Jews learn from the Holocaust and the Jewish Resistance?

First, our most bitter lesson is that a Jew can send no one else to take his place. When it comes down to it, no one except a Jew really cares about Jewish problems

Second, the Holocaust is our history. Young Jews must know their history. They must know their own history before they learn another's.

Third, they must be proud to be a Jew. We must respect every human being; but first of all we must respect ourselves! Our own dignity and our own self-respect must come first!

Reprinted from Davka, *Winter-Spring 1973*

* * * * *

Moshe Flash and Jack Melamedik

Both Moshe Flash and Jack Melamedik live in Montreal today. Flash (called "Ivan") fought the Nazis from September 1942 to February 1944 and was awarded the "Hero of the Soviet Union" medal. (See Photo Section for a picture of Flash and his medal.) Melamedik was a young boy during the war and lost both parents and most of his family. He fought under Captain Yanchikov who was second in command under Colonel Anton Brinsky (called Dyadya Petya during the war). Dyadya Petya was a Russian commander under whose control were such groups as Max, Kruk, Kartukhin, and others. These excerpts of an interview took place in Montreal on August 28, 1974:

What was it like to join the partisans?

Flash: Joining the partisans is like a lottery — one never knows what life will throw you. The important thing is to help your fellow man. We had to take revenge against all the killings. But we knew nothing about fighting. I was a baker before the war. It was Kruk (Nikolai Konishchuk, a Ukrainian partisan leader) who taught us how to fight. He was a mayor of a town there; he knew the people; he knew the forests; we needed him at first, but not later. He wasn't perfect either. He shot a Jew once.

Melamedik: We [Jewish fighters] made Kruk into what he was.

After all the killing and all that you saw, do you still believe in God?

Flash: I don't believe in *Gott* [God].

Melamedik: I believe in something or someone that guides us. I still believe because I survived. It was like a miracle.

Flash: You can't believe in God after seeing young babies shot in the mouth. I'm saying that I believe in Judaism, in the Jewish people, and in Israel, but not in God. Because of God, many Jews died. The religiously orthodox Jews kept the people from fighting. They told us we were guilty of something so that we were being punished. They told Jews not to fight. The religious leaders kept a strong hold on the people. I respect them today but I do not respect the religion. I go to *shul* [synagogue] for the sake of the family, for *yahrtzeit* [memorial services for the dead] ... not to pray to God but for the sake of the memory of my family. A partisan was a *hefker mensch* [Yiddish term]: he did not care about anything. The Jews became partisans to take revenge and to save lives — no politics, no ideology, no nothing. God was on vacation, but I didn't have time for a vacation then. A young Jew must learn to give a *patch* [Yiddish for a "blow"] to those who wish to harm us. I admire [Rabbi Meir] Kahane of the JDL for this. But I don't know. Your father [referring to Jack Nusan Porter's father] came from a religious family and he sat at a *Yiddish tish* [a "Jewish table"], but I was an orphan and I never had a good Jewish education. Maybe if I did I would believe in God today like your father. [See prior interview with my father.]

* * * * *

Morris (Moshe) Kramer

Morris Kramer fought in the Kruk *otryad* (fighting unit) together with my father. They were very close friends both during the after the war, when my father and mother lived in Milwaukee and Moshe Kramer lived in Philadelphia, where he still lives with his second wife, Sophie, and his two children. Kramer's first wife was also in the forests, active in the "family camp" and she had a child who died in the woods. His first wife was killed in a tragic accident in Philadelphia. The interview was carried out in his home in Philadelphia on October 15-16, 1981, but will have to wait for another time to be published. (Sadly, it seems that I have lost this interview.)

* * * * *

Faygeh Marin Puchtik (Faye Porter)

As can be imagined interviewing one's own mother is very difficult, especially concerning the deaths of her two daughters (my sisters) but here it is. My father is referred to by several names: *Tateh* ("Dad" in Yiddish), Srulik, or Yisroel Puchtik. Compare this account with several others in the book. The interview took place in November, 1981 in Boston.

Could you please describe our family's social status before the war?

My father and mother and all my brothers and sisters were religious people. I had four sisters and four brothers; there were sixteen grandchildren and even one great-grandchild. I grew up in Gorodok, a small town near Manevichi, Ukraine, until 1939. We were middle-class. My father Nusan Merin was a teacher before World War I; after the war he had a flax and wool machinery shop, but later, together with my brothers, we built a vegetable oil manufacturing firm. We weren't poor but we weren't rich either. My mother Beyla Merin [née Singerman] was a housewife.

You grew up in a shtetl?

Yes, it was a little *shtetl*, a town, Gorodok, of about 500 people, Ukrainians and Jews. Until 1939. *Erev Yom Kippur* {the evening of the High Holy Day] in September 1939, the Soviet Army came, and they wanted to surrounding the Polish Army which was based in Gorodok. But first they sent planes to drop leaflets asking for their surrender. The Polish Army said no, so the Soviets later came with twenty-five planes and bombed the Polish Army camp, and all the houses, and killed many people. We escaped through a window and fled to the safety of the forests. The next day we returned. Everything was ashes. The only thing alive were the cows, waiting in the fields for us. So we had milk. We sold the cows for clothes and money and moved away to Manevich. I was then living with my husband, Yisroel [Srulik] Puchtik and my parents.

When were you married?

We were married in 1937. We had two children, one daughter Chaya Udel, two years old, and Pesel, born later in Manevichi.

Could you describe them? Did they look like [my son] Gabriel?

No. The oldest one looked like you; the other one like Shlomo [my brother — JNP]. They were both dark, brown-haired but with a light skin. The oldest was dark; the youngest light, but with dark hair and dark eyes.

Were they cute?

Don't ask me too much, please.

Did you encounter anti-Semitism before World War II?

Oh yes, from the Ukrainians. They were anti-Semitic. We had a baker once who lived next door to us. He used to bake white bread and *challah*. One day, a Ukrainian told me: "If I could kill this Jew I'd kill him." No reason. Just like that.

Any other experience with you or Tateh?

Altogether, no. *Tateh* had good relations with all the Ukrainians. They liked him. He was friendly with them. For example, when they needed a *peckel michorkeh* [small packet of smoking or chewing tobacco], he would get it for them. Maybe we were an exception but we had good relations with the Ukrainians.

Let's move on to another issue. When war became imminent, what options were open to you and our family? What did you do in response to the coming war?

I understand the question. When the war started, the Soviets were pushed back by the Germans, and when the Germans started bombing the railroads near our town, I said to my husband: "Srulik, let's rent a horse and wagon and follow the Russians in their retreat. Let's get out of here." So I went to Berl Bronstein [see his memoir in this book] and said, "Berl, you have horses and a wagon, let's go away." But he said no we shouldn't go.

Right away, the Russians started mobilizing people for the war effort and they came for my husband because he had once been in the Polish Army as a "Cavalryist," a member of the Polish Cavalry and he knew about horses. So they wanted to put him on a train which carried horses.

It was a mixed-up crazy situation. We didn't know what to do. My mother- and father-in-law [Srulik's parents] said to Srulik: "You're going and leaving us alone? And your wife and children, too?" So, he felt very guilty and left the horses, and the train went away without him. It was later bombed by the Germans and many people and horses died. So, my husband stayed with us. I guess, in a way, he was lucky he didn't go on that train.

How old were you when the war broke out? I was twenty-eight years old and had been married only one year.

How did news of the war first reach you?

By radio and newspaper.

Polish newspapers?

No, we had a Jewish magazine [a Yiddish magazine]. It was called, I think, the *Tog-Morgen Journal.* We found out what was going on from that.

What was the first change that occurred in your job, your home lie or social life because of the war?

When the Germans arrived, the most important change was that they didn't allow us to slaughter cattle anymore. They said we Jews were "punishing" the cattle, "hurting" them. No *shochet* [ritual slaughter] was allowed to kill even one chicken.

What about your school or job?

I didn't have a job and I didn't go to school. I was a full-time mother and housewife.

Was your religious life disrupted?

From 1939 until September 1942, we had our *shul* [synagogue] and a full religious life — rabbis, services. Only in September 1942 was it disrupted.

And your social life?

Oh, what kind of a social life. What a question.

So, what did you do day to day?

It was a sad life. We just stayed home. We couldn't go out. We had to wear the yellow patches on our clothes [to mark them as Jews]. From the beginning we had a white strap with a *magen david* [Star of David] on it. Then, they made us take off the white straps and we put on yellow patches of cloth — eighteen inches in front and eighteen inches in back … and a fifteen-inch yellow patch on every Jewish house. This was in Manevichi.

When did the patches start?

Right from the start of the German occupation, September 1939.

And your possessions?

They gave permission to the Ukrainians for three days to rob the Jews. For three days. Like an open market. The pillows, the sheets, everything. They came and took it all away.

And what could you do?

Nothing. Nothing at all. They laid us out on the floor and came in and took whatever they wanted. And we had no ammunition to fight them off.

Did you think that this was the end of the world, of your lives? What was in your mind to do?

[Sadly, with head bowed] We didn't know what to do.

Did you have a feeling that the Holocaust, that the killings, were coming?

We had a feeling that things were going to get worse but we didn't think it was going to be such a Holocaust. We didn't believe that because we knew from the Germans during World War I that bad things might happen but they didn't kill us back then. We didn't think they would kill us all now.

What about the Manevichi ghetto? Who were the leaders?

We had a *Judenrat* [a ghetto leadership] set up in the summer of 1940. They were high-class people, many newcomers from Poland, teachers, educated people The first thing the Nazis asked the *Judenrat* to do was collect fur coats, gold, silver, Jewelry as "contributions" for the Third Reich. There were about 2,000 people rushed into Manevichi by then.

Were you surrounded by soldiers?

No.

So, it was easy to escape?

Yes, but you had to wear the yellow patch. If you were caught without a patch … My brother Zisya was caught without a patch one day. He was taken to the police station and beaten black and blue. I don't know how he survived.

How did you get food?

You couldn't go outside the town, and you couldn't buy food openly from Gentiles. But some people hid clothes and jewelry and exchanged them for food. There was a lot of underground smuggling.

And what did Tateh do?

When he found out that the Nazis would take men "out to work" [meaning to kill them — JNP], he ran away to Gorodok, a small town about eight kilometers away, and I was left in Manevichi with the family. He ran away eight days before they took all the men to a place called *Ferdishe Mogiles* ['Horses' Graves'], a field outside of town, and killed all the men. That was in late summer 1941, the third of Elul, 1941. This was the first "action," killing the men.

And the second action? [The second action was where they killed the remaining women, children, and any other men still alive. My two young sisters were killed in this action.]

The second "action" took place around September 23, 1942, about a year later. Some men, like my father, were still in hiding. The Germans, SS, searched for men, including *Tateh*, but didn't find them. *Tateh* heard about the action that very same night, and he went into hiding in Gorodok. They killed all them men — *Judenrat* leaders, rabbis, anyone they could find.

475

How did they kill them?

They lied to them, said they were going to work. They collected them in a kind of dormitory or auditorium first. I saw them take the men out of the houses and collect them in this dormitory.

That's all I saw. Then, they put them on trucks and took them outside the town to a field where pits had already been dug. They forced the Ukrainian peasants to dig the pits. They took *Tateh*'s father [Yankel Puchtik], my brothers Zisya and Yankel, Yehuda Merin's father, and many, many others.

And so they took them out to Ferdishe Mogiles, lined them up, and shot them?

Yes.

Did the men know what was to happen to them?

No. [Long silence]

Did they have to dig their own graves?

Some peasants told us later that they had to dig their own graves in some cases, but pits were dug already by the Ukrainians.

So, they lined them up, killed them, covered them with dirt and lime, and then went onto the next town?

Yes. [Deep silence]

Was there any resistance?

No. Yes, Yehuda Merin's brother-in-law [his sister's husband] fought back before they shot him. There may have been others too but I don't know.

And what happened to Tateh?

They liked him in Gorodok. He was a good shoemaker. Even the mayor of Gorodok liked him and prepared special papers for him to stay, stating that he was needed in Gorodok. The mayor even got permission for us to leave Manevichi and rejoin *Tateh* in Gorodok. There we were re-united. The Laniz family was there; so too the Nesanel family. [My mother then tells me the story of how the two Nesanel boys, age eighteen and twenty, were killed by a Ukrainian policeman and several others. The boys were taken out to a field, told to dig their own graves, and shot for breaking the curfew for Jews. They were out too late at night. Before he shot them, the policeman said: So, you were trying to run away and join the partisans, eh?"]

Did you know the name of the policeman — or the peasants — or anyone who did this?

No. The farmers were good people by and large but their sons became Nazis. Uneducated, stupid boys. The Nazis said shoot people; they shot people. Just followed orders. Most were Ukrainian nationalists, *Banderovtsy*-types.

Did any Ukrainians try to stop this action or even question it?

I don't think so. Maybe some but it happened so fast. I think though we should have asked them for help, but we didn't. They might have saved some Jewish men if we had asked but we didn't ask. That was stupid of us [as Jews] — we didn't ask. We could have done something...

What happened later?

We worked in Gorodok for a while. Then one day, a Ukrainian commandant and police [no Nazis] came and said to take all our things, that we were going back to Manevichi, all three families, the Puchtiks, Lanizs, and Nesanels. We knew then that this was the end. We were going to die.

They drove us from Gorodok on trucks. We wanted to jump from the truck, but our father's mother, Yenta, said no. So, first they took us to a jail, all three families in a little room, and we stayed there overnight. The *Judenrat* heard we were in jail and got us out. They took *Tateh* to work packing hay, very hard labor. Your father asked the Nazis: "What will happen to us?" and the German said: *"Der beste Jude vil zein der letzte"* ("The best Jew will be the last to go"). He worked in the hay fields for two weeks.

The, on Wednesday, September 20, 1942, the police surrounded the entire town and said they were making a ghetto and started pushing people into one street. The *Tateh* said

— "No, I'm not staying. Enough already. I'm going to try to escape." He took of his yellow patch, in fact his whole jacket, and said: "Faye, should I go?", and I said, "Srulik, do what you want. It's up to you."

He went through the police lines disguised as a Ukrainian farmer and fled past a church. A Polish priest saw him and said: "Are you running away from the devil? The devil will catch you!" He saw that Srulik was a Jew because he looked frightened, but luckily nobody else recognized him. He went into the forest, to Slovik's house, and Slovik, a good man, hid him. I too went and took both children to a Polish neighbor and begged her to help me, but she said it was too dangerous. "Go to the barn and hide there." I decided to return to my parents' house.

After Slovik hid him, Srulik walked back to Gorodok and went into hiding. The Ukrainians, even the mayor, couldn't help him anymore. It was just too dangerous so he hid in a Jewish cemetery, slept there, and begged for food at night.

On Saturday evening, September 23, 1942, some Ukrainian friends of his came to the cemetery and told him: "There is no one left alive in Manievich. The are all dead." The *Tateh* started to cry. He went to a friend Ivan, a sympathetic Ukrainian, and said to Ivan: "Give me a gun. I know you have arms. Let me go and take revenge." Ivan gave him a rifle, 150 bullets, and two grenades. He wished him well and my father left; he went into the forests to join the partisans.

Ivan trusted *Tateh* so much he gave him the ammunition. Ivan also told him another Jew Abraham Lerer was also hiding somewhere in an abandoned house in the woods. So *Tateh* went to find his friend Lerer. They hugged and cried. "Now we had to look for others and for a fighting group. We can't stay here any longer." Some Ukrainian friends helped them find Kruk [Nikolai Konishchuk, leader of the Kruk fighting Group] and others from the towns of Griva and Lishnevka.

Who was in that group that's alive today or who I know?

In this group were the Avruchs, the Zweibels, Vova [Zvi] Verba, the Wolpers, the Blansteins, Abba Klurman, Sasha [Charlie] Zarutski, the Zaicheks, and others.

So most of the people who escaped and joined the partisans survived? Isn't there a lesson in this?

Yes, if more would have tried to escape, they'd be alive today. You had a much better chance to survive fighting with the partisans. But people were afraid; some didn't want to go into the forests [it was a hard life]; and many didn't want to leave their families. Better to stay together in the ghetto.

And what of the rabbis? What was their role?

I'm afraid the rabbis were not much help. Some said it was God's will; most shook their head and did nothing; but a few warned us to leave and to fight. One of them, the *Tateh's* rebbe, said: "Yidn, escape to Russia," but few of us listened.

Were there any other stories you failed to tell me?

Yes, there are a few that I remember well. On Wednesday, when the Germans surrounded the *shtetl*, Senka Melamedik, Jack Melamedik's father, tried to spring over a fence and escape. In that minute, a Ukrainian policeman shot him on the spot. Senka was thirty-five years old; Jack was only ten. Chunek Wolper saw it.

My sister Elka, thirty-six years old, had a son, a nice boy by the name of Chunah. He was on his way to work at the parquet [wood] factory. He saw a Ukrainian policeman; he got scared and started running; the policeman shot him. He was only seventeen years old. That was Wednesday, September 20, 1942, a few days before the second action.

Elka's husband, Mordechai Wool, was another example. They lived in a Ukrainian village, Novaya Ruda. The police came one day and said to him: "You're a Communist; we have to take you away." They tied him to a wagon and dragged him on the ground for a half a mile. He died. Elka and her four kids ran away into the woods. Her young son, Shlomo Wool, got so sick in the stomach from the shock the doctors had to come and apply leeches to his body.

The mayor of Novaya Ruda, a good man and a Ukrainian, brought her and her children to Manevichi at our request. That was a big mistake. She should have stayed in the woods hiding. She might be alive today if she had.

Now, Momeh, let's go to your story…

On Wednesday, September 20, 1942, the Germans made a strict ghetto, and on Friday afternoon, they went from house to house, shouting at us to come out and go to the road, about 300-400 of us, and we saw that this was the end. Everyone started crying and praying *Shma Yisrael* [Hebrew prayer for "Hear, O Israel"].

They took us over a railroad track and shoved us into the street and packed us into houses on that street. We didn't know what to do. I was with my sisters Elka and Rivkeh and my two little daughters, Chaya Udel and Pesel.

I noticed that one woman in the crowd had sleeping pills, and I saw her give her child one so she could escape (without the child crying). It was evening and escape was still possible. But she wouldn't give me a pill. It didn't help. Her child woke anyway.

I said to the people let's make a fire and burn down the ghetto and escape, but they didn't listen to me. We knew we would be killed the very next day, Saturday. Still, they wouldn't believe me.

So, I told my sister Rivka that I was going to Velvel Bronstein and Pesel Librant-Bronstein, to their home. [See Pesel's memoir in this book.] I went outside but I was afraid. I didn't go back to the house. Instead, I remembered what the Polish lady told me and I went to the barn. I sat in a corner all night Friday and all day Saturday, in the barn, near the hay. I didn't even cover myself, just sat in the corner alone.

And what was your purpose for doing this?

I don't know. I didn't know what to do. But early in the morning on Sunday, I saw Pesel hiding too, and I said: "This is Faygeh. Show me where you are." And they showed me and I climbed into, like an attic in a house near the barn, and there was Pesel, Velvel, and their four children. It was getting lighter all the time, and the Ukrainian police where looking for us. I saw them but they didn't see me. I said we better escape or they'll come back and find us. So all of us crawled maybe two blocks over the railroad track on our hands and knees and came into the forests. We sat and rested and then went to the forester Slovik. Slovik helped us to hide just like he helped *Tateh*. It was raining. We had no food, no good shelter, and the lice were all over us. It was terrible.

A couple days later, three boys [Vova Verba and two others] from Kruk's group came and told me that my husband was still alive. I begged them to take me to him. But it wasn't easy. On the way, some police started shooting at us, but eventually we came upon a group of twenty-five young people, armed with only one short rifle. They welcomed us. They even had food. I weighed maybe 75-80 pounds. The group had no name. It was outside the town of Lishnevka.

In a few days, the *Tateh* came with Kruk, David Blaustein, and several others. And he found me. The feeling was over-whelming. We hugged and cried. But I felt like falling into a grave. I was so ashamed to be alive.

Did you feel guilty about leaving your two daughters?

Yes, very guilty. Even the *Tateh* felt guilty that he had left me, his children, and mother and father; and I felt guilty for leaving my family.

But, why did you leave your daughters and hide in the barn?

Oh, I only left to see Velvel Bronstein and Pesel Librant. I wanted to go back home, but there were police everywhere. I couldn't go back. [Long pause] … That's what God planned for me …

I eventually joined the Kruk partisan group. However, just two days later, the Nazis and Ukrainians came to the woods and found us. Chunek Wolper however saw them and fired at them. They opened up such a fire on us. When we heard the first round, we scattered everywhere. Later we regrouped and continued the hard partisan life.

And my two little sisters?

You know, Yankele, what happened. Why do you ask? They were taken out on *Shabbos* [Saturday], taken outside the town, only four years old and two, and … I can't speak anymore.

EDITOR'S NOTES

1: - This was the term used by the Germans to denote the mass killings of the Jews — usually men first, the leadership of the ghetto and those able to give the most resistance. The German spelling is "Aktion."

2: - This was an area, a field really, outside Manevichi where horses were buried. Today it is a military cemetery. The editor's family were killed and buried there.

3: - This is Jack Nusan Porter's mother. The original name was Puchtik. Today, Faye Porter lives in Milwaukee, Wisconsin. Her husband was Irving Porter (Yisroel Puchtik, known as Zalonka). She is also a cousin to Yehuda Merin.

4: - Today, he is alive and living in Tel Aviv, Israel, and is a relative to both editors of this book.

5: - These are underground bunkers built in the woods to hide the partisans and their belongings.

6: - *Daven* means praying in Hebrew; *minyan* is a religious quorum of ten men.

7: - *Chametz* means unleavened bread, forbidden on Passover.

8: - The *Banderovtsy* were Ukrainian nationalist partisan groups, feared by Jews, Poles, and Communists alike. They were named after their leader Stefan Bandera.

9: - An *otryad* is a Russian term for a partisan fighting force, often named after its leader.

10: - Atlit is a small seaport in Israel and a prison camp. This story itself should be expanded since this is part of the history of the illegal immigration by Jews into Palestine, then ruled by Great Britain.

11: - The 22nd day of Elul, 5712, is the Hebrew calendar day for September 21, 1942.

12: - Kruk is the *nom de guerre* for the controversial Ukrainian leader of the partisan fighting group described in these pages, Nikolai Konischuk.

13: - Slovik is the family of father Yasenty and his son, Casimir, Polish foresters and farmers, who saved several Jewish lives during the "action" in and around Manevichi. He saved the life of the mother of the editor of this book, Jack Nusan Porter.

14: - It was getting too "hot to handle" for these Russian (Dyadya Petya — Anton Brinsky), Polish (Max — Józef Sobiesiak), and Ukrainian (Kartukhin and Kruk) leaders. Too many collaborators were being executed, and it was becoming too prickly an issue politically.

15: - Blanstein was probably too much of a "Zionist" for the authorities to tolerate. The "escape" was the *Breicha* organization, which helped people immigrate to Israel.

16: - Ethnic Germans living in the Soviet Union, Poland, Ukraine, and other areas.

17: - The masses of Jews were killed in "actions" from May to October 1942.

18: - From the Hebrew term for benevolent Gentiles, non-Jews that treated Jews kindly.

19: - The 19th of Elul corresponds to the thrid week of September in the Hebrew calendar in 1942, the date of the mass killings (the "action" of the Jews in this town.

20: - In Hebrew this is a play on the word "karah." This pun is an example of the "black humor" that developed among partisans, as usually, one would write "zeh karah" meaning "this happened" but here we hear the word "karah," but meaning "torn apart" (killed). Thank you, Ann Abrams, the Hebrew translator.

21: - *Breicha* movement---the movement to rescue Jews from Europe to go to Israel.

22: - A group of friendly partisans led by A. P. Fedorov.

23: - From the Yom Kippur prayer "who shall die by strangulation..."

24: - Mourner's prayer for the dead.

25: - Probably a Displaced Person Camp.

26: - The Jewish community in Israel (Palestine).

APPENDIX

ADDITIONAL COPYRIGHT INFORMATION:

First edition was published by University Press of America in both hardcover and soft-cover: Volume I: ISBN: 0-8191-2180-0 (perfect-binding) and ISBN: 0-8191-2179-7 (cloth); Volume II: ISBN: 0-8191-2538-5 (perfect) and ISBN: 0-8191-2537-7 (cloth).

Portions of this book have previously appeared in *Present Tense, Genesis 2, Davka* and *Yalkut Volyn, Wisconsin Jewish Chronicle, Women's American ORT Reporter,* and *Jewish Combatants of World War II.*

Copyright © 1982 by University Press of America, Inc., with rights resorting back to Jack Nusan Porter after the books went out of print.

LC Catalog Number 81-40258

Translated from the Hebrew by the Magal Translation Institute, Ltd., and based on original Russian, Polish, and Yiddish sources.

Hebrew version: Volume I: Binyamin West (ed.), *Heym Hayu Rabim: Partizanim Yehudim B'brit Ha-moatzot B'milchemet Ha-olam Ha-shniya (They Were Many: Jewish Partisans in the Soviet Union During World War II)*, Tel Aviv, Israel: Archives for the Committee of Russian Jewry, Hapoel Hatzair Publishing Cooperative, 1968, in cooperation with Yad Vashem Memorial Institute, Jerusalem.

Volume I originally published as part of *Partizanskaya Druzhba (Partisan Brotherhood)*, Moscow, USSR: Der Emes Publishing House, 1948; and then later translated into Hebrew by Binyamin West in 1968 as *Heym Hayu Rabim.*

Permission to publish this book was granted by VAAP, the copyright agency of the USSR; by Binyamin West, editor of the Hebrew version of Part 1 of Volume II; the World Union of Volynian Jews in Israel; the Federation of Volynian Jews in the United States; and various authors and friends of my parents for Part 2 of Volume II. Some of the interviews of Volume II were translated from the Yiddish to English by Jack Nusan Porter.

Volume II: Taken in part from *K'Oranim Gavahu: Partizanim Yehudim B'Ya'arot Volyn (Like Tall Pines trees: Jewish Partisans in the Forests of Volyn)*, Givatayim, Israel: Beit Volyn in Givatayim, Israel, Summer, 1980, edited by Natan Livneh.

Volume II translated by Magal Translation Institute, Ltd., of Tel Aviv and by Ann Abrams, Esther Ritchie, and Esther Kluger.

A second edition Copyright © 1997 by The Spencer Press came out in 1997 in a limited paperback edition. ISBN: 0-932270-10-7 (Volume I) and 0-932270-11-5 (Volume II).

Introduction Footnotes

[1]Martha Byrd Hoyle, *A World in Flames: A History of World War II*, New York: Atheneum, 1970, pp. 323-324. These figures reflect civilian deaths with regard to the Chinese and the Jews. For the Russians, approximately seen million out of the twenty million dead were civilians; the rest, thirteen million, were Soviet soldiers.

[2]William B. Helmreich, "How Jewish Students View the Holocaust: A Preliminary Appraisal," *Response: A Contemporary Jewish Review*, Vol. IX, No. 1 (25), Spring 1975, p. 104.

[3]Raul Hilberg, *The Destruction of the European Jews*, Chicago: Quadrangle Books, 1961, pp. 662-669. See also Yuri Suhl (ed.), *They Fought Back: The Story of the Jewish Resistance in Nazi Europe*, New York: Schocken Books, 1975, pp. 3-4. (Originally published by Crown Publishers.)

[4]Hannah Arendt, *Eichmann in Jerusalem: A Report on the Banality of Evil*, New York: Viking Press, 1963, p. 108. See also Jacob Robinson, *And the Crooked Shall Be Made Straight: The Eichmann Trial, the Jewish Catastrophe, and Hannah Arendt's Narrative*, Philadelphia: Jewish Publication Society, 1965, pp. 213-223; and Morris U. Schappes, "The Strange World of Hannah Arendt," *Jewish Currents*, July-August, September and October 1963. Available also in pamphlet form.

[5]Bruno Bettelheim, *The Informed Heart: Autonomy in a Mass Age*, New York: The Free Press, 1960, p. 263. See also Jacob Robinson, *Psychoanalysis in a Vacuum: Bruno Bettelheim and the Holocaust*, New York: YIVO Institute of Jewish Research, A Yad Vashem Documentary Project, 1970, 36 pages.

[6]Ruth Kunzer, "Teaching Literature of the Holocaust," *Davka* (a student review of the UCLA Hillel Foundation), Vol. V, No. 2, Summer 1975, p. 6. George Steiner's quote is from his book *Language and Silence*, New York: Atheneum, 1970.

[7]Reuben Ainsztein, *Jewish Resistance in Nazi-Occupied Eastern Europe*, New York: Harper & Row (Barnes & Noble), 1974, pp. 394 and 396. See also Binyamin Eliav, "Soviet Russia and the Holocaust" in *Israel Pocket Library: Holocaust*, Jerusalem: Keter Publishing House, 1974, pp. 177-179.

[8]Eliezer Berkovits, *Faith after the Holocaust*, New York: KTAV, 1973, p. 36.

[9]See Suhl, *op. cit.*, p. 6. Joseph Goebbels, Hitler's Minister of Propaganda, made these remarks in his diary and thereby paid a grudging tribute to the Warsaw Ghetto uprising of April 1943.

[10]Suhl, *op. cit.*, pp. 239-240.

[11]Quoted in the introduction to the Hebrew version of this book by Binyamin West, *Heym Hayu Rabim*, Tel Aviv: Labor Archives Press, 1968, p. 11. This letter also appeared in Dr. Y. Karmish, "Enemy Sources Tell of Jewish Bravery" (English translation of original Hebrew), *Yediot Ya-Va-Shem* (Yad Vashem Newsletter) No 6-7, Teveth 5727, January 1957.

[12]For further discussion on this theme, see Shaul Esh, "The Dignity of the Destroyed: Towards a Definition of the Period of the Holocaust," *Judaism*, Vol. II, No. 2, Spring 1962.

[13]See Ber Mark, "The Herbert Baum Group: Jewish Resistance in Germany in the Years 1937-1942" in Suhl, *op. cit.*, pp. 55-68

[14]See Abraham Foxman, "Resistance: The Few Against the Many" in Judah Pilch (ed.), *The Jewish Catastrophe in Europe*, new York: American Association for Jewish Education, 1968, pp. 117-119; and especially Suhl, *op. cit.*, pp. 189=195 and 219-225.

[15]The figures in this section are taken from Foxman, *op. cit.*, pp. 122-123.

[16]Again, the figures are from Foxman, *op. cit.*, p. 121. Foxman has quoted from Reuben Ainsztein, "The War Record of Soviet Jewry," *Jewish Social Studies*, January 1966, p. 8. See also Binyamin West, *op. cit.*, p. 9. Some may question the authenticity of these awards because so many were given out by the Russian command both to its soldiers and its partisans in order

to bost morale. This may be true, but great acts of heroism still abounded and these medals reflect that, even though a great many of them were eventually distributed.

[17]See Reuben Ainsztein, "The War Record of Soviet Jewry," p. 14.

[18]For further information on Hannah Senesh, see Marie Syrkin, *Blessed is the Match*, New York: Alfred A. Knopf, 1947.

[19]These are, of course, very rough estimates. See Foxman, *op. cit.*, p. 123; Reuben Ainsztein, *Jewish Resistance in Nazi-Occupied Eastern Europe*, pp. 393-396; Israel Gutman, "Partisans" in *Israel Pocket Library: Holocaust*, Jerusalem: Keter Publishing House, 1974, pp. 114-116.

[20]See Franklin H. Osanka (ed.), *Modern Guerrilla Warfare*, New York: The Free Press, 1962, and his extensive bibliography, pp. 475-508. See also his article "Internal Warfare: Guerrilla Warfare" in *International Encyclopedia of the Social Sciences*, New York: Macmillan Company, 1968, pp. 503-507; Otto Heilbrunn, *Partisan Warfare*, New York: Praeger, 1962. For an analysis of the Soviet partisan movement, see Edgar M. Howell, *The Soviet Partisan Movement*, 1941-1944, Washington, D.C. Department of the Army (Pamphlet 20-244), August 1956.

[21]This is the evaluation of a United States Army officer and historian, Edgar M. Howell, *Ibid.*, p. 203.

[22]These figures were compiled from official German sources and can be found in the chapter by Earl Ziemke, "Composition and Morale of the Partisan Movement" in John A. Armstrong (ed.), *Soviet Partisans in World War II*, Madison, Wisconsin: University of Wisconsin Press, 1964, p. 151.

[23]Reuben Ainsztein, *Jewish Resistance in Nazi-Occupied Eastern Europe*, p. 280. The emphasis is from the original. For a fuller treatment, see his subchapter, "The Size of the Jewish Participation," pp. 393-396.

[24]The background information on these three stages were acquired from three sources: Ainsztein, *Jewish Resistance in Nazi-Occupied Eastern Europe*, pp. 280-281; Howell, *op. cit.*, pp. 204-205; and Ziemke, *op. cit.*, pp. 148-150 and 194-196.

[25]Howell, *op. cit.*, p. 205.

[26]This is the opinion of Ainsztein, *Jewish Resistance in Nazi-Occupied Eastern Europe*, p. 394.

[27]This description of the partisan composition is based on Ziemke, *op. cit.*, pp. 141-146.

[28]Ziemke, *op. cit.*, pp. 147-148.

[29]Ainsztein, *Jewish Resistance in Nazi-Occupied Eastern Europe*, p. 280.

[30]Quoted from Binyamin West's introduction to *Heym Hayu Rabim*, p. 10.

[31]From an interview with Israeli Holocaust researcher and professor at the Bar Ilan University, Dr. M. Diburzchki, *Maariv* (an Israeli newspaper), July 28, 1964. Quoted in West, *op. cit.*, p. 10.

[32]Israel Gutman, *op. cit.*, p. 109. The material in this book was first published in the *Encyclopedia Judaica*.

[33]West, *op. cit.*, pp. 11-12.

[34]Bruno Bettelheim, *The Informed Heart*, *op. cit.*, pp. 252-254.

[35]See Stanley Milgram, *Obedience to Authority*, New York: Harper & Row, 1973, and his article, "The Perils of Obedience," *Harper's Magazine*, December 1973.

[36]Ponchardier is talking of the postwar liberation of France, but his words also apply to the war years themselves. The quote is from Blake Ehrlich, *Resistance: France 1940-1945*, Boston: Little Brown, 1965, p. 272.

[37]Leon Wells, *The Janowska Road*, New York: Macmillan, 1963, p. 190. For further discussion of collective responsibility, see Abraham Foxman's excellent discussion upon which I have elaborated, *op. cit.*, pp. 94-95.

[38]Philip Friedman, "Jewish Resistance to Nazism: Its Various Forms and Aspects" in Jacob Glatstein et al. (eds.), *Anthology of Holocaust Literature*, New York: Atheneum, 1973, p. 276.

[39]This dilemma is graphically portrayed in a play by Arthur Miller, *Incident at Vichy*, in *The Portable Arthur Miller*, New York: Viking Press, 1971, pp. 283-342.

[40]Friedman, *op. cit.*, p. 277. This section on lack of arms and lack of trust relies heavily on Foxman's discussion, *op. cit.*, pp. 123-124.

[41]See Suhl, *op. cit.*, p. 6.

[42]Friedman, *op. cit.*, p. 277.

[43]For a more intensive discussion of this point and others that follow, see Howell, *op. cit.*, pp. 209-213, and Kenneth Macksey, *The Partisans of Europe in the Second World War*, New York: Stein and Day, 1975.

[44]Howell, *op. cit.*, p. 210. However, Howell is not completely correct, since partisan groups play an important role outside of military matters too, but even so, a few partisan movements were quite effective. The most notable was General Tito's partisans in Yugoslavia. About 2,000 Jews took part in his ranks, and Tito's first and closest comrade-in-arms was Moshe Piade, a Jew. Also, the Russian partisan movement played an extremely important role in keeping pressure on the Germans and its allies as the USSR was rebuilding its strength to continue the struggle.

* * * * *

Portions of this essay, the parts dealing with obstacles to resistance, appeared in Byron Sherwin and Susan Ament (eds.), *Encountering the Holocaust*, New York: Impact Press, distributed by Hebrew Publishing Company, 1979, pp. 190-195, reprinted by permission of the editors.

BOOK ONE FOOTNOTES

[1]It is difficult to tell what this is: possibly *banki* sucking cups used for medical treatment in Eastern Europe. (ed.)

[2]The ten Jewish martyrs during the time of Rabbi Akiva who gave their lives rather than desecrate the Torah. (ed.)

[3]According to another version, those Jewish partisans who were not Soviet citizens could begin the oath in the following manner: "I, a free son to my people, and one who has seen enough suffering, volunteer, and hereby join the ranks of the Red (Soviet) partisans. (ed.)

[4]For partisans who were Ukrainian or Byelorussian, the appropriate name of the Soviet state was substituted. The oath was given in the Russian or Ukrainian language depending on the nationality of the partisan. Note the special emphasis in both oaths on loyalty and discipline and its extremely propagandistic and patriotic tone. (ed.)

[5]Soon after "Operation Barbarossa," the German attack on Russia on May 15, 1941, Stalin appealed to the Soviet people to organize guerrilla warfare. Many partisan leaders had also been active in the post-1917 October Revolution civil wars in Russia. (ed.)

[6]An escape from hanging most likely, but this is unclear. (ed.)

[7]World War II. (ed.)

[8]Though acts of cooperation and friendship were numerous, the author does not mention the anti-Semitism ""and the tensions among ethnic groups that did exist. (ed.)

[9]"Jews, right! Jews, left!" (ed.)

[10]Hebrew for "Hear, O Israel," a Jewish prayer, one sometimes reserved for imminent death. (ed.)

[11]In the original Russian, the term used was the "Great Land" or the "Big Land." (ed.)

[12]On October 14, 1943, over 400 inmates of the Sobibor concentration camp led a revolt, killing ten SS men and thirty-

eight Ukrainian guards; nearly half of them survived, broke into six groups, and joined the Soviet partisans shortly afterwards. (ed.)

[13]Another account of Glieder is given later in this book. The film mentioned is probably in the Lenin Library of Moscow. The editor is in the process of having this documentary released to the West. (ed.)

[14]The yellow patch or star distinguished them as Jews. (ed.)

[15]A collective settlement in Russia. (ed.)

[16]N.K.V.D. is the Russian abbreviation for the "People's Commissariat of Internal Affairs." (ed.)

[17]This is a free translation of the song text. (ed.)

[18]Pravda means "truth." (ed.)

[19]Term for Hungarian soldiers who fought at the side of the Germans. (ed.)

[20]This is the town where the editor and his parents grew up. A fuller account of the Kruk partisan group is given in a later chapter. (ed.)

[21]This is about 44 pounds. (ed.)

[22]Raffia shoes were shoes made of soft leather or rubber, somewhat like tennis shoes, for moving quietly through the forest. (ed.)

[23]A non-Jew. (ed.)

[24]This term, "national avenger," is a direct translation — it simply meant those Russians who took revenge for their dead families and friends. (ed.)

[25]From Binyamin West's original Hebrew introduction. (ed.)

[26]To our regret, Vershigora does not tell us the decision of the survivors or what happened to them. (ed.)

[27]This section was added to this book later.

[28]The international Holocaust documentation center based in Jerusalem, Israel. (ed.)

[29]These were, no doubt, Orthodox Jews, whose side-curls (*peyos*) would have given them away. (ed.)

[30]Russian army rank equivalent to colonel. "Uncle Petya" is "Dyadya Petya" in Russian. (ed.)

[31]Ukrainian nationalists, often Nazi collaborators, who preyed on Soviet partisan and Jew alike. (ed.)

[32]From *Einikeit*, June 15, 1944.

[33]His films rest in the archives of the Lenin State Library in Moscow. (ed.)

[34]See his memoirs, *S kinoapparatom v tylu vraga (With a Motion Picture Camera in the Rear of the Enemy), Moscow: Gosknoizdat*, 1947. (ed.)

[35]Again, it is a private hope of the editor that one day these films will be available to Western audiences. (ed.)

[36]It was also in all likelihood one of their last, for the war was to end in several months. (ed.)

[37]Russian equivalent of colonel. (ed.)

[38]Probably *no* relation to the Soviet dissident Andrei D. Sakharov, the noted physicist and father of the Russian A-bomb. (ed.)

[39]Another term for the Germans. (ed.)

[40]Approximately 144 miles, a long march by any standards. (ed.)

[41]By this time, some of the partisans were organized by the Soviet Army, and forests or regions within forests were "allocated" according to military needs, not by whim. (ed.)

[42]See Moshe Flash's partisan documents and medal in the appendix of the book. (ed.)

[43]This is the editor's (my) father. He was awarded the "War of the Fatherland" medal, First Class. (ed.)

[44]Konishchuk is correct: a great many other fighters, both men and women, all of them Jews, could have been added to his list. His group is significant because as noted, it was even labeled by the Germans themselves as a "Jewish Unit"; this was unusual, because most Soviet partisan groups were mixed groups. (ed.)

[45]There were Romanian collaborative police and army personnel working with the Germans. (ed.)

[46]It seems that even military support workers won medals as well. (ed.)

[47]Unless otherwise specified these books are in Russian or Ukrainian and have not been translated into English; I am giving the English equivalent of the title only. (ed.)

SOURCES

For general background information the single most useful source for the English-speaking student and scholar is John A. Armstrong (ed.), *Soviet Partisans in World War II*, Madison, Wisconsin: University of Wisconsin Press, 1964. I have made use of this book in my introduction, especially the sections dealing with the composition of the partisans and their social structure. It is invaluable, especially its index and excellent annotated bibliography of Russian books on partisan warfare. The Lenin Library of Moscow has by far the greatest collection of material on this subject.

Other collections of memoirs and descriptions of Soviet partisan commanders (based on material found in the Armstrong book) are:[47]

V.A. Andreyev, *The People's War*, Moscow, 1952. Andreyev was a teacher of military history who later became a prominent commissar and partisan leader, eventually attaining the rank of major-general in the Bryansk Forest of Byelorussia.

G. Linkov, *The War Behind Enemy Lines*, Moscow, 1951, 1959. Linkov was an engineer and an important Communist Party official before the war who organized and led one of the parachutist detachments that played a major role in reactivating the partisan movement in Byelorussia in 1941-1942.

A. Fedorov, *The Underground Obkom in Action*, two volumes, Moscow, 1947. There are also several other editions, including one in English called *The Underground Committee Carries On*, Moscow: Foreign Languages Publishing House, 1952. "Obkom" is a Communist Party committee at the province level. Fedorov was not only a major partisan leader, but a high official in the Ukrainian Communist Party.

Anton P. Brinsky or Brinskii (known by his *nom de guerre*, "Dyadya Petya," or "Uncle Petya"), *On the Other Side of the Front: Memoir of a Partisan*, Moscow, 1958. An important document by one of the leaders of the organizing teams sent to West Byelorussia and later to the Western Ukraine to revive the partisan movement in those areas.

Nikolai Konischuk ("Kruk"), a leader of a nearly all-Jewish partisan brigade numbering about 300 fighters and support troops in the Volyn region of Western Ukraine, is mentioned in several books, among them Abraham Foxman, "Resistance: The Few Against the Many," in Judah Pilch (ed.), *The Jewish Catastrophe in Europe*, New York: American Association for Jewish Education, 1968, pp. 87-142, and Moshe Kaganovitch, *Di Milchumeh fun di Yidishe Partizaner in Mizrach Europa*, Buenos Aires: Central Union of Polish Jews in Argentina, 1956, Vol. One, pp. 217, 341, and 343, Vol. Two, pp. 283 and 358. Kruk was a village mayor as well as a partisan leader. He was killed by Ukrainian nationalists after the war in revenge for someone Kruk put to death during the war.

Michael (Mikhail) Glieder, the "underground" moviemaker and photographer, wrote his own book called *With a Motion Picture Camera Behind Enemy Lines*, Moscow: Goskinoizdat, 1947. Sheds some interesting light on partisan propaganda in the Ukraine.

Several other books should be mentioned:

Vasily Begma and Luka Kyzya, *The Paths of the Unsubjugeted*, Kiev, Ukraine: Radyanskyi Pysmennyk, 1962.

Sidor Kovpak, *From Putivl to the Carpathians*, ed. E. Gerasimov, Moscow, 1945. Several editions exist including one in English, *Our Partisan Course*, London: Hutchinson, 1947. Kovpak was one of the most famous partisan leaders, and his account is fairly accurate.

Timofei Strokach, *The Partisans of the Ukraine*, Moscow, 1943. Strokach, who is described in the Appendix, was a prominent KNVD official and chief of the Ukrainian Staff of the Partisan Movement, and extremely important figure.

Soviet Partisans: From the History of the Partisan Movement in the Years of the Great Patriotic War, Moscow: Gospolitizdat, 1960. This is, according to Sovietologist John Armstrong, the single most valuable volume on the partisan movement; it is a collection of sixteen very substantial monographs on many aspects of partisanship.

Sputnik Partizana (The Partisan's Traveling Companion), Moscow, 1942. This was the semiofficial Soviet handbook for use by partisans and for partisan training. It was published by the Communist Youth League (Komsomol) Press early in the war.

Individual Chapters

The first version of the partisan oath is taken from a publication of the Der Emes Publishing House, Moscow, 1944; the second oath is taken from Armstrong, *op. cit.*, p. 662, who, in turn, found a copy of it in the German Military Documents Section (GMDS), Federal Records Center, Departmental Records Branch, Alexandria, Virginia.

The tales of Shmuel Persov are taken from the Moscow-based Der Emes Publishing House, 1944, except for the last one, which is found in *Einekeit*, March 1, 1943. For a description of Persov, refer to Alexander Pomerantz, *Die Sovietish Harugai-Malchut (The Soviet Martyrs)*, Buenos Aires: YIVO-Yiddish Scientific Institute, 1962.

"The Partisan Mine," "Abraham Hirschfeld, The Watchmaker," and "Women Spies" are taken from G. Linkov, *The War Behind Enemy Lines*, Moscow, 1959.

"The Davidovich Family" from *Einikeit*, October 21, 1943.

"Remember!" by H. Orland, from the publication *To Victory (Tzum Zig)*, Moscow: Der Emes Publishing House, 1944, pp. 28-30.

"A Civilian Camp in the Forest" is from Pavlo P. Vershigora, *People with a Clear Conscience*, Moscow: Sovietskii Pisatel, 1953 (one of several editions). Vershigora, a motion picture director in Kiev before the war, was an aide to partisan general Sidor Kovpa and later commanded a roving band himself in the Carpathian Mountains. See also his other book, *The Raid on the San and the Vistula*, Moscow, 1960, which deals with his independent operations in Volyn and Poland and is especially revealing on Soviet attitudes toward Communism in Poland.

"Without Fire" by Shirka Gaman is from *To Victory*, Moscow: Der Emes Publishing House, 1944.

"Soviet Jews During and After the War of the Fatherland" by L. Singer, from *The Ressurected People (Dos Oifgerichteh Folk)*, Moscow: Der Emes Publishing House, 1948.

"Our Place" by Ilya Ehrenburg, from *Einikeit*, June 25, 1943. Ehrenburg's works are well known, and his talents as a novelist and journalist were widely noted. He was an official correspondent for the Soviet army and traveled widely under its shield, culminating at the gates of Berlin. See S.K. Shneiderman, *Ilya Ehrenburg*, New York: Yiddisher Kemfer, 1968, for a biography of the man written in Yiddish.

Photographic Sources

Several of the photos are taken from the original Russian edition, *Partizanskaya Druzhba*, Moscow: Der Emes Publishing House, 1948, and from Binyamin West's Hebrew translation of the book plus other sources in his *Heym Hayu Rabim* (1968). The reader should forgive the sometimes grainy quality of some of the photos; they were taken under the most difficult conditions, and some have reproduced in less than excellent shape.

Other sources include two Soviet books, G. Deborin, *Secrets of the Second World War*, Moscow: Progress Publishers, 1971, pp. 144 and 256; and *Soviet Ukraine*, Kiev: Ukrainian Soviet Encyclopedia, Editorial Office, 1970, pp. 148-150 and 153.

Two photos are from Judah Pilch (ed.), *The Jewish Catastrophe in Europe*, New York: The American Association for Jewish Education, 968, pp. 105 and 111. Reprinted by permission of the AAJE.

Most of the photos, however, were contributed by various partisans that the editor interviewed, including Moshe Flash, Berl Lorber, and Irving Porter (Puchtik).

Map and Organizational Chart Sources

The maps of Eastern Europe are taken from Edgar M. Howell, *The Soviet Partisan Movement, 1941-1944*, Washington, D.C.: Department of the Army (Pamphlet 20-244), August 1956. The charts showing the organization of the partisan movement and of the partisan brigade are also from Howell, pp. 138 and 139. The charts of the other partisan organizations (the staff of the Ukrainian partisan movement, an operative group) are taken from Jon Armstrong (ed.), *Soviet Partisans in World War II*, pp. 99, 112, 119 and 343. Reprinted by permission of the Regents of the University of Wisconsin, Copyright 1964.

ANNOTATED BIBLIOGRAPHY ON
JEWISH RESISTANCE DURING THE HOLOCAUST

This bibliography is not meant to be complete, especially with regards to works on the history and sociology of Soviet Jewry or of Holocaust literature in general, but it does contain all major books in English on Jewish resistance. A great many other important books, originally written in Russian Polish, Yiddish, Hebrew, or French, are still waiting to be translated for the benefit of Western readers.

The bibliography is geared specifically to cover Jewish resistance in four major areas: camps, ghettos, forests, and allied forces. The emphasis is on the Jews of *Eastern Europe* (Russia, Poland, Latvia, Ukraine) as opposed to, let us say, France, Holland, or Greece. Most selections are in English, with a few titles in Russian, Yiddish, and Hebrew. There is also a special section on faith and values in the post-Nazi era, another that discusses Jewish "cowardice," and a third on Jews in the Soviet Union.

The Moshe Kahanovitch (or Kaganovich) books mentioned in the bibliography contain additional sources of partisan memoirs written in Russian, Yiddish, and Hebrew; an the comprehensive anthology edited by John A. Armstrong, *Soviet Partisans in World War II*, will direct the reader to original *Russian* memoirs of commanders and fighters, some of whom are also mentioned in this book: for example — Andreyev, Begma, Brinsky (Brinskii), Fedorov (Fyodorov), Moshe (Mikhail) Glieder, Kovpak, Linkov, Petrov, Saburov, Strokach, and Vershigora.

I. General References on the Holocaust and the Nazi Era

Apenszlak, Jakob. *The Black Book of Polish Jewry*. New Yorl: American Federation of Polish Jews, 1943.
    A "memorial book" containing photos, maps, and sources, this volume is one of the first accounts of the destruction

of European Jewry and the Nazi occupation of Poland. It gives lie to the fact that the Allies and American Jewry did not know of the plight of the Jews.

Bloch, Sam E. (ed.) *Holocaust and Rebirth: Bergen-Belsen 1945-1965*. New York and Tel Aviv: Begen-Belsen Memorial Press and World Federation of Bergen-Belsen Associations, 1965.

An impressive and beautifully illustrated *Yizkor* (remembrance) book commemorating the 20th anniversary of the liberation of the Bergen-Belsen concentration camp — and a model for all *Yizkor* books. Written in English, Yiddish, and Hebrew.

Dawidowicz, Lucy S. "Toward a History of the Holocaust." *Commentary*, XLVII, 4 (April 1969), pp. 51-56.

A useful and critical survey of research perspectives and historical problems dealing with the Holocaust.

_____. *The War Against the Jews: 1939-1945*. New York: Holt, Rinehart and Winston, 1975.

One of the most important histories of the Holocaust and clearly one of the best, but not without its biases.

Donat, Alexander. *The Holocaust Kingdom*. New York: Holt, Rinehart and Winston, 1965.

An exceptionally sensitive memoir by a Polish-Jewish survivor and his wife, dealing, among othe things, with the Warsaw Ghetto, the uprising, and the Maidanek concentration camp.

Esh, Shaul. "The Dignity of the Destroyed: Towards a Definition of the Period of the Holocaust." *Judaism*, XI, 2 (Spring 1962), pp. 99-111.

A brief essay attempting to define the Holocaust as a subject of study.

Friedlander, Albert H. (ed.). *Out of the Whirlwind*. New York: Doubleday, 1968.

A fine anthology of Holocaust literature, illustrated in pen and ink by Jacob Landau.

Friedlander, Henry. *On the Holocaust: A Critique of the Treatment of the Holocaust in History Textbooks Accompanied by an Annotated Bibliography*. New York: Anti-Defamation League of B'nai B'rith, 1972, 1973.

A short 30-page booklet with an excellent and very useful bibliography and guide to Holocaust material for both scholar and layman.

Glatstein, Jacob, Israel Knox, and Samuel Margoshes, (eds.). *Anthology of Holocaust Literature*. Philadelphia: Jewish Publication Society, 1968.
One of the best anthologies in existence, with a solid section on Jewish resistance.

Hilberg, Raul. *The Destruction of the European Jews*. New York: Quadrangle Books, 1961, 1971.
A *magnum opus* based mainly on German sources and almost impertinently inadequate in the area of Jewish resistance.

Hilberg, Raul (ed.). *Documents of Destruction, Germany and Jewry 1933-1945*. New York: Quadrangle Books, 1971.
A compilation of official archival German documents and autobiographical Jewish sources. Even after all the criticism heaped upon him, it still contains no documents on Jewish resistance.

The Holocaust and Resistance. Jerusalem: Yad Vashem Remembrance Authority. Israel, 1972.
An illustrated 44-page booklet outlining the history of Nazi-occupied Europe, 1933-1945. Contains numerous photos and documents.

Jewish Black Book Committee. *The Black Book: The Nazi Crime Against the Jewish People*. New York: Duell, Sloan and Pearce, 1946.
One of the earliest documents of the Holocaust, prepared by the Jewish Anti-Fascist Committee of the U.S.S.R., the World Jewish Congress Vaad Leumi, and the Palestine and American Committee of Jewish Writers, Artists, and Scientists. Contains valuable documents and over 100 illustrations.

Katz, Jacob. "Was the Holocaust Predictable?" *Commentary*, 59, 5 (May 1975), pp. 41-48.
A compelling essay that attempts to answer the question: how could people have been so foolish as not to have seen what was in store for them at the hands of Hitler? This question begs another... and what could they have done if they had known?

Katz, Shlomo. "6,000,000 and 5,000,000." *Midstream*, X, 1
(March 1964), pp. 3-14.
   The numbers refer to the Jews living in the United States
   during the Holocaust and the number of Jews killed during
   the Holocaust. The introduction by Katz leads the reader
   to an article by Labor Zionist Leader Hayim Greenberg
   and asks: what could the 5 million have done to save the 6
   million?
Levin, Nora. *The Holocaust: The Destruction of European Jewry,
   1933-1945.* New York: Schocken, 1968, 1973.
   Well-written, well-researched, lively, compassionate,
   and moving. Fairly good section (pp. 317-386) on Jewish
   resistance in the Warsaw Ghetto and in the forests.
Morse, Arthur D. *While Six Million Died: A Chronicle of
   American Apathy.* New York: Random House, 1967, 1968.
   The shocking story of the appalling apathy and callousness
   of the United States government, particularly the State
   Department, in the face of Nazi genocide.
Pilch, Judah (ed.). *The Jewish Catastrophe in Europe.* New York:
   American Association for Jewish Education, 1968.
   An exceptionally well-written and conceived book,
   especially useful for students and teachers. An excellent
   section (pp. 87-142) on Jewish resistance which can serve as
   a useful model for other textbook writers.
Reitlinger, Gerald. *The Final Solution: The Attempt to
   Exerminate the Jews of Europe 1939-1945.* New York: A.S.
   Barnes, 1953-1961.
   An important early work on the Nazi "final solution"; small
   sections (pp. 276-280, 288-292) on resistance; they are
   essentially weak sections, but no better or worse than most
   historical works on the Nazi era, except for Nora Levin's
   book.
Robinson, Jacob (with the assistance of Ada Friedman). *The
   Holocaust and After: Sources and Literature in English.* (12th
   volume in the Yad-Vashem-YIVO Documentary Projects
   Series.) New York and Jerusalem: Yad Vashem and YIVO
   Institute for Jewish Research, 1973.
   The comprehensive bibliography of 6,637 items, listed in
   this 354-page volume, deals with no only the Holocaust,
   but also with political, economic, historical, and cultural life
   in the pre- and post-Holocaust period.

Rutherford, Ward. *Genocide: The Jews in Europe 1939-45*. New York: Ballantine Books Illustrated History of the Violent Century, Human Conflict, No. 4, 1973.
A profusely illustrated, sensitively written booklet.

Schoenberner, Gerhard. *The Yellow Star: The Persecution of the Jews in Europe, 1933-1945*. New York: Bantam Books, 1969, 1973.
An illustrated documentation of genocide with many never-before published photographs. Includes a chapter on Jewish resistance, mainly General Stroop's report on the Warsaw Ghetto (pp. 209-234). Translated from the German by Susan Sweet.

Shirer, William L. *The Rise and Fall of the Third Reich: A History of Nazi Germany*. New York: Simon and Schuster, 1959.
A monumental work, probably *the* definitive work on Nazi Germany, but contains very little on Jewish resistance.

Trunk, Isaiah. *Judenrat: The Jewish Councils in Eastern Europe Under Nazi Occupation*. New York: Macmillan, 1972.
Winner of the National Book Award in 1973, this is the first scholarly attempt to analyze the Jewish Councils that presided over the ghettos of Eastern Europe. Massive and valuable footnotes.

Tsur, Muki, and Nathan Yanai (eds.). *The Holocaust*. New York: American Zionist Youth Foundation, 1970.
A surprisingly effective and useful paperback book with short, strong, forceful statements on various aspects of the Holocaust, including resistance (pp. 49-71).

Zack, Avraham, and Shmuel Razshansky (eds.). *ChurbanAnthologia* (The Holocaust Anthology). Buenos Aires: Ateneo Literario en el Instituto Cientifico Judio, 1970. In the original Yiddish, this is an excellent anthology of prose, poetry, and drama, written by such renowned writers as Itzik Feffer, Chaim Grade, Avraham Reisen, Shmuel Halkin, Joseph Opotashu, and Jacob Glatstein.

II. General References on Jewish Resistance

Ainsztein, Reuben. *Jewish Resistance in Nazi-Occupied Eastern Europe*. New York: Harper and Row, 1974.
One of the most monumental works on Jewish defiance to appear in the English language. Containing nearly 1,000 pages, it ranks with the works of Moshe Kahanovitch in magnitude.

Barkai, Meyer (ed.). *The Fighting Ghettos*. Philadelphia: J.B. Lippincott, 1962. (Available in paperback from Tower Books.) A solid collection of essays on Jewish resistance in the ghettos of Warsaw, Vilna, and Cracow. Long out of print, now available in paperback. Also contains material on resistance in the camps and the forests. Translated from the Hebrew, this is an edited version of *Seifer Milchamot Hagetaot*, published in Tel Aviv by the Ghetto Fighters House and Kibbutz Hameuchad Association.

Bauer, Yehuda. *They Chose Life*. New York: American Jewish Committee, 1973. Illustrated.
A brief (68 pages) overview of Jewish resistance during the Holocaust, dealing with both unarmed and armed resistance, revolts in the ghettos, camps, and forests. Excellent for study groups and students. Bauer, head of the department of Holocaust studies at the Hebrew University in Jerusalem, is also the author of *Flight and Rescue: Brichah*.

Elkins, Michael. *Forged in Fury*. New York: Ballantine Books, 1971 (paperback).
Fast-paced, well-written account of Jewish heroism in Europe and the continued search for Nazi criminals after the war.

European Resistance Movements, 1939-1945. Oxford Pergamon Press, 1960.
The proceedings of the First International Conference on the History of the Resistance movements, held in Belgium, September 14-17, 1958. Contains much valuable information including an article by Philip Friedman on the role of the Jews in the Soviet partisans, titled "Jewish Resistance to Nazism."

Extermination and Resistance. Israel: Ghetto Fighters House, Kibbutz Lochamei Haghetot, 1958.
Collection of essays published by a kibbutz among whose members are many partisans, including Yitzchak Zuckerman and Zivia Lubetkin, leaders of the Warsaw Ghetto uprising.

Foxman, Abraham H. "Resistance: The Few Against the Many" in Judah Pilch (ed.) *The Jewish Catastrophe in Europe*, pp. 87-145, 1968.
An excellent, well documented, and comprehensive overview of Jewish resistance.

Handlin, Oscar. "Jewish Resistance to the Nazis." *Commentary*, 34, 5 (November 1962), pp. 398-407.
The prize-wining Harvard historian criticizes the "sheep to slaughter" perspective of Hilberg and Bettelheim calling it "dangerous," "misleading," "uninformed," and a "defamation of the dead and their culture."

Jewish Heroism in Modern Times. Jerusalem: World Zionist Organization, 1965.
A propaganda book, dealing with Jewish bravery both in Europe and in Palestine. Contains articles by Cholavski, Blumenthal and Karmish, Galili, Yehudah Bauer, and M. Schwartz. Of uneven quality.

Knout, David. *Contribution à l'Histoire de la Résistance Juive in France 1940-1944.* Paris: Editions du Centre, 1947.
This is monograph #3 in a series of studies produced by the Centre de Documentation Juive Contemporaine of Paris. It is 184 ages long and contains photos and documents.

Latour, Anny. *La Résistance Juive en France.* Paris: Stock, 1970.
A fine account of the French resistance, with outstanding photos, documents, and maps.

Nirenstein, Albert. *A Tower from the Enemy: Contributions to a History of Jewish Resistance in Poland.* New York: Orion Press, 1959.
A somewhat disorganized book, with heavy emphasis on the Warsaw, Vilna, Cracow and Bialystok ghettos. Contains photographs. Translated from Polish, Yiddish, and Hebrew by D. Neiman and from the Italian by M. Savillio.

Porter, Jack Nusan. "Jewish Resistance During the
Holocaust." *Wisconsin Jewish Chronicle*, four-part series
(December 1, 15, 22, and 29), 1972.
An impassioned analysis of the myths surrounding Jewish
resistance and a description of the major areas of resistance.
Also includes a short bibliography.

Schwartz, Leo (ed.). *The Root and the Bough: The Epic of an
Enduring People*. New York: Holt, Rinehart and Winston,
1949.
A fine collection of tales by a well-known anthologizer
of heroism in Warsaw, White Russia, and the Western
Ukraine as well as first-person accounts of survivors living
in Israel.

*Sefer Ha-Partizanim Ha-Yehudim (The Book of Jewish
Partisans)*. Merhaviya, Israel: Sifriat Poalim, Workers Book
Guild, and Yad Vashem, 1958, two volumes.
A massive, nicely produced compendium of Jewish
resistance. Each volume is over 700 pages log and includes
maps, documents, memorabilia, etc. Indexed.

Soviet Ukraine. Kiev, Ukraine: Editorial Office of the
Ukrainian Soviet Encyclopedia, Academy of Sciences, no
date, but circa 1960.
A beautifully illustrated single-volume compendium of the
history of sociology of the Soviet Ukraine. The section on
the role of the Ukrainians during World War II contains a
section (pp. 150-154) on partisan warfare that is typically
heroic in style and makes no mention of Jews, but its
valuable background to the general Soviet partisan role in
the war.

Suhl, Yuri (ed. and trans.). *They Fought Back: The Story of the
Jewish Resistance in Nazi Europe* New York: Crown, 1967.
Available also in paperback.
A wide-ranging collection of reprinted and originally
translated pieces covering heroism in the ghettos, and
camps, and the forests. The editor is also a well-known
novelist (*One Foot in America*). Contains photographs.

Tartakower, Aryeh (ed.). *Jewish Resistance During the Holocaust*.
Jerusalem: Yad Vashem Memorial, 1971.
Very valuable papers and commentary by world specialists
in Holocaust literature; they proceedings of a conference

on the subject held in Israel in April, 1968. Translated into English, with three papers in French.

Tenenbaum, Joseph. *Underground: The Story of a People.* Philosophical Library, 1952. Out of print.

III. Specific Areas of Jewish Resistance

A. The Ghettos

Barkai, Mayer. *The Fighting Ghettos*, pp. 9-128.
The struggle of the Jews within the ghetto walls of Warsaw, Bialystok, Grodna, and Brodi.

Foxman, Abraham H. "Resistance." In Judah Pilch (ed.), *The Jewish Catastrophe in Europe*, pp. 95-114.
Deals with the Warsaw and Vilna ghettos, the Glazman affair, and other aspects of resistance.

Friedman, Philip. *Martyrs and Fighters: the Epic of the Warsaw Ghetto.* New York: Praeger, 1954.
Documents of the ghetto, with illustrations, 325 pages.
Goldstein, Bernard. *The Stars Bear Witness.* New York: Viking, 1949. (Dolphin paperback edition in 1961 titled *Five Years in the Warsaw Ghetto.*)
Translated from the Yiddish, this is an important account of life in the ghetto by the leader of the Jewish Socialist Bund.

Goldstein, Charles. *The Bunker.* New York: Atheneum and Jewish Publication Society, 1970.
A moving memoir of a Warsaw ghetto survivor and French partisan activist. Translated from the French.

Kaczerginski, Shmuel. *Khurban Vilne (The Destruction of Vilnius).* New York: The United Vilner Relief Committee, 1947.

Katsh, Abraham I. (ed. and trans.). *The Warsaw Diary of Chaim A. Kaplan* (originally published under the title of *The Scroll of Agony*). New York: Macmillan, Collier Books, 1965, 1973.
A most compelling first-person account of the ghetto, written by a Hebrew scholar and teacher who perished in the Holocaust.

Lazar, Chaim. *Muranowska 7: The Warsaw Ghetto Uprising.* Tel Aviv: Massada-P.E.C. Press, 1966.

The role of the Betar Zionist Youth Movement in the
ghetto. Translated from the Hebrew. Illustrated.

Reiss, Asher. "A Quarter Century of Books on the Warsaw
Ghetto Battle." *Jewish Book Annual*, 26 (1968-69), pp.
23-33.
An excursion into the literature, 1943-1968, of the Warsaw
Ghetto. Quite useful in its bibliography.

Ringelblum, Emanuel. *Notes from the Warsaw Ghetto.* New
York: McGraw-Hill, 1958.
A poignant insider's account of life in the ghetto, written by
its historian and archivist. Edited and translated by Jacob
Sloan. Now also available in paperback from Schocken
Books (New York, 1974).

Suhl, Yuri (ed. and trans.). *They Fought Back*, pp. 51-54,
69-127, 136-143, 148-159, 165-171, and 231-245.
Resistance memoirs, translate from the Yiddish, dealing
with the ghettos of Warsaw, Bialystok, Vilna, Lachwa, and
Minsk.

The Warsaw Ghetto Uprising. New York: Congress for Jewish
Culture, 1974.
Short booklet that includes essays, poetry, ghetto songs,
and photos. Useful for Passover service.

B. The Partisans

Armstrong, John A. (ed.). *Soviet Partisans in World War II.*
Madison, Wisconsin: University of Wisconsin Press, 1964.
A massive and comprehensive 800-page summation of
"Soviet irregular warfare." Though not describing Jewish
participation in great detail, this excellent book does help
the reader in understanding the overall conditions of
partisan life. Contains useful annotated bibliography.

Bakalczuk-Felin, Meilech. *Zikhroynes fun a Yidishn Partizan
(Memoirs of a Jewish Partisan).* Buenos Aires: Central Union
of Polish Jews in Argentina, 1958.
The Central Union should be highly commended for its
diligence and energy in gathering and publishing accounts
of Jewish participation in World War II. These memoirs
are from the regions of Volyn and Polesia in Western
Ukraine.

Barkai, Meyer. *The Fighting Ghettos*, pp. 129-189.
Authentic description of accounts of guerrilla warfare by
Jews, written by Moshe Kahanovitzh, Abba Kovner, Tuvia
Belsky, and Mischa Gildenman, among others.

Deborin, G. *Secrets of the Second World War.* Moscow: Progress
Publishers, 1971.
Translated from the Russian and published by the English
branch of a Russian publishing house, this book contains
material and rare photographs never before seen in
Western countries. See especially the chapter on Soviet
partisans (pp. 195-214, 234-237, and 274-277). No
mention of the role of Jews, and the language is "heroic and
propagandistic"; the question is — are the facts correct?

Foxman, Abraham H. "Resistance." In Judah Pilch (ed.), *The
Jewish Catastrophe in Europe*, pp. 123-137.

Heilbrunn, Otto. *Partisan Warfare.* New York: Praeger, 1962.
A theoretical discussion of partisan resistance with a useful
bibliography dealing with cross-cultural and comparative
guerrilla operations. No stress on the Jewish component in
partisanship.

Howell, Edgar M. *The Soviet Partisan Movement, 1941-1944.*
Washington, DC: Department of the Army, 1956.
Department of the Army Pamphlet No. 20-244.
Prepared after the war in the Office of the Chief of Military
History under the chief of that division, Major Howell.
This is a useful, though boring, account of the partisan
movement in Eastern U.S.S.R. Contains maps and charts of
partisan fighting zones and partisan chain of command.

Kahanovitch, Moshe. *Di Milchumeh fun di Yidishe Partizaner
in Mizrach Europe (The War of Jewish Partisans in Eastern
Europe).* Buenos Aires: Central Union of Polish Jews in
Argentina, 1956. Two volumes, with illustrations, maps,
index, and bibliography.
Written in Yiddish, this is one of the monumental books on
Jewish partisan resistance. Someone should translate this
magnum opus into English. Its Spanish title is *La Lucha de los
Guerrilleros Judios en la Europa Oriental.*

Kahanovitch, Moshe. *Der Yidisher Unteil in ther
PartizanerBevegung fun Soviet Russland (Jewish Participation
in the Partisan Movement in Soviet Russia).* Rome, 1948.

Kahanovitch admits that his Yiddish and/or Hebrew
version of *The War of Jewish Partisans in Eastern Europe* is a
better and more inclusive account of Jewish resistance than
this account. This is not a particularly good source; it is
incomplete in many ways.

Macksey, Kenneth. *The Partisans of Europe in the Second World
War.* New York: Stein and Day, 1975.
An objective but rather dull study of partisan activity.
It comes to the conclusion, shocking to some, that the
partisans had only a marginal impact on the basic military
issues of the war and on the final outcome of the war itself.

Osanka, Franklin M. (ed.). *Modern Guerrilla Wafare: Fighting
Communist Guerrilla Movements.* New York: The Free
Press, 1962.
A most comprehensive collection of articles on
contemporary partisanship, useful for comparative research.
Contains articles of uneven quality on Soviet partisans.
Useful bibliography of English language books and articles.
Has a biased perspective, as the title implies.

Porter, Jack Nusan. "'Zalonka': An Interview with a Jewish
Partisan Leader." *Davka* (UCLA Hillel Foundation), III, 2,
3 (Winter-Spring 1973), pp. 14-20.
A son interviews his father in order to discover his past.

Suhl, Yuri. *They Fought Back*, pp. 160-164, 176-181, 226-230,
246-281.
Original translated accounts of heroism in the forests.
Includes for the first time in English the story of the brave
acts of the Herbert Baum Group, German-Jewish "urban
guerrillas" who defied the Nazis in Berlin; plus accounts of
resistance in Paris, Rome, and Brussels.

_____. *Uncle Misha's Partisans.* New York: Four Winds
Press, 1973.
The editor of *They Fought Back*, a chronicle of Jewish
resistance during the Holocaust, has written an outstanding
children's book (best for ages 10-14) about
the adventures of a twelve-year-old boy who joins

the Jewish partisan brigade of Dyadya Misha (Misha Gildenman), which battled the Nazis in the area of Zhitomer, Soviet Ukraine.

West, Binyamin (ed. and trans.). *Heym Hayu Rabim: Partizaner Yehudim B'brit Hamoatzot B'milchemet Haolam Hashiniyah (They Were Many: Jewish Partisans in the Soviet Union During World War II)*. Tel Aviv: Labor Archives Press, 1968.
Translated from the Russian version, *Partizanskaya Druzhba (Partisan Brotherhood)*, Moscow: Der Emes Government Publishing House, 1948. Personal memoirs and commentary. Contains rare photographs and additional material not found in the Russian version.

C. The Concentration Camps

Adler, H.G. "Ideas Toward a Sociology of the Concentraion Camp." *American Journal of Sociology*, LXIII, 5 (March 1958), pp. 513-522.
One of the few sociological analyses probing methodological problems regarding research into camp life. The concentration camp is seen as the most recent institution of oppression in which prisoners live without rights.

Barkai, Meyer. *The Fighting Ghettos*, pp. 191-251.
Jewish resistance in the concentration camps of Treblinka, Sobibor, Konin, Ponyatov, Trabnik, Ponary, and others by Isaiah Trunk, Yankel Vyernik, A. Petzorsky, Leon Velitzker, and Shlomo Gul.

Foxman, Abraham H. "Resistance" in Judah Pilch (ed.), *The Jewish Catastrophe in Europe*, pp. 114-120.
Compact descriptions of revolts in Auschwitz, Sobibor, and Treblinka.

Levi, Primo. *If This Be a Man*. New York: Orion Press, 1959. Also in Collier paperback, as *Survival in Auschwitz*, 1961. Written by a most eloquent survivor, an Italian Jewish chemist, this is one of the best eyewitness accounts of the extermination camps.

Steiner, Jean-François. *Treblinka*. New York: Simon and
Shuster, 1967.
Translated from the French by Helen Weaver, this is a
powerful account of the revolt by camp inmates. It is,
however, not a very reliable account. The book is basically
fiction, though based on a factual event.

Suhl, Yuri (ed.). *They Fought Back*, pp. 7-50, 128-135, 172-
175, and 182-225.
Descriptions of the revolt in Auschwitz led by Josef
Cyrankiewicz and Rosa Robota, as well as descriptions of
other camp revolts, such as uprisings in Treblinka, Sobibor,
and Koldyczewo.

Wells, Leon. *The Janowska Road*. New York: Macmillan, 1963.
Sensitive report of a young Jewish boy which deals with the
genocide of Jews in Eastern Galicia and with the camp at
Janowska Street in Lvov (Lemberg).

D. The Armed Forces

Ainstztein, Reuben. "The War Record of Soviet Jewry."
Jewish Social Studies, XXVIII, 1 (January 1966), pp. 3-24.
More than 500,000 Jews fought in the Russian Army;
200,000 fell in battle; and about 150,000 of them were
decorated for valor and devotion to duty; more than 100
Jews were named "Hero of the Soviet Union," one of the
Russian army's highest awards. Ainsztein describes the
scope of this participation.

Foxman, Abraham H. "Resistance" in Judah Pilch (ed.), *The
Jewish Catastrophe in Europe*, pp. 120-123.
Thousands of Jews participated in the armed forces of the
Allied Forces; they too should be considered as part of the
resistance forces, in a sense.

E. The Breicha (The Rescue of Jews)

Bauer, Yehudah. *Flight and Rescue: Brichah*. New York:
Random House, 1970.
The gripping tale of the role of the *Breicha*, the movement
for rescuing Jews during and after the war; written by the
Hebrew University social analyst and the author of *They
Chose Life*, an account of Jewish resistance.

Masters, Anthony. *The Summer That Bled: The Biography of Hannah Senesh*. New York: St. Martins Press and Washington Square Press, 1973.
The short but remarkable life of a Jewish paratisan parachutist. Contains photographs.

Senesh, Hannah. *Her Life and Diary*. New York: Schocken Books, 1973.
A poignant story of one woman, a Jewish partisan from Palestine. Her story is now legendary.

Syrkin, Marie. *Blessed is the Match: The Story of Jewish Resistance*. Philadelphia: Jewish Publication Society, 1948.
One of the first accounts of Hannah Senesh's bravery. Also contains examples of other acts of resistance.

IV. The Myth of Jewish Cowardice

Arendt, Hannah. *Eichmann in Jerusalem: A Report on the Banality of Evil*. New York: Viking Press, 1964.
A brilliant and impulsive essay on the Eichmann trial in Jerusalem and a controversial analysis of the *Judenrats* (Jewish councils) as unwilling instruments of the Nazis. Read with caution, however.

Bettelheim, Bruno. *The Informed Heart: Autonomy in a Mass Age*. New York: The Free Press, 1960 (Avon paperbacks, 1971).
An eminent psychotherapist presents a psychological theory of the Jews, maintaining that they were unwilling to realistically evaluate their predicament, thereby becoming passive victims in their own destruction. Again, this book must be read with a critical eye because it too contains many errors of both fact and interpretation.

De Pres, Terrence. *The Survivor*. New York: Oxford University Press, 1976.
A brilliant book and an excellent retort to Bettelheim; an account of the sociology of the death camps.

Donat, Alexander. *Jewish Resistance*. New York: Warsaw Ghetto Resistance Organization, 1964.
This short, 32-page booklet is, in essence, an answer to the post-Eichmann trial myth that all Jews were cowards and "sheep."

Hausner, Gideon. *Justice in Jerusalem.* New York: Schocken
Books, 1968.
Survey of the Holocaust and the Eichmann trial by the
Israeli prosecutor. Should be contrasted with Arendt's book.

Robinson, Jacob. *And the Crooked Shall Be made Straight:
The Eichmann Trial, the Jewish Catastrophe, and Hannah
Arendt's Narrative.* New York: Macmillan, and Jewish
Publication Society, 1965.
A powerful and persuasive attack in Hannah Arendt's book
Eichmann in Jerusalem. Massive and valuable footnotes.

Robinson, Jacob. *Psychoanalysis in a Vacuum: Bruno Bettelheim
and the Holocaust.* New York: YIVO Institute-Yad Vashem
Documentary Projects, 1970.
A rebuttal to the Bettelheim book, *The Informed Heart.*

Schappes, Morris U. *The Strange World of Hannah Arendt.*
New York: *A Jewish Currents Reprint,* 1963 (pamphlet).
Another well-reasoned rebuttal to Hannah Arendt's book
on Eichmann.

Shabbetai, K. *As Sheep to the Slaughter? The Myth of Cowardice.*
New York and Tel Aviv: World Association of the Bergen-
Belsen Survivors Associations, 1963. With a foreword by
Gideon Hausner.
An impassioned and eloquent plea for understanding the
sanity and madness of the Nazi Era and its victims. Written
in response to Arendt, Bettelheim, and Hilberg.

Wiesel, Elie. "A Plea for the Dead" in his *Legends of Our
Time.* New York: Holt, Rinehart and Winston, 1968. Also
Avon, Bard Books, paperback, 1970.
Nearly all of Wiesel's writings are a defense of the victims
of the Holocaust, but this article is one of the most
eloquent of those pleas.

V. Faith and Despair in the Post-Holocaust Era

Berkovits, Eliezer. *Faith after the Holocaust.* New York: KTAV
Publishing House, 1973.
A Talmudic scholar of renown and a distinguished rabbi
and educator, Berkovits intensely analyzes the theological

aspects of man's response to God's "hiding of the face" and his affirmation of faith despite God's mystery.

Cohen, Arthur A. (ed.) *Arguments and Doctrines: A Reader of Jewish Thinking in the Aftermath of the Holocaust.* New York: Harper and Row, 1970.

Twenty-eight essays focus on the internal conflict and ferment of post-Holocaust Jewish religious thought.

Cohen, Elie A. *Human Behavior in the Concentration Camp.* New York: Norton, 1953.

A valuable study of psychological reactions to total institutions like the camps. Translated from the Dutch.

Frankl, Victor. *Man's Search for Meaning.* New York: Pocket Books (Simon and Schuster), 1963. Originally published by Beacon Press, 1959.

A psychiatrist who spent three years in Auschwitz develops his theory of logotherapy, which focuses attention upon mankind's groping for a higher meaning in life. He suggests that love can be an effective means of coping with suffering.

Fackenheim, Emil L. *God's Presence in History: Jewish Affirmation and Philosophic Reflections.* New York: Harper and Row, 1972.

An eminent Jewish theologian from the University of Toronto inquires into the role of the Jewish people; their duty is to survive and prevail as a people and as a moral force.

Halpern, Irving. "Meaning and Despair in the Literature of the Survivors." *Jewish Book Annual,* 26 (1968-69), pp. 7-22.

Halpern examines this "depressing body of literature" from Victor Frankl to Elie Wiesel in order to answer some existential questions about death and hope.

Judaism, special section, "Jewish alues in the Post-Holocaust future," 6, 3 (Summer 1967).

A series of statements and responses that emerged during a symposium on the subject. The contributors include Emil Fackenheim, George Steiner, Richard Popkin, and Elie Weisel. It raised more questions than it answered.

Judaism, special section, "Jewish Faith After Nazism," 20, 3 (Summer 1971), pp. 263-294.

Jewish Partisans of the Soviet Union in WWII

Contributions by Charles Steckel, Seymour Cain, and
Michael Wyschograd examine the Holocaust through the
works of Emil Fackenheim and Richard Reubenstein.

Neusner, Jacob. "Implications of the Holocaust." In his
anthology, *understanding Jewish Theology*. New York: KTAV
and ADL, 1973, pp. 177-193.

Neusner examines the implications of the Holocaust on
Jewish theology and especially its impact on youth. See also
Emil Fackenheim's article "The Human Condition after
Auschwitz," pp. 165-175, in this same anthology.

Reubenstein, Richard L. *After Auschwitz: Radical Theology and
Contemporary Judaism*. Indianapolis: Bobbs-Merrill, 1966
(paperback).

A leading Jewish rabbi confronts the dilemmas within
contemporary religion in the post-Holocaust era.

Wiesel, Elie. "To a Young Jew of Today." In his *One
Generation After*. New York: Random House, 1970. Also,
Avon, Bard Books, 1972.

The themes of faith and despair appear in almost any
Wiesel novel or essay: *Night, The Gates of the Forest, A
beggar in Jerusalem*, and in this essay, addressed to youth of
all religions.

VI. Jews in the Soviet Union

Cang, Joel. *The Silent Millions: A History of the Jews in the
Soviet Union*. New York: Taplinger Publishing House, 1969.
An engrossing history of Soviet Jews from the Revolution
of 1917 to Brezhnev. Contains a very useful bibliography.

Eliav, Arie. *Between Hammer and Sickle*. Philadelphia: Jewish
Publication Society, 1967, 1969.

A prize-winning account of the tragedy of Soviet Jews
written by a member of the Israeli parliament and author of
other books including *Eretz Ha-Tzvi* and *The Voyage of the
Ulua*.

Frumkin, Jacob, et al. (eds.). *Russian Jewry 1860-1917* and
Russian Jewry 1917-1967. Two volumes. New York: A.S.
Barnes and Thomas Yoseloff, 1966 and 1969, respectively.
Collections of articles dealing with historical, sociological,

518

political, and educational areas; also contain two chapters on the Holocaust and Soviet Jews. Sponsored by the Union of Soviet Jews of New York City.

Gilboa, Yehoshua. *The Black Years of Soviet Jewry 1939-1953.* Boston: Little Brown, 1971. Translated from the Hebrew. A well-researched, valuable book, dealing with a crucial period in Soviet Jewish affairs: the Jewish Anti-Fascist Committee, the Stalin purges and "doctor's plots." Written by a leading Israeli journalist.

Goldhagen, Erich (ed.). *Ethnic Minorities in the Soviet Union.* New York: Praeger, 1968. Collected essays read at a symposium held in the fall of 1965 at the Institute of East European Jewish Studies of the Philip Lown School of Near Eastern and Judaic Studies at Brandeis University. Includes bibliographies.

Kochan, Lionel (ed.). *The Jews in Soviet Russia Since 1917.* New York: Oxford University Press, 1970, 1972. An excellent collection of scholarly articles on various aspects of Soviet Jewish life, written by 16 American and British experts in their fields.

Korey, William. *The Soviet Cage: Anti-Semitism in Russia.* New York: Viking Press, 1973. A lucid factual account of Russian anti-Semitism, written by the leading U.S. expert on Soviet Jewish affairs.

Kuznetsov, Anatoly. *Babi Yar.* New York: Dial Press, 1967. A moving account of the famed massacre of thousands of Jews in the Babi Yar ravine in the Ukraine near Kiev.

Meisel, Nachman. *Dos Yidishe Shafen un der Yidisher Shrayber in Sovietfarband (Jewish Creativity and the Jewish Writer in the Soviet Union).* New York: Yiddish Cultural Union-Farband (YKUF) Farlag, 1959. A general overview of Jewish theater, literature and other arts in the USSR from the 1920s to the 1950s.

Shneiderman, S.L. *Ilya Ehrenburg.* New York: Yiddisher Kemfer, 1968. Written in Yiddish soon after the death of this controversial Jewish-Communist novelist, post, and journalist, this is a short biography by a noted expert in the area of Russian-Jewish affairs.

VII. Miscellaneous Material

Berman, Aaron, et al. *Thinking About the Unthinkable: An Encounter with the Holocaust.* Amherst, Massachusetts: Hampshire College, Social Science Division, 1972.
An impressive course outline organized and carried out by students that included speakers and trips to Holocaust sites in Europe. A model for any college or university course in this area.

Breakstone, David. *God in Search of Himself.* Washington, DC: B'nai B'rith Hillel Foundations, 1974.
Called "a passage of respect for the six million," this is the personal quest of a young student from Boston, now living in Israel, which can serve as a basis for further inquiry and is valuable as a teaching and group discussion guide. This dramatic reading is available from the national Hillel Foundations.

Gottlieb, Malke, and Mlotek, Chana (compilers). *Twenty-Five Ghetto Songs with Music and Transliteration.* New York: Workmen's Circle, Educational Department, 1968. Good collection of ghetto songs, with music, from the Yiddish.

Post, Albert. *The Holocaust: A Case Study of Genocide: A Teaching Guide.* New York: American Association for Jewish Education, 1973.
This is a teaching guide and lesson plan for teenagers. Though edited by professionals it is more superficial and inferior in many ways to the Hampshire College outline done by Berman et al., but this guide is geared toward younger ages.

Roskies, David G. *Night Words.* Washington, DC: B'nai B'rith Hillel Foundation, 1973.
Subtitled a "midrash on the Holocaust," this is a very effective reading and commentary on an almost inscrutable event. The author is a young Jewish activist and Yiddishist from Canada.

Sartre, Jean-Paul. *Anti-Semite and Jew.* New York: Schocken, 1948, 1965.
A classic portrait of anti-Semitism, written by a great non-Jewish philosopher and social activist; translated from the French by George J. Becker.

BOOK II
ANNOTATED BIBLIOGRAPHY

A. Books (English)

Ainsztein, Reuben. *Jewish Resistance in Nazi-Occupied Eastern Europe*. New York: Barnes and Noble (Harper and Row), 1974. One of the finest books on the subject; see especially pp. 353-360 and 389-393 for information relevant to this book.

Armstrong, John A. (ed.) *Soviet Partisans in World War II*. Madison, Wisconsin: University of Wisconsin Press, 1964. While Jewish participation is often overlooked, this is still a most valuable compilation of articles on the military and political role of the Soviet partisans during the war.

Barkai, Meyer (ed.). *The Fighting Ghettos*. Philadelphia: J.P. Lippincott, 1962; New York: Tower Publications, 1962.

Bartoszewski, Wladyslaw, and Zofia Lewin. *The Samaritan: Heroes of the Holocaust*. New York: Twayne, 1970. Accounts of Poles who risked their lives to save Jews from death during the Nazi occupation.

They Chose Life — Jewish Resistance in the Holocaust. New York: American Jewish Committee, 1973.

Eckman, Lester, and Chaim Lazar. *The Jewish Resistance: The History of the Jewish Partisans in Lithuania and White Russia under Nazi Occupation, 1940-1945*. New York: Shengold, 1977.

Foxman, Abraham H. "Resistance — The Few Against the Many." In Judah Pilch (ed.), *The Jewish Catastrophe in Europe*. New York: American Association for Jewish Education, 1968. Not only was this one of the first comprehensive accounts of resistance written for students, but also the entire book is an excellent classroom tool.

Friedman, Phillip. *Their Brother's Keepers*. New York: Schocken Books, 1978; Crown, 1957. A moving account of the Christian heroes and heroines who helped Jews during the war. For a section relevant to this book, see pp. 130-142, dealing with the Ukraine, Latvia, Estonia, and Byelorussia.

Guttman, Yisrael. *The Holocaust and Resistance.* Jerusalem: Yad Vashem; see also Yisrael Guttman and Efraim Zuroff (eds.), *Rescue Attempts During the Holocaust*, New York: KTAV, 1979.

Kowalski, Isaac. *A Secret Press in Nazi Europe.* New York: Shengold, 1969, 1972, 1978.

Porter, Jack Nusan (ed.). *Jewish Partisans: Jewish Resistance in Eastern Europe During World War II.* Lanham, Maryland: University Press of America, 1982. Memoirs of non-Jewish Russian and Ukrainian army officers, telling of the bravery of their Jewish soldiers and partisans. This is based on original Russian and Polish sources and is the English version on Binyamin West's Hebrew version. Two volumes.

Prager, Moshe. *Sparks of Glory.* New York: Shengold, 1974. Inspiring tales of the often-overlooked role of Orthodox rabbis and Jews during the Holocaust.

Samuels, Gertrude. *Mottele.* New York: Signet, 1976. A good book for children based on true episodes in the lives of Jewish partisans in Russia and Poland told through the story of a young boy who joins them in their struggle.

Shabbetai, K. *As Sheep to Slaughter?* New York: World Association of Bergen-Belsen Survivors, 1963. A short booklet aimed at discrediting the myth of Jewish cowardice.

Stadler, Bea. *The Holocaust: A History of Courage and Resistance.* New York: ADL/Behrman House, 1974. Another book on the subject geared to young people.

Suhl, Yuri (ed.). *They Fought Back: The Story of the Jewish Resistance in Nazi Europe.* New York: Schocken Books, 1975. A wide-ranging collection of resistance on many fronts and in many countries. One of the best collections around.

Tenenbaum, Joseph. *Underground: The Story of a People.* New York: Philosophical Library, 1957. An early, popular historical account of Jewish resistance in Eastern Europe.

B. Books (Hebrew and Yiddish)

Granatstein, Yehiel, and Moshe Kahanovich. *Lexicon Hagevurah (Biographical Dictionary of Jewish Resistance)*. Jerusalem: Yad Vashem, 1965, Vol. 1, parts 1 and 2. A compilation of names and pictures of Jewish partisans and other fighters in the western Soviet territory.

Kahanovich, Moshe. *Der Idisher Onteyl in der Partizaner Bavegung fun Soviet Rusland*. Rome, 1948.

_____. *Di Milkhome fun di Yishishe Partizaner in Mizrakh-Eyrope*. Two volumes. Buenos Aires, 1956.

_____. *Milchemet Ha-Partizanim HaYehudim B'Mizrach Europa (The Jewish Fighting Partisans in Eastern Europe)*. Tel Aviv: Ayanot Publishers, 1954. These three books are basically the same; some are abridged versions, either in Yiddish or Hebrew, of the role of Jewish partisans. They are probably the best and most comprehensive books on these fighting forces in Hebrew and Yiddish and should be translated into English one day.

Kantarowicz, N. *Di Yidishe Vidershtand-Bavegung in Polin (he Jewish Counter-Movement in Poland)*. New York, 1967.

Livneh, Natan (ed.). *K'Oranim Gavahu: Partizanim Yehudaim B'Yaarot Volyn (Like Pines They Grew: Jewish Partisans in the Forests of Volyn)*. Givatayim, Israel, and New York: World Union of Volynian Jews in Israel and in the USA, 1980.

West, Binyamin (ed.). *Heym Hayu Rabim: Partizanim Yehudim B'brit Hamoazot B'milchemet-Haolam Hashniya (They Were Many: Jewish Partisans in the Soviet Union During the Second World War)*. Tel Aviv: Labor Archives Press, 1968. This is a very rare collection of memoirs of Jewish partisans in Russia written by non-Jewish Soviet army and partisan commanders. See also Porter, *op. cit.*, for the English version.

C. Books (Russian and Polish)

Begma, Vasily, and Luka Kyzya. *Shlyakhy Neskorenykh (The Paths of the Unsubjugated)*. Kiev: 1962. An important partisan memoir, Begma was commander of one of the major roving bands and since the war has occupied key posts in the Communist Party in the Ukraine.

Brinsky, Anton P. *Po tu storonu fronta (On the other Side of the Front: Memoir of a Partisan)*. Moscow, 1958. An important account by one of the leaders of organizing teams sent by the Russian Central Command to organize and revive the partisan movement in West Byelorussia and later to the West Ukraine. He was called "Dyadya Petya" in this book.

Fedorov, A.P. *Podpolny obkom deistvuyet (The Underground Obkom in Action)*. *Two volumes*. Moscow, 1947, plus later editions in 1950 and 1957. An English translation appeared as *The Underground Committee Carries On*, Moscow: Foreign Languages Publishing House, 1952. Valuable memoirs since Fedorov was a high-ranking official of the Communist party of the Ukraine as well as a major partisan leader.

Glieder, Mikhail. *S kinoapparatom v tylu vraga (With a Motion Picture Camera in the Rear of the Enemy)*. Moscow: Goskinoizdat, 1947. Written by a Jewish cameraman working alongside the partisans, this is an interesting account of partisan sidelights and partisan propaganda in the Ukraine. Several partisan films, including those of Jews, were made and are found in Russian archives. Hopefully, they will be brought to the attention of English-speaking countries one day. See his account in Volume I.

Kisielev, K.B. *Zapiski sovetskogo diplomata*. Moscow: Politizdat, 1971.

Kovpak, Sidor. *Ot Putivlya do Karpat (From Putivl to the Carpathians)*, edited by E. Gerasimov. Moscow, 1945. English version: *Our Partisan Course*, London: Hutchinson, 1947. Kovpak was one of the most famous partisan leaders, respected by many Jews as well, and his is a fairly accurate account of military action though not very revealing on political affairs.

Linkov, Gregory. *Voina v tylu vraga (The War in the Rear of the Enemy)*. Moscow, 1951, 1959. Linkov was an engineer and important Communist Party official who organized and led one of the parachutist detachments that played such an important role in reactivating the partisan movement in Byelorussia in 1941-42. He was well liked and admired by Jewish partisans, and he spoke well of them too.

Sobiesiak, Józef, and Ryszard Jegorow. *Ziemla Plonie (The Earth is Burning)*. Warsaw: MON, 1963.

_____. *Burzany (Wild Weeds)*. Warsaw: MON, 1964.

_____. *Brygada Grunwald (The Grunwald Brigade)*. Warsaw: MON, 1964.

_____. *Przebraze*. Warsaw: MON, 1964.

Sobiesiak, called Max or Maks, was the well-known partisan leader in the western Ukraine who made it a point to save as many Jewish lives as possible. A man well respected in Jewish partisan circles, today he is a Polish rear admiral. He worked closely with the Kruk Detachment under Nikolai Konishchuk, a Ukrainian partisan leader also friendly to Jews.

Strokach, Timofei. *Partyzany Ukrainy (The Partisans of the Ukraine)*. Moscow, 1943. Strokach was a prominent NKVD official and Chief of the Ukrainian Staff of the Partisan Movement.

Torzecki, Ryszard. *Kwestia Ukrainska w Polityce III Rzeszy (1933-1945)*. Warsaw: Książka i Wiedza, 1972.

Vershigora, Pavlo. *Lyudi s chistoi sovestuyu (Men with a Clear Conscience)*. Moscow: Sovetsky Pisatel, 1951. Vershigora was a motion picture director in Kiev before the war and an aide to Commander Kovpak. He later commanded a roving band himself, and was sympathetic to the Jewish plight.

_____. *Reid na San i Vislu (The Raid on the San and the Vistula)*. Moscow, 1960. Deals with his operations in Volyn and Poland and is especially revealing on Soviet attitudes toward Communism in Poland.

D. Books (other languages)

Darashczuk, Dymytrii. *Die Ukraina und das Reich*. Leipzig: Verlag Hans Hirzel, 1941.

Iankyvsky, Kost. *Roky Nimetskoi Okupatsii*. New York and Toronto, 1965.

Ilnytskyi, Roman. *Deutschland und die Ukraine 1934-1945*. Munich: Osteuropa Institut, 1958.

Liebrandt, George. *Ukraine*. Berlin: Verlag Otto Stolberg, 1942.

E. Articles

Fein, Barbara. "Not to Go as an Animal," *Wisconsin Jewish Chronicle*, May 5, 1971. A moving account of Irving Porter (Yisroel Puchtik), a partisan leader in the Kruk Detachment in Volyn — his escape, military exploits, and after-thoughts on the struggle.

Janz, William. "Say Shalom to One Who Fought Dearly," *Milwaukee Sentinel*, March 21, 1979, pp. 5-6. Another account, written on the death of Irving Porter, on his life with the Ukrainian and Russian partisans. See also "One Who Fought Back," *Wisconsin Jewish Chronicle*, April 19, 1979, p. 9.

Kahanovich, Moshe. "Why No Separate Jewish Partisan Movement was Established During World War II," *Yad Vashem Studies*, Vol. 1, Jerusalem, 1957. A good analysis of the political and military factors that led to the disbanding of strictly Jewish groups and their merging into the general partisan movement in Russia.

Konishchuk, Nikolai. "They Were Many," in Binyamin West (ed.), *Heym Hayu Rabim, op. cit.*, pp. 143-147. A short description of the Jews who fought in the Kruk Detachment under the author's command.

Porter, Jack Nusan. Four-part series on the Holocaust and resistance, *Wisconsin Jewish Chronicle*, Dec. 1, Dec. 15, Dec. 22, and Dec. 29, 1972.

_____. "Zalonka: An Interview with a Jewish Partisan Leader," *Davka*, 3, 2, Winter-Spring 1973, pp. 14-20. Jack Porter interviews his father Irving Porter (called "Zalonka" in the underground).

_____. "Jewish Women in the Resistance," *Women's American ORT Reporter*, Nov.-Dec. 1978, pp. 7-8.

_____. "Some Social-Psychological Aspects of the Holocaust," in Bryon Sherwin and Susan Ament (eds.), *Encountering the Holocaust: An Interdisciplinary Survey.* New York: Hebrew Publishing Company and Chicago: Impact Press, 1979, pp. 189-222. Treats the impact of the Holocaust on the survivors and their children regarding both psychological and social responses to the traumatic events.

Shuelevitz, I.I. "Der Yichus fun Dem Futer," *Jewish Forward* (NYC), Shabbat, January 13, 1973. Another account of the life of Irving Porter in the Kruk Detachment including the role played by Porter's wife, Faye Merin Porter. Also contains a picture of Porter and his family.

F. Other Sources

Datner, Szymon. "Zydowski Ruch Oporu we Wschodniej Europie w Czasie Okupacju Hitlerowskiej (o Pracy R. Ainsztein)," *Biuletyn Zydowskiego Instytutu Historycznego w Polsce.* Warsaw: Jan.-March 1976, No. 1 (97).

Der Chef der Sicherheitspolizei und des SD, Berlin Ereignissimeldung, UD, SSP, NO. 100 — Oct. 1, 1941; No. 187 — Mozz 30, 1942. Meld (No. 4).

"General Tokarzowski do Gen. Sosnkowskiego", *Armija Krajowa w Dokumentach*, Sept. 1, 1940.

Litopysets (pseudonym). *Ukraintsy ta Zhydy (Kilka Zamitok do Zhydivskii Spravy).* Lvov, 1937.

Samchuk, Ulas. "Zanimaem Mesta." Lutsk, 1941, *Volyn*, No. 1, P. 2.

* * * * *

I am grateful to the following sources for this bibliography: Canadian Jewish Congress, National Holocaust Remembrance Committee, *Holocaust: An Annotated Bibliography*, Montreal, Canada, Jan. 1980; and John A. Armstrong (ed.), *Soviet Partisans in World War II*, University of Wisconsin Press, 1964, bibliography on Soviet publications on anti-Nazi resistance, pp. 770-777.

Compiled by Jack Nusan Porter and Yehuda Merin

NEW BOOKS AND SOURCES
ON JEWISH PARTISANS AND RESISTANCE

New Material or Overlooked Material
since the book was published in 1981

New archives have opened up in the former Soviet Union, in Germany, in Israel, in South America, and in Arab Countries. But the most important are Yad Vashem in Jerusalem, the US Holocaust Memorial Museum, the Wiener Library and Imperial War Museum in London, the archives at Kibbutz Lochamei Hagetaot in the Western Galilee, Kibbutz Yad Mordechai in the Negev in Israel, Yad Volyn Archives in Givatayim, Partisans and Soldiers Archives in Tel Aviv, and the Lenin Library in Moscow.

The field of partisan resistance and resistance in general needs to be grounded in several new paradigms, listed below: in German, Nazi, Soviet, and Shoah backgrounds; in World War I and II history; in multi-ethnic relations; in comparative genocide studies; in women and gender studies, in colonialism and neo-colonialism frameworks, and in mass culture, mobilization, and mass propaganda research. No longer is special pleading acceptable whether it be Ukrainian, Israeli, Jewish, or Soviet. Partisan memoirs were needed at the beginning but today we need to look with sanguine eyes at all the documents, biased as they are in many ways yet still valuable, and thereby open up new ways of thinking about the "final solution" and the resistance to it.

The field is coplex and emotional. One man's victim is another man's enemy; victims became perpetrators and perpetrators became victims. It is difficult to stay focused. One had to fight with people who also hated and mistrusted you; you were not sure who the enemy was; he or she was everywhere, even amongst your own comrades. The following works will be a good start and yet it is mostly works in English. Several languages are needed in this research. It's a big field and constantly growing.

The following encyclopedias have been published: *Encyclopedia Judaica*, second edition (however the 1971 first edition is superior in many ways when dealing with the Shoah); the *Encyclopedia of the Holocaust* (in Russian, editor Ilya Altman), the *Encyclopedia of the Holocaust* (1989, in English, from Israel, editor Israel Gutman); *History of the Holocaust: A Handbook and Dictionary*, (1994, editors Abraham and Hershel Edelheit); the *Encyclopedia of Camps and Ghettos* (2012, editor Martin Dean) the *Encyclopedia of Genocide*, (1999, editor Israel Charny); the *Encyclopedia of Genocide and Crimes Against Humanity* (2005, editor Dinah Shelton); and there are several more.

I have even proposed an *Encyclopedia of Resistance during the Shoah*.

What follows is only a small fraction of the material out there. See more in my other bibliographies or in any of the books mentioned here. My thanks to Gershon Weisenberg, Shoah teacher and collector extraordinaire, who sold me his collection of rare resistance books, among other Holocaust material. Thank you, Gerry.

German and Nazi Background

Editors of Time-Life. *The SS*. Alexandria, VA: Time-Life Books, 1989.

_____. *The New Order*. Alexandria, VA: Time-Life Books, 1989

Herzstein, Robert Edwin, and the editors of Time-Life. *The Nazis*. New York: Time-Life Books, 1980.

Kersten, Felix. *The Kersten Memoirs, 1940-1945*. New York: Macmillan, 1957. Heinrich Himmler's personal doctor brings extraordinary insights into the mind of the relatively unknown architect of the "final solution", and shows surprisingly open comments on homosexuals, Jews, war with Russia, and other topics.

Mollo, Andrew, with an introduction by Hugh Trevor-Roper. *A Pictorial History of the SS 1923-1945*. New York: Stein and Day, 1976.

Rubenstein, Joshua, and Ilya Altman (eds.). *The Unknown Black Book: The Holocaust in the German-Occupied Soviet Territories*. Bloomington, IN: Indiana University Press, 2010, paperback.

Walther, Herbert (ed.). Der Fuhrer. Secaucus, NJ, and
London: Chartwell Books/Bison Books, 1978. See also his
book *Die Waffen SS*, 1977.

Russian, Ukrainian, Polish, and Soviet Background

Berkhoff, Karel C. *Harvest of Despair: Life and Death in
Ukraine Under Nazi Rule*. Cambridge, MA: Harvard
University Press, 2004. Mentions western Volynians, Jews
and non-Jews.

Brandon, Ray, and Wendy Lower (eds.). *The Shoah in Ukraine*.
Bloomington, IN: Indiana University Press and the US
Holocaust Memorial Museum, 2008.

Dobroszycki, Lucjan, and Jeffrey S. Gurock (eds.). *The
Holocaust in the Soviet Union: Studies and Sources, 1941-1944*.
Armonk, NY: E. M. Sharpe, 1993. Also, see the newly
opened Soviet archives available at the US Holocaust
museum and elsewhere.

Kamenetsky, Ihor *Hitler's Occupation of Ukraine (1941-1944)*.
Milwaukee, WI: Marquette University Press, 1956. From a
Ukrainian perspective.

Kennedy, Robert M. *The German Campaign in Poland
1939*. Washington, DC: Department of Army, 1956.
Department of Army Pamphlet No. 20-255. Also see their
other reports on the campaigns in Russia on p. iii.

Rubenstein, Joshua, *Tangled Loyalties: The Life and Times of
Ilya Ehrenburg*. New York: Basic Books, 1996.

Shneiderman, S. L. "Stalin hut Upgeshtelt dem Roif fun
Ehrenburg tzu Nekumeh gegen Deutchen." *The Yiddish
Forward*, November 25, 1980. A newspaper journalist tells
the story of how Ilya Ehrenburg raised the morale of the
Russian people to take revenge against the Germans. See
Shneiderman's own biography of Ilya Ehrenburg, New
York: Yiddisher Kemfer, 1968, written in Yiddish.

Solzhenitsyn, Alexander. *One Day in the Life of Ivan Denisovich*.
New York: Bantam Books, 1963. Good to compare Stalin's
gulags with Hitler's concentration lager.

Snyder, Timothy. *Bloodlands: Europe between Hitler and Stalin*.
New York: Basic Books, 2010. A controversial book that
conflates Hitler and Stalin and the lands in between

Germany and Russia as genocidal sectors. An example
of the new ways to approach the subject. See Donald
Bloxholm's books in comparison.

Thorpe, David. *The Rise and Fall of the Soviet Union: From
Lenin to Trotsky*, a set of 36 cards. Forestville, CA: Eclipse
Enterprises, 1992. A very useful set of trading cards on the
subject.

Westwood, J. N. *Endurance and Endeavour: Russian History
1812-1971*. Oxford, UK: Oxford University Press, 1973. A
most readable history, quite enjoyable. See pp. 341-350 for
an account of the "Great Patriotic War."

Wytwycky, Bohdan. *The Other Holocaust: Many Circles of Hell*.
Washington, DC: The Novak Report, 1982. Again from
the Ukrainian perspective, a "brief account of the 9-10
million persons who died with the 6 million Jews..."
including Russian POWs, Gypsies, Poles, and Ukrainian
civilians.

WW II Background and Post-World War II Escape

Bauer, Yehuda. *Flight and Rescue: ah*. New York: Random
House, 1970. Written by the renowned and prolific Israeli
scholar and teacher, this book details the escape from
Europe to Palestine. (There are many spellings for the
word "Breicha," Hebrew for "flight").

Bethell, Nicholas, and the editors of Time-Life. *Russia
Besieged*. Alexandria, VA: Time-Life Books, 1977.

Dekel, Ephraim. *B'riha: Flight to the Homeland*. New York:
Herzl Press, 1972. Written by a former Haganah
commander (1925-1946), this is about the organized escape
of Jewish refugees and survivors from Eastern Europe to
Palestine and elsewhere.

Editors of Army Times. *Heroes of the Resistance*. New York:
Dodd, Mead, 1967. On resistance throughout Europe
during the war.

Hoare, Robert, edited by R. J. Unstead; special advisor Dr
J. M. Roberts. *World War II*. London: Macdonald and
Company, 1973.

Miller, Russell, and the editors of Time-Life. *The Resistance*.
Alexandria, VA: Time-Life Books, 1979.

Muller, Rolf-Dieter, and Gerd R. Ueberschar. *Hitler's War in the East: A Critical Assessment*, 3rd ed. New York and Oxford, UK: Berghahn Books, 2009. See pp. 232 and 272 for mention of my partisan book.

World War II Remembered, 1941-1945. Washington, DC: US Postal Service, 2005. A history of the war in stamps. Very colorful.

Comparative Genocide

Chalabian, Antranig. *Revolutionary Figures*. Self-published by the translator Dr. Arra S. Avakian, Fresno, CA., 1994. An example of "comparative resistance to genocide." See the works on Musa Dagh below.

Eva Fried (ed.). *Beyond the "Never Agains."* Stockholm: Swedish Ministry of Foreign Affairs, 2005. A picture book on an important conference on genocide held in Stockholm in August of 2005.

Friedman, Ina R. *The Other Victims: First-Person Stories of Non-Jews Persecuted by the Nazis*. Boston, Houghton Mifflin, 1990. Tales of non-Jewish victims of genocide. I am mentioned on p. vi.

Gioseffi, Daniela (ed). *On Prejudice: A Global Perspective*. New York and London: Doubleday/Anchor Books, 1993. While not specifically on genocide, it is a very useful anthology. My essay on gays is on p. 67 and my essay on the history and definition of genocide is on p. 143.

Jacobs, Steven L. (ed.). *Lemkin on Genocide*. New York: Lexington Books, 2012. Provides an annotated commentary on two unpublished manuscripts written by Raphael Lemkin, the Polish-Jewish jurist and lawyer, who coined the word "genocide" in 1944. See Jacob's other books on Lemkin. See Lemkin's other books and articles.

Jones, Adam. *Genocide: A Comprehensive Introduction*. London and New York: Routledge, 2006. This is the best genocide textbook in existence. See p. 16 in the first edition for my pioneering effort and p. 17 in the second edition for my contribution to the definition of genocide. The second edition in 2011 is about 40 percent longer than the first.

Kiernan, Ben. *Blood and Soil: A World History of Genocide and Extermination from Sparta to Darfur*. New Haven, CT: Yale University Press, 2007.

Leven, Mark. *Genocide in the Age of the Nation-State*. Three volumes. London and New York: I. B. Tauris, 2008. See p. IX for mention of me regarding foundational and "ground-breaking" studies (among others) in the field of genocide studies.

Minasian, Edward. *Musa Dagh*. Nashville, TN: Cold Tree Press, 2007. The story of the suppression of Musa Dagh by Hollywood.

Montgomery, Lane H. *Never Again, Again, Again*. New York: Ruder Finn Press, 2007. A picture book of several sites of genocide from Armenia to Bosnia to Cambodia to Darfur to Rwanda to the Holocaust. Very powerful text and photos.

Moses, Dirk A. (ed.). *Empire, Colony, Genocide: Conquest, Occupation, and Subaltern Resistance in World History*. New York and Oxford, UK: Berghahn Books, 2008. Another example of the fresh new approaches to comparative genocide coming out of Europe.

Porter, Jack Nusan (ed.). *Genocide and Human Rights: A Global Anthology*. Lanham, MD: University Press of America, 1982, reissued in 2002 and still in print. This was the first anthology of its kind in genocide studies. It has very useful early bibliographies.

_____. *The Sociology of Genocide/The Holocaust*. Washington, DC: American Sociological association, 1999. The first curriculum guide on the subject.

Power, Samantha. *"A Problem from Hell": America and the Age of Genocide*. New York: Perseus Books/Basic Books, 2002. The classic book on America's abysmal record in stopping genocide in the twentieth century.

Shaw, Martin. *What is Genocide?* Cambridge, UK and Malden, Mass: Polity Press, 2007. An excellent and somewhat controversial short book on genocide.

Totten, Samuel, William S. Parsons, and Israel W. Charny. *Century of Genocide: Eyewitness Accounts and Critical Views*. New York and London: Garland Publishing, 1997. An excellent and very complete collection of eyewitness accounts. Surprisingly, none of my books are mentioned.

Walliman, Isidor, and Michael N. Dobkowski (eds.). *Genocide and the Modern Age*. Syracuse, NY: Syracuse University Press, 1987, 2000. An excellent collection of relevant essays on several genocides. I am mentioned in several essays.

Werfel, Franz. *The Forty Days of Musa Dagh*. Boston: David R. Godine, 2012, originally published in 1933. A famous account of Armenian resistance in 1915 that heavily influenced Jewish fighters in the Shoah and laid the controversy for many years of trying to make a movie about this insurrection against the Turks.

White, Matthew. *The Great Big Book of Horrible Things*. New York: W.W. Norton, 2012. Introduction by Steven Pinker. Answers the question: Was the twentieth century really the most violent in history? This strange yet fascinating book moves across 2,000 years of war and genocide. My book *Genocide and Human Rights* is noted on p. 191 and p. 585.

The Shoah

Alexander, Jeffrey C., et al. *Remembering the Holocaust: A Debate*. New York and Oxford: Oxford University Press, 2009. Alexander's essay is important and should be juxtaposed to the other essays in the book and with Bauman's book below.

Bauman, Zygmunt. *Modernity and the Holocaust*. Ithaca, NY: Cornell University Press, 1989, 2000. The prolific sociologist from England explains the sociological significance of the Shoah and other evils in a postmodern world. An influential book.

Bloxham, Donald. *The Final Solution: A Genocide*. Oxford, UK and New York: Oxford University Press, 2009. Example of the new revisionist analyses of the Shoah from an eminent British historian.

Cargas, Harry James (ed.). *Problems Unique to the Holocaust*, Lexington. KY: University Press of Kentucky, 1999. See p. 51 for my essay on "Holocaust Suicides." I have to agree with Donald Bloxham that these "problems" (suicide, moral dilemmas, grief) are not unique to the Shoah but reflect every genocide.

Friedman, Philip. *Roads to Extinction: Essays on the Holocaust.* Philadelphia, PA: Jewish Publication Society, 1980. Crucial essays by a historian who died much too young. See the chapter on Jewish resistance, pp. 387-408. The book was edited by his wife Ada after his death.

Hilberg, Raul. *Perpetrators, Victims, Bystanders: The Jewish Catastrophe 1933-1945.* New York: HarperCollins, 1992. The late great Hilberg mentions this book on p. 312, referring to a discussion on Alexander Abugov on p. 202. Also see his magnum opus, *The Destruction of the European Jews,* 1973.

Merin, Yehuda (ed.). *Memorial Book (Yizkor Book) for the Communities of Maniewitch, Horodoc, Lishnivka, Trojanovka, Povursk.* Tel Aviv: World Voyhnian Society, and Givatayim: Beit Volyn, 2002. This book is in Hebrew and English.

Porter, Jack Nusan. *The Genocidal Mind: Sociological and Sexual Perspectives.* Lanham, MD: University Press of America, 2006. It bridges the gap between Holocaust studies and genocide studies, delving into the mind of Hitler as well as the sociological and sexual bases of genocide.

Spector, Shmuel. *The Holocaust of Volhynian Jews 1941-1944.* Jerusalem: Yad Vashem, 1990. The best and most comprehensive book on the subject. It gives a background to the Max-Kruk *otryad* and others operating in Voynhia, Ukraine. See the chapter called "The Jews and Partisan Warfare," pp. 257-341, plus the photos following p. 288, plus the next chapter as well, pp. 342-355. Nearly all the people mentioned in this book are mentioned in Spector's book. See also his article in *Yad Vashem Studies,* Vol. XV, 1983, pp. 159-186, plus his essay-review in *Yad Vashem Bulletin,* No. 13, October 1963 on the Kaunas Ghetto uprising.

Jewish Resistance in General

Ajzensztadt, Amnon. *Endurance: Chronicles of Jewish Resistance.* New York: Mosaic Press, 1987

Gill, Anton. *An Honorable Defeat: A History of German Resistance to Hitler, 1933-1945.* New York: Henry Holt, 1994.

Gottlieb, Roger S. "The Concept of Resistance: Jewish Resistance during the Holocaust." *Social Theory and Social Practice*, Vol. 9, No. 1, Spring 1983, pp. 31-49. Written by a philosopher.

Gutman, Israel. *Fighters among the Ruins: The Story of Jewish Heroism during World War II*. Washington, DC: B'nai B'rith Books, 1988. Has a section on "guerilla warfare," pp. 215-244, and the Allied armies, pp. 245-261.

Kohn, Moshe M. (ed.). *Jewish Resistance during the Holocaust: Proceedings of a Conference*. Jerusalem: Yad Vashem, 1971. A classic, early conference in April 1968.Very useful.

Kowalski, Isaac (ed.). *Anthology of Armed Resistance to the Nazis, 1939-1945*. Four volumes. New York: Jewish Combatants Publishing House, 1986. I was a contributing editor to these volumes, and my essays from this book and other places are scattered and reprinted throughout the four volumes.

Krakowski, Shmuel. *The War of the Doomed: Jewish Resistance in Poland, 1942-1944*. New York: Holmes and Meier, 1985.

Langbein, Hermann. *Against All Hope: Resistance in the Nazi Concentration Camps, 1938-1945*. New York: Contiuum (Paragon House), 1994.

Rings, Werner. *Life with the Enemy: Collaboration and Resistance in Hitler's Europe 1939-1945*. Garden City, NY: Doubleday and Company, 1982.

Rohrlich, Ruby (ed.). *Resisting the Holocaust*. New York: Berg, 1998.

Steinberg, Lucien. *Not as a Lamb*. Farnborough, UK: Heath, 1970.

Tec, Nechama. *Jewish Resistance: Facts, Omissions, and Distortions Occasional Paper*. Washington, DC: US Holocaust Memorial Museum, Research Institute, 1997. I disagree with Tec on several points.

Partisan Resistance in particular

Abrahamsen, Samuel. *Norway's Response to the Holocaust*. New York: Holocaust Library, 1991.

Arad, Yitzhak. *The Partisan: From the Valley of Death to Mount Zion*. New York: Holocaust Library, 1979. Written by an important Israeli leader, a brigadier-general and scholar at Yad Vashem.

Armstrong, John A. (ed.). *Soviet Partisans in World War II.* Madison, WI: University of Wisconsin Press, 1964.

Bertelsen, Aage. *October '43.* New York: G. P. Putnam's Sons, 1954. An early account of the resistance in Denmark.

Cohen, Rich. *The Avengers: A Jewish War Story.* New York: Knopf, 2000. Not only the story of Abba Kovner and his partisan group in Vilnius, but the tale of their desire to take revenge by killing Nazis after the war—an act that thankfully was stopped.

Duffy, Peter. *The Bielski Brothers.* New York: HarperCollins, 2003.

Koblik, Steven. *The Stones Cry Out: Sweden's Response to the Persecution of the Jews 1933-1945.* New York: Holocaust Library, 1988.

Kohn, Nahum and Howard Roiter. *A Voice from the Forest: Memoirs of a Jewish Partisan.* New York: Holocaust Library, 1980.

Levi, Primo. *If Not Now, When?* New York: Summit Books, 1985. The famous Italian novelist tells his tale of resistance and rescue.

Levine, Allan. *Fugitives of the Forest: The Heroic Story of Jewish Resistance.* Toronto: Stoddart, 1998. See pp. 175 on the Kruk-Max group.

Merin, Yehuda, and Jack Nusan Porter. "Three Jewish family Camps in the Forests of Volyn, Ukraine, During the Holocaust." *Jewish Social Science*, 156, No. 1, 1984, pp. 83-92. Based on Merin's Master's Thesis from Bar Ilan University in Israel, it describes the three family camps of the Kruk-Max *otryads.*

Novitch, Miriam. *Sobibor: Martyrdom and Revolt.* New York: Holocaust Library, 1980.

Pesce, Giovanni. *And No Quarter: An Italian Partisan in World War II.* Ohio University Press, 1972.

Rautkallio, Hannu. *Finland and the Holocaust: The Rescue of Finland's Jews.* New York: Holocaust Library, 1987.

Tec, Nechama. *Defiance: The Bielski Partisans.* New York: Oxford University Press, 1993. This is the book made into a movie, starring Daniel Craig as Tuvia Bielski. I am mentioned on pp. 222, 225, 242, and 255.

Temchin, Michael. *The Witch Doctor: Memoirs of a Partisan.* New York, Holocaust Library, 1983. Memoir of a doctor.

Werner, Harold. *Fighting Back: A Memoir of Jewish Resistance in World War II.* New York: Columbia University Press, 1992. A tale of a Polish-Jewish resistance fighter.

Woman, Gender, and Sexual Issues

Baumel, Judith Tydor. *Doubleday Jeopardy: Gender and the Holocaust.* London: Vallentine Mitchell, 1998.

Bleuel, Hans Peter. *Sex and Society in Nazi Germany.* Philadelphia and New York: J. B. Lippincott, 1973. A classic book.

Burds, Jeffrey. "Sexual Violence in Europe in World War II," *Politics and Society*, 37, No. 1, March 2009, pp. 35-74.

Cohn, Carol (ed.). *Women and Wars.* Cambridge, UK: Polity Press, 2012. Polity Press has one of the most innovative series on this subject and in cognate areas of war and conflict.

Haste, Cate. *Nazi Women.* London: Channel 4 Books/ Macmillan, 2001. A rare look into the life of Nazi women and the Nazi attitude towards women, sex, and gender.

Jones, Adam (ed.). *Gendercide and Genocide.* Nashville, TN: Vanderbilt University Press, 2004. One of the first anthologies in the field.

Langer, Walter C. *The Mind of Hitler: The Secret Wartime Report.* New York: Basic Books, 1972. A rare insight into the mind of evil, with insights into Hitler's sexual identity.

Laska, Vera. *Women in the Resistance and in the Holocaust.* Westport, CT: Greenwood, 1983. An early book on the subject.

Leatherman, Janie L. *Sexual Violence and Armed Conflict.* Cambridge, UK: Polity Press, 2011.

Meed, Vladka. *On Both Sides of the Wall: Memoirs from the Warsaw Ghetto.* Washington, DC: Holocaust Library, 1993. An early memoir by a famous woman partisan who could pass as an "Aryan" due to her blond hair and blue eyes, and who later became an important witness to resistance in the USA and Israel.

Ofer, Dalia, and Lenore J. Weitzman (ed.). *Women in the Holocaust.* New Have, CT: Yale University Press, 1998.

Porter, Jack Nusan. *The Genocidal Mind: Sexual and Sociological Issues*. Lanham, MD: University Press of America, 2006.

_____. *Sexual Politics in Nazi Germany; The Persecution of the Homosexuals and Lesbians During the Holocaust*. Newton, MA: The Spencer Press, 2011. See bibliography for more material.

_____. "Jewish Women in the Resistance" in Isaac Kowalski (ed.) *Anthology of Armed Resistance to the Nazis*, Vol. 1, pp. 289-295.

Schulman, Faye. *A Partisan's Memoir: Woman of the Holocaust*. Toronto: Second Story Press, 1995. A rare memoir by a female partisan.

Tec, Nechama. *Resilience and Courage: Women, Men, and the Holocaust*. New Haven and London: Yale University Press, 2003. An important book on sex and gender issues in the partisan movement. See pp. 391, 412, 410 for mentions of my work. Tec seems to disagree with me about the lack of "sexism" in the Soviet partisans. There was less than people think, and women were safer in the partisans than at large, facing the Soviet army, where great numbers of rape took place. I came across no instance of rape in the Kruk-Max group. Comprehensive and very useful bibliography and note sections.

Mass Culture, Cinema, Literature, and Poetry

Forche, Carolyn. *Against forgetting: Twentieth-Century Poetry of Witness*. New York and London: W.W. Norton, 1993. One of the finest collections of poetry of witness and injustice.

Friedlander, Albert H. *Out of the Whirlwind: A Reader of Holocaust Literature*. Garden City, NY: Doubleday & Company, 1968. A classic collection.

Glieder, Mikhail (Michael). *With a Motion Picture Camera behind Enemy Lines*. Moscow: Goskinoizdat, 1947. This moviemaker and photographer made several films that should be discovered, given sub-titles, and shown. There are copies in the Lenin Library and elsewhere in Moscow.

Kosinski, Jerzy. *The Painted Bird*. New York: Grove Press, 1965, 1976. A controversial book by a controversial writer but still a powerful literary achievement on the Shoah.

Porter, Jack Nusan. "Holocaust Suicides," in Cargas (ed.) above, pp. 51-66. Porter analyzes a pattern of suicide among six or seven Shoah writers and thinkers in the late 80s and early 90s as well as the entire concept of suicide during and after the war.

_____. *L'matara: For the Purpose: Jewish Partisan Poems and Stories from the D.P. Camps of World War II.* Newton, MA: The Spencer Press, 1997. A rare collection in Yiddish, Hebrew, and Polish poems and stories from the DP camps.

Roskis, David G, and Naomi Diamant. *Holocaust Literature: A History and Guide.* Waltham, MA: Brandeis University Press, 2012. An excellent and very useful collection of essays, reviews, and cover art.

Shrayer, Maxim. *An Anthology of Jewish-Russian Literature.* Two volumes, New York: M.E. Sharpe, 2007.

Teichman, Milton, and Sharon Leder. *Truth and Lamentation: Stories and Poems on the Holocaust.* Urbana and Chicago, Illinois: 1994.

Youngblood, Denise J. *Russian War Films: On the Cinema front, 1914-1945.* Lawrence, KS: University Press of Kansas, 2007. An excellent guide with an excellent bibliography, especially of Russian-language sources, with a section on partisan films but does not mention Mikhail Glieder (see above) surprisingly.

Legacies

Alexander, Jeffrey. *The Dark Side of Modernity.* Cambridge, UK: Polity Press, 2013. This book exposes the "destructive impulses" of post-traditional society.

Beck, Ulrich. *Twenty Observations on a World in Turmoil.* Cambridge, UK: Polity Press, 2012. The world is in a state of turmoil; genocide is only one manifestation. It all began with the Holocaust.

Goldensohn, Leon. *Nuremberg Interviews,* edited by Robert Gellately. New York: Knopf, 2004. Written by a Jewish psychiatrist, this is an extraordinary insight into the mind and thoughts of top Nazis facing almost certain death by hanging at Nuremberg, Germany after the war. Their views will surprise readers.

Helmreich, William B. *Against All Odds: Holocaust Survivors and the Successful Lives They Made in America*. New York: Simon and Shuster, 1992. My mother is quoted on p. 240, part of much longer interview, which I will publish in a companion book to this one.

Lewin, Rhoda G. *Witness to the Holocaust: An Oral History*. Boston: Twayne Publishers, 1990. My mother's story is on pp. 167-169, yet for a very short tale, it contains numerous errors, including the town she is from—Gorodok, Ukraine, not Gorodok, Poland.

Lutz, Thomas (ed.). *Memorial Museums to the Victims of the Nazi Regime*, Berlin: The Topography of Terror Foundation, 1995. An example of listings in Germany but there are many more throughout Europe, and we need more guidebooks like this one.

Ramsbotham, Oliver, et al. *Contemporary Conflict Resolution*, Cambridge, UK: Polity Press, 2011.

Sandole, Dennis J.D. *Peace Building*, Cambridge, UK: Polity Press, 2011. Explores the theory and practice of peace building and conflict resolution.

Stevens, Michael E. (ed.). *Remembering the Holocaust: Voices of the Wisconsin Past*, Madison, WI: State Historical Society of Wisconsin, 1997. While my parents Faye and Irving Porter are not mentioned, many of their friends are, like Walter Peltz.

Weil, Pierre. *The Art of Living in Peace: Guide to Education for a Culture of Peace*. New York: UNESCO Publishing, UN Publications, 2002. A gentle, almost quaint notion that we must educate for peace in this world.

Wieviorka, Michel. *Evil*. Cambridge, UK: Polity Press, 2012. Part of a growing number of sociological works on evil.

GLOSSARY

Breicha — Hebrew for "rescue"; the attempt by Israeli and Jewish leaders to rescue Jews in Europe both during and after the war.

Brigada — Brigades, three to four *otryads*.

Civilian Camps — Refers to those groups of civilians who were part of the partisan bands and were protected by them.

Commissar — Communist party official. Some commissars were also military commanders. At other times there was both a military commander and an ideological and political advisor. His purpose was to teach and enforce party principles and policy.

Diaspora — Greek for "dispersion." The Hebrew equivalent is *Galut*, meaning all lands outside of Israel, the "lands of exile." Also refers to the Jews living in these lands and to their state of mind.

Einikeit — The house organ and newspaper of the Jewish Anti-Fascist Committee of the Soviet Union. The word means "unity" in Russian. The first issue appeared June 7, 1942; the last issue, November 20 1948.

Folk-Shtimme — Yiddish for "People's Voice"; an important Yiddish Communist newspaper in Warsaw.

Genocide — The systematic murder of an entire people, nation, or race. The word comes from two Latin roots: *genus*, people, and *cide*, killing. The word was first coined in 1944 by Polish-Jewish legal scholar Raphael Lemkin. It is a legal as well as a sociopolitical term. (See **Holocaust**.)

Hero of the Soviet Union — The title of the highest-ranking military award given to Soviet citizens for valor in battle. Nearly 150 Jews received such an award.

Holocaust — Literally means "destruction" or "being consumed by flames." It is the term that Jews use to describe the genocide of the Jewish people and the obliteration of the Jewish community and culture(s) during World War II. In Hebrew the term is *Shoah*, and in Yiddish it is the *Churban*. (See **Genocide**)

Kolkhoz — A Communist collective farm found in the U.S.S.R.

Oblast — Russian term for "province"; it is not the American equivalent of a state, but more like a large county.

Oblava — Russian for "encirclement."

Okrug — Russian term for "district."

Otryad — A Company-size Red Army unit or a smaller-size partisan detachment.

Podpolkovnik — Russian term for "lieutenant-colonel."
Pogrom — An organized massacre of helpless people and the looting of property, usually with the tacit support of the local officials; specifically, a massacre of Jews, as originally occurred in Russia or Poland.

Politruk — Political officer attached to a Russian army unit or partisan group. (See **Commissar**.)

Polkovnik — A Russian military rank somewhat equivalent to the American rank of colonel. A *general-polkovnik* is a colonel-general, which in the U.S. Army would be equivalent to the rank of general.

S.S. — Abbreviation of the German word *Shutzstaffel*, meaning "protection squads." These were paramilitary units responsible for guarding the Nazi leaders, terrorizing anti-Nazi individuals and groups, and operating the concentration (death) camps of Nazi Germany. At times they were used, in conjunction with other troops, for putting down resistance, most notably the Warsaw Ghetto uprising of Jews in April, 1943.

Soyedineniye — A brigade-size group about equal to a division by U.S. Army standards.

Zemlyanka — underground bunker, hut or cave where forest partisans or civilians lived.

Zadaniye — Russian for "an action," to get food or supplies.

Jewish Partisans of the Soviet Union in WWII

PHOTOS

Major-General Vasily A. Begma, Russian partisan commander

Sidor A. Kovpak, a former school teacher, was one of the most famous partisan commanders. He led a unit of about 10,000 men near the town of Putivt, Ukraine. As the Germans retreated, Kovpak and his men moved ahead of them, destroying communications. They were later active in Poland. © 1987 V. Karpov, G. Drozdov, E. Ryabko

Polkovnik (colonel) Anton Brinsky, known as "Dyadya Petya," Russian for "Uncle Petya," a widely respected leader, he was liaison to the Soviet Commandant for the Kruk and Max Group around Manievich, Ukraine. See also photo 84 of his statue in the center of present-day Manevichi. © 1982, 2002 Jack Nusan Porter (See photo on page 584 of his statue.)

Captain Józef (Yosef) Sobiesiak ("Max"), a Polish leader of the Max Group, he later became an admiral in the Polish Navy and married Irena Guz. He lived in Warsaw until his death many years after the war. © Jack Nusan Porter

Nikolai (Mikola) Konishchuk, a Ukrainian Communist and village leader, known as "Kruk," he and Max led the well-known partisan group known as the Kruk-Max otryad (fighting group) in the Volyn region of northwest Ukraine. Ironically, he was killed after the war by his wife's brothers for leaving her for a Jewish woman. © 1982, 2002 Jack Nusan Porter

Yasenty Slovik, a "righteous gentile" from the small town of Koninsk/ Okonsk, near Manevichi. He gave Srulik Puchtik ("Zalonka") a rifle and 150 bullets and thus allowed Puchtik to become a leader in a partisan group, the Kruk otryad ("fighting unit" in Russian).

Casimir Slovik, Yasenty's son, another "righteous gentile."

Shimon Mirochnik, from Manevichi, Max's Group. Lived in Israel.

Berl (Dov) Bronstein, from Manevichi, known as "Zhuk" and Bardu. Lived in Israel. See his powerful memoir in this book.

Ze'ev Verba (Raveh) of Israel

Medals awarded Ze'ev Raveh (Verba) for participating in the war of the partisans, on the left, and in Israel's battles (Six-Day War, Yom Kippur War) on the right.

549

Chunek Wolper, Manevichi, fought in Kruk's group. Immigrated to Israel. Lived in Tel Aviv.

Lazin, the Ukrainian deputy to Kruk

David (Dovid) Blanstein

Yehoshua Kanonitz, partisan youth who joined Kruk's unit with a revolver. Left forest at age eighteen. Later murdered in a Lublin hospital by anti-Semitic Polish nationalists.

Irena Sobiesiak (Rivka Guz), Second Lieutenant in the Polish Army. Awarded Virtuti Military Cross, Hero's Cross, Partisan's Cross, and Combat Paratrooper Medal. Married Józef Sobiesiak. Died in Warsaw long after the war.

Moshe Flash of Montreal. See his partisan documents.

Berl Avruch and Yitzchak Zafran

Misha Edelstein, refugee from Kalisz; organized escape to forest; murdered by the Banderovtsy, Ukrainian nationalist groups named after Stefan Bandera.

Alexander (Szika) Grushka (Agas), also known as Sashka, from the Kartukhin Partisan group.

Yosef Zweibel

Shmaryahu Zafran ("Verny")

Yitzchak Kuperberg

Dov Lorber ("Malinka"), a founder and commander of the Volyn partisans, lived in Seattle in USA. Had his own group of twenty-four Jewish fighters.

Lorber after the war

Lorber and a friend

Alexander Abugov commander of a scout unit, and an important founder of Volyn partisans

Zev Avruch, among the youngest of the partisans

Partisan leaders, after the war, group photo. Right to Left, standing: Dichter, Ze'ev Raveh, Yitzchak Kuperberg, and Yitzchak (Isaac) Avruch; sitting right to left: Alexander Abugov and Dov Lorber

Sender (Sam) Lande, photo taken outside DP Camp Bindermichel, Linz, Austria, 1946. Lived in Milwaukee, Wisconsin.

Partisans relaxing in the woods near DP Camp Bindermichel, Linz, Austria circa 1945-1946. Irving and Faye Porter in center with Jack Nusan Porter on his mother's lap. Moshe Kramer to the right of Faye and Jack Porter and his wife Chaya on the left.
© 2013 Jack Nusan Porter

Asher Flash. Drove the horses for Kruk. Lived in Israel.

Susel Shepa of the Kruk Group. Lived in Denver, USA

Yuri (Jack) Melamedik of the Max Group. Lives in Montreal, Canada.

Pinick Berman, a young bemedaled Polish fighter in the Kruk Group, which was under the command of Kruk and Colonel Anton Brinsky.

Partisan Srulik Puchtik (Jack Nusan Porter's father) and Commander Konishchuk (on right) of the Kruk Group.

Partisan cook and "nurse" Faygeh (Faye) Merin Puchtik-Porter (Jack Nusan Porter's mother) in a 1997 picture, at age 88, in Minneapolis, MN.

Youngsters in the Woods. From right to left, Yoseleh Melamed, left forest at age 14, Berl Finkel, left at age 10, and Avrum Finkel, left at age 13.

Moshe Finkel. Left the forest at age 15. Died in 1956 in Israel, in the Galil, by Arab terrorists.

More youngsters. From left to right: Alan Rubin, Jack Melamedik, Berl Finkel

From left to right, Yidele Lorber (Dov Lorber's cousin) and Berl Finkel, from Max's Group. Left the forest at age 10.

Moshe Lanitz from Gorodok, Ukraine. Died in the 1948 Israeli War of Independence.

The boy from Kruk's Group, Vova (Zev) Avruch, worked with explosives.

Joseph Schneider (on the left) from Troyanovka, Ukraine and his friends from Povursk, Ukraine; Rubin Kirzner (Slivka), of Brookline, Mass., is on the right.

Rubin Kirzner (Slivka)

Rubin and Bella Kirzner (Slivka) and their children with Jack Porter, Krakow, Poland 1995

*Partisan Rivka (Irena) Guz and Yitzchak
Sher, before the war, Povursk, Ukraine 1937.*

*Irena Guz (right) with Mr. Slivka and his family,
Warsaw, Poland 1995*

Yehuda Melamedik, on right, left the forest at age 11

Avraham Finkel and Zippora Melamed were 13 when leaving forest.

Hadassah (Feldman) Chernov left with group of orphans for Russia at age 12

The late David Lanitz was 16 on leaving the forest. Fell in battle on Soviet front.

Boy adopted by partisans and called "Synok."

Asher Mirochnik, a Kruk youth scout, was 15 upon leaving the forest.

Micha Gazit. Left forest at age 10.

Yitzchak Puchtik, son of Avrum and Chava Puchtik and brother to Idka Puchtik (Shuster), was 17 upon leaving the forest. Fell in battle during Suez Canal war in 1956.

Idka (Ida) Puchtik (Shuster) was age 15 when she left the forest.

Youths who fought with the partisans in the Volyn forests (Kostyushko Units). Yaakov Shuster, husband of Idka Shuster of Tel Aviv, is on the right.

Partisans at rest (Max Group), Pripyat Marshes area, Volyn, Ukraine. A unit of partisans specializing in exploding mines. Moshe (Morris) Kramer of Philadelphia is on the right, sitting upright, facing camera, with rifle and cap.

Partisans in Kruk's Group placing mines on the railway.

Crossing the River Styr, Volyn region, Ukraine, helping the women cross, during a retreat from German forces.

Partisans on horses crossing the Stokhod River, northwest Volyn.

Show of strength by partisans in Galuziya, Volyn, Ukraine.

General Fedorov addressing partisan unit commanders.

Partisans on their way in the marshes.

Partisan unit on the move through the pine woods of Volyn.

Crossing the river near the Serkhov Woods, Volyn.

Max's sabotage unit derailing tracks

Partisans from the Sidor Kovpak unit. At top right is Zusia Chajuck.

Yiddil Shandlov

Yefim Litvinovsky

Yaakov Vasin

Nehemiah Endlin

Wolf Lussik (right) and his son Lazar

A group of partisans from the Kaunas ghetto.

Destroying rail communications.

Here, a partisan, armed with a Schmeisser submachine gun stolen from the German army, lights the fuse of a bomb planted on a main railway line.

The results. German soldiers inspect a train that has been blown up by partisans. The train may have been an empty train, sent along the rails ahead of one carrying troops or ammunition. To deter partisans, the Germans would sometimes use a train full of Russian prisoners in this way.

A partisan base in the woods. The partisans could rarely light bonfires because of the risk that Germans would see the smoke and track them down.

Zemlyankas—forest bunkers—where partisans ate, worked, and slept.

A partisan stronghold, a type of zemlyanka. Note the "Cossack" style clothes and automatic weapons.

David Keimach.

*Commander of the
Kovno partisans, Leib
Solomon (on right) and
the leader of the Vperyod
(Forward) Brigade, Tziko.*

Michael (Mikhail) Glieder, the partisan filmmaker.

The Soviet flag is raised over the Reichstag, May 2, 1945.

All for the front, all for victory! Soviet Poster.

The Nazi eagle in the dust. Soviet soldiers look on.

Victorious Soviet troops return home.

Yisroel Porter (Puchtik), son Jack (Yaakov Natan/ Jack Nusan) and wife Faygeh nee Merin, Milwaukee, 1950s. © Jack Nusan Porter

After the war. Morris Kramer and Irving Porter in center. Chaya Kramer on right; and their daughters on left, in Philadelphia, 1960s. © Jack Nusan Porter

Faye and Irving Porter with daughter, Bella and son, Sol, Milwaukee, 1962

Three Survivors, Three Friends - from left to right:
Celia (Tzila) Sztundel, Faye Porter, Emma Ertel, Milwaukee, 1997

Irving Porter (on right) singing at
(on left) Jack Porter's Wedding, Sharon, MA - September 18, 1997

Faye Porter and son Jack Porter, St. Louis Park, MN, 2006

Faye Porter, 2006

Avrum Puchtik

Chava Puchtik (Eisenberg)

Statue of Colonel Anton Brinsky in Manevichi center; Dr. Jack Porter standing next to it, 2003. © 2013 Jack Nusan Porter

The railroad tracks in Manevichi, 2003. © 2013 Jack Nusan Porter

Mrs. Cassy Skoronek and Jack Porter, at the Manevichi memorial, site of the Manevichi massacre of Jews, 2003. © 2013 Jack Nusan Porter

The town of Manevichi, Volyn, Ukraine with two locals who remembered, 2003. © 2013 Jack Nusan Porter

The shtetl of Manevichi, with historian Joe Voss (back to photo), Cassy Skoronek, translator Oksana, driver, and Ukrainian man, 2003.
© 2013 Jack Nusan Porter

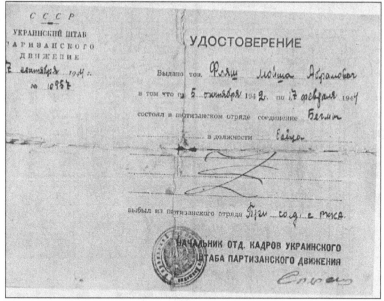

Partisan papers and medal belonging to Moshe Flash of the Kruk and Kartukhin units. He fought in western Ukraine from September 1942 to February 1944. The medal is the "War of the Fatherland." Without the documents, the medal was useless or worse, stolen. Flash, who lived in Montréal, went by the name "Ivan" in the woods.
© 1982, 2002 Jack Nusan Porter

БОЕВАЯ ХАРАКТЕРИСТИКА.

На бойца партизана ххх партизанского соединения Героя Совет-
ского Союза полковника Бринского тов. ФЛЯША
Мойше Абрамовича рождения 1909 года, п/парт/
уроженец с. Молонька Колковского района Волынской области,
тов. Фляш за время пребывания в партизанах с августа 1944 го.
.....кал в организации крушении вражеских эшелонов противника
7 раз, ... 6 раз, ... на
ст. Маневичи Камарск, в засадах против немцев 4 раза, против националистов 3 раза. Участвовал в боях против немцев 6 раз и
против националистов 7 раз где проявил себя смелым бойцом.
Участвовал при уничтожении комендатуры полицейских, а также
при разгроме масло-перегоночных заводов, в разгроме немецких
лавок, принимал участие в уничтожении националистических шпи-
онов, а так же в достаче оружия сам лично достал 13 винтовок.
Кроме этого тов. Фляш выполн спецзадания командования.

себя как дисциплинированого /ца партизана/ за проявленою борьбу
против немцев командованием партизанского отряда представлен
к Правительственной награде.

КОМАНДИР ОТРЯДА ПАРТИЗАНСКОГО
.... Ст. Лейтенант   /Костин/

НАЧАЛЬНИК ШТАБА ПАРТИЗАНСКОЙ БРИГАДЫ № 1
Ст. лейтенант   /Бутко./

Partisan papers and medal belonging to Moshe Flash of the Kruk and Kartukhin units.

Partisan decorations. From Russian and Soviet Military awards. Order of Lenin State History Museum, © 1990.

Nazi officers executing partisans.

*Dr. Jack Porter and a friend at a WW II re-enactment,
Lancaster, PA, 2010.*

MAPS

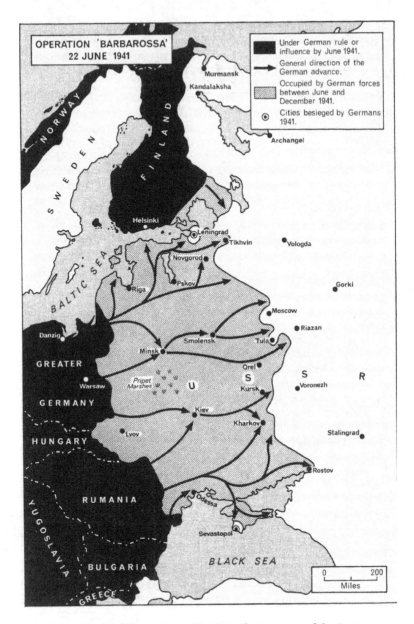

*Operation Barbarossa, June 22, 1941, the invasion of the Soviet
Union and the beginning of partisan warfare. © Martin Gilbert 1972*

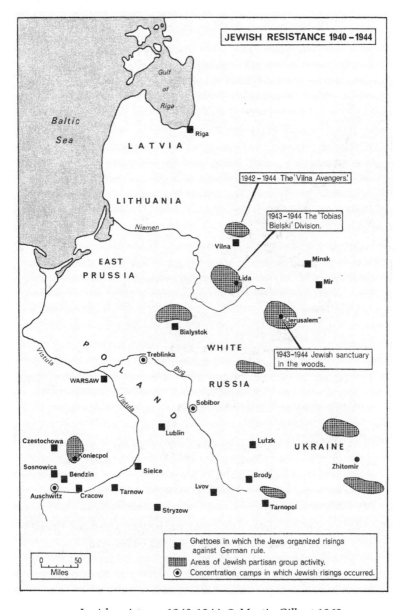

Jewish resistance 1940-1944. © *Martin Gilbert 1969*

Partisans of Eastern Poland, northwestern Ukraine (Volyn and Polesia),
Byelorussia, and Galicia. © Martin Gilbert 1985

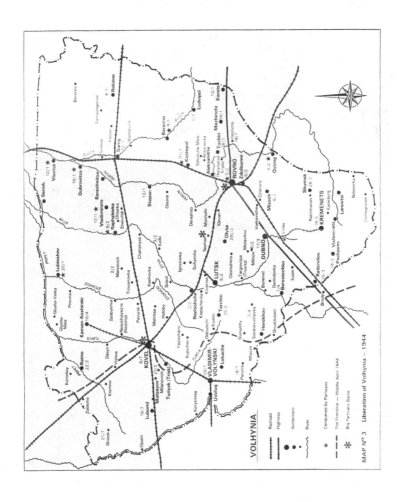

MAP N° 3   Liberation of Volhynia – 1944

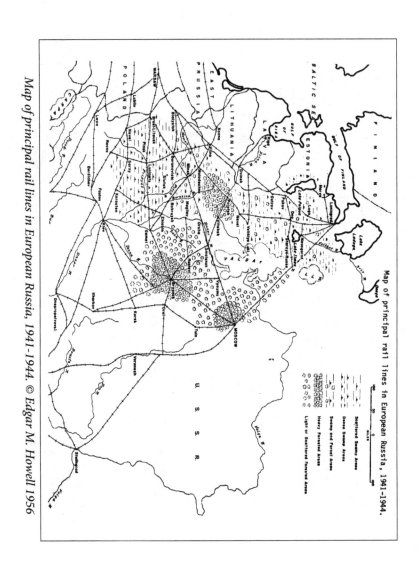

Map of principal rail lines in European Russia, 1941-1944. © Edgar M. Howell 1956

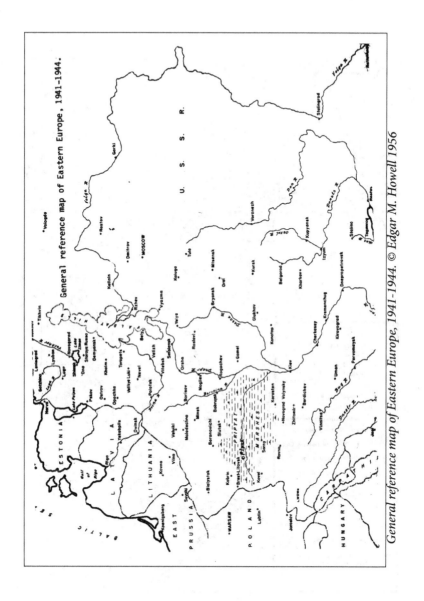

General reference map of Eastern Europe, 1941–1944. © Edgar M. Howell 1956

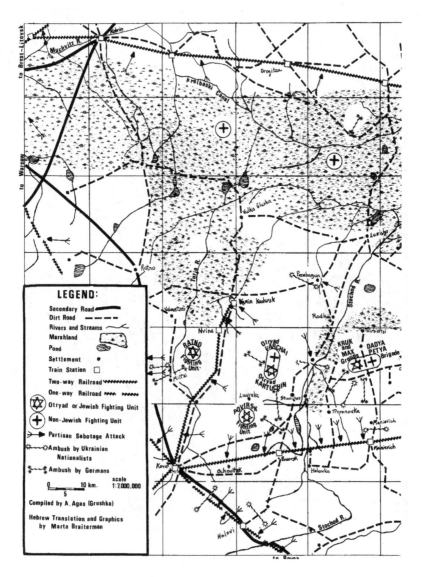

Map of Partisan Movements in Northern Volyn and Polesia,
Northwestern Ukraine, 1941-1944. English version © Jack Nusan Porter
1982, 2002; From the Hebrew version "Like Tall Pine Trees."

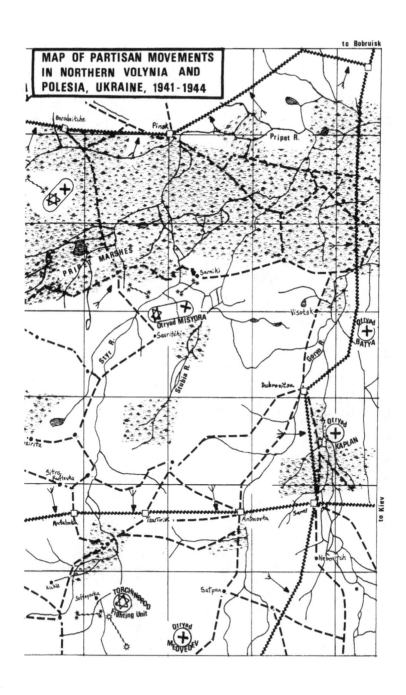

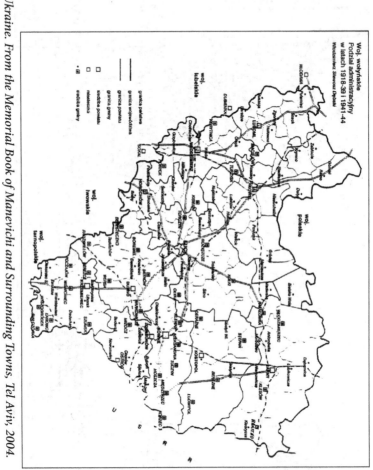

Volyni region, Ukraine. From the Memorial Book of Manevichi and Surrounding Towns, Tel Aviv, 2004.

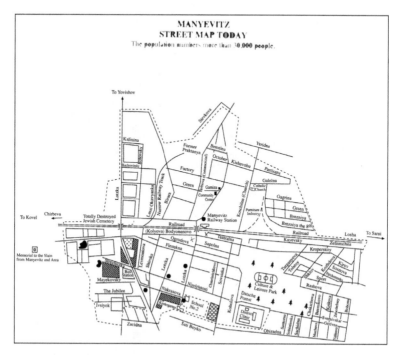

Manevichi Street Map Today, 2003. Population more than 30,000.
From the Memorial Book of Manevichi and Surrounding Towns, Tel Aviv,
2004.

CHARTS

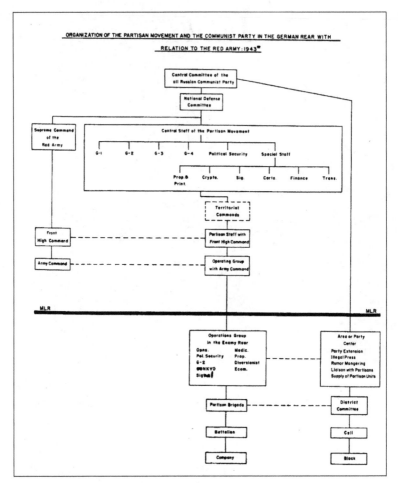

Organization of the Partisan Movement

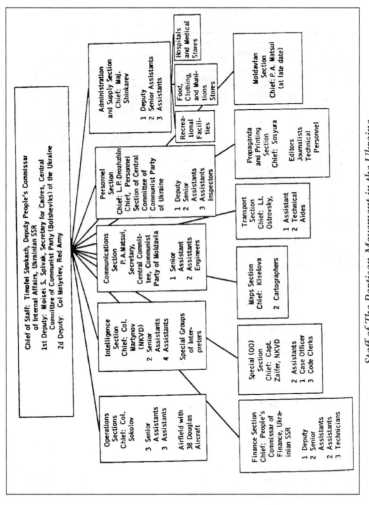

Staff of The Partisan Movement in the Ukraine

Chief of Staff: Timofel Strokach, Deputy People's Commissar of Internal Affairs, Ukrainian SSR
1st Deputy: Moisei S. Spivak, Secretary for Cadres, Central Committee of Communist Party (Bolsheviks) of the Ukraine
2d Deputy: Col Metyelev, Red Army

Operations Sections
Chief: Col. Sokolov

3 Senior Assistants
3 Assistants

Airfield with 38 Douglas Aircraft

Intelligence Section
Chief: Col. Martynov (NKVD)

2 Senior Assistants
4 Assistants

Special Groups of Interpreters

Communications Section
P.A.Matsui, Secretary, Central Committee, Communist Party of Moldavia

1 Senior Assistant
2 Assistants
Engineers

Personnel Section
Chief: L.P. Drozhzhin Chief, Personnel Section of Central Committee of Communist Party of Ukraine

1 Deputy
2 Senior Assistants
3 Assistants
Inspectors

Administration and Supply Section
Chief: Maj. Shinkarev

1 Deputy
2 Senior Assistants
3 Assistants

Hospitals and Medical Stores

Food, Clothing, and Munitions Stores

Recreational Facilities

Finance Section
Chief: People's Commissar of Finance, Ukrainian SSR

1 Deputy
2 Senior Assistants
2 Assistants
3 Technicians

Special (OO) Section
Chief: Capt. Zaifer, NKVD

2 Assistants
1 Case Officer
3 Code Clerks

Maps Section
Chief: Kiselova

2 Cartographers

Transport Section
Chief: Lt. Ostrovsky.

1 Assistant
2 Technical Aides

Propaganda and Printing Section
Chief: Sosyura

Editors
Journalists
Technical Personnel

Moldavian Section
Chief: P.A. Matsui (at late date)

607

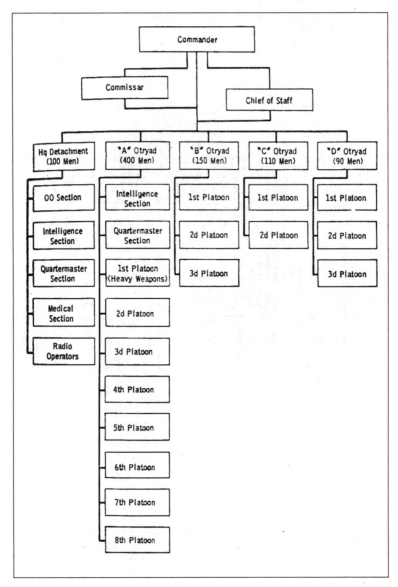

Generalized structure of a partisan brigade

INDEX OF PARTISAN
NAMES & GROUPS

INDIVIDUAL FIGHTERS

Note:
In some cases, only the last name is mentioned; in others
only the first name or the occupation. Such were the times.
I have also included names of relatives of partisan fighters
mentioned in the book.

PARTISAN GROUPS